Lux Presents Hollywood

A Show-by-Show History of the
Lux Radio Theatre *and the*
Lux Video Theatre, *1934–1957*

CONNIE BILLIPS and
ARTHUR PIERCE

Volume 1
(Preface; Lux Radio Theatre History;
Lux Radio Theatre Programs,
First Season–Twelfth Season)

McFarland & Company, Inc., Publishers
Jefferson, North Carolina, and London

The present work is a reprint of the library bound one-volume edition of Lux Presents Hollywood: A Show-by-Show History of the *Lux Radio Theatre* and the *Lux Video Theatre, 1934–1957, first published in 1995 by McFarland.*

Volume 1

LIBRARY OF CONGRESS CATALOGUING-IN-PUBLICATION DATA

Billips, Connie J.
Lux presents Hollywood : a show-by-show history of the Lux radio theatre and the Lux video theatre, 1934–1957 / by Connie Billips and Arthur Pierce.
p. cm.
Includes bibliographical references and index.

2 volume set —
ISBN 978-0-7864-6723-5
softcover : 50# alkaline paper ∞

1. Lux radio theatre (Radio program) 2. Lux video theatre (Television program) I. Pierce, Arthur. II. Title.
PN1991.77.L89B55 2012
791.44'72 — dc20   94-11517

BRITISH LIBRARY CATALOGUING DATA ARE AVAILABLE

Front cover design by David K. Landis (Shake It Loose Graphics)

Manufactured in the United States of America

McFarland & Company, Inc., Publishers
Box 611, Jefferson, North Carolina 28640
www.mcfarlandpub.com

Acknowledgments

The authors are extremely grateful to the following people who worked on the *Lux Radio Theatre* or the *Lux Video Theatre* and without whose help this book would not have been possible: Harry Bartell, Richard Beals, Ralph Bellamy, Joan Bennett, True Boardman, Vanessa Brown, Carroll Carroll, Frank Coghlan, Jr., Fielder Cook, Jeff Corey, Constance Cummings, P.D. ("Dix") Davis, Rosemary deCamp, Larry Dobkin, R.E. Dubé, Jack Edwards, Sam Edwards, Herb Ellis, Dennis Friscia, Betty Lou Gerson, Edward Gilcher, Lillian Gish, Tom Glazer, Jonathan Hole, Gladys Holland, Josephine Hutchinson, Bill James, Ray Kemper, John Milton Kennedy, Buzz Kulik, Joan Banks Lovejoy, Roddy McDowall, Tyler McVey, Loring Mandel, Virginia Mayo, Rosemary and Walter A. Menn, Shirley Mitchell, Hope Cook Noyes, Maureen O'Sullivan, Vincent Price, Cesar Romero, Doris Singleton, Phyllis Thaxter, Willard Waterman, Jane Webb, and George Wells.

The authors would also like to thank the following people and institutions for their invaluable assistance: Doris Bickford-Swarthout and Douglas Swarthout of the Berry Hill Bookshop, CSM H.L. Billips (U.S. Army Ret.), Irmgard Lautenbacher Billips, Joey Billips, Robert Board, Ed Clute, Arthur K. Cook, Fran Carlon, James Cushing, Daniel Dolo, Marion Hirsch and Ellen Gartrell of Duke University Special Collections, Alex Gordon, Geneva Helm, Jay Hickerson, Alfred Kleinen, Nina Klowden, Judy Kolb, Priscilla Lawlor, Kristine Moerler of Lever Brothers, Jay Livingston, Sam Gill and Howard Prouty of the Margaret Herrick Library, Charles Merrill Mount, Randy Myers, William O'Barr, Tom Olson, Martin Halperin and Ron Wolfe of Pacific Pioneer Broadcasters, James Robert Parish, Howard Mandelbaum of Photofest, Beverly Pierce, Clifford Pierce, Carole Potter, Jerry Reed, Terry Salomonson, John Gassman, Larry Gassman, Carolyn Rawski, and Barbara Watkins of SPERDVAC, Margie Schultz, David Siegel, Thomas Whitehead of Temple University Special Collections, Barbara Thomas, Willie White, Mrs. Frank Woodruff, and Gary Yoggy.

Contents

• Volume 1 •

Preface

There is today an entire generation of people who have grown up without ever hearing a radio drama of any sort, and consequently they are not even familiar with the concept of telling a story in dramatic terms without the aid of a visual element. But radio drama of one kind or another was the prevalent entertainment form for most Americans for a period of more than twenty years.

One of the most important and most influential of the radio dramatic anthology series was the *Lux Radio Theatre*, which began in 1934, when radio drama was still developing, and ended in 1955, well into the television era. That it was among radio's finest dramatic series there can be no doubt, as *Lux*'s staff had the efficiency to turn out a polished program every week, and the creativity to make many of these shows brilliantly effective.

In the first part of this book, the authors have set down a general history of the *Lux Radio Theatre*, drawing upon news releases, documents, articles of the period, and interviews and correspondence with some of the people who worked on the program. The next section includes an entry on each show in the series, listing casts and literary sources, with a brief commentary on each week's program. Cast lists were assembled from payroll/expense sheets, when available, which, beginning midway through 1936, list all the actors who participated in the broadcasts, along with the roles they played. The J. Walter Thompson Collection at Duke University has these sheets for most of the show's history but is missing those from 1949 and 1951–55. For those years, cast listings were assembled from scripts and were supplemented with information obtained from listening to recordings of the actual broadcasts. (Unfortunately, the one show that has no cast information available, other than that about the two stars, happens to be the first in the series, "Seventh Heaven," from October 14, 1934.)

It was the authors' intent to listen to as many of the *Lux Radio Theatre* broadcasts as possible. Of the first 82 shows broadcast from New York, only one is presently known to survive ("Dulcy," from October 28, 1935), but the authors were fortunate in being able to locate 655 of the remaining 844

ix

shows. Those shows with entries preceded by an asterisk (*) have not been heard by the authors, and thus the information contained therein comes from sources other than *hearing* the broadcast. (In many cases, the scripts to these missing shows were read, and all director's quotes in the entries come from the director's report, dated the day of the broadcast.)

The *Lux Video Theatre* was an important television dramatic series that ran for seven seasons, from 1950 to 1957. Although at first it resembled the radio series but slightly, it eventually became something of a visual version of the *Lux Radio Theatre,* basing its shows on motion pictures and using stars from the screen to play the leading roles.

Because there are virtually no *Lux Video Theatre* shows readily available (the authors viewed two and heard the soundtrack to one other), there are fewer comments about details of each show. (Though the authors were able to read many of the scripts, it is impossible to discuss in detail television shows one has not seen.)

As in the radio discussion, the first portion of the *Lux Video Theatre* section relates the general history of the series, and the second part contains an entry for each week's show. Also as in the radio section, the listings of film versions of the story under discussion are limited to American and British productions.

Indexing for the two history sections is found in the *History Index (to Pages).* For the convenience of the user, the programs are indexed to entry numbers. Since each programming season has a short introduction that is not part of an entry, page references will follow entry number references in the *Programs Index (to Entries).*

The Lux Radio Theatre: A History

Radio Drama Before the Lux Radio Theatre

Commercial radio was still a new medium when radio drama began in 1922. Generally cited as the first radio station to perform a drama over the air was WGY, in Schenectady, New York, where, on August 3, 1922, *The Wolf*, by Eugene Walter, was enacted. That fall, the *WGY Players* became a regular Friday night feature, offering well-known stage plays such as *Get-Rich-Quick Wallingford*, *The Garden of Allah*, *Seven Keys to Baldpate*, and even occasional classics by the likes of Henrik Ibsen. There was no set running time for each program in the series, but the shows averaged about two and a half hours each and used an orchestra to perform musical bridges.[1] The casts in the shows were not made up of well-known stars but instead featured local amateurs and employees of the station. Other stations across the country followed WGY's lead and began offering their own radio adaptations of plays and, in some cases, even original dramas for the air. Even after the birth of network radio (the National Broadcasting Company began on November 15, 1926, and the Columbia Broadcasting System on September 18, 1927), the dramas that were performed rarely employed celebrities. Most of the network dramas were actually performed as part of variety shows, two early examples being *The Eveready Hour*, which included a dramatic sketch as well as musical numbers and comedy routines, and *The Collier Hour*, which each week dramatized four 15-minute serial segments taken from the pages of *Collier's* magazine.

It was not long after the advent of radio entertainment that the movie industry began to consider the upstart medium a rival, and therefore all the major studios except RKO (which was controlled by RCA, the same company that owned NBC) had, by the early 1930s, policies restricting their stars from appearing on the air, making radio programs featuring motion picture players out of the question.

1

Full-page 1934 Lux Toilet Soap advertisement featuring MGM film star Maureen O'Sullivan. Even before the *Lux Radio Theatre* was created, only glamorous, popular stars were chosen to endorse the internationally acclaimed Lux Toilet Soap (photo: Lever Brothers/Duke University Special Collections).

In the period immediately preceding the birth of *The Lux Radio Theatre*, the most popular shows were the variety programs such as *The Maxwell House Show Boat* and *The Kraft Music Hall,* leaning toward music; and *The Eddie Cantor Show*, Rudy Vallee's *Fleischman Hour,* and *The Jack Pearl Show* (featuring Pearl as Baron Munchausen), leaning toward comedy. All these shows, however, offered one sort of drama or another at least occasionally, and some on a regular basis. Comedy shows, too, successfully introduced audiences to the concept of radio drama with *Amos 'n' Andy,* for example, chronicling the exploits of the two characters for 15 minutes a day, five days a week. *The March of Time*, which began in 1931, even took it upon itself to dramatize events in the news. In February 1934, *45 Minutes in Hollywood* debuted, which succeeded in breaking new ground by managing, through *Photoplay* magazine, to obtain at least a minimum of cooperation from the movie studios. Excerpts from upcoming motion picture releases were dramatized on the show (with anonymous radio players), which also featured interviews with the actual star of the film.[2] During the fall of that same year, the first network show to rely heavily on the participation of film actors was launched. *Hollywood Hotel* began on October 5, 1934, originating from Hollywood, with gossip columnist Louella Parsons using her influence to assure the cooperation of the studios. Though *Hollywood Hotel* was another radio variety show, lengthy scenes from soon-to-be-released films were performed (sometimes taking up nearly half of the hour-long show), with some of the actual stars of the motion pictures playing their screen roles.

The Lux Radio Theatre: The Early Years in New York

Beginning in the 1920s, Lux Toilet Soap used celebrities to endorse the product in magazine advertisements. By the latter part of the decade, the focus of the advertising was already on glamorous motion picture players (and it was in fact during this period that the slogan "Nine out of ten screen stars use Lux Toilet Soap" was invented). Sometime in 1934, the J. Walter Thompson Advertising Agency was successful in persuading its client Lever Brothers to put up the money to record an audition of a proposed hour-long dramatic radio program that would use stars from the stage and screen to perform in the leading roles. In the spring or early summer of that year, an audition recording was made of William Archer's *The Green Goddess*, with Claude Rains as the Rajah of Rukh. Lever Brothers, the manufacturer of Lux products, was intrigued with the idea and agreed to sponsor the new series, which was to be called *The Lux Radio Theatre.*

The first script assembled for *The Lux Radio Theatre* was adapted from the J.M. Barrie London stage success *What Every Woman Knows*, but, perhaps in a wish for a more sure-fire property for the opening program, Austin Strong's famous 1922 love story *Seventh Heaven* was chosen for the October 14, 1934, broadcast. Of course an hour dramatic program could not go on the air without some sort of an introduction, so a host was needed for the show. The fictitious Douglass Garrick, who was referred to as the producer of *The Lux Radio Theatre*, was played by John Anthony that first season, and engaged to lead the orchestra and provide the musical arrangements was well-known radio conductor Robert Armbruster. It was Armbruster's special waltz, composed for the occasion, that was first heard after announcer Ben Grauer's opening declaration on that Sunday afternoon at 2:30 P.M., New York time: "*The Lux Radio Theatre* . . . now playing . . . Miriam Hopkins and John Boles in 'Seventh Heaven.'[3] Anthony as Douglass Garrick briefly chatted about the upcoming play and stars, and was very careful to mention in which current-run pictures they could be seen. Each of the two stars made a brief speech in character, and the curtain was rung up on the first *Lux Radio Theatre* drama.

The show originated from the WJZ studios in Radio City in downtown Manhattan, and, as the broadcasts were coming from New York, it is not surprising that the focus of the series was on Broadway plays. With this in mind, the man engaged to direct the programs was Antony Stanford, a young (born in 1897) native of Dallas, Texas. Stanford was very much a man of the theatre, coming from a theatrical family and having appeared regularly on the stage from his early teens onward. In 1929 he began working in radio regularly, becoming a production director at NBC in 1930 and eventually writing, producing, and acting in CBS's *The March of Time*. His knowledge of theatrical affairs and friendships with Broadway actors were an assurance that *Lux*'s plays would be intelligently selected and cast. Though he was called the director of the show, he actually handled many of the chores that would ordinarily have been assumed by the producer. Although Stanford could request and recommend the plays that were to be performed and the stars who were to appear, it was up to another Thompson employee, Thomas Luckenbill (referred to as the show's producer in the trade journals of the day), to make the booking arrangements. The *Lux* program at this time offered what amounted to condensations of Broadway plays, with little new material added specifically for their radio presentations. It was obviously Stanford's goal to offer a theatrical experience to the multitude of listeners who would never have the opportunity to visit the "Great White Way" in person. Among the radio plays performed that season, all very faithfully adapted from the stage originals, were "The Barker," "Smilin' Through," "Berkeley Square," "Counsellor-at-Law," "The First Year," "Michael and Mary," and "Elmer the Great."

After the first show (in which host Douglass Garrick was joined by a "friend" to discuss the play and the stars prior to the commencement of the drama), the program's format remained fairly consistent throughout that initial season at NBC. Ben Grauer's opening announcement would mention the play and the star or stars (there was often only one featured performer) for the afternoon, after which Garrick would go into his introduction. The play itself was generally in three acts (a few were performed in a four-act format), with commercials coming after the first and second acts. The type of commercial varied. Sometimes Grauer would simply read a straight endorsement of the product; on other occasions either he would be joined by an actor whose words would drive home the point, or a dramatized commercial without Grauer would be performed. Appearing as a regular in each week's show to plug the product was "noted beauty advisor Peggy Winthrop." Actually a fictitious character played by Doris Dagmar, "Peggy Winthrop" had appeared on the air as early as 1931 in an advice-to-listeners program. As in the case of Grauer, Peggy Winthrop's commercials might be done solo or in conjunction with one or more actors in a dramatized segment. A typical example of the latter was heard between the first and second acts of the April 11, 1935, broadcast of "The Broken Wing":

WINTHROP:
It's early evening, around eight o'clock. It's any house . . . perhaps your own. Sis is at her dressing table. She's pretty . . . she's gay . . . she hopes to be eighteen soon . . . and she hasn't a care in the world . . . except an annoying younger brother.
BOY'S VOICE:
Wow! Will you look at Sis! Is that powder and rouge? You think you're grown up, don't you? Well, I'm going to tell . . . (*YELLS*) HEY, M-O-M!
SIS:
Be quiet, Billy. Don't be such a tattle tale . . .
MOTHER:
Billy, what *are* you yelling about? Oh—I know Ruthie uses rouge and powder. All her friends do and she's allowed to use them just as much as she likes. As long as she removes them the *Lux Toilet Soap* way, they won't do her skin one bit of harm. (*FADEOUT*) In fact, Billy, a little Lux Toilet wouldn't *hurt your ears* . . .
WINTHROP:
Lux Toilet Soap is especially made to remove cosmetics thoroughly so they can't *choke your pores.* Choked pores become enlarged . . . and it's then that dullness and tiny blemishes warn you "You've got cosmetic skin!" . . . [4]

After the dramatic portion had concluded, the star(s) would appear out of character for an "informal" (though scripted) chat with Garrick. It was during this segment of the show (which usually included the star's endorsement of the product) that the play and star for the following week's show would be announced.

The many different types of plays performed on Broadway were well reflected in the selection aired on *The Lux Radio Theatre.* "Seventh Heaven" the drama, set in Paris, of a physically and emotionally abused street waif whose life is rebuilt through her love for a carefree street-washer, was, as mentioned, the play that initiated the series, and this sort of sentimental love story was typical of the type of program that found favor with *Lux*'s audience. "The Nervous Wreck," performed on November 11, 1934, is a comedy about a hypochondriac from Pittsburgh who goes west for his health, while "Counsellor-at-Law" is a serious drama about a modern-day New York attorney whose life is in danger of falling apart at the seams.

One feature that made *The Lux Radio Theatre* different from other radio dramatic programs of the period was the presence each week of one or more well-known stars of the stage or screen in the leading parts. Because *The Lux Radio Theatre* aired all over the United States, including isolated areas far from any legitimate theatre, it was thought important to cast players who had national reputations. Therefore, the show gradually began to favor stars of the screen over those of the stage; nonetheless, the first season featured many well-known performers recreating roles they had played on the Broadway stage some years previously. For example, the fourth show in the series cast Jane Cowl in "Smilin' Through," in which she had starred on Broadway some 15 years earlier. (Miss Cowl was also the co-author of the play.) The previous week had seen Walter Huston reprise one of his favorite stage roles in "The Barker," and other shows during that season featured Leslie Howard, Paul Muni, Roland Young, Minnie Dupree, Ina Claire, and Pauline Lord in their original parts. The program of May 12, 1935, brought to the airwaves a play currently running on Broadway, *The Bishop Misbehaves*; the radio version featured virtually the entire cast of the production (led by Walter Connolly, Jane Wyatt, and Alan Marshal) then playing at the Cort Theatre. (This was, according to Garrick, the first time in the history of the broadcast medium that this feat was accomplished.) Such was Stanford's dedication to recreating the flavor of the Broadway originals that in many cases even relatively small supporting roles were filled by the same actors who had created them on the stage. The June 1935 *Stage* article by Ruth Woodbury Sedgwick noted that "stars have stood up to the microphone before, and read lines into the air. But what was attempted in the *Lux Radio Theatre* and, in the main, achieved, was that faithful reproduction of character, story, environment, which transforms a fine play into a living experience."[5]

Preparations for *The Lux Radio Theatre* may well have been greater than for any radio dramatic hour that had preceded it to the air. Acquiring the rights to the plays (a task performed by Thomas Luckenbill) was relatively simple in comparison to securing the services of the starring players. Sedgwick stated:

> It is Mr. Luckenbill's job to buy the stars. Buying a star sounds like a radiant enterprise, but it isn't. The one he wants is usually in South Africa

or the Holy Land. If the star isn't abroad, he is sure to be just going. For instance, when they were casting "Little Women" for the Easter program he had to find four famous actresses known to all America whose gifts and personalities would fit those hallowed and familiar roles.... The first and perfect choice was the Gish sisters. They would have been delighted to do it but were sailing that Saturday for Greece. By practically making over all the spring schedules for trans–Atlantic travel, Mr. Luckenbill arranged for them to take a later boat and still arrive in Greece in time to meet their automobile, which had already been shipped. With two little women snared, he started for the third. Helen Chandler would have loved to play Amy, but she was just off to Spain—her Honeymoon, what could she do about it! It is not easy to convince a bride that to arrive in Spain before Easter is not only foolhardy, but apt to be fatal. Mr. Luckenbill did it, however. Trembling, he then approached Sylvia Field, and nearly collapsed from anti-climax. She was *not* abroad. She only had to upset a theatric engagement and her entire family to be able to play Beth.[6]

The show also received considerably more rehearsal time than most, with Stanford often working with his cast as long as 30 hours in preparation for the hour-long program. Rehearsals could begin as early as Monday, with the first dress rehearsal usually taking place on Friday. Saturday would be the day off, and the final dress rehearsal would take place Sunday morning just prior to the afternoon broadcast. The schedule was flexible and could change depending on the availability of the stars. Because of his stage background, director Tony Stanford preferred to use actors of the legitimate theatre for the supporting roles. Many of the stage performers in New York at that time were also making radio appearances, and, as Broadway had suffered hard times because of the Depression, some had abandoned the stage entirely in favor of the theatre of the air. Still, radio was a relatively new medium, and consequently Stanford found it necessary to give more direction to the actors than would his successors on the West Coast. Writer George Wells recollected that Stanford "gave a lot of direction—he was the boss. They listened to him because nobody knew anything about radio—he did. He was the one-eyed man in a nation of blind men."[7] Jonathan Hole, a stage actor who began performing on radio in 1926, appeared in two New York *Luxes* under Antony Stanford's direction:

> In those days, he was getting mostly stage actors—most of us were from the stage ... and, of course, a lot of them didn't know anything about a microphone.... Most of the actors from the stage were used to projecting, and in radio, you didn't have to project, but he would draw chalk lines around the microphone and tell the actors they could speak normally ... as long as they kept within those marks.[8]

A possible distraction to stage actors appearing on *The Lux Radio Theatre* during this period was the lack of an audience, as no studio audience was admitted to the broadcasts. This may have been particularly unsettling during comedies, but, as Mr. Hole noted, "That was where your experience of the stage came in, because you more or less knew where the laughs should be."[9]

Another important member of the *Lux Radio Theatre* production team was the writer. George Wells was a 24-year-old stage actor (who had also appeared in a few Hollywood films) and the son of successful comedy writer and former vaudeville headliner Billy K. Wells when he began his *Lux* association. Wells, a native New Yorker, recently recalled his start with *Lux*:

> I knew that *The Lux Radio Theatre* was going to do adaptations of plays and I thought I might take a crack at it. And I went over and spoke to somebody I knew there and they didn't want to do it, but they finally let me write a script on speculation (a practice which is forbidden now by the Guild), and they liked my work. They still hadn't opened the show, and they handed me that first show to fix up.[10]

Wells went on to pen the rest of the *Lux* programs that season, and he would stay with the series as principal writer for the next nine years. There is more to adapting a full-length stage play to radio than just cutting it. Purely visual scenes in the theatre which cannot be effectively translated to the nonvisual medium must be replaced by something entirely new if they are essential to the plot, and sound effects play a great part in the telling of a story on the air. A segment of *Lux*'s broadcast of "Counsellor-at-Law" was described in a *New York Times* article of the period:

> The door closed and the unseen audience knew the lawyer was alone in his office. From previous dialogue, the listeners were aware that he was intending to commit suicide, he did not have to tell them directly. Then, after a slight pause, all the listener heard after the door closed was a window raised, traffic noises, and foghorns on the river giving a perfect sound picture of a lofty downtown office. Then the door opened; the window slammed, and before any further dialogue was spoken, the listener knew the window had been closed; that the lawyer had been interrupted by someone entering the room and that he did not jump out of the window. It all happened quickly on the air, but if the sounds had not been skillfully handled, the listener would have been muddled. That is an excellent example of the director's skill where timing is vital.[11]

The same article featured Wells's explanation of how he adapted a play to the air. The drama was broken down into scenes:

> Each time a character enters or leaves the stage, we consider it a scene. Then each scene is checked for its importance. First, has it anything to do with telling the story; does it bear directly on the plot? If so, it is very important. If not, is it a character bit important for the star of the show? It

may act so well that it would be a shame to cut it from the radio performance. All scenes of a good play bear on the plot, therefore, the better the play is written, the closer it is knit, and that makes the adapter's task more difficult.... The man who adapts is a blender. He is not a butcher. He must be extremely skillful, for he will find every script calls for a new bag of tricks. Every play necessitates novel stunts performed by words and all sorts of sounds. There is no single formula to fall back upon. The fact that radio calls for cuts in plays does by no means indicate that broadcasting destroys them. It is merely a transformation from one medium to another; what is essential in one may be utterly worthless in the other, and so to gain the most entertaining performance certain parts can be dropped and never be missed.[12]

It took a great deal of ingenuity to bring some scenes to radio, and the skillful Wells handled these difficulties very successfully. An example of this talent is cited in a *Radio Stars* article from 1936. Referring to *Lux*'s broadcast of "The Bishop Misbehaves," author Dora Albert said,

In the original play, a woman holds up the Bishop, saying to him: "Hold up your hands!" She didn't have a gun or anything else to hold him up with, but the Bishop, who was holding up a gang of desperadoes, meekly obeyed. Over the air, that would sound just silly. Mr. Wells hit on the idea of having the woman hold up the Bishop by prodding his back with a monkey-wrench. Thinking it's a gun, he puts up his hands. Later he discovers he was held up with a monkey-wrench. "An old trick but a useful one," says the woman, grinning. When Mr. Golden, producer of the play, heard this scene over the air, he said, "For heaven's sake, why didn't I do that!"[13]

Unlike the television programs of today, *The Lux Radio Theatre* was produced not by the network but by the advertising agency; NBC (and later CBS) was merely the means of conveyance and was paid by the sponsor for leasing the airtime. No one individual served as producer of *Lux*; instead these duties were divided among several people. As previously noted, Antony Stanford suggested the plays and stars and cast the supporting roles, while Thomas Luckenbill handled the booking arrangements. The vice president of Thompson's West Coast operations was Danny Danker, who was in charge of making the arrangements with the Hollywood studios for *Lux* to borrow their stars, and his influence was even more advantageous after the show moved to California and began using picture players on a weekly basis. Putting together a weekly live radio program, in fact, required the participation of a great many people who never appeared on the air. Despite the meticulous planning that went into each week's production, occasional unforeseen circumstances could cause some last-minute scurrying about. One such instance occurred in connection with the broadcast of "Peg o' My Heart" on February 3, 1935. Margaret Sullavan was scheduled to play the title role in Hartley Manner's comedy that Sunday and had rehearsed the show all week, but on the morning of the broadcast (which was to go on the air at 2:30) Stanford got word that Sullavan had been stricken with laryngitis and could not go on. Immediately, he telephoned Helen Hayes, who expressed an interest in the project until she discovered that the program was to be performed that very afternoon. Shortly afterward, Stanford received a call from Hayes's husband, Charles MacArthur, notifying him that she had reconsidered and would be there as soon as possible. As a precautionary measure, in the event that Hayes did not arrive in time, Helen Chandler was called in to stand by if needed. By the time Hayes arrived at the NBC studios in Radio City, it was well past the noon hour, and her nervousness was compounded when she discovered that she had left home without her eyeglasses. Borrowing her husband's spectacles, Hayes and the cast plunged into the dress rehearsal, which, with the show slated to begin in about an hour and a half, would be the only run-through the star would be allowed. Meanwhile, out of respect for Helen Hayes, Margaret Sullavan had arrived to apologize for the inconvenience that Hayes was being put through. The show came off without a hitch and was described by Stanford as "a fine performance under great difficulties."[14] Sullavan remained throughout the broadcast and said a few words at the end of the show.

Well before the end of the 1934-35 season, it was evident that *The Lux Radio Theatre* was a critical success. It was, in fact, presented with the Radio Editors of America Award for the best dramatic program of the year. Although the cost of putting the show on (averaging over $4,000 per week before network costs) was but a fraction of what the weekly budget would be after the move to Hollywood, the series was still relatively expensive to produce. Lever Brothers felt that, for the money they were spending, they would like a larger listening audience. *Lux*'s Crossley rating of 17.1 (indicating that 17.1 percent of American homes with radios were tuned in to the program on any given Sunday) was very good for its time slot and a respectable rating for any time of the day, but both the client and the agency felt that a move to a more favorable time slot would boost listenership tremendously. The rival Columbia Broadcasting System was willing to make available the nine o'clock Monday evening time slot, and this became the hour during which *The Lux Radio Theatre* would be heard for the next 18 years.

The second season began on July 28, 1935, with Helen Hayes in "Bunty Pulls the Strings," a comedy by Graham Moffatt. The format of the series at CBS was basically the same as it had been on NBC, the minor changes being a new announcer in the person of Art Millett, the deletion of the Peggy Winthrop character (though Doris Dagmar continued to appear in commercials now and then), and a new Douglas Garrick. In March 1935, auditions had been held for a new actor to portray *Lux*'s producer-host.

Those trying out for the role of Garrick were Edwin Jerome, Harry Neeley, and Albert Hayes; Parker Fennelly also auditioned at that time, not for Garrick but for *Lux* host under his own name. Albert Hayes, a stage actor with radio experience (he had appeared in a *Lux* commercial during the first season), was awarded the job of portraying the fictitious Mr. Garrick (though Ed Jerome did appear as an anonymous master of ceremonies one week when Hayes was indisposed). The new season brought much the same mixture of comedies and dramas as had the old, but as the year progressed, it became evident that a new emphasis was being placed on casting motion picture players. Among the film stars making their *Lux* debuts that season were Joan Crawford, Joan Bennett, Douglas Fairbanks, Jr., Clark Gable, Edward G. Robinson, and Bette Davis. Highlights included the 80-year-old William Gillette portraying the title character in the radio version of his own 1899 play, "Sherlock Holmes," and Lillian Gish and Richard Barthelmess recreating their screen roles in a broadcast of "Way Down East" (which, however, was based on the stage play, *not* on the film). The April 20 broadcast was a foreshadowing of things to come as the offering for that date was an adaptation for radio of the 1935 movie *Harmony Lane*—the first *Lux* broadcast based on a motion picture property. As the season wore on, writer George Wells began to add more and more new material to the stage plays that he adapted to the air:

> I kept pushing for what I called "motion picture technique," to open up the story, not to tell it the way the stage tells it. The old plays had a butler on the telephone: "Oh, the master had been very ill, sir, and he has this big deal coming, of course, but cannot tend to it now. He's becoming quite irritable." That sort of thing . . . so you knew what was happening before the master showed up. That was a pretty flimsy way to tell a story, and they were stuck with it in the theatre. [Antony Stanford] had a great love for theatre. He'd been an actor, his wife had been an actress, they had played stock half their lives . . . He was full of the tradition, and it was very nice to be that way, but when you carry it into a modern form of entertainment, you have to do things with it. It all started with "Alias Jimmy Valentine" [aired September 30, 1935], that was the one I had the big problem with . . . you didn't even have the crutch, which is a door opening and closing to allow people to enter a scene . . . you had a lobby, and that's where it was played. I said, "I can't do that, I can't do the opening . . . where people tell stories about him" . . . It was agony, and I couldn't make it understandable for radio. I wanted to show him getting out of prison—it seemed so logical. Not a brilliant scene, just a good way of telling a story. Motion pictures had a good technique, and you could use the same thing in radio.[15]

Wells eliminated the scene in the hotel lobby entirely, and *Lux*'s "Alias Jimmy Valentine" opened with a quiet scene in a restaurant between the recently pardoned safecracker and the tenacious detective who continues to hound him. This brief opening sequence not only succeeds in introducing two of the main characters to the audience, but it also explains all the audience needs to know of the title character's past.

The *Lux* broadcasts performed prior to "Alias Jimmy Valentine" (as well as many that followed it) took little advantage of the radio medium's potential. The adaptations faithfully translated the originals, down to retaining the settings, although a radio drama could easily be set virtually anywhere that was desired without any additional expenditure. Though radio, like any medium, has its limitations, Wells felt that there was no reason why radio should inherit the limitations of the stage. Music in the *Lux* broadcasts during the seasons in New York also contributed to creating a theatrical atmosphere, for it was rarely used except during the show's opening and closing and at the beginning and conclusion of each act. Even musical bridges, which would later (in Hollywood) be so effectively used to indicate transitions in time or place between scenes, were only occasionally employed. "Tony didn't like musical interludes," George Wells explained. "He wanted straight action."[16]

After the "Alias Jimmy Valentine" program (which, incidentally, Antony Stanford described as a "splendid adaptation"),[17] Wells began to interject original material more frequently into his scripts and to exercise his new (relative) freedom, more often employing locales that would have been impossible in the theatre. The more modern-style scripts also called for greater and more imaginative use of sound effects, which had always been kept to a minimum prior to this. In "Song and Dance Man" (performed on March 23, 1936), George M. Cohan, the author of the play and the man who had played the title role in the stage production 13 years earlier, had a scene in which he converses with the heroine of the piece while doing a dance routine. Cohan noticed that this sequence in the radio script indicated "*SOUND:* Tap Dance." Inquiring about the direction's meaning, he was informed that it was nothing for him to worry about, as the sound effects man would create the sound of the tap steps. Cohan insisted, however, that since he had done his own tap dancing when playing the part in the theatre, he would do it in the broadcast as well. So, at his request, a special sounding board was brought in and placed over the carpet, and a microphone was fastened down at the star's feet, and he did indeed perform the unheard-of act of creating his own sound effects during the scene.[18]

As *Lux*'s second season progressed, two things became apparent: that the added competition in the 9:00 P.M. time slot hurt *Lux*'s ratings (the 1935-36 season's rating was actually down 3.5 points from that of the first season), and that the producers favored employing well-known motion picture actors over Broadway stars. It was often with great difficulty that movie stars were persuaded to travel the 3,000 miles to New York for a single radio broadcast, and if this usage of motion picture players was to continue, it would be much to *Lux*'s advantage to move the show to the movie capital.

Beginning in February 1936, John Gilman, the Lever Brothers head of advertising, began conferring with people at J. Walter Thompson about revamping *The Lux Radio Theatre*. At a meeting on Febrary 4, the idea of changing the format of the program entirely, possibly to that of a musical variety show, was suggested. Whether *Lux* remained a dramatic program or not, a decision was made that the fictitious "Douglass Garrick" feature would be dropped. Lever decided a "personality" was needed as master of ceremonies—"not necessarily a famous name. But could have a famous name."[19] Persons suggested to fill this important position were: George M. Cohan, D.W. Griffith, Cecil B. DeMille, Charles Winninger, Leading Man of *One Man's Family* (J. Anthony Smythe), Leslie Howard, John Boles, Walter Huston, Walter Connolly, Wallace Beery, Frank Morgan, Conrad Nagel, Kenneth MacKenna, Osgood Perkins, George Bancroft, Noah Beery, Fred Stone, Rupert Hughes, Irvin S. Cobb, Guy Bates Post, and Frank Crummit. Other suggestions were made about the program, such as possibly interpolating the commercials into the drama itself, à la the Jack Benny program ("Can't kid about Lux Toilet Soap or Lux, however").[20] Methods of getting the audience involved in the program were considered, such as having one promising young player in the cast about whom the audience could vote, with a possible reward of a year's scholarship; offering play-writing contests; or presenting "acting contests in 500 towns, with winners on *Lux* show. Like little theatre tournaments . . . listeners would vote on those members of the cast they thought were outstanding. Award membership in *Lux Radio Theatre* Guild."[21] It was even suggested that stars could perform the first two acts of the drama and a group of amateurs could do the third act. Fortunately, the basic format of the show remained much the same, but the location would definitely change.

The Move to Hollywood

> Hollywood California—Monday, June 1, 1936. Ladies and gentlemen, we have grand news for you tonight, for *The Lux Radio Theatre* has moved to Hollywood and here we are in a theatre of our very own. The Lux Radio Theatre, Hollywood Boulevard, in the motion picture capital of the world. The curtain rises![22]

These words opened the *Lux Radio Theatre* broadcast from its new home in Hollywood, California. Now the Lux Radio Theatre was a real place, the 965-seat Music Box Theatre on 6126 Hollywood Boulevard (today known as the Henry Fonda Theatre). Audiences, which were not admitted to the program when it was in New York, were very much a part of the revamped West Coast version of *The Lux Radio Theatre*, and in the first few shows from California, dignitaries present in the audience were often identified for those listening in at home. The production team was almost entirely different from that in New York, with only writer George Wells resuming his position. The new musical director (in charge of conducting the orchestra and preparing the musical scores) was an Academy Award–winning composer-conductor for motion pictures, Louis Silvers. With music playing a more important part in the Hollywood *Luxes*, his skills would be much used. The new program director was Frank Woodruff, a Columbia, South Carolina, native (born in 1906), who had come to Hollywood a year earlier to direct Al Jolson's *Shell Chateau*. It took a man of unique talents to handle the more temperamental stars, some of whom might possibly resent taking orders from a young man they had never even heard of before. But, as Woodruff's widow recently commented:

> He didn't have an awful lot of trouble with stars because, having been an actor, he understood actors. And there is a difference with a lot of people—Frank loved actors and that was why he could always understand them, get along with them. If they didn't like something, he'd say, "Let's try it your way..." Almost every big star of that time wrote a letter thanking him for the opportunity of working on *Lux*, because they wanted to work in radio and they wanted to do *Lux—Lux Radio Theatre* was the finest dramatic program always in its day.[23]

Another important addition to the Hollywood staff was Sanford Barnett, who had been transferred from Thompson's New York office to write the framework of the show (the portions of the show other than the dramatic—that is, the commercials, introduction, curtain call, and intermission spots). Barnett, a scholarly young man who was born in 1908, began at Thompson in 1930 as a copywriter, having worked previously as a reporter on the *Newark Evening News* and the *New York Times*, and as an office assistant at WOR radio in New York. Barnett would also be responsible for penning a new feature especially created for the Hollywood *Lux*— the intermission spot. Beginning with that first West Coast *Lux* on June 1, special guests would appear after Acts 2 and 3 to chat with the host. These guests were generally associated with the motion picture industry and were often in one way or another connected to the play being presented that particular week. That first show featured producer Jesse Lasky and Paramount casting director Fred Datig, and following weeks would see the likes of silent screen actress Theda Bara, illustrator James Montgomery Flagg, motion picture producer-directors D.W. Griffith and Hal Roach, Hollywood cartoonist Feg Murray, columnist Sheilah Graham, and MGM portrait photographer George Hurrell. The presence of these Hollywood luminaries contributed greatly to bringing the flavor of the movie capital to listeners across the United States. The procedure for the creation of these spots was for Barnett to interview the guests, write the dialogue for them and for host Cecil B. DeMille, and then submit it to the subjects for their approval. Barnett also saw to it that at least one of these talks per show contained an enthusiastic endorsement of Lux Toilet Soap of Lux Flakes.

Two announcers were used for the show: Frank Nelson announced the play and the stars at the very opening of the program, and Melville Ruick, who handled the regular announcer's duties, took over for the remainder of the show. Undoubtedly one of the most exciting additions to the new version of *Lux* was the presence of a new host, one of the most influential producer-directors in the motion picture industry and a man whose name was well known even among casual moviegoers: Cecil B. DeMille.

DeMille, who was born on August 12, 1881, in Ashfield, Massachusetts, came from a theatrical family and got his first experience before the footlights when he made his acting debut in 1900. He continued to act while occasionally writing plays with his brother, William C. deMille (who retained the original lower-case *d* of the family name), until starting up a motion picture firm (which would eventually become Paramount Pictures) with Jesse Lasky in 1913. His first directorial effort was 1914's *The Squaw Man* (codirected by Oscar Apfel), shot in and around his new headquarters, a barn in the then-rural community of Hollywood, California; other movies quickly followed. By the late 'teens the young man was one of filmdom's best-known behind-the-scenes figures, having already turned out such artistic triumphs as *The Cheat* (1915), *Joan the Woman* (1917), *Romance of the Redwoods* (1917), and *The Whispering Chorus* (1918), as he worked toward such unforgettable epics as *The Ten Commandments* (1923), *The King of Kings* (1927), *The Sign of the Cross* (1932), and *The Crusades* (1935).

Lux's new host, like the spurious Douglass Garrick before him, was credited on the air as the "producer," but actually these duties were still being distributed among several persons in the J. Walter Thompson agency. It would, of course, have been impossible for the exceedingly busy DeMille to take on the assignment of producing a weekly radio show (a full-time job in itself), but the mere mention of Cecil B. DeMille was synonymous with quality and integrity in the movie business, and his association with *The Lux Radio Theatre* was extremely beneficial to the program. DeMille proved to be the perfect on-the-air host as well, actually sounding the way many people assumed an important and dignified producer should sound, and his obvious sincerity gave him the ability to get the full dramatic effect out of his lines without sounding flowery. Cecil B. DeMille clearly took great pride in his new position, saying of the show in his 1959 autobiography that

> it meant families in Maine and Kansas and Idaho finishing the dishes or
> the schoolwork or the evening chores in time to gather around their radios.
> It meant the shut-ins, the invalid, the blind, the very young, and the very

Lux Radio Theatre publicity photo of host Cecil B. DeMille, circa 1940.

old who had no taste of the theater. It meant people, not in the mass, but individuals, who did me the honor of inviting me into their homes, people to whom I was no longer a name filtered through the wordage of imaginative press agents, but a person whom they knew. And I would be less human than even my critics would allow, if I were not touched when people, recognizing me on trains or in stores or on the street in almost any city I visited, told me that they liked those Monday evenings, and the little comments I made between the acts of the *Lux* plays, and my "greetings" and "goodnight."[24]

It mattered little that, due to his extremely tight schedule, DeMille did not arrive until dress rehearsal; to listeners, Cecil B. DeMille was synonymous with *The Lux Radio Theatre*.

Stories of DeMille's activities on *Lux* quickly moved into the realm of folklore. Ralph Bellamy recalled the director's mode of attire for his air appearances as "a hunting jacket, puttees and riding britches."[25] Actor Jeff Corey remembered a 1940s incident that clearly displayed the director's strong feelings for his radio work:

> There were some terrible rainstorms and he was at his ranch (in Riverside County), and he got on a horse and he went through the muck and the floods and all that, and then got transportation and came to the theatre for the performance in his mud-splattered puttees and riding crop in hand.[26]

The new location brought the availability of new supporting players. Lou Merrill and Frank Nelson quickly became fixtures of the Hollywood *Lux*, appearing nearly every week in a wide variety of roles, and persons primarily known as movie character actors, such as Ynez Seabury, Chester Clute, Byron Foulger, and Rolfe Sedan, graced many a cast in *Lux's* early West Coast years. As expected, most, though not all, of the Hollywood *Luxes* were based on motion pictures, and it was the desire of J. Walter Thompson and Lever Brothers that the original screen stars be cast in the radio versions whenever possible. Consequently, such stories as "The Jazz Singer," with Al Jolson, "Elmer the Great," with Joe E. Brown, "The Virginian," with Gary Cooper, "Captain Blood," with Errol Flynn and Olivia deHavilland, "Magnificent Obsession," with Irene Dunne and Robert Taylor, and "Death Takes a Holiday," with Fredric March, were among those shows performed that first season from Hollywood. Among the stage plays adapted for the air were *Irene*, with Jeanette MacDonald, *The Brat*, with Marion Davies and Joel McCrea, *The Curtain Rises*, with Ginger Rogers and Warren William, and *Dulcy*, with George Burns and Gracie Allen. The cooperation between J. Walter Thompson and the movie studios was now of the utmost importance. Stars, of course, could not appear on any radio program without the permission of their studio, nor could any motion picture be adapted without the consent of the company that produced it. These motion picture radio rights were sometimes leased to *Lux* for a fee (rarely exceeding $1,000) and were sometimes presented to *Lux* gratis in exchange for publicity on the air. Paramount, for example, offered *Lux* the right to produce *The Gilded Lily* on the air, specifying that, in return, their current releases *Maid of Salem* and *Champagne Waltz* would be mentioned during the course of the program. It was apparent from the start that *Lux's* intelligent adaptations and excellent productions found favor with the studios, who trusted the artistic judgment of those in charge of putting the shows on the air.

The studios generally did not ask for and did not receive permission to examine the radio adaptations of their properties prior to their going on the air, nor did they make an issue of who would be cast in them, as a rule. "They didn't think radio was very important," George Wells explained. "They ignored radio to begin with except for the publicity they could get out of it—just as they ignored television in the early days."[27] One exception was the conscientious producer David O. Selznick, who not only read the script prior to the broadcast but also proposed some worthwhile changes.

Many of the stars appearing in *The Lux Radio Theatre* were motion picture players with little or no experience whatsoever in the legitimate theatre. Consequently, those stars finding themselves on a stage in front of a microphone with a studio audience of nearly 1,000 people looking on and countless millions more listening in, with nothing more to assist them in their characterizations than a printed script, might well have been overwhelmed by the magnitude of the situation. Nearly all gave thoroughly capable performances, but some positively excelled in this challenging medium, giving truly memorable performances. Among the stars who proved themselves splendid radio performers in that ground-breaking first Hollywood season were Maureen O'Sullivan, Marion Davies, Jean Harlow, Robert Taylor, Pat O'Brien, Jean Arthur, Joan Crawford, and Bette Davis.

The Artistic Development

As *The Lux Radio Theatre* progressed, it began to take even greater advantage of the audio medium. Unfortunately today, just as many discount the value of silent films because of their inability to speak, there are some people who assume that radio is somehow inferior to talking pictures and television because of its lack of a visual element. This judgment, however, is decidedly not the case. All media are limited in one way or another; clever people working in those media have the ability not only to work around these limitations, but actually to use them to their advantage. The translation of a motion picture into a radio play is every bit as legitimate as the translation of a novel into a film. Far from being a mere condensation for the airwaves, the radio adaptation of a movie is an art form in itself. That is not to say that all pictures translate equally well to radio, but some (especially those damaged by substandard production values) are actually improved as an audio production.

One trick in telling a story on the air is to make dialogue seem natural even when describing an action that would need no description in a visual medium. *Lux*'s adapters were especially skilled at this art, nearly always avoiding obvious lines such as "Oh, you've got a gun!" or "Hey, you slapped me!" George Wells, in recalling a thriller program that he heard when he was *Lux*'s principal writer, described a scene in which there were two men locked in a room with a tiger, "and one man would describe every action of the tiger: 'He's getting on the table . . . look out! He's on the table . . . be careful! . . . Oh, he's crouching down!' Finally, it reached the climax and he said, 'He's springing through the air!'"[28]

Obviously, this kind of dialogue was to be avoided at all costs. There is a scene in the 1951 Warner Bros. picture *Goodbye, My Fancy* in which the Frank Lovejoy character kisses the Joan Crawford character against her will, and she forcefully pushes him away. There is no dialogue to describe the events, and there is no need for any. The obvious line to insert in a radio adaptation would be the oft-used (on other programs), "Oh, you kissed me!" *Lux*'s Sandy Barnett, however, gave the man the line "Sorry I smeared your lipstick," which not only tips the listener off as to what has transpired, but is in keeping with the character of the wisecracking newspaperman who said it *and* is a good piece of dialogue as well. It all passes very quickly and was perhaps hardly noticed by listeners, but is typical of the manner in which *Lux*'s adapters avoided clumsy and unnatural-sounding dialogue.

While radio is technically a nonvisual medium, it is the job of the production team, including the scripter, composer, sound effects man, and the actors, to assist listeners in creating an image in their minds. When these artists are as adept at their craft as those of *The Lux Radio Theatre* were, the results often add up to a powerful listening experience.

With the first Hollywood show beginning late in the season, 1936 turned out to be the only year, save for the special series in 1953, that *Lux* ran through the summer. No expense was spared in assembling the *Lux* Hollywood shows. Though it was considered a costly show to put on when it originated from New York, the tab for the California *Lux*es regularly ran three or four times as much as those from the East Coast. The top salary for stars, which had been established during the first season in New York, remained $5,000, but the additional expenditures greatly expanded the weekly payroll. There was, for instance, rarely more than one top-salaried star per cast in the New York shows, whereas in Hollywood there were always at least two stars, who were often joined by two, three, or even more featured players. Add DeMille's salary of $2,000 (later $2,500) to the already hefty weekly payroll and the total could reach as much as $20,000—and this did not even include the network's bill for their airtime. The higher budget paid off, however, for the stellar casts and the presence of DeMille created considerable prestige for the product and gave the program a tremendous increase in listenership. (The 1936-37 rating of 25.1 was nearly double that of the previous season.)

Lux started off as a smoothly produced series in Hollywood, and it became even more polished as it progressed. The format remained basically the same until the 1939-40 season, when the intermission guest spot was dropped in favor of a standard commercial, as was the second announcer (Frank Nelson), who, after the opening fanfare (which was also deleted), had heralded the date, title, and stars of the show. Now, Melville Ruick opened each show with the proclamation "Lux presents Hollywood" (which had formerly come at a later point in the introduction); this was followed by the same theme that had been used in every *Lux* show since the beginning. At the end of the 1938-39 season, director Frank Woodruff, who had so effectively served the series since its move to Hollywood, left to become a motion picture director at RKO, and writer George Wells was offered the position. Wells was an independent artist, not an employee of the J. Walter Thompson Agency, and consequently his was a higher-paying job than that of director, so, as much as he liked the idea of directing the show, he turned down the offer. The next obvious person to ask was Sandy Barnett, who had been writing the show's framework for the past three years, and who accepted the position. Junior Coghlan, who appeared in several *Luxes* during this period, compared the styles of the two men:

> Woodruff was an actor's director and Sandy was more of a writer's director. Frank was much more flamboyant, and if he did give you instructions, he'd act it out for you. Sandy was very low-key. He stood at his little stand and looked at his script and pointed his finger at you for a cue but very rarely did he give you dramatic input like Woodruff would.[29]

Although *Variety*'s "Hobe." noted in his review of "The Awful Truth," *Lux*'s opener for the 1939-40 season, that "Actual producer is Sandy Barnett, of the J. Walter Thompson staff, who is turning in his first important production job on this show,"[30] the change went unheeded by most listeners as the series continued on its usual course. *Variety* referred to the show's director as its producer, which he was, as much as any one man could lay claim to the title on *The Lux Radio Theatre,* and it was he who was responsible for assembling the show every week, hiring the supporting players, and so forth. But as George Wells recalled,

> The stars themselves were a matter of whether we could get them. And Sandy and Frank and the rest of them, they couldn't be involved in that. We would give them our preference as to which stars we should try to get, but very often we had to settle for [someone else].[31]

In the position of booking the stars (a job later called "talent buyer") were, at one time or another in Hollywood, Paul Rickenbacher, Norm Blackburn, and Harry Kerr. (Harry Kerr began his association with the program as framework writer, filling that vacancy after Sandy Barnett became director.) "We tried to match stars with the vehicle that they had played but . . . we weren't always successful," explained Wells.[32]

Some of the properties were acquired in an arrangement similar to the block-booking system of silent picture days, in which several screenplays were purchased at once for one price. In August 1938, for example, *Lux* took advantage of Warner Bros.' offer to select any 12 movies from a list of 20 for $10,000. This deal gave *Lux* the exclusive air rights to the stories up to October 1, 1939, after which time they could not be broadcast without further arrangements with the studio. These block-booking deals were the exception rather than the rule, however, and most properties were acquired one at a time. This meant considerable behind-the-scenes activity to prepare each week's program, with several staff members of J. Walter Thompson working furiously to secure the broadcast rights of the plays, sign up the often elusive stars, and get approval from the client (Lever Brothers) for everything.

Assuming "Pygmalion" from November 27, 1939, to be typical in format (if not in story matter), a *Lux* show from the period usually progressed in something like the following manner:

> RUICK: Lux presents Hollywood.
>> (*THEME IN*)
>
> The Lux Radio Theatre brings you Jean Arthur and Brian Aherne in "Pygmalion."
>> (*PAUSE*)
>
> Ladies and gentlemen, your producer . . . Mr. Cecil B. DeMille.
>> (*THEME: UP AND OUT*)
>> (*APPLAUSE*)[33]

DeMille's introduction, always preceded by his "greetings from Hollywood, ladies and gentlemen," would touch on the play and the stars, and would naturally contain a brief plug for Lux Toilet Soap or, in this case, Lux Flakes:

> From the standpoint of the woman, "Pygmalion" is pure Cinderella . . . and that gives it a special appeal for every woman. The story of Cinderella will never grow old because it expresses the longing of all women to be more beautiful. Of course, the pumpkin coach and glass slippers are a little out of date. Present day Cinderellas who want to catch the eye of some handsome prince are more likely to depend on that fresh out of the bandbox look and are sure there's a good supply of Lux Flakes on hand. In fact, I suppose a modern Cinderella considers Lux Flakes standard equipment.[34]

DeMille himself serves as narrator, setting the scene for Act 1, and the play is under way. George Bernard Shaw's familiar story of a cockney flower girl who is transformed into a lady by an elocution professor proceeds until

18 minutes and 45 seconds into the show, when DeMille returns and introduces announcer Melville Ruick and a singing trio (the Modernettes). After a few words from Ruick, the trio sings a version of "Whistle While You Work" from the Walt Disney animated feature *Snow White and the Seven Dwarfs*, but with new words that point out the marvelous effectiveness of Lux Flakes.

The conclusion of the commercial finds DeMille back at the microphone to introduce and set the scene for Act 2 of the play.

Forty-one minutes and ten seconds into the show marks the spot for the second commercial, this time featuring Ruick and *Lux*'s "Hollywood reporter," Libby Collins, another purely fictional character in the tradition of "beauty expert" Peggy Winthrop from the New York years. On this occasion, Libby (played by Margaret Brayton) cannot resist telling Ruick about Barbara Stanwyck's sweater collection, and the announcer points out that one can "get more pleasure and longer wear out of your sweaters by caring for them with gentle Lux Flakes." Then Libby adds, "Just the way the leading studios here in Hollywood do. They use Lux because it's so dependable. It does a grand job of keeping all washables bright and new-looking."[35]

The play comes to a conclusion 55 minutes and ten seconds into the program, at which point Ruick performs a dialogue with another running commercial character, Sally (here played by Julie Bannon). After they deliver the message that "about a penny's worth of Lux will wash your stockings *four* times. Or your underthings *three* times," DeMille returns to interview the evening's stars. Their brief chat concentrates on the mythological origins of "Pygmalion," until Brian Aherne brings the conversation to an abrupt close with the question, "What's the bill for next week?"

DEMILLE:
Next Monday night, Brian . . . we're going to present Bob Burns and Anita Louise in "A Man to Remember," one of the most heart warming stories to come from the screen in several years. It's the drama of a country doctor . . . one of those truly great men who are known and loved in every small American community . . . and Bob Burns as our country doctor will be "A Man to Remember."

ARTHUR:
A very moving play and a fine cast, Mr. DeMille. Good night.

AHERNE:
So long, C.B.

DEMILLE:
Goodnight . . . and a feather in both your caps.
(*APPLAUSE*)
(*MUSIC: THEME IN*)[36]

DeMille's farewell, "This is Cecil B. DeMille saying goodnight to you from Hollywood," is followed by Ruick's invitation to "enjoy the popular

Lux daytime program — *The Life and Love of Dr. Susan*," and a quick reading of the supporting cast, after which he reminds the listeners that

> Jean Arthur's current picture is the Columbia hit, "Mr. Smith Goes to Washington." Brian Aherne will be seen in the forthcoming Edward Small production, "My Son, My Son," which is the film version of the best selling novel by Howard Spring.
> Our music was directed by Louis Silvers.
> (*MUSIC*)
> (*APPLAUSE*)
> This is the COLUMBIA . . . BROADCASTING SYSTEM.[37]

With that announcement ending at precisely 59 minutes and 30 seconds after the program began, the broadcast has concluded. Such was a normal *Lux Radio Theatre* of the period, with the dramatic portion of the show running between 45 and 48 minutes and the framework taking up the remaining 12–15 minutes. (During *Lux*'s first seasons in Hollywood, when each show included two intermission guests, the dramatic portion would typically run only about 40 minutes.)

Since June 1, 1936, all the *Lux* shows had originated from the Music Box Theatre on Hollywood Boulevard, and "not in a very fashionable section of Hollywood Boulevard," George Wells remembered. He described the Music Box as "a very bad theatre . . . it was a long, narrow theatre—very old-fashioned."[38]

The program of May 6, 1940, was the final *Lux* performed in the old theatre; the next week found the show coming from the more spacious Vine Street Playhouse (seating nearly 2,000) on 1615 Vine Street (today known as the Doolittle Theatre). "The other theatre was such an improvement over that Music Box," continued Wells,

> we were all delighted with it. There was a green room downstairs, and the dressing rooms were better. The other theatre was strictly movie—it didn't have decent dressing rooms. This one at least had dressing rooms, even to having one stage dressing room for stars . . . just in the wings near the stage door. It was much more of a theatre: they had legitimate plays in there.[39]

The new theatre, like the old,

> was used exclusively for *Lux*. . . . It was not rented out . . . the sponsor didn't want the Lux Radio Theatre associated with anything else. Although it was used for rehearsals, that was only a small part of the week, really . . . They could have put other shows in there, but they didn't because the sponsor wouldn't have stood for it—they were very jealous of our show.[40]

The Vine Street Theatre, which was the *Lux Radio Theatre*'s home from 1940 to 1953, pictured here circa 1937, while CBS's *Hollywood Hotel* originated from the building (photo: Photofest).

Dix Davis, a child actor at the time, vividly recalled the Vine Street Playhouse after the *Lux* program took it over:

> The whole thing was kind of different because we were doing it in a real theatre instead of a broadcast studio. Right across the street was NBC and, a few blocks away, CBS, but those were regular, new radio studios, and this was an old theatre, so they had to build a control booth and so forth. They had to remodel it, they had to wire the whole thing for radio. The stage was sort of cut in half depthwise—they only used the front part of the stage. Then there was a backdrop, and then there was a long line of ordinary, card-playing chairs along the back, where all of us sat—sat there for the whole performance and we got up when we had a line coming and came back and sat down. DeMille sat stage right over in the corner next to the proscenium. And this hanging mike was in the center with this unusual stand underneath it, and the control booth was on the left. The stars would come and go from the left, and we [the supporting players] would be sort of all lined up in the back, facing the audience.[41]

The stand underneath the hanging mike in center stage, which would eventually be given the nickname "Oscar," was there for the stars—some of whom had a tendency to be nervous—to hang on to. (This would ensure that they did not grab the mike itself for support.) As Davis indicated, DeMille did not perform center stage but had his own microphone stage right, where he sat at a card table. The actual broadcast was preceded by a brief warm-up show in which the audience was instructed on how to behave and the cast was introduced. Everyone, stars and supporting players, was on stage at the time the program began and remained there throughout the show. Even an actor whose part was finished by the end of the first act was required to remain on stage for the entire length of the broadcast. There was an additional microphone offstage, where some of the commercials were performed. Adults playing children, humans imitating animals—anything that might generate an unwelcome laugh from the studio audience—also originated from this offstage mike. The orchestra was placed behind a curtain, with only conductor Louis Silvers (later Rudy Schrager) visible to the audience through a windowlike opening in the curtain—this allowed the orchestra leader to accept cues from the director. Initially, the sound effects man, Charlie Forsyth, worked on the stage, but he was eventually given his own platform above the main stage, supposedly to avoid distracting the actors and the studio audience.

The elaborate production methods and the presence of the glamorous screen idols made *The Lux Radio Theatre* a show to which tickets were much sought after. Hours before airtime a line would begin forming in front of the theatre as fans requested tickets (which were given away). Seating space was of course limited, and on occasion it was estimated that 1,000 people had to be turned away. At times these disappointed fans could get unruly, and police guards were employed to keep would-be gatecrashers outside. According to a CBS press release, 100 policemen were detailed to keep those turned away from "Madame Sans-Gene," with Jean Harlow and Robert Taylor, in check in December 1936, but

> the overflow crowd would not disperse and finally crashed through the cordon of police right into the theatre while the show was going out over the air. The noise was thunderous but listeners were unaware that anything unusual had happened, for at the very moment the riot had started, the script called for a mob scene.[42]

To avoid any trouble, the stars were hustled out a side entrance and into a waiting automobile the moment the broadcast was completed, but tenacious fans, unaware of this, would wait outside the theatre for autographs. "We had to push our way through them every night coming out, especially if we had a big star on," George Wells recalled.

> And they would run up to you as you came through the alley. I'd be walking out with Sandy, and we'd be discussing things, and these kids would

A typical Monday evening gathering in front of the CBS Vine Street Theatre, circa 1944 (photo: Berry Hill Bookshop).

come running up saying, "Can we have your autograph?" Then they would look at us and say, "Oh, they're nobody!" We always laughed—we thought it was kind of funny, kind of cute. "They're nobody!" they'd announce to the whole bunch behind them.[43]

The expertise of the Thompson employees handling the *Lux* program assured a continuously smooth operation under normal circumstances, but unforeseen and unavoidable events could sometimes create problems. Since 1922, ASCAP (the American Society of Composers, Authors, and Publishers), the most powerful popular music group in the country, had been involved in a running battle with radio stations playing its music. A court decision ruled that any radio station that played ASCAP music had to pay a licensing fee to that organization, and the broadcasters grudgingly complied. With existing licensing agreements due to expire on December 31, 1940, ASCAP announced a major rate increase, to which all four networks objected. Preparations were made to hold out against ASCAP by refusing to pay the new rates, meaning that any ASCAP tune played over a station involved in the rebellion would be subject to a fine. Foreseeing just such a situation, the National Association of Broadcasters had recently formed BMI (Broadcast Music, Inc.), an alternate group of publishers, which based its catalogue on old songs, foreign compositions, and works by non–ASCAP (and generally not well-known) composers. Beginning with the new year (January 1, 1941), the ASCAP ban was on. Needless to say, the ban affected some shows more severely than it did others, and several musical programs actually went off the air entirely because of it. *Lux*'s theme, by Robert Armbruster, was a non–ASCAP composition and was thus unaffected, but musical director Louis Silvers was an ASCAP composer, meaning that none of his music could be performed on the air for the duration of the ban, although he *could* continue to conduct the orchestra. The problem was solved by having Maestro Silvers's young assistant, Rudy Schrager (a pianist in the orchestra), compose the necessary original music for the show, supplemented with non–ASCAP arrangements of pre-existing music. To avoid any trouble with ASCAP, Rudy Schrager signed a statement each week stating that he composed all the original music himself with no assistance from anyone, and Louis Silvers signed a statement that he had no hand whatsoever in writing the score. This procedure continued until the ban was lifted in the late spring of 1941, though many of Rudy Schrager's original themes would be used in Louis Silvers's incidental music for the next nine years, when he turned over his baton to Maestro Schrager.

The Lux Radio Theatre Goes to War

With the attack by the Japanese on the American naval base at Pearl Harbor, Hawaii, on December 7, 1941, and President Roosevelt's declaration of war on Germany and Japan the following day, the United States entered the Second World War. Scheduled for the *Lux* broadcast on December 8 was a frivolous comedy, "The Doctor Takes a Wife." George Wells recalled the hectic events surrounding that production:

That was a night—the night before that! All lines were down between New York and the Coast, and it was murder. We had a very fussy sponsor—he was a tyrant . . . and he had to be notified of every word that was changed—it didn't mean anything, but he had to be notified. . . . And I remember on that Monday night after Pearl Harbor, we had been up all night with the show—all sorts of problems. And we had some stinking little comedy, it was an awful thing to do on such a day, and we apologized for it [in DeMille's introduction], which was written by all of us the night before. And we couldn't get to Cambridge [Lever Brothers' headquarters] with it . . . and finally, just before the show went into its final rehearsal, a long Teletype came through—it must have taken 30 minutes to send it—"Changes suggested by the sponsor." This is an hour or so before we went on the air! I can still remember, because my message to Cambridge was "Forget it!" We just went ahead and did it our way.[44]

The program opened, not with the usual *Lux* theme but with the national anthem, after which, Cecil B. DeMille, sounding more solemn than usual, made his introductory remarks:

Throughout America tonight this inspired music lifts every heart to new patriotism, as all of us join all of you in pledging full allegiance to our country. We've asked the Columbia Broadcasting System to interrupt our program tonight with any important news developments. We here in *The Lux Radio Theatre*, as well as you who are listening, want to keep in touch with any and all events bearing upon this national emergency. In the meantime, this theatre carries on as usual which, as you know, is one of the oldest and finest traditions of the theatre.[45]

Midway through the second act of "The Doctor Takes a Wife," an interruption *did* occur, as CBS reporter John Daly was heard from New York giving an update on the war situation, mentioning during his five-minute talk that a late bulletin reported that 50 unidentified aircraft were seen heading toward San Francisco. "Oh, we were going crazy," George Wells insisted.

We were warned that they may take up 20 minutes or they may take up three minutes. All these words kept coming through from the O.W.I. (Office of War Information), and how much time they were going to do it, whether it would come from New York or here, we had no idea. And it kept changing every half hour—we had to prepare for five, ten different eventualities.[46]

The show, of course, could not run over, and at 7:00 P.M. Pacific Standard Time (10:00 on the East Coast) it had to be completed, which meant that Wells, along with Sandy Barnett and Harry Kerr, had quickly to abridge the remainder of the broadcast. The problem was that, until the special news bulletin was over, they had no idea as to how much of the show had to be trimmed. "We had a bad night," Wells recalled.[47]

The Lux Radio Theatre continued unabated through the war years, now serving to keep up the morale of the millions of anxious listeners on the homefront. With gasoline rationing in effect, entertainment outside the home, especially for those not living in the city, became an uncommon luxury, and the radio became more important than ever. Barbara Thomas, a young radio fan at the time, recently recalled an incident of the sort that is unique to the war period:

> Our little family lived in Queens on the 4th floor of an apartment building. One of the weekly highlights of our lives was listening to the Lux Radio Theater—we would gather around the radio and be transported by the broadcast of the theater. As the war intensified—so too the air raids—they would usually take place as soon as it got dark enough which meant there could be no lights anywhere. You can imagine our surprise when one evening, in the middle of an air raid, the warden yelled out "Lights out on the 4th floor apartment." My mother, brother and myself had been in the kitchen listening to the Lux Radio Theater on our radio which was powered by lighted tubes. We were loath to turn it off but had no choice, we certainly didn't want to see the city of N.Y. go up in flames from the bombers honed in to the light from our radio. My mother solved the problem by covering the kitchen table with blankets that went to the floor and we all crawled into this makeshift dark room and finished listening to the program without uttering a sound.[48]

Lux offered much the same sort of entertainment that it had before the outbreak of the hostilities, though the war story, which had been a rarity on the series, began to be booked fairly regularly. Throughout *Lux*'s history, however, this sort of change merely reflected the changes in the type of motion pictures being produced, which, after all, is whence *Lux* drew most of its material.

Lux Flakes and Lux Toilet Soap were still hawked during the commercials, but added to the chores of announcer John Milton Kennedy (who took over when Melville Ruick joined the military in the summer of 1942) were pleas for housewives to preserve their waste cooking fats:

> Waste fats and greases from your kitchen contain glycerin—one of the things that goes into the making of explosives. No amount is too small to save. Think of it this way, one man doesn't make an army, yet together, millions of individual Americans make up the finest army in the world. If every American housewife turns in one pound of waste household fats a month, together that will make five hundred and forty million pounds of smokeless powder a year! Now, here's what our government asks us to do: strain waste fats and greases into a can—any clean, smooth-edged can. Don't use glass or paper containers because they break or leak. The cans you use will be salvaged later. Keep the can in a cool place and, when it's full, take it to your local meat dealer. He'll pay you cash for each pound of fat. Try to do this early in the week when he's not so busy as weekends.

> Remember, only waste fats and oils are wanted, not anything you can use
> or re-use yourself. Every bit is precious — save it carefully. Within twenty-
> one days of the time you turn it in to your butcher, it will be on its way
> to send your message to the axis.
> (SOUND: EXPLOSIONS)[49]

With this sort of announcement common on the airwaves during the
war, the radio was really not the place to go to escape the realities of everyday life. Even when the story was far removed from the throng of battle,
as many continued to be, one was bound to be reminded of the situation
somewhere in the show, such as in the curtain call:

> DEMILLE:
> . . .the Treasury Department and pictures seem to keep you both pretty
> busy. How many miles have you gone this last month, Veronica?
> LAKE:
> About eighteen thousand or so, Mr. DeMille. I started out after finishing
> "The Glass Key" at Paramount and sold bonds in eighteen cities. Where
> have you been, Ralph?
> BELLAMY:
> Well, the Victory Committee asked me to go to the Middle West. I guess
> I hit about thirty different places.
> DEMILLE:
> The two of you seem to have covered most of the country.
> LAKE:
> Everywhere except home. A little while ago I moved my home to a place
> near Seattle where my husband is stationed with the Army Engineers but
> I haven't been able to go back to see him since.[50]

During the early part of the conflict, there was some hesitancy on the
part of the networks to saturate the airwaves with war dramas, and *Lux's*
plans to air "The Bugle Sounds" on June 29, 1942, were vetoed by CBS
(which usually did not interfere with the series) out of fear that a story of
sabotage might alarm the public. (The previously presented "The Champ"
was quickly substituted.) Yet by the time the play was aired six months later
(on January 4, 1943), this sort of inspirational, patriotic battle drama had
gained great approval from the public, the government, *and* the networks.

Mr. DeMille's Exit

Toward the end of the war, another series of events occurred that were
destined to affect the remainder of *The Lux Radio Theatre's* run. In the summer of 1944, the American Federation of Radio Artists (AFRA), the union
that everyone had to join before working on network radio in a professional

capacity, decided to fight a proposition scheduled to appear on the ballot in California's general election in November. This Proposition 12, popularly known as "the right of employment" amendment, would, if carried, have allowed every Californian to obtain a job without first joining a union. The plans of AFRA to help defeat the proposition involved assessing each of its members one dollar, with which they would demonstrate the "dangers" of this plan to the public. On August 16, Cecil B. DeMille received a letter informing him that, as a member of AFRA, he would be required to pay the one-dollar fee. Upon receiving the notification, DeMille immediately set out to investigate Proposition 12 and

> decided to vote for it. And here my union was demanding that I pay $1 into a political campaign fund to persuade other citizens to vote against Proposition 12: was demanding, in a word, that I cancel my vote with my dollar. Even if I were opposed to Proposition 12, I asked myself, did my union have the right to impose a compulsory political assessment upon any citizen, under pain of the loss of his right to work?[51]

DeMille refused to pay the dollar, would not allow anyone to pay it for him, and took the matter to the Superior Court, where the union's right to assess its members the fee was upheld. Meanwhile, the deadline to make the payment, originally set at September 1, was extended several times, but *Lux*'s host still held out, realizing full well that his continued refusal to give in would cause him to lose his status as a member in good standing with AFRA and could force him off the air. On the program, things were much as usual, and few listeners realized on Monday evening, January 22, 1945, that Cecil B. DeMille was saying "goodnight to you from Hollywood" for the last time on a *Lux Radio Theatre* broadcast. January 29 saw Lionel Barrymore assuming the host's duties, "in the absence of my good friend, C.B. DeMille,"[52] but DeMille continued his fight and was allowed to speak over the air on the *March of Time* program of February 1, not in his professional capacity but as "a citizen in the news." DeMille was permitted three minutes to express his views. "I am a union man," he insisted,

> but this is no question of unionism or non-unionism. It has to do with the abuse of power, for I cannot concede that the union by-laws take precedence over the Constitution of the United States or the Constitution of a state. At no time did I agree to an assessment for a political purpose.... A union that operates a closed shop becomes a monopoly of labor. It controls the lives, fortunes, and happiness of all, for all must join it in order to work. Therefore, it has a responsibility to the public just as a water company, which controls all the water of a community. The courts, the legislatures and the congress also have a responsibility—to see that the rights and freedom of the *people* are protected as well as the welfare of the union. Thomas Jefferson said, and I quote, "To compel a man to furnish contributions of money for propagation of opinions which he disbelieves

and abhors is sinful and tyrannical." (Well, there's one great American statesman who sees it my way.) To preserve our freedom we must fight for it and our weapon is the ballot. You elected the legislature and the congress. Ask them to protect the freedom of that ballot and so guarantee your liberty . . . a power has been built up in this country that is antagonistic to individual liberty and constitutional government. When freedom of individual choice in an election is taken from us, the right to support what people and propositions we choose with our money or our voice or our vote; when that is taken from us because of our convictions, and we are arbitrarily denied the right to work and make a living, then the cornerstone of government by the people is removed, and the whole structure of liberty collapses.[53]

Speaking on behalf of AFRA over the Mutual network two weeks later, radio announcer Ken Carpenter, national vice president of that organization and president of the Los Angeles local (filling in for Orson Welles, who was "unable to appear . . . due to his unfortunate illness"), gave the union's side of the story. Carpenter claimed that Proposition 12 would, if passed, "destroy organized labor in this state and would result in disastrous industrial chaos." He went on to say that

> AFRA . . . was convinced that it had not only the right but the obligation of resisting this malicious threat to its very existence. So here was a group of some 2,000 men and women in the Hollywood chapter of AFRA who have never chosen to take political action in the name of their union, even refusing to endorse candidates, but who are now forced to combat a measure appearing on the ballot which directly threatened the life of their organization. Mr. DeMille says our action constituted political action, Judge Emmett Wilson of the Los Angeles Superior Court says it was *not* political action, that it was an effort of the members to combat what we were convinced was a threat to our union's existence and a threat to our economic well-being.[54]

It was, according to Carpenter, only after union members present voted that any necessary action should be taken to fight Proposition 12, that the board of directors unanimously voted to

> levy an assessment of $1 per member on educational campaigns through which the implications of the proposition might be explained to the public. . . . But, Mr. DeMille refused to pay his dollar, charging that we were abridging his political freedom and interfering with his right to vote. We did not attempt to interfere with Mr. DeMille's right to vote in any way he saw fit. It was the unanimous opinion of the membership that the union was threatened by this bill, and the men and women of AFRA, believing that Mr. DeMille was a good union man, believed further that he would not hesitate to help defend his union. As an individual citizen, Mr. DeMille could vote any way he chose; as a member of AFRA, according to the sound principles of American democracy, he was bound by a decision of the

majority of the members when they decided that their union should contribute funds to help fight Proposition 12. Is Mr. DeMille right and some 2,000 of the rest of us wrong?[55]

One point that Carpenter touched upon undoubtedly surprised some listeners, for he stated that despite DeMille's title of "producer" of the show, he was a "narrator on the program."[56] This remark had nothing to do with the matter at hand, and must have discomfited those persons in charge of assembling *The Lux Radio Theatre*, since, even as Carpenter denied that the host of the show was the actual producer, that week's guest "producer" was preparing to read his part over the air. It was, after all, not DeMille's part to deny that he produced *The Lux Radio Theatre* when he was, in fact, paid to enact that very role in the same sense that an actor is engaged to essay a character.

The public support DeMille received was, in his own words,

> overwhelming. No motion picture, with the exception of *The King of Kings* and *The Ten Commandments* (1956), has brought me so many letters. They came from every part of the country and from every fighting front where Americans were still at war. They were from Democrats and Republicans, rich and poor, men, women, and even children in all walks of life. Many of the most touching of them came from union members or their wives. The gist of them all was much the same: "Do something to keep what has happened to you from happening to the rest of us."[57]

What it all amounted to was that Cecil B. DeMille would unfortunately no longer be a part of *The Lux Radio Theatre* on Monday evenings; and an era, which had begun nearly nine years earlier, had ended. The show never seemed the same after DeMille's departure, as none of those engaged to fill his shoes, first-rate emcees though many of them were, had the same sort of charming rapport with the audience or the guests, or the sense of drama as *Lux*'s first Hollywood host. John Milton Kennedy, *Lux*'s announcer at the time, recently recalled, "It really was a very deep, deep cut to Cecil B. DeMille because he regarded his influence as a result of being on radio every week for so many weeks a year as more important to him emotionally than some of his contributions to motion pictures."[58]

The Post-DeMille Period

Meantime, the business of creating a *Lux Radio Theatre* broadcast every week became more complex without a permanent host, for now a guest host had to be engaged for each show. Initially it was thought likely that Cecil B. DeMille would eventually return to the program, and, to avoid antagonizing the man still regarded as *Lux*'s host, he was actually consulted before some of the guest "producers" were hired. (DeMille's own favorite was Preston Sturges, whom he hoped *Lux* would use every Monday evening until his return.) Most of the guest hosts appeared for only one week, though Brian Aherne was heard for two consecutive weeks and Lionel Barrymore appeared a total of three times (including the first two weeks after DeMille left) and would undoubtedly have been used again if MGM (his studio) had not forbidden it.

The idea of having a host appropriate to each evening's offering was toyed with (William Powell, Robert Benchley, or Leo McCarey, for example, for a comedy; Paul Muni, Warner Baxter, or Donald Crisp for a drama) but ultimately rejected. The fact that the voices of many well-known motion picture producers and directors were not known to the advertising executives at Lever Brothers created some problems, as they insisted on knowing what a potential host sounded like prior to signing him. This necessitated considerable scrambling about on the part of the *Lux* people in attempts to find often elusive and sometimes nonexistent recordings of these men. When it became obvious that DeMille would not be permitted to return to the show, the search for a new permanent host was begun, with several serious candidates being invited to make audition recordings for the sponsor, while many of the guest hosts who were appearing were actually auditioning for the permanent position, sometimes unaware of the fact. Some of those who were offered the opportunity to appear once (with the obvious but unspoken possibility of an offer to become regular host) had no interest in it or were not available. (Frank Capra, Sam Wood, Howard Hawks, and John Ford were among those in this group.) Otto Kruger and Brian Aherne were both considered to be very good in their guest host appearances, but neither was available due to commitments with other programs. Frank Borzage, George Cukor, Frank Lloyd, D.W. Griffith, Raymond Massey, and Hal Roach were others who were at least momentarily considered for the assignment. What the client was still hoping for was "a voice with character, personality, dignity though not stuffy."[59] A memo from Virginia Spragle of Thompson's New York office entitled "Lux Radio Theatre Guest Producers" included in its listing:

> *Kighley* [sic], *William* — they are recording him today, and the coast feels quite hopeful about him. He just got out of the Army and has signed a contract with Paramount to do one picture a year with them.[60]

William Keighley, born in Philadelphia in 1889, had been an actor and director on the stage before beginning his career as a movie director in 1932. Though his name may not have been as well known with the general public as that of his colleague Cecil B. DeMille, Keighley was a very successful director, first at Warner Bros., then at Paramount, turning out such pictures as *Babbitt* (1934), *G-Men* (1935), *Brother Rat* (1938), *Each Dawn I Die* (1939), and *The Man Who Came to Dinner* (1942). His first *Lux* guest host assignment came on September 17 and caused Miss Spragle to wire Hollywood that "Cambridge and we thought show was excellent last night and that Keighley's performance was very good."[61] He guested again on October 1, and, realizing they had found their man, Lever Brothers approved him as permanent host, which he became with the November 5, 1945, broadcast. Keighley's cultured speaking voice, relaxed delivery, and high degree of professionalism made him a good choice for the job, which he would fill for the next seven seasons.

The show was now written by Sandy Barnett, who had stepped down from his position of director when George Wells left to write for MGM at the beginning of 1944. Fred MacKaye, who had been a regular on *Lux* as a supporting actor and "a sort-of assistant to Sandy Barnett,"[62] in the words of John Milton Kennedy, was now directing the program. Like all of *Lux*'s directors, MacKaye was a young man (born in 1906). He was fairly quiet, especially considering his life in the theatre (he had been a professional actor from the age of 18) and, like Sandy Barnett, gave relatively little direction. "Fred just kind of floated around the stage," actor Sam Edwards recalled.[63] Radio performer Willard Waterman remembered that

> he did a very good job of setting the scripts in proportion so that you knew where you were going — what was going to happen in the show. And he had a very good hand with the star people. He knew how to make them comfortable and get them interested in what they were doing.[64]

Radio actress Betty Lou Gerson agreed: "He was a very capable, very talented man, and marvelously easy to work with. He'd put you completely at ease."[65]

Fred MacKaye's ability to keep calm in a moment of crisis was perhaps most effectively put to the test on May 24, 1948, when "I Walk Alone," starring Burt Lancaster and Lizabeth Scott, was scheduled. After completing the afternoon dress rehearsal, Lancaster returned to his studio dressing room to shave and clean up. Fifteen minutes before airtime, the star had not returned to the theatre, and at 5:52 P.M. MacKaye made a decision: radio actor Ira Grossel (who would later attain movie fame under the name of Jeff Chandler) would be made ready to go on in his place. A brief portion of the previous day's dress rehearsal (which had been recorded) was played back so the actor could study Burt Lancaster's speech patterns, while, at 5:58, a telephone call was made to Universal Studios to see if the elusive star was there. After being told he had just left, MacKaye, realizing that Lancaster could never make the theatre by the 6:00 airtime (it was about a 15-minute trip), decided there was nothing else to do but have Ira Grossel

Publicity photo of *Lux Radio Theatre* host William Keighley, circa 1946 (photo: Photofest).

fill in until the star got there, while he himself would play Grossel's role in the broadcast. Lancaster, who for some reason believed the show was to begin at 6:30, arrived at 6:12 and was horrified to discover that the program was already in progress. He took over his part at an appropriate moment, and reportedly even the sponsors did not know about the incident until they were later told.[66]

A typical week in *The Lux Radio Theatre* at this time might run as follows. Thursday: Sound rehearsal with sound effects artist Charlie Forsyth, engineer Ed Whittaker, and director Fred MacKaye, lasting approximately two hours. Friday: Two hours' rehearsal with the supporting cast (and stand-ins for the stars), followed by a two-and-a-half-hour rehearsal with the full cast (including stars). Saturday was a day off. Sunday: Rehearsal beginning at 10:30 A.M. and lasting two hours; lunch break at 12:30, during which the orchestra rehearsed; and after lunch, a one-hour dress rehearsal, which was recorded by a studio on Hollywood Boulevard. As soon as the dress rehearsal was completed, a messenger rushed over with the record, which was then played back for the director and cast. (Later in *Lux*'s history the recordings were made by Radio Recorders in Hollywood, where the record would be played back and piped into the *Lux* control booth.) Monday: Cast and crew arrived at 3:30 P.M. and rehearsed until 5:00, when there was an hour break before 6:00 airtime.

Stories of troubled ex–G.I.'s such as "I'll Be Seeing You" and "Pride of the Marines" were now commonplace on *Lux*, as were psychological dramas such as "Love Letters," "Spellbound," and "The Seventh Veil." A dark, gritty side of life, barely touched upon before, or even during the war, was examined in "Whistle Stop," "None but the Lonely Heart," and "From This Day Forward." This does not mean that the bright comedy or carefree musical was now perennially absent from the *Lux* stage, but the focus had definitely changed with the times.

Another alteration that had been gradually taking place since the early 1940s was that *Lux* was now getting more of its stories from 20th Century–Fox than from any other studio. The reason was simple: 20th Century–Fox was especially cooperative, usually offering their properties at no charge (in exchange for publicity) and often more than willing to loan out the star or stars who had appeared in the screen version. More than ever before, in fact, this period saw the original stars reunited with their screen vehicles, which was usually the goal all along. As the 1940s progressed, there began to be more and more repeats on the show — not in the present-day sense of replaying a recorded program but offering a second (or even a third) performance of a play that had been done previously. Many of these old favorites were repeated by audience request, such as "Seventh Heaven," voted the story *Lux*'s listeners most wanted to hear for the show's tenth anniversary program on October 16, 1944, and "The Jazz Singer," which brought Al Jolson back in one of his most fondly remembered vehicles on June 2, 1947. Names of players who had not even been heard of a few years earlier began to appear on the *Lux* marquee, and such newcomers to the screen as John Hodiak, Van Johnson, Richard Conte, Jeanne Crain, and Ella Raines all made their debuts on the show in the second half of the 1940s.

At the end of the 1949-50 season, Fred MacKaye left the show due to ill health and was replaced by Thompson employee Earl Ebi. Ebi, who was born in Fresno, California, in 1903, had begun his show business career as an actor and had gone into radio as a staff producer at WWJ Detroit in 1937, later becoming staff producer for NBC in Chicago and Hollywood. Prior to becoming *Lux*'s director, starting with the 1950-51 season, he had directed such shows as *Vic and Sade* and *The Charlie McCarthy Show.*

The 1953 Summer Series

Although Earl Ebi would be *Lux*'s director for the next four years, a special summer series of shows in 1953 was turned over to CBS producer-director Norman Macdonnell. *The Lux Radio Theatre* had run through the summer only once, during the first season in Hollywood in 1936, but *this* series, called *The Lux Summer Theatre*, would be something different. Budgeted at a mere $4,250 each, the shows would originate not from the Vine Street Playhouse but from the regular CBS studios, and though some of the 14 shows would be adapted from movies, most would be based on other (unfilmed) properties, and a few would be original radio plays. With Norman Macdonnell at the helm, the shows were far removed from the regular *Lux* programs, using actors from what sound man Bill James called Macdonnell's "stock company,"[67] many of whom had appeared infrequently or not at all in the regular series. The different broadcast location (first in CBS Studio B, later in Studio A) even contributed to this different flavor, offering an acoustic with noticeably less reverberation, which, when combined with the considerably smaller audience, created a more intimate effect. The prerecorded music (by Earl Towner) was not always appropriate to the situations, and many of the same themes were used over and over again.

One of the trademarks of a Norman Macdonnell production from this stage of his career was the emphasis on sound effects. Fans of Macdonnell's *Gunsmoke* series, which had begun the year before, had learned to identify certain characters by the sound of their footsteps and even discovered that Marshal Matt Dillon's gun had a "bigger" sound than those of the other characters. This attention to sound gave the Macdonnell productions their special character, and he brought two of his regular sound men, Ray Kemper and Bill James, in to work the *Lux* summer series. Kemper recently said that

> Norm was the one who always gave us the time to do it right, and he always said, "Sound effects are a very important part of any show I do," and we all loved him for that. . . . Those were the years that I call the golden years of radio, where sound effects kind of came into their own, and I think Norm Macdonnell had a lot to do with that because he allowed the sound men to really be an artistic part of each show, and it was so important and

so unusual. . . . And it *did* make a difference, it made a difference to you
inside, it made you feel good about doing the job.[68]

Demonstrating Macdonnell's attention to detail, Kemper explained the
difference between the sound of beer being poured and that of liquor:

> You have a bottle of soda pop for the beer, and you give it a little shake
> and you pour the soda pop and it's got a fuzzy sound to it. And for the liquor
> you just pour out water; it's got a harder sound to it. . . . That's the sort of
> thing Norm let us do and *wanted* us to do.[69]

Each show used one featured star, all of whom had appeared on the
regular *Lux* series several times, and cast opposite the star in the leading
masculine or feminine part was a player usually limited to supporting roles
on the air, but more than capable of carrying a starring part when the occasion arose. Thus, William Holden's leading lady was Georgia Ellis, Miss
Kitty on radio's *Gunsmoke,* while John Dehner played opposite star Virginia
Mayo the following week. Other radio actors who performed splendidly in
leading roles in the summer series included Sammie Hill (opposite Fred
MacMurray), William Conrad (opposite Dorothy McGuire), and Betty Lou
Gerson (opposite Herbert Marshall). The final element to set *The Lux Summer Theatre* apart from the regular season shows was the choice of stories,
for such unusual fare as Maxwell Anderson's decidedly odd play *High Tor*
or Molière's seventeenth-century farce *The Physician in Spite of Himself,*
had never and would never be performed on *The Lux Radio Theatre.*
Highlights of the replacement series included two charmingly quiet
original comedies by Kathleen Hite, "The Fall of Maggie Phillips" and
"Romance to a Degree," and an adaptation of Mildred Cram's engrossing
character study, "Cynara." Daphne du Maurier's "The Birds" received its
first radio presentation on July 20 in a play produced and directed by Fred
MacKaye, who took over for Macdonnell for one week only. Ray Kemper
remembered the show vividly:

> It was a very difficult sound effects show to do, with all these thousands
> and thousands of birds pecking away at things to try to get in at these peo-
> ple, and it was kind of spooky, and Bill [James] and I really worked
> ourselves into a froth getting that show done. Now keep in mind that we're
> doing a radio show — I'm perfectly aware that it's a radio show — and after
> the show was over the hair was standing up on the back of my neck
> because that was such a spooky show! And I walked out of the studio with
> Bill, and I said, "Bill, the hair's standing up on the back of my neck; did
> that make *you* feel funny?" And he said, "Are you kidding? Look at the hair
> on my arms!" and it was standing straight up![70]

The fact that each week's show was rehearsed and performed all in the
same day, receiving but a fraction of the rehearsal time that would have

been dedicated to a regular *Lux* show, was never noticeable in the work of the production crew or in the performances of the supporting cast. Harry Bartell, who worked often with Macdonnell and appeared in four of the *Lux* summer shows, recalled that "Norman usually worked with a comparatively small company of actors, and those actors got so used to playing with each other that they could practically anticipate character touches, timing, and things of this nature."[71]

The host for seven of the shows was Ken Carpenter, who had become the regular *Lux* announcer when John Milton Kennedy left to do television the season before, and Don Wilson filled in for seven weeks when Carpenter took a vacation. The programs were all performed live and aired during the regular 6:00 P.M. time slot on the West Coast (9:00 P.M. on the East Coast) until the regular series resumed on September 7.

The Final Seasons

The Lux Radio Theatre had undergone a few important personnel changes beginning with the 1952-53 season, including the previously mentioned new announcer, Ken Carpenter, a new "Hollywood Reporter," the real-life movie publicist Frances Scully, who functioned much as the Libby Collins character had (whom she replaced), and a new host. William Keighley, who had effectively served the series for seven years, was about to retire from picture work, after which he and his wife, actress Genevieve Tobin, would move to Paris. His replacement was a director who had already retired, Irving Cummings. Born in New York City in 1888, Cummings had broken into show business as a stage actor before entering films in 1909, where he became a popular star. He started his career as a director (also occasionally producing) in 1922, and between that time and his retirement in 1951 he turned out 69 pictures, among them *The Johnstown Flood* (1926), *Behind That Curtain* (1929), *Curly Top* (1935), *The Story of Alexander Graham Bell* (1939), *Lillian Russell* (1940), *Springtime in the Rockies* (1942), and *The Dolly Sisters* (1945). He began his new job on *The Lux Radio Theatre* on September 8, 1952, one month and one day before his sixty-fourth birthday. Though clearly uncomfortable at first, Cummings soon proved a suitable choice for the assignment, and his cultured, almost British-sounding voice quickly became a familiar part of the series.

By the time of the 1953-54 season, *Lux*'s rating had dipped to 6.2 (which actually was respectable when compared with the ratings other shows received). *Jack Benny* and *Amos 'n' Andy* tied for the lead that season, bringing in 8.2 apiece. The reason for radio's severe slump was no mystery, as more and more Americans were acquiring televisions and turning their backs on the audio-only medium. Television destroyed radio with incredible

A 1943 publicity photo of motion picture director Irving Cummings, who became host of the *Lux Radio Theatre* in 1952 (photo: Photofest).

rapidity, and *Lux* had gone from a rating of 28.6 in 1948-49 (when it led all programs in the ratings department) to a mere fraction of that just five years later. Lever Brothers, aware that the end was just a matter of time, had begun sponsoring *The Lux Video Theatre* in the fall of 1950, which was now commanding the lion's share of that company's advertising budget. Since CBS Studio A had served the *Lux Summer Theatre* effectively enough, it was

Interior of NBC Studios (photo: Photofest).

decided to abandon the Vine Street Playhouse and move the regular series to that location with the beginning of the fall season in 1953. At the end of the season, *Lux* left CBS altogether, opting to move back to the network on which it had started in 1934, the National Broadcasting Company.

Clearly proud of its new possession, NBC began a large-scale publicity campaign to promote *The Lux Radio Theatre* and *The Lux Video Theatre*, which had also moved to the older network, often combining promotions for both series in one advertisement. The slogan "Now . . . Lux Presents Hollywood . . . on NBC" was seen in newspapers and magazines, and it was heard on such radio shows as *Fibber McGee and Molly* and on such television programs as *Dragnet* and *Art Linkletter's House Party*. A featured part of the 1954-55 season would be the presentation of "20 Greats": radio adaptations of "20 of the greatest Hollywood pictures."[72] This idea also succeeded in saving money on new scripts, because all of the 20 shows in question used scripts that had already been performed on *Lux*, some as far back as 1938. The staff now included the J. Walter Thompson vice president of West Coast operations, Cornwell Jackson, now listed as "executive producer," who had actually served for several years in the position that Danny Danker had filled until his death in 1944. Other members of the *Lux* team were Irving Cummings as "producer," Rudy Schrager leading the orchestra

Candid of (left-right) Irving Cummings, Rudy Schrager, Ken Carpenter, Len White (of J. Walter Thompson's radio and television production department), executive producer Cornwell Jackson, Walter Pidgeon, and Fred MacKaye, circa 1953 (photo: Photofest).

(and also serving as musical director of *The Lux Video Theatre*), Ken Carpenter as announcer, and Frances Scully handling the "Hollywood Reporter" chores in the commercials. Earl Ebi, who had directed a few of *The Lux Video Theatre* shows the season before, now left the radio series to devote all his time to the television equivalent. Hired to direct the radio show was none other than Fred MacKaye, whose partial recovery from his illness had allowed him to return to occasional *Lux* acting assignments during the previous few seasons. Still not in the best of health, MacKaye courageously took the helm from Ebi and managed to get through the season. "Everybody helped him, of course," actor Herb Ellis recalled. "Everybody loved him — he was a terrific guy."[73] Writer Sandy Barnett also left for the *Video Theatre*, though most of the "20 Greats" actually used his old scripts. Milton Geiger worked as script supervisor and writer for the first two months, with Lenard St. Clair taking over the position in November. (In the season of 39 shows, there were only 20 new scripts to produce, anyway.) The series would now originate from Studio A in NBC's Radio City in Hollywood, and the network, mindful of *Lux Radio Theatre* tradition, created a new green room in their studios. The season began on September 14 with "Wuthering Heights," the first of the "20 Greats," which featured Merle Oberon in her 1939 movie role and a special appearance by Samuel Goldwyn, the producer of the picture, in the curtain call. "So Big" and "How Green Was My Valley" followed, and it was not until October 5 that the first story new to *Lux*, "The Turning Point," was performed.

Despite the expenditure cutbacks and the meagerness of the material (a reflection of the artistic decline of motion pictures), the series still offered expertly produced radio dramas, with such shows as "War of the Worlds" and "Shane" standing out in that season. By the end of 1954 the programs often included only one featured star—another cost-saving procedure— and, with the ratings continuing to slip, it seemed very unlikely that the series would run for another season. The final program, "Edward, My Son," the last of the "20 Greats," aired on June 7, 1955, with Walter Pidgeon as the sole featured star. Although Irving Cummings did not actually say it in the curtain call, the very vagueness of his closing message suggested the show would not be back in the fall:

> Now, Walter, it's time to say goodbye. This is the last broadcast of The Lux Radio Theatre for the season. But we hope our wonderful audience that has been with us for over twenty years will go right on with us by watching the Lux Video Theatre. The Lux Video Theatre will be on all summer and will continue to bring you the finest entertainment that Hollywood has to offer. So ... for now ... this is goodbye ... and thanks again, Walter, for making this an evening to remember.[74]

Its fate hung in the balance for the next two months as J. Walter Thompson and Lever Brothers examined the practicality of continuing the series, but in August it was made official: *The Lux Radio Theatre*, after an incredible run of 21 years as the most consistently outstanding dramatic program on the air, had rung down the curtain for the last time.

The Writers

One of the most important elements of any radio drama is the script, and *The Lux Radio Theatre* was fortunate in having two excellent writers who, between them, provided virtually all the adaptations for 20 years: George Wells, from 1934 to 1943, and Sanford H. ("Sandy") Barnett, from 1944 to 1954. Both of these men would eventually find their way into the motion picture business, where both would end up winning Academy Awards, George Wells for best original screenplay for 1957's *Designing Woman*, and Sandy Barnett for best original story for 1964's *Father Goose*. Wells brought a new style of adaptation to the air early in *Lux*'s history, using what he terms "motion picture technique" to "open up" the stage plays he was translating to the radio, and taking advantage of the medium's potential. "I began to feel very restless in that thing of just taking a stage play and kind of cutting it and fixing it," Wells explained, "and I found that some of the stage plays we were trying to do on the radio just did not translate."[75] When the show was in New York, Wells did most of his writing at home, but with the move to Hollywood in 1936, he was given an office at J. Walter Thompson (though he was not a Thompson employee). He was not just the principal writer, he was also what would now be termed "script supervisor," making necessary changes in the script during rehearsals, which he often attended. After the first rehearsal, the supporting cast would be let go, "then Frank Woodruff, the director, and I would sit around with the [stars]—talk about it and see what they felt about it."[76] Wells found that adapting the scripts from motion pictures, rather than from stage plays, made his job much easier as it was no longer necessary to open up the stories. Still, some important movie scenes simply did not adapt to the nonvisual medium and had to be substantially altered or completely rewritten.

Two key scenes in the 1941 Preston Sturges movie *Sullivan's Travels*, for example, are completely silent except for the musical score. The first sequence, which lasts about seven minutes, chronicles the hero and heroine's travels among the impoverished as they learn the meaning of "trouble." The second (and shorter) sequence, which follows soon after, shows how the hero comes mistakenly to be thought dead, an event around which the remainder of the story revolves. *Lux*'s writer got around the seemingly insurmountable problem of bringing these segments to the air by simply creating an entirely new scene that uses events from both but is actually a piece of entirely original writing. In most cases Wells was so successful in capturing the flavor of the original that virtually no one realized that any changes had been made. "I've had people come to me and say, 'Boy, that was a great show, it was exactly like the movie!' It wasn't like the movie, but they *thought* it was."[77]

Alterations that were necessary for radio sometimes puzzled the stars, recalled Wells:

> In those days radio was a new thing for them. They had no idea why they were called upon to do some things, and we had to explain it to them, or why we had to cut out one of their favorite scenes. Not that they were necessary to the piece, but they were their favorites for one reason or another, usually for some sort of visual piece of business which could not translate. It all took explanation and a little tact and a little diplomacy.[78]

Wells holds that

the adaptation field was a kind of crazy one. It didn't matter how good a writer you were, but what mattered was something else: whether you could tell a story in 52 minutes, whether you could do that picture, or that story, and make it sound like it was all of a piece instead of depending entirely on announcers. It was a very peculiar kind of a thing. It was imitating the style, it was catching the mood of a picture or a story. And some people had it—I had it, I think—but it doesn't necessarily make you a great writer.[79]

Even though George Wells had virtually a free hand in doing the adaptations, the client had the final say in all matters. Most of the objections, when there were any, would concern the vehicles that were proposed for radio presentation, as Lever Brothers did not want their product associated with certain kinds of stories. "If it had overtones of real tragedy," Wells explained, "they were very leery about it. They didn't want the soap associated with tragedy."[80] The network interfered very little with *Lux*:

The only thing they had to say about a script was whether it fit their code, which was that you didn't give publicity to any sponsor in the script—things like that. The agency themselves would sometimes try to censor certain lines in a script. A classic one was not on the *Lux* show but some show that was done by the agency which handled the Chevrolet account. There was a show with that agency that had a line in it which said, "We'll camp here and ford the river tomorrow." They didn't want that line because of the *ford*.[81]

Many of the early Hollywood *Luxes* were based on pictures released prior to the 1934 Code of Decency restrictions or on stage plays, and it was sometimes necessary to severely alter aspects of the story to avoid risqué situations. *Polly of the Circus*, for example, as a play and twice as movies, told of a small town minister who creates a scandal when he takes an injured female circus performer into his home, but *Lux*'s version (broadcast on November 30, 1936) changes the leading man's profession to that of a doctor. *Only Yesterday*, as a 1933 Universal film, concerns a woman who gives birth to a child out of wedlock, and the baby's father who returns from the war and, forgetting the victim of his brief fling, marries another woman. *Lux*'s broadcast of November 6, 1939, had the couple marrying secretly early in the story but kept the other events intact, demonstrating that Lever Brothers evidently preferred to have the hero commit bigamy rather than see the heroine bear an illegitimate baby. As the series continued and the radio plays were more and more often based on very recent films, these sorts of alterations in the story line became less frequent, and very few issues tackled in the 1940s and 1950s movies that were adapted for *Lux* had to be sidestepped. (Part of the reason for this, however, was the fact that radio was becoming ever more permissive.)

There were, over the years, several attempts to lighten George Wells's workload by hiring writing assistants, but none stayed for long. At times, an outside writer would be allowed to submit a script, which Wells would alter during rehearsals, often substantially rewriting it. True Boardman, principal writer for the CBS series *The Silver Theatre*, remembered, however, that at least one of his *Lux* scripts, "Broadway Bill," "got on very much the way I wrote it."[82]

Shows featuring popular radio comedians often found the comics' writers contributing gags or writing the entire interview spot during the curtain call (which was ordinarily the task of, first, Sandy Barnett, and later Harry Kerr, during the years George Wells was with *Lux*). Some, such as Jack Benny, were glad to have a chance to act in a legitimate role and wanted to avoid an excess of gags in the story. As Wells recalled,

> Very often, when we finished a script, particularly with Jack, I would ask him if he wanted his men in on it and he would say, "Not too much — I will tell them what I think." He didn't want the thing full of jokes, like Bob Hope would. Bob Hope's men did come in and do considerable joking up. They never did any of the building of scenes or anything, the production of the scenes or the choosing of the scenes, but they did hoke it np a little bit.[83]

Looking for the opportunity of creating entirely original radio plays for a change, George Wells received permission to do a little outside writing toward the end of his *Lux* stay, contributing a couple of scripts to *The Silver Theatre* and turning out a particularly memorable story for *Suspense* called "The Sisters."

When he left at the end of 1943, *Lux* was lucky to have another fine writer, Sandy Barnett, already working on the show. As framework writer (for commercials and interview spots), Barnett had served the series for three years, before becoming director in 1939. With the better-paying position now open, he resigned from Thompson and was transferred to what was known as the "talent budget." (The adapter was a freelance artist, not an employee of the agency.) Barnett began as principal writer with the first show of 1944, turning out consistently excellent scripts for the next ten and a half years, making truly outstanding radio plays out of the likes of *Berkeley Square* (on December 18, 1944), *Union Station* (on April 7, 1952), and *Phone Call from a Stranger* (on January 5, 1953). Barnett left the radio series at the end of the 1953–54 season to devote his talents exclusively to *The Lux Video Theatre*, but the "20 Greats" gimmick during the final year allowed *The Lux Radio Theatre* to present 19 previously used scripts written by him or George Wells, while five of the remaining shows (including one of the "20 Greats") were adapted by top-notch radio writer Milton Geiger and the other 15 by the equally capable Lenard St. Clair.

The Commercials

Both J. Walter Thompson and Lever Brothers took pride in their *Lux Radio Theatre*, seeing it not only as an effective means of selling their product, but also as an artistic achievement that created a considerable amount of good-will. Nevertheless, it was necessary to promote their wares, and the advertisement became an integral part of the show. Brief commercial announcements could come anywhere during the course of the program, but, right from the earliest shows in New York, the dramatized sketch became a popular way to plug Lux Toilet Soap or Lux Flakes. Actress Hope Cook, who appeared in two commercials in 1935, remembers that these miniature dramas often consisted of "two young women who talked in a rather disparaging way of the poor social life of a third young woman (who was not present) because she never washed her lingerie in Lux."[84] A good example of this type of commercial involved Cook and another actress between the acts of "Adam and Eva" on May 3, 1935:

JANE:
> Poor Amy! Everybody noticed she wasn't having a good time! It's a shame. After all, Amy *is* quite pretty...

SUE:
> And the men like her, really. Why, my brother says he'd go for Amy in a big way if it weren't for her complexion—

JANE:
> No, really, did he? Gee—let's *help* Amy! Let's send her some Lux Toilet Soap—

SUE:
> And I'll put in a note about how it guards against Cosmetic Skin. That's all the hint she needs...[85]

Sometimes these spots were remarkable in the amount of story they could tell in about 60 seconds, often involving emotional conflict and suspense, all leading to the inevitable happy ending. In the late 1930s audiences were often invited to listen in on the doings of the Browning family, consisting of two teenage daughters, a troublesome younger brother, and a set of parents. In the broadcast of October 17, 1938, the girls are having a hard time convincing a visiting aunt of Lux's wonders. As the older woman prepares, at her insistence, to wash the dishes, the drama begins:

AUNT CYNTHIA: *(IN A BRISK, AUTHORITATIVE VOICE)*
> Come now ... where d'ye keep your soap?

DOT:
> Here it is, Aunt Cynthia.

AUNT CYNTHIA:
> Humph! That box! Young lady, I don't hold with any of these new-fangled tricks. Haven't you got a cake of good strong soap?

DOT:
> But, Aunt Cynthia—Lux is wonderful! It leaves your hands looking just sparkie!

AUNT CYNTHIA:
> What's that, young lady?

DOT:
> Swell to look at, Aunt Cynthia.

BOBBY: *(PAUSE)*
> Like rose petals, she means, Aunt Cynthia. Thass what Archie Smith calls 'em.

AUNT CYNTHIA: *(SEVERELY)*
> Young man, I don't hold truck with such nonsense. My hands are quite adequate, I'm sure.

MIDGE:
> Aw, come on, Aunt Cyn. Be modern! All we want you to do is try Lux. Look... *(SOUND OF WATER RUNNING INTO DISHPAN WHILE SHE POURS IN FLAKES)* Bet you never saw suds like that! All bubbly and sparkly!

AUNT CYNTHIA:
> Humph!

DOT: *(ACCOMPANIED BY SOUND OF WASHING DISHES)*
> And look at the dishes! They just sparkle, too!

AUNT CYNTHIA: *(GRUDGINGLY)*
> They seem quite satisfactory.

MIDGE:
> Satisfactory! Migosh, Aunt Cynthia, they're a wow!

AUNT CYNTHIA: *(SEVERELY)*
> I wouldn't go so far as to say that, Margaret. *(PAUSE, THEN WEAKENING)* Let me try it. *(SOUND OF DISHES BEING WASHED)*

AUNT CYNTHIA:
> Very adequate, I should say. *(CHUCKLES SOFTLY TO HERSELF)* Sparkie hands, eh!

BOBBY:
> Gosh, Archie Smith'll he holdin' *your* hands next, Aunt Cynthia.

AUNT CYNTHIA: *(BRIDLING)*
> Robert—that'll be enough from you.[86]

As previously mentioned, Sandy Barnett, a Thompson employee since 1930, had been sent to Hollywood for the express purpose of working on the show when it moved there in 1936. His job was to write the framework, which included the commercials, intermission spots, and introduction— everything, in fact, other than the drama itself. Most shows during the first two seasons would feature a special guest after Act 2 and another after Act 3. Some of the best-known dignitaries, such as Jack Warner, D.W. Griffith, or King Vidor, were not called upon to promote the product, but one could be sure that at least one of the guests of the evening would have a kind word to say about Lux Toilet Soap or Lux Flakes. Not only would a costume designer, makeup artist, or wardrobe mistress bring Lux into the conversation, but so would as unlikely a personage as gold prospector Ted Atmore, as in the December 21, 1936, show:

. . .and I'll tell you what I'll do. The next claim I find, I'll name it Lux, on account of being here tonight. And I hope there'll be as many flakes of gold in it, as there are flakes of soap in a box of Lux. And don't think I don't know about Lux. After fifty years of washing my own clothes, I can tell plenty of women a thing or two.[87]

On occasion a commercial could be genuinely inspired, as was the one entitled "No, Junior," a very amusing one-woman dialogue performed by radio actress Alice Frost on the December 19, 1938, program. As DeMille explained, "Miss Frost now gives her impression of a young mother who, at the end of a long day, accompanied by her small son, Junior, . . . is shopping in a department store":

FROST:

No, Junior, you may *not* pull Santa Claus' whiskers. Why? Because Santa Claus doesn't like you to pull his whiskers. Wait 'til we get home and you can pull Grandpa's. Oh, I want six cakes of Lux Toilet Soap, please. Junior, come back here. Yes, six cakes, please. Who, Junior! *Where?* No, that's not cousin Lily. Cousin Lily wears black. Because poor Uncle Charlie went on a long, long journey. No, not to Newark, he went to heaven. Junior, you mustn't point. No, that lady isn't freckled . . . She just doesn't have a nice complexion . . . Sh-h-h-h, it's a friend of Mother's. . . . Oh, hello Eleanor. *(NERVOUS LAUGHTER)* Merry Christmas. Junior, say Merry Christmas to Mrs. Edwards. I'm buying myself a Christmas present, Eleanor. Lux Toilet Soap. I *always* use it. Yes, just like the screen stars! It has ACTIVE lather, you know. . . .[88]

The host's interview with the star or stars was almost always bound to contain an endorsement of the product, a tradition that began with the first program and continued until the series ended. The curtain calls during the New York years generally kept a serious tone unless the star being interviewed was a comedian, and there was little attempt at subtlety in working in the plug, as is evidenced by this excerpt from the October 14, 1935, show with Joan Crawford:

GARRICK:

Miss Crawford, you have every right to speak as an authority on beauty . . . and on beautiful complexions. Won't you tell us what you think of Lux Toilet Soap?

CRAWFORD:

I'm only too glad to. I've used Lux Soap for years, and I love it. When I go on a long trip, or whenever I go any place where I'm out of touch with the stores, I make sure that I have plenty of Lux Toilet Soap with me. I came East with a make-up bag full of it, so you can see how I depend on it. The reason why, of course, is because I like the way it keeps my skin![89]

The move to Hollywood brought a smoother approach to the same problem, demonstrated in the August 3, 1936, curtain call, with Fred MacMurray and Barbara Stanwyck:

DEMILLE:
> Personally, I think you're a fine actor, even if you do play the saxophone.

MACMURRAY:
> Well, I think you're about nine of the ten best directors in Hollywood, Mr. DeMille — and I like your soap, too.

STANWYCK:
> Who doesn't?

MACMURRAY:
> Well, speaking of soap reminds me of the Indian Chief down in New Mexico. He told me that he always bathes in a hole full of hot rocks. He said he fills the hole with water and the rocks give off steam — just like a Turkish bath.

DEMILLE:
> That was probably the original "open plumbing." It's a good idea for a bathtub, too. I'll probably steal it for my next picture.

STANWYCK:
> Well, personally, I never *tried* hot rocks and steam as a beauty cure, but I can recommend soap, water and sunshine — if a third of the combination is Lux Toilet Soap. I know about *that* because I use Lux Soap all the time.[90]

Beginning with the show of November 20, 1939, a new recurring character was added to the commercial lineup. The fabricated "Hollywood reporter" Libby Collins, who was in the tradition of the equally fictitious "beauty expert" Peggy Winthrop from the first season in New York, chatted with the announcer about various happenings in the movie capital, never failing to work Lux into the conversation. The character, first played by Margaret Brayton, would be played by a number of other actresses, including Ynez Seabury, Doris Singleton, Dorothy Lovett, and, on one occasion, even Eve Arden, before being dropped in 1952 (when real-life movie publicist Frances Scully took over). Many listeners assumed Collins was a real person, and Doris Singleton recalled that there were drawbacks to playing the part:

> I was delighted with the Libby Collins role, but unfortunately since Libby was portrayed as a real personality I could no longer be cast in acting roles because all of us sat on stage during the broadcast in full view of the audience. However, like any actress, I was happy to have a steady job and be under contract, plus the opportunity to work with C.B. [DeMille] and Wm. Keighley — both charming men.[91]

Later the Libby commercials were performed on the offstage microphone "and then I was able to play a variety of parts," Singleton declared.[92]

When Sandy Barnett became *Lux*'s director in 1939, Harry Kerr became the framework writer, with that position eventually going to Sam Carter after Kerr was elevated to the job of the show's talent buyer. The intermission guest spot was deleted after the 1938-39 season, but another version of it returned in the 1944-45 season via the host's interview with a promising young starlet between acts. The starlet spot was actually little more than a glorified commercial, and the girls rarely had anything to discuss other than their studio's latest release (in which they might or might not have appeared) and Lux. Several of these hopefuls went on to successful careers in movies, among them Janet Leigh, Nancy Gates, Martha Hyer, Marilyn Monroe, Debra Paget, and Debbie Reynolds. The starlet interview continued through the 1953-54 season, when it was dropped in favor of a straight commercial.

The Directors

Obviously one of the most important people involved with the assemblage of a radio show was the director. In the case of *The Lux Radio Theatre*, the director was the one responsible for hiring the supporting cast, suggesting the stars, and generally overseeing the production. The five men who served in this capacity on *Lux* during the show's 21-year history were among radio's best, beginning with Antony Stanford, who was at the helm for the first 82 broadcasts in New York. Stanford was something of a pioneer in the young medium, having started in radio in 1929, and his guidance was much sought after by performers who were just making their acquaintance with the microphone. A 1935 magazine article reported that

> air directing, Mr. Stanford has found, comes straight back to the theatre. Timing, pacing, tempo, showmanship — all have the same relationship to produce a good show that they have on Broadway. His first care has been to throw microphone tradition out of the window and make his actors feel comfortable and authentic in their characterizations. Wallace Beery played *The Old Soak* with his shirt open at the neck and his suspenders hanging down. Paul Muni had a coat rack put beside the microphone so that he could actually grab his coat, jam on his hat, and rush away in *Councellor-at-Law*. Mr. Stanford always, when it is possible, has his players do their own doors, having learned from long experience in the theatre that sometimes the way a door is closed can become a telling dramatic climax.[93]

Stanford's radio productions never totally escaped their stage origins, nor did he desire them to. Unfortunately, only one of the New York *Luxes* is known to have survived on record ("Dulcy," from October 28, 1935), but in it one can hear all the actors perform very much in the tradition of the theatre that Antony Stanford loved.

Frank Woodruff, *Lux's* first director after the move to Hollywood, came to the show from *The Shell Chateau*, which starred Al Jolson. Another former actor, Woodruff quickly established a reputation for being an expert in the handling of movie stars, many of whom made their radio debuts under his tutelage. As far as actual direction of a performance went, it was not necessary for him to give a great deal. Junior Coghlan remembers:

> We were all pros, and we read the script and we thought we knew how to do it and, in many cases, we had seen the movie, so he didn't have to give us an awful lot of hands-on direction. But, of course, if we were doing something wrong he'd tell us so. And I enjoyed Woodruff, he was such a charming guy.[94]

A CBS publicity release of the period quoted Frank Woodruff's explanation of one of the director's chief responsibilities:

> Timing is the big problem. The whole script has to be carefully checked, trimmed or expanded here and there. Almost every word is scheduled to a precise second. Yet none of this careful timing must interfere with the dramatic quality of the play.[95]

When Frank Woodruff left in 1939 to direct pictures at RKO, Sandy Barnett took over. Barnett, who had never been an actor, went about his job more quietly than the often demonstrative Woodruff. Actor Tyler McVey remembered him as "kind of introspective.... He was cerebral because he was a thoughtful guy, and he wasn't flamboyant at all. He was a good director."[96]

By the late thirties there was a stable of actors who made their living almost exclusively in radio, and, with the movie stars also becoming more comfortable in front of the microphone, players simply did not expect to receive a great deal of direction. *Lux*'s two remaining directors, Fred MacKaye and Earl Ebi, were also both ex-actors (MacKaye, in fact, went back to acting for a brief time after stepping down as *Lux* director in 1950) and, as in the case of Barnett, gave little performance instruction to the actors. "You had to bring in your characterization," Vanessa Brown explained. "That was one of the big factors in radio is that you had to bring in your characterization and you had to work on your own."[97] As far as the supporting players went, the director was so familiar with the works of most of them that, in the words of Sam Edwards, "he almost knew how they would play a part before he cast them."[98]

The fact that the director offered little guidance did not mean that his job was easy. As the general overseer of the program, he had a great responsibility. Buzz Kulik, who has since gone on to a lucrative career as a motion picture and television director, was a Thompson employee who had directed several *Lux Video Theatre* shows when, in 1954, he was asked to fill in for regular *Lux Radio Theatre* director Earl Ebi for two weeks. The first show he was to preside over was "What a Woman!" for the May 31 broadcast. Kulik discovered that a radio director's job was anything but simple:

> Cummings came to me and said, "Listen, do you mind if I wear this hat? It's part of a gag that we do right away, and it might grab the audience and pull the audience with us in the house," and I said, "No, not at all." I'd played the aircheck that had been done before [the show had previously been performed on March 14, 1949], and I talked to Sandy and a couple other people because it was almost like a lark that I was doing this . . . and they said, "We'll allow so many minutes for laughter and so on for 'spread,'" as we called it, "and then judge it as you go, and you'll be fine." So we rehearsed it, and then we went on the air . . . . Almost immediately he did the thing with the hat, I can't remember what it was, but the audience fell down and started to laugh and never stopped laughing for the whole hour. Now there was an assistant director who was, I think, a CBS employee, who was in the booth — I was on the stage. And I had a headset and he was saying to me, "Buzz, you're losing time — your spread is going!" By the end of the first act, the audience was simply howling. These were two such good performers and they'd gotten off to such a rollicking start that by the end of the first act I'd eaten up about three-quarters of the spread and I had two acts to go, so I went to these two actors and I said to them, "Listen, you've got to ride through these laughs because we're losing time!" "Don't worry." Well, you know two actors getting those kinds of laughs on a live stage, they're not about to slow down, and by the end of the second act I'd lost all my spread and I was sweating. And again I went to them while the commercials were going on and I said, "Listen, you've *got* to pick it up or we'll never get off the air!" By the time we finished the third act, we were about two minutes over, and they had to cut a lot of stuff at the end — the interview, whatever, and when we finished, I want to tell you, I was a wreck beyond compare, and I think that was maybe the most difficult experience I've ever had in my career.[99]

The Actors

Lux's supporting casts throughout its history boasted the best actors radio had to offer. The first shows in New York included mostly thespians from the stage, with director Antony Stanford using players from the original production whenever possible in even the smallest roles. Some of the actors whose performances boosted many an East Coast *Lux* production included Alma Kruger, Burford Hampden, Raymond Bramley, James Jolley, Wilfred Lytell, Eric Dressler, John F. Hamilton, and Averell Harris. Frequent *Lux* performers such as Hanley Stafford, Santos Ortego (later Ortega), Carleton Young, and Wright Kramer, primarily associated with the theatre at this time, would later become popular players in West Coast radio programs. Future leading ladies Betty Field, Rosemary deCamp, and Rita Johnson all acted in *Lux* commercials at least once during 1935 or 1936. DeCamp, a

Publicity portrait of Lou Merrill, frequent *Lux* supporting player (photo: Photofest).

busy New York radio actress at the time, recalled, "We got about $15 for a broadcast, and if you ran from Madison Avenue CBS over to Radio City and, if you made the lights all right, you could get two shows in an hour—but you had to be quick on your feet."[100]

The records of popular singer Billy Murray were more than likely in many households across America when he made his series debut as a grocer in a *Lux* commercial on March 31, 1935, later going on to appear in several more *Luxes* before the show deserted New York for Hollywood. Both of the actors to play host Douglass Garrick, John Anthony and Albert Hayes, were also veterans of the Broadway stage, as was Doris Dagmar, who played the recurring role of beauty adviser Peggy Winthrop in commercials during the first season.

In Hollywood *Lux* had a new stable of supporting players from which to draw, and the early programs from the West Coast found many familiar movie character actors in their casts, with the likes of Eddie Kane, Byron Foulger, Clara Blandick, Chester Clute, and Rolfe Sedan often playing much the same sorts of roles they did on the screen. Two performers who were to become fixtures on the show, Lou Merrill and Frank Nelson, appeared in the first program from Hollywood and in virtually every other for the next three years. Lou Merrill became the unofficial assistant to Frank Woodruff and later Sandy Barnett, and directed the crowd scenes. A very versatile actor, as were many radio performers, Merrill might be cast in anything from the tiny role of a street vendor or a judge to an important part, such as that of comically naive Texas oilman Dan Leeson in "The Awful Truth" (Ralph Bellamy's picture role) or sophisticated movie executive Oliver Niles in "A Star Is Born" (Adolphe Menjou's screen character). He appeared only occasionally after the early 1940s but continued to be an active performer on the air, and he was especially memorable in his dryly comic characterization of host "Thomas Highland" in CBS's brilliant *Crime Classics* program of 1953-54. Frank Nelson's voice was the first heard on each of the *Lux Radio Theatre* shows from June 1, 1936, to July 10, 1939, as it was his job to make the opening announcement of date, play, and stars prior to the entrance of regular announcer Melville Ruick. Nelson usually played a role in the drama as well and sometimes doubled in two small parts, which was a common practice in the Hollywood shows. His roles were almost always of the minor variety, such as a newsboy, a reporter, or a radio announcer, but once in a while he would be given the chance to perform in a substantial part and even received featured billing in "The Green Light" on January 31, 1938. After departing as a regular, Nelson never appeared on a *Lux* again, but continued his successful career as a radio and later television actor, making a special niche for himself in comedy roles, especially as Jack Benny's nemesis on that comedian's program.

Eddie Marr, who acted in most of the *Lux* programs between his first appearance on June 14, 1937, and the final show on June 7, 1955, certainly holds the record for most appearances on the series. His talent for portraying Brooklyn cabbies, newsboys, and carnival barkers meant that he too was often heard in small roles, but his occasional opportunities to play important supporting parts were worth waiting for, and he made lasting impressions portraying such characters as Max, a rowdy from the newspaper circulation department in "Nothing Sacred" (Maxie Rosenbloom's movie role) and the cab driver in "Close to My Heart" (his own screen part). Eddie Marr also served as an unofficial assistant to *Lux*'s directors and in the 1950s took over from another *Lux* regular, Charles Seel, as director of the crowd scenes. Some actors specialized in certain kinds of roles, and thus Earl Keen and Lee Millar were often called on to play dogs, cats, or cows, and even, in one case, a trained seal, and Duane Thompson or Leone Ledoux (both adult women) were usually the actresses tapped if there was an infant or young child character in the script. Others who were semiregulars during *Lux*'s first decade on the West Coast included Ynez Seabury, Victor Rodman, Ross Forrester, Earle Ross, Eric Snowden, Julie Bannon (who had a regular role as "Sally" in commercials for a time), and Fred MacKaye (whose frequent acting appearances stopped when he became the show's director in 1944).

The Lux Radio Theatre was generally considered the best dramatic show on the air, and actors looked forward to getting a call from the director's office to do the show. As then child actor Dix Davis recalled, "Everybody who worked it loved it because the paycheck was about twice as much as the average other show like *Theatre Guild* or *Silver Theatre*."[101] The reason for the larger salary was that there were more rehearsals than on other shows, as Davis explained:

Fred MacMurray in front of *Lux*'s "Cups of Fame," which began in 1950 (photo: Photofest).

It was the most rehearsed radio show in the business, not only because it was long (an hour, and not too many of them were that long), but they simply spent a lot of money on the show and they insisted on more rehearsals. . . . The average [other] show would have . . . the early rehearsal, the run-through, the first mike rehearsal, and then the writers would go back and make changes and all that. Then you'd come back, two days later, maybe, and there might be another mike rehearsal, then a dress rehearsal, and that would be it. Say, two afternoons or two evenings. *Lux* went on for about five days.... Rehearsals were scheduled on more days—twice as many days, I would say—as other shows.[102]

The period surrounding the Second World War saw several other actors join the *Lux* stock company, some of whom had previously appeared on infrequent occasions. Bea Benaderet, probably best remembered today for her comic characterizations such as the telephone operator Gertrude on *The Jack Benny Program*, and on television as neighbor Blanche Morton on *The George Burns and Gracie Allen Show*, and as the star of *Petticoat Junction*, played both comedy and dramatic roles on *Lux* with equal effectiveness (standing out as the kindly grandmother in both presentations of "Love Affair" and as the heroine's cruel mother in the second broadcast of "Remember the Night"). Verna Felton was almost always heard in comedy roles but was a convincingly vengeful Madame Defarge in "A Tale of Two Cities" on January 12, 1942. Arthur Q. Bryan, famous as the voice of Elmer Fudd in the Warner Bros. cartoons, was another familiar radio actor who frequently appeared on *Lux*, often as comic bosses and the like, and was especially effective as the hammy defense attorney in "Remember the Night" on December 22, 1941. Griff Barnett and Norman Field made effective grandfather types or bankers, and Barnett was sometimes on hand to reprise his movie characterizations, as he was in "To Each His Own" (as the heroine's understanding father) and for both broadcasts of "Apartment for Peggy" (as the wise Dr. Conway). Field, who started as a professional actor around the turn of the century, became an expert on radio and in 1940 was put in charge of the radio dramatic division of the UCLA Extension Department, teaching radio courses in Berkeley and Alameda, California, high schools. Joseph Kearns was one of the members of the postwar *Lux* company; an excellent actor in virtually any sort of role, he gave especially compelling performances in the Claude Rains screen part of the Nazi agent and husband of the leading lady in "Notorious," and in the Edward G. Robinson role of the immigrant father in "Our Vines Have Tender Grapes." Alan Reed was another performer primarily associated with comedies (and was the poet Falstaff Oppenshaw on *The Fred Allen Show*) and was heard to best advantage as bombastic fathers of the Edward Arnold type, as in "Dear Ruth" (which he performed twice), but he could give a quiet characterization when called upon to do so and was a regal Sir Thomas Gainsborough in "Kitty." (He later became the voice of Fred Flintstone in the animated television series *The Flintstones*.) Bill Johnstone appeared in all sorts of roles, but made a specialty of police inspectors (crooked or honest) and later starred as one in CBS radio's *The Lineup*. Herb Butterfield was at his best in roles of flustered college presidents or pig-headed politicians, and he was particularly memorable as the title character in "The Wizard of Oz" and as Uncle Thaddeus in "The Bachelor and the Bobby Soxer." Noreen Gammill was usually called upon to play old ladies (eccentric or otherwise), and Betty Lou Gerson often played the second female lead in *Lux* productions such as "The Man Who Came to Dinner" (where she was Lorraine), and she sometimes got the leading lady role, as in "Cheaper by the Dozen," opposite Clifton Webb. Others gracing *Lux* casts on several occasions at this time included silent movie stars Herbert Rawlinson and Frances X. Bushman, and soon to be a motion picture star Jeff Chandler (formerly Ira Grossel).

Oftentimes a supporting actor was asked, in addition to playing his assigned role, to appear as well in the crowd scenes, as Jeff Corey explained:

> Sometimes we doubled and sometimes we did what they call "omnes" — all the voices together.... Lou Merrill used to be in charge of that, later Charlie Seel. Sandy Barnett used to use Lou Merrill for all his miscellaneous voices, then Charlie Seel did it when Fred MacKaye directed.... We were all pretty good at it. We had an attitude about the characters in the crowd and so forth. We weren't just making "ruba, ruba, ruba," we were really talking and improvising pretty good dialogue. We got pretty skilled ... Charles Seel didn't have to direct us. If he came close to the mike, we came close to the mike, if he walked away, we walked away — it was really very uncomplicated.[103]

A 1951 CBS publicity release features Eddie Marr's comments on the importance of these scenes, after he had taken over as crowd director from Charles Seel:

> It is our job to establish the scene in which the leads are enacting the major drama. Take, for instance, "Lux's" recent broadcast of "That Forsyte Woman." During that show, the respective settings of a restaurant, a bookstore, an art gallery, a dance and a street scene had to be established behind the dialogue of the principal players. This was accomplished by the changing ad-libs of the supporting performers, which were as carefully planned and rehearsed as the written dialogue. It is this consciousness of background detail that is an important contributing factor to the "Lux Radio Theatre's" long-time success.[104]

The late forties and fifties saw such old standbys as Eddie Marr and Tyler McVey make more appearances, while a new crowd, including Howard McNear (who had actually appeared on *Lux* occasionally in the early 1940s), Jack Kruschen, Ed Begley, Eleanor Audley, George Neise, and Ruth Perrott, became an important part of the show. William Conrad continued to play key roles on *Lux* even after establishing himself as Marshal Matt Dillon on radio's *Gunsmoke* in 1952, and Parley Baer, the Chester of that same series, was heard in all sorts of roles in *Lux*'s final seasons after his debut in 1953.

Some actors were understandably nervous about appearing before an unseen audience of 30 million plus, according to Sam Edwards: "Some of them were terrified—they really were."[105] Of course, the prospect of appearing on the air did not affect all people the same way, but all of those appearing were thorough professionals and rarely did any of their nervousness come through in a performance. Any stage fright an actor might have was an indication of how seriously he was taking the engagement, and they *did* take their radio appearances seriously—none of the stars brought a condescending attitude to rehearsals with the idea that this was in some way less important than picture work. "I think they enjoyed it enormously," Jeff Corey said.[106]

Corey remembered an incident involving Bette Davis during a rehearsal for *All This and Heaven, Too,* in which he played a very aggressive prosecuting attorney, which displays Davis's commitment to her art under even the most uninspiring conditions:

> We were doing a recording for the Sunday show so this was, I believe, a dress rehearsal. . . . Bette was hungry, so they quickly delivered to her a wonderful Brown Derby hamburger with everything on it, and she proceeded to eat it as we acted. And I was badgering her as the attorney and . . . it wasn't the onions, she was crying real tears—she was acting and munching the hamburger. . . . She just loved to act.[107]

Josephine Hutchinson recalled an event that took place on another series, *The Gulf Screen Guild Show,* where, before the broadcast of a story called "Bridge of Mercy" on March 5, 1939, another artist's serious regard for the medium was displayed:

> [Paul] Muni played the part of a man going to the electric chair, and I was his wife. A number of important business executives in their conservative three-piece suits came to the studio and passed out carnations to everyone, including cast members. Offered a carnation for his lapel, Muni indignantly exclaimed, "I can't wear a carnation; *I'm* going to the electric chair!" Even though this was a broadcast and he would not be seen, his dedication to work and his role was complete, as usual.[108]

One attractive feature of *The Lux Radio Theatre* for listeners as well as for the actors was that it sometimes allowed stars to work together who had never appeared together on screen because they were contracted to different studios. Some of the most interesting of these teamings include Maureen O'Sullivan and Ronald Colman in "Berkeley Square," Veronica Lake and Ralph Bellamy in "Sullivan's Travels," Marlene Dietrich and Clark Gable in "The Legionnaire and the Lady," Grace Moore and Peter Lorre in "Trilby," Janet Gaynor and William Powell in "Mayerling," Fredric March and Jean Arthur in "The Plainsman," and Lupe Velez and Herbert Marshall in "Under Two Flags."

Any *Lux Radio Theatre* was an event for the cast, the listeners, and the large studio audience in attendance, and the actors were required to wear formal dress, as Vanessa Brown recalled: "We had an audience and they expected us to look like movie people—movie *stars.*"[109] Ralph Bellamy remembered his feelings before airtime: "We were all as nervous as a first night on stage or the first day of a picture, before stepping up to the mike...."[110]

There was, at that time, a glamour and even a mystique surrounding the stars which do not prevail in the business today, and many oft-repeated stories concerning *Lux* stars have circulated over the years. One such tale concerns Constance Bennett and her cocker spaniel, Chips. Bennett, during rehearsals of "I Found Stella Parish" (to be broadcast on July 4, 1938), brought her dog along but for obvious reasons left him home on the day of the actual performance. During the broadcast the actress was shocked to see her pet approaching her from the wings. A 1940 article described the scene that supposedly followed:

> Chips . . . ambled over to her and sat up amiably, his fore paws dangling in front of him, honest brown eyes beseeching reward. And then it was that Connie nearly had a fit. You who listened to her that night didn't know it, but all the while she was acting in that very dramatic story, she was frantically pushing at the bewildered Chips, trying to get him away from her, but at the same time motioning others bent on eliminating him, to stand back. The general effect was gymnastic to say the least. And when the "curtain" finally went down Connie was a wreck. "When he sits up, he barks," she gasped, "especially if he's interfered with before he gets his dog biscuit." However, perhaps bewildered by the unfamiliar behavior of his mistress, or perhaps silenced solely by the grace of the god of radio, he hadn't barked on this occasion. He had just sat there. But it was a near thing.[111]

Another incident that has been described often occurred prior to the beginning of the *Lux* production of "The Letter," when Bette Davis, moments before airtime, announced that she had just taken poison. Upon being questioned, Davis reported that she had asked her maid or chauffeur (accounts differ) to bring her a glass of water with a few drops of spirits of ammonia in it, and the servant, attempting to comply with her request, had brought her a tumbler of water with *household* ammonia in it. The actress recovered sufficiently to appear on the program, and disaster was once again narrowly avoided.

One story told in an official J. Walter Thompson publicity release and retold in countless articles about *Lux* which is definitely *not* true reports that "Random Harvest" contained a sound cue for a squeaking gate. According to the story, sound man Charlie Forsyth had a terrible time getting the gate to squeak exactly as required:

> After dress rehearsal, Charlie told his assistant to clean up the sound booth, and in doing so, the assistant methodically oiled every hinge on the gate, so that it swung noiselessly. When Ronald Colman appeared at his imaginary cottage, Charlie Forsyth received his cue from the director and opened his gate. There was the most thunderous crash of silence the sound man had ever heard. The show was saved by Colman, who quietly ad-libbed "I see you have oiled the gate!"[112]

The supposed incident makes a good story, but the fact is that neither of *Lux*'s broadcasts of "Random Harvest" (both of which use the same script) contain any such scene.

One of the most frequently encountered yarns about *any* radio show concerned an incident that was also supposed to have happened on *Lux*. According to a 1970 item in *Variety*, it occurred as Joseph Cotten was handed a slip to read at the close of a broadcast, announcing the following week's show. Cotten allegedly read the line this way: "Hollywood's newest sensation and a new talent personality, SONNY TUFTS?"[113] This statement in the form of a question is supposed to have "broken up" the studio audience, but in fact Sonny Tufts made only one appearance on *The Lux Radio Theatre* and Joseph Cotten *did not* appear on the previous week's show. Besides, as regular *Lux* listeners knew, it was on extremely rare occasions that a star would announce the following week's players, as that task was regularly undertaken by the show's host. Tufts's one *Lux* assignment came in the November 1, 1943, broadcast of "So Proudly We Hail"; the preceding week's stars were Lana Turner and Victor Mature, and the coming attraction announcement on October 25 went as follows:

TURNER:
Now, what's your play next week, Mr. DeMille?
DEMILLE:
One of the big successes of the current screen, Lana. It's the Paramount hit, "So Proudly We Hail." And the stars are Claudette Colbert, Paulette Goddard, Veronica Lake and Sonny Tufts—the same stars you saw in the picture—one of the finest casts we've ever had. And the play is in keeping with the cast, an heroic story of Bataan, with Claudette Colbert, Paulette Goddard and Veronica Lake as the Army nurses of "So Proudly We Hail."
MATURE:
I think you can hail that one very proudly, sir. Good night.
TURNER:
Good night.
DEMILLE:
Good night, goodbye. You two certainly make good listening![114]

The *Variety* account even goes so far as to say that the play being promoted during the incident was "The Major and the Minor," with Joan Fontaine as Mr. Tufts's costar; that story *was* performed on *Lux*, but with Ginger Rogers and Ray Milland.

Sound Effects

An extremely important person on the production team of a radio drama is the sound man, whose sound effects help to create the illusion of reality. When radio drama started during the 1920s, the actors were expected to provide their own sound effects, but as the art of the microphone play developed, sound effects became more sophisticated and were created by a man specifically employed for the purpose. *Lux*'s New York shows were done with a minimum of production, and sound cues were relatively sparse, but once on the West Coast this aspect of the presentations developed quickly and considerably. Charlie Forsyth started his show business career as a musician, playing the clarinet and the drums, before making the creation of sound effects his life. He joined *Lux* with the first Hollywood show and remained until the last, 19 years later, in that time providing over 65,000 different effects. Sound was more than a job with Forsyth, it was a hobby as well, and he spent much of his free time traveling about the country recording interesting and unusual sounds that might later be used on the air. ("He's been attacked by enraged hogs, buzzed by a swarm of bees, lunged at by rattlesnakes," reported a CBS news release.)[115] A description of some of the sound man's effects was contained in an early press release:

> Charlie shows us how, during the Marlene Dietrich–Clark Gable show "The Legionnaire and the Lady" he achieved the sound of a car door closing by gently shutting a traveling bag.... The realistic explosion was achieved by bouncing a rubber ball full of shot, the ball being supported by rubber bands. A wireless key, tapped just the right way, gives the sound of a whining shell in "The Dark Angel."[116]

Charlie Forsyth was passionately dedicated to his work, which he took very seriously. Scriptwriter George Wells recalls that "he always got me aside and asked, 'What's in the script for next week? What's in the script?' I had to describe each sound to him."[117] A period article (credited to William Keighley) illustrated his resourcefulness in the face of disaster:

> During a show guest-starring Bob Burns, the script called for, in the order named, a music bridge, the sound of an automobile pulling away, another music bridge denoting lapse of travel time, the sound of crickets, indicating new surroundings, and lastly the sound of the same car coming in at full swell and then halting. After the second music bridge, Charlie put the needle down on the records on which he had captured the sound of the approaching halting car and the sound of crickets. The disc was dead. The amplifier tube had blown out. "I felt," Forsyth revealed later, "like a man on the top of a hill who applies his brakes and finds there aren't any." Charlie quickly fell back on another found prop, a car door. He slammed it with relish, following which he simulated footsteps. Thus with different sounds he established the same effect.[118]

As radio production increasingly sought to create a realistic atmosphere, more of the sound effects used became recordings of the actual source, and fewer were mechanical imitations. In 1953 Charlie Forsyth's collection (which belonged to him personally) was estimated to contain 2,000 recorded sides for a total of 8,000 sound effects, and was said to be worth $25,000. Beginning in the 1940s Forsyth's son Eugene often assisted, but Charlie remained *the Lux* sound man until the series went off the air in 1955.

Everything on radio had to be conveyed with sound, of course, and the importance of Forsyth's contribution cannot be overstated. "Jeopardy," for example, which aired on March 15, 1954, concerns a woman's desperate attempts to secure help in freeing her trapped husband from a collapsed pier on the ocean shore. As the story progresses, one can *hear* that the tide is coming in, and that the water is getting closer and closer to enveloping the helpless man. There is, of course, discussion of the events among the characters, but it is the sound of the rising tide, as the volume level of the splashing water steadily increases, that paints the horrifying picture in the mind of the listener better than any word description could, whether he is consciously aware of it or not.

Music

Music is one more feature of dramatic radio production which is essential in creating or reinforcing images in the listener's mind. The scripts to the New York shows indicate that they contained far fewer music cues than did those programs originating from Hollywood, and "Dulcy," the one show known to survive on record from this period, bears this out. It would undoubtedly be a mistake to assume that all the New York broadcasts followed the same pattern, but we can probably surmise that this production's use of music was fairly typical. Here Robert Armbruster's themes are used sparingly, with music heard only at the beginning of each act (during the host's scene-setting narration) and at the close of the act. There are no musical bridges whatsoever during the dramatic portion of the broadcast, and the only other music heard is the opening and closing theme (by Robert Armbruster), which is played at a faster tempo and with considerably more lilt than it would be on the Hollywood shows. There were certainly instances in which Maestro Armbruster was given a better chance to display his talents for composing and arranging, as was noted in a 1935 article:

> One of the best things about this program ... is Robert Armbruster's music. For the first time in the history of radio every play presented has its own original score. As soon as the script is ready Mr. Stanford turns it

over to Mr..Armbruster with annotations as to how he is handling each
scene; and Mr. Armbruster composes harmonic backgrounds which set
the mood for the entire broadcast. In obvious cases like *Smilin' Through*
and *Lilac Time* he has used familiar tunes, but what he did for *Berkeley
Square* with his mysterious, eerie melodies was an arresting prophecy of
how this sort of radio scene designing can be developed.[119]

When *The Lux Radio Theatre* moved to Hollywood, Robert Armbruster remained in New York, but the popular composer-conductor eventually made his way to the West Coast where he continued his prolific radio
career.

The musical director selected for the Hollywood *Lux* had no previous
radio experience at all. Louis Silvers, formerly a busy staff composer-
arranger-conductor at Warner Bros. and Columbia (where he was awarded
the first Oscar for film scoring for 1934's *It Happened One Night*), was, by
1936, an equally busy musical director at 20th Century–Fox. He accepted
Lux's offer to provide the music for the first Hollywood season with some
misgivings but soon proved himself an immensely effective radio composer,
and he remained with the program for the next 14 seasons. Incidental music
in radio drama functions differently from the way it does in film, and Silvers
clearly understood this from the outset. Music's primary purpose in *The Lux
Radio Theatre* (and in most other radio dramas of the period) is to tie
together scenes. A musical bridge between scenes can depict a change in
time or place which, when properly combined with the appropriate sound
effects (when necessary), will leave no doubt in the listener's mind that a
transition has occurred. A Louis Silvers bridge will generally reflect the
mood of the scene that has transpired and, if a deviation is required, will
alter its character midway to prepare the audience for the mood of the
scene that is about to occur. Music during actual dialogue among characters
is relatively uncommon, but sometimes a bridge will overlap into the beginning of a conversation or commence toward the end of a scene, and then,
following the conclusion of the passage of dialogue, swell up and take the
story into the next scene. Very brief scenes often contain music throughout,
especially if their function is to punctuate or tie together two more important scenes in the drama, and scenes set in a nightclub or café usually
feature an orchestra playing in the background to create atmosphere. Occasionally, however, Silvers would depart from this formula, as he often did
during love scenes, where music under the dialogue could greatly enhance
the sequence. One broadcast where this was used to great effect was
"Desire" (aired on March 15, 1937), where Debussy's "Reverie" is played
(with the melody taken by a solo violin) during the first real love scene of
the leading couple (portrayed by Marlene Dietrich and Herbert Marshall).
The sensual melody leaves no doubt in the mind of the listener that this man
and woman are absolutely sincere in their declarations of love for one another,

which is especially important in this story as the woman had earlier only pretended to have a romantic interest in the man for her own purposes. (Those scenes tellingly contained no musical underscoring.) Use of music in this manner is probably not something most members of the listening audience were conscious of, but it very much affected their emotional reactions to the story and characters. *Lux*'s musical director often took advantage of interesting dramatic situations by scoring them in an unusual manner, as in Leora's death scene in "Arrowsmith" (October 25, 1937), which he accompanies with a chorus's wordless chant.

Louis Silvers eventually built up a substantial library of musical themes, some of his own compositions and some his arrangements of pre-existing pieces. These tunes would be used over and over again in appropriate situations (and the same music sometimes fit scenes of widely varied mood), so that although some shows required entirely new scores others could be successfully scored almost entirely from music already in the collection. Thus, when "Portrait of Jenny," the film of which had used several compositions by Claude Debussy in its score, was presented on October 31, 1949, Silvers merely returned to that same "Reverie" and put it to use as the main theme. And though it was not one of the Debussy themes used in the film version, its impressionistic melody is very characteristic of the French composer, and it successfully assisted the broadcast in recapturing the mood of the picture.

One of Silvers's own themes of which he made liberal use was the waltz that had been used over the opening credits of his 1934 Columbia pictures, *It Happened One Night* and *Twentieth Century*. It was heard frequently in thirties *Lux* shows (and occasionally in forties shows) and even found itself in the story it was created for when "It Happened One Night" was presented on March 20, 1939. A great many neutral cues were also pressed into service on frequent occasions, such as one entitled "Downstream" (so named to reflect its descending scale pattern) and a sprightly, somewhat mocking theme called "Joy," which brought many a *Lux* comedy's first or second act to a fitting conclusion.

During the Second World War it was necessary to come up with themes appropriate to war stories, so Silvers created cues entitled "Menace" and "Attack," and a piece especially useful in depicting Nazi activities, "Foreboding," which briefly quotes "Siegfried's Funeral March" from Wagner's opera *Götterdämmerung* and "The Ride of the Valkyries" from the same composer's *Die Walküre*. It was, of course, common practice during this period to interpolate Wagner into music representing the Führer's army. These two pieces were quoted in countless movie scores, but rarely were they woven into a new composition with more subtlety or effectiveness than they were by *Lux*'s musical director.

Announcer John Milton Kennedy remembered Lou Silvers as

Publicity photo of musical director Rudy Schrager circa 1952 (photo: Photofest).

one of those guys that it took me a long time to become acquainted with. . . . I thought he had no sense of humor until one time in rehearsal I was in the midst of doing a commercial [offstage] and Lou Silvers gave me a hot foot. . . . That softened me up in my attitude towards him. I knew from then on that the guy really had a sense of humor and was a delightful person.[120]

The musicians in the *Lux* orchestra (which generally consisted of between 16 and 24 members during the Hollywood years) had to be very versatile, playing everything from symphonic music to swing, and many were capable of making a good showing as soloists on a concert stage.

When Louis Silvers stepped down as musical director at the end of the 1949-50 season, *Lux* was fortunate in having an extremely able replacement already on the payroll. Rudolph ("Rudy") Schrager, a native of Czernowitz, Austria (where he was born in 1905), had functioned as an assistant to Lou Silvers from the start, often working as rehearsal pianist and playing in the orchestra as well. During the ASCAP ban in 1941, Maestro Silvers was not allowed to use his own music (though he still conducted), so the young Mr. Schrager stepped in and composed and arranged the show's music for the next several months, at times providing original themes even after the ban was lifted. (The *Lux* "Between the Acts" theme was a 1938 collaboration between Rudy Schrager and Lou Silvers.) Beginning with the 1950-51 season Rudy Schrager took over as the show's full-fledged musical director, carrying on in the tradition of his predecessor. Although Schrager's own music can at times have a slightly modernistic edge to it, it is still firmly fixed in the Romantic style. Schrager's compositions lean toward the Germanic school, differing in this respect from Silvers's music, which has more of a general European flavor.

When *The Lux Video Theatre* moved to Hollywood in September 1953, Rudy Schrager was made musical director of that series as well, performing, incredibly, in both positions until the radio series ended in 1955. When it was decided that a new *Lux Radio Theatre* signature tune was in order for the program's move to NBC in 1954, Schrager was asked to provide it. Publicized as a new composition, it actually went back as far as 1942 when it served as the music for a concert sequence in "City for Conquest" on February 9. Its soaring, optimistic Rachmaninoff-like theme served to represent the flavor of the series well, however, and its slightly bittersweet quality was especially appropriate to what many surmised would be the show's final season.

Lux's Rivals

The popularity of *The Lux Radio Theatre,* beginning with the first Hollywood season in 1936, inspired others to create programs based more or less on *Lux's* successful formula. *The Silver Theatre,* which was recently described by that show's principal writer, True Boardman, as, "the junior *Lux,*"[121] used the same guest star format and even billed its host, Conrad Nagel, as "director," reminiscent of Cecil B. DeMille's title of "producer" on *Lux.* One difference between the shows was that *Silver Theatre's* 30-minute dramas were originals (often by Boardman or Grover Jones) or were based on unfilmed stories. Some of the plays were presented in two parts (always of 30 minutes each) early in the series' history, and the premiere story, "First Love," even ran for three weeks (October 3, 10, and 17, 1937).

Another interesting series in the *Lux* tradition was *The Gulf Screen Guild Show,* which premiered on CBS on January 9, 1939, offering 30-minute variety shows but soon began alternating these with original dramas. Beginning on November 26 the series was called *The Gulf Screen Guild Theater* and now presented half-hour adaptations of movies, with occasional originals or variety programs thrown in. *The Screen Guild,* which began its run Sunday nights at 7:30, was produced for the benefit of the Motion Picture Relief Fund, and all the salaries that would have gone to the stars were instead donated to that organization for the construction and maintenance of the Motion Picture Country Home. This tie-in with such a worthy cause meant that *Screen Guild's* star-filled casts often rivaled *Lux's,* but the half-hour radio versions of full-length feature films often had a breathless quality and could rarely do full justice to a story. When Gulf dropped its sponsorship at the end of the 1941-42 season Lady Esther cosmetics took over, and the series was called *The Lady Esther Screen Guild Players* starting with the 1942-43 season and was even given the Monday evening ten o'clock time slot immediately following *Lux.* In the fall of 1947 the sponsorship was changed again, and now the show was called *The Camel*

Screen Guild Players; the final season found the show sponsorless on ABC, expanded to an hour, and entitled simply *The Screen Guild Players*. After running a single season as a sustainer, *Screen Guild* was canceled.

One of the best of the dramas was the short-lived *The Campbell Playhouse*, which was really Orson Welles's *Mercury Theatre* with a sponsor (Campbell's Soup) and the 9:00 P.M. Friday time slot of the now defunct *Hollywood Hotel* (which had also been sponsored by Campbell's). *The Mercury Theatre of the Air*, which had run for 22 weeks on CBS beginning July 11, 1938, was an often brilliant series that strove to take full advantage of the audio medium in one-hour adaptations of classics of literature, such as *Dracula, Treasure Island, Julius Caesar*, and *The War of the Worlds*. The excellent casts featured many of the Mercury Players who would later attain fame, such as Orson Welles, Ray Collins, Joseph Cotten, Agnes Moorehead, Everett Sloane, and Paul Stewart. When the show became *The Campbell Playhouse*, Orson Welles, who was the show's director, host, star, and coproducer (with John Houseman), found himself with a larger budget to work with and a sponsor interested in attaining higher ratings. Therefore, the revamped Mercury show featured lighter and often more modern fare (sometimes based on recent movies) and included a celebrity to costar opposite Welles in each week's production. As was the case with the *Mercury Theatre* programs, the new series was highlighted by the inspired scores of musical director Bernard Herrmann, whose music played a large part in the artistic success of the presentations. Among the genuinely memorable programs performed on *The Campbell Playhouse* were several plays that were also performed on *Lux*, and the often very different treatments of the same material make fascinating comparisons. When Orson Welles discovered after scheduling "Wuthering Heights" for his September 24, 1939, broadcast that *Lux* intended to present its version of the same story on September 18, he announced that he had changed his plans and would air the play on September 17. Reason prevailed, however, and Welles dropped "Wuthering Heights" entirely and never did broadcast his version. By early 1940 Welles was busy with his motion picture work, and his *Campbell Playhouse* participation ended with the March 31, 1940, broadcast, though the program continued for another season without him. Orson Welles was to have several more radio series in the next decade, but none ever approached the overall artistic merit of *The Mercury Theatre* or *The Campbell Playhouse*.

Some of the many other dramatic anthology programs to follow in *Lux*'s footsteps were *The Theatre Guild of the Air* (also known as *The U.S. Steel Hour*), *The Screen Director's Playhouse, Academy Award*, and *The Ford Theatre*. Excellent though some of their presentations were, few of the shows were as consistently entertaining as those of *The Lux Radio Theatre*, and no other "prestige drama" series ever approached *Lux* in terms of ratings or longevity.

Notes

1. Erik Barnouw, *A Tower in Babel* (New York: Oxford University Press, 1966), p. 136.

2. _____, *The Golden Web* (New York: Oxford University Press, 1968), pp. 103–4.

3. *Lux Radio Theatre*, October 14, 1934.

4. *Lux Radio Theatre*, April 11, 1935.

5. Ruth Woodbury Sedgwick, "Our Unseen Theatre," *Stage*, June 1935, p. 42.

6. *Ibid.*

7. George Wells, interview with Arthur Pierce, January 31, 1993.

8. Jonathan Hole, interviews with Arthur Pierce, September 15, 1990, and February 22, 1993.

9. *Ibid.*, February 22, 1993.

10. George Wells, interview with Arthur Pierce, August 23, 1992.

11. Orrin E. Dunlap, Jr., "Sleight of Hand with Drama," *New York Times*, July 28, 1935, sec. 10, p. 11.

12. *Ibid.*

13. Dora Albert, "Secrets of the Lux Radio Theatre," *Radio Stars*, December 1936, p. 74.

14. Antony Stanford, J. Walter Thompson Program Report, February 3, 1935.

15. George Wells, interview with Arthur Pierce, January 31, 1993.

16. *Ibid.*

17. J. Walter Thompson Program Report, September 30, 1935.

18. George Wells, interview with Arthur Pierce, April 1, 1993.

19. "Notes on radio meeting with Mr. Gilman," February 4, 1936, p. 2.

20. *Ibid.*, p. 3.

21. *Ibid.*, p. 4.

22. *The Lux Radio Theatre*, June 1, 1936.

23. Mrs. Frank Woodruff, interview with Arthur Pierce, September 15, 1990.

24. Cecil B. DeMille, *Autobiography* (Englewood Cliffs, N.J.: Prentice Hall, 1959), p. 347.

25. Ralph Bellamy, letter to Arthur Pierce, February 7, 1990.

26. Jeff Corey, interview with Arthur Pierce, April 13, 1993.

27. George Wells, interview with Arthur Pierce, August 20, 1992.

28. *Ibid.*, January 31, 1993.

29. Junior Coghlan, interview with Arthur Pierce, December 15, 1992.

30. "Hobe.," *Variety*, September 13, 1939, p. 24.

31. George Wells, interview with Arthur Pierce, April 1, 1993.

32. *Ibid.*, August 20, 1992.

33. *Lux Radio Theatre*, November 29, 1939.

34. *Ibid.*

35. *Ibid.*

36. *Ibid.*

37. *Ibid.*

38. George Wells, interview with Arthur Pierce, April 1, 1993.

39. *Ibid.*

40. *Ibid.*

41. Dix Davis, interview with Arthur Pierce, June 2, 1990.
42. CBS press release, undated.
43. George Wells, interview with Arthur Pierce, February 27, 1993.
44. *Ibid.*, January 31, 1993.
45. *Lux Radio Theatre*, December 8, 1941.
46. George Wells, interview with Arthur Pierce, January 31, 1993.
47. *Ibid.*
48. Barbara Thomas, letter to Arthur Pierce, June 25, 1993.
49. *Lux Radio Theatre*, February 8, 1943.
50. *Lux Radio Theatre*, November 9, 1942.
51. DeMille, *Autobiography*, p. 385.
52. *Lux Radio Theatre*, January 29, 1945.
53. *The March of Time*, February 1, 1945.
54. Mutual network, February 15, 1945.
55. *Ibid.*
56. *Ibid.*
57. DeMille, *Autobiography*, p. 387.
58. John Milton Kennedy, interview with Arthur Pierce, June 25, 1990.
59. Virginia Spragle, telegram to *Lux* group, August 20, 1945.
60. *Ibid.*, August 23, 1945.
61. *Ibid.*, September 18, 1945.
62. John Milton Kennedy, interview with Arthur Pierce, June 25, 1990.
63. Sam Edwards, interview with Arthur Pierce, December 7, 1992.
64. Willard Waterman, interview with Arthur Pierce, January 16, 1993.
65. Betty Lou Gerson, interview with Arthur Pierce, February 13, 1993.
66. CBS publicity release, undated.
67. Bill James, interview with Arthur Pierce, February 27, 1993.
68. Ray Kemper, interview with Arthur Pierce, January 21, 1993.
69. *Ibid.*
70. *Ibid.*
71. Harry Bartell, interview with Arthur Pierce, January 22, 1993.
72. NBC press release, undated.
73. Herb Ellis, interview with Arthur Pierce, April 18, 1993.
74. *Lux Radio Theatre*, June 7, 1955.
75. George Wells, interview with Arthur Pierce, August 20, 1992.
76. *Ibid.*
77. *Ibid.*, November 29, 1992.
78. *Ibid.*, August 20, 1992.
79. *Ibid.*, January 31, 1993.
80. *Ibid.*, August 20, 1992.
81. *Ibid.*
82. True Boardman, interview with Arthur Pierce, February 18, 1993.
83. George Wells, interview with Arthur Pierce, November 29, 1992.
84. Hope Cook Noyes, interview with Arthur Pierce, June 7, 1993.
85. *Lux Radio Theatre*, May 3, 1935.
86. *Lux Radio Theatre*, October 17, 1938.
87. *Lux Radio Theatre*, December 21, 1936.
88. *Lux Radio Theatre*, December 19, 1938.
89. *Lux Radio Theatre*, October 14, 1935.

90. *Lux Radio Theatre,* August 3, 1936.

91. Doris Singleton, letter to Arthur Pierce, November 29, 1991.

92. *Ibid.*

93. Ruth Woodbury Sedgwick, "Our Unseen Theatre," *Stage,* June 1935, p. 43.

94. Junior Coghlan, interview with Arthur Pierce, December 15, 1992.

95. CBS publicity release, 1936.

96. Tyler McVey, interview with Arthur Pierce, November 17, 1991.

97. Vanessa Brown, interview with Arthur Pierce, November 10, 1992.

98. Sam Edwards, interview with Arthur Pierce, December 7, 1992.

99. Buzz Kulik, interview with Arthur Pierce, May 4, 1993.

100. Rosemary deCamp, interview with Arthur Pierce, June 6, 1993.

101. Dix Davis, interview with Arthur Pierce, June 2, 1990.

102. *Ibid.*

103. Jeff Corey, interview with Arthur Pierce, April 13, 1993.

104. CBS publicity release, 1951.

105. Sam Edwards, interview with Arthur Pierce, December 7, 1992.

106. Jeff Corey, interview with Arthur Pierce, June 6, 1993.

107. *Ibid.*

108. Josephine Hutchinson, letter to Arthur Pierce, February 14, 1990.

109. Vanessa Brown, interview with Arthur Pierce, November 10, 1992.

110. Ralph Bellamy, letter to Arthur Pierce, February 7, 1990.

111. Marian Rhea, "Secrets of the Lux Radio Theatre," *Radio and Television Mirror,* March 1940, p. 39.

112. J. Walter Thompson publicity release, 1949.

113. *Variety,* June 10, 1970.

114. *Lux Radio Theatre,* October 25, 1943.

115. CBS news release, October 29, 1953.

116. CBS press release, July 1936.

117. George Wells, interview with Arthur Pierce, January 31, 1993.

118. William Keighley, "Curtain at 9," *Radio Mirror,* November 1948, p. 87.

119. Ruth Waterbury Sedgwick, "Our Unseen Theatre," *Stage,* June 1935, p. 43.

120. John Milton Kennedy, interview with Arthur Pierce, June 25, 1990.

121. True Boardman, interview with Arthur Pierce, February 18, 1993.

Lux Radio
Theatre Programs
(October 14, 1934–June 7, 1955)

First Season
(October 14, 1934–June 30, 1935)

National Broadcasting Company (Blue Network), Sunday, 2:30–3:30 P.M. WJZ, Studio 3H, Radio City, New York. *Host*: John Anthony (as Douglass Garrick). *Announcer*: Ben Grauer. *Director*: Antony Stanford. *Musical Director*: Robert Armbruster. *Adaptations*: George Wells. "Peggy Winthrop" (in *Lux* commercials) played by Doris Dagmar.

*1. "Seventh Heaven," 10/14/34
Based on the play by Austin Strong (1922).
Cast: Miriam Hopkins (Diane), John Boles (Chico).
Lux Radio Theatre producers decided to start their series of Sunday afternoon broadcasts with "Seventh Heaven," Austin Strong's tremendously successful love story of a Paris street-washer and a downtrodden waif. The Broadway production opened at the Booth Theatre on October 30, 1922, where, with a cast headed by Helen Menken and George Gaul, it ran for 704 performances. Miriam Hopkins and John Boles were the stars of *Lux*'s radio adaptation—a straight dramatic production without a vocal presentation of "Diane," the hit signature tune of the 1927 screen version. For the only time in a *Lux Radio Theatre* program, host Douglass Garrick's duties were shared by a "friend," Louise Otis, who chatted with Garrick about the play and the product before each act. Another quickly discarded feature of this first show had each of the two stars setting the mood by delivering a few lines of dialogue in character prior to the beginning of the drama. (Curiously, a visual version of this device would be used to introduce the characters on *The Lux Video Theatre* in the late 1950s.) *Variety* noted on October 16, 1934, that "'Seventh Heaven' served as okay

73

October 13, 1934, advertisement announcing the premiere of the *Lux Radio Theatre* (photo: Lever Brothers/Duke University Special Collections).

getter-offer stuff for the *Lux* launching," while the program's director, Antony Stanford, called the debut "a smooth dramatic performance," with "both stars excellent as were supporting cast" (JWT program report, October 14, 1934).

Fox's fondly remembered and brilliantly executed 1927 film of *Seventh Heaven* marked the first teaming of Janet Gaynor and Charles Farrell and was directed by Frank Borzage, while Henry King directed Simone Simon and James Stewart in 20th Century–Fox's talking remake ten years later.

"Seventh Heaven" became one of the most frequently heard of all plays on the air, being performed countless times on several series. (Mary Pickford was to present her version on NBC a mere four months after the *Lux* airing.) *The Lux Radio Theatre* alone was to offer the story a total of four times, with other broadcasts of "Seventh Heaven" coming on October 17, 1938, October 16, 1944, and March 26, 1951.

Film versions: Fox, 1927; 20th Century–Fox, 1937.

***2. "What Every Woman Knows,"
10/21/34**

Based on the play by Sir James M. Barrie (1908).

Cast: Helen Hayes (Maggie Wylie), Kenneth MacKenna (John Shand), and Selina Hall, John Gregg, Buford Hampton, Charles Coburn, Sheila Hayes, Vera Hurst, and Harry Merrill.

J.M. Barrie's *What Every Woman Knows* opened at the Duke of York's Theatre in London, with Hilda Trevelyan and Gerald du Maurier, on September 3, 1908, and reached Broadway with a cast led by Maude Adams and Richard Bennett on December 23 of the same year. *Lux*'s program on October 21 featured the stars of the 1926 Broadway revival, Helen Hayes and Kenneth MacKenna, and related the story of a spinster who, through a series

of unusual circumstances, is forced onto an ambitious young man with a future in politics.

Fred W. Durant was at the helm of the 1917 British film of *What Every Woman Knows*, with the leading role taken by Hilda Trevelyan, and William C. deMille directed Paramount's 1921 effort, which starred Lois Wilson and Conrad Nagel. The stars of MGM's 1934 film were Helen Hayes and Brian Aherne, under Gregory LaCava's direction.

Film versions: British, 1917; Paramount, 1921; MGM, 1934.

*3. "The Barker," 10/28/34

Based on the play by Kenyon Nicholson (1927).

Cast: Walter Huston (Nifty Miller), Betty Garde (Lou), Marjorie Wood (Carrie), Owen Davis, Jr. (Chris), Harlan Briggs (Hap), Ray Bramley (Doc Rice), and John Milton (Colonel Gowdy).

Kenyon Nicholson's *The Barker* opened at Broadway's Biltmore Theatre on January 18, 1927, and starred Walter Huston, Claudette Colbert, and Norman Foster. The story of a lifelong circus man who tries to keep his son from following in his footsteps was a particular favorite of Huston's, and he recreated the title part in *Lux*'s broadcast of October 28 and also in the *Lux* program from Hollywood on July 20, 1936. (This first broadcast also included Ray Bramley of the original cast.)

In 1928, Warner Bros. released the First National film version of the play, a part-talkie that was directed by George Fitzmaurice and starred Milton Sills, Betty Compson, and Douglas Fairbanks, Jr. The 1933 Fox talkie is entitled *Hoopla* and starred Preston Foster, Clara Bow, and Richard Cromwell, under Frank Lloyd's direction.

Film versions: Warner Bros.–First National, 1928; Fox, 1933 (*Hoopla*).

*4. "Smilin' Through," 11/4/34

Based on the play by Allan Langdon (pseudonym of Jane Cowl and Jane Murfin) (1919).

Cast: Jane Cowl (Kathleen Dungannon/Moonyean Clare), Wilfred Seagram, George Graham, Florence Edney, Alfred Shirley, and Richard Whorf.

Smilin' Through opened at New York's Broadhurst Theatre on December 30, 1919, and told the strange story of an embittered old man who is haunted by a past love, and a young couple whose engagement he violently opposes. Jane Cowl, the leading lady and coauthor of the first production, recreated her role for *Lux*'s broadcast of November 4. (Vincent Youmans wrote the songs for *Through the Years*, a musical version of *Smilin' Through* that played on Broadway in 1932.)

Sidney Franklin directed the first two film versions, in 1922 at First National (with Norma Talmadge), and at MGM in 1932 (with Norma Shearer). Frank Borzage was assigned to direct MGM's second version in 1941 (with Jeanette MacDonald).

Film versions: First National, 1922; MGM, 1932; MGM, 1941.

*5. "The Nervous Wreck," 11/11/34

Based on the play by Owen Davis (1923), in turn based on the novel by E.J. Rath (1923).

Cast: Ernest Truex (Henry Williams), June Walker (Sally Morgan), John Milton (Jud Morgan), John Brewster (Chester Underwood), Florida Friebus (Harriet Underwood), Alfred Swenson (Jerome Underwood), G. Underhill Macy (Andy Nabb), Wilfred Lytell (Mort), and Charles W. Dingle (Bob Wells).

The Nervous Wreck, Owen Davis's comedy of a jittery clerk from Pittsburgh who goes west for his health, premiered at the Sam H. Harris Theatre in New York on October 9, 1923, with Otto Kruger and June Walker. Walker was on hand to reprise her stage characterization for *Lux*'s broadcast of November 11, with Ernest Truex cast opposite her as the title character.

A film version for Christie was released in 1926, with direction by Scott Sidney and starring performances by Harrison Ford and Phyllis Haver. *Whoopee!,* the better-remembered musical version of *The Nervous Wreck* (by Gus Kahn and Walter B. Donaldson), opened on Broadway in 1928 and was filmed twice: for United Artists in 1930 (with Eddie Cantor and Eleanor Hunt), and (with a new score) as *Up in Arms* in 1944 (with Danny Kaye and Dinah Shore).

Film versions: Christie/PDC, 1926; United Artists, 1930 (*Whoopee!*); Goldwyn, 1944 (*Up in Arms*).

*6. "Rebound," 11/18/34

Based on the play by Donald Ogden Stewart (1930).

Cast: Ruth Chatterton (Sara Jaffrey), Earle Larimore (Bill Truesdale), Franc Hale (Evie Lawrence), Jeanne Owen (Liz Crawford), Frank Thomas (Les Crawford), Wright Kramer (Henry Jaffrey), Alma Kruger (Mrs. Jaffrey), and Walter Abel (Johnnie Coles).

Donald Ogden Stewart's comedy *Rebound* opened at Broadway's Plymouth Theatre on February 3, 1930, with Hope Williams and Donn (Donald) Cook. Ruth Chatterton was supported by Earle Larimore in the *Lux* program of November 18, which tells what happens when a young man, having been jilted by the girl he loves, marries one whom he does not.

The RKO/Pathé film version of 1931 was directed by Edward H. Griffith and starred Ina Clare and Robert Ames.

Film version: RKO/Pathé, 1931.

Ernest Truex and June Walker in "The Nervous Wreck," November 11, 1934 (photo: Berry Hill Bookshop).

*7. "Mrs. Dane's Defense," 11/25/34
Based on the play by Henry Arthur Jones (1900).
Special Guest: Alexander Woollcott (before Act 1).
Cast: Ethel Barrymore (Mrs. Dane), Hugh Buckler (Sir Daniel), Florence Edney (Lady Eastney), Jessamine Newcomb (Mrs. Bulsom-Porter), Alfred Shirley (Risby), Victor Beecroft (Fendick), and Harry Neville (Butler).
Mrs. Dane's Defense was originally produced at Sir Charles Wyndham Theatre, London, on October 9, 1900, with Miss Lena Ashwell portraying Mrs. Dane, and Sir Charles himself playing Sir Daniel. (The first production on Broadway opened at the Empire Theatre on December 31, 1900, and starred Margaret Anglin and Charles Richman.) The drama of a society lawyer who is determined to terminate the engagement of the title character to his foster son by exposing her past was broadcast by *Lux* on November 25, with Ethel Barrymore supported by Hugh Buckler. Alexander Woollcott, star of *The Town Crier* on "another network" (CBS), appeared prior to Act 1 and introduced Barrymore.
Paramount's 1918 screen version of *Mrs. Dane's Defense* was directed by Hugh Ford and starred Pauline Fredrick and Frank Losee.
Film version: Paramount, 1918.

*8. "Let Us Be Gay," 12/2/34
Based on the play by Rachel Crothers (1929).
Cast: Tallulah Bankhead (Kitty Brown), Bert Lytell (Bob Brown), James Jolley (Whitman), Rita Vale (Diedre Lessing), Edward Woods (Bruce Keen), Gerald Oliver Smith (Townley Town), and Alma Kruger (Mrs. Boucicault).
Let Us Be Gay was originally produced by John Golden at the Little Theatre on Broadway on February 19, 1929, and had in its cast Francine Larrimore and Warren William. The play concerns a sophisticated divorcée who is called in by an elderly friend to break up a romance, only to discover that the man involved is her ex-husband.
Lux's December 2 broadcast featured Tallulah Bankhead, the star of the 1930 London production of the comedy, along with Bert Lytell and, repeating her part from the Broadway staging, Rita Vale.
In 1930 MGM's motion picture version reached the screen, with a cast headed by Norma Shearer and Rod La Rocque, under Robert Z. Leonard's direction.
Film version: MGM, 1930.

*9. "Berkeley Square," 12/9/34
Based on the play by John Balderston (1929), in turn based on the story "A Sense of the Past," by Henry James.
Cast: Leslie Howard (Peter Standish), Helen Chandler (Helen Pettigrew), Lucy Beaumont (Mrs. Barwick), Freida Inescort (Kate Pettigrew), Mary Michael (Marjorie), Charles Romano (Major Clinton), Horace Braham (Tom Pettigrew), William Podmore (Throstle), and Fred Eric (Ambassador).
John Balderston based his intriguing fantasy *Berkeley Square* on an unfinished Henry James story entitled "A Sense of the Past." The play tells the story of a present-day Londoner whose fascination with an earlier era is tested when he finds that he has somehow been transported to the eighteenth century. *Berkeley Square* opened at St. Martin's Theatre in London on October 6, 1926, and received its American premiere on November 4, 1929. Leslie Howard, the star of the 1929 London revival and the first Broadway production (Lawrence Anderson starred in the original London staging), also led the cast of *Lux*'s radio performance on

December 9, with Helen Chandler as his leading lady (the part played by Jean Forbes-Robertson in London and by Margalo Gillmore on the New York stage), and two players repeating their roles from the Broadway cast, Lucy Beaumont and Charles Romano. *Variety* stated on December 11, 1934, that "Berkeley Square" "seemed one of the best things *Lux* has offered on its ambitious Sabbatarian hour-long drama festivals."

John Balderston adapted his play for the screen for Fox in 1933. That film starred Leslie Howard and Heather Angel and was directed by Frank Lloyd. A later version entitled *I'll Never Forget You* was released by 20th Century–Fox in 1951, with Roy Baker directing a cast that included Tyrone Power and Ann Blyth.

Lux again presented Balderston's play on December 17, 1944, as well as on September 22, 1952 (as "I'll Never Forget You").

Film versions: Fox, 1933; 20th Century–Fox, 1951 (*I'll Never Forget You*).

*10. "Turn to the Right!" 12/16/34

Based on the play by Winchell Smith and John E. Hazzard (1916).

Cast: James Cagney (Joe Boscom), Walter Kinsella (Muggs), Anthony Burger (Gilly), Harry Humphrey (Deacon Tillinger), Clyde Franklin (Callahan), Josephine Fox (Mrs. Bascom), Franc Hale (Elsie), Florence Baker (Betty), David Stewart (Sam), and Bruno Wick (Waiter).

James Cagney was the star of *Lux*'s December 16 broadcast of the comedy "Turn to the Right!," which had premiered on Broadway at the Gaiety Theatre on August 18, 1916, with Forrest Winant in the lead (Harry Humphrey, who played Callahan in the original production, became Tillinger for the *Lux* adaptation).

The story, which had been filmed in 1922 by Metro, with Jack Mulhall under Rex Ingram's direction, concerns a young man just out of prison who returns home to find his family in financial difficulty and his girl engaged to another man.

Film version: Metro, 1922.

*11. "The Goose Hangs High," 12/23/34

Based on the play by Lewis Beach (1924).

Cast: Walter Connolly (Bernard Ingals), Eric Linden (Bradley Ingals), Garson Kanin (Ronald Murdoch), Frances Starr (Eunice Ingals), Greta Kvalden (Lois Ingals), Harold Gould (Noel Derby), Matt Briggs (Leo Day), and Jessie Busley (Mrs. Bradley).

Lewis Beach's *The Goose Hangs High* received its first New York performance at Broadway's Bijou Theatre on January 29, 1934, with a cast that included Norman Trevor, Eric Dressler, and Katherine Grey. The drama of a couple who make great sacrifices while catering to every whim of their seemingly selfish grown children was brought to *The Lux Radio Theatre* on December 23 (the play is set during the Christmas season), with Walter Connolly, Eric Linden, and Frances Starr in the leads.

Paramount released a screen version of *The Goose Hangs High* in 1925. Directed by James Cruze, this production starred George Irving, Constance Bennett, and Myrtle Stedman. Frank Tuttle directed the same studio's 1932 sound version, *This Reckless Age*, the cast of which included Richard Bennett, Charles ("Buddy") Rogers, and Frances Starr (who repeated her role in *Lux*'s broadcast).

Film versions: Paramount, 1925; Paramount, 1932 (*This Reckless Age*).

*12. "Daddy Long Legs," 12/30/34

Based on the play by Jean Webster

(1914), in turn based on her own novel (1912).

Cast: John Boles (Jervis Pendleton, aka Daddy Long Legs), Helen Chandler (Judy Abbott), May Buckley (Miss Pritchard), Katherine Revner (Julia Pendleton), Phillip Truex (Jimmy McBride), Lorna Elliot (Mrs. Lippett), John F. Hamilton (Cyrus Wykoff), Clarence Belliar (Griggs), Ethel Barrymore Colt (Sallie McBride), and Jimmy Donnelly, Katherine Hutchinson, and Janet Lee Hutchinson.

Jean Webster's successful stage version of her own novel, *Daddy Long Legs*, opened at New York's Gaiety Theatre on September 28, 1914, and starred Charles Waldron and Ruth Chatterton. The delightful sentimental comedy of an orphan who falls in love with her benefactor was brought to *The Lux Radio Theatre* on December 30, with John Boles and Helen Chandler.

The first film version, released by First National in 1919, served as a vehicle for Mary Pickford, and featured Mahlon Hamilton as the title character (Marshall Nielan directed). Warner Baxter and Janet Gaynor were the stars of Fox's wonderful 1931 version, which was directed by Alfred Santell. John Boles (the star of the *Lux* production) and Shirley Temple were the leading players of *Curley Top*, 20th Century–Fox's 1935 free adaptation, directed by Irving Cummings. A final rendering (in this case with singing and dancing) was released in 1955, with Fred Astaire and Leslie Caron under the direction of Jean Negulesco.

Film versions: First National, 1919; Fox, 1931; 20th Century–Fox, 1935 (*Curley Top*); 20th Century–Fox, 1955.

*13. "The Green Goddess," 1/6/35

Based on the play by William Archer (1921).

Cast: Claude Rains (the Rajah of Rukh), Dorothy Gish (Lucilla Crespin),

Victor Beecroft (Watkins), Eustace Wyatt (Major Attorney Crespin), Charles Romano (Dr. Basil Traherne), Burford Hampden (Lieutenant Denis Cardew), and Maurice Barrett (the High Priest). Additional cast (commercials or crowd): Helen Hedeman, Horace Braham, and Virginia Morgan.

The Green Goddess premiered at the Booth Theatre in New York in 1921, with George Arliss as the Rajah of Rukh, an educated but unscrupulous ruler of a small country who holds two Englishmen and an Englishwoman hostage in retaliation for the forthcoming execution of one of his subjects (Olive Wyndham was the leading lady of that first cast). *Lux*'s attempts to secure the services of Arliss for its broadcast version of January 6 were unsuccessful, and Claude Rains appeared in his place. Starring opposite Rains was Dorothy Gish (filling in for the previously announced Fay Bainter).

George Arliss, who became closely identified with the play, also starred in the first two film versions: the 1923 Metro productions, directed by Sidney Olcott, and the 1930 talkie remake for Warner Bros., directed by Alfred E. Green (Alice Joyce costarred on both occasions). Warner Bros.' 1943 D. Ross Lederman–directed release *Adventure in Iraq* changed the locale but retained the story; it starred Paul Cavanagh and Ruth Ford.

Film versions: Metro, 1923; Warner Bros., 1930; Warner Bros., 1943 (*Adventure in Iraq*).

*14. "Counsellor-at-Law," 1/13/35

Based on the play by Elmer Rice (1931).

Cast: Paul Muni (George Simon), Louise Prussing (Cora Simon), Carlton Macy (Charles McFadden), Albert Hayes (Herbert Weinberg), Charles La Torre (John Tedesco), Gladys Feldman (Bessie Green), Jack Leslie (Roy Dar-

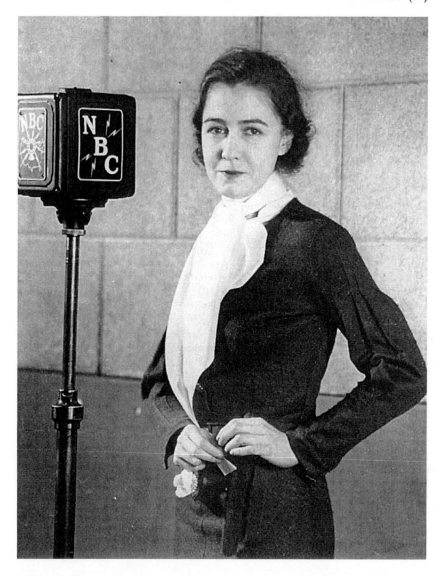

Publicity photo of Dorothy Gish, about the time she appeared on *Lux*'s January 6, 1935, broadcast of "The Green Goddess" (photo: Photofest).

win), Ross Forrester (Johann Breitstein), Walter Scott (Peter J. Malone), and Beatrice Miller (Regina Gordon).

Elmer Rice's hit play *Counsellor-at-Law* opened at New York's Plymouth Theatre on November 6, 1931, with a cast led by Paul Muni, Anna Kostant, and Louise Prussing. When Muni turned down Universal's offer to star in the 1933 film version, John Barrymore was given the role. (Also cast in the William Wyler–directed picture were Clara

Langsner, Doris Kenyon, and Melvyn Douglas.)

Lux's January 13 broadcast repeated the story of a Jewish lawyer of modest background whose brilliant career as well as personal life teeters on the verge of collapse. Paul Muni was once again cast in the title role, and also resuming their parts from the play were Jennie Moscowitz (as his mother), Louise Prussing (as his wife), and Jack Leslie (as his wife's lover). Gladys Feldman, who played Zedorah Chapman on stage, took the role of receptionist Bessie Green in the radio play.

Film version: Universal, 1933.

*15. "The Late Christopher Bean," 1/20/35

Based on the play *Prenez Garde a la Peinture,* by René Fauchois, as adapted by Sidney Howard (1932).

Cast: Pauline Lord (Abby), Walter Connolly (Dr. Haggett), Ernest Lawford (Davenport), George Coulouris (Tallant), Eva Condon (Mrs. Haggett), Adelaide Bean (Susan Haggett), Katherine Revner (Ada Haggett), Joseph Greenwald (Rosen), and David Stewart (Warren Creamer).

Commercial: Anthony Grey, William Boren.

When it is discovered that a now famous (and deceased) painter had, in his days of obscurity, roomed with a doctor and his family in a small New England town, a trio of art vultures descends on the household to procure any of his works that may have been left behind. The *Lux broadcast of Sidney Howard's comedy The Late Christopher Bean* starred Pauline Lord and Walter Connolly, creators of the roles of Abby and Dr. Haggett in the original New York production, which opened at Henry Miller's Theatre on October 31, 1932 (three other members of the original cast, Ernest Lawford, George Coulouris, and Adelaide Bean, also

appeared in the radio presentation of January 20).

The broadly comic 1933 MGM film version, *Christopher Bean,* was Marie Dressler's final motion picture vehicle. The Sam Wood–directed movie also featured Lionel Barrymore, H.B. Warner, George Coulouris, and Helen Mack.

Film version: MGM, 1933 (*Christopher Bean*).

*16. "The Bad Man," 1/27/35

Based on the play by Porter Emerson Browne (1920).

Cast: Walter Huston (Pancho Lopez), Jacqueline Logan (Lucia Pell), John Marston (Gilbert Jones), Howard Smith (Jasper Hardy), Wilfred Lytell (Bradley), Robert Strauss (Henry Smith), Raymond Bramley (Morgan Pell), and Jack Rigo (Pedro).

Commercial: Peggy Patterson, Mary Howard, John Anthony.

Porter Emerson Browne's comedy *The Bad Man* opened at New York's Comedy Theatre on August 30, 1920, with a cast that included Holbrook Blinn and Frances Carson. Walter Huston, the star of *Lux*'s January 27 adaptation, had appeared in the Warner Bros.–First National film version (directed by Clarence Badger and costarring Dorothy Revier) in 1930. Huston played a notorious bandit who, with his gang of cutthroats, holds a young lady captive (Jacqueline Logan in the broadcast).

First National's 1923 silent picture was directed by Edwin Carewe and featured Holbrook Blinn and Enid Bennett, while the second talkie version had a new setting and a new title, *West of Shanghai.* This John Farrow–directed film starred Boris Karloff and Beverly Roberts. The property was obtained by MGM and released as *Bad Man* in 1941, with Wallace Beery and Laraine Day under the direction of Richard Thorpe.

Film versions: First National, 1923; Warner Bros.–First National, 1930; Warner Bros.–First National, 1937 (*West of Shanghai*); MGM, 1941.

*17. "Peg o' My Heart," 2/3/35
Based on the play by J. Hartley Manners (1912).
Special Guest: Margaret Sullavan (during curtain call).
Cast: Helen Hayes (Peg), Bramwell Fletcher (Jerry), Hilda Spong (Mrs. Chichester), Burford Hampden (Alaric), Clement O'Loghlen (Jarvis), Stanley Harrison (Montgomery Hawkes), Alfred Shirley (Christian Brant), and Louise Prussing (Ethel).

Peg o' My Heart was written by J. Hartley Manners as a vehicle for his wife, Laurette Taylor, and received its first performance at Broadway's Cort Theatre on December 20, 1912. The hit comedy-drama (it ran for 603 performances) of an Irish lass who is taken from her fisherman father to live with a well-to-do British family first appeared on *The Lux Radio Theatre* on February 3. Scheduled to star in the broadcast was Margaret Sullavan, but an attack of laryngitis forced her to drop out in favor of Helen Hayes, who was allowed but one rehearsal. *Lux* director Antony Stanford's comments on the February 3, 1935, JWT program report well describe the situation: "A fine performance under great difficulties—Miss Hayes replaced Miss Sullavan who was ill, on very short notice and did a fine job. The entire cast and staff of J. Walter Thompson cooperated beautifully." Margaret Sullavan appeared briefly at the end of the program, expressing her regret at being unable to go on, and congratulating Helen Hayes on her performance.

Laurette Taylor recreated her stage role in the Metro film of *Peg o' My Heart*, which was directed by King Vidor and released in 1922. A talking remake by MGM ten years later was directed by Robert Z. Leonard and starred Marion Davies (who would perform the role on *Lux*'s November 29, 1937, program).

Famous Players–Lasky shot a version of *Peg o' My Heart* in 1919, with Wanda Hawley and Thomas Meighan under the direction of William C. deMille, but the picture was never released due to a legal dispute with the play's author.

Film versions: Famous Players–Lasky, 1919; Metro, 1922; MGM, 1933.

*18. "The First Year," 2/10/35
Based on the play by Frank Craven (1920).
Cast: Gene Raymond (Tommy Tucker), Lila Lee (Grace Livingston), Maude Blair (Mrs. Livingston), John Milton (Dr. Myron Anderson), Sidney Smith (Dick Loring), Peggy Paige (Hattie), Calvin Thomas (Mr. Barstow), and Helen Carew (Mrs. Barstow).

Frank Craven's comedy *The First Year* opened at New York's Little Theatre on October 20, 1920, and played for a successful run of 725 performances with a cast headed by Craven himself and Roberta Arnold. *Lux*'s retelling of the trials of a young couple's first year of marriage was broadcast on February 10 and starred Gene Raymond and Lila Lee.

Fox's first film version was directed by Frank Borzage in 1926, with a cast headed by Matt Moore and Kathryn Perry, while that same studio's 1932 production starred the popular romantic team of Charles Farrell and Janet Gaynor, under William K. Howard's direction.

Film versions: Fox, 1926; Fox, 1932.

*19. "The Old Soak," 2/17/35
Based on the play by Don Marquis (1922).
Cast: Wallace Beery (Clem Hawley),

Minnie Dupree (Matilda), Isabel Goss (Lucy), Eric Dressler (Tom), Morgan Farley (Clarence), Mark Smith ("Al"), and Harry Humphrey (Cousin Webster).

Commercial: Wilfred Lytell, Albert Hayes.

Harry Beresford and Minnie Dupree played the leading roles in the Broadway production of *The Old Soak*, which opened on August 22, 1922, at the Plymouth Theatre. *Lux*'s February 17 broadcast of the comedy featured Wallace Beery as the title character, an out-of-work family man with a good heart but a weakness for strong drink, and Minnie Dupree, repeating her stage role as his wife.

Universal's 1926 film version was directed by Edward Sloman and starred Jean Hersholt and Lucy Beaumont, while MGM's 1937 remake (called *The Good Old Soak*) allowed Wallace Beery to translate his *Lux* performance to the screen, with Janet Beecher costarring under Walter Reuben's direction. (The play was repeated on *Lux*'s February 16, 1936, broadcast.)

Film versions: Universal, 1926; MGM, 1937 (*The Good Old Soak*).

*20. "Nothing but the Truth," 2/24/35

Based on the play by James Montgomery (1916), in turn based on the novel by Frederick Isham (1914).

Cast: Frank Morgan (Bob Bennett), Nana Bryant (Mrs. E.M. Ralston), Lillian Savin (Sabel Jackson), Elspeth Eric (Mabel Jackson), Tucker McGuire (Ethel Clark), Laddie Seaman (Jimmy), William Shelly (Dick Donnelly), Richard Stevenson (Clarence Van Dusen), Floyd Buckley (E.M. Ralston), and Selena Royale (Gwendolyn Ralston).

Commercial: Julie Cobb, Kirk Ames, Eita Allyn, and William Boren.

James Montgomery's stage comedy

of a man who makes a bet to tell "nothing but the truth" for a period of 24 hours was first presented at the Longacre Theatre in New York on September 14, 1916. *Lux*'s February 24 radio revival of the play starred Frank Morgan, cast in the role created on stage by William Collier.

The three film versions, made for Metro in 1920, and Paramount in 1929 and 1941, starred Taylor Holmes, Richard Dix, and Bob Hope, respectively, and were directed by David Kirkland, Victor Schertzinger, and Elliott Nugent.

Film versions: Metro, 1920; Paramount, 1929; Paramount, 1941.

*21. "Lilac Time," 3/3/35

Based on the play by Jane Cowl and Jane Murfin (1917).

Cast: Jane Cowl (Jeannine), Alfred Shirley (Philip Blythe), Leon Quartermaine (Major Holloway), Louis Hector (Captain Watling), Louis Lebey (Cure), John Halloran (George Smylie), and Michelette Burani (Madame Berthelot). Additional cast (commercial and crowd): George Graham, Frank Curran, George LeGuerre, Fred Kuhnley, Roy Hallee, Crane Calder, and James Davies.

Eighteen years after *Lilac Time*'s February 6, 1917, opening at the Republic Theatre on Broadway, Jane Cowl recreated her starring role for the *Lux* microphone. The wartime story of a French girl's love for an English flyer was made into a successful (silent) film in 1928, with Colleen Moore as star and George Fitzmaurice as director.

Film version: First National, 1928.

*22. "Holiday," 3/10/35

Based on the play by Philip Barry (1928).

Cast: Claudette Colbert (Linda Seton), Eric Dressler (Johnny Case), Eleanor Phelps (Julia Seton), Jonathan

Hole (Ned Seton), Josephine Victor (Susan Potter), Blaine Cordner (Nick Potter), Wright Kramer (Edward Seton), and Reginald Carrington (Henry, the Butler).

Commercial: Arline Blackburn, Katherine Revner.

Hope Williams and Ben Smith starred in the original Broadway production of *Holiday*, which opened on November 26, 1928, at the Plymouth Theatre. The comedy concerns a young man from the middle class who becomes engaged to a young lady of the upper crust, though during the course of the play it becomes increasingly clear that he is actually better suited to his fiancée's older sister. Claudette Colbert starred in *Lux*'s broadcast of March 10 (opposite Eric Dressler).

The first film version was released in 1930, the year after the New York production closed, and was directed by Edward H. Griffith, with Ann Harding and Robert Ames in the leads. The 1938 Columbia film featured Katharine Hepburn and Cary Grant and was directed by George Cukor.

Film versions: Pathé, 1930; Columbia, 1938.

*23. "Her Master's Voice," 3/17/35
Based on the play by Claire Kummer (1933).

Cast: Roland Young (Ned Farrar), Lucille Watson (Aunt Min), Frances Fuller (Quena Farrar), Laura Pierpont (Mrs. Martin), Francis Pierlot (Craddock), Frederick Perry (Mr. Twilling), and Isabel Winlock (Phoebe).

Commercial: Greta Kvalden, Elsie Mae Gordon.

Her Master's Voice opened at Broadway's Plymouth Theatre on October 23, 1933, and featured a cast that included Roland Young (whose mother-in-law, Claire Kummer, had written the play), Laura Hope Crews, and Frances Fuller. Young, Fuller, Francis Pierlot,

and Frederick Perry repeated their stage roles in *Lux*'s broadcast of the comedy, which relates the plight of a man who recently lost his job and, thanks to his wife's interfering aunt, may lose his spouse as well.

Laura Hope Crews, who did not take part in the *Lux* broadcast (where Lucille Watson took her role), appeared in Paramount's 1936 Joseph Santley–directed film version, along with Edward Everett Horton and Peggy Conklin.

Film version: Paramount, 1936.

*24. "Secrets," 3/24/35
Based on the play by Rudolf Bessier and Mary Edinton (1922).

Cast: Irene Dunne (Mary), Walter Abel (John Carlton), and T. Daniel Frawley, Wilfred Lytell, Alfred Corn, Edwin Jerome, Jean Dante, J. Malcolm Dunn, Vera Allen, Sydney Booth, and Evelyn Vaughn.

Commercial: Sally Belle Cox (Woman), Frank Dae (Man).

Ruldof Bessier and Mary Edinton's episodic play *Secrets*, told mostly in flashback, unfolds over a period of 55 years and follows the exploits of a couple which take them from civilized England to the wilds of Wyoming, and finally back to England again. Irene Dunne was the star of *Lux*'s March 24 broadcast, playing the part created during the Broadway run (which opened at the Fulton Theatre on Christmas Day, 1925) by Margaret Lawrence, with Walter Abel as her husband, the Tom Nesbitt stage role.

Norma Talmadge and Eugene O'Brien were the stars of First National's 1924 film *Secrets*, which was directed by Frank Borzage, and Mary Pickford's final screen appearance came in United Artists' 1933 version, which costarred Leslie Howard and was also directed by Borzage.

Film versions: First National, 1924; United Artists, 1933.

*25. "The Romantic Age," 3/31/35
Based on the play by A.A. Milne
(1922).
Cast: Leslie Howard (Gervase
Mallory), Sidney Fox (Melisande
Kuowle), and Molly Pearson, Wallace
Erskine, Lillian Tonge, Sheelagh
Hayes, Gerald Oliver Smith, Walter
Tetley, and John Carmody.
Commercial: Arline Blackburu
(Woman), Billy Murray (Grocer), Janet
Lee Hutchinson (Mary Jane).
A.A. Milne's comedy *The Romantic
Age* opened at London's Comedy
Theatre on October 18, 1920, with Ar-
thur Wontner and Barbara Hoffe in the
leading roles, and had its Broadway
opening on November 14, 1922, at New
York's Comedy Theatre, with Leslie
Howard and Margalo Gillmore. The
whimsical tale concerns a young lady
who is enamored of the knights of old,
and who one day seemingly meets just
such a cavalier. *Lux*'s broadcast of
March 31 featured Leslie Howard and
Sidney Fox, who filled in for the
previonsly announced Helen Chandler.
(Columbia's 1927 film *The Romantic
Age* is not related to the play.)

*26. "The Prince Chap," 4/7/35
Based on the play by Edward Peple
(1905).
Cast: Gary Cooper (William Peyton),
Janet Lee Hutchinson (Claudia as a
child), Sylvia Field (Claudia as a girl),
Lionel Pape (Runyion), James Jolley
(Lord Rodney), Margery Pickard
(Phoebe Puckers), and Ruth Weston
(Alice Travers).
Commercial: Arline Blackburn, Betty
Field.
Gary Cooper made his *Lux Radio
Theatre* debut on the program of April
7 in an adaptation of Edward Peple's
play *The Prince Chap*, which tells of an
American artist in London who is left to
bring up the yonng daughter of his de-
ceased model. The original production

of the play opened at the Madison
Square Theatre in New York on Sep-
tember 4, 1905, with Cyril Scott playing
the title character.
The first film version, a 1916 Selig/
V-L-S-E product, starred Marshall Nie-
lau, who also directed. William C.
deMille directed the 1920 Famous
Players–Lasky release, which cast
Thomas Meighan in the lead.
Film versions: Selig Polyscope/
V-L-S-E, 1916; Famous Players–Lasky/
Paramount Artcraft, 1920.

*27. "The Broken Wing," 4/14/35
Based on the play by Paul Dickey
and Charles W. Goddard (1920).
Cast: Lupe Velez (Inez Villera),
Florence Malone (Quichita), Harold
Gould (Luther Farley), Santos Ortego
(Captain Innocencio Das Santos), Milo
Boulton (Sylvestor Cross), Cynthia
Rodgers (Cecilia Edwards), and Peter
Powers (J. Philip Marvin). Additional
cast (commercial and crowd): Laline
Browne, Tucker McGuire, Norman
Williams.
The Broken Wing was first presented
at New York's 48th Street Theatre on
November 29, 1920, with Inez Plummer as the star and Charles Trowbridge
as her leading man. Lupe Velez starred
in *Lux*'s adaptation, which related the
tale of a Mexican girl who prays for an
American husband, and who believes
her prayers have been answered when
a "gringo" (Peter Powers in the broadcast) is delivered to her doorstep via an
airplane crash.
Velez had starred in Paramount's
1932 film version as well, where she
was supported by Melvyn Douglas,
while a silent rendering of the drama
featured Miriam Cooper and Kenneth
Harlan in a 1923 Preferred Pictures
release (directed by Tom Forman).
Film versions: B.P. Schulberg/
Preferred Pictures, 1923; Paramount,
1932.

Lupe Velez and Santos Ortego in "The Broken Wing," April 14, 1935 (photo: Berry Hill Bookshop).

*28. "Little Women," 4/21/35

Based on the play by Marian de Forrest (1912), in turn adapted from the novel by Louisa May Alcott (1868).

Cast: Lillian Gish (Jo), Dorothy Gish (Meg), Helen Chandler (Amy), Sylvia Field (Beth), Grace Fox (Hannah), Carlton Young (John Brooke), Sydney Booth (Mr. March), Effie Shannon (Mrs. March), Jessie Busley (Aunt March), Ben Lockland (Laurie), Harry Southard (Professor Frederich), and Sally Belle Cox.

Marian de Forrest's dramatization of Louisa May Alcott's 1868 novel *Little Women*, which chronicles the triumphs and disappointments of a Massachusetts family around the time of the Civil War, was first seen at the Playhouse Theatre on Broadway on October 14,

1912. Produced by William A. Brady as a vehicle for his daughter, Alice (who portrayed Meg), the play also starred Marie Pavey, Beverly West, and Gladys Hulette. *Lux's* April 21 broadcast teamed Lillian and Dorothy Gish as Jo and Meg, with Helen Chandler as Amy and Sylvia Field as Beth (Antony Stanford called it "an excellent show — well adapted and well played").

William Brady also produced the first feature-length American film of *Little Women,* which was shot by World in 1918 and released by Paramount the following year. The large cast featured Dorothy Bernard, Isabel Lamon, Florence Flynn, and Lillian Hall (directed by Henry Knoles). A British version had preceded it to the screen in 1917, produced by G.B. Samuelson, directed by Alexander Butler, and featuring Ruby Miller, Mary Lincoln, Daisy Burrell, and Muriel Myers. Talkie remakes were released in 1933 and 1949, the first by RKO, with Katharine Hepburn, Frances Dee, Joan Bennett, and Jean Parker, under George Cukor's direction; the second by MGM, with June Allyson, Janet Leigh, Elizabeth Taylor, and Margaret O'Brien, under the direction of Mervyn LeRoy. (None of the film versions credits the Marian de Forrest stage adaptation as its source.) *Lux* brought a radio adaptation of the MGM version to the airwaves on March 13, 1950.

Film versions: G.B. Samuelson, 1917; Paramount, 1919; RKO, 1933; MGM, 1949.

*29. "Ada Beats the Drum," 4/28/35
Based on the play by John Kirkpatrick (1930).

Cast: Mary Boland (Ada Hubbard), Ruth Nugent (Leila Hubbard), Calvin Thomas (Ed Hubbard), Polly DeLoos (Jacqueline), Marcel Journet (the Guide), Hal Thompson (Bow-Tie),

Margaret Mower (Nadine Wentworth), Arvid Paulson (Dmitri), and Santos Ortego (Alonzo). Additional cast (commercials and crowd): John Milton, Francis Pierlot, Doris Easton, Elsie Mae Gordon, and Wilfred Lytell.

John Kirkpatrick's comedy *Ada Beats the Drum* was first produced at the Golden Theatre, opening there on May 8, 1930, and relating the exploits of an American family who go to Europe to get culture. Mary Boland, the star of the Broadway production, repeated her role of the domineering mother of the clan for *Lux's* April 26 program.

At the time of the *Lux* broadcast the play had not been filmed, but in 1937, MGM released its George B. Seitz–directed version, *Mama Steps Out,* with Alice Brady.

Film version: MGM, 1937 (*Mama Steps Out*).

*30. "Adam and Eva," 5/5/35
Based on the play by Guy Bolton and George Middleton (1919).

Cast: Cary Grant (Adam Smith), Constance Cummings (Eva King), Lora Baxter (Julie DeWitt), Stuart Fox (Clinton DeWitt), Richard Sterling (Dr. Dalamater), Gerald Oliver (Lord Andrew Gordon), Frank Kingdon (Horace Pilgrim), and John Milton (James King).

Commercial: Jean Shelby, Hope Cook, Margerie Mitchell.

Adam and Eva, a comedy by Guy Bolton and George Middleton, opened at Broadway's Longacre Theatre on September 13, 1919, where the title characters were portrayed by Otto Kruger and Ruth Shepley. The play relates the story of a wealthy businessman who takes a vacation and leaves a young employee in charge of his irresponsible family. Cary Grant played the substitute "father" in *Lux's* broadcast of May 5, and Constance Cummings took the part of the millionaire's daughter (Richard Sterling recreated his stage role of Dr. Dalamater).

Paramount's 1923 film version starred T. Roy Barnes and Marion Davies; it was directed by Robert Vignola.

Film version: Paramount, 1923.

*31. "The Bishop Misbehaves," 5/12/35

Based on the play by Frederick Jackson (1935).

Cast: Walter Connolly (the Bishop of Broadminster), Jane Wyatt (Hēster Grantham), Effie Shannon (Lady Emily Lyons), A.P. Kaye (Red Eagen), Alan Marshal (Donald Meadows), Reynolds Denniston (Guy Waller), Phyllis Joyce (Mrs. Waller), James Jolley (Collins), Charles Laite (Frenchy), and Edward Broadley (Mr. Brooke).

Commercial: Lillian Savin (Herself).

In the words of Douglass Garrick, as he opened *Lux*'s program of May 12, "Today we are proud to present for the first time in radio history a play which is actually enjoying its first run in a New York theatre right now" (*Lux* script, May 12, 1935).

The play to which *Lux*'s host referred was Frederick Jackson's *The Bishop Misbehaves*, which had opened on February 12, 1935, at the Cort Theatre and was, as Garrick mentioned, in the midst of its 121-performance run at the time of its radio presentation. The comedy-thriller revolves around a bishop with a passion for detective novels who suddenly finds himself involved with real criminals. *Lux*'s broadcast featured a cast largely consisting of players from the Broadway company, led by Walter Connolly and Jane Wyatt. The only members of the radio cast who did not create their roles on the stage, in fact, were Effie Shannon and Edward Broadley, who played the parts taken by Lucy Beaumont and Horace Sinclair in the original.

The delightful 1935 screen version

of *The Bishop Misbehaves* starred Edmund Gwenn and Maureen O'Sullivan and was directed by E.A. Dupont.

Film version: MGM, 1935.

*32. "The Lion and the Mouse," 5/19/35

Based on the play by Charles Klein (1905).

Cast: Ruth Chatterton (Shirley Rossmore), Robert T. Haines (John Burkett Ryder), Carlotta Nillson (Mrs. Rossmore), William Pringle (Judge Stott), Myrta Bellair (the Maid), Katherine Squire (Kate), Philip Tonge (Bagley), Stanley Harrison (Jorkins), Lorna Elliott (Mrs. Ryder), Blaine Cordner (Jefferson Ryder), and George Alison (Judge Rossmore). Additional cast (commercials and crowd): Myrta Bellaire, Josephine Fox, Helen Carew, and Brauer Burgess.

Ruth Chatterton played an author who goes undercover to get the goods on the wealthy financier who is behind the impeachment of her father (a judge) in *Lux*'s May 19 broadcast of Charles Klein's melodrama *The Lion and the Mouse*. The original production opened at Broadway's Lyceum Theatre on November 20, 1905, and played for 686 performances, with Grace Elliston and Richard Bennett in the title roles (Robert T. Haines played Bennett's stage part in the *Lux* adaptation).

Barry O'Neil directed the Lubin film *The Lion and the Mouse* in 1914, with Ethel Clayton and George Soule Spencer, and Tom Terriss was at the helm of Vitagraph's 1919 version, which featured a cast led by Alice Joyce and Anders Randolf. Warner Bros.' part-talkie, which was directed by Lloyd Bacon in 1928, starred May McAvoy and Lionel Barrymore.

The play would be presented again on *Lux*'s March 30, 1936, program.

Film versions: Lubin, 1914; Vitagraph, 1919; Warner Bros., 1928.

*33. "Michael and Mary," 5/26/35

Based on the play by A.A. Milne (1929).

Cast: Elissa Landi (Mary), Kenneth MacKenna (Michael), Eleanor Phelps (Violet Cunliffe), Royal Beal (Harry Price), Alfred Corn (David), Helen Walpole (Romo), Alice Buchanan (Alice), George Anderson (Inspector), and Mark Smith (Sargeant Cuff).

Commercial: William Boren, Fred Sherman.

A.A. Milne's *Michael and Mary* was first produced on Broadway at the Hopkins Theatre on December 13, 1929. It is a romance of a young couple who decide to marry, even though they know the girl's husband (who deserted her) is alive somewhere in the world. When the missing husband pops up many years later, a series of events is set in motion that threatens the couple's happiness and causes them to reconsider their vow that they would always retain their self-respect, whatever happened. Elissa Landi and Kenneth MacKenna were the featured players on *Lux*'s May 26 broadcast, taking the roles created on the stage by Edith Barrett and Henry Hull. The May 29, 1935, issue of *Variety* found Miss Landi was "a pleasant personality to listen to," and noted that "the supporting cast was competent."

The play would be presented on *The Lux Video Theatre* on December 27, 1956, starring Maureen O'Sullivan.

*34. "The Vinegar Tree," 6/2/35

Based on the play by Paul Osborn (1930).

Cast: Billie Burke (Laura Merrick), Conrad Nagel (Max Lawrence), Natalie Shafer (Winifred Mansfield), Greta Kvalden (Leone Merrick), Joseph Allen (Augustus Merrick), and Jonathan Hole (Geoffrey Cole).

Commercial: Peter Powers (Reporter), Myrta Bellair (Miss Jones).

Paul Osborn's *The Vinegar Tree* opened at the Playhouse Theatre on November 19, 1930, and is a comedy centered around a woman in her forties who, dissatisfied with her older husband, dreams of a past romance which she believes is about to be revived. *Lux*'s broadcast version of June 2 cast Billie Burke and Conrad Nagel in the roles played by Mary Boland and Warren William onstage.

*35. "Candle-Light," 6/9/35

Based on the play *Bei Kerzenlicht*, by Siegfried Geyer, as adapted by P.G. Wodehouse (1929).

Cast: Robert Montgomery (Josef), Irene Purcell (Marie), Alfred Shirley (Prince Rudolf Haseldorf-Schlobitten), Frank W. Taylor (Baron von Rischenheim), Lea Penman (Baroness von Rischenheim), and A.P. Kaye (Koeppke, a Chauffeur). Additional cast (commercial and crowd): J. Malcolm Dunn, Gerald Hamer, Grover Burgess.

British humorist P.G. Wodehouse's comedy *Candlelight* (adapted from Siegfried Geyer's German play) debuted on Broadway at the Empire Theatre on September 30, 1929. The story of a valet who poses as his master to impress a lady caller starred Robert Montgomery and Irene Purcell in *Lux*'s June 9 show, playing the roles taken on the stage by Leslie Howard and Gertrude Lawrence.

Universal's 1934 film *By Candlelight* was directed by James Whale and starred Paul Lukas and Elissa Landi.

Film version: Universal, 1934 (*By Candlelight*).

*36. "The Patsy," 6/16/35

Based on the play by Barry Conners (1925).

Cast: Loretta Young (Patricia Harrington), Eric Dressler (Tony Anderson), Calvin Thomas (Mr. Harrington), Josephine Hull (Mrs. Harrington), Peggy

Hovendon (Grace Harrington), and William Boren (Billy Caldwell).

Commercials: Patricia Calvert, Fred C. Barron, Ruth Garland, and Harriett Lorraine.

Barry Conners's farce *The Patsy* was first presented at the Booth Theatre on Broadway on December 22, 1925, with Claiborne Foster as the title character and Herbert Clark as her leading man. *Lux*'s "excellent show," which was "well-played by the entire cast" (according to Antony Stanford), gave Loretta Young the chance to portray the family pest, who, with the help of her sister's ex-boyfriend (Eric Dressler), works to make herself popular.

The charming 1928 MGM film version, which was directed by King Vidor, starred Marion Davies and Lawrence Gray.

Film version: MGM, 1928.

*37. "Polly with a Past," 6/23/35

Based on the play by George Middleton and Guy Bolton (1917).

Cast: Ina Claire (Polly Shannon), Alan Bunce (Rex Van Zile), Wilfred Lytell (Harry Richardson), Mark Smith (Stiles), Allen Fagen (Clay Collum), Aristedes DeLeoni (Petromski), Wright Kramer (Commodore Barker), Alma Kruger (Mrs. Martha Van Zile), Cora Witherspoon (Myrtle Davis), and May Buckley (Mrs. Clementine Davis).

Commercial: Katherine Revner, Rosemary deCamp.

Ina Claire's stage career was launched in *Polly with a Past* when it opened at the Belasco Theatre on September 6, 1917. Claire repeated her role in *Lux*'s June 23 broadcast, playing a minister's daughter who offers to help a lovesick swain (Alan Bunce) win the attentions of a lady welfare worker.

Claire was also the star of Metro's 1920 Leander de Cordova–directed screen version, in which her leading man was Ralph Graves.

Film version: Metro, 1920.

*38. "Elmer the Great," 6/30/35

Based on the play by Ring Lardner (1928).

Cast: Joe E. Brown (Elmer Kane), Lida MacMillan (Mrs. Kane), David Stewart (Nick Kane), Ruth Madison (Nellie Poole), G. Albert Smith (Pinky Doyle), Walter Kinsella (Nosey Noonan), Neil O'Malley (Dave Walker), Betty Garde (Evelyn Corey), Charles Olcott (Sports Announcer), Averell Harris (Walter Crabtree), Marcel Journet (Waiter), Sara Arms (Dolly Williams), and Taylor Graves (Newsboy). Additional cast (commercial and crowd): John D. Hewitt, Henry Landon, Tony Grey, Larry Ellinger, Carleton Young, and Helen Walpole.

Although Walter Huston had played the title role in Ring Lardner's baseball comedy *Elmer the Great* when it premiered at the Lyceum Theatre on September 24, 1928, it is Joe E. Brown who remains most closely associated with the part. Brown's first outing as the cocky pitcher of a small town team who joins the New York Giants was with a road company in 1931, and in 1933 he starred in Warner Bros.' motion picture version (which was directed by Mervyn LeRoy). *Lux*'s season finale gave the actor another crack at the part, casting Lida MacMillan as his mother, the same role she had played on Broadway.

The first film of *Elmer the Great* was released by Paramount in 1929 and entitled *Fast Company*, and it featured Jack Oakie under Edward Sutherland's direction. Warner Bros.' 1939 remake made Lardner's hero a football player (played by Bert Wheeler and directed by Noel Smith) and altered the title to *Cowboy Quarterback*.

Film versions: Paramount, 1929 (*Fast Company*); Warner Bros., 1933; Warner Bros., 1939 (*Cowboy Quarterback*).

Second Season, part 1
(July 29, 1935–May 25, 1936)

Columbia Broadcasting System, Monday, 9:00–10:00 P.M. WABC, Studio 1, New York (except July 28 and August 5, 1935). *Host*: Albert Hayes (as Douglass Garrick). *Announcer*: Art Millett (except July 28, 1935). *Director*: Antony Stanford. *Musical Director*: Robert Armbruster. *Adaptations*: George Wells (except May 4 and May 18, 1936).

*39. "Bunty Pulls the Strings," 7/29/35
Based on the play by Graham Moffatt (1911).
Announcer: William Brenton (from CBS Studio Number 3).
Cast: Helen Hayes (Bunty Biggar), Peter Donald, Jr. (Rab Biggar), Beatrice Terry (Susie Simpson), John McBryde (Thomas Biggar), Lawrence Fletcher (Weelum Sprunt), Molly Pearson (Ellen Dunlop), Margaret Mac-Laren (Teenie Dunlop), Stanley Harrison (Jeems Gibb), and Clement O'Laghlen (Dan Birrel). Additional cast (commercial and crowd): Helen Adair, Marguerite Faust, Loretta Archer, John Hewitt, Larry Ellinger, Edwin Gilcher, Anthony Grey, Bentley Wallace, and Alice Buchanan.
Lux's season opener on July 28 marked the series' move to CBS and the 9:00 P.M. time slot. Graham Moffatt's comedy *Bunty Pulls the Strings* (which premiered in London at the Haymarket Theatre on July 18, 1911) was chosen for the occasion, and Helen Hayes was the actress selected to portray the title character (which was played by Molly Pearson in the Broadway production at the Comedy Theatre on October 10, 1911). The July 31, 1935, issue of *Variety* commented that the radio play was "entirely in thick Scotch dialect."

*40. "Lightnin'," 8/5/35
Based on the play by Frank Bacon and Winchell Smith (1918).

From CBS Studio Number 3.
Cast: Wallace Beery (Lightnin' Bill Jones), Josephine Fox (Ma Jones), Carleton Young (John Marvin), Grover Burgess (Rodney Harper), Phyllis Welch (Mildred Buckley), Walter Greaza (Raymond Thomas), Calvin Thomas (Everett Hammond), Virginia Morgan (Mrs. Jordan), John Milton (Judge), and Frank Dae (Clerk of the Court). Additional cast (commercials and crowd): Loretta Archer, Marguerite Faust, William Boren, John Hewitt, Larry Ellinger, Edwin Gilcher, and Anthony Grey.
Lightnin' opened at Broadway's Gaiety Theatre on August 26, 1918, and is notable as the first play in American history to reach the 1,000 performance plateau, finally closing after a run of 1,291 performances. The star of that historic first production was veteran actor Frank Bacon, and by the time of his death in 1922 he had portrayed the character of Lightnin' Bill Jones more than 2,000 times. *Lux*'s broadcast of August 5 found Wallace Beery in the role of the hard-drinking fabricator of tales, with Josephine Fox playing his wife (the Jessie Pringle stage part).
Jay Hunt and Edythe Chapman appeared in Fox's 1925 film version, which was directed by John Ford, and the 1930 Henry King–directed remake (also for Fox) starred Will Rogers and Louise Dresser.
Film versions: Fox, 1925; Fox, 1930.

*41. "The Man in Possession,"
8/12/35
Based on the play by H.M. Harwood
(1930).
Cast: Robert Montgomery (Raymond
Dabney), Irene Purcell (Crystal Weth-
erby), and George Graham, Katherine Grey, Harold Vermilyea, Selma
Hall, Evelyn Vaughn, and Eustace
Wyatt.
Commercial: Sidney Smith (Man).
H.M. Harwood's farce *The Man in
Possession* relates the tale of an irresponsible young man from a respectable family who becomes a sheriff's
officer and accepts an assignment to
keep an attractive widow under obser-
vation on behalf of her creditors. *The
Lux Radio Theatre* program of August
12 brought Robert Montgomery and
Irene Purcell before the microphone,
taking the roles that had been played by
Raymond Massey and Isabel Jeans in
the first production on January 22,
1930, at the Ambassador's Theatre in
London, and by Leslie Banks and Jeans
in the Broadway premiere at the Booth
Theatre on November 1 of the same
year.
Montgomery and Purcell were also
the stars of MGM's 1931 film version,
which was directed by Sam Wood. The
same studio's 1937 rendering, *Personal
Property*, was directed by W.S. Van
Dyke II and starred Robert Taylor and
Jean Harlow.
Film versions: MGM, 1931; MGM,
1937 (*Personal Property*).

*42. "Ladies of the Jury," 8/19/35
Based on the play by Fred Ballard
(1929).
Intermission Guest: Finette Walker,
Broadway chorus girl (after Act I).
Cast: Mary Boland (Mrs. Livingstone
Baldwin Crane), Lorna Elliott (Lily
Pratt), Helen Walpole (Cynthia Tate),
Hallie Manning (Mayme Mixter), Vir-
ginia Morgan (Mrs. Dace), Marie Hunt

(Mrs. Bridget Maguire), Harold Moffett
(Jay J. Pressley), Hanley Stafford
(Spencer B. Dazey), Irvin Jeffries
(Alonzo Beal), Ralph Locke (Tony
Theodophulus), Walter Kinsella (Steve
Bromm), Horace Sinclair (Andrew
MacKaig), Robert T. Haines (Judge
Fish), Ray Collins (Halsey Van Stye),
Harian Tucker (Rutherford Dale),
Stuart Fox (Dr. Quincy Adams James,
Jr.), Patricia Calvert (Evelyn Snow),
William H. Malone (Clerk of the
Court), Billy Murray (Art Dobbs), and
Andree Caron (Mrs. Yvette Gordon).
Additional cast (commercial and
crowd): William Shelly, Charles Barre.
The *Lux* broadcast of "Ladies of the
Jury" was described by Antony Stan-
ford as "a good comedy well-played by
Boland and the cast," and was based on
the play that had premiered at
Erlanger's Theatre on October 21,
1929. The plot revolves around a
murder trial and one forceful lady juror
who refuses to believe in the defen-
dant's guilt, despite a preponderance of
evidence against her. Mary Boland
starred in the *Lux* adaptation, taking
the role created by Mrs. Fiske on
Broadway, while Hallie Manning,
Marie Hunt, and Walter Kinsella appeared in the parts they originally
played on the stage.
Edna May Oliver starred in RKO's
1932 Lowell Sherman–directed movie
version of *Ladies of the Jury*, and Helen
Broderick played the lead in RKO's
1937 remake, *We're on the Jury*, which
was directed by Ben Holmes.
Film versions: RKO, 1932; RKO, 1937
(*We're on the Jury*).

*43. "A Church Mouse," 8/26/35
Based on the play by Ladislas Fodor
(1931).
Cast: Otto Kruger (Baron Thomas
von Ullrich), Ruth Gordon (Susie
Sachs), Louise Kirkland (Olly Frey),
Wallace Erskine (Count von Talheim),

William Podmore (Jackson), and Eric Dressler (Baron Frank von Ullrich).

Ladislas Fodor's *A Church Mouse*, a comedy concerning a frumpy secretary who spruces up to win the boss's affections, came to *Lux* on August 26 starring Otto Kruger and three members of the original stage cast: Ruth Gordon, Louise Kirkland, and Wallace Erskine. (The first Broadway production at the Playhouse Theatre opened on October 21, 1931, and featured Bert Lytell in the leading masculine role.)

Warner Bros.' 1932 *Beauty and the Boss* was the first film of the play, starring Warren William and Marian Marsh, under the direction of Roy Del Ruth. Warner Bros.' British studio produced the 1935 remake (under the play's original title), which was directed by Monty Banks and featured Ian Hunter and Laura LaPlante.

Film versions: Warner Bros., 1932 (*Beauty and the Boss*); Warner Bros. (British), 1935.

*44. "Whistling in the Dark," 9/2/35

Based on the play by Laurence Gross and Edward Childs Carpenter (1932).

Cast: Charles Ruggles (Wallace Porter), Sylvia Field (Toby Van Buren), and John F. Hamilton, Louis Sorin, Averell Harris, Billy Murray, Ruth Hammond, John A. Butler, and Santos Ortego.

Commercials: Myrl Justiz (Woman), Marcelle D'Arsay (Herself).

Whistling in the Dark, the "melodramatic farce" by Laurence Gross and Edward Childs Carpenter, concerns a meek writer of crime fiction who becomes involved in a real-life adventure when he accidentally stumbles into the hideout of a desperate gang of criminals. Charles Ruggles and Sylvia Fields starred in *Lux*'s production of September 2, taking the roles created by Ernest Truex and Claire Trevor dur-

ing the premiere at the Ethel Barrymore Theatre on January 19, 1932.

Elliott Nugent directed MGM's 1933 film of *Whistling in the Dark*, which starred Ernest Truex and Una Merkel. That studio's 1941 S. Sylvan Simon-directed version changed the hero from an author to a radio actor, and Red Skelton and Ann Rutherford were cast in the leads.

Film versions: MGM, 1933; MGM, 1941.

*45. "Petticoat Influence," 9/9/35

Based on the play by Neil Grant (1930).

Cast: Ruth Chatterton (Peggy Chalfont), Alfred Shirley (Richard), Winfred Monti (Daincourt), J. Malcolm Dunn (Talbot), Horace Sinclair (Lord Algernon), Austin Fairman (Reggie Melcombe), Evelyn Vaughn (Lady Darnaway), and George Graham (Lord Darnaway).

Commercials: William Boren (Man), Edith Atwater.

Neil Grant's comedy *Petticoat Influence*, which demonstrates how a woman schemes to gain a political appointment for her husband, opened at St. Martin's Theatre in London on June 3, 1930, with Diana Wynyard and Frank Allenby in the leading roles. It began its run at New York's Empire Theatre on December 15, where it starred Helen Hayes and John Williams. *Lux*'s broadcast of September 9, 1935, gave Ruth Chatterton the role of Peggy Chalfont and featured Alfred Shirley as her spouse.

*46. "Leah Kleschna," 9/16/35

Based on the play by C.M.S. McLellan (1904).

Cast: Judith Anderson (Leah Kleschna), Conrad Nagel (Paul Sylvaine), Hanley Stafford (Schram), Wright Kramer (General Burton),

Harold Vermilyea (Raoul Berton), Walter Soderling (Reichmann), Bertram Yarbrough (Baptiste), Billy Murray (Officer), and Herbert Ranson (Kleschna).

Commercials: Dorothy Blackburn, James Spotswood, Mary Reilly, Ann Williams, and Lynn Mary Oldham.

C.M.S. McLellan's 1904 Broadway play (which opened December 12) was originally presented at the Manhattan Theatre with a cast that included Mrs. Fiske and John Mason. *Lux's* radio version of "Leah Kleschna" featured Judith Anderson as the woman thief and Conrad Nagel as the man who reforms her.

Famous Players' 1913 film version starred Carlotta Nillson and House Peters and was directed by J. Searle Dawley, while the Famous Players–Lasky remake was entitled *The Girl Who Came Back* and starred Ethel Clayton and Elliott Dexter, under the direction of Robert G. Vignola. Paramount filmed it once more as *The Moral Sinner* in 1924, with Ralph Ince directing Dorothy Dalton and James Rennie.

Film versions: Famous Players, 1913; Famous Players–Lasky, 1918 (*The Girl Who Came Back*); Paramount, 1924 (*The Moral Sinner*).

*47. "Mary, Mary, Quite Contrary," 9/23/35

Based on the play by St. John Ervine (1923).

Cast: Ethel Barrymore (Mary Westlake), J.W. Austin (Sir Henry Considine), Violet Besson (Mrs. Considine), Patricia Calvert (Sheila Dexter), John Emery (Geoffrey Considine), Mary Seton (Jenny), and A.P. Kaye (Mr. Hobbs).

Commercial: Harriett Lorraine (Woman).

"Ethel Barrymore in a hokum comedy—in which she kicked off her shoes and went to town," was how Antony Stanford described *Lux's* Sep-

tember 22 broadcast of "Mary, Mary, Quite Contrary." Barrymore played the part of a famous London actress who creates a stir when she visits a country town, the role created by Mrs. Fiske in the original New York production (Belasco Theatre, September 11, 1923).

*48. "Alias Jimmy Valentine," 9/30/35

Based on the play by Paul Armstrong (1910), in turn based on the story "A Retired Reformation," by O. Henry (1903).

Cast: Richard Barthelmess (Jimmy Valentine), Eleanor Phelps (Rose Lane), Janet Lee Hutchinson (Kitty), Walter Tetley (Bobby), and John Milton, Alice Fleming, Anthony Burgher, Edward J. McNamara, Blanche Hutchinson, and Billy Murray.

Commercial: Doris Dagmar (Woman).

Paul Armstrong's stage adaptation of a famous O. Henry story about an ex-safecracker who cannot escape his past, received its New York opening at Wallack's Theatre on January 21, 1910. *Lux* producers were able to secure the services of Richard Barthelmess for the September 29 adaptation to play the part taken by H.B. Warner in the original stage version (Antony Stanford judged the show to be "a splendid adaptation—well-played").

World filmed the play in 1915, with Robert Warwick starring in the Maurice Tourneur–directed production, and Bert Lytell starred in the Metro version of 1920, which was directed by Edmund Mortimer and Arthur D. Ripley. William Haines assumed the title role in MGM's 1928 Jack Conway–directed remake, a part-talkie that was that studio's first film to contain dialogue.

Lux performed "Alias Jimmy Valentine" again on November 9, 1936.

Film versions: World, 1915; Metro, 1920; MGM, 1928.

*49. "The Wren," 10/7/35

Based on the play by Booth Tarkington (1921).

Cast: Helen Chandler (Seeby Olds), John Beal (Owen Roddy), George Fawcett (Captain Olds), Lea Penman (Mrs. Frazee), Leslie Adams (Mr. Frazee), and Frank Conlon (Francis).

Commercial: Joyce Walsh, Betty Hanna.

The Wren opened at the Gaiety Theatre on Broadway on October 10, 1921, where the stars were Helen Hayes and Leslie Howard. The comedy of a Canadian artist whose interest in the young lady (who serves as general manager of a New England summer resort) is dampened by the arrival of a fascinating married lady, was found by Antony Stanford to be "a charming love story, well-played," as presented on *Lux*'s October 7 program. Helen Chandler and John Beal were the stars of the microphone play, with George Fawcett repeating his stage role of the former's father.

*50. "Within the Law," 10/14/35

Based on the play by Bayard Veiller (1912).

Cast: Joan Crawford (Mary Turner), Raymond Bramley (Joe Garson), Robert T. Haines (Edward Gilder), Ben Lackland (Robert Gilder), Virginia Morgan (Sarah), Frank Wilcox (George Demarest), Charles Slattery (Sergeant Cassidy), John O. Hewitt (Williams), James Jolley (English Eddie Griggs), Edna Hibbard (Agnes Lynch), and Carlton Macy (Inspector Burke).

Commercial: Mary Newton (Woman).

Jane Cowl was the star of *Within the Law* when it opened at the Eltinge Theatre on Broadway September 11, 1912, telling the story of a girl who, having served a term in prison for a crime she did not commit, seeks revenge on the man who put her there. *Lux* director Antony Stanford was clearly pleased with the October 14 broadcast of the play, saying, "One of the best melodramas I know of. Excellent for radio — Joan Crawford did the best job ever done in her life (I believe)."

Crawford also starred in MGM's 1931 film version, *Paid*, which was directed by Sam Wood. Previous renderings were Vitagraph's 1917 release, directed by William P.S. Earle and starring Alice Joyce, and First National's 1923 Frank Lloyd–directed production, featuring Norma Talmadge. Another reworking was produced by MGM in 1939, which was directed by Gustav Machaty and starred Ruth Hussey.

Film versions: Vitagraph, 1917; First National, 1923; MGM, 1931 (*Paid*); MGM, 1939.

*51. "Merely Mary Ann," 10/21/35

Based on the play by Israel Zangwill (1903).

Cast: Joan Bennett (Mary Ann), Kenneth MacKenna (Lancelot), and Richard Stevenson, Marjorie Wood, Franz Bendtsen, Richard Barrows, Myron Paulson, Frank Milan, and Jeanne Owen.

Commercials: Donald Bain, Fred Sherman, and Mary Newton.

Israel Zangwill's *Merely Mary Ann,* which is set in London and chronicles a romance between a scullery maid and a struggling musician, first appeared in New York at the Garden Theatre on December 28, 1903. Starring in *Lux*'s adaptation of October 21 were Joan Bennett, in the part originated in the theatre by Eleanor Robson, and Kenneth MacKenna, in the Edwin Arden stage role.

Vivian Martin and Harry Hilliard led the players in Fox's 1916 John G. Adolfi–directed screen version, and Edward J. LeSaint directed the 1920 remake at the same studio, which featured Shirley Mason and Carson

Ferguson. Fox also produced it as a talkie in 1931, starring Janet Gaynor and Charles Farrell, under Henry King's direction.

Film versions: Fox, 1916; Fox, 1920; Fox, 1931.

52. "Dulcy," 10/28/35

Based on the play by George S. Kaufman and Marc Connelly (1921).

Cast: ZaSu Pitts (Dulcinia Smith), Gene Lockhart (Charles Forbes), Leslie Adams (Gordon Smith), Mary Mason (Angela), James Marr (Blair Patterson), Clifford Walker (Henry), Stuart Fox (Vincent Leech), Harold Vermilyea (Skyler Van Dyck), Donald Foster (Willie), and Mary Newton (Mrs. Forbes).

Commercial: Betty Hanna.

The adaptation of George S. Kaufman and Marc Connelly's 1921 comedy *Dulcy* is the only program of which a recording is known to exist from *Lux*'s New York period. (The Broadway premiere took place at the Frazee Theatre on August 13, 1921, with a cast led by Lynn Fontanne and Wallis Clark.) The plot, such as it is, concerns the scatterbrained wife of a manufacturer of "imitation jewelry" whose attempts to bolster her husband's career lead to trouble for all involved.

To compare this "Dulcy" to *Lux*'s later version (see 3/29/37) is to compare the New York edition of *Lux* to the series after the move to Hollywood. While the second broadcast "opened up" the play by using frequent set changes and appropriate sound effects, the first is content to set all the scenes in one room (as does the stage play), and the orchestra (which is considerably smaller than its Hollywood counterpart) is employed only during Douglass Garrick's scene-setting narration (and at the conclusion of each act). The actors too (in a cast led by ZaSu Pitts and Gene Lockhart) perform their characters in the tradition of the stage, not in the more natural style of the West Coast shows.

Filmed versions of *Dulcy* are the Sidney Franklin–directed 1923 film starring Constance Talmadge and Claude Gillingwater (as Mr. Forbes), MGM's 1929 motion picture *Not So Dumb*, starring Marion Davies with William Holden (not to be confused with the younger actor of the same name), and the 1940 MGM *Dulcy*, directed by S. Sylvan Simon and starring Ann Sothern and Roland Young.

Film versions: First National, 1923; MGM, 1929 (*Not So Dumb*); MGM, 1940.

*53. "The Milky Way," 11/4/35

Based on the play by Lynn Root and Harry Clork (1934).

Cast: Charles Butterworth (Barleigh Sullivan), Helen Lynd (Anne Westley), Edward Butler (Gabby Sloan), Jack Davis (Davis Pinchforth), Bradley Barker (Slim Lincoln), Franz Bendtsen (Wilbur Austin), Billy Murray (Spider McGee), Walter Kinsella (Speed McFarland), and Emily Lowry (May Sullivan). *Commercial*: Virginia Morgan, Rita Johnson.

Hugh O'Connell was the star of *The Milky Way* when it opened at Broadway's Cort Theatre on May 8, 1934, playing a timid milkman who becomes a prizefighter. Charles Butterworth was part of the "good cast" that performed the "very amusing script" (according to Antony Stanford) on *Lux*'s November 4 presentation of the comedy.

Leo McCarey directed Paramount's 1936 film version, which was a vehicle for Harold Lloyd, and ten years later RKO reworked it (with songs) as *The Kid from Brooklyn*, with Danny Kaye, under Norman Z. McLeod's direction.

Film versions: Paramount, 1936; RKO, 1946 (*The Kid from Brooklyn*).

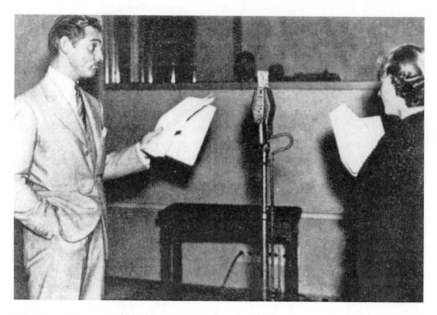

Clark Gable and Lillian Emerson in "The Misleading Lady," November 11, 1935 (photo: Berry Hill Bookshop).

*54. "The Misleading Lady," 11/11/35

Based on the play by Charles W. Goddard and Paul Dickey (1913).

Cast: Clark Gable (Jack Craigen), Lillian Emerson (Helen Steele), Cyril Scott (Boney), Reynolds Denniston (Sidney Parker), Robert Shayne (Stephen Weatherby), Kathryn March (Jane Wentworth), Walter Soderling (Tim), Robert Ashton (Tipple), Grace Fox (Grace Buchanan), Alan Bunce (Keen Fitzpatrick), and Franklyn Fox (Henry Tracey). Additional cast (commercials or crowd): Lottie Gropper, Marguerite Faust, and Loretta Archer.

November 25, 1913, marked the opening of *The Misleading Lady* at New York's Fulton Theatre, a comedy concerning an explorer who kidnaps a society girl in retaliation for a prank that she had pulled on him. *Lux's* November 11 broadcast starred Clark Gable in Lewis Stone's stage role, along with Lillian Emerson, a society debu-

tante who made her acting debut in the program playing the part Joan Cumberland took in the theatre.

Arthur Berthelet directed the first movie version, shot at Essanay in 1916, with Henry B. Walthall and Edna Mayo in the cast, while Bert Lytell and Lucy Cotton starred in Metro's 1920 remake, a production directed by George Irving and George Terwillinger. Paramount made the farce as a talkie in 1932, with Stuart Walker directing Claudette Colbert and Edmund Lowe.

Film versions: Essanay, 1916; Metro, 1920; Paramount, 1932.

*55. "Sherlock Holmes," 11/18/35

Based on the play by William Gillette (1899).

Cast: William Gillette (Sherlock Holmes), Reginald Mason (Dr. Watson), Betty Hanna (Alice Faulkner), Reynolds Denniston (James Larrabee), William Postance (Sid Prince), Charles

Bryant (Moriarty), Roberta Beatty (Madge Larrabee), Harold deBecker (Leary), William H. Barwald (Craigin), Burford Hampden (Billy), Donald Campbell (Parsons), and J. Malcolm Dunn (John Forman).

Commercials: Stuart Fox, Helen Walpole, and Eve March.

Noted American actor William Gillette came out of retirement at age 80 to portray the character for which he was best known, Sherlock Holmes, in the *Lux* adaptation of his own play (which he based on the stories by A. Conan Doyle). Gillette had made his stage debut in 1875, and premiered his *Sherlock Holmes*, with himself as star, at Broadway's Garrick Theatre in 1899. He went on to become the best known Holmes of his time in both the United States and England.

For his *Sherlock Holmes*, Gillette used A. Conan Doyle's famous consulting detective and fashioned something resembling a standard melodrama (involving potentially incriminating letters) from incidents in several Holmes stories, notably "A Scandal in Bohemia."

Six players in *Lux*'s show came from the cast of the November 25, 1929, revival at the New Amsterdam Theatre: William Postance, Roberta Beatty, William H. Barwald, Burford Hampden, and Donald Campbell (Betty Hanna had played Alice Faulkner in the most recent touring production prior to the broadcast).

Though there have been many films featuring literature's famous sleuth, few seem to have been based directly on William Gillette's play. Gillette himself starred in an Arthur Berthelet–directed version for Essanay in 1916, and the Albert Parker–directed production of 1922 (which stars John Barrymore) also credits Gillette's drama as its source. Clive Brook starred in Fox's 1932 *Sherlock Holmes*, which was directed by William K. Howard, and Alfred Werker was at the helm of 20th Century–Fox's *The Adventures of Sherlock Holmes* (the second of the Basil Rathbone–Nigel Bruce teamings), which, though officially based on Gillette's stage version, actually bears scant resemblance to it.

Film versions: Essanay, 1916; Goldwyn, 1922; Fox, 1932; 20th Century–Fox, 1939 (*The Adventures of Sherlock Holmes*).

*56. "Way Down East," 11/25/35
Based on the play by Lottie Blair Parker (1897), as elaborated by Joseph R. Grimser (1898).

Cast: Lillian Gish (Anna Moore), Richard Barthelmess (David Bartlett), Dorothy Gish (Kate), John Milton (Squire Bartlett), Grace Fox (Martha Perkins), Sam Wren (the Professor), Franklyn Fox (Lennox Sanderson), and William A. Norton (Doctor Johnson). Additional cast (commercials or crowd): Vivia Ogden, Peggy Patterson, Tucker McGuire, and Florence Baker.

Way Down East, the famous melodrama of a country girl who is seduced by a wealthy playboy, and the hardships that follow, originally opened at New York's Manhattan Theatre on February 7, 1898, with a cast headed by Phoebe Davis, Howard Kyle, and Minnie Dupree. D.W. Griffith's popular 1920 film version renewed the play's fame and gave memorable roles to Lillian Gish and Richard Barthelmess. *Lux*'s program of November 25 (which was based on the stage play, not on the movie) reunited Gish and Barthelmess, and also featured Dorothy Gish in the part played by Mary Hay in the motion picture.

In 1935, 20th Century–Fox assigned Henry King to direct the next version of *Way Down East,* and cast Rochelle Hudson and Henry Fonda in the leads.

Film versions: United Artists, 1920; 20th Century–Fox, 1935.

*57. "The Swan," 12/2/35

Based on the play by Ferenc Molnar (1914), as translated by Melville Baker (1923).

Cast: Elissa Landi (Princess Alexandra), Alfred Shirley (Agi), Francis Compton (Father Karl), Violet Besson (Princess Beatrice), Wilfred Seagrim (Prince Albert), Roland Bottomley (Colonel Wunderlich), Essex Dane (Princess Maria Dominico), Harold deBecker (Caesar), and Billy and Bobby Mauch (the Twins). Additional cast (commercials and crowd): Marguerite Faust, Lottie Gropper, Loretta Archer, John A. Butler, and Mary Newton.

Elissa Landi starred in *Lux*'s broadcast of "The Swan," playing a princess engaged to marry a foreign monarch though she loves another man. Ferenc Molnar's 1914 comedy made its U.S. debut in 1923, when Melville Baker's translation opened at Broadway's Cort Theatre on October 23, with Eva LeGalliene in the title role.

Paramount filmed *The Swan* in 1925, with Frances Howard starring in the Dimitri Buchowetzki–directed production. Lillian Gish made her talkie debut in United Artists' George Fitzmaurice–directed 1930 release (entitled *One Romantic Night*), and Grace Kelly's final screen appearance came in MGM's 1956 film version, which was directed by Charles Vidor.

Film versions: Paramount, 1925; United Artists, 1930 (*One Romantic Night*); MGM, 1956.

*58. "The Show-Off," 12/9/35

Based on the play by George Kelly (1924).

Cast: Joe E. Brown (Aubrey Piper), Georgie Drew Medum (Mrs. Fisher), T. Daniel Frawley (Mr. Fisher), Helen Carew (Clara), Katherine March (Amy), Charles Barre (Timmons), Francis Pierlot (Mr. Gill), and Glenn Boles (Harry Fisher).

Commercials: Dorothy Daniels, Leighton Carey.

George Kelly's comedy *The Show-Off* was first produced at Broadway's Playhouse Theatre on February 5, 1924. That initial production starred Louis John Bartels as the title character, a loud-mouthed know-it-all who yearns to be someone important, while *Lux*'s December 9 radio rendering featured Joe E. Brown.

Paramount released the first film version of *The Show-Off* shortly after the Broadway production closed, with comic Ford Sterling as star and Malcolm St. Clair as director. A talkie remake followed in 1930 under the title *Men Are Like That,* with Hal Skelly, under Frank Tuttle's direction. The rights were acquired by MGM shortly afterward, and in 1934 MGM produced it, with Spencer Tracy in the lead and Charles F. Reisner directing. Twelve years passed before MGM filmed its second version, which, on this occasion, was directed by Harry Beaumont and featured Red Skelton in the title role (and a screenplay by George Wells, who wrote both this *Lux* adaptation and the one of February 1, 1943).

Film versions: Paramount, 1926; Paramount, 1930 (*Men Are Like That*); MGM, 1934; MGM, 1946.

*59. "The Truth," 12/16/35

Based on the play by Clyde Fitch (1907).

Cast: Grace George (Becky Warder), Francis Compton (Tom Warder), Austin Fairman (Fred Linden), Evelyn Vaughn (Eve Linden), Roberta Beatty (Laura Fraser), Wright Kramer (Stephen Roland), Donald Campbell (Charles the Butler), and Harriett Sterling (Mrs. Genevieve Crespigny).

Commercial: Ruth Thomas, Virginia Gregori.

The Truth premiered on Broadway at the Criterion Theatre on January 7,

1907, with Clara Bloodgood in the starring role of a woman whose penchant for telling little white lies involves her in some serious marital difficulties. Grace George, who starred in the *Lux* adaptation of December 16, first performed the comedy during the 1914 Broadway revival.

Lawrence C. Windom directed Goldwyn's 1920 film of *The Truth*, which starred Madge Kennedy.

Film version: Goldwyn, 1920.

*60. "Applesauce," 12/23/35

Based on the play by Barry Connor (1925).

Cast: Jack Oakie (Bill), Emily Lowry (Hazel Robinson), Josephine Hull (Mrs. Robinson), Charles Dow Clark (Mr. Robinson), Robert Harrison (Mat MacAllister), and Donald Randolph (Rollo Jenkins). Additional cast (commercial and crowd): Alice Buchanan, Elsie Mae Gordon.

According to Antony Stanford, Jack Oakie, the star of *Lux*'s December 23 broadcast of "Applesauce," "turned in a very good show" in the comedy of an unambitious but likable young man who concentrates on spreading good cheer, but shows some spunk when he loses his girl to another. Oakie was playing the role Alan Dinehart created in the Broadway production, which opened at the Ambassador Theatre on September 28, 1925, and Emily Lowry was the leading lady, taking the Gladys Lloyd stage part.

Warner Bros.–First National released a film version of the play in 1936 under the title *Brides Are Like that*, with Ross Alexander and Anita Louise, under William McGann's direction. The 1940 remake by the same studio was directed by Noel Smith and called *Always a Bride*, which featured George Reeves and Rosemary Lane.

Film versions: Warner Bros.–First National, 1936 (*Brides Are Like That*); Warner Bros.–First National, 1940 (*Always a Bride*).

*61. "The Queen's Husband," 12/30/35

Based on the play by Robert E. Sherwood (1928).

Cast: Frank Morgan (King Eric VIII), Gladys Hanson (Queen Martha), Claudia Morgan (Princess Anne), Joseph Curtain (Frederick Granton), Averell Harris (General Northrup), Ian MacLaren (Lord Birten), Harold deBecker (Phipps), William B. Mack (Dr. Fellman), Albert Phillips (Major Blent), and Milton Herman (Mr. Laker). Additional cast (commercials and crowd): Charles Barre, Doris Dagmar, Robert Hall, Rita Johnson, and Dorothy Daniels.

Lux's final program of 1935 featured Frank Morgan as the king of a small country who takes advantage of the domineering queen's absence to assert his authority. Joining Morgan in the Robert E. Sherwood comedy were Gladys Hanson, repeating her role from the first production (which opened January 25, 1928) at the Playhouse on Broadway, and Claudia Morgan (Frank's niece), in the part created on the stage by Katherine Alexander. (Roland Young portrayed the title character during the play's original run.)

*62. "The Third Degree," 1/6/36

Based on the play by Charles Klein (1909).

Cast: Sylvia Sidney (Annie Jeffries), Morgan Farley (Howard Jeffries, Jr.), John T. Dwyer (Howard Jeffries, Sr.), Selena Royale (Mrs. Howard Jeffries, Sr.), Charles Slattery (Captain Clinton), Herbert Ashton (Detective Maloney), Arthur Maitland (Dr. Bernstein), Jay Clark (Newsboy), Charles Barre (Second Newsboy), William H. Malone (Thomas), and A.H. Van Buren (Richard Brewster).

Commercials: Jane Houston, Elisabeth Morgan.

The Third Degree, Charles Klein's melodrama about a young man who confesses to a murder he did not commit and his dedicated wife who tries to clear him, opened at Broadway's Hudson Theatre on February 1, 1909. *Lux's* radio production of January 5 cast Sylvia Sidney and Morgan Farley in the roles created on the stage by Helen Ware and Wallace Eddinger.

Barry O'Neil directed Lubin's 1913 film version of *The Third Degree*, which starred Carlotta Doti and Robert Dunbar, and Alice Joyce and Gladden James led the cast of Vitagraph's Tom Terriss–directed production of 1919. Michael Curtiz made his American directorial debut in Warner Bros.' 1926 remake, which starred Dolores Costello and Jason Robards, Sr.

Film versions: Lubin, 1913; Vitagraph, 1919; Warner Bros., 1926.

*63. "The Boss," 1/13/36

Based on the play by Edward Sheldon (1911).

Cast: Edward G. Robinson (Michael Regan), Lillian Emerson (Emily Griswold), John Milton (James Griswold), Howard Phillips (Donald Griswold), John Wheeler (Mitchell), Donald Cameron (Davis), Walter Kinsella (Porky McCoy), William Ponstance (Gates), Clyde Franklin (Scanlon), Billy Murray (Police Inspector), Frank McCullough (Policeman), and J. Francis Kirk (Archbishop O'Connor).

Commercials: Frances Woodbury (Woman), Alfred Cora (Boy).

The Boss, a drama suggested by the real-life exposés of Lincoln Steffens and Ida Tarbell, opened at Broadway's Astor Theatre on January 30, 1911, with Holbrook Blinn and Lillian Emerson. Blinn also appeared in World's 1915 Émile Chautard–directed film version opposite Alice Brady.

Lux's show of January 12 featured Edward G. Robinson as the title character, a rugged wharf rat who works his way up the ladder of success and becomes one of the most powerful men in the city. Lillian Emerson was Robinson's leading lady in the broadcast.

Film version: World, 1915.

*64. "A Prince There Was," 1/20/36

Based on the play by George M. Cohan (1918), in turn based on the story by Darraugh Aldrich.

Cast: Ricardo Cortez (Charles Martin), Adrienne Ames (Miss Woods), Charles Dow Clark (Bland), Raymond Bramley (Jack Carruthers), Leona Roberts (Mrs. Prouty), Edward Craven (Mr. Shert), Charita Bauer (Confort), Richard Jack (Eddie), and Thomas W. Ross (Mr. Crickett).

Commercials: Rita Johnson, Helen Carew, Doris Dagmar, and Jimmy Donnelly.

George M. Cohan's play *A Prince There Was* opened at New York's Cohan Theatre on December 24, 1918, with Cohan and Ruth Donnelly as stars. *Lux* introduced the comedy to its listeners with a production that starred Ricardo Cortez as a well-to-do young man who becomes a benefactor for the inhabitants of a cheap boarding house, one of whom is the inevitable romantic interest of the tale, played by Adrienne Ames.

Paramount's 1921 film starred Thomas Meighan and Mildred Harris, and was directed by Thomas Forman.

Film version: Paramount, 1921.

*65. "Grumpy," 1/27/36

Based on the play by Horace Hodges and Wigney Percyval (1913).

Cast: Lionel Barrymore (Andrew Bullivant, aka Grumpy), Donald Cameron (Dawson), Kathryn March (Virginia Bullivant), Donald MacDonald

(Ernest), Edith Atwater (Susan), Joseph Granby (Wolf), Leslie King (Dr. MacLaren), James LaCurto (Keble), and Franklyn Fox (Mr. Jarvis).

Commercials: William Boren, Beatrice Miller, and Mary Newton.

According to Antony Stanford, Lionel Barrymore "gave a fine performance" as a crusty old lawyer who becomes involved in tracking down the perpetrator of a diamond robbery in *Lux*'s January 26 broadcast of "Grumpy." The play dates from 1913 when (on November 19) it opened at Wallack's Theatre on Broadway, with C. Cyril Maude as the title character.

William C. deMille directed Paramount's first film of *Grumpy*, which was released in 1923 with Theodore Roberts as the star. The same studio's talkie remake of 1930 was directed by George Cukor and featured the role's creator, Cyril Maude.

Film versions: Paramount, 1923; Paramount, 1930.

*66. "Green Grow the Lilacs," 2/2/36

Based on the play by Lynn Riggs (1931).

Cast: John Boles (Curly McLain), June Walker (Laurey Williams), Maida Reade (Aunt Eller Murphy), John Milton (Elam Peck), John F. Hamilton (Slim), David Stewart (Ed), Woodward "Tex" Ritter (Joe), Virginia Morgan (Ado Annie Carnes), and Ralph Theodore (Jeeter Fry).

Commercial: Katherine Lane, Marguerite Faust.

Lynn Riggs's folk-play *Green Grow the Lilacs,* a romance set in Indian territory that would become Oklahoma, was produced by the Theatre Guild and opened at the Guild Theatre on January 26, 1931, with Franchot Tone and June Walker in the leads. John Boles was the leading man in *Lux*'s broadcast of February 2, and June Walker repeated

her stage role. (Woodward "Tex" Ritter also reprised his Broadway part of Joe.)

Musical numbers (traditional American folk songs except where noted) sung by John Boles were: "Chisholm Trail," "Carry Me Back to the Lone Prairie" (words and music by Carson Robinson, from the motion picture *Stars Over Broadway,* 1935) in Act 1, and "Green Grow the Lilacs" in Act 2.

The play is now best remembered as the basis for the 1943 Oscar Hammerstein II–Richard Rodgers musical version, *Oklahoma!,* which was filmed by Magna Pictures in 1955, with Gordon MacRae and Shirley Jones, under Fred Zimmerman's direction.

Film version: Magna, 1955 (*Oklahoma!*).

*67. "The Bride the Sun Shines On," 2/9/36

Based on the play by Will Cotton (1931).

Cast: Douglas Fairbanks, Jr. (Hubert Burnet), Muriel Kirkland (Psyche Marbury), Robert Harrison (Everett Marbury), Alice John (Mrs. Polly Marbury), Louis Jean Heydt (Alfred), Roland Bottomley (Treloar), James Spottswood (Meredith Lane), and Leona Maricle (Mrs. Lane). Additional cast (commercials and crowd): Katherine Lane, Virginia Spottswood, Marguerite Faust, Lottie Gropper, Muriel Larbater, Frank Curran, and Helen Walpole.

"A very bright comedy" was how Antony Stanford described *Lux*'s February 9 broadcast of "The Bride the Sun Shines On" (originally presented at Broadway's Fulton Theatre on December 26, 1931). The play relates the case of a bride who, an hour before her wedding is scheduled to take place, chances to encounter the man she really loves — the organist for the ceremony. The radio play starred Douglas Fairbanks, Jr., and Muriel Kirkland in the parts played by Henry Hull and Dorothy Gish in the original.

*68. "The Old Soak," 2/16/36

Based on the play by Don Marquis (1922).

Guest Host: Edwin Jerome.

Cast: Wallace Beery (Clem Hawley), Minnie Dupree (Matilda Hawley), Ruth Mateson (Lucy Hawley), Harry Humphrey (Webster Parsons), Donald McFarland (Al the Bootlegger), Morgan Farley (Clarence Hawley), and Donald Foster (Tom Ogden).

"The Old Soak" has the distinction of being the first play to be presented on *Lux* twice. It was first performed on February 17, 1935, also with Wallace Beery and Minnie Dupree (who played Matilda in the stage production) in the leading roles. According to the February 16, 1935, issue of the *New York Times*, Beery recreated his role "in response to 1,700 requests by listeners."

In the absence of Albert Hayes, *Lux*'s regular "Douglass Garrick," Edwin Jerome assumed the host's duties for this program (though he was never referred to by name).

See 2/17/35 for information on the film version.

*69. "Peter Pan," 2/23/36

Based on the play by Sir James Barrie (1904).

Cast: Freddie Bartholomew (Peter Pan), Janet Lee Hutchinson (Wendy), Billy Mauch (Tootles), Bobby Mauch (John Darling), Tommy Donnelly (Michael Darling), Jimmy Donnelly (Curley), Walter Tetley (Slightly), Jackie Jordan (Nibs), Evelyn Vaughn (Mrs. Darling), Bradley Barker (Nana/Jukes), Winfield Hoeny (Cecco), Donald Cameron (Mr. Darling), Tony Burgher (Smee), and Averell Harris (Captain Hook). Additional cast (commercials and crowd): Walter Elliott, John Hewitt, Tom Dawes, Anthony Grey, Charles Crumpton, Taylor Graves, Alice Davenport, and Billy Murray.

Peter Pan, J.M. Barrie's fantasy of the boy who refuses to grow up, received its first London performance at the Duke of York Theatre on December 27, 1904, with Nina Boucicault as star, then came across the Atlantic to Broadway's Empire Theatre on November 6, 1905, where Maude Adams portrayed the title character. *Lux*'s broadcast on February 23 possessed the novel feature of an actual boy as Peter, casting Freddie Bartholomew in the starring role. (Donald Cameron repeated his role of Mr. Darling from the 1928 Broadway revival.)

Herbert Brenon directed Paramount's 1924 film of *Peter Pan*, which starred Betty Bronson, and Bobby Driscoll provided the voice for Peter in Disney's 1953 animated version (directed by Hamilton Luske, Clyde Geronimi, and Wilfred Jackson). (*Lux* performed a radio version of the Disney *Peter Pan* on December 21, 1953.)

*70. "Alias the Deacon," 3/2/36

Based on the play by John B. Hymer and LeRoy Clemens (1925).

Cast: Victor Moore (Tony), Sylvia Field (Phyllis Halliday), Donald Foster (John Adams), Clara Joel (Mrs. Clark), Averell Harris (Luella Gregory), and Richard Jack, Charles W. Dingle, Frank McCullough, Ralph Theodore, James LaCurto, Edward Smith, and Herbert Ashton.

Commercials: Elsie Mae Gordon, Grace Fox, and Arline Blackburn.

Alias the Deacon was first presented at the Sam H. Harris Theatre in New York on November 24, 1925, where it ran for 277 performances. In the cast of that production was Berton Churchill in the title role, with Mayo Methot and Donald Foster supplying the romantic interest. *Lux*'s March 2 broadcast featured Victor Moore as "the Deacon," a cardsharp who helps a family in trouble, with Sylvia Field and Donald

Foster (once again in his stage role) as the young lovers. (Averell Harris, also of the original company, was on hand to reprise her stage part as well.)

Universal acquired the film rights and made three versions: first (as a silent) in 1927, with Jean Hersholt, June Marlowe, and Ralph Graves (directed by Edward Sloman); then as *Half a Sinner* in 1934, with Berton Churchill repeating his stage role, along with Sally Blane and Joel McCrea, in the Kurt Neumann–directed production. The final version was released in 1940 as a vehicle for folksy comedian Bob Burns, and featured Peggy Moran and Dennis O'Keefe in the Christy Cabanne–directed motion picture. (*Lux* was to present their adaptation of the 1940 version on July 1, 1940.)

Film versions: Universal, 1927; Universal, 1934 (*Half a Sinner*); Universal, 1940.

*71. "The Girl of the Golden West,"
3/9/36

Based on the play by David Belasco (1905).

Cast: Eva LeGallienne (Minnie), Kenneth MacKenna (Dick Johnson), Louis Calhern (Jack Rance), Harriett Sterling (Wowkle), and Thomas Gunn, Edgar Nelson, William Shelley, Raymond Bramley, Taylor Graves, and Leo Curley. Additional cast (commercials and crowd): Adele Ranson, Phyllis Welch, John G. Hewitt, Anthony Grey, Tom Davies, and Charles Crumpton.

David Belasco's *The Girl of the Golden West* was first presented in New York at the Belasco Theatre on November 14, 1905 (five years later, Giacomo Puccini's operatic version premiered at the Metropolitan Opera). The story, which is set in a California gold-mining settlement, involves a girl bartender who is in love with an outlaw, and an evil sheriff who pursues them both (in different ways, of course). *Lux*'s broadcast of March 9 offered "a good melodrama well-played," in Antony Stanford's estimation, with the starring roles going to Eva LeGallienne, Kenneth MacKenna, and Louis Calhern. (These parts were taken in the Broadway production by Blanche Bates, Robert Hilliard, and Frank Keenan, respectively.)

Cecil B. DeMille directed the first film version for Famous Players–Lasky in 1915, with a cast headed by Mabel Van Buren, House Peters, and Theodore Roberts, while First National's Edwin Carewe–directed film of the play opened in 1923, with Sylvia Breamer, J. Warren Kerrigan, and Russell Simpson in the cast. John Francis directed the first talking version for Warner Bros. in 1930, with Ann Harding, James Rennie, and Harry Banister, while Robert Z. Leonard directed MGM's musical rendering (with songs by Gus Kahn and Sigmund Romberg) in 1938, which starred Jeanette MacDonald, Nelson Eddy, and Walter Pidgeon.

Film versions: Famous Players–Lasky, 1915; First National, 1923; Warner Bros., 1930; MGM, 1938.

*72. "The Last of Mrs. Cheyney,"
3/16/36

Based on the play by Frederick Lonsdale (1925).

Cast: Miriam Hopkins (Mrs. Cheyney), Leo G. Carroll (Lord Arthur Dilling), George Graham (Charles), J.W. Austin (Lord Elton), Winifred Monti (Lady Jane), Winifred Harris (Mrs. Webley), G. Oliver Smith (Willie Wynton), Harold deBecker (George), Hanley Stafford (Jim), J. Malcolm Dunn (Roberts), and Vera Hurst (Maria).

Commercials: Gladys Thornton, Virginia Morgan, Muriel Harbater, and Katherine Proctor.

Miriam Hopkins was the star of *Lux*'s

"The Last of Mrs. Cheyney," playing a jewel thief who allows love to interfere with a major heist. Leo Carroll was Hopkins's costar for the occasion, the two of them playing the roles created in the London production of the comedy (St. James Theatre, September 22, 1925) by Gladys Cooper and Gerald duMaurier, and played in the Broadway version (Fulton Theatre, November 9, 1925) by Ina Claire and Roland Young. (Winifred Harris recreated the part she played in the Broadway production for the *Lux* broadcast.)

Frederick Lonsdale's play was filmed three times by MGM: under Sidney Franklin's direction in 1929, with Norma Shearer and Basil Rathbone; in 1937, with Joan Crawford and Robert Montgomery starring, under Richard Boleslawski's direction; and finally, as *The Law and the Lady* in 1951, with Greer Garson and Michael Wilding, under the direction of Edwin H. Knopf. (*Lux* performed the play again on May 11, 1942.)

Film versions: MGM, 1929; MGM, 1937; MGM, 1951 (*The Law and the Lady*).

*73. "The Song and Dance Man," 3/23/36

Based on the play by George M. Cohan (1923).

Cast: George M. Cohan ("Hap" Farrell), Emily Lowry (Leola Lane), May Buckley (Mrs. Lane), Georgie Drew Mendum (the Landlady), Joseph Sweeny (Tom Crosby), Reynolds Denniston (Curtis), Edna Holland (Miss Davis), Richard Jack (Jimmy), Edward Butler (Lieutenant Crowley), Walter Gilbert (Joseph Murdock), and Charles D. Brown (Charles B. Nelson).

Commercials: Rita Johnson, Eve March, and William Boren.

George M. Cohan was present on *Lux*'s March 23 broadcast to recreate the starring role in his own play, *The*

Song and Dance Man. The original production on Broadway (Hudson Theatre, December 31, 1923) paired him with Mayo Methot, and *Lux*'s version cast Emily Lowry in the leading feminine role. The comedy-drama concerns a veteran trouper whose assistance to a lady in a financial crisis ends up landing him in hot water.

*74. "The Lion and the Mouse," 3/30/36

Based on the play by Charles Klein (1905).

Cast: Bette Davis (Shirley Rossmore), Robert T. Haines (John Burkett Ryder), and John Milton, May Buckley, Ruth Hammond, Elizabeth Morgan, Gerald Oliver Smith, Reynolds Denniston, Jeane Owen, and Joseph Curtain.

Commercials: Adelaide Klein, William Boren, and Lillian Savin.

At the conclusion of *Lux*'s program of March 23, it was announced that the next week's show would feature Bette Davis in George Broadhurst's marital drama *Bought and Paid For*, but when March 30 rolled around, Davis was present while the promised play was unaccountably absent. Instead, the previously presented "The Lion and the Mouse" was hastily substituted, with Robert T. Haines playing the same role he had in the prior radio rendering.

See 5/19/35 for information on stage and screen versions.

*75. "Kick-In," 4/6/36

Based on the play by Willard Mack (1914).

Cast: Edmund Lowe (Chick Hewes), Ann Sothern (Molly), Raymond Bramley (Whip Fogarty), Averell Harris (Inspector Garney), Anthony Burgher (Tony Habeli), Edward Butler (Sergeant Diggs), Marshall Grant (Charley), Blythe Daly (Myrtle), and Alice Fisher (Mrs. Halleron).

Willard Mack's *Kick-In* premiered on Broadway at the Longacre Theatre on October 15, 1914, and starred John Barrymore and Jane Grey. *Lux*'s radio translation of the story of a criminal who, at the urging of his wife, tries to go straight but finds his gang ties difficult to sever, cast Edmund Lowe and Ann Sothern in the principal roles.

The first film version was shot by Astra and released by Pathé in 1917, with George Fitzmaurice at the directorial helm and William Courtenay and Mollie King in the leads. Fitzmaurice also directed Paramount's 1923 remake, which starred Betty Compson and Bert Lytell. A talking version was released by Paramount in 1931, with Regis Toomey and Clara Bow, under Richard Wallace's direction.

Film versions: Astra/Pathé, 1917; Paramount, 1923; Paramount, 1931.

*76. "Shore Leave," 4/13/36

Based on the play by Hubert Osborne (1922).

Cast: Fay Wray (Connie Martin), Lee Tracy (Bilge Smith), and Carlton Macy, Mrs. Jacques Martin, Edward Craven, Philip Truex, John Butler, David Stewart, Walter Scanlon, Clyde Franklin, John Milton, Frank McCullough, John C. Hewitt, and William Crimmons. Additional cast (commercials and crowd): Loretta Archer, Marguerite Faust, Sylvia Manners, Joseph Curtain, Katherine Lane, and Grace Fox.

Shore Leave, a comedy that depicts a romance between a small town dressmaker and a sailor (with the acts set at two-year intervals), was first produced at Broadway's Lyceum Theatre on August 8, 1922. *Lux*'s microphone version cast Fay Wray and Lee Tracy in the parts created in the theatre by Frances Starr and James Rennie.

First National filmed *Shore Leave* in 1925 (directed by J.S. Robertson), with Dorothy Mackaill and Richard Barthel-

mess, but it is the musical version of the play, *Hit the Deck!* (book by Herbert Fields, lyrics by Leo Robin and Clifford Grey, music by Vincent Youmans), which premiered on Broadway in 1927, that has been filmed more often. The first picture of *Hit the Deck!* reached the screen via RKO, with direction by Luther Reed and performances by Jack Oakie and Polly Walker. Another musical rendering (directed by Mark Sandrich) followed at RKO in 1936, but was remodeled with a new score (by Irving Berlin) and a new title, *Follow the Fleet* (starring Ginger Rogers and Fred Astaire). A final *Hit the Deck!* was released by MGM in 1955 (directed by Roy Rowland), with Jane Powell and Tony Martin.

Film versions: First National, 1925; RKO, 1930 (*Hit the Deck!*); RKO, 1936 (*Follow the Fleet*); MGM, 1955 (*Hit the Deck!*).

*77. "Harmony Lane," 4/20/36

Based on the 1935 Mascot film (screenplay by Elizabeth Meehan and Joseph Santley), taken from *The Life and Songs of Stephen Foster*, by Milton Krims.

Cast: Lawrence Tibbett (Stephen Foster), Selena Royale (Susan Pentland), Edward Fielding (William Foster, Sr.), Grace Fox (Mrs. William Foster), Phyllis Welch (Jane), Donald Cameron (Dunning Foster), A.H. Van Buren (Edwin Christy), Ben Lackland (Andrew Robinson), Lynn Mary Oldham (Marian Foster), Taylor Graves (Tompkins), Robert Harrison (Mr. Knowles), Billy Murray (Mr. Hirsh), Clyde Fillmore (Mr. Pond), Thomas Coffin Cooke (the Doctor), and Walter Scanlon and Carl Mathieu (Singers). Additional cast (commercials and crowd): Bobby Burns, Loretta Archer, Marguerite Faust, and Katherine Lane.

The April 20 broadcast of "Harmony Lane" is the first *Lux Radio Theatre* program to be based on a motion picture rather than on a stage play. The Joseph Santley–directed (and scripted) movie tells of the life of American composer Stephen Foster (1826–64) and features the performances of Douglass Montgomery and Evelyn Venable.

Unlike later Hollywood *Luxes*, which often included at least one, and sometimes several, members of the original film cast, "Harmony Lane" included not a single player who appeared in the picture. Instead, Metropolitan Opera baritone Lawrence Tibbett (a veteran of several films) was cast as Stephen Foster, and Selena Royale played the girl he loves. Musical numbers sung by Lawrence Tibbett during the show (words and music by Stephen Foster) were: "Oh, Susanna!," Act 1; "Old Folks at Home," Act 2; and "Jeannie with the Light Brown Hair," Act 3. Tibbett also performed "I Got Plenty o' Nuttin'" (from George Gershwin's 1935 opera *Porgy and Bess*) in the curtain call.

Film version: Mascot, 1935.

*78. "Under Cover," 4/27/36
Based on the play by Roi Cooper Mergue (1914).
Cast: Sally Eilers (Ethel Cartwright), Richard Barthelmess (Steven Denby), Clyde Franklin (Daniel Taylor), Neil Martin (Monty Vaughn), Sydney Booth (Michael Harrington), Olive Reeves Smith (Mrs. Michael Harrington), Gene Leonard (Marcel Antoine), George Drury Hart (James Duncan), Stanley Harrison (Lambert), and Virginia Morgan (Telephone Operator).
Commercials: Ethel Browning, Muriel Harbater, Alice Wood, and Virginia Curley.
Under Cover opened at the Cort Theatre on August 26, 1914, and recounts the drama of a young lady who is blackmailed by a customs official into spying on a presumed smuggler, with

whom she eventually falls in love. Sally Eilers played the girl in *Lux*'s April 27 broadcast, and Richard Barthelmess canceled a performance of *The Postman Always Rings Twice* at the Lyceum Theatre to take the leading masculine role.

Robert G. Vignola directed a 1916 film version of *Under Cover*, which starred Hazel Dawn and Owen Moore, and was released by Famous Players/ Paramount.
Film version: Famous Players/Paramount, 1916.

*79. "The Music Master," 5/4/36
Based on the play by Charles Klein (1904).
Adapted for radio by Reginald Lawrence.
Cast: Jean Hersholt (Anton von Barwig), Anita Louise (Helene), and Stuart Fox, Taylor Graves, Arthur Maitland, Edward Butler, Harriett Sterling, Averell Harris, Frank Curran, Georgie Drew Mendum, Muriel Harbater, Aristides deLeoni, Louis LeBey, Herbert Ashton, Jr., Billy Murray, Reynolds Denniston, Raymond Bramley, Edward Fielding, John T. Dwyer, Albert Phillips, and Donald Foster.
Commercials: Joseph Curtain, Eleanor Phelps.
"The Music Master," *Lux*'s offering for May 4, was a comedy-drama "well-played by Jean Hersholt and Anita Louise," according to Antony Stanford, and told of a Viennese orchestra conductor who travels to New York City in search of his long-lost daughter. Charles Klein's popular play had its premiere at the Belasco Theatre on September 26, 1904, with David Warfield and Minnie Dupree leading the cast.
The 1927 Fox film of *The Music Master* starred Alec B. Francis and Lois Moran and was directed by Allan Dwan.
Film version: Fox, 1927.

*80. "Bitter Sweet," 5/11/36

Based on the play by Noël Coward (1929).

Cast: Irene Dunne (Sarah Millick), Arthur Pierson (Carl Linden), and Donald Cameron, Helen Walpole, Richard Waring, Josephine Victor, Ralph Sumpter, Malcolm Soltan, Harold deBecker, Walter Soderling, Arnold Korff, and Stuart Fox. Additional cast (commercials and crowd): Lottie Gropper, Marguerite Faust, Loretta Archer, Marjorie Anderson, Helen Carew, Taylor Graves, John G. Hewitt, and Anthony Grey.

Noël Coward's operetta *Bitter Sweet* was first presented at His Majesty's Theatre in London, opening there on July 18, 1929, starring Peggy Wood and George Mataxa, then experiencing another opening night on Broadway (November 5 of the same year), with Evelyn Laye and Gerald Nodin in the principal roles. The romance relates the tale of a young woman who elopes with her music teacher, and chronicles the couple's brief period of happiness and the tragedy that ends it. *Lux*'s May 11 broadcast brought Irene Dunne to the microphone for her first of many appearances on the program, with stage actor Arthur Pierson cast opposite her. Antony Stanford noted that "Irene Dunne did an excellent job with a splendid supporting cast." Musical numbers sung by Dunne during the program (all with words and music by Noel Coward) were: "I'll See You Again," in Act 1; "The Call of Life," in Act 2; and "Zigeuner," in Act 3.

Anna Neagle and Fernand Gravet are the stars of the 1933 British film of *Bitter Sweet*, which was directed by Herbert Wilcox, while Jeanette MacDonald and Nelson Eddy led the cast of MGM's W.S. Van Dyke II–directed version, which was released in 1940.

Film versions: British, 1933; MGM, 1940.

*81. "Get-Rich-Quick Wallingford," 5/18/36

Based on the play by George M. Cohan (1910), in turn based on the novel by George R. Chester (1908).

Adapted for radio by Reginald Lawrence.

Cast: George M. Cohan (Get-Rich-Quick Wallingford), Walter Greson, Eleanor Phelps, David Stewart, Ralph Theodore, Thomas Coffin Cooke, Charles Henderson, Raymond Bramley, Howard Smith, Taylor Graves, and Clyde Franklin.

Commercials: Marcella Shields, Mary Newton.

Hale Hamilton had starred in George M. Cohan's *Get-Rich-Quick Wallingford* when it opened at New York's Gaiety Theatre on September 19, 1910. *Lux*'s producers chose to cast the playwright himself in their May 18 adaptation of the comedy and, as Cohan was appearing on stage in Philadelphia at the time, broadcast from that city to accommodate him.

Although the film was based on Cohan's play, William Haines portrayed G.R. Chester's character in MGM's 1931 Sam Wood–directed release, *The New Adventures of Get-Rich-Quick Wallingford*.

*82. "East Is West," 5/25/36

Based on the play by Samuel Shipman and John B. Hymer (1918).

Cast: Fay Bainter (Ming Toy), Leo Carrillo (Charley Yong), J. Arthur Young, Donald Cameron, Harold deBecker, Walter Soderling, Donald Foster, Raymond Bramley, Wright Kramer, Gladys Hanson, Kathryn March, and J. Malcolm Dunn. Additional cast (commercials or crowd): Helen Kim, Muriel Harbater, Helen Marshall, Lynn Mary Oldham, and Doris Dagmar.

The Lux Radio Theatre bade adieu to the East Coast on May 25 with an appropriately titled melodrama, "East Is West," the Broadway production of which had opened at the Astor Theatre on December 25, 1918. Fay Bainter, the star of that original staging, was back for the broadcast, again cast as a Chinese girl sold into slavery by her father.

Constance Talmadge and Warner Oland starred in the 1922 screen adaptation of *East Is West*, a First National production directed by Sidney Franklin, and the 1930 Monte Bell–directed Universal version starred Lupe Velez and Edward G. Robinson.

Film versions: First National, 1922; Universal, 1930.

Second Season, part 2
(June 1, 1936–July 5, 1937)

Columbia Broadcasting System, Monday, 9:00–10:00 P.M. MUSIC BOX THEATRE, HOLLYWOOD, CALIFORNIA. *Host*: Cecil B. DeMille. *Announcer*: Melville Ruick. *Opening Announcer*: Frank Nelson. *Director*: Frank Woodruff. *Musical Director*: Lou Silvers. *Adaptations*: George Wells. *Sound Effects*: Charlie Forsyth.

83. "The Legionnaire and the Lady," 6/1/36

Based on the play, *Amy Jolly*, by Benno Vigny.

Intermission Guests: Fred Datig, Paramount casting director (after Act 2), and Jesse Lasky of Pickford/Lasky Productions (after Act 3).

Cast: Marlene Dietrich (Amy Jolly), Clark Gable (Tom Brown), Frank Reicher (Adjutant Caesar), Walter Kingsford (Blimey), Crauford Kent (Le-Bessiere), Lou Merrill (Lo Trinto), James Eagles, Ynez Seabury (Spanish Girl), Frank Nelson (Orderly), Karan Faris (the Muzzein), Wally Maher (Sergeant), and Georges Renavent, Kenneth Hansen, Ann Stone, and Margaret Brayton.

Commercials: Frederick Bell, Fred MacKaye, and Billie Bellporte.

"The Legionnaire and the Lady" has the distinction of being the first *Lux Radio Theatre* presentation from Hollywood, with Cecil B. DeMille taking over as host. The radio play is adapted from Benno Vigny's stage drama *Amy Jolly*, which concerns a cynical chanteuse whose pessimistic outlook on life is altered by her love for a legionnaire. Marlene Dietrich is heard in the same role she played in Paramount's Josef von Sternberg–directed 1930 version of the play, *Morocco* (where her leading man was Gary Cooper), and Clark Gable takes the part of the other title character.

Though Dietrich is not given the opportunity to vocalize during the drama, she does sing "Falling in Love Again" in full during the curtain call (accompanied at the piano by the song's composer, Frederick Hollander, with English lyrics by Sammy Lerner). Also, Gable gives the credits for the supporting players, as well as announcing the following week's program.

Film version: Paramount, 1930 (*Morocco*).

84. "The Thin Man," 6/8/36

Based on the 1934 MGM film (screenplay by Albert Hackett and Frances Goodrich), in turn based on the novel by Dashiell Hammett (1934).

Marlene Dietrich and Clark Gable (seen here with host Cecil B. DeMille) starred in "The Legionnaire and the Lady," the first *Lux Radio Theatre* broadcast from Hollywood, on June 1, 1936 (photo: Photofest).

Guest Host: W.S. Van Dyke II.

Intermission Guests: James Seymour, screenwriter and producer (after Act 2), and Theda Bara, silent screen star (after Act 3).

Cast: William Powell (Nick Charles), Myrna Loy (Nora Charles), Minna Gombell (Mimi Wynant), William Henry (Gilbert Wynant), Porter Hall (Herbert McCawley), Barbara Luddy (Dorothy Wynant), Bret Morrison (Chris Jorgenson), Margaret Brayton (Julia Wolf), Thomas Jackson (Inspector Guild), Wally Maher (Joe Morelli),

Ernie Adams (Al Nunheim), Frank Nelson (Radio News Reporter/Police Dispatcher), Michael Fitzmaurice, Glenn Boles, Charles Emerson, Victor Rodman, and Rolfe Sedan.

Commercials: Aline Sholes, Lauretta Puck, and Mary Jane Higby.

The *Lux* broadcast of "The Thin Man" is a fairly faithful adaptation of the brilliant 1934 MGM film of the same name, though several alterations necessary for radio presentation were made. One notable example concerns the character Chris Jorgenson, who is referred to as Mimi's friend, *not* her husband, as he was in the motion picture.

Unlike the previous week's show, which included only one member of the movie cast, the "Thin Man" broadcast featured five actors from the film. Reprising their roles were William Powell as the urbane ex-detective, Myrna Loy as his wealthy socialite wife, who pesters him into investigating the mysterious disappearance of the title character, and Minna Gombell, Porter Hall, and William Henry. Missing principals are Maureen O'Sullivan and Nat Pendleton (as Dorothy Wynant and Inspector Guild). In the *Lux* version, radio actress Barbara Luddy does an imitation of O'Sullivan's style of delivery as a tribute to her delightful screen portrayal, and movie character actor Thomas Jackson (who appeared as a reporter in the film) is promoted to the role of Lieutenant Guild.

The film's director, Academy Award–nominated W.S. ("Woody") Van Dyke II serves as guest host in the absence of Cecil B. DeMille, who was attending the Paramount convention in Chicago.

Film version: MGM, 1934.

85. "Burlesque," 6/15/36

Based on the play by George Manker Watters and Arthur Hopkins (1927).

Intermission Guests: Cora Sue Collins, child actress (after Act 1), George Barnes, Warner Bros. cameraman (after Act 2), and Daniel Frohman, theatrical producer (after Act 3).

Cast: Al Jolson (Skid Brown), Ruby Keeler (Bonny Smith), Wally Maher (Lefty Moore), Victor Rodman (Harvey Howell), Eddie Kane (Bozo), Rita LaRoy (Sylvia Marro), Ynez Seabury (Mazie), Frank Nelson (Telegraph Operator), Lou Merrill (Mr. Kent), and Vicki Vola, Lauretta Puck, Grace Mead, Helen Webster, Mildred Rogers, and Winnie Parker.

Lux's "Burlesque" is a faithful adaptation of the play by George Manker Watters and Arthur Hopkins (which had starred Hal Skelly and Barbara Stanwyck on Broadway), and retains much of the original dialogue. One noticeable alteration in the story of a small-time burlesque performer who is unable to handle success (and this does not substantially affect the plot) is that Skid and Bonny, husband and wife in the stage play, are only engaged to be married in the *Lux* version.

Of course, songs are added for Jolson, who sings two of his standards as part of the drama, "Toot, Toot, Tootsie" (words by Gus Kahn and Ernie Erdman; music by Dan Russo), which he had interpolated into the Broadway musical *Bombo* in 1922 (Act 1), and his recent hit, "Is It True What They Say About Dixie?" (words by Sammy Lerner and Irving Caesar; music by Gerald Marks, 1936), during Act 3. During the curtain call, Jolson is "persuaded" by DeMille to sing again, and he performs Irving Berlin's "A Pretty Girl Is Like a Melody" (from the 1919 edition of the *Ziegfeld Follies*). Although she often sang on the stage and in motion pictures, Ruby Keeler does not vocalize during this broadcast. She does, however, do a dance routine as part of the "Toot, Toot, Tootsie" number.

Burlesque was first filmed in 1929 as *Dance of Life*, with Hal Skelly and Nancy Carroll, under John Cromwell's direction (for Paramount), then with Fred MacMurray and Carole Lombard as *Swing High, Swing Low* (also a Paramount release, directed by Mitchell Leisen, in 1937), and finally in 1948 (directed by Walter Lang for 20th Century–Fox), featuring Dan Dailey and Betty Grable but with a title change to *When My Baby Smiles at Me.*

Film versions: Paramount, 1929 (*Dance of Life*); Paramount, 1937 (*Swing High, Swing Low*); 20th Century–Fox, 1948 (*When My Baby Smiles at Me*).

Swing High, Swing Low was performed on *Lux* on February 26, 1940.

86. "The Dark Angel," 6/22/36

Based on the 1935 Goldwyn/United Artists film (screenplay by Lillian Hellman and Mordaunt Shairp), in turn based on the play by H.B. Trevelyan (1925).

Intermission Guests: Leroy Prinz, Paramount dance director (after Act 2), and James Montgomery Flagg, illustrator (after Act 3).

Cast: Merle Oberon (Kitty Vane), Herbert Marshall (Alan Trent), Rod LaRocque (Gerald Shannon), Zeffie Tilbury (Granny Vane), and Edward Cooper, Lillian Kemble-Cooper, Crauford Kent, Wauna Lidwell, Gwen Mannering, Lionel Pape, Edward Reamers, Charles Romano, Margaret Brayton, Anne Stone, and James Eagles.

Commercials: Margaret Brayton, Anne Stone.

The *Lux* broadcast of "The Dark Angel" offers an effective adaptation of the screenplay of the 1935 Sidney Franklin–directed Goldwyn production. The story tells of a man who, having been severely injured during the First World War, prefers to sacrifice his happiness rather than saddle his fiancée with a blind husband. This film, as well as Goldwyn's 1925 George Fitzmaurice–directed version starring Vilma Banky, Ronald Colman, and Wyndham Standing, concludes with a happy ending, which is a considerable departure from that of the original stage production. In Goldwyn's 1935 rendering, Merle Oberon plays Kitty (the role she recreates for the microphone drama), Fredric March is Alan, and Herbert Marshall plays the part of Gerald, while in *Lux*'s presentation, Marshall interestingly plays the more heroic role of Alan, and Rod LaRocque quite capably undertakes the role of Gerald.

Intermission guest James Montgomery Flagg talks with Cecil B. DeMille on two principal subjects: first, on a little-known series of two-reel satirical comedy films he produced and occasionally acted in during the silent era; and second, on the reason why he is currently in the movie capital (to provide *Photoplay* magazine with illustrations of motion picture actresses for 12 issues of their publication).

Film versions: Goldwyn/First National, 1925; Goldwyn/United Artists, 1935.

87. "Irene," 6/29/36

Based on the musical comedy, book by James Montgomery, lyrics by Joseph McCarthy, and music by Harry Tierney (1919).

Intermission Guests: Mrs. Cora Cobb, Warner Bros. wardrobe mistress (after Act 2), and D.W. Griffith, motion picture producer/director (after Act 3).

Cast: Jeanette MacDonald (Irene O'Dare), Regis Toomey (Donald Marshall), Theresa Maxwell-Conover, Arthur Lake (Bob), Elizabeth Dunn, Victor Rodman, Lou Merrill (Mr. Sweeney), Anne Stone, Margaret Brayton, Frank Nelson (Store Customer/ Clarkson), and Leora Thatcher.

Commercials: Vicki Vola, Maureen Ryan, Claudia Hyams, Charles Emerson, Brett Morrison, and Lee Chadwick.

Lux's first musical production from Hollywood was "Irene," which had starred Edith Day in the Broadway production of 1919. The broadcast version is trimmed of many of the songs, with only three sung in the course of the drama, all by Jeanette MacDonald as the title character. The musical numbers are "Alice Blue Gown" (Act 1), "To Be Worthy of You" (Act 2), and "Castle of Dreams" (which also figures prominently in the incidental music) (Act 3). MacDonald's energetic performance as a girl of the lower classes who is given the opportunity to rise rapidly in the social scale, illustrates that she was capable of much more versatility than her film roles allowed her to display. Movie character actor Regis Toomey is given featured billing as the leading male character, and Arthur Lake has a fairly substantial role as Bob.

During the curtain call, MacDonald presents an encore, "Would You" (words by Arthur Freed, music by Nacio Herb Brown), from her recent MGM motion picture, *San Francisco*. Intermission guest D.W. Griffith (whom Cecil B. DeMille describes as "the greatest genius of his art") and *Lux*'s host discuss some of their artistic and technical innovations.

Irene had been filmed as a silent by First National in 1926, with Colleen Moore and Lloyd Hughes (directed by Alfred E. Green); the only talkie version of the musical followed the *Lux* broadcast four years later when RKO released its rendering (directed by Herbert Wilcox in 1940), featuring Anna Neagle and Ray Milland.

Film versions: First National, 1926; RKO, 1940.

88. "The Voice of Bugle Ann," 7/6/36

Based on the 1936 MGM film (screenplay by Harvey Gates and Samuel Hoffenstein), in turn based on the novel by MacKinlay Kantor (1935).

Intermission Guests: Ruth Waterbury, editor of *Photoplay* magazine (after Act 2), and Hal Roach, motion picture producer and head of Roach Studios (after Act 3).

Cast: Lionel Barrymore (Spring Davis), Porter Hall (Jacob Terry), Anne Shirley (Camden Terry), Kathleen Lockhart (Mrs. Davis), Matt Moore, James Eagles, Louis Mason, Lee Millar, Michael Fitzmaurice, Frank Nelson, Ross Forrester, William Royale, and Lou Merrill (Mr. Tanner/Uncle).

Commercials: Ernie Adams (Tour Conductor), Margaret Brayton (Mother), and Harriet Sterling (Girl).

As the MGM film version of MacKinlay Kantor's novel, *The Voice of Bugle Ann* is a rather talkative affair, and the screenplay adapts well to the *Lux* microphone rendering. The stars of the well-crafted Richard Thorpe–directed 1936 MGM motion picture are Lionel Barrymore (here effectively recreating his performance), Maureen O'Sullivan, and Dudley Diggs in a touching drama of the tragedy that results from a man's love and loyalty for his dog, Bugle Ann. Joining Barrymore in the broadcast are Anne Shirley in O'Sullivan's screen role, and Porter Hall in the part played in the film by Dudley Diggs.

One of the subjects discussed by intermission guest Hal Roach concerns Thelma Todd's replacement in the series of two-reel comedies in which she was appearing with Patsy Kelly at the time of her death. Roach announces that Lyda Roberti has been selected to take the late comedienne's place opposite Kelly.

Film version: MGM, 1936.

"The Brat" (July 13, 1936), with Joel McCrea, Marion Davies, and host Cecil B. DeMille (photo: Photofest).

89. "The Brat," 7/13/36

Based on the play by Maude Fulton (1917).

Intermission Guests: Rose Pedretti of Westmore's Beauty Salon (after Act 1), Orry-Kelly, Warner Bros.' stylist (after Act 2), and Lou Silvers, musical director for 20th Century–Fox and *Lux Radio Theatre* (after Act 3).

Cast: Marion Davies (Peggy MacLaren), Joel McCrea (Stephen Forrester), Gavin Gordon (MacMillan Forrester), Neil Fitzgerald (Timaon), Myra Marsh (Mrs. Forrester), Corinne Ross (Angela), William Royale (Fogarty/Crowd), Norman Field (Judge Henry), Frank Nelson (Court Clerk), Harold Wilson (Officer/Butler), Martha Norton, Duane Thompson, and Charles Carroll (Mob).

Marion Davies made her first appear-

ance on *Lux* in an adaptation of Maude Fulton's 1917 play *The Brat* (Fulton had starred in the Broadway version, with Lewis Stone as MacMillan and Edmund Lowe as Stephen). Though the play offers very little in the way of plot, it is an excellent vehicle for Davies, for she is delightful in the role of an unschooled street waif who is taken in by a society novelist (Gavin Gordon) so that he may use her as inspiration for his latest work (circulating recordings of this program unfortunately lack the final quarter hour).

Herbert Blache directed the first film version of *The Brat*, which was released by Metro in 1919 and stars Nazimova, Charles Bryant (as MacMillan), and Darrell Foss (as Stephen). Fox's talkie of 1931 has John Ford at the directorial helm and features Sally O'Neil, Alan

Dinehart, and Frank Albertson. The 1940 20th Century–Fox offering, called *The Girl from Avenue "A,"* was directed by Otto Brower and retailored to fit the talents of Jane Withers.

Film versions: Metro, 1919; Fox, 1931; 20th Century–Fox, 1940 (*The Girl from Avenue "A"*).

90. "The Barker," 7/20/36

Based on the play by Kenyon Nicholson (1927).

Intermission Guests: Emyle Barrie, script girl to Cecil B. DeMille, Paramount Studios (after Act 2), and King Vidor, Paramount director (after Act 3).

Cast: Claudette Colbert (Lou), Walter Huston (Nifty Miller), Norman Foster (Chris Miller), Harlan Briggs (Hap), Isabelle Withers (Carrie), William Royale (Colonel Gowdy), John Gibson (Doc Rice), Ross Forrester, Margaret Brayton, Vicki Vola, Charles Emerson, and Frank Nelson (Crowd).

Commercials: Ross Forrester, Margaret Brayton, and Vicki Vola.

Walter Huston's second *Lux* performance of "The Barker" reunited him with his Broadway costars Claudette Colbert and Norman Foster, both of whom do very well with their audio portrayals of their stage roles. During the curtain call, it is revealed that Huston wore the same hat that he sported during the stage run (a gift presented to him by a real sideshow barker). (See 10/28/34 for information on the film version.)

Originally announced for this date was "Viva Villa!" but as Wallace Beery and Stuart Erwin were unavailable due to studio commitments, "The Barker" was aired instead (Beery finally appeared in "Viva Villa!" on October 10, 1938, but without Erwin).

Film version: Fox, 1933 (*Hoopla*).

91. "Chained," 7/27/36

Based on the 1934 MGM film (screenplay by John Lee Mahin; original story by Edgar Selwyn).

Intermission Guests: Helen Burgess, Paramount actress (after Act 2), and Oliver Hinsdell, MGM dramatic coach (after Act 3).

Cast: Joan Crawford (Diane Lovering), Franchot Tone (Michael Bradley), Gilbert Emery (Richard Field), Wally Maher (Johnny Smith), Lou Merrill (Mr. Perton/Floorwalker), Frank Nelson (Norris/Steward/Store Clerk/Felix the Waiter), Margaret Seddon (First Spinster), Leora Thatcher (Second Spinster), Walter Soderling (James/Emil), Rosemary deCamp, Lauretta Puck and Henry Hanna (Crowd).

Commercial: Rosemary deCamp, Lauretta Puck.

Clarence Brown directed MGM's 1934 film *Chained,* which stars Joan Crawford, Clark Gable, Stuart Erwin, and Otto Kruger. While the screen drama concerning a young woman who falls in love with a young man but does not wish to hurt her affectionate older husband tends to be slow-moving, the broadcast version effectively condenses what little action there is into an entertaining play. Joining Joan Crawford is Franchot Tone (in the role taken by Clark Gable in the motion picture), and both give excellent portrayals.

Chosen to appear as intermission guest was starlet Helen Burgess, whom Cecil B. DeMille selected to play Louisa Cody in *The Plainsman* (which was in production at the time of this broadcast)—"her first appearance before the camera." Sadly, she was to die of pneumonia in 1937 before reaching her twenty-first birthday, having appeared in only three films for Paramount.

Film version: MGM, 1934.

*92. "Main Street," 8/3/36

Based on the novel by Sinclair Lewis (1924).

Intermission Guests: Clarence Buddington Kelland, author, and Bill Ray.

Cast: Barbara Stanwyck (Carol Kennicott), Fred MacMurray (Doc Kennicott), Edward Woods (Eric Valborg), Ernie Adams (Dave Dyer), Lou Merrill (Sam Clark), Leora Thatcher (Mrs. Clark), Justina Wayne (Mrs. Valborg/ Mrs. Dashaway), Doris Louray (Mrs. Elder), Greta Meyer (Bea), Norman Field (Valborg), Walter Soderling (Miles Bjornstam/Mr. Stowbody), Dink Trout (Chet), Frederick Gierman (Halvor), Ynez Seabury, Ross Forrester, Frank Nelson (Crowd), and Michael Fitzmaurice (Dog Barker).

Commercial: Ynez Seabury, Ross Forrester, and Frank Nelson.

Although a film version of Sinclair Lewis's *Main Street* had been released earlier that year, *Lux*'s August 3, 1936, broadcast used the original 1920 novel as its source. The radio play starred Barbara Stanwyck as a young cosmopolitan bride who envisions bringing culture to her husband's hometown in "the sticks." Fred MacMurray, in his first of many *Lux* appearances, was cast opposite Stanwyck.

Warner Bros. released both film versions of *Main Street*, the first of which was partly inspired by the 1921 Broadway adaptation of the novel. This 1923 motion picture, which was directed by Harry Beaumont, stars Florence Vidor and Monte Blue, while the 1936 Archie Mayo–directed piece (entitled *I Married a Doctor*) stars Josephine Hutchinson and Pat O'Brien.

Film versions: Warner Bros., 1923; Warner Bros., 1936 (*I Married a Doctor*).

*93. "The Jazz Singer," 8/10/36

Based on the play by Samson Raphaelson (1925) and the 1927 Warner Bros. film (screenplay by Alfred A. Cohn).

Intermission Guests: Mrs. Lee Wray Turner, director of the Assistance League of Southern California (after Act 2), and Feg Murray, syndicated newspaper cartoonist (after Act 3).

Cast: Al Jolson (Jack Robin), Karen Morley (Mary), Vera Gordon (Sara), Nat Carr (Yudelson), Howard Lang (Cantor Rabinawitz), William Royale (Lee/Harry/Dr. O'Shaughnessy), Dick LeGrand (Stevens), Margaret Brayton (Eve/Nurse), Frank Nelson (Gene), Charles Emerson (Taxi Driver/Carter), and James Eagles (Jimmy/Telegraph Boy). Chorus: Frank Carpenter, Henry Iblings, Richard Davis, Earl Hunsaker, William Brandt, Kenneth Rundquist, Dudley Kusell, and Floyd Gamble.

Commercial: Myra Marsh (Mother), Dorthy Leslie Parke (Betty).

Al Jolson's second appearance on *Lux* was in an adaptation of the vehicle for which he is probably best remembered: "The Jazz Singer." The 1925 Samson Raphaelson play ran for 303 performances at the Fulton Theatre on Broadway (opening September 14), with George Jessel and Phoebe Foster in the lead roles, before being produced at Warner Bros. as a part-talkie Vitaphone film, with Jolson and May McAvoy. The story of a young Jewish man who chooses the stage over what his cantor father feels is his true calling gave singer Al Jolson the opportunity to perform several musical numbers in the picture, and *Lux*'s first version (which costarred Karen Morley) presumably also featured its share of Jolson specialties (apparently because no recordings of this broadcast survive, and the script does not go into detail about musical numbers, it has not been possible to determine which songs Jolson sings during the dramatic portion of the program).

During the curtain call, Al Jolson sings "April Showers" (which he had interpolated into *Bombo* in 1922), accompanied at the piano by *Lux*'s musical director and the song's composer, Lou Silvers (words by Bud DeSylva).

Film version: Warner Bros., 1927.

94. "The Vagabond King," 8/17/36

Based on the musical production, book, and lyrics by Brian Hooker and W.H. Post, music by Rudolf Friml (1925), in turn based on the play *If I Were King*, by Justin Huntly McCarthy (1901), from his own novel (1901).

Intermission Guests: Geneva Sawyer, 20th Century–Fox dance director (after Act 2), and Robert Riskin, Columbia scenario writer (after Act 3).

Cast: John Boles (François Villon), Evelyn Venable (Lady Katherine), Walter Kingsford (King Louis XI), Lou Merrill (Tristan/Tabarie), Margaret McKay (Huguette), Frank Nelson (Captain of the Guard/Servant), and Wyndham Standing, Brett Morrison, Cecil Elliott (Margot), Ross Forrester (René/Crowd), and Russ Dudley (Astrologer/Crowd). Male Chorus: William Brandt (Manager), Frank Carpenter, Al Garr, Henry Iblings, Freeman High, Richard Davis, Earl Hunsaker, Thad Harvey, Enrico Ricardi, Kenneth Rundquist, Hubert Head, David Knight, Tudor Williams, Dudley Kusell, Ralph Erwin, and Floyd Gamble.

Commercial: Vicki Vola (Molly), Anne Stone (Dorothy).

"The Vagabond King" was the second *Lux* adaptation of a Broadway musical to be presented from Hollywood. (Dennis King and Carolyn Thomas starred in the Broadway production.) In *Lux*'s "The Vagabond King," a fictionalized story of the real-life French poet François Villon (1431–?) and his love for a lady above his social status, each of the songs Boles sings has been shorn of its verse, but the chorus of each is complete. The musical numbers are "Song of the Vagabonds" (Act 1), "Some Day" (Act 2),

"Only a Rose," and "Song of the Vagabonds" (reprise, chorus) (Act 3). Walter Kingsford, who is impressive in the showy role of King Louis XI, was to appear as Tristan in Paramount's 1938 film of the nonmusical version of the story, *If I Were King*.

Robert Riskin, Columbia screenwriter, participates in an amusing routine with Cecil B. DeMille during the third act intermission.

There have been numerous film versions of McCarthy's play *If I Were King*, but only two of the Rudolf Friml musical to date, both of which were released by Paramount. The first, shot in Technicolor in 1930, was directed by Ludwig Berger and featured Dennis King (of the stage production) and Jeanette MacDonald. The 1956 remake was directed by Michael Curtiz, with Kathryn Grayson and Oreste in the leads. (*Lux* presented a second version on December 25, 1944.)

Film versions: Paramount, 1930; Paramount, 1956.

95. "One Sunday Afternoon," 8/24/36

Based on the play by James Hagen (1932).

Intermission Guests: Agnes Ayres, motion picture actress (after Act 2), and Mrs. Evelyn Offield, mother of Jack Oakie (after Act 3).

Cast: Jack Oakie (Biff Grimes), Helen Twelvetrees (Amy Lind), Alan Hale (Hugo Barnstead), Hal K. Dawson (Snappy), Ynez Seabury (Virginia Brush), Frank Nelson (Matt Hughes/ Mullen), Greta Myers (Mrs. Schutzendorf), Justina Wayne (Mrs. Oberstatter), James Eagles (Rowdy/Mob), William Royale (Charlie/Schneider), Mary Lou Fisher (Gladys/Mob), Ross Forrester (Mob), and Margaret Brayton (Mob).

Commercial: Florence Hastings (First Girl), Betty Stewart (Second Girl).

Although James Hagen classified his 1932 play *One Sunday Afternoon* (which starred Lloyd Nolan, Francesca Bruning, and Rankin Mansfield in the Broadway production) as a comedy, there are at least as many dramatic scenes as comedic ones, and *Lux's* August 24 broadcast gave comic Jack Oakie a rare opportunity to appear in a semiserious role. Oakie makes the most of his part as the dentist with a lifelong passion for a shallow blonde who eventually settles for a sensible young lady, as do Helen Twelvetrees as the girl who becomes his wife, and Alan Hale as the loutish Hugo.

Intermission guests Agnes Ayres discusses Rudolph Valentino (with whom she made two motion pictures), since the tenth anniversary of his death had occurred the day before the broadcast. During the curtain call, Jack Oakie sings a chorus from "I Can't Play the Banjo with Susanna on My Knee" (music and lyric by Phil Boutelje, Jack Scholl, and Sam Coslow) from his new picture, *The Texas Rangers*.

One Sunday Afternoon has reached the screen in three versions: first, for Paramount in 1933, with Stephen Roberts directing a cast that includes Gary Cooper, Frances Fuller, Fay Wray (as Virginia), and Neil Hamilton; next, for Warner Bros. in 1941 (entitled *The Strawberry Blonde*), with direction by Raoul Walsh, and James Cagney, Olivia deHavilland, Rita Hayworth, and Jack Carson in the leads (Alan Hale, who plays Hugo in the *Lux* broadcast, portrays James Cagney's father in this version); and finally, as a musical in 1948 (released by Warner Bros.), featuring Dennis Morgan, Dorothy Malone, Don DeFore, and Janis Paige, under Raoul Walsh's direction (songs by Ralph Blane). (*Lux's* version of "Strawberry Blonde" was aired March 23, 1942, and the *Lux Video Theatre* presented "One Sunday Afternoon" on January 31, 1957.)

Film versions: Paramount, 1933; Warner Bros., 1941 (*The Strawberry Blonde*); Warner Bros., 1948.

96. "Cheating Cheaters," 8/31/36

Based on the play by Max Marcin (1916).

Intermission Guests: Donald A. Loomis, MGM fitness expert (after Act 2), and Gloria Swanson, motion picture actress (after Act 3).

Cast: George Raft (Tom Palmer), June Lang (Ruth Brockton), Wally Maher (Mike), Justina Wayne (Mrs. Palmer), Victor Rodman (Mr. Brockton), Lou Merrill (Wilson), Frank Nelson (Phil), Richard LeGrand (Farley), John Lake (Police Officer), Charles Emerson (Police Officer), Ross Forrester (Hanley), Doris Louray (Shipwrecked Woman/Crowd), Barbara Cox (Crowd), and Mary Jane Higby (Crowd).

Commercial: Barbara Cox, Mary Jane Higby.

George Raft made his first *Lux* appearance in an adaptation of Max Marcin's comedy *Cheating Cheaters* (which had starred Robert McWade and Marjorie Rambeau), and although the part of a gangster is a familiar one for him, it is nonetheless a lighter role than he generally undertook. The play tells the clichéd story of a gang of crooks who make the acquaintance of a family with the intention of robbing them of their precious jewels, not knowing that their prey are actually thieves with the same idea themselves.

Intermission guest Gloria Swanson reminisces with her frequent director of the silent era (Cecil B. DeMille) about their days making films together. She also sings Tchaikovsky's "None but the Lonely Heart" (original lyric by Mey, from Goethe).

Cheating Cheaters has appeared on the screen three times since the play opened on Broadway in 1916 (at the Eltinge Theatre). Select Pictures released its version in 1919 (directed by Allan Dwan), with Clara Kimball Young and Jack Holt in the leads, while Universal produced the next two versions. The first, in 1927, was directed by Edward Laemmle and starred Kenneth Harlan and Betty Compson, and the talkie remake, which was directed by Richard Thorpe, starred Cesar Romero and Fay Wray (released in 1934).

Film versions: Select, 1919; Universal, 1927; Universal, 1934.

97. "Is Zat So?," 9/7/36

Based on the play by James Gleason and Richard Taber (1925).

Intermission Guests: Sheilah Graham, Hollywood columnist (after Act 2), and Dr. A.H. Giannini, president/chairman of United Artists Studios (after Act 3).

Cast: James Cagney (Hap Hurley), Robert Armstrong (Chick Cowen), Boots Mallory (Susan Blackburn), Frank Nelson (Referee/Radio Announcer), Kenneth Thompson (Blackburn), Lionel Pape (Major Fitz Stanley), Frank Rowen (Robert Parker), Lou Merrill (Announcer/Duffy), James Eagles (Crowd), Ross Forrester (Handler/Crowd), Margaret Brayton (Crowd), and Maryon Aye (Crowd).

Commercial: Ross Forrester, Margaret Brayton.

The 1925 Broadway hit *Is Zat So?*, which concerns the efforts of a boxing manager who tries to keep his dim-witted skirt-chasing fighter's mind on his upcoming bout, was the piece selected for James Cagney's first Hollywood *Lux* broadcast. The stage stars had been James Gleason (coauthor), Robert Armstrong (who here recreates his role), and Marie Chambers (whose part is taken by Boots Mallory in the radio rendering).

Fox released a film of *Is Zat So?* star-

ring Edmund Lowe, George O'Brien, and Kathryn Perry.

Film version: Fox, 1927.

98. "Quality Street," 9/14/36

Based on the play by J.M. Barrie (1901).

Directed by Antony Stanford.

Intermission Guests: Harold Bucquet, Warner Bros. screen test director (after Act 2), and Mervyn LeRoy, Warner Bros. producer/director (after Act 3).

Cast: Ruth Chatterton (Phoebe Throssel), Brian Aherne (Valentine Brown), Kathleen Lockhart (Susan Throssel), Noel Kennedy (Arthur Wellesley Tomson), Frank Nelson (Lieutenant Spicer), James Eagles (Ensign Beades/Mob), Elspeth Dudgeon (Miss Willoughby), Valentine Sidney (Miss Henrietta), Charles Emerson (Crowd), Mildred Quigley (Crowd), Doris Louray (Crowd), Ynez Seabury (Crowd), Ross Forrester (Crowd), Harriet Sterling (Crowd), and Ralph Kellard (Crowd).

Commercial: Ynez Seabury (Peggy), Ross Forrester (Boy), Harriet Sterling (Mrs. Brown), Ralph Kellard (Mr. Brown).

J.M. Barrie's play *Quality Street*, which concerns a weary schoolteacher who poses as her younger niece in order to recapture the affections of a returning soldier, served as the vehicle that introduced Ruth Chatterton to *Lux Radio Theatre* audiences (at Chatterton's request, Antony Stanford was brought in to direct). Although Chatterton alters her delivery surprisingly little after Phoebe has aged ten years (and considerably more in spirit), she is convincingly flighty as she masquerades as her nonexistent niece, Libby. Filling out the cast are Brian Aherne and Kathleen Lockhart in the roles taken on the Broadway stage (at the Knickerbocker Theatre) by Sydney

Ralph Forbes, Peter Lorre, Grace Moore, and Cecil B. DeMille in "Trilby," September 21, 1936 (photo: Berry Hill Bookshop).

Brough and Helen Lowell (Maude Adams played Phoebe).

Ten seconds of silence are observed at the end of the program to honor the memory of MGM's vice president and supervisor of production, Irving Thalberg, who had passed away at age 37 earlier that day.

*99. "Trilby," 9/21/36

Based on the play by Paul Potter (1895), in turn based on the novel by George DuMaurier (1894).

Intermission Guests: Lloyd Pantages, syndicated Hollywood columnist (after Act 2), and George Hurrell, MGM portrait photographer (after Act 3).

Cast: Grace Moore (Trilby), Peter Lorre (Svengali), Ralph Forbes (Billy Bagot), L'Estrange Millman (Gecko), Ralph Kellard (Taffy Wayne), Vernon Steele (Sandy Laird), Grace Hampton (Mrs. Bagot), Richard Abbott (M. Petard/Manager), Frank Nelson (Boy), Ynez Seabury (First Woman), Anne Stone (Second Woman), John Deering, Ross Forrester, Charles Emerson, Wallace Brasse, Mildred Quigley, and Doris Louray (Crowd).

Commercial: Anne Stone (Mrs. Moran), John Deering (Mr. Kelly).

George DuMaurier's famous tale *Trilby* became a *Lux* play on September 21, undoubtedly a suitable vehicle for opera star Grace Moore. The soprano played the title role opposite Peter Lorre's Svengali, the mysterious professor of voice who establishes a hypnotic hold on the young singer. Musical selections performed by Miss Moore were "Ben Bolt" (words by Thomas Dunn English; music by Nelson Kneass, 1848) (Act 1); "Caprice Viennois" (Act 2); and "Jewel Song," from *Faust* (libretto by Michel Carré and Jules Barbier; music by Charles Gounod, 1859) (Act 3).

Trilby was first filmed by Equitable/

World Film Corporation in 1915, with Clara Kimball Young, Wilton Lackaye, and Chester Barnett, under Maurice Tourneur's direction. James Young directed Andree Lafayette, Arthur Edmund Carewe, and Creighton Hale in the 1923 Richard Walton Tully Productions/Associated First National Pictures rendering; Archie Mayo was at the helm of Warner Bros.' 1931 talkie *Svengali*, starring Marian Marsh, John Barrymore, and Bramwell Fletcher; and Noel Langley directed MGM's 1955 motion picture, with Hildegarde Neff and Donald Wolfit (also entitled *Svengali*).

Film versions: Equitable/World Film Corporation, 1915; Richard Walton Tully Productions/Associated First National Pictures, 1923; Warner Bros., 1931 (*Svengali*); MGM, 1955 (*Svengali*).

100. "The Plutocrat," 9/28/36
Based on the play by Arthur Goodrich (1930), in turn based on the novel by Booth Tarkington (1927).

Intermission Guests: Victor Young, Paramount composer and conductor (after Act 2), and Walt Disney, creator of Mickey Mouse and the "Silly Symphony" cartoons (after Act 3).

Cast: Wallace Beery (Earl Tinker), Clara Kimball Young (Mrs. Tinker), Marjorie Rambeau (Madame Momoro), Cecilia Parker (Olivia Tinker), Eric Linden (Lawrence Ogle), Brett Morrison (Hyacinthe), Frank Nelson (Ship's Steward), Lou Merrill (Second Steward), Ross Forrester (Officer/Crowd), Vicki Vola (Crowd), Margaret Brayton (Crowd), and James Eagles (Crowd).

Commercial: Margaret Brayton, James Eagles.

Wallace Beery, who was to have appeared in "Viva Villa!" on July 27, finally made his Hollywood *Lux* debut as the title character in Arthur Goodrich's "The Plutocrat," an agreeable comedy of an uncultured American industrialist

who is a fish out of water when he mixes with sophisticated Europeans on an ocean voyage. Joining Beery (who plays the role taken on Broadway by Charles Coburn) is silent film star Clara Kimball Young (in Ivah Wills Coburn's stage part), and both are excellent in the leads.

Film composer Victor Young, who appears during the Act 2 intermission, plays (on the violin) his own compositions, "Je vous adore," from Paramount's *Fatal Lady*. The third act intermission is devoted to animator Walt Disney and two of his creations, Mickey Mouse and Donald Duck (Clarence Nash). Their appearance carries into the curtain call, where they perform a routine with Wallace Beery's young daughter, Carol Ann.

101. "Elmer the Great," 10/5/36
Based on the play by Ring Lardner (1928).

Intermission Guests: Carl Hubbell, New York Giants baseball club, Lou Gehrig, New York Yankees baseball club (after Act 2), and Max Reinhardt, theatrical producer (after Act 3).

Cast: Joe E. Brown (Elmer Kane), June Travis (Nellie Poole), Frank Nelson (Jerry Osborn, Radio Sports Announcer), Richard Tucker (Crabtree), Helen Keers (Mrs. Kane), Mia Marvin (Evelyn), Emerson Tracy (Nick Kane), John Gibson (Noonan), Ross Forrester (Doyle), William Royale (Walker), Ynez Seabury (Dolly), Lou Merrill (Radio News Reporter), Anne Stone (Crowd), Margaret Brayton (Crowd), and Charles Emerson (Conductor/Crowd).

Commercial: Anne Stone, Margaret Brayton, William Brandt (Singer).

Joe E. Brown's third *Lux* appearance, and his first in Hollywood, was as Ring Lardner's baseball hero in "Elmer the Great," the same play in which he made his New York *Lux* debut on June 30,

1935. One of the advantages Warner Bros.' 1933 film version with Brown has over the play is the inclusion of several well-staged baseball scenes, during which his athletic ability is nicely showcased. The broadcast understandably eliminates such scenes, though there is a brief description by a sports announcer of the last out of the first game of the World Series.

Heard by remote from New York City during the second act intermission are Carl Hubbell, New York Giants pitcher, and Lou Gehrig, first baseman of the New York Yankees. The Yankees and the Giants were opponents in the 1936 World Series, and both discuss how the series has progressed thus far. (At this point, the Yankees were leading three games to two, and as Gehrig predicts during the broadcast, the Yankees would become World Champions with a victory over the Giants the following day.)

Third act intermission guest Max Reinhardt discusses Shakespeare in films (he had produced and codirected Warner Bros.' *A Midsummer Night's Dream* in 1935) and suggests that no program is better equipped to bring Shakespeare to the air than *Lux Radio Theatre*. (Ironically, in the 21-year history of the program, not one of Shakespeare's works was presented.) (See 6/5/35 for information on film versions.)

Film versions: Paramount, 1929 (*Fast Company*); Warner Bros., 1933; Warner Bros., 1939 (*Cowboy Quarterback*).

102. "The Curtain Rises," 10/12/36
Based on the play by Oskar Rempel (pen name for Benjamin M. Kaye) (1933).
Intermission Guests: Mrs. Leila Rogers, director of RKO's "Little Theatre" and mother of Ginger Rogers (after Act 2), and Doris Kenyon, actress and concert singer (after Act 3).

Cast: Ginger Rogers (Elsa Karling), Warren William (Ronald Phillips), Alan Mowbray (Gregory Matthews), Verree Teasdale (Carol Stewart), Frank Nelson (Stephen/Crowd), John Gibson (Arny), Leora Thatcher (Anna), James Eagles (Call Boy/Porter), Ross Forrester (Train Announcer/Crowd), Margaret Brayton, Claudia Hyams, and Charles Emerson (Crowd).
Commercial: Margaret Brayton, Claudia Hyams.

Ginger Rogers, Warren William (who is given the chance to use his flair for light comedy), Alan Mowbray, and Verree Teasdale star in *Lux*'s "The Curtain Rises," a humorous tale about a shy young lady who takes dramatic lessons for the opportunity to enact love scenes with the handsome actor who is instructing her. (The Broadway production, which debuted at the Vanderbilt Theatre on October 19, 1933, featured Jean Arthur, Donald Foster, and Kenneth Harlan.) With the exception of Elsa Karling, more "American-sounding" names replace the originals in this broadcast (the play takes place in Vienna, while the radio rendering moves the action to New York City). Thus Franz Kermann becomes Ronald Phillips, Wilhelm Meissenger becomes Gregory Matthews, and Thona Landorf is changed to Carol Stewart.

Doris Kenyon, who appears as the Act 3 intermission guest, sings "Thine Alone" (lyric by Henry Blossom), from Victor Herbert's *Eileen*, which she dedicates to the memory of the late composer. (Kenyon made her New York stage debut in Victor Herbert's *The Princess Pat* in 1915.)

103. "Captain Applejack," 10/19/36
Based on the play by Walter Hackett (1921).
Intermission Guests: Albertina Rasch, dance director (after Act 2), and

Cecil B. DeMille, Mitchell Leisen, Maureen O'Sullivan, and Frank Morgan in "Captain Applejack," October 19, 1936 (photo: Connie Billips).

Mitchell Leisen, Paramount director (after Act 3).

Cast: Frank Morgan (Ambrose Applejohn/Captain Applejack), Maureen O'Sullivan (Poppy Faire/Cabin Boy), Zita Johann (Anna Valeska), Akim Tamiroff (Ivan Borolsky), Doris Rankin (Aunt Agatha), Colin Campbell (Lush), Lou Merrill (Lee/Crowd), Frank Nelson (Tom/Crowd), David Kerman (Boots/Crowd), Ross Forrester (Crowd), and Charles Emerson (Crowd).

Commercial: Anne Stone, Mary Arden.

The adaptation of Walter Hackett's enchanting comedy-thriller *Captain Applejack* epitomizes the *Lux Radio Theatre*'s pledge to present imaginative material (especially in evidence in the fanciful dream sequence in which the stars excel). The whimsical situations and dialogue complement Maureen O'Sullivan's wonderful characterizations (as Poppy, the charming ward of the Applejohn family, and, in the dream sequence, the loyal cabin boy) and provide an excellent vehicle for her *Lux Radio Theatre* debut. Frank Morgan's fine characterizations as the ineffectual Ambrose Applejohn and as Captain Applejack, his notorious swashbuckling ancestor, make for an amusing contrast, and Zita Johann and Akim Tamiroff make the most of their roles as well.

Director Frank Woodruff praised the imaginative show and stated, "Morgan and Tamiroff's great sense of comedy values made plausible this fantastic plot. O'Sullivan was splendid."

The play, which opened at the Cort Theatre on December 30, 1921, and starred Wallace Eddinger, Phoebe Foster, Hamilton Revell, and Mary Nash, was filmed twice prior to *Lux*'s broadcast: first, by Louis B. Mayer Productions/Metro in 1923, with Matt Moore, Enid Bennett, Robert McKim, and Barbara LaMarr (directed by Fred

Niblo), under the title *Strangers of the Night*; then by Warner Bros. in 1931, with John Halliday, Mary Brian, Arthur Edmund Carewe, and Kay Strozzi (directed by Hobart Henley).

Film versions: Louis B. Mayer Productions/Metro, 1923 (*Strangers of the Night*); Warner Bros., 1931.

104. "Saturday's Children," 10/26/36

Based on the play by Maxwell Anderson (1927).

Intermission Guests: Frank Richardson, Paramount wardrobe director (after Act 2), and William Koenig, Universal Pictures general manager (after Act 3).

Cast: Robert Taylor (Rims O'Neil), Olivia deHavilland (Bobbie Harrington), Mona Barrie (Florrie), Frederick Perry (Mr. Harrington), Chester Clute (Willie), Leora Thatcher (Mrs. Gorlick/ Old Lady), Lou Merrill (Mr. Mingle/ Storekeeper), Frank Nelson (Keith/ Radio Announcer), Ross Forrester (Bus Conductor/Newsboy), Robert Payton (Crowd), John Lake (Michael/Crowd), Helen Stryker (Crowd), and Margaret Brayton (Crowd).

Commercial: Helen Stryker, Margaret Brayton.

Maxwell Anderson's drama of a newly married romantic couple's struggle with the harsh realities of life is a good vehicle for Robert Taylor and Olivia deHavilland, both of whom do a fine job in their *Lux* debuts. (The stage production, which opened at the Booth Theatre on January 26, 1927, starred Roger Pryor and Ruth Gordon.) Frederick Perry, who was a member of the original stage cast, recreates his role for *Lux*, and Mona Barrie nicely plays the part of Florrie.

First National was first to bring *Saturday's Children* to the screen, with a part-talking version in 1929 that was directed by Gregory LaCava and featured Grant Withers, Corinne Griffith,

and Lucien Littlefield. William McGann directed Warner Bros.' 1935 offering (entitled *Maybe It's Love*), with Ross Alexander and Gloria Stuart, and in 1940, the studio produced a second rendering (with the original title) starring John Garfield, Anne Shirley, and Claude Rains. (*Saturday's Children* was performed on the *Lux Video Theatre* on October 2, 1950.)

Film versions: First National, 1929; Warner Bros., 1935 (*Maybe It's Love*); Warner Bros., 1940.

105. "The Virginian," 11/2/36

Based on the play by Owen Wister and Kirke LaShelle (1904), in turn based on the novel by Owen Wister (1902).

Intermission Guests: Richard Cline, physical culture director of Paramount Studios (after Act 2), and Sidney Skolsky, Hollywood columnist (after Act 3).

Cast: Gary Cooper (the Virginian), Charles Bickford (Trampas), Helen Mack (Molly Wood), John Howard (Steve), Chester Clute (Nebrasky), Hal K. Dawson (Shorty), Earle Ross (Joe), Norman Field (Judge Henry), Ynez Seabury (Nina), Frank Nelson (Jim), Lou Merrill (Greasy), Priscilla Lyon (Little Girl), James Eagles (Baldy), William Brandt (Pedro), and Ross Forrester (Bartender/Crowd).

Commercial: Elvia Allman, Sylvia Farnese.

Gary Cooper's unanimated delivery might well be a disadvantage when coming over the airwaves, but it could not be put to better use than it is in *Lux*'s adaptation of *The Virginian*, Owen Wister's tale of a rugged cowpoke in love with an Eastern schoolmarm, who experiences the usual inner conflicts when his best friend is found guilty of cattle rustling. Charles Bickford, here making his *Lux* debut, is also impressive in his role (as the villainous Trampas).

The famous story is skillfully crafted into a 42-minute drama that includes the best-known scenes and even manages to retain much of the excitement in the final shootout, thanks to a fine cast and skillful use of sound effects.

Cecil B. DeMille directed the first feature film of *The Virginian* for Famous Players–Lasky in 1914, with Dustin Farnum (of the original stage cast), Billy Elmer, and Winifred Kingston. Preferred's 1923 version was directed by Tom Forman and featured Kenneth Harlan, Russell Simpson, and Florence Vidor in the leads, while Paramount's first talking remake (directed by Victor Fleming in 1929) starred Gary Cooper, Walter Huston, and Mary Brian. The most recent rendering was released in 1946 (again by Paramount, under Stuart Gilmore's direction), with Joel McCrea, Brian Donlevy, and Barbara Britton in the leads.

Film versions: Famous Players–Lasky, 1914; Preferred, 1923; Paramount, 1929; Paramount, 1946.

106. "Alias Jimmy Valentine," 11/9/36

Based on the play by Paul Armstrong (1910), in turn based on the story "A Retired Reformation," by O. Henry (1903).

Intermission Guests: Carolyn Newell, Hollywood chorus girl (after Act 2), and Melvyn Purvis, former G-man (after Act 3).

Cast: Pat O'Brien (Jimmy Valentine), Madge Evans (Mary Lane), Allen Jenkins (Red), William Frawley (Doyle), Crauford Kent (Mr. Lane), Myra Marsh (Mrs. Lane), Joan Field (Kitty), Tommy Bupp (Bobby), Sam Flint (the Warden), Rolfe Sedan (Conductor/Smith), Victor Rodman (Nolan/Crowd), Ken Chavelle (Sharp/Crowd), Virginia Stone (Secretary/Crowd), Jean Colbert (Waitress/Crowd), Frank Nel-

son (Guard/Crowd), Charles Emerson, David Kerman, and Ross Forrester (Crowd).

Commercial: Priscilla Lyon, Leora Thatcher.

Approximately 13 months after broadcasting "Alias Jimmy Valentine" from New York, *Lux* gave Pat O'Brien the chance to play the role. Madge Evans was cast opposite him, with Allen Jenkins and William Frawley in the principal supporting parts. O'Brien is splendidly subdued, speaking his lines very softly, thus giving the character of the reformed safecracker an appropriate world-weariness. During the curtain call, O'Brien sings a chorus of the traditional Irish song "The Charlady's Ball."

See 9/29/35 for information about film versions.

Film versions: World, 1915; Metro, 1920; MGM, 1928.

107. "Conversation Piece," 11/16/36

Based on the musical play by Noël Coward (1934).

Intermission Guests: Cotton Warburton, MGM film editor (after Act 2), and Feg Murray, Hollywood columnist (after Act 3).

Cast: Lily Pons (Melanie), Adolphe Menjou (Paul, Duc de Chaucigny-Varennes), Marjorie Gateson (Lady Julia Charteris), George Sanders (the Marquis of Sheere), Elsa Buchanan (Rose), Ben Guy Philips (Footman/ Crowd), Phyllis Coghlan (Lady Harrington), Margaret Brayton (Lady Braceworth), Grayce Hampton (Lady Worth), Lou Merrill (Manager, Le Petit Girondin/Crowd), Evelyn Beresford (Duchess of Beneden), Colin Campbell (Duke of Beneden), Frank Nelson (Crowd), Ross Forrester (Sailor/Crowd), Charles Emerson, and David Kerman (Crowd).

Commercial: Margaret Brayton.

Operatic soprano Lily Pons made her first and only appearance on *Lux* in an adaptation of Noël Coward's *Conversation*

"Conversation Piece" (November 16, 1936), with Adolphe Menjou, Lily Pons, and Marjorie Gateson (photo: Berry Hill Bookshop).

Piece, a comedy of an enterprising but penniless duc (Adolphe Menjou) whose goal is to marry his young protégée off to a man of position. (On the London stage, His Majesty's Theatre, Yvonne Printemps and Noël Coward played the leads for the first time on February 16, 1934, and on Broadway, at the 44th Street Theatre on October 23 of that year, Miss Printemps was joined by Pierre Fresnay.)

Lux's version presents a straightforward abridgement of the stage play, and, as expected, most of the musical numbers have been deleted. The two songs sung by Pons that do remain (both with words and music by Coward) are "I'll Follow My Secret Heart" (which also figures prominently in the incidental music, and is briefly reprised by Pons at the very end of the drama; Act 1), and "Nevermore" (Act 2). In addition, the French soprano sings the concert waltz "O légère hirondelle," from the opera *Mireille* (1864; music by Charles Gounod, text by Michel Carré) in Act 3. Perhaps the

most regrettable musical loss is the lively "Regency Rakes," a witty song delivered by a male quartet in the original. One member of that quartet in both London and New York was George Sanders, who had been cast in the small supporting role of Lord St. Marys. In the *Lux* broadcast, Sanders is given the featured part of the Marquis of Sheere.

108. "The Story of Louis Pasteur," 11/23/36

Based on the 1935 Warner Bros. film (screenplay by Sheridan Gibney and Pierre Collings).

Intermission Guests: William K. Howard, United Artists director (after Act 2), and Adrian, MGM costume designer (after Act 3).

Cast: Paul Muni (Louis Pasteur), Fritz Leiber (Dr. Charbonnet), Crauford Kent (Dr. Radisse), Barbara Luddy (Marie Pasteur), Chester Clute (Roux), Priscilla Lyon (Annette, as a Child), Harriet Russell (Annette, as an Adult), Leo McCabe (the Emperor), Corinne

Ross (the Empress), Ross Forrester (Lacky/Second Man), Edward Woods (Jean Martel), Lee Millar (Chairman/Sheep/Mad Dog), John Lake (Doctor), James Eagles (Visitor), Cy Kendall (Dr. Rossignol), Charles Emerson (Third Doctor/Man), Victor Rodman (Second Doctor), Vicki Vola (Woman/Cecile), Lionel Belmore (Dr. Lister), Frank Nelson (Farmer), Lou Merrill (Dr. Pheifer/Third Man/Russian Ambassador), Henry Hanna (Joseph), and Justina Wayne (Mme. Meister).

Commercial: Emily Williams, Sarah Selby.

The Story of Louis Pasteur, which chronicles the struggles between the innovative French doctor (1822–95) and the established medical community, was brought to *Lux* on November 23, with Paul Muni and Fritz Leiber reprising their roles from the 1936 William Dieterle–directed film.

Film version: Warner Bros., 1936.

109. "Polly of the Circus," 11/30/36
Based on the play by Margaret Mayo (1907).

Guest Host: Lionel Barrymore.

Intermission Guests: Mabel Starke, tiger trainer for the L.G. Barnes circus (after Act 2), and Robert Ripley, "The World's Most Famous Fact-Finder" (after Act 3).

Cast: Loretta Young (Polly), James Gleason (Jim McNally), Gavin Gordon (Dr. John Douglas), John Prince (Toby), David Kerman (Handler), William Royale (Mike), Bob Payton (Ring Master), Georgia Simmons (Mandy), Frank Nelson (Grocer), Leora Thatcher (Mrs. Strong), Elvia Allman (Mrs. Timble), John Gibson (Barber/Crowd/Roustabout), Cy Kendall (Mr. Strong), Chester Clute (Mr. Willis), James Eagles (Ticket Taker), Lou Merrill (Mr. Barker), Ross Forrester (Crowd/Wagon Driver), and Charles Emerson (Crowd/Wagon).

Commercial: Elvia Allman, James Eagles.

Margaret Mayo's 1907 play *Polly of the Circus*, focuses on a female circus star who is brought to the home of a local minister to recover after a serious injury, causing a scandal among the townspeople. Mabel Taliaferro and Malcolm Williams were featured in the leads. In the somewhat unusual *Lux* treatment, the leading man's role is changed to that of a doctor, which alters the focus of the play considerably and somewhat lessens its impact. Also, Polly's circus job in the radio version is as a bareback rider, while in the play the character is an aerialist.

Lionel Barrymore serves as guest host, as Cecil B. DeMille was in New York to preview his latest film, *The Plainsman*. DeMille is still heard, however, by remote, as he introduces Barrymore at the beginning of the show and tells about next week's broadcast at the end.

Polly of the Circus was first seen on the screen in Goldwyn's 1917 version, which was directed by Charles T. Horan and Edwin L. Hollywood and starred Mae Marsh and Vernon Steele in the roles taken by Loretta Young and Gavin Gordon in the broadcast. The talking version was released by MGM in 1932, which was directed by Alfred Santell and starred Marion Davies and Clark Gable.

Film versions: Goldwyn, 1917; MGM, 1932.

110. "The Grand Duchess and the Waiter," 12/7/36
Based on the play by Alfred Savoir (1925).

Intermission Guests: Vince Barnett, motion picture actor (after Act 2), and Mrs. Nathalie Bucknall, MGM research department head (after Act 3).

Cast: Robert Montgomery (Albert), Elissa Landi (Grand Duchess Xenia),

Gene Lockhart (Grand Duke Peter), Alma Kruger (Countess Avaloff), Lionel Pape (Grand Duke Paul), Byron Foulger (Matard), Margaret Brayton (Henrietta), Edwin Max (Russian Waiter), Lou Merrill (Italian Officer), Frank Nelson (Henry), Ross Forrester, David Kerman, Charles Emerson, Betty Stewart, Doris Louray, Ynez Seabury, and Marjorie Winfield (Crowd).

Commercial: Ynez Seabury, Marjorie Winfield.

Lux's version of Alfred Savoir's play *The Grand Duchess and the Waiter* makes a most enjoyable program, largely due to the amusing performances of the cast, especially the two leads. (The Broadway production of the comedy, which charts the relationship between a waiter and the grand duchess of whom he becomes enamored, opened at the Lyceum Theatre, with Basil Rathbone and Elsie Ferguson, on October 13, 1925, while London's premiere at the Globe Theatre on February 10, 1925, featured Lawrence Anderson and Margaret Bannerman.)

The Act 2 intermission guest, movie character actor Vince Barnett, relates stories of practical jokes he played on various stars on occasions when he was disguised as a head waiter.

The first film version of *The Grand Duchess and the Waiter* was the 1926 Paramount release for which Adolphe Menjou (as Albert) achieved popular and critical acclaim. Florence Vidor portrayed the grand duchess in this film, and Malcolm St. Clair directed. Savoir's play surfaced again at Paramount (in 1934) under the title *Here Is My Heart*, which was directed by Frank Tuttle and featured Bing Crosby and Kitty Carlisle. (Songs are by Ralph Rainger and Leo Robin.)

Film versions: Paramount, 1926; Paramount, 1934 (*Here Is My Heart*).

111. "Madame Sans-Gene," 12/14/36

Based on the play by Victorien Sardou and Émile Moreau (1893).

Intermission Guests: Jerome Napoleon Bonaparte, great-great-nephew of the Emperor Napoleon of France (after Act 2), and William Councelman, 20th Century–Fox scenario writer and cartoonist (after Act 3).

Cast: Jean Harlow (Madame Sans-Gene), Robert Taylor (Count de Neipperg), Claude Rains (Napoleon), C. Henry Gordon (Fouché), Lou Merrill (LeFevre), William Royale (the General/Constand/First Patriot), Corinne Ross (Madame Savary), Sarah Selby (Eliza), Phyllis Coghlan (Caroline), Gretchen Thomas (Marie), Frank Nelson (Roustan/Patriot), Ken Chavelle (a Footman/Third Patriot/Second Man), David Kerman (a Guard/Fourth Patriot/Fourth Man), James Eagles (Sergeant/Second Patriot/First Man), Ross Forrester (a Patriot/Third Man), Charles Emerson (Citizen Gervais/Crowd), George Finnie (Citizen DuPrex/Crowd), Viola Moore, Lauretta Puck, and Noreen Gammill (Crowd).

Commercial: Viola Moore, Lauretta Puck, and Noreen Gammill.

Sardou's classic 1893 play *Madame Sans-Gene*, which was cowritten by Émile Moreau, made splendid material for versatile star Jean Harlow's *Lux* debut, and her modern style of delivery creates just the sort of highly effective contrast necessary in her wonderful portrayal of an ex-washerwoman among the high society of Napoleonic France. Also giving fine performances are Robert Taylor as her love interest, Count de Neipperg, and Claude Rains as Napoleon, whom he also played in Warner Bros.' motion picture *Hearts Divided*.

The first (and, to date, only) feature-length version of *Madame Sans-Gene* to be produced in the United States was

C. Henry Gordon, Jean Harlow, Cecil B. DeMille, Claude Rains, and Robert Taylor in the December 14, 1936, broadcast of "Madame Sans-Gene" (photo: Connie Billips).

Paramount's 1925 release, which was directed by Leonce Perret and starred Gloria Swanson, Warwick Ward, and Émile Drain.

Film version: Paramount, 1925.

112. "Gold Diggers," 12/21/36

Based on the 1933 Warner Bros. film *Gold Diggers of 1933* (adaptation by Erwin Gelsey and James Seymour, dialogue by David Boehm and Ben Markson), in turn based on the play *The Gold Diggers*, by Avery Hopwood (1919).

Intermission Guests: Jack Warner, Ted Atmore.

Cast: Dick Powell (Brad Roberts), Joan Blondell (Carol King), Ynez Seabury (Trixie), Harriet Russell (Polly Parker), Chester Clute (Barney Hopkins), John Davidson (J. Lawrence Bradford), J. Donald Wilson (Dugan), Frank Nelson (Call Boy), Claudia

Hyams, Betty Stewart (Crowd), Ross Forrester (Elevator Boy/Crowd), and Charles Emerson (Crowd).

Commercial: Justina Wayne, Verna Felton.

Lux's 1936 "Christmas present" to its listeners was a broadcast pairing the recently wed Joan Blondell and Dick Powell. Since they had appeared together in several musicals at Warner Bros., the logical choice for their vehicle was an adaptation of one of the popular "Gold Digger" films. DeMille announces at the beginning of the program that "this production combines the story of *The Gold Diggers of 1933* and the music of *The Gold Diggers of 1937*." Actually, the plot of the 1933 *Gold Diggers* edition of Broadway chorus girls looking for wealthy husbands is used only as a starting point. Many of the characters from that film are present, and the opening scenes follow the movie fairly closely. From this moment on, however, severe plot alterations are made so that Blondell's and Powell's characters can be romantically united (which is not the situation in the film). Circulating recordings of this show are lacking the entire second half, leaving only the first act and most of the second intact.

One might guess that in an adaptation of a "Gold Diggers" motion picture the songs would come fast and furious, but in the surviving portion of this broadcast, only one song, "Let's Put Our Heads Together," from *The Gold Diggers of 1937* (lyric by E.Y. Harburg, music by Harold Arlen) is actually sung (by Dick Powell, in Act 1). A few other numbers from the 1933 and 1937 "Gold Diggers" (including "With Plenty of Money and You" and "Pettin' in the Park") are, however, played as part of the incidental music.

Warner Bros.' *Gold Diggers of 1933* was directed by Mervyn LeRoy (with musical numbers staged by Busby Berkeley) and starred Dick Powell, Ruby Keeler, and Joan Blondell. Avery Hopwood's play *The Gold Diggers* had been filmed twice previously at that studio: first, under its original title in 1923, with Harry Beaumont directing a cast that included Wyndham Standing, Hope Hampdon, and Louise Fazenda; then as *Gold Diggers of Broadway* in 1929, with William Bakewell and Lilyan Tashman, under Roy Del Ruth's direction. A final rendering was released by Warner Bros. in 1951 entitled *Painting the Clouds with Sunshine.* This version was directed by David Butler and featured Dennis Morgan and Virginia Mayo in the leads.

Film versions: Warner Bros., 1923 *(The Gold Diggers)*; Warner Bros., 1929 *(Gold Diggers of Broadway)*; Warner Bros., 1933 *(Gold Diggers of 1933)*; Warner Bros., 1951 *(Painting the Clouds with Sunshine).*

113. "Cavalcade," 12/28/36

Based on the play by Noël Coward (1930).

Intermission Guest: Noël Coward (after Act 1).

Cast: Herbert Marshall (Robert Marryot), Madeleine Carroll (Jane Marryot), Una O'Connor (Ellen), David Niven (Edward Marryot), Elsa Buchanan (Edith), Douglas Scott (Edward, as a Boy), Leonard Mudie (Bridges), Helena Grant (Flo Snapper), George Kirby (George Snapper), Martin Field (the Older Joe), Ra Hould (the Younger Joe), June Lockhart (the Younger Edith), Jennifer Bruce (Fannie), Wauna Lidwell (Margaret), Ben Guy Phillips (Belder/Crowd), Frederick Sewell (Steward/Man/Crowd), Josephine Brown (a Cook/Crowd), Vernon Steele (Narrator), Frank Nelson (Paper Boy/Crowd), Lou Merrill (Café Manager/Paper Boy), David Kerman, Lauretta Puck, Ross Forrester, Charles Emerson, and Rudy Schrager (Crowd).

Commercial: Margaret Brayton.

Adapting Noël Coward's large-scale production *Cavalcade* to fit a 45-minute radio drama must have been a formidable task, and it is to the credit of *Lux* writer George Wells that all of the integrity and much of the scope of Coward's epic are preserved in the broadcast version. The stage play traces the lives of one family during the first 30 years of the twentieth century (36 years in the broadcast, since it is updated to the present) and contains 21 scenes. Obviously, the *Lux* version can offer little more than highlights of the play, and these memorable moments are very well done. One feature of the stage production that is unfortunately completely absent from the radio drama is the popular music that Noël Coward used so effectively to convey the different cultural climate of each era represented. (Coward also wrote two original songs for the production.)

The playwright himself appears as the sole intermission guest (the first program from Hollywood in which only one intermission guest was heard). He speaks from Broadway's National Theatre, where he was appearing in his own piece, *Tonight at 8:30,* and gives an interesting talk on *Cavalcade* and how it came to be written.

The only film version of *Cavalcade* was released by Fox in 1933. Frank Lloyd directed a predominantly British cast that included Clive Brook, Diana Wynyard, Una O'Connor, John Warburton, and Margaret Lindsay. (This film was the 1932-33 Academy Award winner for best picture.)

Film version: Fox, 1933.

114. "Men in White," 1/4/37

Based on the play by Sidney S. Kingsley (1933).

Intermission Guests: Edith Head, Paramount costume designer (after Act 2), and Victor G. Heiser, physician and author of *An American Doctor's Odyssey* (after Act 3; from New York City).

Cast: Spencer Tracy (Dr. George Ferguson), Virginia Bruce (Laura Hudson), Frances Farmer (Barbara Dennin), Frank Reicher (Dr. Hochberg), Paul Guilfoyle (Dr. Levine), Crauford Kent (Dr. Dunningham), Thomas Mills (Mr. Hudson), Kenneth Hansen (Dr. Michaelson), Brent Sargent (Shorty), Lou Merrill (Dr. Gordon), Ross Forrester (Dr. MacDonald), Frank Nelson (Crowd/Man), Dorothy Gray (Dorothy Smith), David Kerman (Taxi Driver/Intern), Margaret Brayton (Nurse), Sarah Selby (Nurse), Mary Jane Higby (Nurse), and Doris Louray (Nurse).

Commercial: Sarah Selby, William Royale.

The basis for *Lux*'s first broadcast of 1937 was Sidney S. Kingsley's popular tribute to the medical profession, *Men in White.* (On Broadway, the stars were Alexander Kirkland, Margaret Barker, Phoebe Brand, J. Edward Bromberg, and Morris Carnovsky.) Spencer Tracy, in his *Lux* debut, gives a sincere performance as the young doctor, as do Virginia Bruce and Frances Farmer in the roles of the two girls who figure prominently in the physician's life. The stage play's climactic situation, which involves Nurse Dennin's pregnancy by Dr. Ferguson, is altered for obvious reasons in the broadcast version so that the young nurse is severely injured and blinded in an automobile accident for which Dr. Ferguson is responsible.

Metro-Goldwyn-Mayer's 1934 screen version of *Men in White* stars Clark Gable, Myrna Loy, Elizabeth Allan, Jean Hersholt, and Otto Kruger, and was directed by Richard Boleslawski.

Film version: MGM, 1934.

115. "The Gilded Lily," 1/11/37

Based on the 1935 Paramount film (screenplay by Claude Binyon), in turn based on the story by Melville Baker and Jack Kirkland.

Intermission Guests: Janet Riesenfeld, dancer (after Act 2), and Linton Wells, *New York Herald-Tribune* reporter and foreign correspondent (after Act 3).

Cast: Claudette Colbert (Lily David), Fred MacMurray (Pete Dawes), David Niven (Charles Gray), George Chandler (Eddie), C. Montague Shaw (the Duke of Loamshire), Chester Clute (the Editor/Store Clerk), John Gibson (the Bum/Paper Boy/Reporter), Georgie Simmons (Dora/Crowd), Lou Merrill (Nate/Reporter/Crowd), Frank Nelson (the Man/Paper Boy/Reporter), William Royale (Subway Guard/Paper Boy/Photographer), Mary Alden (the Woman/Crowd), Warren McCollum, and Ross Forrester (Newspaper Reporters/Newsboys).

Commercial: Mary Arden, Marilyn Cooper.

Engaged for *Lux*'s broadcast of Paramount's 1935 Wesley Ruggles–directed film *The Gilded Lily* were the picture's two stars, Claudette Colbert and Fred MacMurray. The comedy, which tells of a mercenary young lady who falls for a member of a European royal family, much to the chagrin of the down-to-earth Yankee reporter who also loves her, also features David Niven in the role played onscreen by Ray Milland.

During the curtain call, Fred Mac-Murray sings a chorus from "When Is a Kiss Not a Kiss?" (lyric, Ralph Freed; music, Burton Lane), part of the score of his new Paramount film, *Champagne Waltz.*

The second act intermission guest, dancer Janet Riesenfeld (whose professional name is Rachel Rojas), discusses conditions in war-torn Madrid, whence she recently returned. (She is the daughter of distinguished film composer Dr. Hugo Riesenfeld.)

The Gilded Lily had been filmed once previously at Paramount in 1921, with Mae Murray, Jason Robards, and Lowell Sherman, under Robert Z. Leonard's direction.

Film versions: Paramount, 1921; Paramount, 1935.

116. "Criminal Code," 1/18/37

Based on the play by Martin Flavin (1929).

Intermission Guests: Gladys Lloyd (Mrs. Edward G. Robinson), former stage actress (after Act 2), and Senator James B. Holohan, former warden of San Quentin prison (after Act 3).

Cast: Edward G. Robinson (Martin Brady), Beverly Roberts (Mary Brady), Paul Guilfoyle (Robert Graham), Noel Madison (Galloway), Walter Kingsford (Dr. Rinewulf), Lou Merrill (MacManus/Mr. Parker), Earle Ross (Gleason), William Williams (Kellog/Lew/Crowd), Richard Abbott (Kurtz/Manager of Café/Crowd), Ernie Adams (Runch/Crowd), Justina Wayne (Miss Grady/Crowd), Joe Franz (Jim Fales/Crowd), Hilda Haywood (Gertrude/Crowd), Margaret Brayton (the Operator/Crowd), Ross Forrester (Jerry/Second Waiter/Crowd), David Kerman (the Waiter/the Guard/Crowd).

Commercial: Margaret Brayton, Charles Emerson.

Lux's adaptation of Martin Flavin's play *The Criminal Code* was the occasion on which Edward G. Robinson first appeared in the program's Hollywood series. The radio play, which concerns a prison warden whose controversial trust regarding the inmates is put to the test, also stars Beverly Roberts in the leading lady role and Paul Guilfoyle in a rare heroic part (both of whom give fine performances). Walter Kingsford of the original Broadway production reprises his role of Dr. Rinewulf (the other members of the stage production were Arthur Byron, Anita Kerry, and Russell Hardie). Though the microphone version is for the most part very faithful to the play, a brief scene is added at the conclusion to give the broadcast a (rather unlikely) happy ending.

Columbia released its film version of *The Criminal Code* in 1933, with Walter Huston, Constance Cummings, and Phillips Holmes leading a cast that was directed by Howard Hawks. Like the *Lux* broadcast, the film abandoned Flavin's ending so that all might end happily. (The movie, however, offers a completely rewritten final scene, whereas the *Lux* rendering merely tacks an additional scene onto the play.)

Film version: Columbia, 1933.

117. "Tonight or Never," 1/25/37

Based on the play by Lili Hatvany (1930).

Intermission Guests: Mary Garden, opera singer (after Act 2), and Marcella Napp, MGM casting director (after Act 3).

Cast: Jeanette MacDonald (Nella Vargo), Melvyn Douglas (Jim), Luis Alberni (Rudig), John Davidson (Albert von Gronac), Greta Myer (Emma), Zeffi Tillbury (the Marchesa San Giovanni), Lou Merrill (Doorman/Gendarme), Frank Nelson (Hotel Clerk), John Lake (Callboy), David Kerman, Ross Forrester, and Charles Emerson (Crowd). *Chorus*: Zahuri Elmassian, Emily Beauchamp, Mildred Carroll, Windona Black, Mary Mahoney, Dorothy McCarthy, Cornelia Glover, Frank Carpenter, Alfred Garr, Richard Davis, Russell Horton, Kenneth Rundquist, Tudor Williams, Dudley Russell, William Brandt, and Bernie Altstock. *Commercial*: Jerrie Gail, Jean Colbert.

Lili Hatvany's *Tonight or Never*, a comedy concerning the romance that develops when a persuasive opera company representative attempts to procure the services of a stubborn prima donna, served as the vehicle for Jeanette MacDonald's second *Lux* appearance. In addition to "opening up" the play by presenting scenes in such places as an opera house (the stage play employs only two sets), songs have been added for MacDonald. The musical numbers are "Good Morning, My Dear" (Act 1), "Love, Here Is My Heart" (lyric, Silesu; music, Ross; Act 2), and "Sempre Libera," from Verdi's opera *La Traviata* (Act 3). Melvyn Douglas, who created the role of Jim in the Broadway production, repeats his characterization for the microphone. (Helen Gahagan was his stage costar.)

Former operatic soprano Mary Garden, at this time employed as a talent scout by MGM, tells of the potential for opera on the screen. (Garden herself appeared in two silent films for Goldwyn in 1917–18.)

United Artists' 1931 motion picture of *Tonight or Never* features Gloria Swanson as the prima donna, with both Melvyn Douglas and Ferdinand Gottschalk repeating their stage roles under the direction of Mervyn LeRoy.
Film version: United Artists, 1931.

**118. "Mr. Deeds Goes to Town,"
2/1/37**
Based on the 1936 Columbia film (screenplay by Robert Riskin), in turn based on the story "Opera Hat," by Clarence Buddington Kelland.
Intermission Guests: Fay Gillis, aviator and foreign correspondent for the *New York Herald-Tribune* (after Act 2), and Sidney Skolsky, Hollywood columnist for the *New York Daily News* (after Act 3).
Cast: Gary Cooper (Longfellow Deeds), Jean Arthur (Babe Bennett), Lionel Stander (Cornelius Cobb), Crauford Kent (Judge May), Margaret Seddon (Jane Faulkner), Margaret McWade (Amy Faulkner), Byron K. Foulger (Dr. Fraser), Edgar Norton (Walter), Hal K. Dawson (Mac Goran), John Gibson (Bodyguard/Leader of Band), William Royale (Budington/Bus Conductor), Gretchen Thomas (Mrs. Meredith), Lou Merrill (Waiter/Train Conductor), Frank Nelson (Newsboy/Man), Ross Forrester (Newsboy/Crowd), Margaret Brayton, (First Telephone Operator), and Leora Thatcher (Second Telephone Operator).
Commercial: Margaret Brayton, Leora Thatcher, and Barbara Cox.

Lux producers felt they had made quite a coup in acquiring the broadcast rights to Columbia's popular screen success *Mr. Deeds Goes to Town*. The radio play, which casts Gary Cooper, Jean Arthur, and Lionel Stander in their original roles, retells the adventures of a small town greeting card poet who inherits a fortune and moves to New York City, where those who would take advantage of his naiveté find him a tougher mark than they had imagined. While the broadcast is a straightforward adaptation of the Frank Capra-directed film, much of the movie's charm depends on the many scenes that do not affect the plot. With most of these scenes eliminated (the film runs nearly two hours), the effectiveness of the story is substantially reduced. *Lux* did choose to engage Margaret Seddon and Margaret Mc-Wade of the film cast to reprise their "pixilated" routine over the airwaves, even though their participation is limited to one scene. (The actresses do not receive billing by name but are referred to by DeMille as "the celebrated pixilated sisters.")

The film version of *Mr. Deeds Goes to Town* was directed by Frank Capra (who won an Academy Award) and was released in 1936.

Film version: Columbia, 1936.

119. "Graustark," 2/8/37

Based on the novel by George Barr McCutcheon (1901).

Intermission Guest: Rufus LeMaire, talent scout and executive assistant to Charles Rogers, production head of Paramount (after Act 2).

Cast: Gene Raymond (Glen Lorry), Anna Sten (Princess Yetive), James Gleason (Spud Gervey), Moroni Olsen (Baron Auberlitz), Winifred Harris (Countess), Frank Nelson (Hugo/Secretary/Man), Lee Millar (Higgins), Leo McCabe (Captain Boloroz), Eddie Kane (Lieutenant/Desk Clerk), Lou Merrill (Waiter/Driver/Boy), David Kerman (Soldier/Purser), Ross Forrester (a Footman/Page), Margaret Brayton (Cigarette Girl), Mary Lou Fisher (Hatcheck Girl), and Charles Emerson (Ship Steward/Crowd).

Lux's production of "Graustark," a drama centering around a European princess whose romance with an American reporter forces her to choose between love and duty, features Gene Raymond and (in her only *Lux* appear-

ance) Anna Sten. Though there had been two feature film versions of the story, *Lux*'s rendering is adapted from George McCutcheon's original novel. Character names have been altered for the radio play, with the hero's name changed from Grenfall Lorry to Glen Lorry, for example, and his pal's name changed from Harry Anguish to Spud Gervey.

Fred E. Wright directed Essanay's 1915 rendering of *Graustark*, which featured Francis X. Bushman, Beverly Bayne, and Albert Roscoe, while First National's 1925 remake was directed by Dimitri Buchowetzki and starred Eugene O'Brien and Norma Talmadge.

Film versions: Essanay, 1915; First National, 1925.

120. "Brewster's Millions," 2/15/37

Based on the play by Winchell Smith and Byron Ongley (1906), in turn based on the novel by George Barr McCutcheon (1902).

Intermission Guests: Marjorie Wood and Norbert Janssen, Irish Sweepstakes winners (after Act 2), and William Mondshine, proprietor of Willie's of Hollywood, silk stocking designer for motion picture stars (after Act 3).

Cast: Jack Benny (Jack Brewster), Mary Livingstone (Mary Gray), Crauford Kent (Mr. Grant), Fred Harrington (Mr. Vanderpool), Lee Millar (Mr. Dudley), Margaret Brayton (Barbara Dawn), Helena Grant (Sophie Smith), Helen Keers (Mrs. Gray), John Gibson (Mike Donovan), Hal K. Dawson (Mr. Murphy), Eddie Kane (Slade), Lionel Belmore (Tragedian), Ross Forrester (Gillis), Abe Reynolds (Goldstone), Ynez Seabury (Miss Higgins [Secretary]), Lou Merrill (Skipper), William Royale (Police Officer [Timothy]), Frank Nelson (Stage Manager), and Doris Louray (Crowd).

Commercial: Jean Colbert, Betty Stewart).

For the first time in a Hollywood broadcast, the players engaged for *Lux* were not motion picture stars but popular radio performers. It is true that both Jack Benny and Mary Livingstone had appeared in films, but their fame clearly derived from their participation in *The Jack Benny Program*. Not surprisingly, the *Lux* adaptation of *Brewster's Millions* is tailored better to fit the familiar radio characters of the two stars, and the dialogue has been liberally spiced with wisecracks for both. Still, there is little in the story of man who must spend a small fortune to inherit a larger one to take advantage of Benny's "stinginess," and other aspects of his radio character are also ignored. It is only during the curtain call (written by regular Jack Benny writers Ed Beloin and Bill Morrow) that Mr. and Mrs. Benny become themselves, or, at least, themselves as their radio listeners know them.

There have been several feature-length films of the famous comedy, the first of which was co-directed (with Oscar Apfel) by *Lux*'s own host, Cecil B. DeMille. Starring in that version, which was released by Lasky in 1914, are Edward Abeles (who had created the lead role in the 1906 Broadway production) and Winifred Kingston. Paramount remade *Brewster's Millions* in 1921, on this occasion with Joseph Henabery directing a cast that featured Roscoe ("Fatty") Arbuckle and Betty Ross Clark. The gender of the lead character was changed in Paramount's 1926 film *Miss Brewster's Millions*, which starred Bebe Daniels and Warner Baxter, under Clarence Badger's direction. The first talking version was shot in England and released in the United States by United Artists in 1935. Thornton Freeland directed this musical production, which starred Jack Buchanan, Nancy O'Neil, and Lily Damita. It was not until 1945 that the next version surfaced:

an Allan Dwan–directed Paramount release, with Dennis O'Keefe and Helen Walker. United Artists produced another British version in 1961 entitled *Three on a Spree*, with direction by George Fowler, and Jack Watling and Carole Lesley in the leads. The most recent rendering remolded the play for comedian Richard Pryor and featured Lonette McKee in the 1985 Walter Hill–directed Universal release.

Film versions: Lasky, 1914; Paramount, 1921; Paramount, 1926 (*Miss Brewster's Millions*); United Artists, 1935; Paramount, 1945; United Artists, 1961 (*Three on a Spree*); Universal, 1985.

121. "Captain Blood," 2/22/37

Based on the 1935 Warner Bros. film (screenplay by Casey Robinson), in turn based on the novel by Rafael Sabatini (1922).

Intermission Guests: Charles Courtney, "world's greatest locksmith" (after Act 2), and Douglas MacLean, head of Douglas MacLean Productions and former silent screen star (after Act 3).

Guest Host: Herbert Marshall.

Cast: Errol Flynn (Dr. Peter Blood), Olivia deHavilland (Arabella Bishop), Basil Rathbone (Captain Levasseur), Henry Stephenson (Lord Willoughby), Donald Crisp (Colonel Bishop), Ferdinand Munier (Governor Steed), Vernon Downing (Jeremy Pitt), Leo McCabe (Wolverstone), Ward Dane (Ogle), Eric Snowden (Hagthorpe), Wyndham Standing (Dixon), Vernon Steele (Judge), Edward Cooper (Auctioneer), Eric Lonsdale (Clerk of Court), Lou Merrill (Cahusac), Helen Brown (a Girl of Tortuga), Frank Nelson (Helmsman), Jerry Gail (Crowd), Charles Emerson (Crowd), Robert Payton (Lookout/Man/Crowd), Viola Moore (Crowd), George French (Crowd), David Kerman (Soldier/Aide-de-camp/Crowd), and Ross Forrester (English Lookout/Soldier/Crowd).

Chorus: Kenneth Rundquist, Kirby Hoon, Hubert Head, Richard Davis, Tudor Williams, Dudley Kusell, Harry Stanton, and William Brandt.

Errol Flynn's debut on *Lux* came in an adaptation of his first starring role in an American feature film, Warner Bros.' 1935 production *Captain Blood*. Since the story (which depicts the adventures of a British surgeon who is forced to engage in piracy) features key action sequences that play an important part in the overall effectiveness, the deletion of such a part is naturally noticed, though *Lux*'s rendering is intelligently presented through skillful acting and scripting. Olivia deHavilland, Basil Rathbone, and Henry Stephenson are also from the cast of the Michael Curtiz–directed Warner Bros.' film, while Donald Crisp takes the role Lionel Atwill played in the movie.

Since DeMille was in Louisiana that week shooting scenes for his upcoming picture *The Buccaneer*, Herbert Marshall assumed the duties of host in his place.

Rafael Sabatini's swashbuckling adventure had been filmed once prior to Warner Bros.' 1935 version, as Vitagraph produced a rendering in 1924 (directed by David Smith), with J. Warren Kerrigan, Jean Paige, and James Morrison.

Film versions: Vitagraph, 1924; Warner Bros., 1935.

122. "Cappy Ricks," 3/1/37

Based on the play by Edward F. Rose (1919), in turn based on the story by Peter B. Kyne.

Intermission Guests: Peter B. Kyne, author and creator of "Cappy Ricks" (after Act 2), and Royer, 20th Century–Fox costume designer (after Act 3).

Cast: Charles Winninger (Cappy Ricks), Sally Eilers (Florry), Richard Arlen (Matt), Byron K. Foulger (Skinner), Janet Scott (Lucy Ricks), Kenneth Hansen (Gordon), Frank Coghlan, Jr. (Jimmy), Maureen Roden Ryan (Bridget), Frank Nelson (Crowd), John Lake (Crowd), Lou Merrill (Man/Crowd), Charles Emerson (Crowd), Ross Forrester (Crowd), Elizabeth Ellis (Crowd), and Mary Low (Crowd).

Commercial: Frank Nelson, Elizabeth Ellis, and Mary Low.

"Cappy Ricks," the entertaining tale of a hard-hearted but likeable president of a shipping business who clashes with his daughter (Sally Eilers) over her romantic interest in his bitter rival (Richard Arlen), provides character actor Charles Winninger with a fine vehicle in which to display his talents (William Courtenay, Marion Coakley, and Thomas A. Wise were the stars of the Broadway production, which opened at the Morosco Theatre on January 13, 1919.)

Winninger also appears in Warner Bros.' 1937 version, *The Go-Getter*, which was directed by Busby Berkeley and costarred Anita Louise and George Brent.

Film version: Warner Bros., 1937.

123. "Madame Butterfly," 3/8/37

Based on the play by David Belasco (1900), in turn based on the story by John Luther Long (1897) and the opera (1904; libretto by Giuseppe Giacosa and Luigi Illica, music by Giacomo Puccini).

Intermission Guests: Princess Der Ling of the Chinese royal family and former lady-in-waiting to the empress of China (after Act 2), and Robert Cobb, president of the Brown Derby (restaurant) Corporation (after Act 3).

Cast: Grace Moore (Cio-cio-san [Madame Butterfly]), Cary Grant (Lieutenant B.F. Pinkerton), Pedro deCordoba (the Bonze), Marek Windheim (Goro), Crauford Kent (Sharpless), Maria Hammond (Suzuki), Mary Lansing

(Kathryn Forbes), Lou Merrill (Commander), Frank Nelson (an Officer), Charles Emerson (Crowd), David Kerman (Crowd), and Ross Forrester (Crowd/Sailor).

Commercial: Frank Nelson (Tom), Margaret Brayton.

Lux's "Madame Butterfly" presented operatic soprano Grace Moore with a second opportunity to combine her acting and singing talents (she had appeared in "Trilby" on September 21, 1936). One of Moore's most popular roles at the Metropolitan Opera was that of Cio-cio-san in Puccini's version of *Madame Butterfly*. As she had also performed selections from the opera in Columbia's *One Night of Love*, it is logical that excerpts from Puccini's work should be interpolated into *Lux*'s "Madame Butterfly." Only two of the opera's arias are performed here, however: "Un bel di vedremo" (Act 2), and the lullaby "Dormi, amor mio" (Act 3). Lou Silvers's incidental music does not employ any of Puccini's themes during the familiar story of an American naval officer who marries, then abandons a naive Japanese girl who fruitlessly awaits his return.

David Belasco's one-act play is quite brief, so the *Lux* adaptation also uses scenes from the much longer operatic version. In order to make Cary Grant's character of Pinkerton more sympathetic (he is a complete cad in both stage versions), additional scenes were created for the broadcast. Thus, Pinkerton and Butterfly become the victims of the interference of American consul Sharpless and Pinkerton's fiancée, Kathryn (his wife in the play/opera).

During the curtain call, Grace Moore sings "Ciribiribin," accompanied by Pietro Cimini.

The first film of the famous story and play of *Madame Butterfly* was released by Paramount in 1915 and starred Mary Pickford as Butterfly and Marshall Nielan

as Pinkerton (under Sidney Olcott's direction). Marion Gering directed Paramount's talking version in 1932, which featured Sylvia Sidney and Cary Grant. None of Puccini's music is sung in this version, but themes from the opera are used in the incidental music.

Film versions: Paramount, 1915; Paramount, 1932.

124. "Desire," 3/15/37

Based on the 1936 Paramount film (screenplay by Samuel Hoffenstein, Waldemar Young, and Edwin Justus Mayer), in turn based on the play by Hans Szekely and R.A. Stemmle (1927).

Intermission Guests: Ernst Lubitsch, Paramount producer/director (after Act 2), and Kay Roberta Williamson, hostess of the Hollywood branch of I. Magnin & Company specialty (clothing) shops (after Act 3).

Cast: Marlene Dietrich (Madeleine), Herbert Marshall (Tom Bradley), Otto Kruger (Carlos), Zeffie Tilbury (Aunt Olga), Georges Renavent (Albert), Ward Lane (Mr. Gibson), Ferdinand Munier (Mr. DuValle), Victor Rodman (Antoine), Leo McCabe (Radio Announcer), Lou Merrill (Giuseppe), Frank Nelson (Customs Officer), Ross Forrester, Charles Emerson, and George French (Crowd).

Commercial: Ross Forrester, Betty Stewart, and Sarah Selby.

Marlene Dietrich's return engagement to *Lux* came two and a half months after her debut in the first show from Hollywood, once again in a role she created in a Paramount picture. Frank Borzage directed the 1936 movie *Desire*, which tells of a sophisticated female European jewel thief who makes an unwilling accomplice out of an American automobile executive on a holiday. The influence of the movie's producer, Ernst Lubitsch, is much in evidence in the film's delightfully droll early scenes, which depict Miss Dietrich's

Herbert Marshall, Marlene Dietrich, Cecil B. DeMille, Ernst Lubitsch, and Otto Kruger in "Desire," March 15, 1937 (photo: Photofest).

ingenious theft of an invaluable pearl necklace. These scenes are unfortunately eliminated from the microphone version, with the surviving portions of the story relating a more or less conventional love story. Much of the film's appeal relies on the cultural differences between the continental Dietrich and the American Gary Cooper; with the debonair Herbert Marshall cast in the broadcast version, this contrast is lost, as now both lead characters are sophisticated Europeans. Nevertheless, the stars give engaging performances, as does Otto Kruger in the role of Dietrich's cunning cohort, Carlos.

The Act 2 intermission guest is Ernst Lubitsch, who discusses his working methods with Cecil B. DeMille and briefly talks of his upcoming picture, *Angel* (which was to begin shooting on the day of this broadcast but was delayed so that the film's stars, Marlene

Dietrich and Herbert Marshall, could be made available for *The Lux Radio Theatre*).

Film version: Paramount, 1936.

125. "Death Takes a Holiday," 3/22/37
Based on the play by Alberto Casella, as adapted by Walter Ferris (1929).

Intermission Guests: Walter Ferris, playwright and screenwriter (after Act 2), and Blanche Sweet, silent film star (after Act 3).

Cast: Fredric March (Prince Sirki), Florence Eldridge (Grazia), Kay Johnson (Alda), Arthur Byron (Duke Lambert), Gene Lockhart (Baron Cessrea), Howard Phillips (Corrado), Theresa Maxwell Conover (Stephanie), Daisy Belmore (Fedele), Lou Merrill (Croupier/Radio Announcer), Frank Nelson (Telegraph), Charles Emerson (Telegraph/Second Man/Crowd), Bernard Phillips (Telegraph/Third Man),

Margaret Brayton (Woman/Crowd), and Ross Forrester (Crowd).

Commerical: Gretchen Thomas, Margaret Brayton, and Ross Forrester.

Lux's "Death Takes a Holiday" gave Fredric March the chance to reprise one of his strongest film roles in a fantasy of what occurs when Death takes human form in an attempt to discover why mortals fear him. The scenes in which March appears in the form of Death (as opposed to his human incarnation of Prince Sirki) are actually more effective in the broadcast than they are in the film, as the listener must imagine the physical appearance of the dreaded figure whom the other characters fear. The remaining cast members, including Florence Eldridge, in the sort of role she did not often play in pictures, also give distinguished performances. Due to obvious time restrictions, nearly all of the humorous bits from the play have been omitted. Otherwise, *Lux* presents a very faithful adaptation of Walter Ferris's Broadway version (which starred Philip Merivale, Rose Hobart, Ann Orr, and James Dale) of the Italian play by Alberto Casella.

Paramount's film of *Death Takes a Holiday* (also based on Ferris's version) was released in 1934 and was directed by Mitchell Leisen. In addition to Fredric March, the cast included Evelyn Venable, Katherine Alexander, and Sir Guy Standing.

Film version: Paramount, 1934.

126. "Dulcy," 3/29/37

Based on the play by George S. Kaufman and Marc Connelly (1921).

Intermission Guests: Hedda Hopper, motion picture actress (after Act 2), and Elsa Maxwell, world-renowned party hostess (from New York; after Act 3).

Cast: Gracie Allen (Dulcinea Smith), George Burns (Gordon Smith), Elliott Nugent (William Parker), Wallis Clark (C. Rogers Forbes), Norma Lee (An-gelia Forbes), Howard Lindsay (Vincent Leach), John Davidson (Schuler Van Dyck), Victor Rodman (Blair Patterson), Joe Franz (Henry), and Leora Thatcher (Mrs. Forbes).

Commercial: Helen Ray (Woman's Voice [opening]), Ynez Seabury (Ruth), Herschel Mayall (Betty's husband), Florence Gordon (Betty), and Frank Nelson (Man's Voice).

Having offered "Dulcy" during the final season of *Lux* in New York, the show's producers chose to present a second adaptation a year and a half later in Hollywood, with movie and radio couple Gracie Allen and George Burns. Repeating their roles from the original Broadway production in 1921 are Wallis Clark, Norma Lee, and Howard Lindsay (who also directed). Elliott Nugent, who portrayed Tom Sterrett on the stage (a role deleted from the *Lux* adaptation), plays Dulcy's brother, Willie Parker, in the broadcast.

See 10/28/35, for information on film versions.

127. "A Farewell to Arms," 4/5/37

Based on the novel by Ernest Hemingway (1929).

Intermission Guests: Frank Borzage, motion picture director (after Act 2), and Courtney Riley Cooper, writer and criminologist (after Act 3).

Cast: Clark Gable (Lieutenant Frederick Henry), Josephine Hutchinson (Catherine Barkley), Adolphe Menjou (Rinaldi), Jack LaRue (Priest), Doris Lloyd (Nurse Ferguson), Lionel Belmore (Rudolph), Morton Provinson (Dr. Peters), Lou Merrill (Bonelli), Justina Wayne (Head Nurse), Norman Ainsley (Piani/English Orderly), Frank Nelson (Railway Clerk/Second Man), Cornelia Osgood (the Italian Nurse), Ruth Easton (the Swiss Nurse), Ross Forrester (Man [Coward]/Orderly), Charles Emerson (First Man/Crowd), and Enrico Cucinelli (Singer).

Lux's first presentation of an Ernest Hemingway work was "A Farewell to Arms." Of course, some of the stronger issues dealt with by the author are glossed over on the air, yet the radio version nonetheless presents a grim picture of conditions during the First World War. (The issue of Catherine's pregnancy by Lieutenant Henry is handled by having the couple become husband and wife earlier in the story.)

Clark Gable portrays the cynical ambulance driver in *Lux*'s offering, while Josephine Hutchinson (who gives an excellent performance) is the nurse with whom he falls in love. Adolphe Menjou and Jack LaRue repeat their original screen roles and are equally memorable.

Frank Borzage (who appears as an intermission guest in the broadcast) directed Gary Cooper, Helen Hayes, Adolphe Menjou, and Jack LaRue in Paramount's 1932 film version of *A Farewell to Arms*, while Michael Curtiz was at the helm for Warner Bros.' 1951 reworking, *A Force of Arms*, which updated the action to World War II and starred William Holden, Nancy Olson, and Frank Lovejoy. Charles Vidor directed the 1957 Selznick opus, which featured Rock Hudson, Jennifer Jones, and Vittorio DeSica.

Film versions: Paramount, 1932, Warner Bros., 1951 (*A Force of Arms*); 20th Century–Fox, 1957.

*128. "Dodsworth," 4/12/37

Based on the play by Sidney Howard (1934), in turn based on the novel by Sinclair Lewis (1929).

Intermission Guests: Sidney Howard, author and adapter of *Dodsworth* for stage and screen productions, and Walter Plunkett, costume designer.

Cast: Walter Huston (Sam Dodsworth), Nan Sunderland (Edith Cartright), Fay Bainter (Fran Dodsworth), Gregory Gaye (Kurt), John Carradine

(Arnold Israel), Harlan Briggs (Tubby), Leo McCabe (Lockert), Marion Burns (Emily), Gretchen Thomas (Matey), Beatrice Maude (Mary/Mme. DePenable/Teresa), Lou Merrill (Travel Agent/Second Man/Crowd), Richard Jacks (Page Boy/Third Man/Crowd), Frank Nelson (Ship's Steward/First Man/Crowd), Margaret Brayton (First Woman/Third Woman), and Jerrie Gail (Second Woman).

Commercial: Margaret Brayton, Jerrie Gail, Sheldon Bey, and Dorothy Drew.

Four members of the Broadway production of *Dodsworth* (which opened on February 24, 1934) were on hand to resume their roles on *Lux*'s April 12 program. Walter Huston played the title character. After many years of dedicating his life to his automobile manufacturing business, Dodsworth retires to take a prolonged European vacation, only to learn more about himself and his wife than he does about the world. Nan Sunderland (Mrs. Walter Huston) was Edith Cartright, the woman who understands Sam Dodsworth, Fay Bainter, his vain and selfish wife, and Harlan Briggs, his unsophisticated pal, Tubby.

Sam Goldwyn produced a film version of *Dodsworth*, which was directed by William Wyler and released by United Artists in 1936. (The *Lux* version, however, is adapted from Sidney Howard's stage rendering, *not* the movie.) Starring in that production are Walter Huston, Mary Astor, Ruth Chatterton, Gregory Gaye, Paul Lukas, and Harlan Briggs.

Dodsworth was repeated on *Lux* on October 4, 1937.

Film version: United Artists, 1936.

129. "Alibi Ike," 4/19/37

Based on the 1935 Warner Bros. film (screenplay by William Wister Haines), in turn based on the story by Ring Lardner.

Intermission Guests: Babe Ruth, former baseball player, and Mrs. Babe (Claire) Ruth (from New York City; after Act 2), and Russell Patterson, commercial illustrator and designer (after Act 3).

Cast: Joe E. Brown (Frank Farrell), Helen Chandler (Dolly Stevens), Roscoe Karns (Carey), William Frawley (Cap Finnley), Wally Maher (Mack), Leora Thatcher (Bess Finnley), Cy Kendall (Crawford), Lou Merrill (Club Owner/Umpire), Joe Franz (Lefty), Charles Emerson (Reporter/Train Conductor), Frank Nelson (Radio Announcer/Newsboy), Ross Forrester (Tex), Ingeborg Tillisch (Telephone Operator), and Marion Dennis (Telephone Girl).

Commercial: Leora Thatcher, Ingeborg Tillisch (Helen), and Marion Dennis (Betty).

Six months after *Lux* paid tribute to baseball's World Series by presenting "Elmer the Great," with Joe E. Brown, the comedian was again called upon for a baseball comedy, "Alibi Ike," which focuses upon a small town braggart in his first year in the big leagues. (The occasion for presenting this piece was the opening of the 1937 major league season, officially set for the following day, although four teams saw action on the day of this broadcast.) Like *Elmer the Great, Alibi Ike* was another of Joe E. Brown's successes for Warner Bros. (Ray Enright directed the 1935 release). Also repeating their film roles for the microphone are Roscoe Karns and William Frawley, while Helen Chandler is heard as Dolly, the part played onscreen by Olivia deHavilland.

During the curtain call, Joe E. Brown wishes a speedy recovery to former baseball player Tris Speaker, who had been injured in an automobile accident a few days earlier.

Film version: Warner Bros., 1935.

130. "Magnificent Obsession," 4/26/37

Based on the 1937 Universal film (screenplay by George O'Neill, Sarah Y. Mason, and Victor Heerman), in turn based on the novel by Lloyd C. Douglas (1929).

Intermission Guests: Dr. Lloyd C. Douglas, author (from New York City; after Act 2), and John Arnold, head of MGM's camera department and president of the American Society of Cinematography (after Act 3).

Cast: Irene Dunne (Helen Hudson), Robert Taylor (Bob Merrick), Pedro deCordoba (Randolph), Sara Haden (Nancy Ashford), Barbara Kent (Joyce Hudson), Sam Flint (Perry), Richard Abbott (Dr. Ramsey/German), John Lake (Horace/Pageboy/Crowd), Herschel Mayall (Bank Teller/Crowd), Lou Merrill (Keller/Croupier/RR Clerk), Sarah Selby (Nurse/Maid), and Frank Nelson (Chauffeur).

Commercial: Jean Colbert, Betty Stewart.

Irene Dunne and Robert Taylor returned to the *Lux* microphone to appear in a radio version of their 1935 Universal screen success, *Magnificent Obsession,* the drama of an unlikely romance that develops between an irresponsible playboy and the widow of a prominent doctor for whose death she had unjustly held him responsible. Both stars give sincere and believable performances, as does Sara Haden, who also repeats her film role in the broadcast.

During the curtain call, Irene Dunne sings a song from her RKO picture *High, Wide, and Handsome,* "The Folks Who Live on the Hill" (words, Oscar Hammerstein II; music, Jerome Kern).

John M. Stahl directed the first film version of *Magnificent Obsession,* released by Universal in 1935. Along with Irene Dunne, Robert Taylor, and Sara Haden, the cast included Betty

Furness, Charles Butterworth, and Ralph Morgan. The 1954 rendering (also released by Universal) was directed by Douglas Sirk and featured Jane Wyman, Rock Hudson, Barbara Rush, Otto Kruger, and Agnes Moorehead.

Film versions: Universal, 1935; Universal, 1954.

131. "Hands Across the Table," 5/3/37

Based on the 1935 Paramount film (screenplay by Norman Krasna, Vincent Laurence, and Herbert Fields; original story by Viña Delmar).

Intermission Guests: Sheilah Graham, Hollywood columnist (after Act 2), and Earl Hayes, printer (after Act 3).

Cast: Claudette Colbert (Regi Kane), Joel McCrea (Theodore Drew III), Walter Pidgeon (Allen Macklyn), Gloria Holden (Vivian Snowden), Grace Kern (Nona Gilhooley), Elizabeth Wilbur (Laura), John Gibson (Taxi Driver), Lou Merrill (Peter), Frank Nelson (Waiter), Harold Wilson (Bus Conductor), Kathryn McCune (a Maid), and Ross Forrester (a Barber/Man/Crowd).

Commercial: Kathryn McCune, Marie Hammond.

The occasion of Claudette Colbert's fourth appearance on *Lux*, and the second of leading man Joel McCrea, was an adaptation of Paramount's *Hands Across the Table*, which was directed in 1935 by Mitchell Leisen. (The film's stars are Carole Lombard, Fred MacMurray, Ralph Bellamy, and Astrid Allwyn.) The predictable but entertaining tale of a manicurist who is determined to marry a wealthy man is boosted by the amusing dialogue, which is delivered most engagingly by the two stars. Second leads Walter Pidgeon and Gloria Holden are also given good roles.

Act 3 intermission guest Earl Hayes discusses his unusual occupation of creating prop newspapers to be used in motion picture productions. He also talks briefly about other people with unique movie jobs.

"Hands Across the Table" was also performed on the *Lux Video Theatre* on January 5, 1956.

Film version: Paramount, 1935.

132. "Mary of Scotland," 5/10/37

Based on the play by Maxwell Anderson (1933).

Intermission Guest: Baron Brook, the 7th Earl of Warrick (after Act 2).

Cast: Joan Crawford (Mary Stuart), Franchot Tone (the Earl of Bothwell), Judith Anderson (Elizabeth Tudor), Edward Cooper (John Knox), Kenneth Hunter (Burghley), Vernon Downing (Darnley), Walter Kingsford (Throgmorton), Vernon Steele (Maitland), Leo McCabe (Moray), Phyllis Coghlan (Mary Beaton), James Eagles (Rizzio/Crowd), Wallace Warner (Lord Huntley), Lou Merrill (Lord Ruthven/Duc deChatel Herault), Frank Nelson (Lord Morton/Crowd), Viola Moore (Mary Livingston), Jill Ronney (Mary Fleming), Robert Payton (First Guard/Crowd), and Ross Forrester (Second Guard/Voices).

Commercial: Grace Kerns.

For only the second time since moving to Hollywood, *Lux* offered an adaptation of an historical drama. Chosen for the occasion was Maxwell Anderson's *Mary of Scotland*, which chronicles Mary Stuart's (1542–1587) forced imprisonment and cruel treatment at the hands of Queen Elizabeth I of England for refusing to renounce her Catholic faith. (The stage production at the Alvin Theatre on November 27, 1933, starred Helen Hayes, Philip Merivale, and Helen Menken.) Joan Crawford gives an excellent performance as the Scottish queen, as does Franchot Tone in the role of the Earl of Bothwell. (Tone even provides the character with a convincing accent.)

The sole intermission guest is Baron Brook, the 7th Earl of Warrick, who discusses English nobility. (He was in Hollywood to make his film debut under the name of Michael Brook.)

John Ford directed RKO's 1936 film version of *Mary of Scotland,* which features Katharine Hepburn, Fredric March, and Florence Eldridge in the leads.

Film version: RKO, 1936.

133. "Another Language," 5/17/37

Based on the play by Rose Franken (1932).

Intermission Guests: Mrs. James Roosevelt, mother of Franklin Delano Roosevelt (from New York City; after Act 2), and Janet Henle, head of the women's wardrobe department at Columbia Studios (after Act 3).

Cast: Bette Davis (Stella Hallam), Fred MacMurray (Victor Hallam), John Beal (Jerry Hallam), May Robson (Mrs. Hallam), Margaret Hamilton (Grace Hallam), Hal K. Dawson (Walter Hallam), Edward Keane (Paul Hallam), Myra Marsh (Etta Hallam), Sam Flint (Mr. Hallam), Lou Merrill (Taxi Driver), and Frank Nelson (Waiter).

Commercial: Margaret Brayton, Margaret MacDonald, and Sherry Ardell.

It is definitely not a run-of-the-mill presentation when, as the play opens, the leading man and lady are already husband and wife. Such is the case with "Another Language," and, though the basic plot line bears a resemblance to that of *Main Street* (which was presented on *Lux* on August 3, 1936), the carefully constructed characters and intelligent dialogue give it a uniqueness all its own, proving an excellent vehicle for Bette Davis. Davis, who was often associated with abrasive roles in motion pictures, gives a splendidly subtle per-

formance as the sensitive artist whose tender concern for her nephew is misinterpreted by her uncouth in-laws. Fred MacMurray is heard in Robert Montgomery's screen role, John Beal and Hal K. Dawson repeat their parts from the 1932 stage production (which opened on April 25 at the Booth Theatre), and Margaret Hamilton, who played Helen on stage, is Grace in the broadcast. (Other members of the Broadway production included Dorothy Stickney, Glenn Anders, Margaret Wycherly, and Irene Cattell.)

A film of *Another Language* was released by MGM in 1935, directed by Edward H. Griffith and featuring Helen Hayes, Robert Montgomery, John Beal, and Louise Closser Hale.

Film version: MGM, 1935.

134. "Under Two Flags," 5/24/37

Based on the novel by Ouida (1867).

Intermission Guests: Miss Fanchon, Paramount producer and former producer of Fanchon and Marco stage shows (after Act 2), and Lieutenant Louis Van Den Ecker, motion picture military technical advisor and former member of the French Foreign Legion (after Act 3).

Cast: Herbert Marshall (Sergeant Victor), Olivia deHavilland (Lady Venetia), Lupe Velez (Cigarette), Lionel Atwill (Major Doyle), Lionel Pape (Captain Menzies), Kenneth Hunter (Lord Seraph), Leonard Mudie (Rake), Michael Visaroff (Ivan), Lal Chand Mehra (Sidi Ben Youssiff), James Eagles (Keskerdit/Ferrol), Lou Merrill (Pierre), Frank Nelson (Baron), David Kerman (Officer/Bouche), Warren McCollum (Crowd), Ross Forrester (Grivon), Harold Daniels (Adjutant), Charles Emerson (a Doctor/Legionnaire), and George Webb (Arab).

Commercials: George Webb, Grace Kern, Jerrie Gail, and Helen Brown.

Lux's broadcast of the popular "Under

"Another Language" (May 17, 1937), with **Fred MacMurray and Bette Davis** (photo: Photofest).

Two Flags," a romantic adventure of a suave legionnaire who is torn between his British fiancée and a high-spirited French peasant, features memorable performances by stars Herbert Marshall, Olivia deHavilland, Lupe Velez, and Lionel Atwill. (The play was first produced on Broadway on February 5, 1901, at the Garden Theatre, with Francis Carlyle and Blanche Bates.)

J. Gordon Edwards directed Herbert Hayes, Claire Whitney, Theda Bara, and Stuart Holmes in the first feature film of *Under Two Flags*, which was released by Fox in 1916. Universal's 1922 effort (directed by Tod Browning) cast James Kirkwood, Ethel Grey Terry, Priscilla Dean, and Stuart Holmes in the leads, while 20th Century–Fox's 1936 version starred Ronald Colman, Rosalind Russell, Claudette Colbert, and Victor McLaglen under Frank Lloyd's direction.

Film versions: Fox, 1916; Universal, 1922; 20th Century–Fox, 1936.

135. "The Plainsman," 5/31/37

Based on the 1937 Paramount film (screenplay by Waldemar Young, Harold Lamb, and Lynn Riggs), in turn based on the book *Wild Bill Hickok,* by Frank J. Wilstach, and on the novel *The Prince of the Pistoleers,* by Courtney Riley Cooper and Grover Jones.

Intermission Guests: Sidney Skolsky, Hollywood columnist for the *New York Daily News* (after Act 2), and Marie Osbourne (Baby Marie), stand-in for Ginger Rogers and former child star (after Act 3).

Cast: Fredric March (Wild Bill Hickok), Jean Arthur (Calamity Jane), Porter Hall (Jack McCall), Joan Fontaine (Louisa Cody), Paul Harvey (Yellow Hand), John Patterson (Bill Cody), Anthony Quinn (Painted Horse), Cy Kendall (Lattimer), Earle Ross (Jake), William Royale (Breezy/General Merritt), Lou Merrill (Sergeant/Second Man/Second Negro), Gil Patric (Red/Deckhand), Hal Taylour (Dave/First Man), Eddie Kane (Joe/Third Man/First Private), George Ernst (a Boy), Chief Thundercloud (a Cheyenne), Chief Thunderbird (Cheyenne Charlie/First Cheyenne), Frank Nelson (a Negro/First Man), Elizabeth Ellis (a Woman/Crowd), James Eagles (Second Private/Second Man), Ross Forrester (Joe), and Grace Kerns (Crowd).

Chorus: Alfred Garr, Frank Carpenter, Earl Hunsaker, Myron Niesley, Kenneth Rundquist, Dudley Kusell, Harry Stanton, and William Brandt.

Commercial: Lauretta Puck, James Eagles (Bill), and Rose Mansfield.

At the end of the *Lux* broadcast of May 24, Cecil B. DeMille announces that on the following week an adaptation of his own film *The Plainsman* will be presented, with the original stars,

Jean Arthur (with unidentified player) donned her Calamity Jane costume for a dress rehearsal of "The Plainsman" (May 31, 1937) (photo: Photofest).

Gary Cooper and Jean Arthur. The actual broadcast only features one of the leads, as Gary Cooper, ill with the flu, was forced to drop out of the production the day before, so Fredric March was chosen as his last-minute replacement. Not only was March allowed just one rehearsal with the cast (he had stayed up all night Sunday studying the part and practicing his accent), but he had never seen the film, and had never played the part of an American frontiersman. Nevertheless, he gives a fine performance as the legendary figure of the Old West who attempts to track down the culprits who have been smuggling guns to the Indians, and he even seems to make the character more of an intellectual who acts primarily on instinct. Leading lady Jean Arthur had

also been bitten by the flu bug that week, but she defied her 103-degree temperature to recreate her movie character of Calamity Jane. Her illness does not reveal itself in her energetic portrayal, though she is especially soft-spoken and subdued during the curtain call. (Dr. Carvel James was engaged to attend Arthur onstage during the program.)

Paramount's 1937 film was produced and directed by Cecil B. DeMille and featured a cast that included Gary Cooper, Jean Arthur, James Ellison, Charles Bickford, Helen Burgess, and three actors who repeat their roles in the *Lux* broadcast: Porter Hall, Paul Harvey, and Anthony Quinn. David Lowell Rich directed Universal's 1966 version, which features Don Murray, Abby Dalton, and Guy Stockwell.

Film versions: Paramount, 1937; Universal, 1966.

136. "British Agent," 6/7/37

Based on the 1934 Warner Bros. film (screenplay by Laird Doyle), in turn based on the novel by H. Bruce Lockhart.

Intermission Guests: Nathalie Bucknall, MGM research department head and former secret agent (after Act 2), and Dolly Tree (MGM costume designer (after Act 3).

Cast: Errol Flynn (Stephen Locke), Frances Farmer (Elena), Colin Campbell (Evans), C. Montague Shaw (Sir Walter Carrister), Don Terry (Medill), Joseph Kearns (LeFarge), Cy Kendall (Pavlov), Frank Nelson (Tito Del Val), Lee Millar (Commissioner), Lou Merrill (Mr. X), John Lake (Dmitri), James Eagles (Peter), Ross Forrester (a Newsboy/Russian Newsboy), Harold Wilson (Crowd), George Webb (Russian Soldier/Crowd), Kenneth Hansen (Crowd), and Charles Emerson (Crowd).

Commercial: Margaret MacDonald, Margaret Brayton, Grace Kerns, and Barbara Jean Wong.

"British Agent," which is based on Warner Bros.' 1934 Michael Curtiz–directed film, takes *Lux* into the espionage genre. Although the leisurely pace is common to both the radio play and the film, the broadcast version's climaxes never really approach the drama of the movie's most tense moments. Nevertheless, it is effectively presented, and both Errol Flynn and Frances Farmer give fine performances as two people who fall in love amidst the turbulence of the Russian Revolution. While Kay Francis, the film's leading lady, in no way altered her delivery to suggest that her character was foreign, Farmer does provide Elena with a convincing Russian accent.

Nathalie Bucknall, who had previously appeared on *Lux* to discuss her job as research department head at MGM, relates some of her exploits as a secret agent during the First World War.

After the broadcast, DeMille pays tribute to actress Jean Harlow, who had tragically died at the age of 26 earlier in the day.

Film version: Warner Bros., 1934.

137. "Madame X," 6/14/37

Based on the play *La Femme X . . .*, by Alexandre Bisson (1908), as adapted by John Raphael.

Intermission Guests: Helen Wills Moody, former professional tennis player (after Act 2), and Raymond Mear and his mother, "a Madame X and her son in real life" (after Act 3).

Cast: Ann Harding (Jacqueline Cartwright), James Stewart (Raymond Cartwright), Conway Tearle (Alan Cartwright), Wheaton Chambers (Dr. Chesney), Leora Thatcher (Bessie/Crowd), Joe DuVal (Dean/Second Man), Edward Marr (Tony Phillips), David Kerman (Nick/Court Attendant), Lou Merrill (Keene), Forrest Taylor (Murphy/Trial Judge), L. Stanford Jolly (First Judge/Court Clerk), Galan Galt (Stone), Frank Nelson (Harry), Victor Rodman (Harper), Marjorie Norton (Myrtle), Ross Forrester (Flynn), Justina Wayne (a Woman), and Gil Patric (a Man).

Commercial: Hilda Heywood, Frank Coghlan, Jr.

Ann Harding, James Stewart, and Conway Tearle made their *Lux* debuts in the June 14, 1937, broadcast of "Madame X," which had first been performed at the New Amsterdam Theatre on February 2, 1910, with Dorothy Donnelly, William Elliott, and Robert Drouet in the leads. The story of Alexandre Bisson's play was well known by this time, having served as the basis for several motion pictures, the most recent of which was MGM's version with

Gladys George (released earlier that year). While the original production of the stage play was set in France, *Lux* moves the action to the United States and alters the spelling of several characters' names. Ann Harding is convincing as the woman on trial for murder who refuses to reveal her identity, and James Stewart is given a good role as (unbeknownst to him) the son of the woman he is defending in court.

The first American feature film of *Madame X*, which reached the screen in 1916, was the Henry W. Savage production directed by George F. Marion and featuring Dorothy Donnelly, Ralph Morgan, and John Bowers. Frank Lloyd directed the Goldwyn production of four years later, which has Pauline Frederick, Carson Ferguson, and William Courtleigh in the lead roles. Ruth Chatterton portrayed the title character in MGM's 1929 talkie, with Richard Carle and Lewis Stone under Lionel Barrymore's direction, while Sam Wood was at the helm of the studio's 1937 remake, which starred Gladys George, John Beal, and Warren William. *Madame X* surfaced once again in 1966 as a vehicle for Lana Turner. This Universal production was directed by David Lowell Rich and featured Keir Dullea, John Forsythe, Burgess Meredith, and (in her final film) Constance Bennett.

Film versions: Pathé, 1916; Goldwyn, 1920; MGM, 1929; MGM, 1937; Universal, 1966.

138. "Monsieur Beaucaire," 6/21/37

Based on the play *Beaucaire*, by Booth Tarkington and E.G. Sutherland (1901), in turn based on the novel *Monsieur Beaucaire*, by Booth Tarkington (1901).

Intermission Guests: Evelyn Keyes, Paramount starlet (after Act 2), and Ray Jones, Universal portrait photographer (after Act 3).

Cast: Leslie Howard (Monsieur Beaucaire), Elissa Landi (Lady Mary), Pedro deCordoba (Major Molyneaux), Denis Green (the Duke of Winterset), Keith G. Kenneth (Captain Badger), Lou Merrill (Marquis de Mirepoix), Eric Snowden (François/Fop), Stella Francis (Miss Lucy/Third Lady), Coral Colebrook (Miss Charlotte/Fourth Lady), Leo McCabe (Beau Nash/Mate), Lionel Belmore (Town Crier/Gentleman), Frank Nelson (Thomas/Lackey), Joan Taylor (Second Lady/Crowd), Renee Orsell (First Lady/Crowd), Ross Forrester, Charles Emerson, Doris Louray, George Webb, Betty Stewart, and Helen Ray (Crowd).

Booth Tarkington's *Monsieur Beaucaire* brought Leslie Howard and Elissa Landi to the Hollywood *Lux* for the first time, and both are well cast in their roles of the nobleman posing as a barber and the lady he loves. (Richard Mansfield and Lettice Fairfax starred in the December 2, 1901, Broadway production at the Herald Square Theatre.)

Both films of *Monsieur Beaucaire* were released by Paramount: the first, made in 1924 as a vehicle for Rudolph Valentino, was directed by Sidney Olcott and also featured Doris Kenyon, while a much-altered comedy version, with Bob Hope, reached the screen in 1946. George Marshall directed this film, which also featured Joan Caulfield.

Lux presented a broadcast of the 1946 version on April 14, 1947.

Film versions: Paramount, 1924; Paramount, 1946.

139. "The Front Page," 6/28/37

Based on the play by Ben Hecht and Charles MacArthur (1928).

Intermission Guests: John MacSoud, fabric expert and motion picture technical adviser (after Act 2), and Kathleen Howard, *Photoplay* magazine fashion editor (after Act 3).

Cast: Walter Winchell (Hildy Johnson),

Josephine Hutchinson (Peggy Grant), James Gleason (Walter Burns), John Butler (Wilson), Frank Sheridan (Sheriff), Georgia Kane (Mrs. Grant), Eddie Marr (Murphy), Victor Rodman (Bensinger), Lou Merrill (Schwartz), Matt Moore (Kruger), Eddie Waller (Jacobi), Rolfe Sedan (Pincus), Sidney Newman (Diamond Louie/Taxi Driver), Bud McTaggart (Earl Williams), Ross Forrester (First Policeman), and Frank Nelson (Second Policeman/"a Voice").

Commercials: Grace Kerns, Emily Williams, and James Eagles.

The voice of syndicated newspaper columnist Walter Winchell was known to virtually every radio listener in the United States in 1937 via his nationwide radio commentaries. This, combined with the fact that he had begun his film career that same year (in 20th Century–Fox's *Wake Up and Live*), made him an appropriate choice for the role of Hildy Johnson in *Lux*'s adaptation of *The Front Page*. (The stars of the Broadway production, which opened August 14, 1928, at the Times Square Theatre, were Lee Tracy, Frances Fuller, and Osgood Perkins.) His familiar rapid-fire delivery suits the character of the savvy newspaper man, and James Gleason makes an interesting Walter Burns, the scheming editor who tries to keep from losing his ace reporter to marriage by constantly interfering in his life. Called in as a last-minute replacement was Josephine Hutchinson, who gives a memorable performance as Hildy Johnson's fiancée, Peggy Wilson. (Joan Bennett was originally announced to play this role, but an illness caused her to miss the broadcast.)

Though much of the interplay among the reporters is lost in the radio version, this is nonetheless a good adaptation of the play and has an even quicker pace than the original (or any of the film versions) because of its necessary condensation of plot. The *Lux* approach to the

play creates a somewhat lighter mood, due mostly to the total elimination of the tragic figure of Molly Malloy (who attempts suicide in the play).

Originally announced as an intermission guest was aviator Amelia Earhart, but she had fallen behind schedule on her around-the-world flight, so it was announced during the broadcast that she would be a guest on the following week's show, "if she should have arrived in time."

At the time of the *Lux* broadcast, *The Front Page* had been filmed once, in a 1931 production for United Artists. Lewis Milestone directed this Howard Hughes–produced movie, which starred Pat O'Brien, Mary Brian, and Adolphe Menjou, plus Matt Moore in the role of Kruger, the part he takes in the *Lux* version. Columbia's *His Girl Friday* (released in 1940) reworked the plot of the original and featured Cary Grant, Rosalind Russell, and Ralph Bellamy, under Howard Hawks's direction. Billy Wilder went back to the original for his 1974 Universal production, and the cast included Jack Lemmon, Susan Sarandon, and Walter Matthau. Another rendering of *His Girl Friday* reached the screen in 1988 under the title *Switching Channels*, which shifts the focus to a television newsroom. This most recent attempt features the direction of Ted Kotcheff and the performances of Burt Reynolds, Kathleen Turner, and Christopher Reeve.

"His Girl Friday" was broadcast on *Lux*'s September 30, 1940, program.

Film versions: United Artists, 1931; Columbia, 1940 (*His Girl Friday*); Universal, 1974; Tri-Star, 1988 (*Switching Channels*).

140. "Beau Brummel," 7/5/37

Based on the play by Clyde Fitch (1890).

Intermission Guest: Mrs. Wallace Reid (Dorothy Davenport), associate

July 5, 1937, cast of "Beau Brummel": Leo G. Carroll, Gene and Kathleen Lockhart, Robert Montgomery, Madge Evans, Cecil B. DeMille, Bramwell Fletcher, and Edwin Maxwell (photo: Photofest).

producer for Monogram Studios (after Act 2).

Cast: Robert Montgomery (Beau Brummel), Madge Evans (Mariana), Leo G. Carroll (Mortimer), Bramwell Fletcher (Reginald), Gene Lockhart (the Prince), Kathleen Lockhart (Mrs. St. Aubyn), Edwin Maxwell (Mr. Vincent), Ralph Kellard (Richard Brinsley Sheridan), Doris Lloyd (Kathleen/First Lady), Lou Merrill (Broker/Crowd), Wallis Roberts (Simpson), Frederick Sewell (Lord Manley/Crowd), John Lake (the Doctor/Crowd), Lillian Castle (Landlady), Frank Nelson (First Gentleman), Phyllis Coghlan (Third Lady/Fourth Lady), James Eagles (Fifth Gentleman/Crowd), Margaret Brayton (Second and Sixth Lady), Ross

Forrester (Crowd), Jerrie Gail (Crowd), and Marion Dennis (Crowd).

Commercial: Frank Nelson (Dance Director), Margaret Brayton (Jane).

The final Lux broadcast of the 1936-37 season featured Robert Montgomery as Beau Brummel (1778–1840), the legendary fop of fashion. Though George Bryan Brummel was, of course, a real person, the Lux presentation is based on Clyde Fitch's fictitious stage play, which fancifully moves the title character's period of fame to his years of seclusion. (Richard Mansfield undertook the role in the 1890 Broadway production.) Very little in the way of plot unfolds during the broadcast, but several memorably played scenes help to make the drama very entertaining.

Fitch's play was the subject of two film versions. The first was released by Warner Bros. in 1924, with John Barrymore in the title role and Mary Astor as his leading lady (under the direction of Harry Beaumont). MGM's talking version came 30 years later, with Curtis Bernhardt directing Stewart Granger and Elizabeth Taylor.

Film versions: Warner Bros., 1924; MGM, 1954.

Third Season
(September 13, 1937–July 4, 1938)

Columbia Broadcasting System, Monday, 9:00–10:00 P.M. *Host*: Cecil B. DeMille. *Announcer*: Melville Ruick. *Opening Announcer*: Frank Nelson. *Director*: Frank Woodruff. *Musical Director*: Lou Silvers. *Adaptations*: George Wells. *Sound Effects*: Charlie Forsyth.

141. "A Star Is Born," 9/13/37

Based on the 1937 Selznick International Pictures Corporation/UA film (screenplay by Dorothy Parker, Alan Campbell, Robert Carson, and John Lee Mahin; story by William A. Wellman and Robert Carson).

Intermission Guests: John LeRoy Johnston, managing editor of *Screenbook* and *Hollywood* magazines (after Act 2), and Sid Grauman, founder of Grauman's Chinese Theatre (after Act 3).

Cast: Janet Gaynor (Esther Blodgett [Vicki Lester]), Robert Montgomery (Norman Maine), May Robson (Granny), Lionel Stander (Libby), Lou Merrill (Oliver Niles), Chester Clute (Pop), John Gibson (Danny McGuire), Margaret Brayton (Anita), Edwin Max (M.C.), Forrest Taylor (Judge/Butler), Frank Nelson (Billy Moon/Charlie), Lucille Meredith (Maid/Operator), Grace Kern (a Waitress), Myra Marsh (Miss Philips/Crowd), Sidney Newman (Director), James Eagles (Otto), Gil Patric (Police Officer/Crowd), and Ross Forrester (Photographer).

Commercial: John Deering, Nancy Leach.

The second season of *Lux* in Hollywood opened with an adaptation of the recent David O. Selznick hit, *A Star Is Born*. A more fitting opening broadcast could hardly have been selected, as the drama presents an affectionate, realistic picture of the movie capital itself and gives the *Lux* producers an excellent foundation on which to build their usual tribute to motion pictures. Janet Gaynor offers the same sincere performance as the naive, movie-struck girl determined to break into motion pictures that earned her a well-deserved Academy Award nomination for the film. Her first *Lux* appearance illustrates that she is a splendid radio performer as well. It is also fortunate that May Robson and Lionel Stander were recruited to repeat their film portrayals for the microphone, for, small though their roles may be, their presence contributes enormously to the flavor of the program. Indeed, the supporting roles in the film add a *great* deal of color to the production, and, in addition to Robson and Stander, these roles are capably filled for the broadcast version.

A rehearsal of "A Star Is Born" (September 13, 1937), with Margaret Brayton (seated at left), Janet Gaynor and Robert Montgomery (center), and Lou Merrill (seated at right, closest to camera) (photo: Photofest).

Chester Clute is heard in Edgar Kennedy's screen role, and John Gibson is given the part of the young assistant director who befriends the heroine (Andy Devine in the movie). Radio character actor Lou Merrill, who played supporting roles of varying importance in nearly all the *Lux* broadcasts during the first Hollywood season, is for the first time given a featured part as producer Oliver Niles; he even receives billing *before* the play. (New to the radio version is the suggestion that Oliver Niles may have a romantic interest in his new star.) Leading man Robert Montgomery, who portrays the irresponsible but likable Norman Maine (Fredric March in the film) also gives a thoroughly capable performance.

While certain visual aspects of the film are obviously not easily adaptable to the airwaves, *Lux*'s straightforward radio version does do justice to the excellent screenplay of Dorothy Parker, Alan Campbell, Robert Carson, and John Lee Mahin. During the curtain call, Miss Gaynor thanks producer David O. Selznick and director William Wellman for their part in the creation of the movie. (Woodruff noted, "Smooth show. Gaynor was marvelous.")

Besides the famed 1937 release of the David O. Selznick *A Star Is Born* (which won an Academy Award for best original story as well as a special Oscar for W. Howard Greene for outstanding color photography), there have been two other versions: the George Cukor–directed 1954 Warner Bros. film (with musical numbers), starring Judy Garland (who would appear in *Lux*'s

1942 broadcast) and James Mason; and the 1976 Frank Pierson–directed rendering, with Barbra Streisand and Kris Kristofferson.

Lux's second version was aired on December 28, 1942.

Film versions: Selznick International Pictures Corporation/UA, 1937; Warner Bros., 1954; Warner Bros., 1976.

142. "The Outsider," 9/20/37

Based on the play by Dorothy Brandon (1924).

Intermission Guests: Anne Bauchens, Paramount film editor (after Act 2), and Milton H. Berry, founder and head of the Milton H. Berry Institute for Paralysis Correctment (after Act 3).

Cast: Fredric March (Anton Ragatzy), Florence Eldridge (Lalage Sturdee), Douglass Montgomery (Basil Owen), Donald Crisp (Dr. Sturdee), Marcelle Corday (Madame Klost), Vernon Steele (Dr. Tolley), Ramsey Hill (Dr. Land), Wyndham Standing (Dr. Israel), Coral Colebrook (a Nurse), Maureen Roden Ryan (Telephone Operator), Doris Louray (Crowd), Frank Nelson (Orderly/Crowd), and Lou Merrill (Man/Crowd).

Commercials: Grace Kern (Annie), Margaret Brayton (Elsie), and Ross Forrester (Kim).

Fredric March fans who regretted his absence from the *Lux* broadcast on September 13 were undoubtedly consoled by his appearance the next week in "The Outsider." Dorothy Brandon's 1924 play had been a notable success on Broadway, with Lionel Atwill as the title character and Katharine Cornell as Lalage. (The other principals were Pat Somerset, Lester Lonergran, and Fernanda Eliseu). In the broadcast, Florence Eldridge takes the role of Lalage Sturdee, the cripple who looks to Anton Ragatzy (March) to cure her, despite charges by members of the medical profession (including her own

father) that he is a "quack." The outcome may be predictable, but the fine performances of March, Eldridge, and the supporting cast make the drama entertaining.

Anne Bauchens, who appears as a guest after Act 2, had served as film editor on DeMille's motion pictures since 1918 and would continue to edit all his pictures through his last in 1956. The second intermission guest, Milton H. Berry, was the founder and head of the Institute for Paralysis Correctment (located near Hollywood), and was chosen to appear because of the parallels between his career and that of Anton Ragatzy of the play.

Lou Tellegen and Jacqueline Logan starred in Fox's 1926 Rowland V. Lee–directed film, while the 1931 Cinemahouse/MGM production, directed by Harry Lachman, featured Harold Huth and Joan Barry. Paul Stein directed ABPC's 1939 release, which has George Sanders and Mary McGuire in the leads.

Film versions: Fox, 1926; Cinemahouse/MGM, 1931; Alliance, 1939.

*143. "Cimarron," 9/27/37

Based on the 1931 RKO film (screenplay by Howard Estabrook), in turn based on the novel by Edna Ferber (1930).

Intermission Guests: Edith Gwynn, Hollywood columnist for the *New York Mirror* (after Act 2), and Edna Ferber, author (after Act 3).

Cast: Clark Gable (Yancey Cravat), Virginia Bruce (Sabra Cravat), John Gibson (Jess Rickey), Forrest Taylor (Dr. Hefner), Leora Thatcher (Mrs. Hefner), Lee Prather (Lon Yountiss), Perry Ivins (Pat Leary), Gretchen Thomas (Felice), Grace Kern (Aunt), Noreen Gammill (Aunt), Ross Forrester (a Citizen), Elvia Allman (Mrs. Wyatt), Warren McCollum (Cim/Newsboy), Harold Wilson (Oscar), Lauretta

Puck (Secretary), Victor Rodman (a Prospector), Earle Ross (Red), Lou Merrill (Senator Brown), Frank Nelson (Joe), James Eagles (Lieutenant), John Marshall (Engineer), and James Sylvan (Crowd).

Commercial: Elvia Allman, Lauretta Puck.

Lux's adaptation of *Cimarron*, RKO's episodic Wesley Ruggles–directed picture of the birth and growth of Oklahoma, starred Clark Gable in Richard Dix's movie role of restless wanderer Yancey Cravat and Virginia Bruce in the Irene Dunne photoplay part of the long-suffering wife who patiently holds down the fort during his frequent (and lengthy) absences. Frank Woodruff deemed the broadcast "a good show—stirring and vital at times . . . Gable and Bruce gave sterling performances. Production could have been smoother."

A 1960 version of *Cimarron* was produced by MGM and featured Glenn Ford and Maria Schell, under Anthony Mann's direction. (The 1931 RKO film received an Academy Award for best picture.)

Film versions: RKO, 1931; MGM, 1960.

144. "Dodsworth," 10/4/37

Based on the play by Sidney Howard (1934), in turn based on the novel by Sinclair Lewis (1929).

Intermission Guest: Arthur M. Levy, head stylist and wardrobe manager at 20th Century–Fox (after Act 2).

Cast: Walter Huston (Sam Dodsworth), Nan Sunderland (Fran Dodsworth), Barbara O'Neil (Edith Cortright), Barbara Kent (Emily), Pedro deCordoba (Arnold Israel), Harlan Briggs (Tubby), Martha Wentworth (Madame dePenable/Mary/Theresa), Hugh Huntley (Clyde Lockert), Frank Nelson (Kurt), Gretchen Thomas (Matey), Lou Merrill (Travel Agent/ Second Man/Crowd), Margaret Brayton (First and Third Woman), James Eagles (Page Boy/First Man), and Jerrie Gail (Second Woman).

Commercial: Jerrie Gail, Beverly Cravens.

Less than six months after its first presentation on *Lux*, "Dodsworth" was once again transmitted over the airwaves (as a substitution for the previously planned but unaccountably canceled "Copperhead"). Whereas the earlier broadcast had featured the three stars of the Broadway production (Walter Huston, Fay Bainter, and Nan Sunderland) in their original roles, Bainter does not participate in this revival performance. Instead, Nan Sunderland takes the stage part of Fran, while her stage role of Edith goes to Barbara O'Neil. (A third member of the Broadway cast, Harlan Briggs, reprises his character Tubby for the radio play.)

See 4/12/37 for information on film version.

145. "Stella Dallas," 10/11/37

Based on the 1937 Samuel Goldwyn/United Artists film (screenplay by Sarah Y. Mason and Victor Heerman; dramatization by Harry Wagstaff Gribble and Gertrude Purcell; additional dialogue by Joe Bigelow), in turn based on the 1925 Samuel Goldwyn/United Artists film (screenplay by Frances Marion), in turn based on the novel by Olive Higgins Prouty (1923).

Intermission Guest: T. Keith Glennon, Paramount operations manager (after Act 2).

Cast: Barbara Stanwyck (Stella Dallas), John Boles (Stephen Dallas), Anne Shirley (Laurel Dallas), Barbara O'Neil (Helen Morrison), Lou Merrill (Ed Munn), Bruce Satterlee (Cornelius Morrison), Jack Egger (Lee Morrison), Dickie Jones (John Morrison), Wallace Roberts (Mr. Cooper/Butler), Sada

Cowan (Mrs. Cooper/First Woman), Hudson Faussett (Mr. Chandler/ Crowd), Grace Kern (First Act Girl/Carrie), James Eagles (Charlie/ Third Act Man), Teresa Harris (Edna/ Girl), Frank Nelson (Mr. Morley/Second Man in Act 1), Elia Braca (Secretary/Fourth Girl in Act 3), Margaret Brayton (Lynn/Second Woman in Act 2/Third Girl in Act 3), Joan Taylor (Doris/Second Girl in Act 3), Margaret McKay (Telegraph Girl/ Second Woman in Act 3), Mary Lansing (a Mill Girl/Baby Cries), Ross Forrester (Pullman Porter/ Third Man in Act 1), and Alexander Lockwood (a Man Reading, Act 1/ Policeman).

Commercial: Frank Nelson (Publicity Man), Joan Taylor (Fashion Editor).

Lux's third anniversary show featured a radio version of "Stella Dallas," the drama of a mother who sacrifices her own happiness for the benefit of her cherished daughter. Although the famous story was created by Olive Higgins Prouty for her 1923 best-selling novel, the *Lux* broadcast is actually an adaptation of Samuel Goldwyn's 1937 film, itself a remake of his 1925 motion picture (this first version used the novel as its source). Present from the 1937 photoplay for the microphone drama are Barbara Stanwyck (making her *Lux* debut), John Boles, Anne Shirley, and Barbara O'Neil. Stanwyck's memorable characterization comes across very well over the air, conveying Stella's essential vulgarity, yet always retaining the audience's sympathy. Lou Merrill is the obnoxious (and often intoxicated) Ed Munn. (Supporting players from the film cast include Bruce Satterlee, Jack Egger, and Dickie Jones.)

The 1925 Goldwyn/United Artists release of *Stella Dallas* was directed by Henry King and starred Belle Bennett, Ronald Colman, Lois Moran (in her film debut), Alice Joyce, and Jean Her-

sholt. In 1990, yet another version of the film reached the screen. Entitled *Stella*, the production featured Bette Midler and Trini Alvarado, under the direction of John Erman.

Only two weeks after this *Lux* broadcast, a daytime serial version of *Stella Dallas* began on WEAF in New York. This well-remembered "soap opera" soon began its long run on the NBC network, lasting until 1955.

Film versions: United Artists, 1925; Touchstone Pictures/Gundwyn, 1990 (*Stella*).

146. "Up Pops the Devil," 10/18/37

Based on the play by John Marston and Albert Hackett (1930).

Intermission Guests: Jimmy Starr, Hollywood columnist for the *Los Angeles Herald* and *Express* (after Act 2), and Howard Greer, dress designer (after Act 3).

Cast: Fred MacMurray (Steve Merrick), Madge Evans (Anne Merrick), Janet McLeay (Luella May Carroll), John Marston (Gilbert Morrell), Charles Tannen (Biney Hatfield), Frank Nelson (George Kent), Dink Trout (Laundry Man), Marie Hammond (Mrs. Platt), Lou Merrill (Mr. Platt/Crowd), Anne Morrison (Secretary), Robert Whitney (Head Waiter/ Crowd), Ross Forrester (Stage Doorman/Crowd), Doris Louray, Jean Lennox, Jerrie Gail, David Kerman, and George Webb (Crowd).

Commercial: Anne Morrison (Marsha), Betty Stewart (Jennie).

Fred MacMurray and Madge Evans made return engagements on *Lux* for an adaptation of John Marston and Albert Hackett's play *Up Pops the Devil*, which concerns a budding author who reluctantly agrees to stay home and write while his wife supports him. The radio rendering turns out to be an amusing comedy, helped along by the performances of the cast, which includes Janet McLeay and (co-author) John Marston, who created the roles of Luella May Carroll and Gilbert Morrell in the 1930 Broadway production. (Also appearing in the play, which opened September 1, 1930, at the Masque Theatre, were Roger Pryor, Sally Bates, and Albert Hackett.) An alteration of the original finds Steve and Anne married as the *Lux* version begins, though they were living together in the stage production. (This change is also made in the screenplay of the 1931 film.)

Paramount's 1931 motion picture of *Up Pops the Devil*, which was directed by A. Edward Sutherland, starred Norman Foster, Carole Lombard, Joyce Compton, Theodor von Eltz, and Skeets Gallagher.

Film version: Paramount, 1931.

147. "Arrowsmith," 10/25/37

Based on the 1931 Samuel Goldwyn/ United Artists film (screenplay by Sidney Howard), in turn based on the novel by Sinclair Lewis (1925).

Intermission Guests: Terry Hunt, "physical director of the stars," United Artists Studios (after Act 2), and John R. Kissenger, former U.S. Army private who participated in Dr. Walter Reed's experiments to discover a cure for yellow fever (after Act 3).

Cast: Spencer Tracy (Martin Arrowsmith), Fay Wray (Leora), Helen Wood (Joyce Lanyon), Frank Reicher (Dr. Gottlieb), John Qualen (Henry Novak), Ross Forrester (Terry Wickett), Crauford Kent (Dr. Dewitt Tubbs), Forrest Taylor (Dr. Sondelius), Emory Parnell (Veterinarian), Lou Merrill (Mr. Twyford), Frank Nelson (a Steward/Reporter), Harold Wilson (Olaff/ Reporter), Leora Thatcher (Head Nurse/ Receptionist), Mary Lansing (Switchboard Girl/Baby), James Eagles (Reporter/Deck Steward), and David Kerman (Reporter).

Chorus: Zaruhi Elmassion, Eleanor Colson, Barbara Whitson, Rosalie Barker-Frye, Mildred Carroll, Millie Jewell, Enrico Ricardi, Tudor Williams, George Gramlich, Stewart Bair, George Weatherill, and Martin Provenson.

Commercial: Frank Nelson (Director), David Kerman (Joe), and Mary Jane Falvey (Miss Sherman).

For the second time in four weeks, *Lux* featured a story that originated from the pen of Sinclair Lewis. As with "Dodsworth" of October 4, "Arrowsmith" is based not directly on the novel but on Sidney Howard's adaptation of it (in this case, for the screen). Certain semi-risqué elements of the book have been toned down for the microphone drama; Martin Arrowsmith's relationship with Joyce Lanyon, for example, went from a full-fledged affair in the book, to a flirtation in the film, to something resembling a casual acquaintance in the broadcast (though their final meeting toward the end of the story suggests that there was more between them than we were made aware of).

Ronald Colman portrays the title character in the John Ford–directed movie, while Spencer Tracy is *Lux*'s Dr. Martin Arrowsmith and is quite credible as the dedicated man of science. Fay Wray is his wife, Leora, the role Helen Hayes takes in the film version, while Myrna Loy's film part of other woman Joyce Lanyon and A.E. Anson's role of Dr. Gottlieb (the young doctor's mentor) are filled by Helen Wood and Frank Reicher, respectively. Character actor John Qualen, who plays farmer Henry Novak in the motion picture, repeats his characterization for the broadcast.

In a somewhat unusual departure, a chorus is employed in the program's incidental music, and their wordless chant proves moving in the scene of Leora's death.

"A Free Soul" (November 1, 1937), with (left to right) Jack Arnold, Charles Winninger, Cecil B. DeMille, Ginger Rogers, and Don Ameche (photo: Photofest).

Act 3 intermission guest John R. Kissenger, a former U.S. Army private, nobly permitted himself to be used as a guinea pig to help Dr. Walter Reed find his cure for yellow fever in 1900. (At this time, Dr. Reed was the director of a commission to investigate the cause and transmission of yellow fever in Cuba.)

Film version: United Artists, 1931.

148. "A Free Soul," 11/1/37

Based on the play by Willard Mack (1928), in turn based on the novel by Adela Rogers St. John (1927).

Intermission Guests: William A. Brady, theatrical producer (from New York City; after Act 2), and Adrian, MGM fashion designer (after Act 3).

Cast: Ginger Rogers (Jan Ashe), Don Ameche (Ace Wilfong), Charles Winninger (Stephen Ashe), Jack Arnold

(Dwight Sutro), Claire Whitney (Dorothea), Myra Marsh (Grace), Eddie Marr (Abe), Eddie Kane (Charlie), Lou Merrill (District Attorney), Norman Field (Judge), James Eagles (Officer), Justina Wayne (the Maid), Sally Creighton (Secretary), Frank Nelson (Foreman), Ken Chaville (a Newsboy), Ross Forrester (Newsboy), and George Webb (Newsboy/Tim).

Commercial: Margaret Brayton, Grace Kerns, and Doris Louray.

Ginger Rogers is given another crack at a "serious" role thanks to *Lux*, via its adaptation of Willard Mack's *A Free Soul*, a melodrama about a free-spirited girl who goes against her father's wishes and begins an illicit relationship with an unsavory underworld character. Both she and Don Ameche (in his *Lux* debut) offer professional performances, but it is veteran character actor Charles

Winninger who is given the meatiest role as alcoholic attorney Stephen Ashe. The play's most famous scene, in which the lawyer makes a courtroom speech blaming himself for Dwight Sutro's death, comes toward the end of the final act, and Winninger succeeds in making it the showpiece it was obviously intended to be.

Persons familiar only with MGM's 1931 movie version, which stars Norma Shearer, Clark Gable, Lionel Barrymore, and Leslie Howard, are apt to be in for a surprise upon encountering the *Lux* broadcast, as (except for similar opening scenes) the picture and radio versions are so different from each other that one might not even recognize them as coming from the same source.

The man who produced *A Free Soul* on Broadway in 1928 and who created the part of Stephen Ashe in that production (which opened at the Playhouse Theatre on January 1, 1928, and also featured Kay Johnson, Melvyn Douglas, and Lester Lonergran) was the legendary theatrical figure William A. Brady, who is a guest after Act 2.

Film version: MGM, 1931.

149. "She Loves Me Not," 11/8/37
Based on the 1934 Paramount film (screenplay by Benjamin Glazer), in turn based on the play by Howard Lindsay (1933), from the novel by Edward Hope (1933).

Intermission Guests: Una McClelland, University of Southern California cinematography student (after Act 2), and Molly Merick, Hollywood columnist for the *San Francisco Examiner* (after Act 3).

Cast: Bing Crosby (Paul Lawton), Joan Blondell (Curley Flagg), Nan Grey (Midge Mercer), Barbara Weeks (Frances), Sterling Holloway (Buzz Jones), William Frawley (Gus McNeal), Lou Merrill (Senator Gray/Mr. Jones),

Margaret Brayton (Tess/Martha), Lee Millar (Dean Mercer), Ross Forrester (Mugg), Frank Nelson (Radio Announcer), Justina Wayne (the Mother), Sidney Newman (Mr. Lawton/Third Newsboy), Ernie Adams (a Truckman/Second Newsboy), Jerrie Gail (Telephone Operator/Miss Higley), James Eagles (Newsboy in Acts 1 and 3/Crowd), Patsy Perrin (Taps [sound effects]), and Millie Walters (Singer).

Commercial: Dorothy Scott.

Crooner Bing Crosby, a radio and film star since 1931, made his *Lux* debut on November 8, 1937, in *She Loves Me Not*, a Broadway success (as authored by Howard Lindsay, from Edward Hope's novel) during the 1933-34 season. Paramount purchased the comedy of a college student who reluctantly provides a hideout for a girl who has witnessed a gangland slaying, and tailored it into a musical vehicle for Crosby (with Miriam Hopkins as Curley Flagg) in 1934. (Others in the cast of the Elliott Nugent–directed photoplay are Kitty Carlisle, Judith Allen, Edward Nugent, and Lynne Overman.) Crosby, who appears through the courtesy of his own show, NBC's *Kraft Music Hall*, is given the chance to sing three numbers from the score of the film: "I'm Hummin' (I'm Whistlin', I'm Singin')" (Act 1); "Straight from the Shoulder (Right from the Heart)" (Act 2) (both with words by Mack Gordon and music by Harry Revel); "Love in Bloom" (lyric by Leo Robin, music by Ralph Rainger; Act 3). ("Love in Bloom" is briefly reprised in the finale.) Joan Blondell is amusing as the dim-witted chorus girl on the lam who is forced to disguise herself as a boy, and Nan Grey is fine as Crosby's love interest, Midge. Barbara Weeks, Sterling Holloway, and William Frawley make up the remainder of the featured cast.

Paramount released a version of *She*

Loves Me Not in 1942 entitled *True to the Army.* The musical, which retained only one song ("Love in Bloom") from the earlier film, was directed by Albert S. Rogell and starred Allan Jones, Ann Miller, and Judy Canova. The version of 20th Century–Fox, which was released in 1955 under the title *How to Be Very, Very Popular,* starred Betty Grable (in her last film), Robert Cummings, and Sheree North, under the direction of Nunnally Johnson.

Film versions: Paramount, 1934; Paramount, 1942 (*True to the Army*); 20th Century–Fox (*How to Be Very, Very Popular*).

150. "Come and Get It," 11/15/37

Based on the 1936 Samuel Goldwyn/ United Artists film (screenplay by Jules Furthman and Jane Murfin), in turn based on the novel by Edna Ferber.

Intermission Guest: Helen Rowland, syndicated columnist (from New York City; after Act 2).

Cast: Edward Arnold (Barney Glascow), Anne Shirley (Lotta Bostrom), Walter Brennan (Swan Bostrom), Lew Ayres (Bernie Glascow), Mary Nash (Emma Louise Glascow), Mady Christians (Karie), Marion Burns (Evvie Glascow), Perry Ivins (Mr. Hewitt), Galen Galt (Sid), Louis LeBey (Bengt), Earle Ross (Cookie), James Eagles (a Dealer), Frank Coghlan, Jr. (Chore Boy), Frank Nelson (Minister), Harold Wilson (First Lumberjack), David Kerman (Second Lumberjack), Lou Merrill (Third Lumberjack), Ross Forrester (Fourth Lumberjack), and Mildred Carroll (Singer).

Commercial: Sarah Selby, Sista Axselle, and Lauretta Puck.

Star character actor Edward Arnold made his *Lux* debut in one of his memorable film roles, that of Barney Glascow in *Come and Get It*, which focuses on an ambitious lumberman who climbs the ladder of success, casting aside old friends and values en route. Arnold proved to be an excellent radio performer and would go on to become a popular personality in the medium. (Besides his many guest appearances, he starred in ABC's *Mr. President* series from 1947 to 1953.) Others in Howard Hawks's 1936 movie of Edna Ferber's *Come and Get It* are Frances Farmer, Joel McCrea, Walter Brennan (who won the best supporting actor Oscar for his portrayal of Swan), Mary Nash, and Mady Christians. The latter three actors all repeat their film parts in the *Lux* version.

Despite a painful injury, Arnold performed flawlessly, which prompted Frank Woodruff to comment: "Great performances by a great cast. Arnold handicapped by a bad knee, but trouped magnificently."

Film version: United Artists, 1936.

151. "The Petrified Forest," 11/22/37

Based on the play by Robert E. Sherwood (1934).

Intermission Guests: Charles H. Smith, ranger and superintendent, Petrified Forest National Monument, Arizona (after Act 2), and Nick Janios, proprietor of Café de Paris, studio restaurant at 20th Century–Fox (after Act 3).

Cast: Herbert Marshall (Alan Squier), Margaret Sullavan (Gabrielle Maple), Eduardo Ciannelli (Duke Mantee), Donald Meek (Gramp), Wallis Clark (Mr. Chisholm), Frank Milan (Boze), Wally Maher (Jackie), George Travell (Hank), Martha Wentworth (Mrs. Chisholm/Paula), Margaret Brayton (Doris), Frank Melton (Lineman/State Trooper), Lou Merrill (Doctor/Jones), Frank Nelson (Police Announcer/Radio Announcer), Ross Forrester (Joseph), James Eagles (Bank Teller/Second Lineman/Second Police Announcer), Doris Louray, and Grace Kern (Crowd).

Commercial: Myra Marsh, Margaret McKay.

As *The Petrified Forest* had been a successful play on Broadway in 1934, and a hit movie for Warner Bros. in 1936, it was almost inevitable that Robert E. Sherwood's drama should find its way to *Lux*. (The New York stage production had starred Leslie Howard, Peggy Conklin, Humphrey Bogart, Charles Dow Clark, Frank Milan, and Blanche Sweet.) The Archie Mayo–directed film stars Leslie Howard, Bette Davis, Humphrey Bogart, Charley Grapewin, Dick Foran, and Genevieve Tobin (the only player from either cast to repeat his role in *Lux*'s production is Frank Milan as Boze). Herbert Marshall and Margaret Sullavan give sincere performances as the lovers, Donald Meek makes a convincing Gramp Maple, and Eduardo Ciannelli (the well-known character villain of films and theatre) creates a memorable interpretation of gangster Duke Mantee.

There are a few brief scenes added to the radio play which succeed in "opening up" the production, including one that depicts a bank robbery by Mantee's gang at the very beginning, but the most jarring addition is the incongruous happy ending that is tacked onto the conclusion of the drama.

Warner Bros. released a remake of *The Petrified Forest* in 1945, which updates the action to World War II. Directed by Edward A. Blatt, this version features Helmut Dantine as an escaped Nazi who takes refuge in a desert hotel, while Philip Dorn and Jean Sullivan play the Leslie Howard and Bette Davis characters.

Film versions: Warner Bros., 1936; Warner Bros., 1945 (*Escape in the Desert*).

152. "Peg o' My Heart," 11/29/37

Based on the play by Hartley Manners (1912).

Intermission Guests: Earl Johnson, trainer of motion picture dogs (after Act 2), and Marjorie Williams, director of the Hollywood Studio Club (after Act 3).

Cast: Marion Davies (Peg), Brian Aherne (Sir Gerald Markham), Benita Hume (Ethel), J. Farrell MacDonald (Patrick Seamus O'Connell), Aileen Pringle (Mrs. Chichester), Gerald Oliver Smith (Alaric), Edgar Norton (Jarvis), Edward Broadley (David), Eric Snowden (Christopher Brent), Doris Lloyd (Mrs. Brent), Michael Fitzmaurice (Port Officer/the Dog/Second Guard), Wallace Roberts (Flint), Lou Merrill (Bradley), Frank Nelson (a Guard), Ingeborg Tillisch, Doris Louray (Irish Women), Mary Jane Falvey, and Ross Forrester (Crowd).

Commercial: Renee Orsell, Marion Dennis.

Lux presented J. Hartley Manners's comedy "Peg o' My Heart" for the second time on November 29. Marion Davies, who starred in MGM's delightful film version of the famous play, repeats her splendid characterization of the Irish waif who goes to live with an English family "of quality," and Brian Aherne makes an interesting Sir Gerald. Director Frank Woodruff stated enthusiastically that a "good cast made the most of this play. Davies gave her best performance of series."

The movie's theme song, "Sweetheart Darlin'" (words by Gus Kahn, music by Herbert Stothart), is used by Lou Silvers in the incidental music as the main theme, and Davies also sings a snatch of it early in the program.

Earl Johnson, the second act intermission guest, discusses his occupation of training dogs for motion pictures, and appearing with him is his most famous pupil, Lightning, who participates in a *Lux* commercial. Act 3 intermission guest Marjorie Williams, the

Benita Hume, Brian Aherne, Aileen Pringle, Marion Davies, and Cecil B. DeMille in "Peg o' My Heart" (November 29, 1937) (photo: Photofest).

director of the Hollywood Studio Club (the famous residence for young women starting show business careers), talks of the purpose of the club and mentions some of its most famous tenants.

See 2/3/35 for information on Broadway and film versions.

Film versions: Famous Players–Lasky, 1919 (unreleased); Metro, 1923; MGM, 1933.

153. "These Three," 12/6/37

Based on the 1936 Samuel Goldwyn film (screenplay by Lillian Hellman), in turn based on the play *The Children's Hour,* by Lillian Hellman (1934).

Intermission Guests: The Abbe children (Patience, Richard, and Johnny), authors (after Act 2).

Cast: Barbara Stanwyck (Martha Dobie), Errol Flynn (Joe Cardin), Mary Astor (Karen Wright), Alma Kruger (Mrs. Tilford), Marcia Mae Jones (Rosalie), Helen Parrish (Mary Tilford), Constance Collier (Aunt Lilly), Dorothy Gray (Helen), Helena Grant (Agatha), Lou Merrill (Taxi Driver), Frank Nelson (Conductor), Sidney Newman (Drugstore Clerk), Ross Forrester (Burton's Chauffeur), Estelle Hyman, Lois Lee, and June Smaney (Crowd).

Chorus: Eloise Spann, Mills Jewell, Dorothy Jackson, Nancy Kellogg, Mildred Carroll, June Robbins, Elva Lois Kellogg, Katherine Rue, Barbara Whitson, Winona Black, and Enrico Ricardi.

Commercial: Mary Lansing, Sista Axselle.

These Three, as produced by Samuel Goldwyn and released through United Artists in 1936, is Lillian Hellman's own screen adaptation of her 1934 Broadway play, *The Children's Hour.* Certain aspects of the stage production's plot made a straight film version out of the question, but Hellman's screenplay, far from being a mere shadow of the original, is an outstanding drama in its own right. The movie, which was directed by William Wyler and starred Miriam Hopkins, Joel McCrea, Merle Oberon, Alma Kruger, Marcia Mae Jones, and Bonita Granville, tells the story of two young ladies who operate a successful school for girls and whose lives are shattered by the slanderous accusations of a discontented pupil. In an interesting bit of recasting, the three leads in *Lux*'s adaptation are Barbara Stanwyck, Errol Flynn, and Mary Astor (in her *Lux* debut), all of whom give very good performances. The one-hour radio play necessarily eliminates several scenes (and even alters key character motivations and situations), yet the power of the drama remains intact.

William Wyler also directed United Artists' second version of *The Children's Hour* in 1962 when the more permissive sixties allowed Hellman's play to reach the screen with the original theme unaltered. The lead performers in that motion picture are Shirley MacLaine, James Garner, Audrey Hepburn, Fay Bainter, and a veteran of the earlier production, Miriam Hopkins (as Aunt Lilly).

Film versions: United Artists, 1936; United Artists, 1962 (*The Children's Hour*).

154. "The 39 Steps," 12/13/37

Based on the 1935 Gaumont British film (scenario and adaptation by Charles Bennett and Alma Reville), in turn based on the novel by John Buchan (1915).

Intermission Guest: Major C.E. Russell, formerly of the U.S. Intelligence Service (after Act 2).

Cast: Robert Montgomery (Richard Hannay), Ida Lupino (Pamela), Isabel Jewell (Annabella Smith), Gene Lockhart (Mr. Memory), Leonard Mudie (Professor Bartlett), Reginald Sheffield (Detective), Herbert Evans (Second Detective), Keith Kenneth (Third Detective), Lionel Belmore (Inn Keeper), Vernon Steele (Cart Driver/Doctor), Edgar Norton (Manager of the Music Hall), Eric Wilton (Cockney Traveler/Manager of the Palladium), Raymond Lawrence (Cockney Traveler), Ward Lane (Butler), Eric Snowden, Norman Ainsley (Scotsmen), Sibyl Harris (a Rowdy), Phyllis Coghlan (a Woman), Frank Nelson (Usher), Lou Merrill (Conductor/Doorman), Ross Forrester (Boy/Fourth Rowdy), Edith Craighead, Lillian O'Marra, George Webb, and Grace Kern (Crowd).

Commercial: Gretchen Thomas, Dorothy Gray.

The "39 Steps" broadcast by *Lux* presents the program with another milestone: its first adaptation of a British film. The motion picture version of John Buchan's novel of espionage became a hit in the United States and helped to establish a reputation in America for the man who directed it, Alfred Hitchcock. (The movie relates the plight of a man who is fleeing from the police for a crime he did not commit, and from a group of organized spies for the knowledge he possesses.) It is unfortunate that *Lux* did not return to Buchan's novel for the source of its drama, for in Alfred Hitchcock's film (which bears only the slightest resemblance to the book), the story is told so visually that it adapts rather clumsily to the air in certain sequences. The radio play does, however, offer fine performances by Robert Montgomery and Ida Lupino in the leads (played by

Robert Donat and Madeleine Carroll in the picture), as well as a good supporting cast headed by Gene Lockhart.

The 1959 release featuring Kenneth More and Taina Elg is based on the 1935 film and was directed by Ralph Thomas, while the 1978 Rank/Norfolk production was directed by Don Sharp and featured Robert Powell and Karen Dotrice in the leads.

Film versions: Gaumont-British, 1935; J. Arthur Rank/20th Century–Fox, 1959; Rank/Norfolk International, 1978.

155. "The Song of Songs," 12/20/37
Based on the 1933 Paramount film (screenplay by Leo Birniski and Samuel Hoffenstein), in turn based on the play by Edward Sheldon (1914), which is based on the novel *Das Hohe Lied*, by Hermann Sudermann (1909).

Intermission Guest: Walt Disney, "creator of Mickey Mouse and the Silly Symphonies" (after Act 3).

Cast: Marlene Dietrich (Lily), Douglas Fairbanks, Jr. (Richard Waldow), Lionel Atwill (Baron von Merzbach), Pedro deCordoba (the Art Dealer), Justina Wayne (Mrs. Rasmussen), Margaret Brayton (Miss Volk), Fred MacKaye (Walter), Victor Rodman (Butler), Elizabeth Ellis (Maid/Frau Holden), Eddie Kane (Manager), James Eagles (a Man), Sidney Newman (Station Guard), Charles Emerson (a Porter), Frank Nelson (a Cabbie), Ross Forrester (Conductor), and Lou Merrill (Main Cabbie).

Chorus: George Gramlich, Hubert Head, Morton Provenson, Enrico Ricardi, Bernice Altstock, Mildred Carroll, Catherine Rue, and Clemence Gifford.

Commercial: Marie Hammond, Jerrie Gail, and Betty Stewart.

Marlene Dietrich returned for another visit to *Lux* in an adaptation of her 1933 Rouben Mamoulian–directed film *The Song of Songs*, which focuses upon a naive girl whose life is dramatically altered after she poses for a statue created by a young sculptor. Making his Hollywood *Lux* debut is Douglas Fairbanks, Jr., who portrays the artist (Brian Aherne's screen role) who falls in love with her, and Lionel Atwill reprises his picture characterization as the wealthy older man she marries. All three stars give effective performances, with Miss Dietrich handling her transformation from naive girl to embittered woman most convincingly. Lou Silvers uses the title song, composed for the Paramount film, as part of the incidental music (words by Lucas; music by Moya).

Two film versions of Sheldon's play preceded Paramount's 1933 production: Famous Players–Lasky's photoplay, which starred Elsie Ferguson and Cecil Fletcher, under Joseph Kaufman's direction, and the 1924 Paramount release, *Lily of the Dust*, starring Pola Negri and Ben Lyon in a cast directed by Dmitri Buchowetzki.

Film versions: Famous Players–Lasky/Artcraft, 1918; Paramount, 1924 (*Lily of the Dust*); Paramount, 1933.

156. "Beloved Enemy," 12/27/37
Based on the 1936 Samuel Goldwyn/United Artists film (screenplay by John Balderston, Rose Franken, David Hart, and William Brown Meloney).

Intermission Guests: Walter J. Hoffman, creator of special battle effects for motion pictures (after Act 2), and Ted Lesser, head of the Paramount Studios talent department (after Act 3).

Cast: Brian Aherne (Dennis Riordan), Madeleine Carroll (Helen Attleigh), C. Aubrey Smith (Lord Attleigh), Donald Crisp (Burke), Neil Fitzgerald (Jerry O'Rourke), Lurene Tuttle (Cathleen O'Brian), Jackie Egger (Paedar O'Brien), Crauford Kent (Colonel Loder), Douglas

Gordon (Sergeant Hawkins), Wyndham Standing (Preston/Second Man), Leslie Frances (Perrins/Officer), Michael Fitzmaurice (Hall/Whispering Man), Lou Merrill (an Irish Officer/Third Whispering Man), Vernon Steele (Doctor/Major Domo), Bob Ingersoll (Callahan/Police Officer), Frank Nelson (Irish Officer/Second Whispering Man), Coral Colebrook (English Girl/Crowd), Sibyl Harris (an Englishwoman/Crowd), Sidney Newman (English Soldier/Crowd), Ross Forrester (Second English Soldier), George Webb (English Officer), and Sheldon Bay (Jerring Boy).

Commercial: Frank Nelson (Bob), Sista Axselle (Betty).

The final *Lux* broadcast of 1937 features an adaptation of the Samuel Goldwyn/United Artists film *Beloved Enemy*, which concerns an Irish revolutionary leader who puts his life in danger by falling in love with an Englishwoman. Returning after his appearance in *Lux*'s "Peg o' My Heart" a mere four weeks earlier is Brian Aherne, who recreates his role of Dennis Riordan from the film. Joining him are Madeleine Carroll in Merle Oberon's screen part, C. Aubrey Smith in Henry Stephenson's role, and Donald Crisp, who reprises his characterization from the H.C. Potter–directed movie.

Film version: United Artists, 1936.

*157. "Alice Adams," 1/3/38

Based on the 1935 RKO film (screenplay by Dorothy Yost and Mortimer Offner; adaptation by Jane Murfin), in turn based on the novel by Booth Tarkington (1921).

Intermission Guest: George Hurrell, portrait photographer (after Act 2).

Cast: Claudette Colbert (Alice Adams), Fred MacMurray (Arthur Russell), Walter Connolly (Mr. Adams), Ann Shoemaker (Mrs. Adams), Benny Baker (Walter Adams), Georgette Spelvin [Marsha Hunt] (Mildred Palmer), Winifred Harris (Mrs. Palmer), Lou Merrill (Mr. Lamb), Grace Kern (Ella/Crowd), Verna Felton (Mrs. Dresser), Frank Nelson (Employment Agent), Charles Emerson (Crowd), Jean Lennox (Crowd), David Kerman (Crowd), and Doris Louray (Crowd).

Commercial: Lauretta Puck, Mary Lansing, Lurene Tuttle, and Nancy Leach.

Katharine Hepburn starred in RKO's 1935 film of *Alice Adams*, portraying a middle-class girl who sets her sights on the town's most eligible bachelor. *Lux*'s air version cast Claudette Colbert (who carried on despite illness) as the title character, with Fred MacMurray and Ann Shoemaker repeating their parts from the George Stevens–directed movie, and Walter Connolly and Benny Baker taking the roles that went to Fred Stone and Frank Albertson on the screen. Marsha Hunt made her network radio debut (appearing under the name of Georgette Spelvin) as the character played in the picture by Evelyn Venable. Frank Woodruff described *Lux*'s "Alice Adams" as a "good show that just missed being excellent."

King Vidor directed the first version of *Alice Adams*, which was released by Associated Exhibitors in 1923. Cast in the principal roles were Florence Vidor, Claude Gillingwater, Margaret McWade, and Harold Goodwin.

Film versions: Associated Exhibitors, 1923; RKO, 1935.

158. "Enter Madame," 1/10/38

Based on the play by Gilda Varesi and Dolly Byrne (1920).

Guest Host: Edward Arnold (Cecil B. DeMille is heard during the Act 2 intermission).

Intermission Guests: Lyle Saxon, historian and author (from New Orleans;

after Act 2), and Jean Ellis, 11-year-old protégée of Grace Moore (during curtain call).

Cast: Grace Moore (Madame Lisa Della Robia), Basil Rathbone (Gerald Fitzgerald), Sharon Lynne (Flora), William Frawley (Farnham), James Eagles (Johnnie/Fourth Reporter), Francesca Rotoli (Maria), Eric Wilton (Manager of the Opera/Jones), Lou Merrill (Archimede), Tony Martelli (Dr. Giovanni/Gondolier), Frank Nelson (Stretcher Bearer/Telegraph Operator/Second Reporter), Perry Ivins (Ship's Officer/Third Reporter/Second Telegraph Operator), Sidney Newman (Reporter), Michael Fitzmaurice (Toto), and Gil Patric (Third Reporter).

Chorus: Zaruhi Elmassion, Lois Miller, Lorraine Bridges, Rosalie Frye, Bernice Altstock, Mildred Carroll, Thad Harvey, Russell Horton, Robert Bradford, Enrico Ricardi, Earl Kovert, Hubert Head, Gordon Weatherill, and Tudor Williams.

Commercials: Emily Williams, Barbara Cox (Act 1), and Margaret Brayton (Act 3).

Opera singer Grace Moore returned for a third engagement on *Lux* in an adaptation of Gilda Varesi and Dolly Byrne's play *Enter Madame*. (The Broadway production, which opened at the Garrick Theatre on August 16, 1920, starred Gilda Varesi, Norman Trevor, Jane Meredith, and George Moto.) Basil Rathbone, who plays Moore's romantic leading man, is given the role of the prima donna's ardent suitor, and William Frawley plays the part of the singer's hard-boiled manager. Moore's excursions into song (and these are limited to a brief portion of the third act finale of Friedrich von Flotow's opera *Martha*, here sung in English; original German text by W. Friedrich) are "L'Ultima canzone" (lyric, Francesco Cimmino; music, F. Paolo Tosti) and the title song from her latest Columbia

picture, *I'll Take Romance* (words, Oscar Hammerstein II; music, Ben Oakland).

During the curtain call, Moore's protégée, 11-year-old Jean Ellis, sings Manuel Ponte's "Estralita" ("Little Star") in an English translation.

As DeMille's production *The Buccaneer* received its premiere in New Orleans on January 9, *Lux*'s regular host was unable to be in Hollywood for the January 10 broadcast. He is, however, heard by remote from New Orleans during Act 2 intermission, as he interviews author/historian Lyle Saxon, whose book *Lafitte, the Pirate* was the source on which *The Buccaneer* is based. The substitute host for this week's program is the respected actor Edward Arnold, who succeeds admirably in temporarily filling DeMille's shoes.

Paramount released a film version of *Enter Madame* in 1933, which stars Elissa Landi (whose singing voice was provided by Nina Koshetz), Cary Grant, Sharon Lynne (who repeats her role in the *Lux* production), Lynne Overman, and Frank Albertson, under Elliott Nugent's direction.

Film version: Paramount, 1933.

*159. "Disraeli," 1/17/38

Based on the 1929 Warner Bros. film (screenplay by Julian Josephson), in turn based on the play by Louis N. Parker (1916).

Intermission Guest: Major Bowes (from New York City; after Act 2).

Guest Host: Edward Arnold (Cecil B. DeMille is heard from New York City).

Cast: George Arliss (Disraeli), Florence Arliss (Lady Beaconsfield), David Torrence (Sir Michael Probert), Pat Paterson (Lady Clarissa), G.P. Huntley, Jr. (Charles, Viscount Delford), Ivan Simpson (Hugh Meyer), Walter Kingsford (Foljambe/Agitator), Doris Lloyd (Mrs. Travers), Vernon

Steele (Gladstone), Charles Evans (Bascot), Lou Merrill (Count Borsinov), Eric Snowden (Major Domo/Loafer), Reginald Sheffield (Lord Athleigh/Man/ Speaker of House), Phyllis Coghlan (Duchess), Frank Nelson (a Man), Pauline Gould, David Kerman, Warren McCollum, Doris Louray, Charles Emerson (Crowd), and Ross Forrester (Messenger).

Commercials: Sherry Ardell, Leora Thatcher, Marie Hammond (Act 1), and Myra Marsh (Act 2).

By 1938 George Arliss was well acquainted with playing British statesman and writer Benjamin Disraeli (1804–81), having starred in the first production of Louis N. Parker's play at the Royalty Theatre in London in 1916. He also plays the title role in United Artists' 1921 film version and made his talkie debut in Warner Bros.' 1929 *Disraeli*. It is thus appropriate that his first *Lux* appearance was in one of his most famous vehicles, which concentrates on the wily prime minister's schemes to procure the Suez Canal for England, and to assist Cupid in bringing a young couple together.

Arliss's wife, Florence, enacted the role of Lady Beaconsfield (as she had in both film versions), and three other players — David Torrence, Ivan Simpson, and Doris Lloyd — repeat their parts from the 1929 movie. (Charles Evans, who played Bascot in the broadcast, takes the role of Potter in the picture.) Joan Bennett's film part went to Pat Paterson, and G.P. Huntley, Jr., played Anthony Bushell's screen role.

The 1921 United Artists silent film of *Disraeli* was directed by Henry Kolker, and starred George and Florence Arliss and Louise Huff, while Warner Bros.' 1929 version was under the direction of Alfred E. Green.

Film versions: United Artists, 1921; Warner Bros., 1929.

*160. "Clarence," 1/24/38

Based on the 1937 Paramount film (screenplay by Seena Owen and Grant Garret), in turn based on the novel by Booth Tarkington (1919).

Intermission Guests: Mrs. Tay Garnett (Helga Moray), Hollywood's only movie camerawoman (after Act 2), and Tom English, mayor of Van Buren, Arkansas (during curtain call).

Cast: Bob Burns (Clarence), Gail Patrick (Violet Pinney), Thomas Mitchell (Wheeler), Jane Bryan (Cora), Johnny Downs (Bobby), Aileen Pringle (Mrs. Wheeler), Sarah Selby (Della), Wally Maher (Dinny), Perry Ivins (Tobias), Lou Merrill (Sergeant of Police), and Frank Nelson (Cab Driver).

Commercial: Paula Winslowe, Stuart Buchman.

Comedian Bob Burns was cast as the title character in *Lux*'s adaptation of "Clarence," the story of an ex-soldier who takes a job with a troubled family and quickly finds himself mixed up in their problems. Based on Paramount's 1937 George Archainbaud–directed film, the radio rendering features (besides Burns, who plays Roscoe Karns's screen role) Gail Patrick (in the Eleanor Whitney movie part), Thomas Mitchell (as the character played by Eugene Palette), and Johnny Downs (repeating his original part).

Paramount first filmed the 1919 Booth Tarkington play in 1922, with Wallace Reid, Agnes Ayres, Adolphe Menjou, May McAvoy, Edward Martindell, and Kathlyn Williams, under William C. deMille's direction.

Film versions: Paramount, 1922; Paramount, 1937.

*161. "The Green Light," 1/31/38

Based on the 1937 Warner Bros. film (screenplay by Milton Krims), in turn based on the novel *Green Light*, by Lloyd C. Douglas (1935).

Intermission Guests: Alton Cook, radio editor of the *New York World Telegram* (from New York City), and Dinty Doyle, radio editor of the *New York Journal-American* and columnist for Hearst newspapers (both after Act 2).

Cast: Errol Flynn (Dr. Newell Paige), Olivia deHavilland (Frances Ogilvie), C. Aubrey Smith (Dean Harcourt), Polly Ann Young (Phyllis Dexter), Frank Nelson (Dr. John Stafford), Janet Young (Mrs. Dexter), Roy Gordon (Dr. Endicott), John Lake (Dr. Lane), Lee Millar (Dr. Booth), Lou Merrill (Chairman/Train Conductor), Ethel Wales (Mrs. Howell), Ross Forrester (Chauffeur), Henry Anthony (Police Officer/Butler), Coral Colebrook (Telephone Operator/Crowd), Ingeborg Tillisch (Nurse/Filtered Voice), and James Eagles (Telegraph Operator/Announcer's Voice).

Commercial: Margaret Brayton, Emily Williams, and Henry Anthony.

Warner Bros.' *The Green Light*, which is based on Lloyd C. Douglas's novel, was directed by Frank Borzage and released in 1937. In the broadcast, Errol Flynn repeated his movie role as a dedicated doctor who puts his career in jeopardy when he takes the blame for another surgeon's costly mistake, and Olivia deHavilland, C. Aubrey Smith, and Polly Ann Young were cast in the parts played by Margaret Lindsay, Cedric Hardwicke, and Anita Louise on the screen.

Alton Cooke and Dinty Doyle announce that *Lux* has been awarded Best Dramatic Program on the Air (for the fourth year in a row) by radio editors in the *World Telegram* poll.

Film version: Warner Bros., 1937.

*162. "Anna Christie," 2/7/38

Based on the play by Eugene O'Neill (1921).

Intermission Guest: Albert McCleery, columnist for *Stage Magazine* (after Act 2).

Cast: Joan Crawford (Anna Christopherson), Spencer Tracy (Matt Burke), George Marion (Chris Christopherson), Marjorie Rambeau (Marthy Owen), Frank Shannon (Johnny), Sidney Newman (Joe), Wally Maher (Concessionaire), Hal K. Dawson (a Barker), Frank Nelson (a Vendor), Henry Hanna (a Little Boy), Lou Merrill (a Ticket Seller), Ross Forrester (Barge Man), Charles Emerson, Gil Patric, Lauretta Puck, Emily Williams, and Doris Louray (Crowd).

Commercial (parody on "Bei Mir Bist du Schön"): George Gramlich, Adele Buran.

Anna Christie, Eugene O'Neill's play about an embittered seaman's daughter who revises her pledge to have nothing more to do with the opposite sex when she falls in love with a two-fisted wharf-rat, premiered at Broadway's Vanderbilt Theatre on November 2, 1921. *Lux's* radio adaptation cast Joan Crawford, Spencer Tracy, George Marion, and Marjorie Rambeau in the roles played by Pauline Lord, Frank Shannon, George Marion, and Eugenie Blair on the stage. (Shannon, the Matt of the original production, was on hand to play Johnny in the broadcast, as well as to coach Tracy in his characterization.) Director Frank Woodruff deemed the radio presentation an "excellent show. Crawford, Marion, Rambeau, etc., fine."

Anna Christie first reached the screen in 1923 via the John Griffith Wray–directed First National release, which starred Blanche Sweet, William Russell, George Marion, and Eugenie Besserer. Greta Garbo made her much-heralded talkie debut (and was nominated for an Academy Award) as the title character in MGM's Clarence Brown–directed version in 1930, with the other principal parts going to Charles Bickford, George Marion, and Marie Dressler.

Film versions: First National, 1923; MGM, 1930.

*163. "Brief Moment," 2/14/38

Based on the play by S.N. Behrman (1931).

Intermission Guest: Jimmy Starr, Hollywood columnist for the *Los Angeles Herald-Express* (after Act 2).

Cast: Ginger Rogers (Abby), Douglas Fairbanks, Jr. (Roderick Deane), Louis Calhern (Cass Worthing), Paul Harvey (Manny Walsh), Nigel Bruce (Sigrift), Grace Kern (Gertie/Maid), Ynez Seabury (Mabel/Chorus Girl/Glove Counter Girl), David Kerman (Frank/Gangster), Mary Smith (a Saleslady), James Eagles (Chef/Third Reader), Lou Merrill (Irate Customer/Waiter), Frank Nelson (Gossip Columnist), and Ross Forrester (Fourth Reader).

Commercial: Mary Smith, Mary Lansing.

Brief Moment, S.N. Behrman's comedy concerning a marriage between a discontented millionaire's son and an unconventional musical comedy actress, was adapted for *Lux* and starred Ginger Rogers and Douglas Fairbanks, Jr., with Nigel Bruce as his sharp-tongued friend. Repeating their roles from the 1931 Broadway production (which opened at the Belasco Theatre on November 9 and also featured Francine Larrimore, Robert Douglas, and Alexander Wolcott) were Louis Calhern, as Abby's old flame who refuses to be completely extinguished, and Paul Harvey, as gentleman racketeer Manny Walsh.

Among the subjects discussed by Hollywood reporter Jimmy Starr were some of the stars' requests for personalized license plates for 1938, and D.W. Griffith's plans to remake *The Birth of a Nation*.

The 1933 Columbia film of *Brief Moment* was directed by David Burton and starred Carole Lombard, Gene Raymond, Arthur Hohl, and Monroe Owsley. (There is no Cass Worthing character in the picture.)

Film version: Columbia, 1933.

*164. "Romance," 2/21/38

Based on the play by Edward Sheldon (1913).

Intermission Guest: Walter Wanger, independent motion picture producer (after Act 2).

Cast: Madeleine Carroll (Margherita Cavallini), Herbert Marshall (Thomas Armstrong), Ralph Morgan (Cornelius Van Tuyl), Claire Dodd (Susan), Marga Ann Deighton (Vanucci), Barry Drew (Gerald/Crowd), Sada Cowan (Kate/Woman), Wallace Roberts (Cabman/Man), John Lake (Joseph/Brouder), Lou Merrill (First Hack Driver/Second Young Man), Frank Nelson (Young Man), Ross Forrester (Call Boy/Young Man/Crowd), Doris Louray, Virginia Parker, Jerrie Gail, Sidney Newman, and Charles Emerson (Crowd).

Chorus: Louis Yeckel, Morton Scott, Robert Bradford, Phillip Neely, Ralph Leon, Hubert Head, Abe Dinevitz, Lorraine Bridges, Devona Doxie, Winona Black, Mildred Carroll, and Bernice Altstock. *Soloists*: Zaruhi Elmassion, Enrico Ricardi.

Commercial: Frank Nelson.

In commemoration of the twenty-fifth anniversary of the original Broadway production of *Romance* (which actually opened on February 10, 1913), *Lux* presented an adaptation of Edward Sheldon's drama. The play is told in flashbacks by a bishop who relates the story of some years previous, when he was involved in an affair with a renowned prima donna of the opera. *Lux* chose Madeleine Carroll and Herbert Marshall for the leads, with featured supporting roles going to Ralph Morgan and Claire Dodd. (The first Broadway production starred Doris Keane, William Courtenay, A.E. Anson, and Gladys Wynne.)

Keane recreated her role in the first film version of the play, which was released in 1920. The Chet Whithey–directed movie also features Basil Sydney, Norman Trevor, and Betty Ross Clarke. The 1930 MGM talkie starred Greta Garbo, Gavin Gordon, Lewis Stone, and Florence Lake; Clarence Brown was director.

Film versions: Chet Whithey Productions, 1920; MGM, 1930.

*165. "Forsaking All Others," 2/28/38

Based on the play by Edward Barry Roberts and Frank Cavett (1933).

Intermission Guest: Kathleen Coghlan, "fan magazine contact" for Paramount Pictures (after Act 2).

Cast: Bette Davis (Mary Clay), Joel McCrea (Jefferson Tingle), Anderson Lawlor (Dillon Todd), Leona Maricle (Constance Barnes), Hal K. Dawson (Shepherd Perry), Margaret Brayton (Mrs. Paula LaSalle), Barbara Pelgram (Dottie Winters), Margaret McKay (Susan Thomas), Lou Merrill (Dent), Pauline Haddon (Elinor Branch), Frank Nelson (the Reverend Duncan), Eddie Kane (Headwaiter), Ross Forrester (Taxi Driver), and Mildred Carroll (Singer).

Commercial: Jerrie Gail.

Forsaking All Others, the play by Edward Barry Roberts and Frank Cavett, opened on Broadway at the Times Square Theatre on March 1, 1933, with Tallulah Bankhead and Fred Keating in the leading roles. *Lux*'s radio adaptation features Bette Davis and Joel McCrea in the comedy, which begins with Mary Clay being stood up at the altar by her childhood sweetheart, Dillon Todd, and goes on to tell of her continued infatuation with the man, even though he has married another girl. Meanwhile, Jeff Tingle, the man who has silently loved her for years, stands quietly by. Recreating his stage role of Dillon in the broadcast (which Frank Woodruff called "an excellent show due to superb trouping by Davis and McCrea") was Anderson Lawlor, with Leona Maricle playing the part taken on Broadway by Millicent Hanley.

W.S. Van Dyke II was at the helm of MGM's 1934 film of *Forsaking All Others*, which starred Joan Crawford, Clark Gable, Robert Montgomery, and Frances Drake.

Film version: MGM, 1934.

166. "Poppy," 3/7/38

Based on the 1936 Paramount film (screenplay by Waldemar Young and Virginia Van Upp), in turn based on the play by Dorothy Donnelly (1923).

Intermission Guest: Margaret Graham of the L.G. Barnes Circus (after Act 2).

Cast: W.C. Fields (Professor Eustace McGargle), Anne Shirley (Poppy), John Payne (Billy Farnsworth), Skeets Gallagher (Whiffen), Helena Grant (Mrs. Tubbs), Lou Merrill (Mayor Farnsworth), Gretchen Thomas (Sarah Brown), W.L. Thorn (Manager of the Circus), Frank Nelson (Circus Barker/Second Man [Act 3]), Vangie Beilby (an Irate Woman/Maid), Dink Trout (a Yokel/Third Man), Forrest Taylor (Sheriff/Constable), Ross Forrester (First Man [Act 3]), and George Webb (Crowd).

Commercial: Virginia McMullin, Justina Wayne.

American comedian W.C. Fields made his only appearance on *Lux* in an adaptation of his 1936 Paramount vehicle *Poppy*, which was in turn based on the 1923 play in which he had starred. (The original Broadway production also featured Madge Kennedy, Alan Edwards, and Jimmy Barry.) Fields's comedy relies much on his visual antics, and this aspect of his talent is, of course, lost on the air. His voice and manner of delivery, however, are also a familiar part of his comedic makeup, and he puts these qualities to good use in this yarn of a dishonest sideshow performer who tries to pass his young ward off as a long-lost member of a prominent family. Young Anne Shirley, already making her fourth appearance before the *Lux* microphone since the program's move to Hollywood, takes the part of the title character, which is portrayed by Rochelle Hudson in the film. Character actor Skeets Gallagher is the Professor's shady cohort, Whiffen (played by Lynne Overman in the movie), while John Payne (who had recently married Miss Shirley) takes the relatively small role of Poppy's wealthy suitor, Billy Farnsworth (played on the screen by Richard Cromwell).

Paramount's 1936 film of *Poppy* (which was directed by A. Edward Sutherland) was not the first production in which Fields played the Professor onscreen, as the studio had previously released a version in 1925 under the title *Sally of the Sawdust*. D.W. Griffith directed a cast that featured, in addition to Fields, Carol Dempster and Alfred Lunt.

Film versions: Paramount, 1925 (*Sally of the Sawdust*); Paramount, 1936.

*167. "The Boss," 3/14/38
Based on the play by Edward Sheldon (1911).

Intermission Guest: Dorothy Dix, syndicated newspaper columnist (from New Orleans; after Act 2).

Cast: Edward Arnold (Mike Regan), Fay Wray (Emily Griswold), H.B. Warner (Archbishop), Howard Philips (Donald Griswold), Frank Shannon (Parky McCoy), Eric Wilton (Mitchell/Third Man), Earl Gunn (Scanlon), Lou Merrill (the Inspector), Dwight Kramer (Mr. Griswold), Frank Nelson (Davis/Man/Second Newsboy), David Kerman (Dave/Guard [off]), Sidney Newman (Gates/Newsboy), Eddie Kane (Officer), and Ross Forrester (Second Man/Third Newsboy).

Commercial: Sally Creighton.

The Boss, Edward Sheldon's 1911 play about the rise of a crooked businessman, received a revival on *Lux* on March 14. Edward Arnold portrayed the title character, with Fay Wray, H.B. Warner, Howard Philips, and Frank Shannon taking the remainder of the featured parts. (Bill Luckenbill noted, "Arnold, Wray, Warner excellent. Support good. This made an entertaining evening.")

See 1/12/36 for information on stage and film versions.

*168. "The Man Who Played God," 3/21/38
Based on the 1932 Warner Bros. film (screenplay by Julien Josephson and Maude Howell), in turn based on the play *The Silent Voice*, by Jules Eckert Goodman (1914), which was founded on a story by Gouverneur Morris (1912).

Intermission Guest: Leo McCarey, motion picture director (after Act 2).

Cast: George Arliss (Montgomery Royale), Florence Arliss (Mildred Miller), Dolores Costello (Grace Blair), Elisabeth Risdon (Florence), Ivan Simpson (Battle), Leonard Willey (Mr. Appleby), Evelyn Keyes (Girl in Park), Reginald Sheffield (Boy in Park), Vernon Steele (the King), Frank Nelson (Harold), Michelette Burami (Madame LaVelle), Charles Evans (Usher), Lou Merrill (Manager/Man), James Eagles (Aide to King), Edith Nestier (French Girl), Lou Lorraine (French Girl), Elizabeth Wilbur (Second Woman), Georgia Kane (Third Woman), and Ross Forrester.

Commercial: Mary Lansing, Victor Rodman.

George Arliss was back on *Lux*'s

March 21 broadcast in another of his well-remembered vehicles, *The Man Who Played God*. This program was based on Warner Bros.' 1932 John Adolfi–directed movie, which also featured Violet Heming in the role played by Florence Arliss on *Lux*, as well as Bette Davis, whose part was taken by Dolores Costello on the air. (Elisabeth Risdon played the Louise Closser Hale movie part, and Ivan Simpson repeated his screen role.)

The radio play told of a concert pianist who, having lost his hearing, dedicates his existence to reconstructing the shattered lives of others. (Frank Woodruff commented that the show featured a "great Arliss performance and good support.")

United Artists released the George Arliss production of the silent *Man Who Played God*, which was directed by Harmon Wright in 1922 (and also featured Florence Arliss and Ann Forrest), while Gordon Douglas was at the helm of that studio's 1955 version. Entitled *Sincerely Yours*, the film featured Liberace as the pianist.

Film versions: United Artists, 1922; Warner Bros., 1932.

*169. "Naughty Marietta," 3/28/38
Based on the 1910 musical production (book and lyrics by Rida Johnson Young; music by Victor Herbert).

Intermission Guest: A.B. Oldfield, film critic for the *Nebraska State Journal*, who saw every film released in the United States in 1936 and 1937 (944 motion pictures) (after Act 2).

Cast: Lawrence Tibbett (Captain Richard Warrington), Helen Jepson (Marietta), Ian Maclaren (Count d'Altena), Ralph Kellard (Governor of Louisiana), Ferdinand Munier (Rudolpho), Otis Harlan (Watchman), Richard Abbott (Captain), Edwin Max (Mate/Man), Gay Seabrook (Josephine), Margaret McKay (Lizette), Grace Kern

(Nanette), James Eagles (François/ Crowd), Lou Merrill (Town Crier/ Sergeant), Frank Nelson (Man/Second Man), Gaughan Burke (Soldier/Crowd), Sidney Newman, Bob Burleson, Emily Williams, Marion Dennis, and Edward Kogan (Crowd).

Chorus: Morton Scott, Thad Harvey, Louis Yackel, George Gramlich, Paul Sautter, Phil Neely, Don Goodenough, Earl Kovart, Allan Watson, Abe Dinevitz, Delos Jewkes, Tudor Williams, Enrico Ricardi, and Ross Forrester. *Chorus Coach*: Rudy Schrager.

Commercial: Margaret Brayton.

Naughty Marietta, probably the best known of Victor Herbert's long string of popular operettas, received its official opening at Broadway's New York Theatre on November 7, 1910, in a production by Oscar Hammerstein with a cast headed by Orville Hannold and Emma Trentini (both stars of Hammerstein's Manhattan Opera Company). The W.S. Van Dyke–directed version was released in 1935 by MGM, and made a popular team of Jeanette MacDonald and Nelson Eddy, whose first film together it was. On March 28, 1938, it was *Lux*'s turn to present the tuneful musical, which concerns the love story (set in eighteenth-century New Orleans) between a princess, disguised as a husband-seeking coquette who is running away from a prearranged marriage in France, and a rugged leader of a backwoods team of soldiers. Metropolitan Opera singers Lawrence Tibbett and Helen Jepson (both of whom had also achieved success in Hollywood) were cast in *Lux*'s version, which, while officially crediting the stage production as its source, receives considerable inspiration from the MGM movie as well.

Only four different vocal numbers (of the original score's 18) were heard in the broadcast: Act 1: "Naughty Marietta" (Jepson), "Tramp, Tramp, Tramp" (partial, with dialogue; Tibbett and

Male Chorus), and "Tramp, Tramp, Tramp" (reprise); Act 2: "Ah, Sweet Mystery of Life" (partial; Jepson), "Italian Street Song" (Jepson and Male Chorus), and "I'm Falling in Love with Someone" (Tibbett); Act 3: "Ah, Sweet Mystery of Life" (finale; Jepson and Tibbett).

Lux presented another rendering on June 12, 1944.

Film version: MGM, 1935.

*170. "Dark Victory," 4/4/38

Based on the play by George Brewer, Jr., and Bertram Bloch (1934).

Guest Host: Edward Arnold.

Intermission Guest: Nina Roberts, United Artists hairstylist (after Act 2).

Cast: Barbara Stanwyck (Judith Traherne), Melvyn Douglas (Dr. Frederick Steele), Crauford Kent (Dr. Parsons), Margaret Brayton (Martha), Gretchen Thomas (Jenny), Ted Osborne (Leslie Clarke), Coral Colebrook (Alice), Lou Merrill (Harvey), Frank Nelson (Chairman of Horse Show), Ross Forrester (Guest/Crowd), James Eagles (Groom), Joan Taylor, Phyllis Coghlan, Leonard Willey, George Webb, and Doris Louray (Crowd).

Commercial: Sally Creighton.

Dark Victory, the play by George Brewer, Jr., and Bertram Bloch, premiered at the Plymouth Theatre in New York on November 7, 1934, with Tallulah Bankhead cast as a spoiled society girl who discovers she is dying of a brain tumor, and Earle Larrimore as the doctor with whom she falls in love. (The radio adaptation found Barbara Stanwyck in the role of Judith Traherne and Melvyn Douglas as Dr. Frederick Steele.)

According to Edmund Goulding, who appeared as an intermission guest on October 31 (approximately seven months after this broadcast), it was *Lux*'s production of "Dark Victory" (which Frank Woodruff called a "mov-

ing drama of victory of the spirit") which brought the property to the attention of Hal B. Wallis and himself. The film, which was released in 1939 by Warner Bros., starred Bette Davis and George Brent.

Due to illness, DeMille's duties as host are given to Edward Arnold.

The British Mirisch/Barbican production (released by United Artists in the United States) was entitled *Stolen Hours* and featured Susan Hayward and Michael Craig, under Daniel Petrie's direction.

Lux's broadcast of "Dark Victory" on January 8, 1940, was based on the Warner Bros. film.

Film versions: Warner Bros., 1939; Mirisch/Barbican/United Artists, 1963 (*Stolen Hours*).

*171. "Mary Burns, Fugitive," 4/11/38

Based on the 1935 Paramount film (screenplay by Gene Towne, Graham Baker, and Louis Stevens).

Guest Host: Edward Arnold.

Intermission Guest: Travis Banton, Paramount fashion designer (after Act 2).

Cast: Miriam Hopkins (Mary Burns), Henry Fonda (Alec MacDonald), Mary Astor (Goldie), Paul Guilfoyle (Don Mason), Earl Gunn (Cameron), Sibyl Harris (the Matron), Eddie Marr (Luigi), Justina Wayne (Miss Jennings), Perry Ivins (Steve/Minister), Roger Drake (Joe), Lou Payton (Jeremiah), Lou Merrill (District Attorney/Announcer), Frank Nelson (Judge/Clerk), David Kerman (Second Customer/Third Newsboy), Sidney Newman (First Customer/Second Newsboy), and Ross Forrester (First Newsboy).

Commercial: Helen Crow.

Mary Burns, Fugitive, Paramount's 1935 melodrama of an innocent girl whose unwilling involvement with a gangster leads to her eventual imprisonment, was on tap for *Lux*'s April 11 show. The title role, portrayed by Sylvia Sidney in the William K. Howard–directed motion picture, was undertaken by Miriam Hopkins on the air, with the remaining principal parts going to Henry Fonda, Mary Astor, and Paul Guilfoyle (as the gangster), which are played in the movie by Melvyn Douglas, Pert Kelton, and Alan Baxter.

Frank Woodruff found the radio play "an excellent melodrama which seemed to make good."

For the second week in a row, Edward Arnold filled in for an ailing Mr. DeMille.

172. "Mad About Music," 4/18/38

Based on the 1938 Universal film (screenplay by Bruce Manning and Felix Jackson), in turn based on a story by Marcella Burke and Frederick Kohner.

Guest Host: Walter Huston.

Intermission Guest: Mrs. Kellaphene Morrison of the Adult Education Department of the Los Angeles Public Schools (teacher of motion picture child stars) (after Act 2).

Cast: Deanna Durbin (Gloria), Herbert Marshall (Richard Todd), Gail Patrick (Gwen Taylor), William Frawley (Dusty), Jackie Moran (Tommy Gray), Christian Rub (Pierre), Helen Parrish (Felice), Marcia Mae Jones (Olga), Edgar Norton (Tripps), Margaret Brayton (Miss Fusenot/Telephone), Marie Hammond (Miss Louise), Jo Ann Ransom (Dorothy), Suzanne Ransom (Catherine), Jerrie Gail (Lisette), Sherry Ardell (Crowd), Shirley Karne (Student/Crowd), Lois Lee (Crowd), Pauline Gould (Crowd/Second Woman), Ross Forrester (Reporter Number One), Eric Wilton (Reporter Number Three/Crowd), Lou Merrill (Reporter Number Two/Second Man), and Frank Nelson (Man).

Commercial: Frank Nelson.

The popularity of Universal's teenage singing star Deanna Durbin was taken advantage of in *Lux*'s adaptation of one of her films, *Mad About Music*, which concerns a spirited American girl in a Swiss boarding school. Neglected by her mother, she creates a make-believe father and convinces a suave author to play the part. During this pleasant comedy with music, Durbin is given the chance to sing three selections: Act 1: "Ave Maria" (by Bach/Gounod); Act 2: "Chapel Bells"; and Act 3: "Serenade to the Stars" (both with words by Harold Adamson and music by Jimmy McHugh).

Joining Durbin are seven members of the film (which was directed by Norman Taurog): Herbert Marshall, Gail Patrick, William Frawley, Jackie Moran, Christian Rub, Helen Parrish, and Marcia Mae Jones.

Cecil B. DeMille's illness once again kept him from the *Lux* microphone, so Walter Huston was recruited to fill in for him on this week's program.

Universal produced another version of *Mad About Music* in 1956. Directed by Jerry Hopper, this rendering changed the gender of the child, played by Tim Hovey, and featured Jeff Chandler and Laraine Day in the roles played by Herbert Marshall and Gail Patrick.

Film versions: Universal, 1938; Universal, 1956 (*Toy Tiger*).

*173. "Dangerous," 4/25/38

Based on the 1935 Warner Bros. film (screenplay and original story by Laird Doyle).

Intermission Guest: Thelma Saxton, hand double (after Act 2).

Cast: Madeleine Carroll (Joyce Heath), Don Ameche (Don Bellows), Heather Angel (Gail Armitage), Ted Osborn (Gordon), Ethel Wales (Mrs. Williams), Frank Nelson (Ted/Third Newsboy), Lou Merrill (George Sheffield), Sarah Selby (Mrs. Linder/Nurse), James Eagles (Carlos/Newsboy), Galan Gault (Mr. Melton/Doorman), David Kerman (Waiter), Phyllis Coghlan (Secretary/Voice), Bob Burleson (Cabby/Second Newsboy), and Ross Forrester (Mr. Elmsby/Newsboy).

Commercial: Katherine Carleton.

Dangerous, which was directed by Alfred E. Green and released by Warner Bros. in 1935, tells the story of a down-on-her-luck actress who is taken under the wing of a well-meaning fan, and the complications that result from their subsequent love affair. *Lux* cast Madeleine Carroll in the part Bette Davis plays onscreen (which won the latter an Academy Award), while Don Ameche portrays the Franchot Tone movie character, and Heather Angel is given Margaret Lindsay's picture role. Director Frank Woodruff commented that the broadcast was "very moving and suspense was great."

174. "Prisoner of Shark Island," 5/2/38

Based on the 1936 20th Century–Fox film (screenplay by Nunnally Johnson).

Intermission Guest: Mrs. Nettie Mudd Monroe, daughter (and youngest of nine children) of Dr. Samuel Mudd, who authored *The Life of Dr. Samuel A. Mudd* in 1906.

Cast: Gary Cooper (Dr. Samuel Mudd), Fay Wray (Peggy), Walter Connolly (Colonel Dyer), John Carradine (Sergeant Rankin), Ernest Whitman (Buck), Ted Osborn (David E. Herold), Albert Van Dekker (Sergeant Henderson), John Deering (Lieutenant Lovett), Victor Rodman (General Ewing/Third Voice in Act 1), Lee Millar (Dr. McIntyre/Third Witness), Frank Shannon (Judge Advocate/General Holt/Corporal O'Toole), Lou Merrill (Judge Maiben/Fourth Witness/First Voice in Act 1), Earl Gunn (Major Stone/Commandant/Second Voice), Warren Mc-

Collum (Orderly/Third Voice in Act 2), Frank Nelson (Prosecutor Hunter/Rathbone/First Witness), Cracker Henderson (Druggist), Libby Taylor (Rosabelle), Jester Hairston (Corporal/Boy in Act 1/Third Negro in Act 3), Clarence Hargrave (Field Boy), Jack Carr (Sentry), and Ross Forrester (Signalman/Crowd).

Commercial: Helen Crow, Jo Ann Ransom, Dorothy Grey, and Harriett Bennett.

Lux's "The Prisoner of Shark Island," which was based on the factual story of Samuel Mudd, the doctor who was imprisoned for treating the injured John Wilkes Booth after the 1865 assassination of President Abraham Lincoln, was presented with Gary Cooper in the role Warner Baxter effectively played onscreen. The remaining members of the cast include Fay Wray as Mrs. Mudd (Gloria Stuart's film role in the John Ford–directed 1936 20th Century–Fox movie), Walter Connolly as her feisty father (Claude Gillingwater in the motion picture), and John Carradine and Ernest Whitman repeating their photoplay parts as the sadistic prison guard and faithful friend, respectively. (Originally announced to play Peggy was Joan Bennett, but illness prevented her from appearing.)

The radio version tones down the aspect of Dr. Mudd's being railroaded into the conviction by his accusers (members of the U.S. government)—even the victim himself holds no ill feeling toward those who are responsible for his plight (this is accomplished primarily by leaving out portions of the screenplay).

Lippet Pictures released a version featuring Sterling Hayden and Joan Leslie under Charles Marquis Warren's direction in 1952 (entitled *Hellgate*).

Film versions: 20th Century–Fox, 1936; Lippet Pictures, 1952 (*Hellgate*).

William Powell, Carole Lombard, and Eddie Kane during a rehearsal of "My Man Godfrey" (May 9, 1938) (photo: Photofest).

175. "My Man Godfrey," 5/9/38

Based on the 1936 Universal film (screenplay by Morrie Ryskind and Eric Hatch), in turn based on the novel by Eric Hatch (1935), in turn based on his *Liberty* story, "Irene, the Stubborn Girl" (1935).

Intermission Guests: Madalynne Fields, Carole Lombard's friend and personal business manager (after Act 2), and Eric Hatch, author of *My Man Godfrey* and coauthor of the screenplay (after Act 3).

Cast: William Powell (Godfrey), Carole Lombard (Irene Bullock), Gail Patrick (Cornelia Bullock), Mischa Auer (Carlo), David Niven (Tommy Gray), Wallis Clark (Alexander Bullock), Elvia Allman (Angelica Bullock), Ynez Seabury (Molly), Edwin Max (Mr. Guthrie), Frank Nelson (George), Lou Merrill (a Detective), David Kerman (Clarence), Eddie Kane (Mayor Courtland), Ernie Adams (a Waiter), Eleanor Mitchell (Girl), Elia Braca (Second Girl), and Ross Forrester (Jon).

Commercial: George Gramlich.

Gregory LaCava's brilliant "screwball comedy" *My Man Godfrey* found its way to *Lux* with four of the delightful stars from the film version: William Powell, Carole Lombard, Gail Patrick, and Mischa Auer. Powell portrays a derelict (whose address is the city dump) who is engaged as the butler of a highly amusing eccentric family, and Lombard plays the impressionable younger daughter of the clan who fancies she has fallen in love with the new prize. Gail Patrick repeats her role as sophisticated troublemaker Cornelia Bullock, and Mischa Auer recreates his characterization as Mrs. Bullock's free-loading musical protégé, Carlo.

David Niven makes another *Lux*

appearance, here as Tommy Gray, a role taken in the film by Alan Mowbray, while radio character comedian Elvia Allman does an approximate imitation of Alice Brady's delightful film portrait of Mrs. Bullock.

During the curtain call, DeMille asks *Lux* listeners to send in their votes as to whether they would like to see a sequel to "My Man Godfrey" (to date, there has not been one!).

Henry Koster directed Universal's 1957 version, with David Niven and June Allyson in the leads.

Lux remounted the play on November 9, 1954.

Film versions: Universal, 1936; Universal, 1957.

*176. "The Girl from Tenth Avenue," 5/16/38

Based on the 1935 First National/ Warner Bros. film (screenplay by Charles Kenyon), in turn based on the play *The Outcast*, by Hubert Henry Davies.

Intermission Guest: Emily Post, etiquette authority (from New York City; after Act 2).

Cast: Loretta Young (Miriam Brady), George Brent (Geoffrey Sherwood), Beulah Bondi (Mrs. Martin), Mona Barrie (Valentine), Eric Snowden (John Marland), Lou Merrill (Mr. French/ Train Announcer), Eddie Marr (the Waiter), Eddie Waller (a Reporter/ Conductor), Rolfe Sedan (Hotel Clerk/ Porter), Harold Wilson (a Policeman), Frank Nelson (Hugh Williams), Kenneth Hansen (Tony/Third Newsboy), Jessica Wells (Miss Mansfield), Edward Kogan (First Newsboy), Ross Forrester (Second Newsboy), Betty Stewart, Marion Dennis, Margaret McKay, and Paul Frohman (Crowd).

Commercial: Adele Burton (Singer).

Alfred E. Green directed the 1935 Warner Bros.–First National picture *The Girl from Tenth Avenue*, which

offered principal roles to Bette Davis, Ian Hunter, Allison Skipworth, and Katherine Alexander. The story concerns a successful attorney who goes on a drinking binge after his intended bride marries another man. The next morning, he awakens to find himself married to a young lady who is a stranger to him. *Lux*'s production (of which Frank Woodruff said, "Fine performances of rather 'thin' script") cast George Brent as the lawyer, Loretta Young as the girl he marries, Beulah Bondi as their landlady, and Mona Barrie as the former fiancée.

*177. "The Letter," 5/23/38

Based on the play by W. Somerset Maugham (1927).

Intermission Guests: Carweth Wells, author and explorer, and his wife, Zetta Wells (after Act 2).

Cast: Merle Oberon (Leslie Crosbie), Walter Huston (Robert Crosbie), Ralph Forbes (Geoffrey Hammond), Eric Snowden (Howard Joyce), Leonard Mudie (Coroner Bentley), Raymond Lawrence (Sergeant Jenkins), Lou Merrill (Chung), Celeste Rush (Li-Ti), Sybil Harris (the Matron), Frank Nelson (Foreman), and Ross Forrester (Judge).

Commercial: Hattie Thompson, Paul Frohman, Sidney Newman, Mary Arden, and George Webb.

W. Somerset Maugham's play *The Letter* premiered on *Lux* on May 23. Merle Oberon was cast as a woman who shoots a family friend to death, claiming he had attacked her, which her husband accepts until a letter surfaces that indicates there was more between the woman and her victim than has been admitted. Filling the remainder of the roles were Walter Huston as the husband, Ralph Forbes as the victim, and radio actor Eric Snowden as the lawyer who fights to save his client (Nigel Bruce had previously been announced to play the part).

The Letter was first produced at the Playhouse Theatre in London on February 24, 1927, with a cast headed by Gladys Cooper, and the Broadway production at the Morosco Theatre followed on September 26, with the starring roles taken by Katharine Cornell, J.W. Austin, Burton McEvilly, and Allan Jeayes. Paramount released the first filmed version in 1929, which was directed by Jean DeLimur and starred Jeanne Eagles, Reginald Owen, Herbert Marshall, and O.P. Heggie. The 1940 Warner Bros. movie (on which *Lux's* broadcasts of April 21, 1941, and March 6, 1944, were based) was directed by William Wyler and featured Bette Davis, Herbert Marshall (now playing the husband), David Newell, and James Stevenson.

Film versions: Paramount, 1929; Warner Bros., 1940.

*178. "I Met My Love Again," 5/30/38

Based on the 1938 Wanger/United Artists film (screenplay by David Hertz), in turn based on the novel *Summer Lightning*, by Allene Corliss (1936).

Intermission Guest: Jimmy Starr, Hollywood columnist for the *Los Angeles Herald-Express* (after Act 2).

Cast: Joan Bennett (Julie Weir), Henry Fonda (Ives Towner), May Robson (Aunt William), Margaret Hamilton (Mrs. Towner), Louise Platt (Brenda), Genee Hall (Joan Shaw), Frank Nelson (Michael Shaw), Florence Baker (Carol), Margaret Brayton (Agatha), Warren McCollum (Budge Williams), Barbara Palgram (Miss Taylor/Second Woman), James Eagles (Hubert), Pauline Haddan (Coed/First Woman), Jerrie Gail (Coed/Third Woman), and Ross Forrester (College Student).

Commercial: Coral Colebrook, Mary Lansing, and Sally Creighton.

I Met My Love Again (1938), the Walter Wanger–produced picture re-

leased through United Artists, marked the movie directorial debuts of both Arthur D. Ripley and Joshua Logan. The story concerns a young lady who impulsively leaves her fiancé and runs off to Europe to marry another, but after she is widowed, she returns home and discovers that her affection for her former beau has not diminished.

Joan Bennett and Henry Fonda repeat their screen roles in *Lux's* broadcast, with the parts played in the film by Dame May Whitty and Dorothy Stickney assigned to May Robson and Margaret Hamilton. Also reprising their movie characterizations were Louise Platt and child actress Genee Hall.

*179. "A Doll's House," 6/6/38

Based on the play *Et Dukkehjem*, by Henrik Ibsen (1879).

Intermission Guest: Frances Manson, chief story editor for Samuel Goldwyn Productions (after Act 2).

Cast: Joan Crawford (Nora Helmer), Basil Rathbone (Thorvald Helmer), Sam Jaffe (Krogstad), Nedda Harrington (Mrs. Linden), Vernon Steele (Dr. Rank), Celeste Rush (Ellen), John Russell (Ivar Helmer), Jackie Horner (Emmy Helmer), Frank Nelson (a Messenger), Eleanor Mitchell (Leah), Ross Forrester (Waiter), Lou Merrill, and David Kerman (Crowd).

Commercial: Lurene Tuttle, Mary Lansing, Sally Creighton, and Kathryn Carlton.

Henrik Ibsen's oft-produced play *A Doll's House* was *Lux's* presentation on June 6. The drama of a submissive wife who rebels after her husband chastises her for some slightly shady dealings she had performed (for his benefit) several years before, gave meaty roles to Joan Crawford and Basil Rathbone, and good supporting parts to Sam Jaffe (repeating his role from the Morosco Theatre production, which had recently

May Robson, Henry Fonda, Joan Bennett, and Cecil B. DeMille in "I Met My Love Again" (May 30, 1938) (photo: Berry Hill Bookshop).

closed on Broadway), Nedda Harrington, and Vernon Steele. Frank Woodruff noted that the broadcast was highlighted by "superb and superior performances by all the cast," and he singled out Miss Crawford's Nora, saying it "had the quality of muddle-headedness that is more Nora than the usual chirping soubrette interpretation."

Famous Players–Lasky produced the first U.S. feature film of *A Doll's House* in 1918. Directed by Maurice Tourneur, this picture starred Elsie Ferguson, H.E. Herbert, Alex K. Shannon, Ethel Grey Terry, and Warren Cook. United Artists was next with its Charles Bryant–directed production, in which the featured roles went to Nazimova (the movie's producer), Alan Hale, Wedgewood Nowell, Florence Fisher, and Nigel Bruler. Two British productions were made in 1973: the first, which was released by Paramount and directed by Patrick Garland, featured Claire Bloom, Anthony Hopkins, Den-

holm Elliott, Anna Massey, and Ralph Richardson, while the second (which went straight to television in the United States) included Jane Fonda, David Warner, Edward Fox, Delphine Seyrig, and Trevor Howard in a cast directed by Joseph Losey.

Film versions: Famous Players–Lasky, 1918; United Artists, 1922; Paramount, 1973; World Film Services, 1973.

*180. "Theodora Goes Wild," 6/13/38

Based on the 1936 Columbia film (screenplay by Sidney Buchman), in turn based on a story by Mary McCarthy.

Intermission Guest: Gwen Dew, Hollywood writer (after Act 2).

Cast: Irene Dunne (Theodora Lynn), Cary Grant (Michael Dane), Kathleen Lockhart (Aunt Mary), Sarah Haden (Rebecca Perry), Noreen Gammill (Aunt Elsie), Lou Merrill (Mr. Stevenson), Myra Marsh (Ethel Stevenson),

Joe DuVal (Jed Waterbury), John Fee (Mr. Dane), Helen Christian (Agnes), Lee Millar (Uncle John Lynn), Sybil Harris (Mrs. Hanks), Mary Lansing (Secretary), Tris Coffin (Tony), Jack Morrison (Newsboy), Frank Nelson, Sidney Newman, and David Kerman (Reporters). *Commercial*: Patsie deSousa, Mary Arden.

Theodora Goes Wild, Columbia's comedy of a proper small town girl from a respectable family who secretly pens a scandalously racy novel, was directed by Richard Boleslawski and featured Irene Dunne, Melvyn Douglas, Elisabeth Risdon, and Margaret McWade in the leading roles. The *Lux* adaptation recast Dunne as the title character, with Cary Grant, Kathleen Lockhart, and Sarah Haden rounding out the quartet of stars.

*181. "Manslaughter," 6/20/38

Based on the 1930 Paramount film (screenplay by George Abbott), in turn based on the story by Alice Duer Miller.

Intermission Guest: George Abbott, Broadway producer who adapted and directed the talking picture *Manslaughter* (from New York City; after Act 2).

Cast: Fredric March (Dan O'Bannon), Florence Eldridge (Lydia Thorne), James Gleason (Connie), Charlotte Treadway (Aunt Ethel), Grace Kern (Miss Evans), Arthur Van Slyke (Captain Frazer), Ted Osborn (Albee), Lurene Tuttle (Elinor Roberts), David Kerman (Detective Harvey), Lou Merrill (the Judge), Frank Nelson (Officer Drummond), John Lake (Higgins), Ross Forrester (Clerk), Marie Hammond (Secretary), Eddie Kane (an Officer), Charles Emerson (a Witness), Justina Wayne (a Matron), Patsie deSousa (Crowd), Margaret Brayton (Matron Number Two), and George Webb (Morson).

Commercial: Margaret MacDonald, Margaret Brayton.

Paramount's *Manslaughter*, the 1930 film on which *Lux's* June 20 broadcast was based, concerns a D.A. of humble beginnings who falls in love with the wealthy young lady he is prosecuting for recklessly running down a motorcycle cop. Fredric March recreated his role from the George Abbott–directed movie, while Florence Eldridge played the Claudette Colbert part and James Gleason the character taken in the picture by Pat G. Collins. Of this production, *Variety's* "Bert." noted (on June 22, 1938), "Cast was good, with Miss Eldridge strutting off with top honors."

Lux's host, Cecil B. DeMille, directed the first version of *Manslaughter* for Paramount in 1922, with a cast led by Thomas Meighan, Leatrice Joy, and Jack Mower.

Film versions: Paramount, 1922; Paramount, 1930.

*182. "Jane Eyre," 6/27/38

Based on the novel by Charlotte Brontë (1847).

Intermission Guest: Albert McCleery, columnist for *Stage* magazine (after Act 2).

Cast: Helen Hayes (Jane Eyre), Robert Montgomery (Edward Fairfax Rochester), Mary Nash (Mrs. Fairfax), Brandon Tynan (Mr. Briggs), Esther Dale (Grace Poole), Albert Van Dekker (St. John Rivers), Marion Burns (Diana Rivers), Martha Wentworth (Bertha Mason/Lady Lynn/Old Lady), Lou Merrill (Richard Mason), Marga Ann Deighton (Hannah/Miss Temple), Ted Osborn (Mr. Brocklehurst), Josette Deegan (Adele Varens/Third Girl), Sarah Selby (Leah), Perry Ivins (John), Greta Gould (Lady Ingram), Paula Winslowe (Blanche Ingram), Frank Nelson (Mr. Dent), James Eagles (an Agent), Ann Howard (Amy), Lois Lee (Ella), Paul Monroe (a

North Countryman), Marie Hammond (First Woman/Crowd), Mary Arden (Second Woman/Crowd), Vallarie Morgan (First Girl/Crowd), Jerrie Gail (Betty/Crowd), Margaret McKay (Jane/Crowd), and Ross Forrester (Another Man/Crowd).

Commercial: James Eagles, Frank Nelson, Marie Hammond, Mary Arden, Valarie Morgan, Jerrie Gail, and Margaret McKay.

Charlotte Brontë's famed novel *Jane Eyre* found its way onto *Lux* for the first time (of three) on June 27. The broadcast retold the story of a naive young lady who is engaged as a governess in the home of the mysterious Mr. Rochester. Helen Hayes was cast in the title role, with Robert Montgomery as her brooding employer (a part he would repeat on *Lux* ten years later), and Mary Nash, Brandon Tynan, and Esther Dale in supporting roles. Frank Woodruff found that the program's "adroit mixture of eerie melodrama and love story made good air material." (*Lux* would present "Jane Eyre" again on June 5, 1944, and June 18, 1948.)

The oft-filmed *Jane Eyre* was first seen as a feature motion picture in an anonymously directed production released in 1914 and starring Lisabeth Blackstone and Dallas Tyler. Alice Brady and Elliott Dexter were the stars of *Woman and Wife*, which was directed by Edward José and released by Select Pictures in 1918. Hugo Ballin's 1921 film featured his wife, Mabel Ballin, and Norman Trevor, while Monogram's 1934 production starred Virginia Bruce and Colin Clive, under Christy Cabanne's direction. Joan Fontaine and Orson Welles led the cast of the Robert Stevenson–directed 20th Century–Fox offering, which was released in 1944.

Film versions: Whitman Features/Blinkhorn Photoplays, 1914; Select,

1918 (*Woman and Wife*); Hugo Ballin, 1921; Monogram, 1934; 20th Century–Fox, 1944.

*183. "I Found Stella Parish," 7/4/38

Based on the 1935 First National/Warner Bros. film (screenplay by Casey Robinson; original story by John Monk Saunders).

Intermission Guest: Mrs. Grace Noll Crowell, of Dallas, Texas, who was "recently chosen the American Mother of 1938" (after Act 2).

Cast: Constance Bennett (Stella Parish), Herbert Marshall (Keith Lockridge), George Brent (Stephen Norman), Lucile Watson (Nana), Josette Deegan (Gloria), Edward Broadley (Morton/Third Man), Lou Merrill (Clifton Jeffords), Eric Snowden (Stage Manager/Fourth Man), Frank Nelson (the Voice), David Kerman (Joe Burns), Clive Halliday (Call Boy/Second Man), Eddie Kane (Costumer/Reporter), Forrest Taylor (Manager/Steward), Pauline Gould (Mabel), Sybil Harris (a Gossip), Phyllis Coghlan (Second Woman), Wallace Roberts (Man), and Gil Patric (Crowd).

Commercial: Frank Nelson.

Mervyn LeRoy directed the First National/Warner Bros. motion picture *I Found Stella Parish*, which relates the tale of an actress who tries to conceal her unsavory past from her young daughter. Constance Bennett, Herbert Marshall, George Brent, and Lucille Watson starred in *Lux*'s production, taking the roles played on the screen by Kay Francis, Ian Hunter, Paul Lukas, and Jessie Ralph. Frank Woodruff noted that "Bennett gave an excellent performance as did Marshall, Brent, and all," and pronounced the show "a good ending for an excellent season."

Fourth Season
(September 12, 1938–July 10, 1939)

Columbia Broadcasting System, Monday, 9:00–10:00 P.M. *Host*: Cecil B. DeMille. *Announcer*: Melville Ruick. *Opening Announcer*: Frank Nelson. *Director*: Frank Woodruff. *Musical Director*: Lou Silvers. *Adaptations*: George Wells. *Sound Effects*: Charlie Forsyth.

*184. "Spawn of the North," 9/12/38
Based on the 1938 Paramount film (screenplay by Jules Furthman and Talbot Jennings; story by Barrett Willoughby), in turn based on a novel by Barrett Willoughby (1932).
Intermission Guest: Will H. Hays, head of the Motion Picture Producers and Distributors of America (after Act 2).
Cast: George Raft (Tyler), Fred MacMurray (Jim), Dorothy Lamour (Nicky), John Barrymore (Windy Turlon), Akim Tamiroff (Red Skain), Helen Wood (Diane Turlon), Chester Clute (Jackson), Forrest Taylor (Skagg), Fred Harrington (Grant), Frank Nelson (Tom), Lou Merrill (Lefty), David Kerman (Erickson), Gil Patric (Gregory), Ross Forrester (Davis), Charley Lung (the Seal), Dorothy Farrar, Sidney Newman, and Elaine Miller (Crowd).
Commercial: Elvia Allman, Jerry Tucker, Gloria Fisher, and Monica Ward.
With the cooperation of Paramount Pictures, *Lux* opened its fourth season with an adaptation of that studio's current release, *Spawn of the North*. Henry Hathaway directed the large-scale movie, which relates the rivalry between American and Russian salmon fishermen in Alaska. *Lux*'s cast included four members of the original cast, George Raft, Dorothy Lamour, John Barrymore, and Akim Tamiroff, with Fred MacMurray playing Henry Fonda's film part and Helen Wood portraying the character created on the screen by Louise Platt.
Paramount filmed *Alaska Seas*, another version of *Spawn of the North*, in 1954; this Jerry Hopper–directed effort starred Robert Ryan, Jan Sterling, and Brian Keith.
Additional film version: Paramount, 1954 (*Alaska Seas*).

*185. "Morning Glory," 9/19/38
Based on the 1933 RKO film (screenplay by Howard J. Green), in turn based on the play by Zoë Akins.
Intermission Guest: Zoë Akins, playwright and screenwriter (after Act 2).
Cast: Barbara Stanwyck (Eva Lovelace), Melvyn Douglas (Joseph Sheridan), Ralph Bellamy (Lewis Easton), C. Aubrey Smith (Robert Hedges), Elaine Barrie (Rita Vernon), Ynez Seabury (Secretary/Marie/Second Woman), Byron Stevens (Stage Manager/Second Man), Lou Merrill (Seymour), Frank Nelson (Charley/First Man/Man), Margaret Brayton (Vivian Hall/Ella/Second Girl/Woman Two), Eddie Kane (Butler/Man), Rolfe Sedan (a Waiter), James Eagles (Call Boy/Second Man), Elia Braca (Cleo/Third Girl), Ross Forrester (Counterman), Raye Ellis (First Girl/Woman), George Webb (Sailor/Crowd), and Paul Marion (Crowd).
Commercial: Joyce Rippe.
Morning Glory, which had been a Katharine Hepburn film at RKO in

1933, became a Barbara Stanwyck radio play on September 19. Also starring in the tale of a naive girl's struggle to become a stage actress were Melvyn Douglas and Ralph Bellamy in the parts played by Douglas Fairbanks, Jr., and Adolphe Menjou in the Lowell Sherman–directed movie, with C. Aubrey Smith recreating his film role and Elaine Barrie in the Mary Duncan motion picture part.

RKO/Buena Vista called its 1958 Sidney Lumet–directed production *Stage Struck*. Susan Strasberg, Christopher Plummer, Henry Fonda, Herbert Marshall, and Joan Greenwood were cast in the leading roles.

Lux presented a second rendering on October 12, 1942.

Additional film versions: RKO/Buena Vista, 1958 (*Stage Struck*).

186. "Seven Keys to Baldpate," 9/26/38

Based on the play by George M. Cohan (1913), in turn based on the novel by Earl Derr Biggers (1913).

Intermission Guest: Efrem Zimbalist, violinist (after Act 2).

Cast: Jack Benny, Mary Livingstone, Cecil B. DeMille (Themselves), Margaret Brayton (Rita), Ted Osborn (Hermie), Ross Forrester (Bland), Gale Gordon (Morgan/Third Man), Lou Merrill (Kennedy), John Fee (Sergeant), Eddie Waller (Jed/Second Prisoner), Martha Wentworth (Belinda), Joe Kearns (a Prisoner), Victor Rodman (Bollister), Mary Lansing (Telephone Operator/Second Girl), Frank Nelson (Oakley), Dorothy Griwatz (Miss Cole), and Katherine Carlton (a Girl).

Commercial: Forrest Taylor, Monica Ward, and Gloria Fisher.

Earl Derr Biggers conceived his novel *Seven Keys to Baldpate* as a straight melodrama; George M. Cohan's stage play is a parody of the very sort of work the novel represents, and *Lux*'s

adaptation is even more comedic than Cohan's version. The reasoning behind this is that the production was assembled as a vehicle for its stars — Jack Benny and Mary Livingstone. Unlike the earlier "Brewster's Millions" (February 15, 1937), which also featured the radio couple, the lead characters in "Seven Keys to Baldpate" *are* their radio characters (which undoubtedly served as an effective plug for NBC's *The Jack Benny Program*, which was to return to the air after its summer break on the following Sunday).

Lux's version of the comedy-drama opens and closes in the offices of Cecil B. DeMille, where the director promises Jack Benny that he will star in a motion picture if he can pen a successful play in 24 hours. DeMille even offers him a quiet place to work: a deserted inn on isolated Baldpate Mountain. (The scenes that follow in which Benny attempts to live up to his end of the agreement are only loosely based on Cohan's stage work.)

For the first and only time in a *Lux* broadcast, DeMille performs in the dramatic portion of the show, and because he is so busily involved in his acting chores (which he handled splendidly), some of his host duties are assumed by Melville Ruick, who sets the scene for each act and interviews that week's intermission guest, violinist Efrem Zimbalist. Zimbalist performs Franz Schubert's "The Bee" (accompanied by Theodore Saidenberg at the piano), which is the piece that started the famed "feud" between Jack Benny and fellow radio comedian Fred Allen.

Seven Keys to Baldpate has a long history on the screen, with the first version produced by Cohan Feature Film Corporation/Artclass in 1917. The stars of that Hugh Ford–directed movie are George M. Cohan and Anna Q. Nilsson, while Douglas MacLean and Edith

Roberts head the cast of Paramount's 1925 Fred Newmeyer–directed effort. RKO produced the first talkie of Cohan's play in 1929, with Reginald Barker directing Richard Dix and Miriam Seegar, and in 1935 RKO gave the story another go-round with Gene Raymond and Margaret Callahan under the direction of William Hamilton and Edward Killy. It was filmed once more by RKO in 1947, and though it credits the novel *and* the play as its source, actually it departs drastically from both. Featured in that Lew Landers–directed opus are Phillip Terry and Jacqueline White. Pete Walker was at the helm of the most recent attempt, a 1983 Cannon (British) release starring Desi Arnaz, Jr., and Sheila Keith, and entitled *House of the Long Shadows*.

Film versions: Cohan Feature Film Corporation/Artclass, 1917; Paramount, 1925; RKO, 1929; RKO, 1935; RKO, 1947; Cannon, 1983 (*House of the Long Shadows*).

*187. "Another Dawn," 10/3/38

Based on the 1937 Warner Bros. film (screenplay by Laird Doyle).

Intermission Guest: Beatrice Fairfax, syndicated newspaper columnist (from New York City; after Act 2).

Cast: Madeleine Carroll (Julia Ashton), Franchot Tone (Dennis Roark), George Brent (Colonel John Wister), Joan Garstin (Grace Roark), Denis Green (Hawkins), Evan Thomas (Charlie Benton), Wyndham Standing (Dr. Forbes/Waiter), Eric Snowden (Wilkins), C. Ramsay Hill (Victor Sardler), Frank Nelson (Nichols), Louis Merrill (Orderly), Jo Anne Ransom, Carolyn Newell, David Kerman, Sidney Newman, George Webb, and Ross Forrester (Crowd).

Commercial: Gwenn Walters.

Warner Bros.' *Another Dawn*, a 1937 William Dieterle–directed production, focuses on a lady married to a colonel in the British military and her love for a dashing captain who reminds her of a former (lost) beau. Kay Francis is the star of the film, while *Lux*'s dramatization features Madeleine Carroll in her role, with Franchot Tone and George Brent as the gentlemen in her life (played onscreen by Errol Flynn and Ian Hunter). Frank Woodruff called the show "a great melodrama with nice heart tug," and commented on the cast's fine performances—especially Madeleine Carroll, Franchot Tone, and Brent."

*188. "Viva Villa!," 10/10/38

Based on the 1934 MGM film (screenplay by Ben Hecht), in turn suggested by the book by Edgcumb Pinchon and O.B. Stade (1933).

Intermission Guest: James Wong Howe, Hollywood cameraman (cinematographer for *Viva Villa!*) (after Act 2).

Cast: Wallace Beery (Pancho Villa), Edmund Lowe (Johnny Sykes), Leo Carrillo (Sierro), Noah Beery (President Madero), Eduardo Ciannelli (General Pascal), Ellen Drew (Rosita), Edward Marr (Calloway), Walter White (the Attorney/First Statesman), Celeste Rush (Peon Woman), Tito Renaldo (Teller/Operator), Raoul deLeon (Bandit/Guard), Walter Gering (Lopez/Second Peon/Third Peon), Roger Joseph (Statesman/Second Bandit), David Kerman (Captain/Soldier), Lou Merrill (Politico/Third Statesman), Ross Forrestser (Peon), George Webb (Captain/Soldier), Harry Vejar (Peon/Man/Waiter), and Enrico Ricardi (Singer).

Commercial: Gretchen Thomas (Mother), Betty Jean Hainey (Midge), Eric Forsyth Burtis, Jr. (Bobby), and Elia Braca (Dot).

After a delay of more than two years (it had originally been announced for the July 20, 1936, show), MGM's *Viva Villa!* reached the airwaves on October 10.

The romanticized adventures of Mexico's bandit and revolutionary leader Pancho Villa (1887–1923) made entertaining screen fare in the excellent 1934 Jack Conway–directed production, and two members of that motion picture's cast, Wallace Beery and Leo Carrillo, reprised their characterizations in *Lux*'s radio version. Also appearing on the program were Edmund Lowe, Noah Beery, Eduardo Ciannelli, and Ellen Drew, playing roles created by Stuart Erwin, Henry B. Walthall, Joseph Schildkraut, and Ellen Drew herself in the movie. (The Fay Wray picture character of Teresa was deleted from the broadcast.)

Variety's "Edga" said of the program (on October 12, 1938) that the "performance of 'Viva Villa!' by the cast, and the job done on trimming the opus down from its film antecedents were first rate."

*189. "Seventh Heaven," 10/17/38
Based on the play by Austin Strong (1922).
Intermission Guest: Marjorie Hillis, author (after Act 2).
Cast: Jean Arthur (Diane), Don Ameche (Chico), Jean Hersholt (Father Chevillon), Lionel Belmore (Papa Boul), Barry McCollum (Sewer Rat), Lou Merrill (Brissac), Ynez Seabury (Nana), Geraldine Peck (Madame Gobin), Paul Gryar (Captain/Second Gendarme), James Eagles (Third Gendarme/Officer), Sybil Harris (Arlette), Gil Patric (Crowd), Sidney Newman (Voice of Machine), George Webb, Margaret MacKay, Marie Hammond (Crowd), Noreen Gammill (Crowd), Frank Nelson (Gendarme/Man/Voice), Jerrie Gail (Crowd), and Eric Burtis (Crowd).
Commercial: Jane Loffaourrow (Aunt Cynthia), Colleen Ward (Dot), Henry Hanna (Bobby), and Betty Jean Hainey (Midge).

Lux's fourth anniversary was celebrated on October 17 with a revival of the play that opened the series on October 14, 1934, Austin Strong's poignant love story, *Seventh Heaven*. Leading lady Jean Arthur, who played Diane in the broadcast, was also celebrating a birthday at the time, as DeMille pointed out. Featured opposite Arthur was Don Ameche as Chico, with Jean Hersholt as Father Chevillon.

Other *Lux* "Seventh Heaven" broadcasts aired on October 14, 1934, October 16, 1944, and March 26, 1951; see 10/14/34 for information on stage and film versions.

Film versions: Fox, 1927; 20th Century–Fox, 1937.

*190. "Babbitt," 10/24/38
Based on the 1934 First National/Warner Bros. film (screenplay by Mary McCall, Jr.; adaptation by Tom Reed and Niven Bush), in turn based on the novel by Sinclair Lewis (1922).
Intermission Guest: Jimmy Starr, Hollywood columnist for the *Los Angeles Evening Herald and Express* (after Act 2).
Cast: Edward Arnold (George Babbitt), Fay Bainter (Myra), Claire Dodd (Mrs. Judique), Johnny Downs (Ted), Victor Rodman (Mr. Earthorne), Joe DuVal (Mr. Gurnee), Stanley Farrar (Virgil Gunch/Salesman), Georgia Simmons (Rosalie), Jo Ann Ransom (Miss McGowan), Ross Forrester (Newsboy), Eddie Kane (Irate Citizen), Lou Merrill (Kendall/Conductor), Frank Nelson (Waiter/Second Man), Pauline Gould (Second Woman), Elizabeth Wilbur (First Woman), and George Gramlich (Man).
Commercial: Frank Nelson, Sally Creighton.

Sinclair Lewis's *Babbitt*, the tale of an average businessman and his normal American town, became considerably more melodramatic in Warner Bros.' 1934 William Keighley–directed film version, and it was this picture that was adapted for *Lux*'s October 24 broadcast. Edward Arnold starred in the Guy Kibbee film role, Fay Bainter played his wife (Aline MacMahon in the movie), Claire Dodd recreated her screen part, and Johnny Downs played the Glen Boles picture role.

Warner Bros.' first *Babbitt* was directed by Harry Beaumont in 1924 and starred Willard Louis, Mary Alden, Carmel Myers, and Raymond Kee.

Additional film version: Warner Bros., 1924.

*191. "That Certain Woman," 10/31/38

Based on the 1937 First National/ Warner Bros. film (screenplay by Edmund Goulding), in turn based on the United Artists 1929 film *The Trespasser* (screenplay by Edmund Goulding, Laura Hope Crews, and Gloria Swanson).

Intermission Guest: Edmund Goulding, motion picture director (after Act 2).

Cast: Carole Lombard (Mary Donnell), Basil Rathbone (Lloyd Rogers), Jeffrey Lynn (Jack Merrick), Montague Shaw (Norton Merrick), Elizabeth Wilbur (Amy), Lurene Tuttle (Jean), George Pembroke (Tilden/Englishman), Galan Galt (Dr. Hartman), Bobby Larson (Jackie), Frank Nelson (Virgil Whittaker), Louis Merrill (Commissioner Finley/Frenchman), Mary Lansing (Telephone Operator), Sada Cowan (Secretary), James Eagles (Newsboy/ Reporter), Ross Forrester (Newsboy/ Elevator Boy), Edward Marr (Reporter/ Italian), James Robbins (Reporter), and David Kerman (Newsboy/Reporter/ German).

Commercial: Mary Lansing.

That Certain Woman is a 1937 motion picture concerning a woman who becomes involved with an attorney and a ne'er-do-well playboy while trying to live down her past life (during which she was married to a gangster). Edmund Goulding, who is *Lux*'s intermission guest, scripted and directed both the Warner Bros. movie and the 1929 United Artists film on which it is based. The 1937 photoplay cast Bette Davis, Ian Hunter, and Henry Fonda in the roles that were played in *Lux*'s 1938 broadcast by Carole Lombard, Basil Rathbone, and Jeffrey Lynn. *The Trespasser* of 1929 was the first talkie for Gloria Swanson, who costars with Robert Ames.

Additional film version: Swanson/ United Artists, 1929 (*The Trespasser*).

*192. "Next Time We Love," 11/7/38

Based on the 1936 Universal film (screenplay by Melville Baker), in turn based on the novel *Say Goodbye Again*, by Ursula Parrott (1935).

Intermission Guests: Linton Wells and Fay Gillis Wells, newspaper correspondents (after Act 2).

Cast: Margaret Sullavan (Cicely Tyler), Joel McCrea (Christopher Tyler), Colin Tapley (Tommy Abbott), Lou Merrill (Carteret/Train Announcer), Marga Ann Deighton (Madame Donato/a Woman), John Lake (Mr. Kane/German Conductor), John Fee (Otto), Harold Wilson (Conductor/ Man Number Two), Sidney Newman (Third Man/Joe), Carolyn Newell (Telephone Operator/First Woman), Gil Patric (Doorman/Second Man), Ross Forrester (Taxi Driver/a Man), Eric Burtis (Small Boy), George Webb (Taxi Driver/Man Number Three/ Guard), Mary Lansing (Baby Cries/ Woman), and Cracker Henderson (Redcap/General Utility).

Commercial: Jane Morgan (Mother), Eric Burtis, Jr. (Bobby), John Fee (Dad), and Marilyn Stuart (Dot).

Universal's *Next Time We Love* was directed by Edward H. Griffith and rehashes the familiar situation of a married couple, the woman a budding stage actress and the man a reporter, who find their separate careers pulling them in opposite directions. Margaret Sullavan played her screen part in the *Lux* broadcast, while Joel McCrea was cast in James Stewart's picture role.

193. "The Buccaneer," 11/14/38

Based on the 1938 Paramount film (screenplay by Edwin Justis Mayer, Harold Lamb, and C. Gardner Sullivan; adaptation by Jeanie Macpherson), in turn based on the book *Lafitte, the Pirate,* by Lyle Saxon (1930).

Intermission Guest: Rupert Hughes, author (after Act 2).

Cast: Clark Gable (Jean Lafitte), Olympe Bradna (Gretchen), Akim Tamiroff (Dominique), Gertrude Michael (Annette de Remy), Clara Blandick (Aunt Charlotte), Edmond Elton (Governor Claiborne), John Fee (General Andrew Jackson), Lou Merrill (Senator Crawford), Eddie Waller (Mr. Peavey/Beluche), Montague Shaw (Captain McWilliams/Third Man in Act 3), Reginald Sheffield (Captain Lockyer/Major Hinds), Harry Humphrey (Colonel Butler), George Pembroke (Collector of Port/Mouse/Second Man), Lois Collier (Roxanne/Woman/Second Woman), Earl Gunn (Brown/Man in Act 2/Victory Voice/Second Man in Act 3), Vic DeMourell (Jacques/Third Man in Act 2/Monsieur Villier), Earle Ross (Fish Hook/Fourth Man in Act 3), Frank Nelson (Councilman/Man in Act 3), Tony Paton (Baratarian/Lobo), Jack Carr (Scipio/Major Domo), Libby Taylor (a Nurse), Geraldine Peck (Woman), Cracker Henderson (Butler), Ross Forrester (Miguel), Lee Millar (Dog), and Perry Ivins (Gramby).

Commercial: Marilyn Stuart (Dot), Betty Jean Hainey (Midge), John Fee (Dad), and Jane Morgan (Mother).

Since host Cecil B. DeMille frequently referred to his film *The Buc-* *caneer* while it was in production, the story was a natural choice to be presented on *Lux*. The broadcast, which chronicles the adventures of pirate Jean Lafitte (1780–1826?) and his patriotic acts to help his adopted country during the War of 1812, features Clark Gable in the title role, Olympe Bradna (who turns in a fine performance in her only *Lux* appearance), and Akim Tamiroff, who repeats his film portrayal of Lafitte's right-hand man, Dominique. Though Gable may not be totally convincing as the swashbuckling European and does not attempt a French accent, he nevertheless brings a certain amount of strength to the part, and his speech to convince his band of pirates to fight for America is effectively rendered. (The motion picture features Fredric March as Jean Lafitte and Franciska Gaal as Gretchen.)

The main theme from George Antheil's film score is quoted briefly at the beginning of each act in Lou Silvers's incidental music.

Cecil B. DeMille produced Paramount's 1958 version of *The Buccaneer,* which was directed by Anthony Quinn and starred Charlton Heston, Claire Bloom, Yul Brynner, and Charles Boyer.

Additional film version: Paramount, 1958.

*194. "Confession," 11/21/38

Based on the 1937 First National/Warner Bros. film (screenplay by Julius J. Epstein and Margaret LeVino), in turn based on the 1935 Tempelhof (German) film *Mazurka Tragika* (screenplay by Hans Rameau).

Intermission Guest: Dr. Herman Lissauer, head of Warner Bros.' research department (after Act 2).

Cast: Miriam Hopkins (Vera Kowalska), Claude Rains (Michael Michailov), Richard Greene (Leonide), Anne Shirley (Lisa), Cy Kendall (Prosecutor), Margaret Brayton (Stella Maloff), Louis

Merrill (Gregori Stern), Ted Osborn (Counsel/Man), Arthur Van Slyke (Judge), Myra Marsh (Mrs. Koslov), Ethel Sykes (Xenia Salkow), Frank Nelson (Stephens), Edwin Max (an Officer), David Kerman (a Clerk), Elia Braca (Elaine Martine), Jerrie Gail (Hildegarde), Justina Wayne (a Maid), Teresa Carmo (a Nurse), James Eagles (Court Reporter), Sarah Selby (Woman), Jo Ann Ransom (Girl), Mildred Carroll (Singer), and Ross Forrester (Foreman).

Commercial: Rosemary deCamp (Joan), Virginia McMullen (Second Girl), James Eagles (Bill), Jo Ann Ransom (First Girl).

Joe May directed First National/ Warner Bros.' visually arresting motion picture *Confession*, which stars Kay Francis, Basil Rathbone, Ian Hunter, and Jane Bryan. On November 21, *Lux* presented the melodrama about a café singer who shoots a licentious scoundrel to death to keep him away from her daughter, with Miriam Hopkins, Claude Rains, Richard Greene, and Anne Shirley in the leads.

Willi Forst directed the 1935 German production *Mazurka Tragika*, on which First National's later *Confession* was based. Starring in this motion picture were Pola Negri, Albrecht Schoenhals, and Ingeborg Theek.

Additional film version: Tempelhof (German), 1935 (*Mazurka*).

*195. "Interference," 11/28/38

Based on the play by Roland Pertwee and Harold Dearden (1927).

Intermission Guest: Captain Michael Fiaschetti, private detective (after Act 2).

Cast: Herbert Marshall (Philip Voaze), Leslie Howard (Sir John Marlay), Mary Astor (Deborah Kane), Gail Patrick (Faith Marlay), Frederick Worlock (Inspector Haines), Denis Green (Childers), Eric Snowden (Fred/ Third Reporter), Herbert Evans (Mr.

Cleaver/First Reporter), Edith Mason (Woman Reporter), Louis Merrill (Robert), Frank Nelson (Fourth Reporter), Ross Forrester (Second Reporter/Crowd), and George Webb (Sergeant of Police).

Commercial: Betty Jean Hainey (Midge), Jane Morgan (Mother), John Fee (Dad), and Marilyn Stuart (Dot).

Interference, the play by Roland Pertwee and Harold Dearden (which opened at the Empire Theatre in New York on October 18, 1937), is a melodrama concerning a prominent London physician who discovers that his wife's first husband, thought killed in the war, has turned up alive, and that an insidious female blackmailer is holding the fact over her. Herbert Marshall was the star of *Lux*'s production, cast in the role of the first husband, with Leslie Howard as Sir John Marlay, M.D., Mary Astor as the blackmailer, and Gail Patrick as Lady Marlay. (These roles were played in the original Broadway production by A.E. Matthews, Arthur Wontner, Kathlene MacDonell, and Phoebe Foster.)

Interference, which was Paramount's first all-talking picture (released in 1928), starred William Powell, Clive Brook, Evelyn Brent, and Doris Kenyon and was directed by Roy Pomeroy. (Lothar Mendes shot a silent version of the film simultaneously.)

Film version: Paramount, 1928.

*196. "The Princess Comes Across," 12/5/38

Based on the 1936 Paramount film (screenplay by Walter DeLeon, Francis Martin, Frank Butler, and Don Hartman; story by Philip MacDonald), in turn based on the novel by Louis Lucien Rogger.

Intermission Guest: Phil Baker, radio comedian (from Toronto; after Act 2).

Cast: Madeleine Carroll (Princess Olga), Fred MacMurray (King Mantell),

Mary Boland (Lady Gertrude), Roscoe Karns (Benton), Robert Warwick (Captain Nichols), Georges Renavent (Inspector Lorel), Egon Brecher (Dr. Steindorf), Ramsay Hill (Inspector Cragg), Victor Rodman (Darcy), Raymond Lawrence (Purser), Louis Merrill (Morevitch), Hugo Borg (Mr. Gustavson), Eddie Marr (a Cameraman), David Jordan (a Steward/Man), John Lake (the Doctor/Reporter), Ralph Nelson (Master of Ceremonies/Film Man), Frank Nelson (Second Reporter/Newsreel), James Eagles (Third Reporter).

Commercial: James Eagles (Bill), Jerry Hausner (Joe), Ralph Nelson (Bob), and Dorothy Ohrt [formerly Dorothy Meade] (Betty).

The William K. Howard–directed comedy-mystery *The Princess Comes Across* was released by Paramount in 1936. *Lux*'s version features Madeleine Carroll in Carole Lombard's movie role of a Brooklyn girl masquerading as a Swedish princess, and Fred MacMurray in his original role of a band leader who falls for her. Their shipboard romance is complicated by the presence of an escaped killer and an international group of detectives who attempt to discover his true identity. (Frank Woodruff called the radio presentation a "rather pleasing comedy" and noted that "Carroll [was] very good.")

197. "The Scarlet Pimpernel," 12/12/38

Based on the 1935 London Films/United Artists film (screenplay by Robert Sherwood, Arthur Wimperis, Sam Berman, and Lajos Biro), in turn based on the novel by Baroness Orczy (1905) and on the play by Baroness Orczy and Montagu Barstow (1905).

Intermission Guest: Madame Hilda Grenier, motion picture technical advisor and former royal dresser to Queen Mary of England (after Act 2).

Cast: Leslie Howard (Sir Percy Blakeney), Olivia deHavilland (Lady Marguerite Blakeney), Denis Green (Monsieur Chauvelin), Walter Kingsford (Sir Andrew Foulkes), Vernon Steele (Romney), Ramsay Hill (Armand St. Just), Reginald Sheffield (Count deTournay/Lackey), Eric Snowden (the Prince of Wales/Sergeant), Gerald Cornell (Innkeeper), Keith Kenneth (Brinker), Lou Merrill (a Barber), George Pembroke (Lord Hastings/Second Man), John Toti (a Voice), Dave Roberts (a Guard), Geraldine Peck (a Lady/Woman), Ethel Sykes (Second Woman), Coral Colebrook (Second Girl), Betty Sutter (Girl), Carolyn Newell (Second Lady), Ross Forrester (Man), Frank Nelson (Third Man), and Dave Roberts (Guard).

Commercial: Marilyn Stuart (Dot), Betty Jean Hainey (Midge), Jane Morgan (Mother), and Eric Burtis, Jr. (Bobby).

In *Lux*'s "The Scarlet Pimpernel," Leslie Howard recreated one of his most famous film roles of a seemingly inconsequential dandy who assumes a secret identity to free members of the French aristocracy from the clutches of the bloodthirsty revolutionaries during the late eighteenth century. Howard's performance for the microphone serves as a good reminder of his witty characterization in the 1935 Harold Young–directed film, and he is clearly able to distinguish between the foppish Percy Blakeney and the courageous Scarlet Pimpernel entirely in the manner of his delivery. (Robert Montgomery had previously been announced to play the role.) Olivia deHavilland is very effective in her role as Sir Percy's estranged wife, Lady Marguerite, and even provides the character with an appropriate French accent (which Merle Oberon does not do in the movie).

Fox was the first studio to release a feature film of *The Scarlet Pimpernel,* which it did in 1917. Starring in this Richard Stanton–directed production were Dustin Farnum, Winifred Kingston, and William Burgess. British Lion came out with a version in 1950, which was directed by Michael Powell and Emeric Pressburger, and featured David Niven, Margaret Leighton, and Cyril Cusak. Entitled *The Elusive Pimpernel,* the motion picture was originally shot as a musical but was released without the songs.

Additional film versions: Fox, 1917; British Lion, 1950 (*The Elusive Pimpernel*).

198. "Kid Galahad," 12/19/38

Based on the 1937 Warner Bros.–First National film (screenplay by Seton I. Miller), in turn based on the novel by Frances Wallace (1936).

Intermission Guests: Jack Dempsey (from Buffalo, New York) and Gene Tunney (from New York City), former heavyweight boxing champions (after Act 2).

Additional Guest (in *Lux* commercial): Alice Frost, radio actress (after Act 1).

Cast: Edward G. Robinson (Nick Donati), Joan Bennett (Fluff), Wayne Morris (Kid Galahad), Andrea Leeds (Marie Donati), Cy Kendall (Turkey Morgan), Edwin Max (Chuck McGraw), Chester Clute (Silver), Ross Forrester (Buzz), Frank Nelson (Radio Announcer/Redcap), Joe Cunningham (a Reporter), Louis Merrill (Referee/Radio Announcer/Announcer Number Two), Galan Galt (Fight Announcer), David Kerman (Judge/Man/Second Reporter), Joe Frenz (Barney), George Pembroke (Handler/Third Man), Ruth Weston (Blonde), Eddie Kane (Second Judge/Man), Stewart Wilson (Second Man), Cracker Henderson, Margaret McKay, Celeste Rush, Pauline Gould (Crowd), George Webb (Third Reporter).

Even though Warner Brothers' *Kid Galahad* relies heavily on its action scenes for much of its impact, the story is compelling enough for an entertaining radio drama. Edward G. Robinson, the star of the 1937 film (which was directed by Michael Curtiz), repeats his role of fight manager Nick Donati, while Wayne Morris recreates his celluloid part of the title character, a hick bellboy converted into a heavyweight champ. The leading feminine roles, played in the motion picture by Bette Davis and Jane Bryan, are played on the air by Joan Bennett and Andrea Leeds.

In an interesting departure, the usual sort of *Lux* commercial after the first act is bypassed. Instead, actress Alice Frost (heard from New York City), at that time the star of CBS's daytime serial drama *Portia Faces Life,* performs an entertaining one-woman routine promoting the sponsor's product.

Roy Enright directed Warner Bros.' 1941 version of *Kid Galahad,* which had a new title, *The Wagons Roll at Night,* and a new setting in a circus. Humphrey Bogart (who plays Morgan in the original) is featured, along with Sylvia Sidney, Eddie Albert, and Joan Leslie. United Artists filmed the story once again in 1962 under its original title, with direction by Phil Karlson and a cast which included Gig Young, Lola Albright, Elvis Presley, and Joan Blackman.

Additional film versions: Warner Bros., 1941 (*The Wagons Roll at Night*); United Artists, 1962.

199. "Snow White and the Seven Dwarfs," 12/26/38

Based on the 1937 Walt Disney/RKO animated production (screenplay by Ted Sears, Otto Englander, Earl Hurd, Dorothy Ann Blank, Richard Creedon, Dick Rickard, Merrill deMaris, and Webb Smith), in turn based on Grimm's

Fairy Tales, "Schneewittchen," in *Kinder und Haus-marchen,* by Jakob Ludwig Karl Grimm and Wilhelm Grimm (1812).

Intermission Guest: Walt Disney (after Act 2 and during curtain call).

Cast: Thelma Hubbard (Snow White), James Eagles (Prince), Roy Atwell (Doc), Billy Gilbert (Sneezy), Rolfe Sedan (Happy), Jack Smart (Bashful), Moroni Olsen (Mirror), Stuart Buchanan (Grumpy/Huntsman), Paula Winslowe (Queen), Gloria Gordon (Witch), Eddie Davis (Whistler/ Bird One), Louise Burnett (Whistler/ Bird Two), Marie Green (Echo), Lou Merrill (Sleepy), and Ross Forrester (Special Effects/Ad Lib).

Singers: Richard Davis, Myron Neely, Kenneth Rundquist, Harry Stanton, Freeman High, Dudley Kusell, Robert Stevens (the Prince), and Enrico Ricardi.

Lux's holiday offering on December 26 was a well-crafted radio production of the 1937 animated Walt Disney feature, *Snow White and the Seven Dwarfs.* (Directors credited are Perce Pearce, Larry Morey, William Cottrell, Wilfred Jackson, and Ben Sharpsteen.) Four members of the unbilled cast, Roy Atwell, Billy Gilbert, Moroni Olsen, and Stuart Buchanan, reprise their voice characterizations of the film version, while the leading roles of Snow White and the Prince (which use the voices of Adriana Caselotti and Harry Stockwell on the screen) are taken on the air by Thelma Hubbard and James Eagles. (The Prince's singing voice is provided by Robert Stevens.)

As visual as the motion picture is, the radio play is successful in capturing its spirit and effectively retells the familiar fairy tale. Songs from the film score (words by Larry Morey, music by Frank Churchill) heard in the broadcast are: Act 1: "I'm Wishing" (Snow White and Echo), "One Song" (Prince Charming),

"Whistle While You Work" (Snow White), "Dig, Dig, Dig, Dig, Dig, Dig, Dig" (the Seven Dwarfs), "Hi-Ho" (the Seven Dwarfs); Act 2: "Dwarf's Song" (the Seven Dwarfs), "Some Day My Prince Will Come" (Snow White); Act 3: "Hi-Ho" (reprise); finale: "Some Day My Prince Will Come" (Snow White and Prince Charming).

"Snow White," the first Hollywood *Lux* that does not have a studio audience, uses recorded applause at the beginning and end of each act.

200. "The Perfect Specimen," 1/2/39

Based on the 1937 Warner Bros. film (screenplay by Norman Reilly Raine, Lawrence Riley, Brewster Morse, and Fritz Falkenstein), in turn based on the novel by Samuel Hopkins Adams (1936).

Intermission Guest: Dr. Floyd L. Ruch, associate professor of psychology, University of Southern California, and author of *Psychology and Life* (after Act 2).

Cast: Errol Flynn (Gerald Wickes), Joan Blondell (Mona Carter), May Robson (Grandma Wickes), Byron K. Foulger (Alfred Gratton), Lindsay MacHarrie (Killegrewe Shawe), Alma Lloyd (Alicia), Clem Bevans (Professor Carter), Eddie Waller (Sheriff Snodgrass/Man), Ross Forrester (Pinky), Gay Seabrook (Clarabelle), Billy Bletcher (Conley), Frank Nelson (Jink Carter), Lou Fulton (Hooker), Earle Ross (Hotel Clerk/Flight Announcer), Lou Merrill (Announcer), Bob Burleson (Referee/Clerk), Eddie Marr (Butler/ Voice), Caroline Frasher, Raoul DeLeon, Gil Patric, David Kerman, and Margaret Brayton (Crowd).

Commercial: Lou Merrill (Grocer).

Warner Bros.' *The Perfect Specimen,* another feature in the "screwball" comedy genre, was showcased on the two-hundredth broadcast of *The Lux Radio*

Theatre. The plot concerns a "perfect specimen" kept in a carefully controlled environment who ventures into the outside world where he meets life for the first time. Cast in the radio play are Errol Flynn, Joan Blondell, and May Robson, all of whom reprise their roles from the 1937 Michael Curtiz–directed motion picture.

Evidently, the one-woman *Lux* commercial that took place on the December 19 broadcast met with good response, for the commercial after the first act on this program is done in the same style. Instead of a featured performer, however, *Lux* regular Lou Merrill (who is not credited) is the actor involved.

201. "Mayerling," 1/9/39
Based on the 1936 Nero film (screenplay by Joseph Kessell and Madame J.V. Cube), in turn based on the novel *Idyll's End,* by Claude Anet (1930).
Intermission Guest: Don Eugene Plummer, "Hollywood's oldest citizen" (after Act 2).
Cast: Janet Gaynor (Marie Vetchera), William Powell (Prince Rudolf), Alma Kruger (Countess Vetchera), Robert Barrett (Count Taffe), Frank Reicher (Emperor Franz Josef), Verna Felton (Mimi), Doris Lloyd (Countess Larische), Clarence Derwent (Herr Szeps), Eddie Woods (George), Ethel Wales (Nounou), Eric Snowden (Commissioner), Bud McTaggart (Karl Semmering), J. Donald Wilson (an Officer), Joseph Kearns (Loschek), John Lake (an Aide), Barbara Willett (Irma), Paula Winslowe (Empress Elisabeth), Lou Merrill (an Agent), Leone LeDoux (a Puppet), Frank Nelson (Flirtatious Gentleman), Ben Wright (Devil Puppet), Gaughan Burke (a Secret Agent), Geraldine Peck, and Celeste Rush (Ladies of the Court).
The January 9, 1939, broadcast of *Lux*

marked the first time the program featured an adaptation of a foreign language film. (The Nero production of *Mayerling* was made in France in 1936.) This Anatole Litvak–directed motion picture caused a considerable stir when it was released in the United States, which helped to establish a reputation for its stars, Charles Boyer and Danielle Darrieux. (Others in the cast include Suzy Prim and Jean Dax.) Engaged to create the lead roles in the *Lux* version are Janet Gaynor and William Powell, both of whom give sincere and touching performances in the drama concerning the real-life love story of Prince Rudolf of Hapsburg and Marie Vetchera, which ended tragically in a much-publicized double suicide in 1881. (Frank Woodruff noted that the broadcast contained "sensitive performances by all of cast in an emotionally stirring show.")

Eighty-six-year-old Don Eugene Plummer, "Hollywood's oldest citizen" and a resident of the community for 72 years, tells fascinating tales about the area before it became the motion picture capital.

Terrence Young directed a British-Pathé version of *Mayerling* in 1969, which starred Omar Sharif, Catherine Deneuve, James Robertson Justice, James Mason, and Ava Gardner.
Additional film version: British-Pathé, 1969.

202. "Front Page Woman," 1/16/39
Based on the 1935 Warner Bros. film (screenplay by Roy Chanslor, Lillie Hayward, and Laird Doyle), in turn based on the story "Women Are Bum Newspapermen," by Richard Macauley (1934).
Intermission Guest: Floyd Gibbons, newspaper reporter (from New York City; after Act 2).
Cast: Fred MacMurray (Curt Devlin), Paulette Goddard (Ellen Garfield), Roscoe Karns (Toots), Ynez Seabury

(Olive Wilson), Margaret Brayton (May LaRue), Lindsay MacHarrie (Officer Hollohan/Foreman), John Fee (Maitland Coulter/Norris), Lee Millar (Marvin Stone/Hartmett), Lou Merrill (Spike Kiley/Roma), Rolfe Sedan (Robert Chinard/Harrow), Abe Reynolds (a Tailor/Vance), Frank Nelson (Robert Cordoza), Mary Jane Karns (Inez Cordoza), Ted Osborn (District Attorney/Charovski), Edward Marr (Laundryman/Second Reporter/Noyes), David Starling (a Chinese Cleaning Boy/Phillips), Harry Humphrey (Judge/Warden), Joe Franz (Bailiff/Sergeant), Elizabeth Wilbur (a Nurse), Elinor Harriett (Telephone Operator), Sidney Newman (Taxi Driver/Newsboy/Stacey), Ross Forrester (Warburton), James Eagles (Newsboy Number Two/Barclay), and James Robbins (a Reporter/Newsboy Number Three/Smith).

Commercial: Marilyn Stuart (Dot), Jane Morgan (Mother), and Eric Burtis, Jr. (Bobby).

The source for *Lux*'s broadcast of "Front Page Woman" was a Warner Bros. feature (directed by Michael Curtiz) that starred Bette Davis, George Brent, and Roscoe Karns and was released in 1935. Fred MacMurray and Paulette Goddard give appealing performances as rival newspaper reporters, as does Roscoe Karns (of the film cast), who plays MacMurray's wisecracking photographer.

During the curtain call, it is revealed that DeMille has been deliverying his lines from a stretcher, the result of an accident on the *Union Pacific* set.

203. "Cardinal Richelieu," 1/23/39

Based on the 1935 20th Century/United Artists film (adaptation by Cameron Rogers, screenplay by Maude Howell, and dialogue by W.P. Lipscomb), in turn based on the play by Sir Edward Bulwer-Lytton (1839).

Intermission Guest: Edward P. Lambert, motion picture costume designer (after Act 2).

Cast: George Arliss (Cardinal Richelieu), Florence Arliss (Marie deMedici), Cesar Romero (Andre dePons), Heather Angel (Lenore), Montagu Love (King Louis XIII), Douglass Dumbrille (Barabas), Ivan Simpson (Joseph), Doris Lloyd (Queen Anne), Walter Kingsford (Gaston/Duc D'Orleans), David Torrence (Marshall LeMoyne), John Burton (Brugnon), Denis Green (Lorraine), Eric Snowden (Olivares), Frank Nelson (Guard/Man), Lionel Belmore (Second Innkeeper), John Toti (Coachman), Lou Merrill (Usher/Second Man), Dorothy Lloyd (the Cat), David Kerman (Third Man), Geraldine Peck (Second Woman), Marga Ann Deighton (Woman), Sidney Newman, Bob Burleson, Ross Forrester (Crowd), and George Webb (Innkeeper/Crowd).

Commercial: Jane Morgan (Mother Browning), Betty Jean Hainey (Midge), and Eric Burtis, Jr. (Bobby).

Lux's "Cardinal Richelieu" once again gave George Arliss the opportunity to reprise one of his most memorable film characterizations. The adaptation, which focuses upon the cardinal's (1585–1642) efforts to thwart an attempt to dethrone King Louis XIII in favor of his unscrupulous brother, also features Florence Arliss as the king's scheming mother. Heather Angel is heard as Cardinal Richelieu's ward, Lenore, the role created by Maureen O'Sullivan in the 1935 Rowland V. Lee–directed 20th Century/United Artists film, and Montagu Love takes Edward Arnold's movie part of King Louis XIII. Repeating their screen characterizations are Cesar Romero as Andre and Douglass Dumbrille as the treasonous Duke Barabas.

204. "The Arkansas Traveler," 1/30/39

Based on the 1938 Paramount film

(screenplay by Viola Brothers Shore and George Session Perry), in turn based upon the story by Jack Cunningham.

Intermission Guest: Hugh Park, editor and publisher of the *Van Buren Press Arkas* (from Little Rock, Arkansas; after Act 2).

Cast: Bob Burns (Traveler), Fay Bainter (Mrs. Martha Allen), Jean Parker (Judy Allen), Dickie Moore (Benny Allen), James Eagles (Johnny Daniels), Frank Nelson (Matt), Eddie Waller (Constable), Earle Ross (Trainman), Harry Humphrey (Homer Daniels), Lou Merrill (a Voter/Hobo/Man), Walter White (Citizen Number Two/Hobo Number Four/Man), Gil Patric (Citizen Number Three/Hobo Number Two/Man Number Three), Stanley Farrar (Citizen Number Four/Hobo/Man Number Four), and Ross Forrester (Grocer/Crowd).

Commercial: Lou Merrill (Mr. Billings), Pauline Haddon, and Frank Coghlan, Jr.

Bob Burns, the Arkansian purveyor of "folksy" humor, came to *Lux* in an adaptation of one of his motion picture successes, *The Arkansas Traveler*. The country comedian gives an engaging performance in the quiet tale of a likable stranger who arrives in a small town and solves everyone's problems; he is joined by three other members of Paramount's 1938 Alfred Santell–directed film: Fay Bainter, Jean Parker, and Dickie Moore.

205. "The Count of Monte Cristo," 2/6/39

Based on the novel by Alexandre Dumas, *père* (1845), and the play by Charles Fletcher (1873).

Intermission Guest: Alton Cooke, columnist for the *New York World Telegram* (after Acts 2 and 3).

Cast: Robert Montgomery (Edmond Dantes), Josephine Hutchinson (Mercedes), Lewis Stone (Abbé Ferrier), Lloyd Nolan (Dunlar), Sidney Blackmer (Mondaigo), Paul Lukas (DeVeilfons), Walter Byron (Giacopo), Barry Drew (Halvey), Victor Rodman (Monsieur Maurel), Frank Nelson (Helmsman/Guard/Doctor), Wright Kramer (Nortier), Joe Franz (Jacques/Sailor), Perry Ivins (Jules/Lackey), John Fee (Napoleon), Rolfe Sedan (Manouse/Lackey), Louis Merrill (Judge/Guard/Clerk), Raoul DeLeon (Officer), Stanley Schewd (Brabant), Paul Bryer (Major Domo), Gaughan Burke (Sailor), Ross Forrester (Servant), and Maryon Aye (Crowd).

Commercials: Caroline Frasher, Jane Morgan (Mother Browning), Marilyn Stuart (Dot), and Lorraine Edwards.

"The Count of Monte Cristo" presented *Lux* adapter George Wells with the formidable task of condensing Alexandre Dumas's rather lengthy novel into a radio drama of approximately 47 minutes. It is a chore well executed, for the temptation of squeezing as much plot as possible into the drama has been resisted. Instead, each act effectively focuses on a few scenes from the novel, with the first working as the exposition, the second depicting the protagonist's unjust imprisonment and subsequent escape, and the third concentrating on his long-awaited revenge on his enemies. Robert Montgomery makes a good Dantes, creating a proper transformation in the young hero between the first two acts. The remaining players are relegated to what amounts to supporting roles, but Josephine Hutchinson as Dantes's fiancée and Lewis Stone as the fellow prisoner who aids his escape give fine performances.

Between Acts 2 and 3, radio columnist Alton Cooke reminisces briefly on *The Lux Radio Theatre*'s beginnings and reports that his newspaper, the *New York World Telegram*, has conducted a poll that ranks *Lux* as the number one radio program of 1938.

Lionel Barrymore and Maureen O'Sullivan, who starred in *Lux*'s broadcast of "The Return of Peter Grimm" (February 13, 1939) (photo: Connie Billips).

James O'Neil brought his well-known stage characterization of Edmond Dantes to the screen in the first feature film of *The Count of Monte Cristo*, which was released by Famous Players in 1913 and was directed by Edwin S. Porter. Other film versions include a 1922 Fox picture called *Monte Cristo*, which was directed by Emmett J. Flynn and starred John Gilbert, and a 1934 British talkie with Robert Donat, which was directed by Rowland V. Lee.

Film versions: Famous Players, 1913; Fox, 1922 *(Monte Cristo)*; British, 1934.

206. "The Return of Peter Grimm," 2/13/39

Based on the play by David Belasco and Cecil B. DeMille (1911); suggested from an idea by Cecil B. DeMille.

Intermission Guest: Cecil B. DeMille, coauthor of the play *The Return of Peter Grimm*.

Cast: Lionel Barrymore (Peter Grimm), Maureen O'Sullivan (Catherine), Edward Arnold (Dr. MacPherson), Peter Holden (William), Gavin Muir (Frederick), Alan Ladd (James), Greta Meyer (Marta), Lou Merrill (Clown), Martha Wentworth (Mrs. Bartholomey/Woman), Lee Millar (Mr. Bartholomey/Toby the Dog), Frank Nelson (Man), Ross Forrester (Man in Crowd), Ethel Sykes (Woman in Crowd), and Maryon Aye (Crowd).

The presentation of "The Return of Peter Grimm" on *The Lux Radio Theatre* was something of a unique event, as the 1911 drama was written by Cecil B. DeMille and David Belasco. Actually, the intriguing tale was first put to paper in 1910, when Belasco commissioned young playwright Cecil B. DeMille to write a play for presentation on the stage. The former then took the latter's manuscript of *The Return of Peter Grimm,* made a few alterations, and produced it in 1911 at the Belasco

Theatre with David Warfield and Janet Dunbar on October 17, where it was a success. Lionel Barrymore, who had played the title role in RKO's 1935 motion picture, directed by George Nicholls, Jr., is splendid in the part of a man who returns from the dead to right some potentially disastrous wrongs, as is Maureen O'Sullivan, whose sincerity makes for a moving performance as Catherine, the young ward who loyally casts aside personal happiness to make her beloved uncle's last moments on earth pleasant. Edward Arnold is a likable Dr. MacPherson, and Alan Ladd makes his *Lux* debut as Peter Grimm's secretary (and Catherine's romantic interest), James. Director Frank Woodruff was extremely pleased with the broadcast, calling it "one of the best of the series—all performances excellent."

The first screen version of *The Return of Peter Grimm* was released by Fox in 1926 and was directed by Victor Schertzinger. Alec B. Francis, Janet Gaynor, John St. Polis, and Richard Walling were the stars of that production. The 1935 RKO remake, directed by George Nicholls, Jr., featured Lionel Barrymore, Helen Mack, Edward Ellis, and Allen Vincent.

Film versions: Fox, 1926; RKO, 1935.

207. "Stage Door," 2/20/39

Based on the 1937 RKO film (screenplay by Morrie Ryskind and Anthony Veiller), in turn based on the play by Edna Ferber and George S. Kaufman (1936).

Intermission Guest: George Pierce, stage doorman of the Empire Theatre (New York) (after Act 2).

Cast: Ginger Rogers (Jean Maitland), Rosalind Russell (Terry Randall), Adolphe Menjou (Anthony Powell), Eve Arden (Linda Shaw), Florence Lake (Ann), Lurene Tuttle (Kaye Hamilton), Leona Roberts (Mrs. Orcutt), Gloria

Adolphe Menjou and Ginger Rogers in "Stage Door" (February 20, 1939) (photo: Photofest).

Gordon (Mrs. Ann Luther), Gerald Cornell (Carmichael/Man Number Three), Tyler McVey (Bill), Frank Nelson (Ellsworth/Man Number Four), Ynez Seabury (Eve), Jeanette McLeay (Mary Lou), Margaret Brayton (Judy), Colleen Ward (Susan), Sara Selby (Operator/Woman), Martha Wentworth (Mother [in play]), Lou Merrill (Korovsky/Father [in play]), Edward Marr (Usher/Man), James Eagles (Harcourt/Waiter), David Kerman (Reporter/Man Number Two), Crauford Kent (Henry Sims), and Ross Forrester (Man).

Commercial: Mary Lansing.

Ginger Rogers returned to *Lux* in an adaptation of one of her RKO films, *Stage Door,* the story of the residents of a theatrical boarding house and their various triumphs and disappointments.

The broadcast is a reasonably good rendering of the picture, though it does not entirely succeed in creating the film's atmosphere of the second-rate boarding house. To a large extent, this is caused by the elimination of much of the banter among the girls of the Footlights Club, which was understandably excised due to time limitations.

Others from the film cast are Adolphe Menjou as impresario Anthony Powell, and Eve Arden, here playing Gail Patrick's screen role of the venomous Linda Shaw (though in the motion picture she was cast in the smaller part of Eve). Rosalind Russell, given Katharine Hepburn's movie part of Terry Randall, offers a portrayal quite different from that of her predecessor, and Leona Roberts repeats her stage role of Mrs. Orcutt. (Others in the 1937 Gregory La-Cava–directed film include Ann Miller, Andrea Leeds, and Elizabeth Dunne.)

208. "Ceiling Zero," 2/27/39

Based on the 1935 Warner Bros./ Cosmopolitan film (screenplay by Frank Wead), in turn based on the play by Frank Wead (1934).

Intermission Guest: Major Carl A. Cover, senior vice president and general manager of the Douglas Aircraft Company (after Act 2).

Cast: James Cagney (Dizzy Davis), Ralph Bellamy (Jake Lee), Stuart Erwin (Texas Clark), Boots Mallory (Tommy Thomas), Jeanne Cagney (Lou Clark), James Bush (Buzz Gordon), Mary Lansing (Mary Lee), Martha Wentworth (Mama Gini), Edward Marr (Doc Wilson), Lou Merrill (Alan Stone), Joseph DuVal (Joe Allen), Frank Nelson (Tay Lawson), Ross Forrester (Mike Owens), and John Gibson (Smiley Johnson).

Commercial: Jane Morgan (Mother Browning), Betty Jean Hainey (Midge), and Marilyn Stuart (Dot).

Ceiling Zero, a drama of a cocky pilot who is constantly at odds with his superior, was the offering for the *Lux* broadcast of February 27, though the flying scenes take a back seat to the dramatic portions on the ground in the radio adaptation of the Warner Bros. film. This moving of the emphasis away from the aviation sequences does not damage the story, as, after all, the 1935 motion picture (directed by Howard Hawks) *is* based on Frank Wead's stage play, which, naturally, had no flying scenes whatsoever. (The stars on Broadway were John Litel, Osgood Perkins, G. Albert Smith, Margaret Perry, and Hope Lawder.) James Cagney and Stuart Erwin both repeat their film roles, while Ralph Bellamy and Boots Mallory take the parts played by Pat O'Brien and June Travis in the picture. James Cagney's sister, Jeanne, whose film debut would come in 1940, is given the role of Lou Clark, which in the motion picture went to Isabel Jewell.

The intermission guest, Major Carl A. Cover, is not present in the studio but rather speaks to DeMille and the listening audience from a Royal Dutch Airlines DC-3 airplane flying above the *Lux Radio Theatre*.

Ceiling Zero was reworked by Warner Bros. in 1941 and titled *International Squadron*. This Lothar Mendes–directed production starred Ronald Reagan, James Stephenson, Cliff Edwards, and Julie Bishop.

Additional film version: Warner Bros., 1941 (*International Squadron*).

209. "One Way Passage," 3/6/39

Based on the 1932 Warner Bros. film (screenplay by Wilson Mizner and Joseph Jackson; original story by Robert Lord).

Intermission Guest: Commander Carl A. Allen of the steamship *Calvin Coolidge* of the American Presidents Line (after Act 2).

Cast: William Powell (Dan Hardesty), Kay Francis (Joan Ames), William Gargan (Steve Burke), Marjorie Rambeau (Countess Barihaus [Barrel House Betty]), John Fee (Dr. Bolton), Ross Forrester (Skippy), Lee Millar (Mike/Purser), Lou Merrill (Dick/Steward), David Kerman (Captain Mallory/Officer), Bobby Larson (Child), Myron Gary (Coolie/Mexican Bartender), Raymond Lawrence (Second Steward/Sailor Number Three), Charles Emerson (Tours/Sailor), Gaughan Burke (Sailor Number Two/Man), Geraldine Peck (Woman in Act 1/Woman in Act 3), and Frank Nelson (Barman/Man [in Singapore]).

Commercial: Elia Braca (Betty), Alan Ladd (Betty's husband).

At the conclusion of the February 29 *Lux* broadcast, DeMille announced that the following week's offering would be a version of that fondly remembered Warner Bros. love story *One Way Passage*. The stars, he noted, would be

William Powell, repeating his movie role, and in her *Lux* debut, Norma Shearer. Shearer's subsequent illness, however, caused an alteration in casting, and Kay Francis, who had been Powell's leading lady in the 1932 Tay Garnett–directed picture, stepped into the part. This *was* the *Lux* debut for Francis, while listeners had to wait two years (until May 11, 1942) for Norma Shearer to make her first (and only) appearance before the *Lux* microphone. Both stars give touching performances in this famed story of a shipboard romance between a woman with a fatal heart condition and a man on his way to the electric chair, and the second leads are capably handled by William Gargan (a more serious detective than Warren Hymer of the film) and Marjorie Rambeau (taking Aline MacMahon's movie role). Frank Woodruff called the show "excellent," noting that "Kay Francis proves great value as [a] radio personality."

The year following the *Lux* "One Way Passage" broadcast saw the release of a Warner Bros. remake of the story. Entitled *Til We Meet Again*, this version was directed by Edmund Goulding and featured a cast that included George Brent, Merle Oberon, Pat O'Brien, and Binnie Barnes. (On June 10, 1940, *Lux* presented its adaptation of "'Til We Meet Again," while on March 7, 1957, the *Lux Video Theatre* presented an adaptation of "One Way Passage.")

Additional film version: Warner Bros., 1940 (*'Til We Meet Again*).

210. "So Big," 3/13/39

Based on the 1932 Warner Bros. film (screenplay by J. Grubb Alexander and Robert Lord), in turn based on the novel by Edna Ferber (1924).

Intermission Guest: Mrs. Sarah Delano Roosevelt, mother of Franklin Delano Roosevelt (from New York City; after Act 2).

Cast: Barbara Stanwyck (Selina Peake Dejong), Preston Foster (Dirk Dejong), Fay Wray (Julie), Otto Kruger (Pervus Dejong), Billy Cook (Dirk, as a Young Boy), Ted Osborn (Rolf Poole), Jackie Kelly (Rolf, as a Young Boy), Ferdinand Munier (Mr. Hempel/Auctioneer), Janet Young (Maartje Poole/Ayla), Lou Merrill (Klaus/Cop), Frank Nelson (Johannes/Tom), Harry Humphrey (the Reverend Dekker), Mary Lansing (Secretary/Dirk, as a Baby), Walter White (Doctor), Harold Wilson (Farmer), Gil Patric (Second Man), Lurene Tuttle (Julie Hempel), and Ross Forrester (Crowd).

Commercial: Jerrie Gail (Betty), Lorraine Edwards (Marion).

The William A. Wellman–directed feature *So Big* starred Barbara Stanwyck (who re-enacts her role for the broadcast) in an episodic story of a tenacious schoolteacher in a Midwestern farming community who strives to lead her misguided son down the right path. The entire production has a quiet, subdued atmosphere, which is especially appropriate to the story, and if the characters are given little chance to develop in the hour drama the fine performances of the cast always manage to hold the interest. (George Brent was second billed in the movie cast, playing young sculptor Ralph Poole, a character that is given only minor involvement in the broadcast.) Contributing significantly to the rustic atmosphere in the story's early scenes, and reminding listeners of the characters' roots in the latter portion of the drama is Lou Silvers's incidental music, which makes interesting use of themes from the largo movement of Dvorak's "New World" Symphony.

First National released the first film of Edna Ferber's *So Big* in 1925, with Colleen Moore heading a cast that also included Ben Lyon and John Bowers and was directed by Charles Brabin. Warner Bros. filmed the novel a third time in 1953, with Robert Wise directing Jane Wyman, Steve Forrest, Nancy Olson, and Sterling Hayden.

Additional film versions: First National, 1925; Warner Bros., 1953.

211. "It Happened One Night," 3/20/39

Based on the 1934 Columbia film (screenplay by Robert Riskin), in turn based on the story "Night Bus," by Samuel Hopkins Adams (1933).

Intermission Guest: Harold Burnham, bus driver of the Pacific Greyhound Lines (after Act 2).

Cast: Clark Gable (Peter Warne), Claudette Colbert (Ellie Andrews), Walter Connolly (Mr. Andrews), Roscoe Karns (Shapeley), John Gibson (Bus Driver), Chester Clute (Mr. Dike/Man), Eddie Waller (Mr. Dobbs), Lou Merrill (Harry Gordon), Walter Tetley (a Newsboy), Maryon Aye (Telephone Operator), and Frank Nelson (a Detective).

Commercials: Betty Jean Hainey (Midge), Marilyn Stuart (Dot), Elia Braca, and Miami Campbell.

Five years after its initial release, Frank Capra's Academy Award–winning picture *It Happened One Night* was presented on *Lux*, with four players from the original cast: Clark Gable, Claudette Colbert, Walter Connolly, and Roscoe Karns. The comedy of a runaway heiress who teams up with a cynical reporter on a cross-country bus trip contains many memorable visual moments (such as the "walls of Jericho" and hitchhiking sequences), and these are cleverly used in the broadcast thanks to the skills of writer George Wells.

It Happened One Night was filmed on two more occasions by Columbia, both times as musicals. The first was *Eve Knew Her Apples*, a 1945 release that was directed by Will Jason and featured William Wright and Ann Miller. *You*

Can't Run Away from It reached the screen in 1956, with the lead roles in the Dick Powell–directed production going to Jack Lemmon and June Allyson.

Additional film versions: Columbia, 1945 (*Eve Knew Her Apples*); Columbia, 1956 (*You Can't Run Away from It*).

212. "A Man's Castle," 3/27/39

Based on the 1933 Columbia film (screenplay by Jo Swerling), in turn based on the play by Lawrence Hazard.

Intermission Guest: Father Edward J. Flanagan, founder and director of Boy's Town (from Omaha, Nebraska; after Act 2).

Cast: Spencer Tracy (Bill), Loretta Young (Trina), Arthur Hohl (Bragg), Martha Wentworth (Flossie), Perry Ivins (Ira), Margaret Brayton (Fay LaRue), Paul Hilton (a Small Boy), Frank Nelson (Waiter), Lou Merrill (Restaurant Manager), Sybil Harris (a Mother), and Ross Forrester (Waiter).

Commercial: John Lake, James Eagles, and Walter White.

Spencer Tracy and Loretta Young made return engagements to *Lux* in an adaptation of their 1933 Columbia film *A Man's Castle*, a tale of a hapless girl taken under the wing of an abrasive dump dweller who refuses to be defeated by the Depression. Though the movie's earthy story and unpolished characters may seem a bit too severe to meet *Lux*'s wholesome standards, surprisingly little is done to soften the original drama's harsh approach. There are naturally some modifications; for example, Bill and Trina's (excellently portrayed by Tracy and Young) marriage takes place much earlier in the radio version than it does in the film (long *before* Trina's announcement that she is expecting a baby). Also, the character of Bill is made somewhat more sympathetic for the broadcast, with several hints that he is not as cynical as he pretends. Arthur Hohl also repeats his screen role, while the characters played by Marjorie Rambeau and Walter Connolly in the Frank Borzage–directed motion picture are taken by radio actors Martha Wentworth and Perry Ivins.

Since Spencer Tracy had recently received an Academy Award for his performance in *Boy's Town* (1938), the man he portrayed in that photoplay, Father Edward J. Flanagan, speaks (from Omaha, Nebraska) during the second act intermission.

213. "Silver Dollar," 4/3/39

Based on the 1932 Warner Bros./ First National film (screenplay by Carl Erickson and Harvey Thew), in turn based on a story by David Karsner.

Intermission Guest: Mrs. Ruth Bryan Owen Rhoday, former congresswoman and U.S. ambassador to Denmark (from New York City; after Act 2).

Cast: Edward Arnold (Yates Martin), Anita Louise (Lily), Marjorie Rambeau (Sarah Martin), Joe DuVal (Colonel Stanton/Grocer), Forrest Taylor (William Jennings Bryan/Hook), Perry Ivins (Slick/Clerk), Lee Millar (a Doctor), Ynez Seabury (Porker Annie), Lou Merrill (Adams/Newsboy), David Kerman (Rische/Doorman), Walter White (Contractor), Mary Lansing (Secretary/Baby), Frank Nelson (Stony/Mark, as a Grown Man), Eric Burtis, Jr. (Mark, as a Boy), and Ross Forrester (Crowd).

Commercial: Betty Jean Hainey (Midge), Marilyn Stuart (Dot), Lois Collier, and Sally Creighton.

Silver Dollar, as released by Warner Bros. in 1932, is the thinly disguised story of silver king Horace A.W. Tabor. Besides having had a colorful career in politics, he is also well remembered for his construction of the Denver, Colorado, opera house that bears his name. (His story was later the basis for Doug-

las Moore's opera *The Ballad of Baby Doe.*)

Edward Arnold gives an effective performance as Yates Martin, the role taken by Edward G. Robinson in the Alfred E. Green–directed motion picture, while Marjorie Rambeau is heard as his wife, Sarah. Rambeau's radio portrayal is far less sympathetic than that of Aline MacMahon's of the film, while Lily, the woman for whom Yates Martin casts aside his spouse, who is portrayed (by Bebe Daniels) as calculating and manipulative in the screen version, is remolded into a relatively good woman for the broadcast (where she is essayed by Anita Louise).

The intermission guest, heard from New York City, is Mrs. Ruth Bryan Owen Rhoday, daughter of William Jennings Bryan (who is a character in the play) and herself a distinguished stateswoman.

214. "The Lives of a Bengal Lancer," 4/10/39

Based on the 1935 Paramount film (screenplay by Grover Jones, William Slavens McNutt, Achmed Abdullah, Waldemar Young, and John Balderston), in turn based on the novel by Francis Yeats-Brown (1930).

Intermission Guest: General Hugh Samuel Johnson, former NRA administrator and columnist of the Scripps-Howard newspapers (after Act 2).

Cast: Errol Flynn (Lieutenant McGregor), Brian Aherne (Lieutenant Forsythe), C. Aubrey Smith (Colonel Stone), Jackie Cooper (Lieutenant Stone), Douglass Dumbrille (Mohammed Khan), Ian McLaren (Major Hamilton), C. Montague Shaw (Sir Thomas Woodley), Nancy Leach (Tanya), Lal Chand Mehra (Vizier/Native), Eric Snowden (Captain Hendrickson/Orderly), Ian Purvis (Dawson/Officer), Lou Merrill (Muzzein), Frank Nelson (Soldier), and Ross Forrester (Crowd).

Commercial: Jane Morgan (Mother Browning), Betty Jean Hainey (Midge), Marilyn Stuart (Dot), and Katherine Carlton.

Paramount's 1935 Henry Hathaway–directed adventure *The Lives of a Bengal Lancer* made for an entertaining broadcast as well, thanks to the engaging performances of the stars. Errol Flynn, Brian Aherne, and Jackie Cooper (in the roles taken by Gary Cooper, Franchot Tone, and Richard Cromwell on the screen) play British soldiers defending the northwest frontier from villainous Douglass Dumbrille (of the movie cast) and his throng of rebellious natives, and C. Aubrey Smith, who plays Major Hamilton in the film, is here promoted to Colonel Stone.

215. "Bullets or Ballots," 4/17/39

Based on the 1936 Warner Bros./First National film (screenplay by Seton I. Miller; original story by Martin Mooney and Seton I. Miller).

Intermission Guest: Frank B. Gomphert, criminologist in charge of the research lab of Los Angeles County and motion picture technical advisor (after Act 2).

Cast: Edward G. Robinson (Johnny Blake), Mary Astor (Lee Morgan), Humphrey Bogart (Bugs Brenner), Otto Kruger (Al Kruger), Wallis Clark (McLaren), Edward Marr (Joe Vinci), Lindsay MacHarrie (Ward Bryant), Chester Clute (Herman), Wally Maher (Crail), Galan Galt (Doorman/Waiter), Lou Merrill (Thorndyke/Newsboy), Earle Ross (Officer Donlan), Frank Nelson (McAllister), and Ross Forrester (Louie/Newsboy).

Edward G. Robinson repeats his film characterization of the detective who goes undercover to infiltrate and disband a notorious crime ring in *Lux*'s adaptation of Warner Bros./First National's *Bullets or Ballots* (which was

directed by future *Lux* host William Keighley and released in 1936). Joining him from the motion picture cast is Humphrey Bogart (making his *Lux* debut), while Mary Astor takes the role played onscreen by Joan Blondell, and Otto Kruger plays Barton MacLane's movie character of gang leader Al Kruger.

216. "Broadway Bill," 4/24/39

Based on the 1934 Columbia film (screenplay by Robert Riskin), in turn based on the story by Mark Hellinger (1933). Adapted for radio by True Boardman.

Intermission Guest: Alfred G. Vanderbilt, racehorse breeder and president of the Maryland Jockey Club (from New York City; after Act 2).

Cast: Robert Taylor (Dan Brooks), Frances Dee (Alice Higgins), Gail Patrick (Margaret Brooks), Raymond Walburn (Colonel Pettigrew), Ernest Whitman (Whitey), Lou Merrill (J.L. Higgins), Elvia Allman (Mrs. Peterson), Victor Rodman (Mr. Winslow), Eddie Kane (Mr. Earley/Cop), Willis Claire (Eddie North), Hal K. Dawson (Roberts/Happy), Niles Andres (Mel), Frank Nelson (Announcer/Deputy), Fredrick Shields (Morrow/Collins), Myra Marsh (Matilda/Maid), Joe DuVal (Veterinarian/Joe), James Eagles (Ted Williams/Boy in Act 1), and Ross Forrester (Guy).

Commercials: Marilyn Stuart (Dot), Sarah Selby (Aunt Cynthia), and Vyola Vonn (Woman).

Columbia's 1934 Frank Capra–directed film *Broadway Bill*, which stars Warner Baxter, Myrna Loy, Helen Vinson, and Raymond Walburn, and was one of that studio's most popular motion pictures of the season, made for a charming radio play as well. (The broadcast was adapted by True Boardman, who was on an excursion away from his head writer duties on CBS's *Silver Theatre*.)

Lux's four stars are well cast (with Walburn repeating his movie role), and Robert Taylor gives an especially engaging performance as an unwilling business executive who would much rather spend his time with his beloved racehorse, Broadway Bill, instead of at the office.

Frank Capra filmed a 1950 version at Paramount under the title *Riding High*, which features songs by Johnny Burke and Jimmy Van Heusen and stars Bing Crosby, Coleen Gray, Frances Gifford, and Raymond Walburn.

Additional film versions: Paramount, 1950 (*Riding High*).

217. "Lady for a Day," 5/1/39

Based on the 1933 Columbia film (screenplay by Robert Riskin), in turn based on the story "Madame La Gimp," by Damon Runyon.

Guest Host: Leslie Howard.

Intermission Guest: Florence Farley, "a real-life lady for a day" (interviewed by Cecil B. DeMille from New York City; after Act 2).

Cast: May Robson (Apple Annie), Warren William (Dave the Dude), Guy Kibbee (Judge Blake), Jean Parker (Louise), Lou Merrill (Happy/Frank), Margaret Brayton (Missouri Martin), James Eagles (Smiley/Weasel), Wally Maher (Steve/Long Chin), Frank Nelson (Carlos/Louie), Chester Clute (Oscar/Cheesecake), Ross Forrester (Shakespeare), John Gibson (Police Captain), David Kerman (Harry the Horse), John Fee (the Mayor/Officer), Walter White (Count Alfonso Romero/Waiter), Joe Franz (Murphy/Joe), Earl Gunn (Inspector/Governor), and Edgar Norton (a Butler).

Commercial: Jane Morgan (Mother), Betty Jean Hainey (Midge), Marilyn Stuart (Dot), and Lee Millar (Dog).

Lux's May 1 broadcast offered an adaptation of Columbia's 1933 Frank Capra–directed film *Lady for a Day*, starring May Robson, Warren William, Jean Parker, and Guy Kibbee in their original screen roles. The story concerns a collection of soft-hearted underworld rogues who are banded together by a charming racketeer to assist an apple peddler in deceiving her daughter into thinking she is a society matron so that the girl's upcoming nuptials can take place.

As DeMille was in New York for the premiere of his latest picture, *Union Pacific*, Leslie Howard assumes the host's duties for this program. He is heard during the second act intermission, however, as he interviews Florence Farley, "a real-life lady for a day."

Frank Capra was at the directorial helm of *Pocket Full of Miracles*, the 1963 United Artists version of *Lady for a Day*. Bette Davis was the impoverished apple peddler in this production, while the other principal roles went to Glenn Ford, Thomas Mitchell, and Ann-Margret.

Additional film version: United Artists, 1963 (*Pocket Full of Miracles*).

218. "The Life of Émile Zola," 5/8/39

Based on the 1937 Warner Bros. film (screenplay by Heinz Herald, Geza Herczeg, and Norman Reilly Raine; original story by Heinz Herald and Geza Herczeg).

Guest Host: Leslie Howard.

Intermission Guest: William Dieterle, motion picture director (after Act 2).

Cast: Paul Muni (Émile Zola), Josephine Hutchinson (Alexandrine Zola), Robert Warwick (Anatole France), Ted Osborn (Paul Cézanne), Henry Brandon (Captain Alfred Dreyfus), Nigel DeBruille (Chief Censor/Advocate), Verna Felton (Mme. Zola), Ferdinand Munier (Monsieur Charpentier), Denis Green (Major Dort/Editor), Crauford Kent (Colonel

San Dherr/President), John Fee (Minister of War), Cy Kendall (Chief of State), Frank Nelson (Major Picquart/ Man), Lee Millar (Maître Labori), Lou Merrill (Police Agent/Second Man), Victor Rodman (Georges Clemenceau/ LaRue), Rolfe Sedan (a Clerk/Man Number Three), Vernon Steele (Mr. Richards), Mary Alice Sheffield (Helen Richards), Stanley Farrar (Albert), Gil Patric (a Soldier/Orderly), Celeste Rush (Woman), Geraldine Peck (Woman), and Ross Forrester (Editor).

Commercial: Jane Morgan (Mother), Betty Jean Hainey (Midge), and Marilyn Stuart (Dot).

Warner Bros. Productions' *The Story of Louis Pasteur* and *The Life of Émile Zola* (both of which starred Paul Muni) proved that serious biographical material could attract all types of audiences. Having aired "Louis Pasteur" with its original star during the first *Lux* season in Hollywood (November 23, 1936), the program now offered "Émile Zola," also with Muni in the title role as the nineteenth-century French writer who diligently comes to the defense of Captain Alfred Dreyfus (who was accused of treason against his country). As in the motion picture, the famous Dreyfus case proves to be the centerpiece of the story, and it extends through the final two acts. The presence of Josephine Hutchinson (who plays the role taken by Gloria Holden in the film) is most welcome, though her role as Madame Zola is unfortunately little more than a supporting bit.

The Life of Émile Zola received the Academy Award for best picture, as well as Oscars for Joseph Schildkraut (best supporting actor) and best screenplay.

The *Lux Video Theatre* presented a version on March 10, 1955.

219. "Tovarich," 5/15/39

Based on the 1937 Warner Bros. film (screenplay by Casey Robinson; adapted by Robert E. Sherwood), in turn based on the novel by Jacques Deval.

Intermission Guest: Grand Duchess Marie of Russia (from New York City; after Act 2).

Cast: William Powell (Prince Mikhail Alexandrovitch Ouratieff), Miriam Hopkins (Grand Duchess Tatiana Petrovna), C. Henry Gordon (Commissar Gorotchenko), Lawrence Grossmith (Charles Dupont), Heather Thatcher (Madame Dupont), Florence Baker (Madame Helene Dupont), Gene O'Donnell (Monsieur George Dupont), Helen Geddes (Olga/Madame Van Hemert), Lou Merrill (Admiral Soukhomine/Concierge), Frank Nelson (Gendarme), and Ilis Khmara (Guitar Player).

Commercial: Margaret McKay, Tyler McVey.

Warner Bros.' intelligent comedy *Tovarich* (which was directed by Anatole Litvak in 1937) made its way to the screen with Charles Boyer and Claudette Colbert as the usurped royalty of Imperial Russia whose unfortunate circumstances force them to go into domestic service abroad. William Powell and Miriam Hopkins are interestingly cast in the leads in *Lux*'s entertaining radio production, and Hopkins even has the opportunity to sing the traditional Russian song "Black Eyes," which she renders most charmingly.

220. "Angels with Dirty Faces," 5/22/39

Based on the 1938 Warner Bros. film (screenplay by John Wexley and Warren Duff; original story by Rowland Brown).

Intermission Guest: Courtney Riley Cooper (after Act 2).

Cast: James Cagney (Rocky Sullivan), Pat O'Brien (Jerry Connelly), Gloria Dickson (Laurie Ferguson), Frank Nelson (Frazier), Lou Merrill

Gloria Dickson, Pat O'Brien, and James Cagney in "Angels with Dirty Faces" (May 22, 1939) (photo: Photofest).

(Mac Keefer), Frankie Darro (Soapy), Cy Kendall (a Guard/Man), Ross Forrester (Steve/Newsboy), James Eagles (Hunky/Newsboy), Frank Bealen (Crab), Joe Brown, Jr. (Johnny/Newsboy), Harris Berger (Bim), Jackie Morrow (Red), Forrest Taylor (Kennedy/Croupier), Ethel Sykes (a Girl), and Paul Marion (Convict/Waiter).

Singers: Betty Rome, Elva Kellogg, Pauline Deigert, Grace Nielson, Joe Campbell, Marie Green, Vivian Edwards, Devona Doxie, Vera Gilmer, and Enrico Ricardi.

Commercial: Elia Braca (Nancy), Eric Burtis (Bobby).

The Warner Bros./First National film *Angels with Dirty Faces* was directed in 1938 by Michael Curtiz and teamed James Cagney and Pat O'Brien for the second time (adding the Dead End Kids for good measure). *Lux*'s microphone version of the story features the pictures costars resuming their characterizations of boyhood pals, one of whom grows up to be a notorious public enemy; the other, a respected priest. Though none of the original Dead End Kids are present in the broadcast, *Lux*'s recruits (headed by Frankie Darro) make a convincing gang of young punks. (Harris Berger, who has a bit role as a basketball captain in the motion picture, takes Leo Gorcey's part of Bim in the broadcast.) Gloria Dickson is given Ann Sheridan's screen role of Laurie, while *Lux* regulars Frank Nelson and Lou Merrill handle the parts played in the film by Humphrey Bogart and George Bancroft.

221. "Only Angels Have Wings," 5/29/39

Based on the 1939 Columbia film (screenplay by Jules Furthman; story by Howard Hawks).

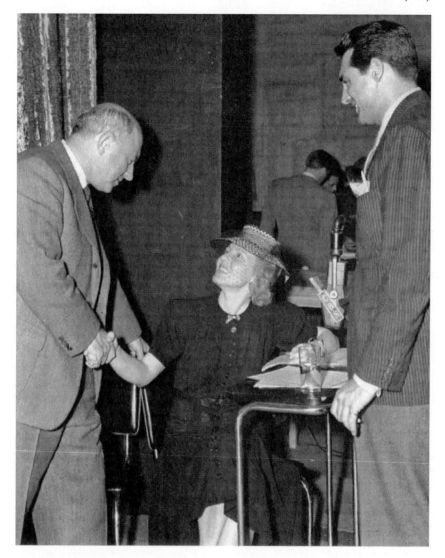

Cecil B. DeMille, Jean Arthur, and Cary Grant during a rehearsal for "Only Angels
Have Wings" (May 29, 1939) (photo: Photofest).

Intermission Guest: Captain Arthur
E. LaPorte (after Act 2).

Cast: Cary Grant (Geoff Carter), Jean
Arthur (Bonnie Lee), Richard Barthel-
mess (Bat McPherson), Rita Hayworth
(Judith), Thomas Mitchell (Kid Dabb),
Noah Beery, Jr. (Joe Souther), Victor

Killian (Sparks), Donald Barry (Tex
Gordon), Lou Merrill (Dutchy), Alan
Ladd (Les Peters), John Allen (Gent
Shelton), Herb Vigran (Mike), Frank
Nelson (Pancho), Ross Forrester (Grant
Haywood), and Bob Burleson (Crowd).
"Only Angels Have Wings" was

presented on *Lux* only two weeks after the release of Columbia's 1939 Howard Hawks–directed motion picture. Present for the broadcast were eight players from the movie cast: Cary Grant, Jean Arthur, Richard Barthelmess, Rita Hayworth, Thomas Mitchell, Noah Beery, Jr., Victor Killian, and Donald Barry. (The only three screen members missing are Sig Rumann, Allyn Joslyn, and John Carroll, and their roles are capably handled by Lou Merrill, Alan Ladd, and John Allen.) The plot centers around a showgirl, stranded in a South American seaport, who falls for the brassy boss of an operation of American mail flyers, and is effectively adapted to the airwaves through brisk pacing.

222. "The Prisoner of Zenda," 6/5/39

Based on the 1937 Selznick International/UA film (screenplay by John L. Balderston; from Wells Root's adaptation of Edward Rose's dramatization), in turn based on the novel by Edward Hope (1894).

Intermission Guest: Colonel Ivar Enhorning (after Act 2).

Cast: Ronald Colman (Rudolf Rassendyll/Rudolf V), Douglas Fairbanks, Jr. (Rupert of Hentzau), Benita Hume (Princess Flavia), C. Aubrey Smith (Colonel Zapt), Ralph Forbes (Black Michael), Peter Wills (Captain Fritz von Tarlenheim), Ian McLaren (the Cardinal), Paula Winslowe (Antoinette), Eric Snowden (Josef), Lou Merrill (Detchard/Guard), Frank Nelson (Kraftstein), Ross Forrester, Bob Burleson, Gaughan Burke, James Eagles, Bob Payton, Noreen Gammill, Charles Emerson, Ethel Sykes, and Galan Galt.

Commercials: Jane Morgan (Mother Browning), Betty Jean Hainey (Midge), and Mary Lansing.

Selznick International's 1937 swashbuckling romantic adventure *The Pris-*

oner of Zenda was performed on *Lux* with Ronald Colman, Douglas Fairbanks, Jr., and C. Aubrey Smith all reprising their screen roles. Rounding out the impressive radio cast are Benita Hume, Ralph Forbes, and Peter Wills in the parts played in the motion picture by Madeleine Carroll, Raymond Massey, and David Niven (who were directed by John Cromwell). The plot centers around a Briton, vacationing in a mythical European kingdom, who is unexpectedly pressed into service when his look-alike distant cousin is kidnapped on the eve of his coronation.

The first feature-length American film of *The Prisoner of Zenda* was Metro's 1923 release, which was directed by Rex Ingram and starred Lewis Stone, Alice Terry, and Ramon Novarro; MGM retold the story in 1952 with Richard Thorpe at the directorial helm and Stewart Granger, James Mason, and Deborah Kerr in the leads.

Additional film versions: Metro, 1923; MGM, 1952.

223. "White Banners," 6/12/39

Based on the 1938 Warner Bros. film (screenplay by Lenore Coffee, Cameron Rogers, and Abem Finkel; story by Lloyd C. Douglas).

Cast: Fay Bainter (Hannah), Lewis Stone (Paul Ward), Jackie Cooper (Peter Trimble), Betty Jean Hainey (Sally Ward), Elizabeth Wilbur (Marcie Ward), Richard LeGrand (Bradford), Frank Nelson (Taxi Driver/Telegraph Operator), Lou Merrill (Dr. Thompson/ Milkman), Ross Forrester (Butcher), and Mary Lansing (Baby Gurgles).

Commercial: Florence Lake (Sue), Alan Ladd (Tom).

White Banners, a 1938 Edmund Goulding–directed Warner Bros. film about a lady stranger who goes into domestic service and immediately sets about bettering the lives of the members of her troubled household, was presented effectively on *Lux* due to the performances of Fay Bainter, Lewis Stone (in Claude Rains's movie part), and Jackie Cooper.

224. "The Ex–Mrs. Bradford," 6/19/39

Based on the 1936 RKO film (screenplay by Anthony Veiller), in turn based on a story by James Edward Grant.

Intermission Guest: Dr. Ronald F. MacCorkell (after Act 2).

Cast: William Powell (Doctor Bradford), Claudette Colbert (Paula Bradford), John Archer (Nick Martel), Alice Eden (Mrs. Summers), Norman Field (Mr. Summers), Colin Campbell (Stokes), Ray Appleby (Mike North/ Justice), Ross Forrester (Mr. Frankenstein), Frank Nelson (Morgue Attendant/Radio Announcer), John Fee (Mr. Hutchins), Martha Wentworth (Mrs. Hutchins), Edwin Max (Mr. Strand), David Kerman (Patrolman/Mr. Pender), Lou Merrill (Inspector Corrigan), and Bob Burleson (Mr. Curtis).

Commercial: Verna Felton (Mother), Eric Burtis, Jr. (Brother), and Lora Marlo (Sue).

The comedic murder mystery *The Ex–Mrs. Bradford* (one of the RKO's attempts to cash in on the enormously successful 1934 MGM film *The Thin Man*) made its way to *Lux* with one original cast member: William Powell. Powell reprises his screen role as the suave doctor who puts his sleuthing skills to work regarding the mysterious death of a healthy jockey, and Claudette Colbert plays the part of the charmingly meddlesome title character, which was portrayed by Jean Arthur in the Stephen Roberts–directed motion picture.

225. "Mrs. Moonlight," 6/26/39

Based on the play by Ben W. Levy (1930).

Intermission Guest: Walter B. Pitkin, author of the best-selling book *Life Begins at 40* (after Act 2).

Cast: Janet Gaynor (Sarah Moonlight), George Brent (Tom Moonlight), Janet Young (Minnie), Jane Gilbert (Jane), Ted Osborn (Willie Ragg), Claire Verdera (Edith), James Eagles (Peter), Eric Snowden (Percy Middling), Lou Merrill (Heinrich/Station Manager), Frank Nelson (Bonelli/Creg), Jane Morgan (Frau Mudler/Mrs. A), Eddie Kane (Ticket Agent), Geraldine Peck (Mrs. B), Sybil Harris (Mrs. C), and Ross Forrester (LaJoie).

Commercials: Jane Morgan (Mrs. Browning), Marilyn Stuart (Dot), Betty Jean Hainey (Midge), and Marilyn Cooper (Straight Commercial).

Seemingly selected as a vehicle for Janet Gaynor, "Mrs. Moonlight" actually makes few demands on her dramatic abilities, although her youthful voice is especially appropriate to the character of a girl whose pre-wedding wish that she never age is granted, with tragic results. (The basis for the broadcast was Ben W. Levy's 1930 play, which had starred Edith Barrett and Guy Standing on Broadway.) Though the leading male role is not especially large (at least in this adaptation), George Brent is effectively cast, and he handles the gradual aging of his character very convincingly.

226. "Bordertown," 7/3/39

Based on the 1935 Warner Bros. film (screenplay by Laird Doyle and Wallace Smith), in turn based on the novel by Carroll Graham (1934).

Intermission Guest: H.V. Kaltenborn (after Act 2).

Cast: Don Ameche (Johnny Ramirez), Joan Bennett (Dale Elwell), Claire Trevor (Marie Roark), Celeste Rush (Mrs. Ramirez), Lou Merrill (Charlie Roark), Jerry Mohr (Brook Manfille), Lee Millar (Mr. Elwell), Dick LeGrande (Padre), Frank Nelson

(Manuel/Defense Lawyer), Ted Bliss (Commissioner/Alberto), Eddie Marr (Hernandez/Man), David Kerman (Pedro/Dave), Forrest Taylor (Judge), Philip Van Zandt (Attorney/Officer), Victor Rodman (Judge J. Rufus Barnswell/Butler), John Fee (Doctor/Judge), Ross Forrester (Ed), and Kay Sutton (Second Woman).

Commercials: Jane Morgan (Mother), Marilyn Stuart (Dot), Mary Lansing (Mrs. Smith), and Jerry Hausner.

Bordertown, Warner Bros.' successful 1935 Archie Mayo–directed melodrama chronicling the struggles of a young Mexican lawyer determined to conquer financial as well as personal adversity, was performed without its original stars, Paul Muni, Margaret Lindsay, and Bette Davis. For the radio rendering, Don Ameche is cast as the attorney, while Joan Bennett and Claire Trevor perform the roles enacted by Lindsay and Davis in the motion picture (as the sophisticated socialite Dale Elwell and the fanatically obsessed and married woman Marie Roark, respectively).

In an intriguing departure, *Lux* adapter George Wells completely alters the film's ending, in which Dale is run down by an automobile and killed; instead, it is Johnny who is hit while successfully saving Dale (though it is deliberately ambiguous, presumably Johnny dies at the story's conclusion).

Bordertown was partially reworked by Warner Bros. in 1940 for its film *They Drive by Night* (the second portion of the former is used in this drama). Featured in the motion picture are George Raft, Ann Sheridan, Ida Lupino, and Humphrey Bogart, with direction by Raoul Walsh.

Additional film version: Warner Bros., 1940 (*They Drive by Night*).

227. "Ruggles of Red Gap," 7/10/39
Based on the 1935 Paramount film

(screenplay by Walter DeLeon, Harlan Thompson, and Humphrey Pearson), in turn based on the novel by Harry Leon Wilson (1915).

Intermission Guest: Herbert Peacock, "one of the most famous real-life butlers" (after Act 2).

Cast: Charles Laughton (Ruggles), ZaSu Pitts (Mrs. Judson), Charlie Ruggles (Egbert Floud), Eric Snowden (Lord Burnstead), Lelah Tyler (Effie Floud), Hal K. Dawson (Belknap Jackson), Verna Felton (Ma Pettingill), Stanley Farrar (Jeff Tuttle), Earle Ross (Sam), Joe DuVal (Jake Henshaw/ Waiter), Mary Cecil (Mrs. Tiflin/Mrs. A), Frank Nelson (Mr. Bainbridge/ Hank), Margaret Brayton (Mrs. Jackson/Mrs. C), Myron Gary (Willy Lung/ Joe), Georgia Simmons (Maizie), Marie Hammond (Mrs. B), Frank Marton (Harry), and Ross Forrester (Agent/ Man).

Commercials: Marilyn Stuart (Dot), Florence Baker (Janey), Jane Lauren (Second Woman and First Woman), Maryon Aye (Second Woman), and Justina Wayne (First Woman and Third Woman).

Lux's last broadcast of the 1938-39 season presented Charles Laughton not just in his *Lux* debut, but in his first appearance in any radio drama in the United States. As well known as the British actor was for his dramatic portrayals, his characterization of the title figure in Paramount's 1935 comedy *Ruggles of Red Gap* was also fondly remembered. If the story is weakened somewhat by the condensation, this is at least made up for by the performances of the fine cast. Laughton shines as the proper English valet who is an unwilling import to the frontier town of Red Gap, Washington, while ZaSu Pitts and Charlie Ruggles are also delightful playing their original roles from the Leo McCarey–directed film.

A popular screen property, *Ruggles of Red Gap* was filmed twice before Paramount's 1935 opus: first, by Essanay in 1918, with Lawrence C. Windom directing a cast that included Taylor Holmes, Virginia Valli, and Frederick Burton; then by Paramount, in a 1923 James Cruze–directed production that featured Edward Everett Horton, Lois Wilson, and Ernest Torrence in the cast. A slapstick version of the story was assembled by Paramount in 1950; entitled *Fancy Pants*, this film was directed by George Marshall and featured Bob Hope, Lucille Ball, and Jack Kirkwood. ("Fancy Pants" was presented on *Lux* on September 10, 1951.)

Additional film versions: Essanay, 1918; Paramount, 1923; Paramount, 1950 (*Fancy Pants*).

Fifth Season
(September 11, 1939–July 8, 1940)

Columbia Broadcasting System, Monday, 9:00–10:00 P.M. Music Box Theatre, Hollywood, California, September 11, 1939–May 6, 1940; Vine Street Playhouse, Hollywood, California, May 13, 1940–July 8, 1940. *Host*: Cecil B. DeMille. *Announcer*: Melville Ruick. *Director*: Sanford Barnett. *Musical Director*: Lou Silvers. *Adaptations*: George Wells. *Sound Effects*: Charlie Forsyth.

228. "The Awful Truth," 9/11/39

Based on the 1937 Columbia film (screenplay by Viña Delmar), in turn based on the play by Arthur Richman (1922).

Cast: Claudette Colbert (Lucy Warriner), Cary Grant (Jerry Warriner), Phyllis Brooks (Barbara Vance), Lou Merrill (Dan Leeson), Gale Gordon (Frank/Mr. Vance), Ynez Seabury (Aunt Patsy), Rolfe Sedan (Armand Luvall), John Fee (Judge), Verna Felton (Mrs. Leeson), Forrest Taylor (a Lawyer/Caretaker), Mary McDonald (Dixie Belle Lee), Ted Bliss (Joe/M.C.), Lee Millar (Edwards/Mr. Smith), Mollie Jo Duncan (Gladys), Anna Lisa (Celeste), Ross Forrester (Hank), and Gloria Gordon (Mrs. Vance).

Commercial: Grace Nielson, Jo Campbell, and Vivian Edwards (Modernettes Trio).

The 1939–40 season began with an adaptation of Columbia's bright comedy *The Awful Truth*. The Leo McCarey–directed film presented Irene Dunne and Cary Grant as the warring couple who continue their stormy relationship after their separation, while *Lux* casts Claudette Colbert opposite Grant. Phyllis Brooks plays the supporting role of Barbara, and *Lux* regular Lou Merrill is given one of his most important parts on a *Lux* broadcast to date, that of Oklahoma oilman Dan Leeson (played in the motion picture by Ralph Bellamy).

Frank Nelson, who previously announced the date of the program immediately following the opening fanfare, is absent, and the show now begins with Melville Ruick's familiar declaration of "Lux Presents Hollywood!"

Columbia reworked *The Awful Truth* in 1953 as a musical. Appropriately entitled *Let's Do It Again*, this Alexander Hall–directed film stars Jane Wyman, Ray Milland, and Aldo Ray.

Other *Lux* productions of "The Awful Truth" aired on March 10, 1941, and January 18, 1955.

Additional film version: Columbia, 1953 (*Let's Do It Again*).

229. "Wuthering Heights," 9/18/39

Based on the 1939 Goldwyn/United Artists film (screenplay by Ben Hecht and Charles MacArthur), in turn based on the novel by Emily Brontë (1848).

Cast: Barbara Stanwyck (Cathy), Brian Aherne (Heathcliffe), Ida Lupino (Isabella), Sarita Wooten (Cathy, as a Child), Douglas Scott (Hindley, as a Child), Rex Downing (Heathcliffe, as a Child), Thomas Freebairn Smith (Edgar Linton), Kemble Cooper (Hindley), Marga Ann Deighton (Ellen), Clarence Derwent (Mr. Earnshaw), Reginald Sheffield (Dr. Kenneth), Eric Snowden (Mr. Lockwood), Lou Merrill (Joseph), and Lee Millar (Servant/Dog).

Commercials: Grace Nielson, Jo Campbell, Vivian Edwards (Modernettes Trio), and Catherine Carleton (straight commercial).

According to DeMille at the beginning of this broadcast, it was the many letters from *Lux* listeners asking for "Wuthering Heights" that convinced him to put it on the air. As Samuel Goldwyn had produced his popular screen version earlier that year, the radio production is based on that film.

The motion picture, which was directed by William Wyler, stars Merle Oberon, Laurence Olivier, and Geraldine Fitzgerald, while *Lux* cast Barbara Stanwyck, Brian Aherne, and Ida Lupino in the roles of the indecisive Cathy, brooding Heathcliffe, and hapless Isabella. (The latter was to play Cathy in *Lux*'s second "Wuthering Heights," which was presented the following season.) Recruited from the film cast were Sarita Wooten, Douglas Scott, and Rex Downing, who recreate their performances of the principal characters as children.

A British motion picture of *Wuthering Heights*, with Anna Calder-Marshall, Timothy Dalton, and Hilary Dwyer (directed by Robert Fuest), was released in 1970.

"Wuthering Heights" was broadcast twice more by *Lux*, on November 4, 1940, and September 14, 1954.

Additional film version: AIP (British), 1970.

230. "She Married Her Boss," 9/25/39

Based on the 1935 Columbia film (screenplay by Sidney Buchman), in turn based on a story by Thyra Samter Winslow.

Cast: Ginger Rogers (Julia Scott), George Brent (Richard Lenning), Edith Fellows (Annabel), Frederic MacKaye (Jerry Edwards), Marian Free (Gertrude Lenning), Lurene Tuttle (Martha Pryor), Vangie Bielby (Miss Fitzpatrick), Margaret Brayton (Agnes), Lou Merrill (Hoyt/Old Man), John Lake (Russell/Newsboy Number One), Kay Sutton (Marie/Helen), Galan Galt (Franklin/Handyman), Jessie Huston (Teacher/Operator), Dick Ryan (Watchman/Newsboy), James Eagles (Carter/Photographer), and Ross Forrester (Taxi Driver).

Commercials: Grace Nielson, Jo Campbell, Vivian Edwards (Modernettes Trio), Elwood Rainey (Straight Commercial), and Dorothy Meller (Straight Commercial).

The Columbia film *She Married Her Boss* was directed by Gregory LaCava and released in 1935. An entertaining comedy as a motion picture, it makes an equally engaging broadcast, which focuses upon an efficient, straightforward secretary and the employer she weds. Edith Fellows is the only member of the motion picture cast to appear in the radio version, repeating her portrayal of the title character's spoiled brat daughter, while Ginger Rogers and George Brent nicely play the parts taken by Claudette Colbert and Melvyn Douglas onscreen.

231. "You Can't Take It with You,"
10/2/39

Based on the 1938 Columbia film
(screenplay by Robert Riskin), in turn
based on the play by George S. Kaufman and Moss Hart (1936).

Cast: Edward Arnold (Mr. Kirby),
Walter Connolly (Grandpa), Fay Wray
(Alice), Robert Cummings (Tony),
Nedda Harrigan (Mrs. Kirby), Lee
Patrick (Penny), Lou Merrill (Kolenkhov), Sally Payne (Essie), Edward
Marr (Ed), Rolfe Sedan (Poppins/First
G-Man), Wally Maher (Henderson),
Griff Barnett (Hughes/Judge), Gil
Patric (Secretary/Moving Man), Abe
Reynolds (DePinna), John Fee (First
Associate/Second G-Man), Victor Rodman (Blakely), Jane Morgan (Secretary/
Maggie), Libby Taylor (Rheba), Harry
Humphrey (Paul), and Earle Ross
(Guard/Second Associate).

Commercial: Grace Nielson, Jo
Campbell, Vivian Edwards (Modernettes Trio), and Vivian Edwards (wrote
original music for trio).

Columbia's Academy Award-winning 1938 Frank Capra-directed film
You Can't Take It with You was adapted
by Robert Riskin from the George S.
Kaufman/Moss Hart Broadway play,
which focuses on a household of freespirited eccentrics who refuse to relinquish their property to an unfeeling
businessman.

Lux's large cast includes only Edward Arnold from the movie and
features Walter Connolly, Fay Wray,
Robert Cummings, Nedda Harrigan,
and Lee Patrick in the parts played
onscreen by Lionel Barrymore, Jean
Arthur, James Stewart, Mary Forbes,
and Spring Byington.

Considering that the motion picture
runs for 126 minutes, it is to the credit
of *Lux* writer George Wells that the
radio play of roughly 50 minutes
manages to retain much of the flavor of
its source.

232. "The Sisters," 10/9/39

Based on the 1938 Warner Bros. film
(screenplay by Milton Krims), in turn
based on the novel by Myron Brinig
(1938).

Cast: Irene Dunne (Louise Elliott),
David Niven (Frank Medlin), Gavin
Gordon (Mr. Benson), Florence Baker
(Grace), Kathleen Fitz (Helen), Forrest
Taylor (Ned/First Sailor), Verna Felton
(Rose Elliott), Ted Bliss (Tom Knivel/
Second Sailor), Stanley Farrar (Sam
Johnson/Captain), Celeste Rush
(Flora), Lou Merrill (Tim), Griff
Barnett (Doctor/First Man), Chester
Clute (Bartender/Second Man), Frank
Nelson (Election Announcer/Second
Man [Act 2]), James Eagles (Bill/First
Man [Act 2]), Jean Vander Pyl (Miss
Ortel), Ethel Sykes (Nurse), Mary Lansing (Baby), and Anna Lisa (Ad Lib).

Commercials: Grace Nielson, Jo
Campbell, Vivian Edwards (Modernettes Trio), Pauline Gould, and Lois
Collier.

"The Sisters," based on Warner
Bros.' 1938 Anatole Litvak-directed
film, was presented on *Lux* with Irene
Dunne in the leading feminine role
(which was played by Bette Davis in the
motion picture). The bulk of the story
takes place in early twentieth-century
San Francisco (with the inevitable
earthquake sequence), and one of the
film's strong points is the convincing
period atmosphere which the *Lux* crew
vividly recreates. Heard in Errol
Flynn's picture part is David Niven as
the discontented and undependable
(but likable) husband whose irresponsible ways cause his long-suffering wife
endless grief.

Interestingly, a single reference to
DeMille's obvious case of laryngitis is
cleverly written into his introduction to
the drama.

233. "If I Were King," 10/16/39

Based on the 1938 Paramount film

Douglas Fairbanks, Sr., stops by to visit Douglas Fairbanks, Jr., Frances Dee, and Cecil B. DeMille during a rehearsal of "If I Were King" (October 16, 1939) (photo: Berry Hill Bookshop).

(screenplay by Preston Sturges), in turn based on the play by Justin Huntley McCarthy (1901), from his own novel (1901).

Cast: Douglas Fairbanks, Jr. (François Villon), Frances Dee (Katherine), Cedric Hardwicke (Louis XI), Anna Lisa (Huguette), Wallis Roberts (Tristan), Barry McCollum (René), Frederick Shields (Father Villon), Tony Martelli (Oliver), Guy Repp (Captain), Lou Merrill (General DeLau/ Third Soldier), Howard McNear (Turgis/De La Poucette), Frank Nelson (Casin/Herald), Gloria Gordon (Queen), Marjorie MacGregor (Colette), Lee Millar (D'Aussigny/Nantoullet), Robert Warrick, Sr. (a General), Kenneth Lawton (Watchman), Tyler McVey (First Soldier), Sidney Newman (Second Soldier), Gaughan Burke (Driver), and Josephine McLean (Ad Libs).

Commercials: Grace Nielson, Jo Campbell, Vivian Edwards (Modernettes Trio), and Eva Nixon.

Paramount's 1938 Frank Lloyd–directed film version of Justin Huntley McCarthy's famed novel *If I Were King* provided the material for *Lux's* broadcast of October 16. Douglas Fairbanks, Jr., makes an excellent François Villon, who is played by Ronald Colman in the motion picture, and Frances Dee, the Katherine of the movie cast, is on hand to recreate her role. Rounding out the cast is Cedric Hardwicke, who portrays Basil Rathbone's photoplay character of King Louis XI.

Lux presented two additional broadcasts on August 17, 1936, and December 25, 1944; see the former for information on film versions.

Additional film versions: Fox, 1920; United Artists, 1927 (*The Beloved Rogue*).

234. "Invitation to Happiness," 10/23/39

Based on the 1939 Paramount film (screenplay by Claude Binyon; original story by Mark Jerome).

Cast: Fred MacMurray (King Cole), Madeleine Carroll (Eleanor), Cy Kendall (Hank Hardy), Harry Humphrey (Mr. Wayne), Eric Burtis (Jimmy), Frank Nelson (First Sports Announcer), Lou Merrill (Second Sports Announcer/ Second Cab), Tristram Coffin (Judge), James Eagles (Referee/First Cab), Ross Forrester (Newsboy/Mugg), Robert Warrick, Sr. (Lawyer), Kathleen Fitz (Telegraph Girl), Thomas Graham, David Kerman, Sidney Newman, Jessie Huston, and Ethel Sykes (Crowd).

Commercials: Grace Nielson, Jo Campbell, Vivian Edwards (Modernettes Trio), and Eve Nixon.

"Invitation to Happiness," *Lux*'s October 23 offering, tells the tale of a prizefighter whose career keeps him away from his wife and son. Repeating his portrayal from the 1939 Wesley Ruggles–directed Paramount picture (based on the true story of pugilist King Cole) is Fred MacMurray, who gives a convincing performance, and Madeleine Carroll is also heard to good advantage in Irene Dunne's screen role as the fighter's neglected but understanding wife.

Tenaciously sticking to his duties as host despite a lingering and rather severe case of the flu is Cecil B. DeMille, who once again jokingly refers to his malady during his precurtain talk.

235. "The Old Maid," 10/30/39

Based on the 1939 Warner Bros. film (screenplay by Casey Robinson), in turn based on the play by Zoë Akins (1935), from the novel by Edith Wharton (1924).

Special Guest: Zoë Akins, playwright (after Act 3).

Cast: Loretta Young (Charlotte Lovell), Miriam Hopkins (Delia Lovell), Helen Wood (Tina), Juanita Quigley (Tina, as a Child), Doris Lloyd (Nora), Jack Lewis (Dr. Lanskell), Fred Shields (Clem Spender), Fred MacKaye (Joseph Ralston), Harold Daniels (Lanning Halsey), John Fee (Clergyman/Tutor), Lou Merrill (First Mate/ Harvey), Howard McNear (Seaman), Marga Ann Deighton (Brigid), Janice Hood, Jackie Horner, Paul Hilton (Crowd), and Bobby Larson (Boy/ Crowd).

Commercials: Grace Nielson, Jo Campbell, Vivian Edwards (Modernettes Trio), Emma Redding Saunders, Marie Hammond, Genevieve Olson, and Margaret McKay.

The Old Maid, Warner Bros.' 1939 film (which was directed by Edmund Goulding), provides Bette Davis with one of her most memorable roles, that of a self-sacrificing mother who allows her fatherless child to be brought up by her wealthy sister. Loretta Young succeeds in adapting the character to her own style in the broadcast, and Miriam Hopkins is highly effective (in her original screen role) as the scheming but ultimately sympathetic Delia.

The film screenplay adds the character of Clem Spender (played by George Brent in the movie), who is a pivotal figure in the play and is talked about, but he never appears on stage. The motion picture, which transfers the action some 30 years ahead to the Civil War period, eliminates any anticipation on the audience's part that Clem Spender will return by neatly disposing of him in the war. The *Lux* version, which is based on the film, retains the Spender character and kills him off (though in a different manner, and only after he has *wed* Charlotte, which he does not do in either the play or the motion picture) yet returns the story to its original time period.

236. "Only Yesterday," 11/6/39

Based on the 1933 Universal film (screenplay by William Hurlbut, Arthur Richman, and George O'Neil), in turn based on the book by Frederick Lewis Allen (1931).

Cast: Barbara Stanwyck (Mary), George Brent (Jim Emerson), Dorothy Peterson (Julia), Jacqueline Wells (Blanche), Eric Burtis, Jr. (Jimmy), Gavin Gordon (David/Doctor), Gloria Gordon (Mrs. Lane), Victor Rodman (Mr. Lane), Toni Tree (Deborah/Nurse), Harry Walker (Butler), James Eagles (Messenger/Cabby), Emma Saunders (Mother), Frank Martin (Soldier/Newsboy), Bernice Pilot (Abby), Lou Merrill (Mr. Fairchild/Father), George Webb (Crowd), Ethel Sykes (Ad Lib), and Dora Browner (Ad Lib).

Commercial: Grace Nielson, Jo Campbell, and Vivian Edwards (Modernettes Trio).

Univesal's 1933 film *Only Yesterday*, in which Margaret Sullavan made her screen debut, tells the story of Mary Lane, a young woman who meets and falls in love with soldier Jim Emerson during the period of the First World War. Before the couple are able to carry out their plan to wed, Jim's regiment is called for duty, and Mary gives birth to his baby (unbeknownst to him). Jim returns from the war, wounded, and has no recollection of Mary. Soon afterward, he marries another woman, and Mary is forced to accept the fact that she and Jim will never be happily reunited. Following the policy of allowing no child to be born out of wedlock in any of their stories, *Lux*'s producers are careful to inform their listeners that the couple were secretly wed just prior to Jim's tour of duty. While this may succeed in making Mary an honest woman and her son legitimate, it also changes the complexion of the story by making Jim a bigamist. Nonetheless, Barbara Stanwyck (in Margaret Sulla-

van's film role) and George Brent (taking John Boles's screen part) manage to make the characters sympathetic, and the radio play proves quite entertaining. Taking the roles played by Billie Burke and Benita Hume in the John M. Stahl–directed film are Dorothy Peterson and Jacqueline Wells (Julie Bishop).

The story is given a nostalgic treatment by the *Lux* crew, which adds greatly to the play's effectiveness, and Lou Silvers even uses the 1915 song "Memories" (lyric by Gus Kahn, music by Egbert Van Alstyne) as the main musical theme.

237. "The Champ," 11/13/39

Based on the 1931 MGM film (screenplay by Leonard Praskins; original story by Frances Marion).

Cast: Wallace Beery (Andy Purcell ["The Champ"]), Josephine Hutchinson (Linda Carlson), Noah Beery (Tony Carlson), Bobby Larson (Dink), Lou Merrill (Sponge), Stymie Beard (Jonah), Gale Gordon (Louie/Announcer), Eddie Marr (Photographer), Griff Barnett (Doctor/First Promoter), Wally Maher (Guard/Referee), Earle Ross (Dealer), John Lake (Jose), Walter White (Second Promoter), Lou Lauria (Bookie), Ethel Sykes (Mary), Sidney Newman (Street Vendor/Man [Act 3]), Gaughan Burke (Racetrack Steward/Second Man [Act 3]), and Sally Payne (Crowd).

Commercial: Grace Nielson, Vivian Edwards, Jo Campbell (Modernettes Trio), and Vivian Edwards (composer of original music for the trio).

MGM's 1931 release *The Champ* (directed by King Vidor) was a fondly remembered motion picture about a former boxing champion who makes a gallant effort at a comeback to impress his young son. Wallace Beery, who won the Best Actor Academy Award for his performance (actually, he shared the award with Fredric March), is back for the *Lux* version, and once again he shows how well suited he is to the role. Jackie Cooper had one of his best film parts as Dink, the Champ's loyal little boy. Because he was "about seven years too old for the part now" (as DeMille points out), he was allegedly asked to suggest a child to play what amounts to the largest part in the play, and he chose Bobby Larson. Josephine Hutchinson once again does all she can with what amounts to a featured supporting role, that of the Champ's ex-wife and mother of Dink (played in the film by Irene Rich), while Wallace Beery's brother, Noah, takes the character of her present husband (Neil Hamilton in the motion picture).

Although "The Champ" is not really a boxing tale, it does feature the inevitable comeback bout near the broadcast's conclusion, and in an interesting departure from the standard procedure (a blow-by-blow description of the match by a sports announcer), we have only the reactions of the characters viewing the fight to tell us how it is progressing.

A version of *The Champ* was produced by MGM in 1953 under the title *The Clown*, with the boxer switched to a comedian. Red Skelton, Jane Greer, and Tim Considine starred in this film, which was directed by Robert Z. Leonard. The most recent version was released in 1979 and featured Jon Voight, Faye Dunaway, and Ricky Schroder, under Franco Zeffirelli's direction. "The Champ" was broadcast again on June 29, 1941.

Additional film versions: MGM, 1953 (*The Clown*); MGM, 1979.

238. "Goodbye, Mr. Chips," 11/20/39

Based on the 1939 MGM film (screenplay by R.C. Sherriff, Claudine West, and Eric Maschwitz), in turn based on the novel by James Hilton (1934).

Intermission Guest: James Hilton, author and screenwriter (after Act 2).

Cast: Laurence Olivier (Mr. Chipping), Edna Best (Katherine), Alan Napier (Wetherby/Sir John), Clifford Severn (Linford), Ronald Sinclair (Cooley), Frederic Worlock (Ralston), Lillian Kemble-Cooper (Martha), Mary Gordon (Mrs. Wickett), C. Montague Shaw (a Doctor [Act 3]/Innkeeper), Eric Snowden (Bowden/Doctor [Act 2]), Ian MacLaren (Meldrum), Douglas Scott (Boy Number One), Harry Duff (Boy Number Two), Tommy Martin (Boy Three), Bobby Mauch (Boy Four), Brian Kellaway (Boy Five), Ernest Carlson (Boy Six), Cliff Oland (Boy Seven), Bill Martin (Boy Eight), Bob Stevens (Boy Nine), Edwin Mills (Boy Ten), Bobby Winkler (Boy Eleven), and Richard Clucas (Boy Twelve).

Commercials: Emma Redding Saunders, Lois Collier, and Margaret Brayton (Libby Collins).

Robert Donat won an Oscar for his portrayal of the title character in MGM's 1939 Sam Wood–directed drama *Goodbye, Mr. Chips,* but he preferred to work in his native England (where the film was shot) and thus would never appear on *Lux*. In his absence, fellow Briton Laurence Olivier was engaged to play the role of the beloved schoolmaster, Mr. Chipping, known to his students as Mr. "Chips." The Chips character so dominates the story that little chance remains for any of the other figures to have lengthy scenes, yet Edna Best (also in her *Lux* debut) makes a fine impression as Katherine, the role Greer Garson plays on the screen.

The character of gossip columnist "Libby Collins" (here played by Margaret Brayton) makes her first appearance on the program and plugs the product after the third act. This fictional figure would become a major part of Lux's advertising on the show and would go on to appear in hundreds of additional broadcasts.

A musical rendering of *Goodbye, Mr. Chips* was released by MGM in 1969, with Peter O'Toole and Petula Clark, under Herbert Ross's direction.

Additional film version: MGM, 1969.

*239. "Pygmalion," 11/27/39

Based on the play by George Bernard Shaw (1913).

Cast: Jean Arthur (Eliza Doolittle), Brian Aherne (Henry Higgins), Alan Napier (Colonel Pickering), Jack Lewis (First Bystander/Footman), Eric Snowden (Mr. Doolittle), Mary Gordon (Mrs. Pearce), Evelyn Beresford (Mrs. Ensford), Mary Taylor (Miss Ensford), Thomas Freebairn-Smith (Freddy/ Cabbie), Louis Merrill (Ambassador), Margaret Brayton (Parlour Maid), Janet Young (a Young Woman), Thomas Mills (Second Bystander/Man), and Gloria Gordon (Mrs. Higgins).

Commercials: Grace Nielson, Vivian Edwards, Jo Campbell (Modernettes Trio), and Margaret Brayton (Libby Collins).

George Bernard Shaw's popular play about an uncouth cockney flower girl who gradually blossoms into a refined young lady under the tutelage of a determined professor was first produced in Vienna in 1913 at the Hofburger Theatre, starring Lilly Marberg and Max Paulsen (German translation by Siegfried Trebitsch). His Majesty's Theatre in London was the site (on April 11, 1914) for the first British version, which featured Mrs. Patrick Campbell and Herbert Tree. Six months later (on October 12, 1914) the play made its way to Broadway, with Mrs. Patrick Campbell and Philip Merivale. *Pygmalion* reached the screen in 1938 as a British production directed by Anthony Asquith and Leslie Howard, with Howard as Henry Higgins and Wendy Hiller as Eliza; *Lux*'s adaptation of the story paired Jean Arthur and Brian Aherne in the leads. An Academy Award–winning musical version was produced by Warner Bros. in 1964 (directed by George Cukor), starring Rex Harrison and Audrey Hepburn, based on the Alan J. Lerner/Frederic Loewe Broadway play.

Film versions: Gabriel Pascal (British), 1938; Warner Bros., 1964 (*My Fair Lady*).

240. "A Man to Remember," 12/4/39

Based on the 1938 RKO film (screenplay by Dalton Trumbo), in turn based on the story by Katharine Haviland-Taylor.

Cast: Bob Burns (John Abbott), Anita Louise (Jean), Harold Daniels (Dick), Granville Bates (George Sykes), Harlan Briggs (Homer Ramsey), Lou Merrill (Jode Harkness), John Fee (Clyde Perkins), Earle Ross (Howard Johnson), Clara Blandick (Mother), Eric Burtis, Jr. (Dick, as a Boy), Victor Rodman (Dr. Robinson), Griff Barnett (Minister), Rolfe Sedan (Superintendent), James Eagles (Howard Sykes), Edward Marr (Dr. Palmer), Celeste Rush (Baby/Woman), Josette Doogan (Little Girl), and Josephine McLean (Ad Lib).

Commercials: Grace Nielson, Vivian Edwards, Jo Campbell (Modernettes Trio), Alyn Lockwood, and Sherry Ardell.

A Man to Remember, the 1938 RKO drama (directed by Garson Kanin) that proved to be the surprise hit of the season, was actually a version of the same studio's 1933 release, *One Man's Journey*, which stars Lionel Barrymore. In an interesting bit of casting, rustic comedian Bob Burns plays the serious part of the title character (which was undertaken by Edward Ellis on the screen), a small town doctor whose poor business sense is more than compensated for by his kind heart. Anita Louise takes the role of the doctor's

adopted daughter, played by Anne Shirley in the film, while Harold Daniels is heard in Lee Bowman's movie role of the doctor's son, Dick. (Granville Bates and Harlan Briggs repeat their motion picture parts for the *Lux* broadcast.)
Additional film version: RKO, 1933 (*One Man's Journey*).

241. "In Name Only," 12/11/39
Based on the 1939 RKO film (screenplay by Robert Sherman), in turn based on the novel *Memory of Love*, by Bessie Breuer (1939).
Cast: Cary Grant (Alec Warren), Carole Lombard (Julie Eden), Kay Francis (Maida Warren), Julie Bannon (Suzanne), Jean Arden (Laura), Peggy Ann Garner (Ellen), Clara Blandick (Mrs. Warren), Wright Kramer (Dr. Grayson), Lou Merrill (Mr. Warren), Wheaton Chambers (Dr. Muller), Harry Walker (Hotel Manager), and Gil Patric (Groom).
Commercials: Margaret Brayton (Libby Collins). Brown Derby Episode: Gil Patric (Waiter), Wheaton Chambers (Man), Kathleen Fitz (Sally), and Ynez Seabury (Woman).
Although RKO's 1939 production *In Name Only* (directed by John Cromwell) may be a relatively routine drama of a vengeful wife trying to hold on to the husband she does not love, it is boosted immeasurably by the performances of the three stars. Such is the case in the broadcast of December 11, as those same three players, Cary Grant, Carole Lombard, and Kay Francis, were all present to repeat their memorable portrayals for *Lux*. (Also reprising her original role is child actor Peggy Ann Garner.)
Curiously, the names of two of the characters have been altered for the microphone version: Alec Walker becomes Alec *Warren*, and Dr. Gateson is referred to as Dr. *Grayson*.

***242.** "Four Daughters," 12/18/39
Based on the 1938 Warner Bros. film (screenplay by Lenore Coffee and Julius Epstein), in turn based on the Fanny Hurst story "Sister Act."
Cast: John Garfield (Mickey), Priscilla Lane (Ann Lemp), Rosemary Lane (Emma Lemp), Leota Lane (Kay Lemp), Lola Lane (Thea Lemp), Jeffrey Lynn (Felix), Wallis Clark (Father), Clara Blandick (Aunt Etta), Hal K. Dawson (Ben), Lou Merrill (Ernest), and Harry Humphrey (Doctor).
Commercials: Emma Redding Saunders (Grandmother), Eric Burtis, Jr. (Boy), Julie Bannon (Sally), Kathleen Fitz (Girl), Celeste Rush (Woman in Act 2), and Martha Wentworth (Woman after Act 3).
Michael Curtiz's 1938 film *Four Daughters*, the first entry in the Warner Bros. series that focuses on four small town girls and their various trials and tribulations in love and life, was brought to *Lux* with five original cast members: John Garfield, Priscilla Lane, Rosemary Lane, Lola Lane, and Jeffrey Lynn. Leota Lane, the real-life sibling of the aforementioned young ladies, rounds out the cast as the fourth sister (played onscreen by Gale Page).

243. "Pinocchio," 12/25/39
Based on the 1940 Walt Disney/RKO animated film (screenplay by Ted Sears, Webb Smith, Joseph Sabo, Otto Englander, William Cottrell, Erdman Penner, and Aurelius Battaglia), in turn based on the story "Le Avventure di Pinocchio" ("The Adventures of Pinocchio"), by Carlo Collodi (1893).
Cast: Walter Catlett (Honest John [Fox]), Stuart Buchanan (Gideon/Barker Number Two), Dickie Jones (Pinocchio), Charles Judels (Stromboli/Coachman), Frankie Darro (Lampwick), Cliff Edwards (Jiminy Cricket), Christian Rub (Geppetto), Evelyn Venable (Blue Fairy), Grace Nielson

(Blue Fairy Singing Voice), Earl Hodgins (Barker Number One), Florence Gill (Cuckoo/Figaro), Joe Pennario (Alexander), Clarence Straight (Donkey/Barker Number Three), Ernest Carlson, Jean Forsyth, Eric Burtis, Jr., and Jackie Morrison (Ad Libs).

Commercials: Bobby Larson (Little Boy after Act 1), Barbara Jean Wong (Little Girl after Act 1), Fred Shields (Man after Act 1), Nancy Leach (Woman after Act 1), Eric Burtis, Jr. (Ad Libs after Act 1), Jackie Morrison (Ad Libs after Act 1), Julie Bannon (Sally), Margaret Brayton (Libby Collins).

Lux's 1939 "Christmas gift" to its listeners was an adaptation of Walt Disney's animated feature *Pinocchio*. Actually, the broadcast precedes the release of the film, which would premiere in January 1940. In keeping with the Disney policy of the time, none of the players is billed, although it is evident that most of the actors taking part in the broadcast created the voices for the film (where, of course, they are also unbilled). Perhaps to retain the anonymity of the cast, there is no studio audience for this program, and recorded applause is inserted for DeMille's entrance and at the end of each act.

The audio adaptation is successful even with the necessity of abridgment, and the slight modifications (such as Jiminy Cricket providing narration to describe characters and to tie together scenes) play very well over the air. Adding to the show's entertainment is the inclusion of the original incidental music and most of the songs from the film score (lyrics by Ned Washington, music by Leigh Harline). Heard in various degrees of completeness are: Act 2: "When You Wish Upon a Star" (Jiminy Cricket), "Little Woodenhead" (Geppetto), "When You Wish Upon a Star" (reprise, the Blue Fairy), "Give a Little Whistle" (Jiminy Cricket and Pinocchio), "Hi-Diddle-Dee-Dee (An

Actor's Life for Me" (Honest John and Pinocchio); Act 2: "I've Got No Strings" (Pinocchio), "Hi-Diddle-Dee-Dee (An Actor's Life for Me)" (reprise, Honest John and Pinocchio); Act 3: "When You Wish Upon a Star" (reprise, Jiminy Cricket).

244. "Sorrell and Son," 1/1/40
Based on the novel by Warwick Deeping (1926).

Cast: Herbert Marshall (Stephen Sorrell), Richard Carlson (Kit), Karen Morley (Dora), Clifford Severn, Jr. (Kit, as a Boy), Eric Snowden (Roland), Vernon Steele (Buck), Mary Gordon (Mrs. Marks), Claire Vedera (Mrs. Palfrey), Kathleen Fitz (Molly), Thomas Mills (Mr. Palfrey/Minister), Gloria Gordon (Mrs. Verity/Anna), Jack Lewis (Samfitz/Headmaster), Clifford Severn, Sr. (Dr. Harvey/Trainman), Thomas Freebairn-Smith (Hotel Clerk/Voice), and Lou Merrill (Man in Act 2).

Commercials: Julie Bannon (Sally), Sally Payne (Young Woman's Voice).

Although it had been filmed twice, this week's play, "Sorrell and Son," was adapted from Warwick Deeping's 1926 novel. It tells of a former Army captain's attempts to retain his dignity in the eyes of his son, despite having to struggle to eke out a living. The controversial mercy-killing that concludes the novel has been softened for the broadcast; instead of receiving an intentional overdose of morphine from his son, Captain Sorrell dies in the microphone version simply because he has refused the operation that would save his life but leave him an invalid.

Herbert Marshall's sophisticated delivery is perfect for the character of Captain Stephen Sorrell, and he gives a fine performance, as do Richard Carlson as his son and Karen Morley as his ex-wife.

The first film version of *Sorrell and Son* was released by United Artists in

1927, with H.B. Warner, Nils Asther, and Anna Q. Nilsson in the starring roles. Warner was also given the chance to star in a talking version of the story in 1934, which was shot in England and released by United Artists in the United States. This production was directed by Jack Raymond and also featured Hugh Williams and Winifred Shotter.

Film versions: United Artists, 1927; British and Dominions/United Artists, 1934.

245. "Dark Victory," 1/8/40

Based on the 1939 Warner Bros. film (screenplay by Casey Robinson), in turn based on the play by George Emerson Brewer, Jr., and Bertram Bloch (1934).

Cast: Bette Davis (Judith Traherne), Spencer Tracy (Dr. Frederick Steele), Lurene Tuttle (Ann), Fred Shields (Michael), Wright Kramer (Dr. Parsons), Martha Wentworth (Miss Wainwright), Clara Blandick (Martha), Lou Merrill (Mantle/Waiter), Nancy Leach (a Nurse), George Webb (Ad Libs), Carol Browner (Ad Libs), and Ray Lithgow (Telegraph Sound Effect).

Commercials: Julie Bannon (Sally), Emma Redding Saunders (Woman), Celeste Rush (Woman), and Griff Barnett (Grocer).

The featured attraction of the second *Lux* broadcast of the new year was the presence of the Academy of Motion Picture Arts and Sciences' choices for best actress and best actor of 1937: Bette Davis and Spencer Tracy. The play chosen for this occasion was one of Davis's hits from the previous season, Warner Bros.' Edmund Goulding–directed drama *Dark Victory*, which concerns a wealthy young woman's struggle against a deadly brain tumor and her relationship with the doctor who is treating her. The program offers the usual high production values and

serves as a good vehicle to reunite Bette Davis and Spencer Tracy, who last appeared together in the 1933 film *20,000 Years in Sing-Sing*.

Stolen Hours was the title chosen for the 1963 British version of *Dark Victory*. This altered rendering was directed by Daniel Petrie and features Susan Hayward and Michael Craig in the leads.

The *Lux Video Theatre* presented a version on February 14, 1957.

Additional film version: Mirisch/Barbican/United Artists, 1963 (*Stolen Hours*).

246. "Sing, You Sinners," 1/15/40

Based on the 1938 Paramount film (screenplay by Claude Binyon).

Cast: Bing Crosby (Joe), Ralph Bellamy (David), Elizabeth Patterson (Mrs. Beebe), Jacqueline Wells (Martha Randall), Charles Peck (Mike), Arthur Q. Bryan (Ringner), Lou Merrill (Announcer), Emery Parnell (Manager/Leader), Edward Marr (Pete/Cab Driver), Jack Carr (Filter/Porter), James Eagles (Steward/Waiter), and Frank Coghlan, Jr. (Telegraph Boy).

Commercials: Gloria Gordon (Mrs. Aldrich), Julie Bannon (Sally), Celeste Rush (Woman/Ad Lib), and Thomas Freebairn-Smith (Scientist's Voice).

Bing Crosby's second appearance on *Lux* once again found him recreating his role from a Paramount picture. *Sing, You Sinners*, a 1938 release that was produced and directed by Wesley Ruggles, features Crosby as a chronic gambler whose irresponsibility in dealing with life causes considerable trouble for his level-headed family. Rounding out the excellent cast are Ralph Bellamy and Charles Peck as Bing Crosby's brothers (played in the film by Fred MacMurray and Donald O'Connor), Jacqueline Wells in Ellen Drew's screen part of Martha, and Elizabeth Patterson, who recreates her movie role as the boys' mother. Three of the songs from the motion picture are performed by Bing Crosby in the broadcast: Act 1: "I've Got a Pocketful of Dreams" and "Don't Let That Moon Get Away" (both with words by Johnny Burke, music by James V. Monaco); Act 2: "Small Fry" (words by Frank Loesser, music by Hoagy Carmichael); Act 3: "I've Got a Pocketful of Dreams" (reprise).

247. "Bachelor Mother," 1/22/40

Based on the 1939 RKO film (screenplay by Norman Krasna; original story by Felix Jackson).

Cast: Ginger Rogers (Polly Parrish), Fredric March (David Merlin), Frank Albertson (Frank Miller), Lou Merrill (J.B. Merlin), Bea Benaderet (Mrs. Weiss), Emery Parnell (Investigator/Third Man), Edward Marr (Jerome/Announcer), Martha Wentworth (Matron/Shopper), Rolfe Sedan (Hargroves), Thomas Mills (Butler), Kenneth Lawton (Clerk/Jones), Walter White (Detective/Second Man), Celeste Rush (Matron/Baby), Audrey Reynolds (Louise/Girl), and Frank Martin (First Man).

Commercials: Justina Wayne (Girl after Act 1), Julie Bannon (Sally).

The 1939 Garson Kanin–directed light comedy *Bachelor Mother* concerns a department store clerk whose life is turned upside down after she finds a baby on her doorstep. Ginger Rogers, the star of RKO's picture, also appears in *Lux*'s amusing broadcast as the girl who finds it impossible to convince anyone that she is not the child's mother, while Fredric March proves a good choice for the David Niven movie part of the store owner's stuffy son who becomes unwillingly entangled in the proceedings. (Joel McCrea was originally announced, but an illness kept him from appearing.) Frank Albertson of the screen cast repeats his droll performance as the heroine's co-worker, Frank Miller (changed from *Freddie* Miller in the picture).

A musical version of *Bachelor Mother*, entitled *Bundle of Joy*, was produced by RKO in 1956, with Norman Taurog directing Debbie Reynolds, Eddie Fisher, and Tommy Noonan.

Additional film version: RKO, 1956 (*Bundle of Joy*).

*248. "Intermezzo," 1/29/40

Based on the 1939 Selznick International/UA film *Intermezzo: A Love Story* (screenplay by George O'Neil), in turn based on the 1936 Swedish film (screenplay by Gosta Stevens and Gustav Molander; original story by Gustav Molander).

Cast: Herbert Marshall (Holger Brandt), Ingrid Bergman (Anita), Gail Patrick (Margit Brandt), Vernon Steele (Thomas Stenborg), Douglas Scott (Eric), Ann Todd (Anne Marie), Lou Merrill (Charles/"Vienna"), Kenneth Lawton (Doctor/Waiter), Clara Blandick (Emma/Woman), Clarence Straight, (Conductor/Dog), Barry Stall ("England"/Cab Driver), and Rolfe Sedan ("Paris"/Man).

Commercials: Julie Bannon (Sally), Lois Collier (First Girl), and Ynez Seabury (Second Girl).

The Gregory Ratoff–directed David O. Selznick film *Intermezzo: A Love Story* served to introduce Swedish actress Ingrid Bergman to American audiences in 1939 (Bergman also appeared in the original Swedish version, *Intermezzo*, in 1936, with Gosta Ekman and Inga Tidblad). *Lux*'s first radio rendering gave the star a chance effectively to recreate her part of the impressionable young pianist who falls in love with a well-known (and already married) violinist, played by Herbert Marshall in Leslie Howard's screen role. The microphone play also features Gail Patrick in the Edna Best movie part, and child actors Douglas Scott and Ann Todd reprising their film characters.

Lux also aired a version on June 4, 1945.

Additional film version: Swedish, 1936 (*Intermezzo*).

*249. "The Young in Heart," 2/5/40

Based on the 1938 United Artists film (screenplay by Paul Osborn; adaptation, Charles Bennett), in turn based on I.A.R. Wylie's serialized story "The Gay Banditti" (1938).

Cast: Don Ameche (Richard), Ida Lupino (George-Ann), May Robson (Miss Ellen Fortune), Helen Wood (Leslie), Eric Snowden (Sahib), Fred Shields (Duncan), Lelah Tyler (Marmy), Thomas Mills (Butler/Doctor), Phillips Tead (Conductor/Man), and Lou Merrill (Anstruther).

Commercials: Julie Bannon (Sally), Lois Collier (Woman after Act 1), Nancy Leach (Woman after Act 2), and James Eagles (Man after Act 2).

Richard Wallace's 1938 film *The Young in Heart*, a splendidly executed drama revolving around a charmingly misdirected family of con artists who are taught a valuable lesson through the unconditional love lavished on them by a kindly spinster, made its way to *Lux* almost a year and a half after its theatrical release. Don Ameche and Ida Lupino portrayed the scheming siblings delightfully played by Douglas Fairbanks, Jr., and Janet Gaynor in the film, while May Robson enacts the character memorably played by Minnie Dupree in the motion picture.

250. "The Sidewalks of London," 2/12/40

Based on the 1939 Mayflower film *St. Martin's Lane* (released in the United States by Paramount in 1940 as *The Sidewalks of London*) (screenplay by Clemence Dane).

Cast: Charles Laughton (Charlie), Elsa Lanchester (Libby), Alan Marshal (Harley Prentice), Claude Allister (Gentry), Gloria Gordon (Ma), Jack Lewis (Pa/Clerk), Phillips Tead (Arthur), Eric Snowden (Doggie/Policeman), Thomas Freebairn-Smith (Magistrate), Thomas Mills (Second Policeman), Tommy Martin (Julian), Audrey Reynolds (Girl), Adelaide Irving (Girl), Lou Merrill (Strang/Voice), Robert Tait (Soloist), and Robert Bradford (Group).

Commercials: Kathleen Fitz (Sally), Ynez Seabury (Martha), Nancy Leach (Woman), James Eagles (Man), and Barbara Jean Wong (Little Child).

The 1939 Tim Whelan–directed British production *St. Martin's Lane* was released the following year by Paramount under the title *The Sidewalks of London*. In fact, the film was playing in American cinemas as the radio version was being broadcast by the *Lux Radio Theatre* on February 12. Charles Laughton reprises his role of a London sidewalk performer (a "busker") who takes a stagestruck street waif under his wing and helps her realize her ambition. Elsa Lanchester plays the girl created in the motion picture by Vivien Leigh, and Alan Marshal makes his Hollywood *Lux* debut in Rex Harrison's film role.

This program was broadcast on Abraham Lincoln's birthday, and to commemorate the occasion Charles Laughton recites Lincoln's Gettysburg Address (as he did in the film *Ruggles of Red Gap*) during the curtain call.

251. "Made for Each Other," 2/19/40

Based on the 1939 Selznick-International film (screenplay by Jo Swerling), in turn suggested by a story by Rose Franken.

Cast: Carole Lombard (Jane Mason), Fred MacMurray (Johnny Mason), Verna Felton (Mrs. Mason), Lou Merrill (Judge Doolittle), Hal K. Dawson (Mr. Carter/Denver), Rosemary deCamp (Eunice Doolittle), Edward Marr (Conway), Wheaton Chambers (Dr. Healy),

John Fee (Murphy/Chief), Robert Gray (Hatton), Bernice Pilot (Annie), Mary Lansing, Marjorie MacGregor (Nurses), Griff Barnett (Butler), Howard McNear (Allentown), and Jackie Morrison (Boy).

Commercials: Ynez Seabury (Woman after Act 1), Julie Bannon (Sally), Lois Collier (Woman after Act 2), and James Eagles (Man).

Cecil B. DeMille describes "Made for Each Other" as a story of "the married life of two average, healthy, young Americans." It is these qualities in Jo Swerling's screenplay of the 1939 Selznick-International production, combined with John Cromwell's sensitive direction and the performance of Carole Lombard, James Stewart, Lucille Watson, and Charles Coburn, that create such an engaging film. Lombard gives an equally sincere, moving performance in the radio version and is entirely convincing as the young wife. Fred MacMurray of the broadcast tends to emphasize the weak will of the husband's character more than does James Stewart in the film, but this is due partly to the script, as many of the picture's scenes displaying a stronger side of Johnny's character are missing from the microphone adaptation. (Radio actors Verna Felton and Lou Merrill are given the important roles of Johnny's disapproving mother and his cold, business-minded boss.)

Ironically, when Carole Lombard and Fred MacMurray ask what is on the agenda for next week's show, they are informed that it will be an adaptation of their 1937 film Swing High, Swing Low.

252. "Swing High, Swing Low," 2/26/40

Based on the 1937 Paramount film (screenplay by Virginia Van Upp and Oscar Hammerstein II), in turn based on the play Burlesque, by George Manker Watters and Arthur Hopkins (1927).

Cast: Rudy Vallee (Skid Johnson), Virginia Bruce (Maggie King), Una Merkel (Ella), Roscoe Karns (Harry), Martha Wentworth (Murphy), Corinne Miller (Cynthia), Bill Wright (Harvey), Harold Daniels (Miguel/First Backslapper), Lou Merrill (Georgie/First Guide), Walter White (Judge/Third Backslapper), Tristram Coffin (Don/ Second Backslapper), Ted Bliss (Second Guide/Man), Frank Coghlan, Jr. (Elevator Boy/Cabin Boy), Edward Marr (Commentator), Josephine McLean (a Girl), Frank Martin (Waiter/ Voice), Enrico Ricardi (First Crooner), and Marlene Schools (Cynthia's Singing Voice).

Commercials: Lois Collier, James Eagles, and Julie Bannon (Sally).

Although Paramount's 1937 film Swing High, Swing Low is officially based on Burlesque, by George Manker Watters and Arthur Hopkins, the motion picture differs substantially from the famous 1927 play. ("Burlesque" was presented on Lux on June 15, 1936.) The picture, which was directed by Mitchell Leisen, concerns an irresponsible trumpet player (Fred MacMurray) and his adoring wife (Carole Lombard), but in the broadcast version the leading man is given the occupation of crooner, which enables Rudy Vallee to vocalize. Also in the cast are Virginia Bruce as the wife, Una Merkel in Jean Dixon's film role, and Roscoe Karns in the Charles Butterworth movie part.

Vallee is given the chance to sing four hit songs of the period: Act 1: "Adios" (lyric by Eddie Woods, music by Enric Madriguera), "I Didn't Know What Time It Was" (lyric by Lorenz Hart, music by Richard Rodgers; from the Broadway production Too Many Girls); Act 2: "All the Things You Are" (lyric by Oscar Hammerstein II, music by Jerome Kern; from the Broadway production Very Warm for May), "Careless" (words and music by Dick

Jurgens, Eddy Howard, and Lew Qualding); Act 3: "All the Things You Are" (reprise, finale).

At the end of the program, Melville Ruick announces that "Rudy Vallee will star in a new radio series, to begin March 7."

253. "Trade Winds," 3/4/40

Based on the 1939 Walter Wanger/United Artists film (screenplay by Dorothy Parker, Alan Campbell, Frank R. Adams; original story by Tay Garnett).

Cast: Errol Flynn (Sam Wye), Joan Bennett (Kay Kerrigan), Mary Astor (Jean), Ralph Bellamy (Detective Blodgett), Lou Merrill (Chief of Detectives/Radio Announcer), John Lake (Thomas Bruhm II), Wally Maher (Nightclub Owner/Second Newsboy), Earle Ross (Detective/Mr. Cornell), Rosemary deCamp (Hopsing/First Girl), Edward Marr (Third Newsboy/Faulkner), Nancy Leach (Mrs. Cornell/Blonde), Earl Gunn (Man), Stanley Whitman (Bartender/Clerk), and Lois Collier (Second Girl).

Commercial: Julie Bannon (Sally).

A pleasant comedy/drama of a woman accused of murder and the detective pursuing her was the offering for March 4. "Trade Winds" was based on the 1939 Walter Wanger/United Artists production, which was directed by Tay Garnett (who also wrote the original story) and starred Fredric March, Joan Bennett, Ann Sothern, and Ralph Bellamy. Bennett is charming in her role as the fugitive, and Bellamy delightfully recreates his motion picture part as the comically dim-witted police detective who "assists" the hero. Errol Flynn nicely plays the Fredric March screen part, and Mary Astor gives a good portrayal as the private detective's wisecracking secretary (Ann Sothern's movie role).

254. "My Son, My Son," 3/11/40

Based on the 1940 Edward Small/United Artists film (screenplay by Lenore Coffee), in turn based on the novel by Howard Spring (1938).

Cast: Brian Aherne (William Essex), Madeleine Carroll (Livia Vaynol), Louis Hayward (Oliver Essex), Josephine Hutchinson (Nellie), Kathleen Fitz (Maeve), Warren Ashe (Dermott), Scotty Beckett (Oliver, as a Child), Ted Bliss (Rory), Eric Snowden (Colonel), Jack Lewis (Sergeant), Lou Merrill (Paper Boy), Barry Steele (Call Boy), Thomas Mills (Butler/Innkeeper), and Celeste Rush (Baby Cry).

Commercials: Ynez Seabury (Anne), Margaret Brayton (Sue), and Julie Bannon (Sally).

"My Son, My Son" gave *Lux* another chance to "preview" a motion picture—that is, to broadcast an adaptation of a film not yet in general release. As DeMille states in his introduction to the play, which is an interesting blend of sacrifice, selfishness, and unconditional parental love, "The picture will be released nationally by United Artists in a few weeks." He also notes that the four principal players from the Charles Vidor–directed film are present for the broadcast: Brian Aherne, Madeleine Carroll, Louis Hayward, and Josephine Hutchinson. (Scotty Beckett, also of the movie cast, is present to reprise his role of Oliver as a child.)

255. "The Rains Came," 3/18/40

Based on the 1939 20th Century–Fox film (screenplay by Philip Dunne and Julien Josephson), in turn based on the novel by Louis Bromfield (1937).

Intermission Guest: Loretta Francel, Carole Lombard's hairdresser (after Act 2).

Cast: Kay Francis (Lady Esketh), George Brent (Tom Ransome), Jean Parker (Fern), Jim Ameche (Major Safti), Martha Wentworth (the Maharani),

Verna Felton (Mrs. Simon), Lou Merrill (Smiley), Jack Lewis (Lord Esketh), Lal Chand Mehra (Rashid/Messenger), Wyndham Standing (the Maharajah), Thomas Mills (Bates), John Fee, James Eagles, and Melville Ruick (Ad Libs).

Singers: Morton Scott, Bill Daye, George Gramlich, Enrico Ricardi, Phil Neely, Robert Bradford, Ralph Leon, John Oliver, Clifford Lilliquist, Abe Dinovitz, Devona Doxie, Winona Black, and Winnie Parker.

Commercials: Duane Thompson (Nettie), Kathleen Fitz (Jean), Lois Collier (Anne), and Margaret Brayton (Pauline).

Even though the vivid earthquake and flood sequences of 20th Century–Fox's *The Rains Came* (directed by Clarence Brown) are de-emphasized in the *Lux* production, the dramatic situations in the story of an English lady's doomed love for an Indian physician make for an interesting broadcast. The fine cast includes Kay Francis in Myrna Loy's screen role, George Brent repeating his film characterization, and Jean Parker in Brenda Joyce's motion picture part. Radio actor Jim Ameche is heard as Major Safti, the role played by Tyrone Power in the photoplay, while Lal Chand Mehra, who was cast in the small part of a chant singer in the motion picture, is given the part taken onscreen by William Royle.

In 1955, 20th Century–Fox released a version of *The Rains Came* under the title *The Rains of Ranchipur*. The film, which was directed by Jean Negulesco, featured Lana Turner, Fred MacMurray, Joan Caulfield, and Michael Rennie in the leads.

Additional film version: 20th Century–Fox, 1955 (*The Rains of Ranchipur*).

256. "Remember the Night," 3/25/40

Based on the 1940 Paramount film (screenplay by Preston Sturges).

Cast: Barbara Stanwyck (Lee Leander), Fred MacMurray (John Sargent), Beulah Bondi (Mrs. Sargent), Elizabeth Patterson (Aunt Emma), Sterling Holloway (Willie), Lou Merrill (O'Leary), Jack Carr (Rufus), John Fee (Judge), Edward Marr (Tom/Leader), Wally Maher (District Attorney), Celeste Rush (Mother/Matron), Arthur Q. Bryan (Mike/Meyer), Walter White (Clerk/Waiter), Sidney Newman (Cassidy), Ann Lee (Secretary), Warren Rock (a Policeman/Guard), and Clarence Straight (Dog).

Commercials: Rosemary deCamp (Thought Voice), Kathleen Fitz (Libby).

The recently released Paramount film *Remember the Night* was the drama for the March 25 broadcast. The very entertaining motion picture was produced and directed by Mitchell Leisen and features a sensitive, intelligent screenplay by Preston Sturges. The focus is an embittered shoplifter who learns the true meaning of love when she spends Christmas with the family of the D.A.'s assistant who will prosecute her for her crime. The five principals who helped to make the picture such a memorable production — Barbara Stanwyck, Fred MacMurray, Beulah Bondi, Elizabeth Patterson, and Sterling Holloway — are all on hand for the radio version to recreate their excellent screen characterizations.

Lux presented "Remember the Night" for a second time on December 22, 1941, and on the *Lux Video Theatre* on May 5, 1955.

257. "Love Affair," 4/1/40

Based on the 1939 RKO film (screenplay by Delmer Daves and Donald Ogden Stewart; original story by Mildred Cram and Leo McCarey).

Cast: Irene Dunne (Terry McKay), William Powell (Michael Marnet), Gale Gordon (Kenneth), Bea Benaderet (Grandmother), Lou Merrill (Courbé/

Radio Announcer), Frank McGlynn (Superintendent), Linda Douglas (Lois), Warren Ashe (a Doctor/Manager), Sara Selby (Miss Lane/Woman), Phillips Tead (a Painter/Englishman), James Eagles (Elevator Boy/Page Boy), Tony Martelli (a Photographer/Second Man), Rolfe Sedan (a Guide/Frenchman), Edward Marr (Taxi Driver), Griff Barnett (a Priest/Steward), Doris Bryan, Gwenn Bryan, Betty Bryan (Trio/Ad Libs), Barbara Jean Wong, Bobby Larson, and Joe Pennario (Children).

Commercials: Kathleen Fitz (First Girl), Julie Bannon (Second Girl), Lois Collier (Third Girl), Margaret McKay (Fourth Girl), Ynez Seabury (Fifth Girl), Carol Brenner (Sixth Girl), Nancy Leach (Sally), James Eagles (Man), and Celeste Rush (Baby).

Love Affair, the popular 1939 RKO production, starred Irene Dunne and Charles Boyer as the star-crossed lovers whose relationship is tested by a series of unexpected occurrences. Dunne was present to recreate her polished film portrayal for *Lux* and was given the opportunity to sing two new songs: "Sing, My Heart" (lyric by Ted Koehler, music by Harold Arlen), and "Wishing" (lyric and music by B.G. DeSylva). While only a brief snatch of the former is heard in the broadcast (during Act 1), the latter receives a charming rendition by Dunne and the Bryan Sisters in the third act. Heard opposite Dunne is William Powell, who plays the Charles Boyer film role.

Leo McCarey, who directed the 1939 *Love Affair*, shot another version in 1957 under the title *An Affair to Remember*, which featured Deborah Kerr and Cary Grant.

Lux redid "Love Affair" on July 6, 1942.

Additional film version: RKO, 1957 (*An Affair to Remember*).

258. "Mama Loves Papa," 4/8/40

Based on the 1933 Paramount film (screenplay by Arthur Kober, Nunnally Johnson, Douglas McLean, and Keene Thompson), in turn based on the play by Jack McGowan and Mann Page (1926).

Cast: Fibber McGee [Jim Jordan] (Wilbur Todd), Molly [Marion Jordan] (Jessie Todd), Lou Merrill (Mr. MacIntosh), Celeste Rush (Mrs. MacIntosh), Arthur Q. Bryan (O'Leary), Emory Parnell (Mr. Kirkwood), Linda Douglas (Miss Baydecker), Warren Ashe (Dr. Payne/Norman), Hal K. Dawson (Burke/Joe), Rolfe Sedan (Clerk/Second Copy), Abe Reynolds (Sid/Émile), Victor Rodman (Thomas), Edward Marr (Soapbox Orator/First Boy), John Fee (First Photographer/Mayer), James Eagles (Attendant/Photographer), Kay Sutton (Gwennie/Second Woman), Barbara Jean Wong (Little Girl/Kid), Duane Thompson (Mother/Third Woman), Wally Maher (Policeman), and Phillips Tead (Grogan/Second Boy).

Commercials: Nancy Leach (Mrs. D), Barbara Jean Wong (Child Ad Libs), Bobby Larson (Tommy), Joe Pennario (Child Ad Libs), Sheila Sheldon (Child Ad Libs), Lois Collier (Ann), Ann Lee (Marie), and Julie Bannon (Barbara).

The husband-and-wife comedy team of Jim and Marion Jordan had been on the air as Fibber McGee and Molly for five years at the time they made their *Lux* debut. (The Paramount film version of the story on which the broadcast is based dates from seven years earlier and starred Charles Ruggles and Mary Boland.) The comedy of a menial office worker who gets more than he bargained for when he is unexpectedly given the job of city park commissioner presents a change of pace for *Lux* and gives listeners a rare chance to hear the Jordans in roles other than those for which they were famous.

Mama Loves Papa was filmed again

by RKO in 1945, with Leon Errol and Elisabeth Risdon, under the direction of Frank Strayer.

*259. "The Under-Pup," 4/15/40

Based on the 1939 Universal film (screenplay by Grover Jones; original story by I.A.R. Wylie). Directed by George Wells.

Cast: Gloria Jean (Pip-Emma), Nan Grey (Priscilla), Robert Cummings (Dennis), C. Aubrey Smith (Grandpa), Beulah Bondi (Miss Thornton), Barbara Jean Wong (Janet Cooper), Shirley Mills (Cecilia), Ann Gillis (Betty Lou), Duane Thompson (Mrs. Binns), Edward Marr (Dan), Lou Merrill (Mr. Layton), Emory Parnell (Superintendent/Doctor), Wally Maher (Mr. Binns), Sherry Ardell (Edna), Priscilla Lyon, Ann Howard, Sharon Sedan, and Naomi Stevens (Ad Libs).

Singers: Alice Tyrell, Annese Reese, Betty Lou Walters, Betty Bryan, Gwen Bryan, Doris Bryan, Nancy Kellogg, Betty Rome, June Clifford, and Enrico Ricardi.

Commercials: Ann Lee, Rosemary deCamp, Marie Osbourne, Kathleen Fitz (First Girl after Act 2/Ad Libs after Act 1), Julie Bannon (Second Girl after Act 2/Ad Libs after Act 1), Lois Collier (Third Girl after Act 2/Ad Libs after Act 1), Margaret McKay (Fourth Girl after Act 2/Ad Libs after Act 1), Ynez Seabury (Fifth Girl after Act 2/Ad Libs after Act 1), and Carol Brenner (Sixth Girl after Act 2/Ad Libs after Act 1).

Child star Gloria Jean put her acting and singing talents to fine use in Universal's 1939 Richard Wallace–directed motion picture *The Under-Pup*, which centers around an impoverished city girl who wins an all-expense-paid trip to an exclusive summer camp populated by wealthy peers. Though the broadcast uses five of the original cast members—Gloria Jean, Nan Grey, Robert Cummings, C. Aubrey Smith,

and Beulah Bondi—it is most unfortunate that the picture's two remaining stars, Margaret Lindsay and Paul Cavanagh, were not present to recreate their touching performances as the parents of a despondent little rich girl who befriends the emotionally secure, feisty Pip-Emma. (Their characters are, in fact, eliminated in the radio play.)

As *Lux*'s regular director, Sandy Barnett, had fallen ill, adapter George Wells stepped in and directed for the first and only time in his nine years with the show. Sandy Barnett noted that the "show worked out all right . . . cast all did well."

260. "Abe Lincoln in Illinois," 4/22/40

Based on the play by Robert E. Sherwood (1938).

Cast: Raymond Massey (Abe Lincoln), Fay Bainter (Mary Todd), Otto Kruger (Ninian Edwards), Calvin Thomas (Josh Speed), Ted Bliss (Billy Herndon), Lurene Tuttle (Ann Rutledge), Cy Kendall (Sturveson), Warren Ashe (Mentor Graham), Forrest Taylor (Judge Bowling Green), Claire Verdera (Elizabeth Edwards), Earle Ross (Jack Armstrong), Lou Merrill (Ben), Verna Felton (Nancy), Harry Humphrey (First Man in Act 1/Second Man in Act 3), and Marcella Powers (Maid).

Commercials: Sherry Ardell (Girl), Julie Bannon (Sally).

In a departure from the weekly broadcast adaptations of Hollywood motion pictures, the April 22 show recalls the earlier policy of presenting radio versions of Broadway plays. Raymond Massey had won popular acclaim for his portrayal of the title character (1809–65) in Robert E. Sherwood's Pulitzer Prize–winning drama, *Abe Lincoln in Illinois*, which focuses on the early years of the future president. (The stage production also featured Muriel

Kirkwood and Lewis Martin.) Fay Bainter and Otto Kruger appear as Mary Todd and Ninian Edwards in the radio play, which also features Calvin Thomas repeating his New York stage role of Josh Speed.

At the time of the broadcast, Raymond Massey had already starred with Ruth Gordon, Harvey Stephens, and Minor Watson in the John Cromwell–directed film for RKO, which was released earlier that year.

The *Lux Video Theatre* presented a version on February 12, 1951.

Film version: RKO, 1940.

261. "Smilin' Through," 4/29/40

Based on the play by Allan Langdon (pseudonym of Jane Cowl and Jane Murfin) (1919).

Cast: Barbara Stanwyck (Kathleen O'Hara/Moonyean Clare), Robert Taylor (Kenneth Wayne/Jerry Wayne), H.B. Warner (John Carteret), Eric Snowden (Dr. Owen), Frank Martin (Willie Ainsley), Julie Bannon (Mary), Lou Merrill (Doctor), Martha Wentworth (Ellen), Justina Wayne (Jane), James Eagles (Jimmy), and Sidney Newman (Ad Libs).

Commercial: Kathleen Fitz (Sally).

Lux's second broadcast (of three) of the popular play "Smilin' Through" served as a vehicle for the recently wed actors Barbara Stanwyck and Robert Taylor, both of whom give good performances in their dual roles (Stanwyck even supplies Moonyean Clare with an appropriate Irish accent). Character actor H.B. Warner is also given a strong part as John Carteret, whom he plays as both a young and an older man.

Lux would air "Smilin' Through" once more on January 5, 1942; see 11/4/34 for information on stage and screen productions.

262. "Our Town," 5/6/40

Based on the 1940 Sol Lesser/United Artists film (screenplay by Thornton Wilder, Frank Craven, and Harry Chandlee), in turn based on the play by Thornton Wilder (1938).

Cast: Frank Craven (Newton Morgan), William Holden (George Gibbs), Martha Scott (Emily Webb), Fay Bainter (Mrs. Gibbs), Beulah Bondi (Mrs. Webb), Thomas Mitchell (Dr. Gibbs), Guy Kibbee (Mr. Webb), Stuart Erwin (Howie Newsome), Virginia Sale (Mrs. Soames), Lou Merrill (Dr. Ferguson), Barbara Jean Wong (Rebecca Gibbs), Bobby Winkler (Wally Webb), James Eagles (Bob/Young Man), Sidney Newman (Si), Duane Thompson (First Woman in Audience), Walter White (Man in Audience), and Mary Lansing (Second Woman in Audience/Baby Cry).

Singers: Morton Scott, Lyman Patterson, Robert Bradford, Larry Murphy, Ralph Leon, Winona Black, Catherine Rue, and Betty Rome.

Commercials: Julie Bannon (Sally), Fred Shields (Man), and Margaret McKay (Woman).

Our Town, Thornton Wilder's moving play of everyday life in a typical American town, opened at the Henry Miller Theatre in New York on February 4, 1938, and featured a cast headed by Frank Craven, John Craven, Martha Scott, Evelyn Varden, Helen Carew, Jay Fassett, Thomas W. Ross, and Tod Fadden. On May 23, 1940, the premiere of the Sol Lesser/United Artists film took place in Boston, while 17 days before that event, *Lux* aired "Our Town" with eight members of the original screen cast. Frank Craven and Martha Scott reprise their characterizations from the Broadway production, while William Holden, Thomas Mitchell, Fay Bainter, Guy Kibbee, Beulah Bondi, and Stuart Erwin make equally effective contributions. Frank Craven's Mr. Morgan/Stage Manager-Narrator part was altered for the film better to fit that medium, and it is adjusted once again for the broadcast. The clever manner in which Mr. Morgan's narration is worked into the *Lux* format adds considerably to the production, as he exchanges dialogue with Cecil B. DeMille and Melville Ruick, comments on the ritual of the station break, and so forth. Even the curtain call sustains the mood of the play, as each of the eight stars tells from which city or town in the United States he or she hails. Aaron Copland's outstanding score for the film is unfortunately absent from the *Lux* version, but Lou Silvers's accompaniment nicely captures the intended atmosphere. "Our Town" was the final *Lux* broadcast to originate from the Music Box Theatre on Hollywood Boulevard.

263. "True Confession," 5/13/40

Based on the 1937 Paramount film (screenplay by Claude Binyon), in turn based on the play *Mon Crime*, by Louis Verneuil and Georges Berr (1934).

Cast: Loretta Young (Helen Bartlett), Fred MacMurray (Kenneth Bartlett), Ruth Donnelly (Daisy), Lou Merrill (Charley Jasper), Wally Maher (Darsey), Arthur Q. Bryan (Otto Krayler/Second Newsboy), Edward Marr (Bill Collector/First Newsboy), Warren Ashe (Butler), Earle Ross (Prosecutor), Jack Lewis (Detective), Celeste Rush (Matron/Second Woman), and Bernice Pilot (Ella).

Commercials: Kathleen Fitz (Libby/First Woman after Act 1), Martha Wentworth (Second Woman after Act 1), Duane Thompson (Third Woman after Act 1), and Julie Bannon (Sally).

"True Confession," a 1937 Paramount farce (which was directed by Wesley Ruggles), is an amusing play as done by *Lux*. Loretta Young's fine portrayal of a girl whose chronic lying involves her in a murder case succeeds in making the character sympathetic and

interesting, and Fred MacMurray has a few droll lines as her lawyer-husband, the same part that he played in the film (opposite Carole Lombard), while Ruth Donnelly takes the role Una Merkel played onscreen (the heroine's pal, Daisy). *Lux* regular Lou Merrill is saddled with the unpleasant character of Charley, which John Barrymore tackled in the photoplay version.

"True Confession" was the first show to be broadcast from *Lux*'s new home, the Vine Street Theatre.

264. "Midnight," 5/20/40

Based on the 1939 Paramount film (screenplay by Charles Brackett and Billy Wilder), in turn based on a story by Edwin Justus Mayer and Franz Schylz.

Cast: Claudette Colbert (Eve Peabody), Don Ameche (Tibor Czerny), Gale Gordon (Georges Flammarion), Fred MacKaye (Jacques Picot), Rosemary deCamp (Helene Flammarion), Rolfe Sedan (Marcel), Lou Merrill (Judge/Gendarme), Warren Ashe (Lebon/First Taxi Driver), Ted Bliss (Leon/Clerk of Court), Tony Martelli (Butler/Second Taxi Driver), John Lake (Doorman/Chauffeur), James Eagles (Hotel Clerk/Footman), and Victor Rodman (Porter).

Commercials: Kathleen Fitz (Libby), Thomas Freebairn-Smith (Narrator), and Jo Campbell (Girl).

Midnight, Paramount's very funny comedy involving mistaken identity in Paris (directed by Mitchell Leisen), is not quite as amusing in its *Lux* presentation. Nevertheless, the radio version is an interesting play and benefits greatly from the performances of Claudette Colbert and Don Ameche, both of whom repeat their film roles. Sorely missed is John Barrymore, who is particularly delightful in the motion picture, but Gale Gordon does a good job in a more or less straight performance of the part. (Fred MacKaye and Rosemary deCamp are cast in Francis Lederer and Mary Astor's screen roles.)

Dorothy Lamour and Arturo deCordova starred in Paramount's 1945 rendering of the film (also directed by Mitchell Leisen), the title of which was altered to *Masquerade in Mexico.*

Additional film version: Paramount, 1945 (*Masquerade in Mexico*).

*265. "Vigil in the Night," 5/27/40

Based on the 1940 RKO film (screenplay by Fred Guidl, P.J. Wolfson, and Rowland Leigh), in turn based on the novel by A.J. Cronin.

Cast: Olivia deHavilland (Anne Lee), Herbert Marshall (Dr. Prescott), Helen Chandler (Lucy Lee), Frederic Worlock (Mr. Bowley), Ethel Griffies (Matron East), Ynez Seabury (Norah), Eric Snowden (Dr. Caley), Martha Wentworth (Mrs. Bowley), Claire Verdera (Mrs. Sullivan/Woman), Lou Merrill (Coroner/Dr. Hassall), Helena Grant (Nurse Gregg), Marie Blake (Glennie), Gloria Gordon (Mrs. Merchant/Matron Leonard), Lee Congden (Nurse), Thomas Mills (Farmer/Clerk), Dick Ryan (Man/Bobby), Douglas Scott (Newsboy), Joe Pennario (Boy), Paul Hilton (Matt), and Barbara Jean Wong (Child).

Commercials: Julie Bannon (Sally), Betty Jean Hainey (Midge), Lois Collier (Dot), Jane Morgan (Mother), Duane Thompson (Woman), and Kathleen Fitz (Libby).

George Stevens's 1940 RKO film *Vigil in the Night* popped up on *Lux* with Olivia deHavilland, Herbert Marshall, and Helen Chandler playing the roles taken by Carole Lombard, Brian Aherne, and Anne Shirley onscreen. (Ethel Griffies was the lone member of the film cast to repeat her portrayal.) The story, which takes place in Manchester, England, concerns a conscientious nurse who willingly shoulders the blame for a child's death that was caused by her younger sister's irresponsibility.

266. "Alexander's Ragtime Band," 6/3/40

Based on the 1938 20th Century–Fox film (screenplay by Kathryn Scola, Lamar Trotti, and Richard Sherman).

Cast: Alice Faye (Stella Kirby), Ray Milland (Alexander [Rod Grant]), Robert Preston (Charlie Dwyer), Hal K. Dawson (Snapper), Nancy Leach (Jerry), Wally Maher (Davey/Cop), Lou Merrill (Manager [Mack]), Warren Ashe (Eddie/Driver), Earle Ross (Third Barker/Man), Fred Shields (Joe/Leader), Walter White (Stage Doorman), Dick Ryan (Second Barker/Jim), Lois Collier (Girl), and James Eagles (Announcer).

Commercials: Jane Morgan (Woman), Lois Collier (Girl), James Eagles (Boy), Kathleen Fitz (Libby), and Philip Neely (Singer).

Irving Berlin's music is the featured attraction of the 1938 20th Century–Fox film *Alexander's Ragtime Band,* and no fewer than 23 of the popular songwriter's compositions are performed during the course of the photoplay. Even counting the brief snatches of some of the tunes heard in the *Lux* broadcast, only seven different Berlin songs are used. Some of the movie's musical numbers feature the vocal talents of Ethel Merman, Jack Haley (as Jerry and Davey — nonsinging roles in the *Lux* adaptation), Wally Vernon, and Chick Chandler, but the only singing in this radio version is done by Alice Faye, repeating her screen role. (The slight plot focuses on the career of a cocky bandleader and his turbulent romance with the orchestra's vocalist.) Only three of the songs heard in the picture were especially created for the occasion, with the remainder of the score made up of numbers from earlier in Berlin's career. Performed in the *Lux* version (by Alice Faye unless noted) are: Act 1: "Alexander's Ragtime Band" (1911), "Now It Can Be Told" (1938 film), "Alexander's Ragtime Band" (reprise, partial); Act 2: "Blue Skies" (1927, interpolated into *Betsy*); Act 3: "What'll I Do?" (partial, interpolated into the 1923 edition of *The Music Box Revue*), "Say It with Music" (partial; instrumental; 1921 *Music Box Revue*), "A Pretty Girl Is Like a Melody" (partial; instrumental; 1919; *The Ziegfeld Follies*), "Remember" (1925), "Say It with Music" (reprise; instrumental), Finale: "Alexander's Ragtime Band" (all with words and music by Irving Berlin).

Tyrone Power and Don Ameche are Faye's leading men in the Henry King–directed film; *Lux*'s able replacements (who, as in the case of Alice Faye, make their *Lux* debuts here) are Ray Milland and Robert Preston.

A second *Lux* broadcast of "Alexander's Ragtime Band" aired on April 7, 1947.

267. "Till We Meet Again," 6/10/40
Based on the 1940 Warner Bros. film (screenplay by Warren Duff), in turn based on the 1932 Warner Bros. film (screenplay by Wilson Mizner and Joseph Jackson; original story by Robert Love).
Cast: Merle Oberon (Joan Ames), George Brent (Dan Hardesty), Pat O'Brien (Steve Burke), Mae Clarke (the Countess), Kathleen Fitz (Bonnie), Lou Merrill (Doctor), Wally Maher (Rocky), Celeste Rush (Louise [Maid]/Woman), Clara Blandick (Mrs. Hester), Eric Snowden (Sir Harold), Ted Bliss (Freddy/First Barman), Fred Shields (Officer/Third Barman), James Eagles (Jimmie Coburn), Earle Ross (Steward), Warren Ashe (Sailor), and Lee Millar (Dog/Second Barman).
Commercials: Lois Collier (Dot), Margaret McKay (Peggy), and Julie Bannon (Sally).
Warner Bros.' 1940 film *Till We Meet*

Again, a remake of that same studio's 1932 success *One Way Passage*, was presented on *Lux*'s June 10 broadcast. The radio drama stars Merle Oberon, George Brent, and Pat O'Brien in the roles they played in the motion picture, and Mae Clarke in the Binnie Barnes screen part.

See 3/6/39 for information on the earlier film version.

268. "After the Thin Man," 6/17/40
Based on the 1936 MGM film (screenplay by Frances Goodrich and Albert Hackett).
Intermission Guest: Mary Belle Porter, debutante and representative of the American Cotton Industry (after Act 2).
Cast: William Powell (Nick Charles), Myrna Loy (Nora Charles), Julie Bannon (Selma), Fred MacKaye (David), Edward Marr (Abrams), Mary Lou Simpson (Polly), Warren Ashe (Dancer), Wally Maher (Lum Kee), Arthur Q. Bryan (Party Guest), Ynez Seabury (Prison Matron), Lou Merrill (Detective Malloy), Abe Reynolds (Fingers), Walter White (Waiter/First Reporter), Tristram Coffin (Phil), Eric Snowden (Henry/Fourth Man), Russell Fillmore (Peters/Second Reporter), and Fred Shields (Robert/Third Reporter).
Commercial: Thomas Freebairn-Smith (Narrator), Kathleen Fitz (Woman), Duane Thompson (Woman), and Lee Millar (Dog).
The first film in MGM's very popular *Thin Man* series was adapted for *Lux* and presented as the second show from Hollywood on June 8, 1936; four years passed before the second motion picture in the series, *After the Thin Man*, reached the *Lux* microphone with William Powell and Myrna Loy again in the roles they portray in the 1936 W.S. Van Dyke II–directed photoplay. The plot of the entertaining radio mystery of June 17 is set in motion when Nora

Charles succeeds in convincing her husband, Nick, to put his sleuthing skills to work in order to clear up some mysterious happenings occurring within her own family.

During the next curtain call, William Powell and Myrna Loy reveal that the next *Thin Man* entry is entitled *The Shadow of the Thin Man* (released by MGM in 1941).

269. "Show Boat," 6/24/40

Based on the 1927 musical production (book and lyrics by Oscar Hammerstein II, music by Jerome Kern), in turn based on the novel by Edna Ferber (1926).

Cast: Irene Dunne (Magnolia/Kim), Allan Jones (Gaylord Ravenal), Charles Winninger (Cap'n Andy), Verna Felton (Parthy), Hal K. Dawson (Frank), Ynez Seabury (Ellie), Gloria Holden (Julie/Sister), Tristram Coffin (Steve/Jim), Earle Ross (Sheriff/Hotel Clerk), Edward Marr (Jake/Rubber Face), Barbara Jean Wong (Kim, as a Child), Arthur Q. Bryan (Card Player/Drunk), James Eagles (Radio Announcer), and Sarah Selby (Mrs. O'Brien).

Singers: Robert Bradford, Kenneth Rundquist, Elaine Schwitzer, Stuart Bair, Devona Doxie, Katherine Rue, Elva Kellogg, Morton Scott, Dick Dennis, Bill Reeves, Delos Jewkes, Tudor Williams, and Enrico Ricardi.

Commercials: Gloria Gordon, Sarah Selby, and Julie Bannon (Sally).

The famed musical *Show Boat* was first presented on *Lux* on June 24, almost 13 years after it opened at the Ziegfeld Theatre on Broadway (December 28, 1927), with Norma Terris, Howard Marsh, Charles Winninger, and Edna Mae Oliver in the principal roles. Universal filmed *Show Boat* in 1929, with Harry A. Pollard directing a cast headed by Laura LaPlante, Joseph Schildkraut, Otis Harlan, and Emily Fitzroy, and although the part-talkie

was conceived as an adaptation of Edna Ferber's novel, the Hammerstein-Kern score was so well known that sequences (including a prologue with stars from the Broadway production) featuring songs from the show were quickly added prior to its release. Universal's 1936 James Whale–directed film was based directly on the musical, though Mr. Hammerstein's screenplay made several changes, most notably in the ending. By 1940 the show was probably familiar to most of *Lux*'s listeners, and Irene Dunne, Allan Jones, and Charles Winninger, the stars of the radio presentation, were well versed in the work, having appeared in it in various stage productions in addition to the 1936 film. The character of Joe, who sings "Ol' Man River" in this show, is deleted; thus the best-known number is reduced to an imposing piece of incidental music performed by a chorus.

Also, the important character of Julie has been shrunk to a minor (nonsinging) part, and her secret is changed to her being an illegal alien who spent time in prison in Martinique! Such an alteration is foreign to the Hammerstein-Kern work and succeeds in weakening the presentation, as does the fact that the score is heavily cut, which adds to the overall rushed effect of the broadcast.

The musical numbers presented in the *Lux* broadcast are as follows: Act 1: "Ol' Man River" (partial; chorus), "Make Believe" (Irene Dunne, Allan Jones), "Ol' Man River" (reprise; chorus humming), "Can't Help Lovin' Dat Man" (chorus); Act 2: "Why Do I Love You?" (Dunne, Jones), "Make Believe" (reprise; Jones); Act 3: "Can't Help Lovin' Dat Man" (Dunne), "Ol' Man River" (chorus).

A remolded version of *Show Boat* was produced by MGM in 1951, starring Kathryn Grayson, Howard Keel, Joe E. Brown, and Agnes Moorehead, under the direction of George Sidney.

The MGM *Show Boat* was adapted for the *Lux* broadcast of February 11, 1952.

Film versions: Universal, 1929; Universal, 1936; MGM, 1951.

270. "Alias the Deacon," 7/1/40

Based on the 1940 Universal film (screenplay by Nat Perrin and Charles Grayson), in turn based on the play by John B. Hymer and LeRoy Clemens (1925).

Cast: Bob Burns (Deacon Caswell), Helen Wood (Phyllis), Fred MacKaye (Johnny), Duane Thompson (Mrs. Clark/Woman), Lou Merrill (Cunningham), Arthur Q. Bryan (Sullivan/Man at Fair), Griff Barnett (Sheriff/Yokel), Bobby Winkler (Willie), Rolfe Sedan (André), Wally Maher (Bull), Martha Wentworth (Mrs. Gregory/Baby Cry), Celeste Rush (Mrs. Howley), Maxine March (Mildred Gregory), Edward Marr (Station Master/Handler), and Warren Ashe (Police Chief/Announcer).

Commercials: Julie Bannon (Sally), Lois Collier (Dot), Betty Jean Hainey (Midge), Jane Morgan (Mother), Ann Tobin (Second Woman), and Kathleen Fitz (Woman).

Bob Burns made his second appearance of the season in *Lux*'s "Alias the Deacon" on July 1. The 1925 play by John B. Hymer and LeRoy Clemens starred Berton Churchill in the title role on Broadway, but Universal's 1940 film (directed by Christy Cabanne) added a few elements that reflected the personality of Burns. In the *Lux* broadcast, he is given the chance to concentrate on one of his specialties — telling stories of his relatives. Also, he gets to play a brief solo on the instrument he invented, the bazooka. Others in the

cast of this comedy include Helen Wood in Peggy Moran's film role, and *Lux* semiregular Fred MacKaye, who is given the part played onscreen by Dennis O'Keefe.

See 3/2/36 for information on stage and film versions.

271. "To the Ladies," 7/8/40

Based on the play by George S. Kaufman and Marc Connolly (1922).

Cast: Helen Hayes (Elsie), Otto Kruger (Leonard), Arthur Q. Bryan (Kincaid), Edward Marr (Chester), Gloria Holden (Mrs. Kincaid), Tristram Coffin (Baker), Lou Merrill (Toastmaster/Chief), Stanley Farrar (Truckman/Henrici), Wally Maher (Truckman), Ann Tobin (Miss Fletcher/Girl), and James Eagles (Elevator Boy/Boy).

Commercials: Thomas Freebairn-Smith (Narrator), Jo Campbell (Girl), Rosemary deCamp (Woman), Mary Virginia Palmer (Younger Woman), and James Eagles (Man).

The closing production of the 1939-40 *Lux Radio Theatre* season was a vehicle, as DeMille stated, for "the first lady of the American Theatre." Eighteen years prior to the *Lux* broadcast, Helen Hayes had starred in George S. Kaufman and Marc Connolly's *To the Ladies* on Broadway, and she seems to take a special delight in reprising her part for radio, where she gives a fine performance as the clever wife who advances the career of her slightly dim-witted husband. Otto Kruger, often cast in serious roles in film, had been the leading man of that 1922 production, and he gets a chance on this occasion to display his effective flair for comedy. Director Sandy Barnett deemed the final broadcast of the season "very good. Kruger excellent and Hayes lived up to all expectations."

Sixth Season
(September 9, 1940–July 7, 1941)

Columbia Broadcasting System, Monday, 9:00–10:00 P.M. *Host*: Cecil B. DeMille. *Announcer*: Melville Ruick. *Director*: Sanford Barnett. *Musical Director*: Lou Silvers. *Adaptations*: George Wells. *Sound Effects*: Charlie Forsyth.

272. "Manhattan Melodrama," 9/9/40

Based on the 1934 MGM film (screenplay by Oliver T. Marsh, H.P. Garrett, and Joseph L. Mankiewicz; original story by Arthur Caesar).

Cast: William Powell (Jim Wade), Myrna Loy (Eleanor), Don Ameche (Blackie), Tony Hughes (Father Pat), Lou Merrill (Malone), Kane Whitman (Snow), Edward Marr (Spud), Earle Ross (Judge), Jim Bannon (Attorney), Ruth Rickaby (Miss Adams), Tommy Lane (Young Jim), Bobby Winkler (Young Blackie), Bud McCallister (Newsboy), Byron Shores (Announcer), Tristram Coffin (Ticket Seller), Wally Maher (Second Man [Waiter]), Franklin Parker (Policeman/Third Man), and Joseph Pope (First Man).

Commercials: Lois Collier (Betty), Nancy Leach (Gladys).

W.S. Van Dyke's popular 1934 MGM film *Manhattan Melodrama* chronicles the lives of two orphans who take distinctly different paths on the road of life and wind up on opposite sides of the law. *Lux*'s effectively assembled production stars William Powell and Myrna Loy from the original screen cast and Don Ameche in the role taken by Clark Gable in the film.

A Western version of *Manhattan Melodrama*, entitled *Northwest Rangers*, was offered by MGM in 1942, starring William Lundigan, Patricia Dane, and James Craig, under Joseph Newman's direction.

Additional film version: MGM, 1942 (*Northwest Rangers*).

*273. "Love Is News," 9/16/40

Based on the 1937 20th Century–Fox film (screenplay by Harry Tugend and Jack Yellin), story by William R. Lipman and Frederick Stephani.

Cast: Bob Hope (Steve), Madeleine Carroll (Tony), Ralph Bellamy (Canavan), Lou Merrill (Uncle Cyrus), Ann Tobin (Lois), Eddie Waller (Judge), Stuart Buchanan (Findlay), Charles Seel (Brady), Fred MacKaye (Count Tonelli), Barbara Moyer (Secretary), Ray Montgomery (Leston), Noreen Gammill (Landlady), Wally Maher (Salesman), Earl Gunn (Police Officer), Sally Payne (Tessie), James Eagles (First Reporter/Second Newsboy), Jack Bruskoff (Second Reporter/First Newsboy), Russell Williams (Office Boy/Joe), and Harold Daniels (First Man/Announcer).

Commercials: Jo Campbell, Kathleen Fitz, and Julie Bannon (Sally).

This 20th Century–Fox Tay Garnett–directed comedy concerning a wealthy girl who weds a brash newshound to teach him a lesson for his unscrupulous reporting practices was presented on *Lux* with Bob Hope, Madeleine Carroll, and Ralph Bellamy in the roles taken by Tyrone Power, Loretta Young, and Don Ameche onscreen. The studio filmed a second version in 1948 (which was directed by Robert B. Sinclair), once again featuring

Portrait of William Powell in "Manhattan Melodrama" (September 9, 1940) (photo: Photofest).

Tyrone Power, along with Gene Tierney and Reginald Gardiner.

Additional film version: 20th Century–Fox, 1948 (*That Wonderful Urge*).

274. "The Westerner," 9/23/40
Based on the 1940 Samuel Goldwyn/

United Artists film (screenplay by Jo Swerling and Niven Busch; original story by Stuart Lake).

Intermission Guest: Vera Gilmer, "the modern cameo girl" (after Act 1).

Cast: Gary Cooper (Cole Hardin), Walter Brennan (Judge Roy Bean), Doris

Davenport (Jane Ellen Matthews), Lou Merrill (Chickenfoot), Fred Shields (Wade), Harry Humphrey (Caliphet), Donald Curtis (Blackjack), John Deering (Shad Wilkins), Brooks Benedict (Bart), Jay Michael (Evans), Ted Arthurs (Hod), Hal K. Dawson (Theatre Manager), Forrest Taylor (Farmer), and Gloria Holden (Lily Langtry).

Commercial: Julie Bannon (Sally).

"The Westerner" is the first Western presented on *Lux* since November 2, 1936, when "The Virginian" was aired. It happens that Gary Cooper, whose appearances before the microphone were relatively infrequent, starred in both broadcasts. The Samuel Goldwyn motion picture had premiered only the week before *Lux*'s radio version, which also features Gary Cooper in the role of a drifter who falls in love with a landowner's daughter and helps her battle the tyrannical hanging judge who controls the territory. Walter Brennan, who was to win a Best Supporting Actor Oscar for his performance as the real-life character Judge Roy Bean, also reprises his part for the radio play, and Doris Davenport, who made her only film appearance in the screen version, likewise repeats her picture role.

A guest during the Lux Toilet Soap commercial after Act 1 (introduced by DeMille but interviewed by Melville Ruick) is Vera Gilmer, a photographer's model who was chosen "the modern cameo girl" by commercial artist Russell Patterson.

275. "His Girl Friday," 9/30/40

Based on the 1940 Columbia film (screenplay by Charles Lederer), in turn based on the play *The Front Page*, by Ben Hecht and Charles MacArthur (1928).

Intermission Guest: Kolma Flake, western fashion editor for *Motion Picture* magazine (after Act 2).

Cast: Claudette Colbert (Hildy Johnson), Fred MacMurray (Walter Burns), Jack Carson (Bruce Baldwin), Arthur Q. Bryan (Sheriff Hartwell), Edward Marr (Louie), Lou Merrill (Mayor), Chester Clute (Pettibone), Warren Ashe (McCue), Charles Seel (Murphy), Edwin Max (Endicott), Verna Felton (Mrs. Baldwin), Tony Hughes (Earl Williams), Sherman Nichols (Duffy), Kathryn Keys ("Bangle Dame"), and Hal Gerarde (Gus/Cooley/Policeman).

Commercial: Julie Bannon (Sally).

His Girl Friday, Columbia's 1940 release, interestingly reworks the famous newspaper play *The Front Page* (changing one of the main characters from male to female and another from female to male) without altering the basic theme or message of the original. Howard Hawks directed the film, and Charles Lederer wrote the screenplay, which retains large portions of dialogue from Hecht and MacArthur's *The Front Page*. *Lux*'s version, like the motion picture, is entertaining, with Claudette Colbert taking Rosalind Russell's screen character and presenting an engaging Hildy. Fred MacMurray seems a somewhat more human Editor Burns than does Cary Grant of the photoplay, and Jack Carson is delightful as Hildy's patient fiancé, which Ralph Bellamy plays splendidly on the screen. As in *Lux*'s "The Front Page," the darker aspects of the story are avoided to some extent by eliminating the character of Molly Mallory.

See 6/28/37 for information on stage and screen versions.

276. "Wings of the Navy," 10/7/40

Based on the 1939 Warner Bros. film (screenplay by Michael Fessier).

Cast: George Brent (Cass Harrington), Olivia deHavilland (Irene Dale), John Payne (Jerry Harrington), Tristram Coffin (Harry White), Lou Merrill (Mack), Gale Gordon (Speaker),

Stuart Buchanan (Dr. Harper), Earle Ross (Captain Brown), Stanley Farrar (Captain March), Wally Maher (Reporter), Frank Richards (Steve), and James Eagles (Ormsby).

Commercials: Rolfe Sedan, Lois Collier, Martha Wentworth, Duane Thompson, and Sarah Selby.

The highlights of Warner Bros.' 1939 film *Wings of the Navy* are the aviation sequences, but even lacking this element (except in brief audio equivalents), *Lux*'s adaptation of the Lloyd Bacon–directed motion picture is an interesting drama (revolving around two brothers in love with the same girl). The stars of the film, George Brent, Olivia deHavilland, and John Payne, give solid performances in the broadcast as well.

277. "The Littlest Rebel," 10/14/40

Based on the 1935 20th Century–Fox film (screenplay by Edwin Burke).

Cast: Shirley Temple (Virgie Cary), Claude Rains (Captain Cary), Preston Foster (Colonel Morrison), Leigh Whipper (Uncle Billy), Frank McGlynn (Abraham Lincoln), Bea Benaderet (Mrs. Cary), Avonne Jackson (Sally Ann), Warren Ashe (Union Officer), Lou Merrill (Dudley), Jack Carr (Tom), Bernice Pilot (Rosabelle), Walter White (Corporal), Griff Barnett (Ticket Agent), Edwin Max (Sentry), Bobby Larson, Barbara Jean Wong, Tommy Lane, Dix Davis (Children), Harriet Flowers, Donald Brown, Pauline James (Ad Libs), Charles Seel (Man), and Duane Thompson (a Guest).

Commercial: James Eagles, Nancy Leach.

Shirley Temple made her *Lux* debut in an adaptation of one of her screen vehicles, 20th Century–Fox's *The Littlest Rebel* (1935), which was directed by David Butler. Costarring with the 12-year-old actress in the story of a young Confederate girl who desperately

tries to save her imprisoned father are Claude Rains in the part John Boles plays in the film, and Preston Foster as Jack Holt's screen character. In supporting roles are Leigh Whipper, playing Bill Robinson's photoplay part, and Frank McGlynn, who repeats his motion picture characterization as Abraham Lincoln. Sandy Barnett noted that the broadcast was "very good ... Temple missed all rehearsals until Sunday due to illness, but was excellent."

278. "Lillian Russell," 10/21/40

Based on the 1940 20th Century–Fox film (screenplay by William Anthony McGuire).

Cast: Alice Faye (Lillian Russell [Helen Leonard]), Edward Arnold (Diamond Jim Brady), Victor Mature (Alexander Moore), Stuart Buchanan (Jesse Lewisohn), Noreen Gammill (Marie), Beatrice Maude (Cynthia), Jay Michael (Tony Pastor), Frederic MacKaye (Teddy Solomon), Verna Felton (Lillian's Grandmother), Earle Ross (Leonard), Lou Merrill (Damrosch), Dorothy Farrar (Edna McCauley), Bob Burleson (Jeweler), John Barry (Coachman/Doorman), Norman Ainsley (a Doorman), and James Eagles (an Usher/a Boy).

Commercials: Julie Bannon (Sally), Ynez Seabury (Libby).

Alice Faye returned to *Lux* on October 21, on this occasion in a biography of stage star Lillian Russell (1860–1922). The 1940 20th Century–Fox production *Lillian Russell* was directed by Irving Cummings and starred Faye, along with Edward Arnold, who repeats his Diamond Jim Brady characterization for the broadcast. Don Ameche was actually second-billed in the motion picture, but here the Terry Solomon character is de-emphasized and given to radio actor Fred MacKaye, while Victor Mature is heard in the role Henry Fonda played in the film.

Faye vocalizes two period songs in Act 1: a portion of "After the Ball" (1892, words and music by Charles K. Harris), and a number closely associated with Russell, "Come Down, Ma Evenin' Star" (1902, words and music by John Stromberg). In Act 2, she performs two songs she introduced in the film: "Adored One" (lyric by Charles Henderson, music by Alfred Newman), and "Blue Love Bird" (lyric by Mack Gordon, music by Alfred Newman). Act 3 features a reprise of "Blue Love Bird."

279. "Strike Up the Band," 10/28/40

Based on the 1940 MGM film (screenplay by John Monks, Jr., and Fred Finklehoff).

Guest Host: William C. deMille (regular host Cecil B. DeMille is heard from New York City).

Cast: Mickey Rooney (Jimmy Connors), Judy Garland (Mary Holden), John Scott Trotter (Paul Whiteman), Louis Silvers's Orchestra (Paul Whiteman's Orchestra), Larry Nunn (Willie), Charles Peck (Philip), Betty Jean Hainey (Barbara), Frederic Worlock (Mr. Morgan), Jane Morgan (Mrs. Connors), Griff Barnett (Mr. Judd), Byron Kane (Booper), Duane Thompson (Mrs. Hodges), Lou Merrill (the Barker), Harry Humphreys (the Doctor), Noreen Gammill (Miss Pink), Lucille Garland (Annie), Bud McAllister, Dick Koger, and Annese Reese (Ad Libs).

Commercials: Julie Bannon (Sally), Ynez Seabury (Libby).

Popular teenage stars Mickey Rooney and Judy Garland made their *Lux* debuts together in an adaptation of their current motion picture, *Strike Up the Band* (MGM), the story of an enterprising small town band leader who dreams of catapulting his group into the big time. Busby Berkeley directed the film, which bears no relation to the 1930 Broadway show of the same name,

though it does borrow Ira and George Gershwin's title number for its patriotic finale. (The song is never performed in the *Lux* broadcast, except as part of the incidental music.) Third-billed in the motion picture is Paul Whiteman, who plays himself and conducts an orchestra that includes some of his "boys." (Actually, the Paul Whiteman Orchestra had disbanded just prior to making the film, though they would later regroup.) In Whiteman's absence, John Scott Trotter is cast in the radio version, not as himself but as Paul Whiteman; thus we have the rather absurd situation of one famous bandleader portraying another! (John Scott Trotter's Orchestra does not take part in the broadcast; the billing credits Louis Silvers's Orchestra as Paul Whiteman's Orchestra. It makes little difference, as the only selection that "Paul Whiteman's Orchestra" plays in the broadcast is a chorus of "Wonderful One" [lyric by Dorothy Terriss, music by Paul Whiteman and Ferde Grofé], and this serves only as a piece of incidental music.)

The musical numbers engagingly performed by Garland and Rooney are: Act 1: "Our Love Affair" (Judy Garland and Mickey Rooney); Act 2: "Nobody" (which makes reference, in a clever line change, to Lux Toilet Soap and Cecil B. DeMille; Garland); Act 3: "The Drummer Boy" (Garland); Finale: "Our Love Affair" reprise (Rooney and Garland) (all with lyrics and music by Roger Edens, except "Our Love Affair," which has a lyric by Arthur Freed and music by Mr. Edens).

DeMille was in New York City during the week of October 28 for that city's premiere of *Northwest Mounted Police*. He is, however, still heard in the introduction of the drama, and during the curtain call, where he tells about the following week's broadcast. The remainder of the host's duties are assumed

William C. deMille with his brother, Cecil B. DeMille (October 28, 1940) (photo: Photofest).

by his brother, director, playwright, and screenwriter William C. deMille.

280. "Wuthering Heights," 11/4/40

Based on the 1939 Samuel Goldwyn/United Artists film (screenplay by Ben Hecht and Charles MacArthur), in turn based on the novel by Emily Brontë (1848).

Cast: Ida Lupino (Cathy), Basil Rathbone (Heathcliff), Martha Wentworth (Ellen), Rosemary deCamp (Isabella), Fred MacKaye (Edgar Linton), Fred Shields (Hindley), Larry Nunn (Heathcliff, as a Boy), Barbara Jean Wong (Cathy, as a Child), Douglas Scott (Hindley, as a Child), Eric Snowden (Lockwood), J. Anthony Hughes (Dr. Kenneth/Earnshaw), Lou Merrill (Joseph), and Lee Millar (Servant/Dog).

Commercial: Ynez Seabury (Libby).

Less than 14 months after the first appearance of "Wuthering Heights" on *Lux*, Emily Brontë's famous romance was back again. The same script that was used in the September 18, 1939, broadcast is again employed, but it takes an interestingly different complexion in the hands of a new cast. On this occasion, it is Ida Lupino who plays Cathy, having graduated from the role of Isabella which she played in *Lux's* first presentation of the tale, while Basil Rathbone portrays the cruel and embittered Heathcliff.

Lux would present "Wuthering Heights" once more, on September 14, 1954; see 9/18/39 for information on film versions.

281. "Nothing Sacred," 11/11/40

Based on the 1937 Selznick-International/United Artists film (screenplay by Ben Hecht), in turn based on the story by William Street.

Cast: Douglas Fairbanks, Jr. (Wally Cook), Joan Bennett (Hazel Flagg), Eddie Waller (Enoch), Lou Merrill (Mr. Stone), Edward Marr (Max/Newsboy), Charles Seel (Dr. Egglehoffer/Man in Act 1), Ann Tobin (Nurse), Edwin Max (Bushwick), Arthur Q. Bryan (Fight Announcer/Reporter), Jack Carr (Ernest), Warren Ashe (Taxi Driver/Conductor), and Bernice Pilot (Mammy).

Commercial: Ynez Seabury (Libby).

The David O. Selznick Technicolor production *Nothing Sacred* was directed by William Wellman in 1937, and it focuses upon a much-publicized trip to New York by a small town New England girl who is supposedly dying of an incurable disease. *Lux*'s version features an excellent adaptation of Ben Hecht's script, which has been tightened to such an extent that the brisker pace is actually more consistently amusing than the film. The performances of the two stars also contribute greatly to the broadcast, as both are delightful in the roles of hard-boiled newspaper reporter Wally Cook and "terminally ill" Hazel Flagg. (Bennett's "voice of doom" delivery is very funny and illustrates her skill for radio comedy.)

Nothing Sacred was retailored into a vehicle for Dean Martin and Jerry Lewis (with Janet Leigh as the reporter) in 1954. Entitled *Living It Up*, this Paramount release was directed by Norman Taurog.

Additional film version: Paramount, 1954 (*Living It Up*).

282. "The Rage of Manhattan," 11/18/40

Based on the 1938 Universal film *The Rage of Paris* (screenplay by Bruce Manning and Felix Jackson).

Cast: Tyrone Power (Jim Trevor), Annabella (Nicole), Tristram Coffin (Bill/Man in Act 1), Ruth Rickaby (Gloria), Lou Merrill (Mike), J. Arthur Young (Rigley/Waiter in Act 1), Charles Seel (Pops/Man in Act 1), Stanley Farrar (Wright), Julie Bannon (Secretary), Rolfe Sedan (Hotel Manager/Steward), Jean Scott (Model), and James Eagles (Elevator Boy/Man in Act 3).

Commercials: Ynez Seabury (Libby), Lois Collier, Nancy Leach, Margaret McKay, Sarah Selby, Duane Thompson, and Ann Tobin.

Universal's 1938 Henry Koster–directed release *The Rage of Paris* presented French actress Danielle Darrieux with a tailor-made story. With the change in setting reflected in the new title, *Lux*'s "The Rage of Manhattan" serves as the vehicle for the debut of Tyrone Power and Annabella (Mrs. Power) in an amusing tale of an enterprising girl who pretends to be wealthy in hopes of landing a rich husband.

Film version: Universal, 1938 (*The Rage of Paris*).

283. "Jezebel," 11/25/40

Based on the 1938 Warner Bros. film (screenplay by Clements Ripley, Abem Finkel, and John Huston), in turn based on the play by Owen Davis (1933).

Cast: Loretta Young (Julie Morrison), Jeffrey Lynn (Preston Dillard), Brian Donlevy (Buck Cantrell), Verna Felton (Aunt Belle), Eugene Francis (Ted/Third Man in Act 3), Lurene Tuttle (Amy), Griff Barnett (Dr. Stone/Second Man in Act 1), Earle Ross (General Bogardus), Lou Merrill (DeLautrec/First Man in Act 1), Jack Carr (Uncle Cato), Claire Verdera (Mrs. Kendrick), Ann Tobin (Molly), Rolfe Sedan (Third Man in Act 1/Second Man in Act 3), and Byron Shores (Jenkins/First Man in Act 3).

Commercials: Ynez Seabury (Libby), Julie Bannon (Sally).

Jezebel, the 1938 William Wyler–directed Warner Bros. film for which

Bette Davis won an Oscar, was done on *Lux* without Davis. If Loretta Young's softer approach to the role of the spoiled and manipulative Southern belle removes much of the character's sting, it is nevertheless a distinguished performance. Jeffrey Lynn, who had played Henry Fonda's movie role of Preston Dillard on radio only a month before (October 27) in the *Gulf Screen Guild Theater*'s adaptation of "Jezebel" (with Jean Arthur and Walter Pidgeon), takes the same part here, while Brian Donlevy makes an intelligent and sympathetic character of Buck Cantrell, played in the film by George Brent.

284. "Knute Rockne—All American," 12/2/40

Based on the 1940 Warner Bros. film (screenplay by Robert Buckner), in turn based on the December 1938 *Cavalcade of America* broadcast.

Cast: Pat O'Brien (Knute Rockne), Ronald Reagan (George Gipp), Donald Crisp (Father Callahan), Fay Wray (Bonnie Rockne), Griff Barnett (Father Newland/Man in Act 3), Ted Bliss (Dorais/Announcer), Charles Seel (Doctor/Lars), Earle Ross (Chairman of Investigating Committee/Train Porter), Lou Merrill (Announcer/Scoreboard), Arthur Q. Bryan (Announcer/Crowd/Scoreboard), Edwin Max (a Reporter/a Clerk), James Eagles (O'Flaherty/Second Player), Fred Shields (a Professor/Friend of Rockne), Harold Daniels (First Player/Attendant in Act 1), Forrest Taylor (Doctor/Assistant in Act 3), Bob Burleson (Crowley/Messenger in Act 3), Joe Pennario (Rockne, as a Boy), and Celeste Rush (Marta).

Commercials: Julie Bannon (Sally), Duane Thompson (First Woman), Verna Felton (Second Woman), Jane Morgan (Third Woman), and Martha Wentworth (Fourth Woman).

The 1940 Lloyd Bacon–directed Warner Bros. biography of famed Notre Dame football coach Knute Rockne (1888–1931) was a current-run motion picture at the time *Lux* presented its version on December 2. As in the movie, Pat O'Brien takes the title role (one of the best-remembered portrayals of his distinguished career), and Ronald Reagan plays star halfback George Gipp. Though second-billed, his participation is unfortunately limited to the second half of Act 1, but he is given the chance to deliver his memorable "win one for the Gipper" line. Another of the film's stars, Donald Crisp, plays Father Callahan, and Fay Wray is heard in Gale Page's screen role of Knute Rockne's wife, Bonnie.

285. "My Favorite Wife," 12/9/40

Based on the 1940 RKO film (screenplay by Sam and Bella Spewack; original story by Sam and Bella Spewack and Leo McCarey).

Cast: Rosalind Russell (Ellen Arden), Laurence Olivier (Nick Arden), Gail Patrick (Bianca), Arthur Q. Bryan (Judge/Desk Clerk at Club), Warren Ashe (Burkett), Verna Felton (Ma), Dix Davis (Timmy), Mary Lou Harrington (Chinch), Lou Merrill (Hotel Clerk/Detective), Charles Seel (Court Clerk/Waiter), Hal K. Dawson (Johnson), Ferdinand Munier (Doctor), Bud McAllister (Pageboy/Boy in Act 2), Edwin Max (Truck Driver in Act 2), and Rolfe Sedan (Desk Clerk).

Commercials: Nancy Leach (Janey/Roommate), Betty Jean Hainey (Midge/Goldilocks), Lois Collier (Dot), Jane Morgan (Mrs. Hammond), and Julie Bannon (Sally). Trio: Jay Barris, Austin Grant, and Henry Kruse.

The Garson Kanin–directed comedy *My Favorite Wife* was released by RKO in 1940 to popular success. *Lux*'s version is also a delight, even if certain amusing scenes and lines of dialogue are lost through the necessity of abridgment. Rosalind Russell is a fine Ellen, taking Irene Dunne's screen part of the presumably deceased wife who pops up after having been shipwrecked on an island for seven years. Laurence Olivier and Gail Patrick also give good performances as her perplexed husband, Nick (Cary Grant in the film), and Nick's new wife, Bianca (which she also plays onscreen). Also present from the picture cast is child actor Mary Lou Harrington, who is heard as the daughter of the temporarily estranged couple.

My Favorite Wife was reworked by 20th Century–Fox in 1963 as *Move Over, Darling*, which features Doris Day, James Garner, and Polly Bergen under Michael Gordon's direction.

Additional film version: 20th Century–Fox, 1963 (*Move Over, Darling*).

286. "Fifth Avenue Girl," 12/16/40
Based on the 1939 RKO film (screenplay by Allan Scott).

Cast: Ginger Rogers (Mary Gray), Edward Arnold (Timothy Borden), John Howard (Tim), Joan Perry (Katherine), Claire Verdera (Mrs. Borden), J. Arthur Young (Higgins), Tristram Coffin (Michael), Lou Merrill (Terwillinger), Fred MacKaye (Hopkins/Sailor), Verna Felton (Cook), Rolfe Sedan (Peanut Vendor/Waiter), Sally Payne (Miss Watson/Girl), Allan Wood (Skippy/Boy), Jeanne Webb (Second Girl), and Bob Burleson (Chinese/Cop).

Commercials: Julie Bannon (Sally), Nancy Leach (Libby), and Phil Neely (Singer).

Lux's broadcast of "Fifth Avenue Girl," which is adapted from the Gregory LaCava–directed RKO film, is an amusing play principally due to the performances of the two stars — Ginger Rogers and Edward Arnold. Rogers repeats her movie role of the down-on-her-luck girl whose applied common sense works wonders on a wealthy but misguided family, and Edward Arnold is heard in Walter Connolly's screen part as the unappreciated patriarch of the household. Rounding out the cast are John Howard and Joan Perry in the roles filled by Tim Holt and Kathryn Adams in the motion picture.

287. "Young Tom Edison," 12/23/40
Based on the 1940 MGM film (screenplay by Bradbury Foote, Dore Schary, and Hugo Butler).

Cast: Mickey Rooney (Tom), Beulah Bondi (Mrs. Edison), Virginia Weidler (Tammy), Griff Barnett (Mr. Edison), Lou Merrill (Mr. Nelson), Earle Ross (Mr. McCarney), Warren Ashe (Captain Brackett/Second Man in Acts 1 and 3), Arthur Q. Bryan (Hodges/Man on Train in Act 1), Stanley Farrar (Dr. Pender), Noreen Gammill (Miss Howard), Jack Lewis (Miller), Clarence Straight (Bill), Charles Seel (Dingle/Man), Celeste Rush (Train Passenger in Act 2), and Phillips Tead (Man in Act 3).

Commercials: Jane Morgan (Mother), Lois Collier (Dot), and Betty Jean Hainey (Midge).

The entertaining MGM screen version of the early years in the life of Thomas A. Edison (1847–1931) was adapted for *Lux*, with Mickey Rooney reprising his film role as the engaging young inventor, and this radio rendering successfully captures the motion picture's most memorable scenes. Also from the cast of the photoplay (which was directed by Norman Taurog) is Virginia Weidler as Tom's kid sister, Tammy, while Beulah Bondi takes the role of Tom's mother, which is played by Fay Bainter in the film.

*288. "A Little Bit of Heaven," 12/30/40
Based on the 1940 Universal film (screenplay by Daniel Taradash, Gertrude Purcell, and Harold Goldman; original story by Grover Jones).

Cast: Gloria Jean (Midge), C. Aubrey Smith (Grandpa), Frank Albertson

(Bob), Helen Parrish (Janet), Lou Merrill (Tony), Arthur Q. Bryan (Harrington), Verna Felton (Mom/Mrs. Schultz), Charles Seel (Pop), Alan Reed (Dan), Edwin Max (Cotton/Uncle Pete), Tristram Coffin (Pinky/Uncle Pat), Bobby Winkler (Jerry), Stanley Farrar (Orchestra Conductor/Uncle Jack), Rolfe Sedan (François), Warren Ashe (Uncle Ed), and Duane Thompson (Mrs. Mitchell/Miss Brown).

Commercials: Julie Bannon (Sally), Jane Morgan (Woman), Lois Collier (Girl), and Celeste Rush (Third Woman after Act 2/Dora).

Child star Gloria Jean and C. Aubrey Smith were reunited as granddaughter and grandfather (having performed together in *The Under-Pup* in 1939) in Andrew Marton's 1940 Universal film *A Little Bit of Heaven*. They were also on hand for the *Lux* adaptation aired the same year. The radio play, which centers around a young vocalist who supplements her family's income by using her singing talents, also features Frank Albertson and Helen Parrish in the roles taken by Robert Stack and Nan Grey in the film. Songs were performed by Gloria Jean in the broadcast, but unfortunately the script of this missing show does not give the titles.

289. "Vivacious Lady," 1/6/41

Based on the 1938 RKO film (screenplay by P.J. Wolfson and Ernest Pagano), in turn based on the story by I.A.R. Wylie.

Cast: Alice Faye (Francey), Don Ameche (Peter), Frederic MacKaye (Keith), Lou Merrill (Mr. Morgan), Verna Felton (Mrs. Morgan), Jane Drummond (Helen), Rolfe Sedan (Clerk), Betty Jean Hainey (June), Sally Payne (Hatcheck Girl), Arthur Q. Bryan (Elmer), Celeste Rush (Elmer's Wife), Wally Maher (Charlie/Policeman), Jack Carr (Pullman Porter), and Bob Burleson (Culpepper).

Commercials: Julie Bannon (Sally), Kathleen Fitz (Libby), Duane Thompson (Woman), and Tristram Coffin (Man).

The 1938 George Stevens–directed RKO comedy *Vivacious Lady* stars Ginger Rogers and James Stewart in a story of a timid college professor who finds himself unable to break the news to his stuffy family (as well as his fiancée) that he has recently wed a gregarious nightclub singer.

Lux performed the story on January 6, with Alice Faye and Don Ameche offering fine characterizations that differ from those of the motion picture's stars (though the script is a straight adaptation of the movie).

Rudy Schrager, an excellent arranger and pianist in the orchestra, took over from Lou Silvers the duties of composing *Lux*'s incidental music beginning with this broadcast. Silvers, as a member of ASCAP (American Society of Composers, Authors, and Publishers), was consequently unable to have his music performed on the air during the duration of the ban. He was allowed to continue as the show's conductor, however, and would resume the composer/arranger's duties after the ban was lifted.

With the ASCAP ban having begun as of midnight, January 1, 1941, the opening scene of this play, which is set in a nightclub, begins with a jazz band playing an arrangement of the non–ASCAP piece "Frenesi" (music by Alberto Dominguez). In the film, Ginger Rogers sings the one number written especially for the motion picture, "You'll Be Reminded of Me" (words and music by George Jessel, Jack Meskill, and Ted Shapiro). That song, an ASCAP piece, is of course missing from the radio version, and in its place Faye performs part of the 1940 BMI (Broadcast Music, Inc.) selection "There I Go" (lyric by Hy Zaret, music by Irving Weiser).

290. "Libel!," 1/13/41

Based on the play by Edward Wooll (1935).

Cast: Ronald Colman (Sir Mark Loddon), Otto Kruger (Foxley), Frances Robinson (Lady Enid Loddon), Vernon Steele (Sir Wilfred), Alec Harford (Buckingham), Jeff Corey (Dr. Flordon), Eric Snowden (Judge), Jack Lewis (His Associate), Noreen Gammill (Waitress), Lou Merrill (Miles), Duane Thompson, Bob Burleson, and Joe DuVal (Ad Libs).

Commercials: Duane Thompson (Woman), Sarah Selby (Woman), and Julie Bannon (Sally).

Edward Wooll's play *Libel!* is especially well suited to the airwaves, with much of the story set in the courtroom. Ronald Colman is an excellent choice for the role of Sir Mark Loddon (which Colin Clive played on Broadway at the Henry Miller Theatre beginning December 20, 1935), who finds himself in the unusual position of having to prove his identity after an unscrupulous scoundrel charges that the real Sir Mark died in the war. Frances Robinson is his wife, Lady Enid (Joan Marion's stage part), while Otto Kruger is the brutal prosecutor (which Wilfrid Lawson played on stage).

Libel! was not filmed until 1959, when Anthony Asquith directed Dirk Bogarde, Olivia deHavilland, and Robert Morley in the British MGM release.

Lux repeated "Libel!" on March 15, 1943.

Film version: MGM (British), 1959.

291. "The Cowboy and the Lady," 1/20/41

Based on the 1938 Samuel Goldwyn/ United Artists film (screenplay by S.N. Behrman and Sonya Levien; original story by Leo McCarey and Frank R. Adams).

Cast: Merle Oberon (Mary Smith), Gene Autry (Stretch Willowby), Eddie Waller (Hannibal), Lou Merrill (Mary's Father), Gloria Blondell (Katy), Fred MacKaye (Buzz), Verna Felton (Ma Hawkins), Arthur Q. Bryan (Henderson), Janet Waldo (Elly/Second Woman), Rolfe Sedan (Chester/Announcer), Julie Bannon (Dinner Guest), Charles Seel (Sugar/Announcer), Joe DuVal (Detective/Man), Stanley Farrar (Captain), and Dick Reinhart (Whistler [accompanied Gene Autry's singing]).

Commercials: Margaret McKay (First Girl), Lois Collier (Second Girl), and Kathleen Fitz (Libby).

Samuel Goldwyn's 1938 comedy *The Cowboy and the Lady* (which was directed by H.C. Potter) was tailored by *Lux* into a vehicle for cowboy star Gene Autry, who gives an engaging performance in the Gary Cooper screen role of a rodeo performer who falls for a society lady. The two songs that are added for the radio version and are sung by Autry are "I'd Love a Home in the Mountains" (words and music by Gene Autry and Smiley Burnette, 1935), in Act 1, and "Roamin' Around the Range," in Act 2. Despite the title, the story is not a Western (at least in the conventional sense), and the larger of the two starring roles goes to the leading lady, Merle Oberon, who repeats her screen portrayal.

292. "Captain January," 1/27/41

Based on the 1936 20th Century–Fox film (screenplay by Sam Hellman, Gladys Lehman, and Harry Tugend), in turn based on the novel by Laura E. Richards (1890).

Cast: Shirley Temple (Star), Charles Winninger (Captain January), Gene Lockhart (Captain Nazro), Duane Thompson (Mrs. Easton), Verna Felton (Mrs. Morgan), Griff Barnett (Mr. Winthrop), Bobby Winkler (Gerald), Earle Ross (Mr. Easton), Lou Merrill (Judge Hardrow/Old Sailor), Charles Seel

Charles Winninger, Shirley Temple, and Gene Lockhart in "Captain January" (January 27, 1941) (photo: Photofest).

(Storekeeper), and Bob Burleson (Doctor/Man).

Commercials: Sarah Selby (First Woman), Lois Collier (Second Woman), Nancy Leach (Mary), and Julie Bannon (Sally).

Shirley Temple's return engagement to *Lux* starred her in another adaptation of one of her 20th Century–Fox films, *Captain January*, which was directed by David Butler and released in 1936. As in the case of *Lux's* "The Littlest Rebel," the story, which focuses upon a lighthouse caretaker's struggle to maintain custody of the foundling he raised to girlhood, was appropriately altered to reflect the years Temple had aged since the film was made. Charles Winninger plays Guy Kibbee's movie role, while Gene Lockhart is heard in Slim Summerville's photoplay part.

A silent version of *Captain January* was released by Principal Pictures in 1924, with Baby Peggy, Hobart Bosworth, and Lincoln Stedman under Edward F. Cline's direction.

Additional film version: Principal Pictures, 1924.

*293. "Rebecca," 2/3/41

Based on the 1940 Selznick International film (screenplay by Robert E. Sherwood and Joan Harrison; adapted by Philip MacDonald and Michael Hogan), in turn based on the novel by Daphne DuMaurier (1938).

Cast: Ronald Colman (Maxim), Ida Lupino (Mrs. DeWinter), Judith Anderson (Mrs. Danvers), Roland Drew (Frank), Denis Green (Favell), Verna Felton (Mrs. Van Hopper), Frederic Worlock (Colonel Julius), Hans Conried (Doctor Baker/Ben), Lou Merrill (Coroner), and Lee Millar (Dog/Crowd).

Commercials: Betty Jean Hainey

(Midge), Jane Morgan (Mother), and Julie Bannon (Sally).

Lux's first radio rendering of the 1939 Alfred Hitchcock–directed Selznick International drama *Rebecca* starred Ronald Colman and Ida Lupino in the mystery concerning a temperamental young man tortured by memories involving his deceased first wife. His loyal second spouse is plagued by the consequences of her husband's earlier ill-fated marriage. Colman (who had turned down the film part) and Lupino took the roles played by Laurence Olivier and Joan Fontaine in the motion picture, and Judith Anderson resumed her original screen part as the neurotic Mrs. Danvers. (On November 6, 1950, Olivier would reprise his role for *Lux* opposite his wife, Vivien Leigh.)

294. "The Moon's Our Home," 2/10/41

Based on the 1936 Paramount film (screenplay by Isabel Dawn and Boyce DeGaw), in turn based on the novel by Faith Baldwin (1936).

Cast: Carole Lombard (Cherry Chester), James Stewart (Anthony Amberton), Clara Blandick (Lucy), Verna Felton (Boycie), Hans Conried (Horace), Lou Merrill (Holbrook), Charles Seel (Justice of the Peace/Conductor), Rolfe Sedan (Abner/Bartender), Stanley Farrar (Coachman/Cop), Gloria Blondell (Hilda/First Woman), James Eagles (Hotel Clerk/Newsboy), Jack Carr (Porter), Celeste Rush (Miss Manning), and Noreen Gammill (Mrs. Simpson/Second Woman).

Commercials: Julie Bannon (Sally), Duane Thompson (Woman after Act 2).

Lux's "The Moon's Our Home," which was adapted from the 1936 Paramount William A. Seiter–directed film, stars Carole Lombard and James Stewart in the comedy of the unlikely romance between a temperamental

movie actress and a conceited author-explorer. (The screen cast is headed by Margaret Sullavan and Henry Fonda.)

295. "Johnny Apollo," 2/17/41

Based on the 1940 20th Century–Fox film (screenplay by Philip Dunne and Rowland Brown), in turn based on a story by Samuel G. Engel and Hal Long.

Cast: Dorothy Lamour (Lucky), Edward Arnold (Richard Kane, Sr.), Burgess Meredith (Dick Kane, Jr. [Johnny Apollo]), Warren Ashe (Mickey Dwyer), Hans Conried (Brennan), Lou Merrill (McLaughlin/Warden), Earle Ross (Prison Trustee), Arthur Q. Bryan (District Attorney/Floor Show M.C.), Richard Beach (Prison Guard/Charlie), Charles Seel (Other Prison Guard/Man), Griff Barnett (Judge/the Doctor), Edwin Max (Harry/First Man), Ted Bliss (Bates/Second Boy), and Janet Waldo (Secretary).

Commercials: Duane Thompson (Mary), Ann Tobin (Betty), and Julie Bannon (Sally).

Johnny Apollo, 20th Century–Fox's crime drama, was directed by Henry Hathaway (and released in 1940), and *Lux's* February 17 version features two members of the film cast, Dorothy Lamour and Edward Arnold, who are joined by Burgess Meredith. Meredith, who makes his *Lux* debut in Tyrone Power's screen role, portrays a young man whose disillusionment upon discovering that his revered father is a criminal causes him also to turn to underworld activity.

296. "The Whole Town's Talking," 2/24/41

Based on the 1935 Columbia film (screenplay by Jo Swerling and Robert Riskin).

Cast: Fibber McGee [Jim Jordan] (Wilbur Jones), Molly [Marian Jordan] (Jessie), Paul Guilfoyle (Killer Manion),

Arthur Q. Bryan (District Attorney), Dewey Robinson (Red), Edwin Max (Harry), Rolfe Sedan (Seaver), Lee Millar (J.G. Carpenter), Jeff Corey (Boyle), Ann Tobin (Miss Baedecker), Dick Ryan (Newsboy), Don Brodie (Policeman/Russell), Ted Bliss (Policeman/Man), and Gloria Blondell (Waitress).

Commercials: Julie Bannon (Sally), Lois Collier (First Woman), Jane Morgan (Second Woman), Duane Thompson (Third Woman), and Fred Shields (Man).

Those who had seen Columbia's 1935 comedy *The Whole Town's Talking* might have been surprised upon hearing *Lux*'s adaptation, as the story receives a drastic retailoring as a vehicle for Fibber McGee and Molly. The whole production has been built around Jim and Marian Jordan's characters (the motion picture stars Edward G. Robinson and Jean Arthur), and though they may be called "Wilbur" and "Jessie," they are really playing the same couple who appeared (via the radio) every Tuesday night. In the film (which was directed by John Ford), Robinson plays both the timid office worker Wilbur Jones and the look-alike gangster for whom he is mistaken, but the radio production casts movie character actor Paul Guilfoyle as the public enemy.

297. "My Bill," 3/3/41

Based on the 1938 Warner Bros. film (screenplay by Vincent Sherman and Robertson White), in turn based on the play *Courage* by Tom Barry (1928).

Cast: Kay Francis (Mary Colebrook), Warren William (John Rudlin), Dix Davis (Bill), Claire Verdera (Aunt Caroline), Janet Waldo (Muriel), Sidney Miller (Reggie), Barbara Jean Wong (Gwen), Verna Felton (Mrs. Crosby), Edward Arnold, Jr. (Linn), Bernice Pilot (Beulah), Lou Merrill

(Truck Driver/Prospective Employer), Ferdinand Munier (Doctor/Jenner), Shirley Ward (Woman), Alair Omstead (Miss Kelly), James Reed (Barnes), and Tommy Lane (Mike).

Commercials: Duane Thompson (Woman), Kathleen Fitz (Libby).

My Bill, the 1938 motion picture starring Kay Francis, also served as a vehicle for her in *Lux*'s broadcast three years later. The touching Warner Bros.' motion picture was directed by John Farrow and also featured John Litel and Dickie Moore in the story of a self-sacrificing mother who is deserted by all but one of her children when a financial crisis strikes. Francis gives a fine performance, as do Warren William as the man in her life and Dix Davis as her fiercely loyal son. DeMille states that the role is "one of the best parts we've ever had for a boy actor, and I believe you'll hear more about the lad who's playing it tonight."

Warner Bros.' first film version, entitled *Courage*, was released in 1930 with a cast that included Belle Bennett, Don Marion, and Rex Bell, under Archie Mayo's direction.

Additional film version: Warner Bros., 1930 (*Courage*).

298. "The Awful Truth," 3/10/41

Based on the 1937 Columbia film (screenplay by Viña Delmar), in turn based on the play by Arthur Richman (1922).

Cast: Bob Hope (Jerry Warriner), Constance Bennett (Lucy), Ralph Bellamy (Dan), Bea Benaderet (Aunt Patsy), Fred MacKaye (Armand), Vivian Janiss (Barbara/Gladys), Sally Payne (Dixie Belle Lee/Celeste), Verna Felton (Mrs. Leeson), Gloria Gordon (Mrs. Vance), Robert Strange (Mr. Vance), Lou Merrill (Judge/M.C.), Wally Maher (Hank/Houseboy), Lynn Martin (Singer [Soloist]), Tris Coffin (Butler/Frank), Charles Seel (Lawyer/

Caretaker), Edwin Max (Joe), and Earl Edward Keen (Dog).

Commercials: Betty Jean Hainey (Mabel), Ann Tobin (Sue), Duane Thompson (Girl/Woman), and Fred Shields (Man).

A year and a half after *Lux*'s first airing of "The Awful Truth," a second adaptation of the 1937 Columbia film was featured. While the story line is the same, on this occasion the script has been generously peppered with wisecracks for comedian Bob Hope. Thankfully, Constance Bennett and Ralph Bellamy (who appears in his original screen role) are given the chance to display their delightful comedic talents, and the quips written for them are especially amusing. Repeating her role from the previous *Lux* version is Verna Felton as Dan's mother, while Lou Merrill, who played Dan in the earlier broadcast, is here heard as the judge. ("The Awful Truth" would be done once more on *Lux*, on January 18, 1955.)

See 9/11/39 for information on film and stage productions.

Additional film version: Columbia, 1953 (*Let's Do It Again*).

299. "Cheers for Miss Bishop," 3/17/41

Based on the 1941 Richard A. Rowland/United Artists film (screenplay by Stephen Vincent Benét, Adelaide Heilbron, and Sheridan Gibney), in turn based on the novel *Miss Bishop* by Bess Streeter Aldrich (1933).

Cast: Martha Scott (Ella Bishop), William Gargan (Sam Peters), Mary Anderson (Amy), Griff Barnett (Corcoran), Fred MacKaye (Del), Fred Shields (John Stevens), Shirley Warde (Mrs. Bishop), Kathleen Fitz (Gretchen), Betty Jean Hainey (Hope), Ann Tobin (Minna/Student), Hans Conried (Radchek/Cecco), Lou Merrill (Watts/Doc-

tor), Bob Burleson (McCrae/Student), Earle Ross (Crowder/Man), and Celeste Rush (Stena).

Commercials: Sarah Selby (First Woman), Nancy Leach (Second Woman), Duane Thompson (Third Woman), and Julie Bannon (Sally).

Lux's "Cheers for Miss Bishop" is another adaptation of a film then playing in theatres across the country, and it chronicles the lengthy career of a small town schoolmarm. (The motion picture, directed by Tay Garnett, was produced by Richard A. Rowland and released by United Artists in 1941.)

The broadcast, being an abridgment of the screenplay, takes on an episodic quality that does not allow the characters to develop gradually as they do in the movie, but the radio version does include several of the picture's most memorable scenes. Martha Scott takes the same part she plays on the screen, and William Gargan also repeats his motion picture role as her perpetually unsuccessful suitor, while Mary Anderson is heard in the part played by Marsha Hunt in the film.

300. "Flight Command," 3/24/41

Based on the 1940 MGM film (screenplay by Wells Root and Commander Harvey Haislip; original story by Commander Harvey Haislip and John Sutherland).

Cast: Robert Taylor (Alan Drake), Walter Pidgeon (Bill Gary), Ruth Hussey (Lorna), Tristram Coffin (Jerry), Ted Bliss (Dusty), Fred MacKaye (Martin), Bob Burleson (Stitchy), Edward Marr (Spike/Sparks), Robert Strange (Lloyd/Doctor), Lou Merrill (Officer), Wally Maher (Jung), Griff Barnett (Admiral), Charles Seel (Mechanic), and Ann Tobin (Waitress).

Commercials: Stanley Farrar (Joe), Betty Jean Hainey (Mary), Celeste Rush (Secretary), Duane Thompson (Housewife), and Margaret McKay (Model).

The 1940 adventure-drama of the air, *Flight Command* was released by MGM under the direction of Frank Borzage, and it recounts the exploits of a cocky but likable Navy flyer whose brashness complicates his personal as well as his professional life. Robert Taylor gives a fine recreation of his motion picture portrayal, and he is joined by Ruth Hussey and Walter Pidgeon, also of the film cast.

301. "Stablemates," 3/31/41

Based on the 1938 MGM film (screenplay by Leonard Praskins and Richard Maibaum; original story by Reginald Owen and William Thiele).

Cast: Wallace Beery (Doc Terry), Mickey Rooney (Jimmie), Fay Wray (Mrs. Shepard), Noah Beery (Barney), Verna Felton (Beulah), Griff Barnett (Steward/Bartender), Lou Merrill (Announcer), Sidney Miller (Cliff), Wally Maher (Gale), Warren Ashe (Pete/Watchman), and Jack Carr (Groom).

Commercials: Julie Bannon (Sally), Lois Collier (Sue), Kathleen Fitz (Betty), and Stanley Farrar (Man).

The horse-racing movie *Stablemates* successfully teamed Wallace Beery with youngster Mickey Rooney, under Sam Wood's direction in 1938. The plot line concerning a young jockey and his colorful guardian is relatively routine, but the drama is made compelling by the performances of the two stars. Fay Wray is cast in the surprisingly small role (limited to the last act) of Mrs. Shepard, which Marjorie Gateson plays in the film, and Noah Beery is Barney, the track detective, a character played by Arthur Hohl on the screen.

302. "Stand-In," 4/7/41

Based on the 1937 Walter Wanger/United Artists film (screenplay by Gene Towne and Graham Baker), in turn based on a story by Clarence Budington Kelland (1937).

Cast: Warner Baxter (Attaberry Dodd), Joan Bennett (Lester Plum), Hans Conried (Koslovsky), Dorothy Knox (Cherie), Charles Seel (Quintain), Edward Marr (Potts), Lee Millar (Mr. Pennypacker), Barbara Jean Wong (Elvira), Rolfe Sedan (Hotel Manager), Lou Merrill (Mr. Nassau), Eleanor Stewart (Girl), Alan Wood (Junior/Newsboy), Earl Keen (Third Man/Trained Seal), Gloria Gordon (Elvira's Mother), Stanley Farrar (Taxi Driver), Edwin Max (First Man), and Noreen Gammill (Mrs. Mac).

Commercials: Kathleen Fitz (Libby), Celeste Rush (Woman, Mrs. Anywife), and Ted Bliss (Man).

Stand-In, Walter Wanger's satire on the motion picture industry, was directed by Tay Garnett and released by United Artists in 1937. *Lux*'s radio version is considerably milder than the original (more of a parody than a satire) and is also amusing. Warner Baxter finally makes his debut in this broadcast, playing an impersonal but ultimately sympathetic banker who takes over the leadership of a financially unstable film studio. The dependable Baxter demonstrates his considerable talent for comedy, and Joan Bennett is also enjoyable as the stand-in of the title who becomes his secretary. During the course of the story, she manages to thaw her boss. (The stars of the movie are Leslie Howard and Joan Blondell.)

303. "Dust Be My Destiny," 4/14/41

Based on the 1939 Warner Bros. film (screenplay by Robert Rossen), in turn based on the novel by Jerome Odlum.

Cast: John Garfield (Joe Bell), Claire Trevor (Mabel), Arthur Q. Bryan (Prosecutor), Rex Heath (Judge), Tony Martelli (Nick), Earle Ross (Mike/Magistrate), Pat Collins (Pete/Second Warden), Edward Arnold, Jr. (Hank/Policeman), Spec O'Donnell (Jimmy/

Operator), Adelaide Irving (Matron), Lou Merrill (Charlie), James Eagles (Jimmy/Newsboy), George Yesner (Guard/Jailer), Bruce Payne (First Detective), Earl Keen (Cow), Griff Barnett (Defense Lawyer), Warren Ashe (Venetti/Radio), Charles Seel (Clerk/Second Detective), and Paul O. Irving (Warden/Doctor).

Commercials: Duane Thompson (Sue), Ann Tobin (Mary), and Fred Shields (Man).

Lux's April 14 broadcast features a microphone adaptation of Warner Bros.' 1939 Lewis Seiler–directed gritty melodrama *Dust Be My Destiny*. John Garfield reprises his screen role of a hapless victim of circumstance on the lam for a crime he did not commit, and Claire Trevor, also from the motion picture, plays the downtrodden girl who helps him reconstruct his life. George Wells's adaptation captures the feel of the film especially well, and his sensitive scripting even softens the bitterness to an extent.

304. "The Letter," 4/21/41

Based on the 1940 Warner Bros. film (screenplay by Howard Koch), in turn based on the play by W. Somerset Maugham (1927).

Cast: Bette Davis (Leslie Crosbie), Herbert Marshall (Robert Crosbie), James Stephenson (Howard Joyce), Sen Yung (the Lawyer's Assistant), Richard Davis (Withers), Charlie Lung (Head Boy), Gloria Holden (the Woman), Wally Maher (Policeman/Chung Hi), Eric Snowden (Party Guest/Fireman), Lou Merrill (Judge), Suzanne Kaaren (Dorothy), Eleanor Stewart (Adele), and Leila Hyams McIntyre (Matron).

Commercials: Nancy Leach (Sally), Verna Felton (Mrs. Millar).

Lux's second production of Warner Bros.' *The Letter* reunited four cast members from the 1940 William Wyler film: Bette Davis, Herbert Marshall,

James Stevenson, and Sen Yung. (Other *Lux* presentations were broadcast on May 23, 1938, and May 6, 1944; see the former for information concerning stage and film versions.)

305. "Wife, Husband, and Friend," 4/28/41

Based on the 1938 20th Century–Fox film (screenplay by Nunnally Johnson), in turn based on the story by James M. Cain.

Cast: George Brent (Leonard), Priscilla Lane (Doris), Gail Patrick (Cecilia Carver), Verna Felton (Mrs. Blair), Hans Conried (Hugo), Gale Gordon (Craig), Edward Marr (Operator/Taxi Driver), Lou Merrill (Major Blair), Abe Reynolds (Jaffe), Thomas Mills (Fisher), Stanley Farrar (Doctor/Stage Manager), Hal K. Dawson (Motel Manager), Mildred Carroll (Singer [double for Priscilla Lane]), Paul Keast (Singer [double for George Brent]), and Lynne Davis (Singer [double for Gail Patrick]).

Commercials: Alyn Lockwood [Julie Bannon] (Sally), Duane Thompson (Woman), Fred Shields (Man), Ann Tobin (Woman after Act 2), and Fred MacKaye (Man after Act 3).

James M. Cain's story "Wife, Husband, and Friend" was the basis for the 1938 Gregory Ratoff–directed 20th Century–Fox comedy of the same title, which in turn was translated into *Lux*'s version and presented on April 28. George Brent manages very well Warner Baxter's movie role of a businessman who discovers that he has an operatic voice. Priscilla Lane as his wife (Loretta Young's screen part) and Gail Patrick as the opera singer who tries to come between them (Binnie Barnes in the film) give good performances as well. The script is amusing, though the abridgment of some of the photoplay's funniest scenes (highlighted by Warner Baxter and Loretta Young) robs them of some of their humor.

Edmund Goulding directed 20th Century–Fox's 1949 version of *Wife, Husband, and Friend,* which is entitled *Everybody Does It* and features Paul Douglas, Celeste Holm, and Linda Darnell.

Additional film version: 20th Century–Fox, 1949 (*Everybody Does It*).

306. "Kitty Foyle," 5/5/41

Based on the 1940 RKO film (screenplay by Dalton Trumbo), in turn based on the novel by Christopher Morley (1939).

Cast: Ginger Rogers (Kitty Foyle), Dennis Morgan (Wyn Stafford), James Craig (Mark), Eddie Waller (Pop), Lou Merrill (Giono), Verna Felton (Wyn's Grandmother), Gloria Holden (Delphine), Rosemary deCamp (Veronica), Claire Verdera (Mrs. Stafford), Mary Treen (Pat), Vivian Janiss (Mollie), Ann Tobin (Girl), Bobby Larson (Wyn, Jr.), Fred MacKaye (Radio/Orchestra Leader), Gale Gordon (Waiter/Doorman), Bruce Payne (Kannett), Thomas Mills (Butler), Gloria Gordon (Grandmother), and Celeste Rush (Baby Cry).

Commercials: Julie Bannon (Sally), Kathleen Fitz (Libby).

On May 5 Ginger Rogers was back on *Lux,* this time repeating her portrayal of Kitty Foyle from the Sam Wood–directed RKO film of the same name. (She was given an Academy Award for her performance.) Joining Rogers in the story of a working girl's romantic attachments are Dennis Morgan and James Craig in their screen roles of the men she must choose between.

307. "Craig's Wife," 5/12/41

Based on the play by George Kelly (1925).

Cast: Rosalind Russell (Harriet Craig), Herbert Marshall (Walter), Beulah Bondi (Miss Austin), Jane Morgan (Mrs. Harold), Betty Moran (Ethel), Virginia Gordon (Maizie), Duane Thompson (Mrs. Frazier/Operator), Phillips Tead (Birchmire/Boy), Charles Seel (Grover), and Lou Merrill (Captain Catelle).

Commercials: Nancy Leach (Girl), Ann Tobin (Anne).

George Kelly's play *Craig's Wife,* the drama of a woman fanatically obsessed with her house, made an interesting *Lux* broadcast on May 12. Rosalind Russell, in the role created on Broadway by Chrystal Hearne (who first played the part on October 12, 1925, at the Morosco Theatre), paints a vivid portrait of a conniving woman, and also giving a good performance is Herbert Marshall as her much put-upon husband (taken onstage by Charles Trowbridge).

The broadcast is a straightforward adaptation of the play (though the action begins a bit further along in the story), but the climactic events in this abridgment occur too closely together for the conclusion to ring true.

Russell stars in Columbia's 1937 Dorothy Arzner–directed film *Craig's Wife,* which also features John Boles. The same studio's 1950 version, *Harriet Craig,* was directed by Vincent Sherman and starred Joan Crawford and Wendell Corey.

The *Lux Video Theatre* presented a version on December 2, 1954.

Film versions: Columbia, 1937; Columbia, 1950 (*Craig's Wife*).

308. "Model Wife," 5/19/41

Based on the 1941 Universal film (screenplay by Charles Kaufman, Horace Jackson, and Grant Garrett).

Sound Effects Assistant: Paul Horby.

Cast: Dick Powell (Fred Chambers), Joan Blondell (Joan Chambers), Fred MacKaye (Ralph), Verna Felton (Madame Benson), Chester Clute (Milo), Edward Marr (Telegram Delivery Boy/Joe), Lou Merrill (Policeman), Paula

Francis (Mabel), Julie Bannon (Girl), Stanley Farrar (Mailman), Edwin Max (Butler), Gloria Blondell (Gloria), and Adele Rowland (Woman).

Commercials: Kathleen Fitz (Libby), Sarah Selby (Woman), Jane Morgan (Mrs. Robeson), and Betty Jean Hainey (Ann).

Universal's current release, *Model Wife* (directed by Leigh Jasper), was presented on *Lux* with its original stars, Dick Powell and Joan Blondell. This enjoyable comedy, in which a female employee must go to great lengths to keep her recent nuptials a secret in order to keep her job, is aided even further by the enthusiastic performances of Powell and Blondell.

309. "Virginia City," 5/26/41

Based on the 1940 Warner Bros. film (screenplay by Robert Buckner).

Cast: Errol Flynn (Terry Bradford), Martha Scott (Julia), Warren Ashe (Hurrell), Frank McGlynn (Abraham Lincoln), Gale Gordon (Vance), Griff Barnett (Dr. Cameron), Edwin Max (Marblehead), Lou Merrill (Olaf), Theodore von Eltz (General), Forrest Taylor (Drewry/Bartender), Charles Seel (Blacksmith/Taylor), Stanley Farrar (Spike/Officer), Edward Arnold, Jr. (Driver/Sergeant), James Eagles (Soldier in Acts 1 and 3), and Mildred Carroll (Singer).

Commercials: Julie Bannon (Sally), Duane Thompson (Mrs. Fraser), and Lois Collier (Mary).

Virginia City, Warner Bros.' 1940 Michael Curtiz–directed production set during the Civil War, is an adventure about a Yankee spy's attempts to discover the whereabouts of a sequestered cache of gold in the possession of the Rebels. The radio rendering of May 26, which features Errol Flynn and Martha Scott in their original roles, is not quite as exciting as the film, as it lacks the fairly elaborate action sequences that were skillfully woven into the plot. Frank McGlynn is cast as Abraham Lincoln, and character actor Gale Gordon is heard in Randolph Scott's screen part of Captain Vance Irving.

*310. "They Drive by Night," 6/2/41

Based on the 1940 Warner Bros. film (screenplay by Richard Macaulay and Jerry Wald), in turn based on the novel *The Long Haul*, by A.I. Bezzerides (1938).

Cast: George Raft (Joe Fabrini), Lana Turner (Cassie), Lucille Ball (Marie), Tony Hughes (Paul), Lou Merrill (Eddie), Edward Marr (Irish), Rosemary deCamp (Pearl), Arthur Q. Bryan (District Attorney/Man), Paul Dubov (Pete), Bea Benaderet (Operator/Landlady), Theodore von Eltz (Defense Attorney), Tristram Coffin (Harry/Guard), Earle Ross (Williams/Bailiff), Joe DuVal (Driver/Man), and Betty Moran (Maid/Girl).

Commercials: Duane Thompson (Woman), Julie Bannon (Sally).

Raoul Walsh directed the 1940 Warner Bros. film *They Drive by Night*, a story of two truck-driving brothers and the adventures they have on the road.

Lux's adaptation featured George Raft of the motion picture cast, who was joined by Lana Turner (taking over for Ida Lupino, who had previously been announced to repeat her film role), and Lucille Ball (in the Ann Sheridan screen part). Brian Donlevy was slated to portray the Humphrey Bogart photoplay character, but radio actor Tony Hughes played the role in his absence. (Though the first part of the picture is based on A.I. Bezzerides's novel *The Long Haul*, the second half is actually based on incidents from Warner Bros.' 1935 film *Bordertown* (which was adapted by *Lux* on July 3, 1939).

"Mr. and Mrs. Smith" (June 9, 1941), with Bob Hope and Carole Lombard (photo: Berry Hill Bookshop).

311. "Mr. and Mrs. Smith," 6/9/41
Based on the 1941 RKO film (screenplay by Norman Krasna).

Cast: Carole Lombard (Ann Smith), Bob Hope (David Smith), Bill Goodwin (Chuck Benson), Jack Arnold (Jeff), Verna Felton (Mrs. Krausheimer), Bea Benaderet (Gertie), Rolfe Sedan (Manager), Griff Barnett (Mr. Custer), Jane Morgan (Mrs. Custer), Sally Payne

(Gloria/Lily), Pat Collins (Policeman), Jerry Hausner (Cab/Boy), Ann Tobin (Secretary), Claire Verdera (Martha), Earl Keen (Cat/Man), and Lou Merrill (Restaurant Proprietor/Store Detective).

Commercials: Julie Bannon (Sally), Duane Thompson (Mrs. Jones), and Fred Shields (Mr. Jones).

The 1941 film *Mr. and Mrs. Smith* is a rarity in at least one respect—it is a comedy directed by Alfred Hitchcock. Otherwise, it is a good-natured movie concerning the events that follow a couple's discovery that their marriage of several years before is invalid, and it is elevated by the performances of its three stars: Carole Lombard, Robert Montgomery, and Gene Raymond. Lombard is the sole member of the trio who appears in the *Lux* broadcast, and she once again gives a glowing performance. In this version, her husband is played by Bob Hope, and, as in his previous *Lux* shows, this character has been retailored somewhat to fit his style. Rounding out the cast are Bill Goodwin (the announcer on Hope's weekly NBC show at the time) in Jack Carson's screen part and Jack Arnold in Gene Raymond's film role.

312. "The Lady from Cheyenne," 6/16/41

Based on the 1941 Universal film (screenplay by Kathryn Scola and Warren Duff), in turn based on the story "The First Woman Voter," by Jonathan Finn and Theresa Oaks.

Cast: Loretta Young (Annie Morgan), Robert Preston (Steve Lewis), Edward Arnold (Jim Cork), Forrest Taylor (Hank Freeman), Jane Morgan (Mrs. McGinnis), Vivian Janiss (Elsie), Lou Merrill (Billy), Ferdinand Munier (Ike Fairchild), Warren Ashe (Barney), Buck Woods (George), Stanley Farrar (Dunbar/Mr. Lloyd), Gale Gordon (the Governor/Judge), Dix Davis (Edward),

Gloria Blondell (Gertie), Bruce Payne (Clark/Conductor), Celeste Rush (Landlady), Tyler McVey (Reporter/Man), Dick Ryan (Leo/Noisey), Barbara Jean Wong (Girl), Betty Jean Hainey, Betty Moran, and Julie Bannon (Ad Libs).

Commercials: Betty Jean Hainey (Dot), Betty Moran (Jean), and Julie Bannon (Sally).

Frank Lloyd directed Universal's 1941 release *The Lady from Cheyenne*, a Western that focuses on a young lady schoolteacher's attempts to win the vote for women so that they may then be allowed to serve on a jury and convict a tyrannical land baron of his crimes. Loretta Young of the screen cast presents a strong characterization of the schoolmarm, while the film's two male stars, Robert Preston and Edward Arnold (as the villain of the piece), give equally solid performances.

313. "The Shop Around the Corner," 6/23/41

Based on the 1939 MGM film (screenplay by Samson Raphaelson), in turn based on the play by Nikolaus Làszlò.

Cast: Claudette Colbert (Karen), Don Ameche (Martin), Felix Bressart (Peters), Leo Cleary (Matachek), Fred MacKaye (Harvey), Ann Tobin (Lily/Woman), Bea Benaderet (Miss Baker), Charles Peck (Joey), Verna Felton (Shopper/Grandmother), Lou Merrill (Detective), Arthur Q. Bryan (Waiter), Ferdinand Munier (Officer), Jessie Arnold (Lady), and Bruce Payne (Santa).

Commercials: Kathleen Fitz (Libby), Stanley Farrar (Man), Duane Thompson (Girl), and Julie Bannon (Sally).

The Shop Around the Corner, an Ernst Lubitsch–directed comedy released by MGM in 1939, was presented on *Lux* with Claudette Colbert and Don Ameche (in Margaret Sullavan and James Stewart's screen roles) in the story of two co-workers who ironically become each other's secret pen pals. (Character actor Felix Bressart repeats his film part as Peters.)

In the Good Old Summertime, MGM's 1949 reworking of *The Shop Around the Corner*, was directed by Robert Z. Leonard and starred Judy Garland, Van Johnson, and Clinton Sundberg.

Additional film version: MGM, 1949 (*In the Good Old Summertime*).

314. "I Love You Again," 6/30/41

Based on the 1940 MGM film (screenplay by Charles Lederer, George Oppenheimer, and Harry Kurnitz), in turn based on the novel by Leon Gordon and Maurine Watkins (1937).

Cast: Cary Grant (Larry Wilson), Myrna Loy (Kay), Frank McHugh (Doc Ryan), Arthur Q. Bryan (Duke Sheldon/Bellboy), Jack Arnold (Herbert), Jane Morgan (Mother), Dix Davis (Corporal Belenson), Ferdinand Munier (Mayor Carver), Rolfe Sedan (Mr. Billings), Earle Ross (Steward/Mr. Littlejohn), Tyler McVey (Employee), Betty Ventura (Miss Sting), and Lou Merrill (Mr. Harkspur).

Commercials: Julie Bannon (Sally), Kathleen Fitz (Libby), and Betty Jean Hainey (Ann).

MGM's comedy *I Love You Again* is another teaming of the popular screen couple William Powell and Myrna Loy, but *Lux*'s version of the W.S. Van Dyke II–directed film features only the feminine half of the team, as Cary Grant is given the role of a racketeer whose previous bout with amnesia causes amusing complications with his exasperated wife. Frank McHugh reprises his film role of the hero's sidekick, and Dix Davis is heard in his screen part of Ranger Scout Corporal Belenson.

315. "Algiers," 7/7/41

Based on the 1938 Walter Wanger/United Artists film (screenplay by John Howard Lawson and James M. Cain), in turn based on the 1937 French film *Pepe Le Moko* (screenplay by Henri Jeanson and Roger D'Ashelbe), from the novel by Detective D'Ashelbe.

Cast: Charles Boyer (Pepe Le Moko), Hedy Lamarr (Gaby), Alan Napier (Inspector Slimane), Bea Benaderet (Ines), Hans Conried (Regis/Gendarme), Bruce Payne (Grandpère), Frederic Worlock (Janvier/Man), Jeff Corey (L'Arbi), Leo Cleary (André), Lou Merrill (Carlos), Virginia Gordon (Marie/Girl), Paul Dubov (Pierrot), Noreen Gammill (Aicha), and Howard McNear (Max).

Commercials: Miss Litaker (Stewardess), Charles Seel (Man), and Jane Morgan (Woman).

Both Charles Boyer and Hedy Lamarr made their *Lux Radio Theatre* debuts in the broadcast of "Algiers" on July 7—the finale for the 1940-41 season. (In fact, as DeMille noted, it was Lamarr's "first appearance at any microphone.") The radio play is based on the 1938 Walter Wanger/United Artists John Cromwell–directed film, which focuses upon a brash yet sophisticated thief and his cat-and-mouse games with the law, and in its condensed form, it moves along at a relatively brisk clip. Boyer and Lamarr reprise their original roles for the broadcast, and Alan Napier is heard in Joseph Calleia's screen part of the inspector.

Universal released a musical version of *Algiers* in 1948. Entitled *Casbah*, this production was directed by John Berry and featured Tony Martin, Marta Toren, and Peter Lorre.

Lux presented another version on December 14, 1942.

Additional film versions: French, 1937 (*Pepe Le Moko*); Universal, 1948 (*Casbah*).

Seventh Season
(September 8, 1941–July 13, 1942)

Columbia Broadcasting System, Monday, 9:00–10:00 P.M. *Host*: Cecil B. DeMille. *Announcer*: Melville Ruick. *Director*: Sanford Barnett. *Musical Director*: Lou Silvers. *Adaptations*: George Wells. *Sound Effects*: Charlie Forsyth.

316. "Tom, Dick, and Harry," 9/8/41
Based on the 1941 RKO film (screenplay by Paul Jarrico).
Cast: Ginger Rogers (Janie), George Murphy (Tom), Alan Marshal (Dick), Burgess Meredith (Harry), Arthur Q. Bryan (Justice of the Peace/Fourth Man), Joe Cunningham (Pop/Third Man), Noreen Gammill (Ma), Gloria Blondell (Gertrude), Priscilla Lyon (Butch), Edward Marr (Ice Cream Vendor/Second Baby), Fred MacKaye (Actor on Screen/Second Man), Bea Benaderet (Actress on Screen/Marge), Allen Wood (First Baby/Photographer), and Tyler McVey (Third Baby/Announcer).
Commercials: Duane Thompson (Mary), Ann Tobin (Gladys), and Julie Bannon (Sally).
The Garson Kanin–directed 1941 RKO comedy *Tom, Dick, and Harry*, which concerns an eccentric girl who struggles to decide which of her three distinctly different beaus she will wed, was performed on *Lux* with the film's four stars: Ginger Rogers, George Murphy, Alan Marshal, and Burgess Meredith. The bizarre dream sequences of the motion picture cannot be translated literally to the airwaves, but *Lux* succeeds in creating a sort of audio equivalent (with Arthur Q. Bryan as the Justice of the Peace providing the necessary narration).

317. "Lost Horizon," 9/15/41
Based on the novel by James Hilton (1933).

Cast: Ronald Colman (Robert Conway), Donald Crisp (the High Lama), Lynne Carver (Lo-Tsen), Denis Green (Mallinson), Cy Kendall (Chang), Dennis Hoey (Rutherford), Jill Esmond (Miss Brinklow), Dick Elliot (Barnard), Charlie Lung (Pilot), and Peter Leeds (Rudolf Sieveking).
Singers: Robert Bradford, Stewart Bair, Paul Keast, George Gramlich, Morton Scott, Phil Neely, Hubert Head, Tudor Williams, Allan Watson, and Enrico Ricardi.
Commercials: Howard McNear (Man), Don Thompson (Groom), Virginia Gordon (Woman), Lois Collier (Girl), and Julie Bannon (Sally).
Though James Hilton's novel *Lost Horizon* was adapted into a successful 1937 Frank Capra–directed Columbia film starring Ronald Colman, the *Lux* broadcast ignores the picture and bases its script directly on Hilton's work, which focuses upon a world-weary man who discovers an isolated utopian society in the Himalayas. The radio play is a well-crafted abridgment of the book and features solid performances by Ronald Colman (in his screen part), Donald Crisp, Lynne Carver, and Denis Green. (It is also interesting to hear movie heavy Cy Kendall in a rare sympathetic role.)
The stars of the 1937 Columbia film, in addition to Colman, were Jane Wyatt (as Sandra, a character created for the photoplay), Sam Jaffe (as the High Lama), and Margo (as Maria, the motion

picture's equivalent of the book's Lo-Tsen). Charles Jarrott directed Columbia's 1973 musical version, which featured Peter Finch, Liv Ullman, and Sally Kellerman.

Additional film version: Columbia, 1973.

318. "Lydia," 9/22/41

Based on the 1941 Alexander Korda/United Artists film (screenplay by Ben Hecht and Samuel Hoffenstein; original story by Julien Duvivier and Ladislaus Bus-Fekete).

Cast: Merle Oberon (Lydia McMillian), Edna Mae Oliver (Granny), Alan Marshal (Richard), Joseph Cotten (Michael), George Reeves (Bob), Bruce Payne (James), Dix Davis (Johnny), Verna Felton (Granny's Companion), Barbara Jean Wong (Ruthie), Thomas Mills (Driver), Una White (Secretary/Mary), Stanley Farrar (Speaker/Butler), Ferdinand Munier (Doctor), Jeff Corey (Frank), Priscilla Lyon (Ad Libs), Mary Lou Harrington (Ad Libs), and Joe Pennario (Ad Libs).

Commercials: Ben Alexander (Announcer), Fred MacKaye (Man), and Bea Benaderet (Woman).

Another current picture, the Julien Duvivier–directed Alexander Korda/UA production *Lydia* was presented on *Lux* with five stars from the photoplay: Merle Oberon, Edna Mae Oliver, Alan Marshal, Joseph Cotten, and George Reeves. The tightly constructed radio adaptation, which chronicles an introspective woman's life and the men who played a role in shaping it, proves effective and is aided even more by the impressive performance of the wonderful character actress Edna Mae Oliver.

319. "Third Finger, Left Hand," 9/29/41

Based on the 1940 MGM film (screenplay and original story by Lionel Houser).

Cast: Douglas Fairbanks, Jr. (Jeff Thompson), Martha Scott (Margot Sherwood), Howard McNear (Phillip), Ferdinand Munier (Mr. Sherwood/Martin), Hans Conried (August), Ernest Whitman (Sam), Arthur Q. Bryan (Flandrin/Dad), Dick Elliot (Merton/Joe), Fred MacKaye (Huey/Steward), Charles Seel (Mate/Minister), Helene Costello (Jane), Lee Millar (Judge Kelland), Thomas Mills (Butler), Una White (First Girl/Second Girl), Duane Thompson (Mrs. Kelland), and Leila Hyams McIntyre (Jeff's Mother).

Commercials: Ann Tobin (Marie), Julie Bannon (Sally), and Betty Jean Hainey (Doris).

Lux's broadcast of "Third Finger, Left Hand" was supposed to be a vehicle for William Powell and Myrna Loy, but with both actors down with a touch of flu, Douglas Fairbanks, Jr., and Martha Scott were quickly recruited as replacements. Metro-Goldwyn-Mayer's 1940 comedy, which centers around an unmarried editor who attempts to repel potential suitors by pretending to be married to a small town Ohio boy, was directed by Robert Z. Leonard and features Myrna Loy and Melvyn Douglas.

320. "Unfinished Business," 10/6/41

Based on the 1941 Universal film (screenplay by Eugene Thackeray).

Cast: Irene Dunne (Nancy), Don Ameche (Tommy), Gale Gordon (Steve), Dick Elliot (Elmer), Bea Benaderet (Sheila/Sarah), Virginia Gordon (Nell), Verna Felton (Mrs. Hatch), Fred MacKaye (Richard), Arthur Q. Bryan (Ross), Jean Rhea (Helen), Jack George (Conductor/Walter), Betty Ventura (Girl), Munro Brown (Man), and Leone Ledoux (Baby).

Commercials: Julie Bannon (Sally), Nancy Bickell (Patty), James Eagles (Bill), Jo Campbell (Singer, First Girl), and Sally Mueller (Singer, Second Girl).

Top: (Left to right) Adapter George Wells, Myrna Loy, director (and later writer) Sandy Barnett, and framework writer Harry Kerr, probably photographed during rehearsals for "Third Finger, Left Hand" (September 29, 1941), the broadcast of which Miss Loy missed due to illness (photo: Berry Hill Bookshop). *Bottom:* One of *Lux*'s fine supporting casts during rehearsal of "Third Finger, Left Hand" (September 29, 1941). Those identified are Fred MacKaye (standing at far left), Ferdinand Munier (fourth from left), Arthur Q. Bryan (fourth from right), Hans Conried (third from right), and Howard McNear (far right) (photo: Berry Hill Bookshop).

Universal's 1941 film *Unfinished Business* (produced and directed by Gregory LaCava) turns out to be a disappointingly empty comedy in its radio version, detailing the complications caused by a "spite marriage." What it does have to its advantage is a good cast, led by Irene Dunne of the film and Don Ameche in Robert Montgomery's screen part. (William Powell had been announced as Dunne's leading man at the close of the previous week's broadcast, but no explanation is made for his absence.) Dunne even gets to sing "When You and I Were Young, Maggie" (1866; words by George Johnson, music by J.A. Butterfield).

321. "Buck Privates," 10/13/41

Based on the 1941 Universal film (screenplay by Arthur T. Hornman).

Cast: Bud Abbott (Herbie), Lou Costello (Smitty), Benny Rubin (Sergeant Collins), Lynne Carver (Judy), Gene O'Donnell (Bob), Fred MacKaye (Randy Parker), Warren Ashe (Officer), Wally Maher (Corporal), Frank Penny (First Man), Edwin Max (McGonicle), Howard McNear (Soldier/ Announcer), Boyd Davis (Parker), Griff Barnett (General), Harry Lang (Williams), Eddie Marr (Second Man), Ann Tobin (Patty).

Commercials: Jo Campbell (Singer), Sally Mueller (Singer), and Julie Bannon (Sally).

Universal's film *Buck Privates* (directed by Arthur Lubin) bills Lee Bowman and Alan Curtins (in roles played here by Gene O'Donnell and Fred MacKaye) ahead of Bud Abbott and Lou Costello, who are used as comic relief in the routine story of a spoiled rich young man who learns responsibility in the army. While the *Lux* version keeps some of the film's main plot line, Abbott and Costello's antics are prominently featured. Character actor Benny Rubin is heard in Nat Pendleton's

screen role, and Lynne Carver takes Jane Frazee's photoplay part.

322. "Blood and Sand," 10/20/41

Based on the 1941 20th Century–Fox film (screenplay by Jo Swerling), in turn based on the novel by Vicente Blasco Ibàñez (1908).

Cast: Tyrone Power (Juan), Annabella (Carmen), Kathleen Fitz (Dona Sol), Bea Benaderet (Juan's Mother), Gale Gordon (Pablo), Jeff Corey (Garabato), Lou Merrill (Curro), Howard McNear (Captain Martinez), Bruce Payne (Padre/El Milquetoast), Walter Tetley (Juan, as a Boy), Anne Stone (Encarnacion), Eric Rolf (Manolo), Paul Dubov (Antonio), Elsa Brand (Woman), Nick Toms (Pulga/ Second Man), and Lester Sharpe (Man/ Waiter).

Commercials: Ben Alexander (Announcer), Julie Bannon (Sally), Nancy Bickell (Jane), and Lois Collier (Sister).

Blood and Sand, 20th Century–Fox's 1941 remake of the famed Rudolph Valentino bull-fighting film, was broadcast on *Lux* with well-thought-out performances by Tyrone Power (in his screen role) and Annabella (essaying the Linda Darnell movie part). The radio play, which focuses on the personal struggles of a vain and ignorant man who neglects his loyal wife for a calculating seductress, also features *Lux* semiregulars Kathleen Fitz (in Rita Hayworth's motion picture role) and Bea Benaderet (as Nazimova's movie character). The Rouben Mamoulian-directed photoplay won an Oscar for Technicolor cinematography (Ernest Palmer and Ray Rennahan).

Paramount's 1922 *Blood and Sand* was directed by Fred Niblo and starred Rudolph Valentino, Lila Lee, and Nita Naldi.

Additional film version: Paramount, 1922.

*323. "Her First Beau," 10/27/41

Based on the 1941 Columbia film (screenplay by Gladys Lehman and Karen DeWolfe; original story by Florence Ryerson).

Cast: Jane Withers (Penny), Jackie Cooper (Chuck), Edith Fellows (Milly Lou), Duane Thompson (Mrs. Wood), Sidney Miller (Roger), Charles Peck (Mervyn), Virginia Sale (Office), Boyd Davis (Mr. Harris), Betty Jean Hainey (Julie), Charles Seel (Mr. Wood), Betty Ventura (Ad Libs), Ann Tobin (Ad Libs), and Herbert Vigran (Announcer).

Commercials: Lois Collier (Patty), Virginia Gordon (Ellen), Julie Bannon (Sally), and Stanley Farrar (Man).

The homespun adventures of two small town adolescents are the basis for the 1941 Theodore Reed–directed Columbia film *Her First Beau,* and *Lux*'s radio version reteamed the motion picture's stars Jane Withers and Jackie Cooper.

*324. "Hired Wife," 11/3/41

Based on the 1940 Universal film (screenplay by Richard Connell and Gladys Lehman), in turn based on a story by George Beck.

Cast: William Powell (Stephen), Myrna Loy (Kendal), Arthur Q. Bryan (Van Horn), Edgar Barrier (Ferdie), Torey Carleton (Phyllis), Ferdinand Munier (Justice), Forrest Taylor (McSab), Doris Sederholm (Secretary), Bruce Payne (William), and Bernard Kerry (Hudson/Driver).

Commercials: Ann Tobin (First Girl), Betty Jean Hainey (Second Girl), Anne Stone (Third Girl), Bea Benaderet (Fourth Girl), Duane Thompson (Fifth Girl/Woman), Julie Bannon (Sixth Girl), and Stanley Farrar (Jim).

William A. Seiter's 1940 Universal film *Hired Wife* concerns the comedic situations that arise when an executive weds his highly efficient secretary for business reasons only. For *Lux*'s pro-

duction, William Powell and Myrna Loy are heard in the roles taken by Rosalind Russell and Brian Aherne onscreen.

325. "Hold Back the Dawn," 11/10/41

Based on the 1941 Paramount film (screenplay by Charles Brackett and Billy Wilder), in turn based on the story by Ketti Frings.

Cast: Charles Boyer (Georges Iscoveseu), Paulette Goddard (Anita), Susan Hayward (Emmy), Edgar Barrier (Hammock/Mechanic), Tony Martelli (Flores), Fred MacKaye (McAdams/Man), Griff Barnett (Official/Doctor), Dix Davis (Tony), Robert Lehman (Assistant), Jose Perez (Ox Cart Driver), Dorothy Griwatz (Herself), Barbara Jean Wong (Ad Libs), Priscilla Lyon (Ad Libs), Joe Pennario (Ad Libs), and Cecil B. DeMille (Director).

Commercials: Duane Thompson (Mrs. Martin), Don Thompson (First Man), Stanley Farrar (Second Man), and Charles Peck (Boy).

Paramount's 1941 Mitchell Leisen–directed *Hold Back the Dawn,* one of the hit films of the season, was presented on *Lux* on November 10. Charles Boyer, who stars in the motion picture version as an opportunistic Frenchman who marries a trusting American schoolteacher to gain access to the United States, is back to repeat his role in the broadcast, as is Paulette Goddard as the venomous Anita, while Susan Hayward is cast in Olivia deHavilland's film part as the sympathetic young wife of Boyer. The script is intelligent, and the performances of the stars make "Hold Back the Dawn" a very entertaining broadcast. (The *Lux Video Theatre* presented it on September 16, 1954.)

For the second time in a *Lux* broadcast, Cecil B. DeMille appears in the play. (His first acting assignment for the airwaves came in "Seven Keys to Baldpate" on March 26, 1938.) Here he plays the director to whom Charles Boyer tells the story, which allows him to participate in the scene-setting narration much as usual. (This part was taken by director Mitchell Leisen in the film.)

326. "Merton of the Movies," 11/17/41

Based on the play by George Kaufman and Marc Connelly (1922), in turn based on the novel by Harry Leon Wilson (1922).

Cast: Mickey Rooney (Merton Gill), Judy Garland (Phyllis Wayne), Ferdinand Munier (Mr. Gasreiler), Warren Ashe (Mack), Arthur Q. Bryan (Mr. Baird), Charles Seel (Weller/Second Man), Eddie Marr (Joe/First Man), Brian Conway (Elmer/Frank), Betty Jean Hainey (Tessie/Second Girl), Joe Cunningham (Detective/Third Man), Fred MacKaye (Walberg), Tony Martelli (Nick), Jeanette Reid (Mother/Third Girl), Verna Felton (Landlady), Sarah Berger (First Girl/Car Hop), and Jack Carr (Porter).

Commercials: Julie Bannon (Sally), Duane Thompson (Woman), Joe Pennario (Boy), and Leone Ledoux (Baby Cry).

Lux's updated version of *Merton of the Movies* (which starred Glenn Hunter and Florence Nash in the 1922 Broadway production) makes an appropriate vehicle with which to capitalize on the successful motion picture teaming of Mickey Rooney and Judy Garland. The MGM stars turn in excellent performances as the emotional young star-struck ham and his kindhearted young actress "guardian."

In Act 3, Judy Garland is given the chance to perform "The Peanut Vendor" (which is based on the Latin American song "El Marsiero"; words by Marion Sunshine and L. Wolte Gilbert, music by Moises Simon, 1931), and in the curtain call, Mickey Rooney joins her in a duet, "How About You?" (words by Ralph Freed, music by Burton Lane), from their latest film, *Babes on Broadway*.

Merton of the Movies first reached the screen in the 1924 Paramount version, in which James Cruze directed Glenn Hunter (of the original stage production) and Viola Dana. Paramount's 1932 remake was directed by William Beaudine and entitled *Make Me a Star*, with Stuart Erwin and Joan Blondell in the leads. The most recent offering is MGM's 1947 photoplay, with Red Skelton and Gloria Grahame under Robert Alton's direction.

Film versions: Paramount, 1924; Paramount, 1932 (*Make Me a Star*); MGM, 1947.

327. "Maisie Was a Lady," 11/24/41

Based on the 1941 MGM film (screenplay by Betty Reinhart and Mary C. McCall, Jr.).

Cast: Ann Sothern (Maisie), Lew Ayres (Bob), Maureen O'Sullivan (Abby), Henry Stephenson (Walpole), Gene O'Donnell (Link), Torey Carleton (Diana), Boyd Davis (Cap), Griff Barnett (Judge), Charles Seel (Doc), Eddie Marr (Mack), Warren Ashe (Hudkins/Doctor), and Dick Ryan (Cop).

Commercials: Ann Tobin (Girl), Don Thompson (Man), Virginia Gordon (Woman), and Julie Bannon (Sally).

The character of Maisie Ravier first reached the screen in 1939, and MGM's popular series would continue until 1946. *Lux* brought Ann Sothern (in her debut on the show) and Maisie to its microphone with the pleasing entry "Maisie Was a Lady" (the film of which was directed by Edwin L. Marin in 1941). The success of this faithful adaptation was assured, as the film's splendid stars Maureen O'Sullivan and Lew Ayres also return to give their moving performances as the emotionally fragile

18-year-old Abby Rawlston and her irresponsible brother Bob, whose drunken antics result in his hiring the loyal, outspoken Maisie as the family maid. Rounding out the cast is Henry Stephenson as Walpole the butler, which C. Aubrey Smith plays in the motion picture.

328. "A Man's Castle," 12/1/41

Based on the 1933 Columbia film (screenplay by Jo Swerling), in turn based on the play *Manhattan Melody,* by Lawrence Hazzard (1932).

Cast: Spencer Tracy (Bill), Ingrid Bergman (Trina), Arthur Hohl (Bragg), Mady Correll (Fay), Edgar Barrier (Ira), Bea Benaderet (Flossie), Duane Thompson (Mother), Dix Davis (Joey), Warren Ashe (Manager), Edward Marr (Eddie), Dick Ryan (Spud), Don Thompson (Waiter), Tyler McVey (Man), and Maureen O'Connor (Café Singer).

Commercials: Kathleen Fitz (Mary), Torey Carleton (Sue/Woman), Virginia Gordon (First Woman), Stanley Farrar (Man), and Ann Tobin (Suzanne).

Having presented "A Man's Castle" on March 27, 1939, with the stars of the 1933 Fox film (Spencer Tracy and Loretta Young) in their original roles, *Lux* brought the play back on December 1, 1941, to introduce Ingrid Bergman to its audience. Bergman's *Lux* debut is a complete success, as her innocent voice and timid delivery suit the Trina character perfectly and make for an excellent performance. Spencer Tracy once again plays Bill in the softened *Lux* version (which includes an interpolated marriage ceremony for Bill and Trina *early* in the story) and does a fine job. Arthur Hohl, also of the cast of the film and the earlier *Lux* broadcast, plays Bragg, and Edgar Barrier is heard in Walter Connolly's film role of Ira.

See 3/27/39 for information on film version.

329. "The Doctor Takes a Wife," 12/8/41

Based on the 1940 Columbia film (screenplay by George Seaton and Ken Englund), in turn based on the story by Aleen Leslie (1937).

Cast: Melvyn Douglas (Tim), Virginia Bruce (June), Lynne Carver (Marilyn/ Woman), Edgar Barrier (John Pierce), Ferdinand Munier (Tim's Father), Verna Felton (Mrs. Neilson/Customer), Dix Davis (Boy/Billy), Gene O'Donnell (Cop/Man), Fred MacKaye (First Reporter), Edward Marr (Reporter/ Attendant), Charles Seel (Clerk/Farmer), Torey Carleton (First Operator/Woman), Suzanne Kearen (Second Operator/Maid), Griff Barnett (Burkhardt), Frank Penny (Second Man), and Boyd Davis (Man).

Commercials: Kathleen Fitz (Libby), Bea Benaderet (Woman), Betty Jean Hainey (Girl), Duane Thompson (Second Woman/Third Woman), and Julie Bannon (Sally).

Alexander Hall directed Columbia's 1940 comedy *The Doctor Takes a Wife,* which stars Ray Milland, Loretta Young, Gail Patrick, and Reginald Gardiner, while *Lux*'s version uses Melvyn Douglas, Virginia Bruce, Lynne Carver, and Edgar Barrier, who make what they can of the predictable but entertaining tale of a doctor's marriage to an author.

As the United States had declared war against Germany and Japan earlier that day, it is natural that this situation would take precedence over all the others. This broadcast opens not with the usual theme music but with the playing of the national anthem, and during his precurtain talk DeMille makes a statement that would become very familiar to listeners over the next few years: "We've asked the Columbia Broadcasting System to interrupt our play tonight with any important news developments." He goes on to explain that "in the meantime, this theatre carries on as usual, which, as you know, is one of the oldest and finest traditions of the theatre."

The play *is* interrupted in Act 2 for a news bulletin by CBS reporter John Daly, which updates the situation and lasts approximately five minutes. The drama stops during the special broadcast and resumes after it has concluded. (An obvious quick abridgment of the remainder of the play follows.) At the conclusion of the show, DeMille advises listeners that their purchases of war bonds and stamps are needed to win the war.

330. "All This, and Heaven, Too," 12/15/41

Based on the 1940 Warner Bros./ First National film (screenplay by Casey Robinson), in turn based on the novel by Rachel Lyman Field (1938).

Cast: Bette Davis (Henriette de-Porte), Charles Boyer (Duc dePraslin), Bea Benaderet (the Duchess), Edgar Barrier (Broussais/Marshal), Jeff Corey (DeLangle/Porter), Grena Sloane (Mlle. Maillard), Bobby Larson (Raynald), Jacques Vanaire (the Doctor/Gendarme), Janet Beecher (Mme. La Maire), Robert Davis (Charpentier), Betty Jean Hainey (Agnes), Ann Tobin (Emily), Bruce Payne (Pierre), Sherry Ardell (Louise [in classroom]), Charlotte Munier (Kate), Shirley Coates (Isabelle), Velma Patey Berg (Louise [Praslin]), and Mary Lou Harrington (Berthe).

Commercials: Don Thompson (Man), Duane Thompson (Woman), Earl Keen (Dog Bark), and Lois Collier (Girl).

The 1940 period drama *All This, and Heaven, Too* (set in nineteenth-century France) was directed by Anatole Litvak and released by Warner Bros. Recreating their memorable screen characterizations for the *Lux* adaptation are Bette Davis and Charles Boyer in a story

focusing upon a kind-hearted governess whose innocent love for a wealthy family results in tragedy.

As in the case of the previous week's broadcast, this show is shortened by the war situation. (Evidently, a special broadcast held up the start of the program, as there are no interruptions in the show.)

331. "Remember the Night," 12/22/41

Based on the 1940 Paramount film (screenplay by Preston Sturges).

Special Guests (during curtain call): Bob Hope and Rita Hayworth.

Cast: Jean Arthur (Lee Leander), Fred MacMurray (Jack Sargent), Beulah Bondi (Jack's Mother), Verna Felton (Aunt Emma), Felix Vallee (Willie), Arthur Q. Bryan (O'Leary), Griff Barnett (Judge), Buck Woods (Rufus), Bea Benaderet (Mother/ Matron), Edward Marr (Tom/Leader), Audrey Reynolds (Secretary), Warren Ashe (District Attorney), Edwin Max (Cassidy/Clerk), Lee Millar (Waiter/ Dog), and Bernard Zanville (Cop/ Guard).

Commercials: Julie Bannon (Sally), Kathleen Fitz (Voice), Don Thompson (Man), Duane Thompson (Woman), and Barbara Jean Wong (Girl).

Lux's December 22 broadcast brought back Columbia's sentimental drama *Remember the Night*, with Fred MacMurray and Beulah Bondi once again playing their film parts. New to the role of Lee Leander is Jean Arthur, who gives a subdued and moving performance. The adaptation is virtually identical to the earlier broadcast (though a few minutes shorter), except that a slightly greater emphasis on Christmas has been added. (For example, the second act song, "A Perfect Day" in the earlier show and film, becomes "Silent Night" for this radio rendering.)

The usual sort of curtain call has been

abandoned in favor of a brief plea by DeMille, MacMurray, and Arthur to support the Red Cross, and a spot for special guests Bob Hope and Rita Hayworth, who are presented with awards for being "the most photo-generous people in Hollywood" on behalf of the Hollywood News Photographers.

*332. "The Bride Came C.O.D.," 12/29/41

Based on the 1941 Warner Bros. film (screenplay by Julius J. and Philip G. Epstein), in turn based on a story by Kenneth Earl and M.M. Musselman.

Cast: Bob Hope (Steve Collins), Hedy Lamarr (Joan Winfield), Gene O'Donnell (Allen), Wally Maher (Keenan), Ferdinand Munier (Jones's Uncle), Eddie Marr (PeeWee/Pilot), Warren Ashe (Man/Reporter), Torey Carleton (Gertie), Edwin Max (Hinkle/Announcer), Griff Barnett (Sheriff), and Felix Vallee (Judge).

Commercial: Kathleen Fitz (Libby).

William Keighley's 1941 Warner Bros. film *The Bride Came C.O.D.* aired on *Lux* with Hedy Lamarr and Bob Hope portraying the roles taken by Bette Davis and James Cagney on-screen (those of a fleeing socialite intent upon marrying a bandleader, and the brash flyer hired by her disapproving father to kidnap her).

The *Lux Video Theatre* produced a version on July 28, 1955.

333. "Smilin' Through," 1/5/42

Based on the 1941 MGM film (screenplay by Donald Ogden Stewart and John Balderston), in turn based on the play by Allan Langdon (pseudonym of Jane Cowl and Jane Murfin) (1919).

Cast: Jeanette MacDonald (Kathleen O'Hara/Moonyean Clare), Brian Aherne (John Carteret), Gene Raymond (Kenneth Wayne/Jerry Wayne), Dennis Hoey (Owen), Ann Todd (Kathleen, as a Child), Fred MacKaye (Willie Ainsley), Verna Felton (Ellen), Betty Hill (Mary), Anthony Marsh (Young Man), Eric Snowden (Doctor), and Howard McNear (Soldier).

Commercials: Julie Bannon (Sally), Don Thompson (Man), Ann Tobin (Girl), Betty Jean Hainey (Mary), and Lois Collier (Sue).

The third and final *Lux* version of "Smilin' Through" (based on the 1941 MGM remake) teams Jeanette Mac-Donald with husband Gene Raymond as the star-crossed lovers. MacDonald performs "The Kerry Dance" (words and music by J.L. Mallory) and "Drink to Me Only with Thine Eyes" (old English air, words by Ben Johnson) in Act 1, and "Smilin' Through" (words and music by Arthur A. Penn) in Act 2.

Other *Lux* productions of "Smilin' Through" were aired on November 4, 1934, and April 29, 1940. See 11/4/34 for information on stage and film versions.

Additional film versions: First National, 1922; MGM, 1932.

334. "A Tale of Two Cities," 1/12/42

Based on the novel by Charles Dickens (1859).

Cast: Ronald Colman (Sydney Carton), Edna Best (Lucie Manette), Halliwell Hobbes (Mr. Lorry), Denis Green (Charles Darnay), Verna Felton (Madame Defarge), Griff Barnett (Dr. Manette), Ferdinand Munier (Judge/Coachman), Arthur Q. Bryan (Jerry/Juryman), Jane Morgan (Miss Pross), Torey Carleton (Seamstress), Kathleen Fitz (Lisette), Alec Harford (Barsad), Victor Rodman (Stryver), Edwin Max (Defarge/Jailer), Boyd Davis (Attorney General), Jeff Corey (Gabelle), Thomas Mills (Innkeeper), Don Thompson (Leader/Sergeant), Charles Seel (Joe/Guard), and Eric Snowden (Judge).

Commercials: Julie Bannon (Sally), Ann Tobin (Girl).

The splendid 1935 David O. Selznick–produced, Jack Conway–directed MGM film *A Tale of Two Cities* was presented on *Lux* with Ronald Colman recreating his film role of Sydney Carton. The *Lux* version of the story is adapted not from the film but directly from the novel. It begins just before Carton's execution and is told by him to the seamstress who will soon share his fate. This flashback approach allows Colman to serve as narrator of Charles Dickens's story of the French Revolution — another role for which he is especially well suited.

The adaptation of the fairly lengthy novel never seems rushed, and despite the absence of many of the book's scenes, it even avoids being episodic.

Edna Best, Halliwell Hobbes, Denis Green, and Verna Felton join Colman in contributing to the genuine atmosphere that is present throughout.

Frank Lloyd directed what seems to be the first American feature film of *A Tale of Two Cities* in 1917, with William Farnum (as both Darnay and Carton), Jewel Carmen, Marc Robbins, and Resita Marstini. *The Only Way*, a 1925 British release, starred John Martin Harvey and Betty Faire, under Herbert Wilcox's direction, while J. Arthur Rank's 1958 film has Dirk Bogarde and Dorothy Tutin (directed by Ralph Thomas).

Lux presented "A Tale of Two Cities" for the second time on March 18, 1946.

Film versions: 1917; British, 1925 (*The Only Way*); J. Arthur Rank, 1958.

335. "The Devil and Miss Jones," 1/19/42

Based on the 1941 RKO film (screenplay by Norman Krasna).

Cast: Lionel Barrymore (John P. Merrick), Lana Turner (Mary Jones), Frederic MacKaye (Joe), Ferdinand Munier (George), Arthur Q. Bryan (Hooper), Leo Cleary (Allison), Verna Felton (Store Shopper), Edward Marr (Store Detective), Victor Rodman (Man), Frank Penny (Eddie), Boyd Davis (Waldron), Bruce Payne (Carl), Charles Seel (Love), Eve McVey (Girl), Stephanie Toler (Little Girl), and Betty Ventura (Woman/Secretary).

Commercials: Jane Morgan (Woman), Stanley Farrar (Man), Betty Jean Hainey (Girl), William Ray Melton (Boy), and Julie Bannon (Voice of Loretta Young).

After an absence of two and a half years, Lionel Barrymore made a return engagemeut on January 19, in an adaptation of RKO's comedy *The Devil and Miss Jones*. The picture, which was directed by Sam Wood, stars Charles Coburn and Jean Arthur in the title roles, Coburn as a millionaire who secretly goes to work in his own department store to investigate various complaints, and Arthur as a worker in the shoe department. The adaptation is relatively sluggish and even clumsy at times, and the deletion of the Spring Byington character, which provided several amusing moments on the screen, also works against the broadcast. Lana Turner makes her *Lux* debut as Miss Jones, and Fred MacKaye is heard in Robert Cummings's movie part of her rabble-rousing boyfriend, Joe.

336. "Here Comes Mr. Jordan," 1/26/42

Based on the 1941 Columbia film (screenplay by Seton I. Miller and Sidney Buchman), in turn based on the play *Heaven Can Wait*, by Harry Segall.

Cast: Cary Grant (Joe), Claude Rains (Mr. Jordan), Evelyn Keyes (Betty), James Gleason (Max), Howard McNear (the Messenger), Bernard Zanville (Tony), Torey Carleton (Julia), Thomas Mills (Sisk), Edward Marr (Messenger/Newsboy), Charles Seel (Voice/Announcer), Warren Ashe (Charles/Lefty), and Eugene Forsyth (Second News-boy).

Commercials: Kathleen Fitz (Libby), Jane Morgan (Mrs. Martin), Betty Jean Hainey (Nancy Martin), Julie Bannon (Voice of Claudette Colbert), and Bill Felton (Bill).

Columbia's 1941 fantasy *Here Comes Mr. Jordan* (directed by Alexander Hall), which concerns a recently deceased boxer who must find a new body when he dies prior to his scheduled time due to a heavenly error, makes a particularly appropriate story for radio, as it calls upon the listeners' imaginations to a great extent. Though Cary Grant is cast in Robert Montgomery's screen role, *Lux*'s version is able to retain much of the flavor of the film by casting three players in their original parts: Claude Rains as the title character, Evelyn Keyes in the leading feminine role, and James Gleason as Joe's manager, Max.

Warren Beatty and Buck Henry directed the 1978 version of *Here Comes Mr. Jordan*, which took the title of the play on which the original was based, *Heaven Can Wait* (not related to 20th Century–Fox's 1943 film of the same name), but changed the hero from a boxer to a football player. Beatty is featured in the production, along with James Mason, Julie Christie, and Jack Warden.

Additional film version: Paramount, 1978 *(Heaven Can Wait)*.

337. "Skylark," 2/2/42

Based on the 1941 Paramount film (screenplay by Allan Scott), in turn based on the play by Samson Raphaelson (1939).

Cast: Claudette Colbert (Lydia Kenyon), Ray Milland (Tony), Brian Aherne (Jim Blake), Wally Maher (George), Thomas Mills (Theodore), Torey Carleton (Myrtle), Leo Cleary (Clerk/Judge), Dick Elliott (Mr. Vantine/Conductor),

Edward Marr (Waiter/Bartender), and Doris Sederholm (Receptionist/Telegraph Girl).

Commercials: Julie Bannon (Sally), Ann Tobin (Jane), and Stanley Farrar (Bill).

Mark Sandrich directed Paramount's 1941 comedy *Skylark*, which stars Claudette Colbert, Ray Milland, and Brian Aherne. The same trio of principals are present for *Lux*'s version, which illustrates the situations that occur when an amorous suitor tries to steal the wife of a hard-working business executive.

Interestingly, the broadcast begins with the opening notes of Beethoven's Fifth Symphony—the U.S. theme for victory during the war—prior to Melville Ruick's announcement of "Lux Presents Hollywood!"

338. "City for Conquest," 2/9/42

Based on the 1940 Warner Bros. film (screenplay by John Wexley), in turn based on the novel by Aben Kandel (1939).

Cast: Alice Faye (Peggy Nash), Robert Preston (Danny Kenny), Cy Kendall (Scotty), Edward Marr (Mutt), Warren Ashe (Murray), Howard McNear (Eddie), Bea Benaderet (Mrs. Nash/Gladys), Dewey Robinson (Referee/Dance Hall Proprietor), Mary Virginia Palmer (Lilly), Edwin Max (Reporter), Charles Seel (Checker/Other Leader), Frank Penny (Bouncer/Googi), Earl Ebi (Baron), Charles Hutchinson (Doctor), Ann Tobin (Ad Libs), and Bill Melton (Ad Libs).

Commercials: Kathleen Fitz (Libby), Julie Bannon (Sally).

Warner Bros.' *City for Conquest*, a 1940 release directed by Anatole Litvak, stars James Cagney and Ann Sheridan in the story of an amateur dancer who dreams of fame and the unambitious truck driver whose love for her propels him into the prize-fighting

Musical director Lou Silvers and Claudette Colbert during rehearsals of "Skylark" (February 2, 1942) (photo: Berry Hill Bookshop).

racket. *Lux*'s version of the intriguing boxing drama recasts the leads, giving Alice Faye and Robert Preston the chance to display their dramatic abilities. Faye is also given the opportunity to sing "I Don't Want to Walk Without You" (words by Frank Loesser, music by Jule Styne), the hit number from Paramount's 1941 film *Sweater Girl* (which does not feature Faye in its cast). Two members of the supporting cast who play interesting parts are Cy Kendall, once again in a sympathetic role as the hero's tough but kindly fight manager, and Howard McNear as the boxer's musician brother. (Max Steiner's fine score, which plays an important part in the motion picture, is not used in the radio drama.)

339. "Blossoms in the Dust," 2/16/42
Based on the 1941 MGM film (screenplay by Anita Loos; original story by Ralph Wheelwright).
Cast: Greer Garson (Edna Gladney), Walter Pidgeon (Sam Gladney), Felix Bressart (Dr. Breslar), Bea Benaderet (Charlotte), Marga Ann Deighton (Mrs. Kahly), Griff Barnett (Mr. Eldridge), Bobby Larson (Tony), Verna Felton (Mrs. Gilworth), Aileen Pringle (Mrs. Keith), Tommy Cook (Sammy), Leo Cleary (Dr. West), Buck Woods (Zeke),

Lillian Randolph (Cleo), Ann Tobin (Secretary/Girl), Jacqueline DeWitt (Hilda), John Roche (Man/Copy), Doris Sederholm (Nurse/Secretary), Warren Ashe (Allen/Third Man), Gene O'Donnell (Dannon), Ferdinand Munier (Dr. West), Mary Lou Harrington (Little Girl), Charles Seel (Second Man), Sarah Berner, Mary Jane Croft, and Leone Ledoux (Baby Cries).

Commercials: Jane Morgan (Woman), Julie Bannon (Sally), and Kathleen Fitz (Sally).

Inspired by the real-life story of Edna Gladney, who founded a care center for orphans in Texas, MGM's *Blossoms in the Dust* was directed by Mervyn LeRoy and released in 1941. At the time of the *Lux* broadcast of the story, the stars of the film, Greer Garson and Walter Pidgeon, were working on *Mrs. Miniver* at MGM, but this did not prevent them from recreating their parts of Edna and Sam Gladney. (Felix Bressart, also of the motion picture cast, appears as Dr. Breslar.)

During the curtain call, DeMille reads a congratulatory telegram from Edna Gladney herself.

340. "Appointment for Love," 2/23/42

Based on the 1941 Universal film (screenplay by Bruce Manning and Felix Jackson), in turn based on the story "Heartbeat," by Ladislaus Bus-Fekete.

Cast: Myrna Loy (Jane Alexander), Charles Boyer (André Cassille), Edgar Barrier (Michael), Arthur Q. Bryan (Hastings), Torey Carleton (Nancy), Charles Seel (Timothy), Mary Virginia Palmer (Edith), Verna Felton (Martha/Woman in Audience), Thomas Mills (Leary), Griff Barnett (Dr. Gunther), Duane Thompson (Nora), Eddie Marr (Elevator Boy [Gus]), Frank Penny (Waiter/Pete), Dick Ryan (Intern/Sadler), Bill Melton (Usher/Page Boy),

Eugene Forsyth (Boy/Second Newsboy), and Stanley Farrar (Second Waiter/Man).

Commercials: Julie Bannon (Sally), Lynne Martin (Singer), and Anne Stone (Girl).

Universal's 1941 motion picture *Appointment for Love* stars Margaret Sullavan and Charles Boyer and was directed by William A. Seiter. The *Lux* presentation of February 23 finds Myrna Loy teamed with Charles Boyer in the comedy of a playwright and a doctor who find it nearly impossible to spend time together because of their completely different work schedules.

Lux presented the story again on May 1, 1944.

341. "The Great Lie," 3/2/42

Based on the 1941 Warner Bros. film (screenplay by Lenore Coffee), in turn based on the novel *Far Horizon*, by Polan Banks (1936).

Cast: Loretta Young (Maggie), George Brent (Pete), Mary Astor (Sandra), Ruby Dandridge (Violet), Griff Barnett (Colonel Harriston), Verna Felton (Aunt Ada), Buck Woods (Jefferson), Charles Seel (Jock Thompson), Leone Ledoux (Baby/Maid), Leo Cleary (Doctor), Boyd Davis (Doctor), and Arthur Gillmore (Page Boy/Man's Voice).

Commercials: Julie Bannon (Sally), Duane Thompson (Mrs. X), Jane Morgan (Neighbor), and Kathleen Fitz (Libby).

Warner Bros.' 1941 film *The Great Lie* (directed by Edmund Goulding) served as a popular vehicle for Bette Davis, but *Lux*'s broadcast of March 2 features Loretta Young in the starring role. This drama of a young woman who agrees to claim the illegitimate child of a heartless concert pianist as her own finds George Brent and Mary Astor repeating their movie characterizations. (Astor was awarded, on February 26,

1942, the Best Supporting Actress Oscar for her screen performance.)

The *Lux Video Theatre* aired a version on March 21, 1957.

342. "The Lady Eve," 3/9/42

Based on the 1941 Paramount film (screenplay by Preston Sturges; original story by Monckton Hoffe).

Cast: Barbara Stanwyck (Jean), Ray Milland (Charles Pike), Charles Coburn (Colonel Harrington), Keith Hitchcock (Sir Alfred), Eric Snowden (Gerald), Ferdinand Munier (Pike), Verna Felton (Mrs. Bullock), Doris Sederholm (Myrtle), and Warren Ashe (Man).

Commercials: Mary Virginia Palmer (Mary), Julie Bannon (Sue), Ann Tobin (Voice of Rita Hayworth), and Stanley Farrar (Bill).

Cecil B. DeMille begins the March 9 show with an announcement that because of the president's speech (scheduled to begin at 9:45 P.M. EST), the program will be trimmed to 45 minutes in length. This abridging of "The Lady Eve" hurts the play, for Preston Sturges's film characters are carefully developed with the comic situations building one atop another. *Lux*'s production of the farce, which deals with a cynical chiseler who attempts to sink her hooks into a wealthy, scatterbrained explorer, has a rushed feel to it, damaging both the characters and the situations.

The film version of *The Lady Eve* (written and directed by Preston Sturges) was released by Paramount in 1941 and includes Barbara Stanwyck and Charles Coburn in the cast, both of whom recreate their roles for the broadcast, while Ray Milland plays Henry Fonda's motion picture part.

343. "Manpower," 3/16/42

Based on the 1941 Warner Bros. film (screenplay by Jerry Wald; original story by Fred Niblo, Jr.).

Cast: Edward G. Robinson (Hank), Marlene Dietrich (Fay), George Raft (Johnny), Warren Ashe (Omaha), Edwin Max (Culley), Griff Barnett (Pop), Bea Benaderet (Nurse/Matron), Charles Seel (Second Lineman), Howard McNear (Clerk/Bartender), Torey Carleton (Telephone Operator), and Frank Penny (Orderly/First Lineman).

Commercials: Stanley Farrar (Man), Ann Tobin (Voice of Loretta Young), and Duane Thompson (Sally).

Manpower, a routine drama of two linemen and the embittered girl whose presence complicates their friendship, is highly predictable from the start, but the broadcast, like the film, is enjoyable thanks to the talents of its three stars: Edward G. Robinson, Marlene Dietrich, and George Raft. Dietrich, who sang two numbers by Frank Loesser and Frederick Hollander in the motion picture (directed by Raoul Walsh for Warner Bros.), does not sing in the radio adaptation.

344. "Strawberry Blonde," 3/23/42

Based on the 1941 Warner Bros. film (screenplay by Julius J. and Philip G. Epstein), in turn based on the play *One Sunday Afternoon*, by James Hagen (1933).

Cast: Don Ameche (Biff Grimes), Rita Hayworth (Amy), Gail Patrick (Virginia), Luis Alberni (Nick), Jack Mather (Hugo), Edward Marr (First Man), Charles Seel (Second Man [Act 1]/Treadway), Leo Cleary (Warden/Second Man [Act 2]), Bob Nelson (Third Man/Butler), Arthur Gilmore (Young Man/Cop), Betty Ventura (Girl), and Fritzie Dugan (Josephine).

Commercials: Duane Thompson (Sally), Lois Collier (Girl), and Stanley Farrar (Johnny).

Warner Bros.' 1941 Raoul Walsh–directed production *Strawberry Blonde* is a relatively straightforward adaptation

Writer S.H. ("Sandy") Barnett and Loretta Young during a rehearsal of "The Great Lie" (March 2, 1942) (photo: Berry Hill Bookshop).

of James Hagen's 1933 Broadway play *One Sunday Afternoon* and stars James Cagney, Olivia deHavilland, Rita Hayworth, and George Tobias. Hayworth, who plays the title character in the film, is promoted to the larger (and more sympathetic) role of Amy in the broadcast, and she does an excellent job, as do Don Ameche as Biff and Gail Patrick as Virginia. (Originally, Virginia Bruce was announced to portray this latter character.)

DeMille was in New York during the week of the "Strawberry Blonde" broadcast but is still heard, though his participation is limited to introducing the play and interviewing the stars dur-

ing the curtain call. (The narration at the beginning of each act and the introductions to Acts 2 and 3 are handled by Melville Ruick.)

This is the second *Lux* version of *One Sunday Afternoon*; the first (which had the original title) was a feature of *Lux's* first Hollywood season on August 24, 1936. (A third rendering was presented on September 4, 1950, and the *Lux Video Theatre* aired a version on October 2, 1950.)

See August 24, 1936, for information on film versions.

Additional film versions: Paramount, 1933 (*One Sunday Afternoon*); Warner Bros., 1948 (*One Sunday Afternoon*).

345. "I Wanted Wings," 3/30/42

Based on the 1941 Paramount film (screenplay by Frank Wead, Eleanore Griffin, Beirne Lay, Jr., Richard Maibaum, and Sig Herzig), in turn based on the novel by Lieutenant Beirne Lay, Jr. (1937).

Cast: Ray Milland (Jeff), William Holden (Al), Veronica Lake (Sally Vaughn), Lynne Carver (Carolyn), Warren Ashe (Captain Mercer), Griff Barnett (Judge/Third Officer), Edward Marr (Masters), Howard McNear (Mike/Charlie [Mechanic]), Leo Cleary (Announcer/Officer), Boyd Davis (Colonel), Arthur Gillmore (Tom/Second Mechanic), and Lynne Martin (Singer [double for Veronica Lake]).

Commercials: Duane Thompson (Sally), Eve McVey (Girl), Stanley Farrar (a Sailor), and Bea Benaderet (Voice of Madeleine Carroll).

Paramount's flying drama *I Wanted Wings* is notable as the production in which Veronica Lake made her screen debut as a featured player, and *Lux*'s adaptation of the 1941 Mitchell Leisen–directed film accordingly presents Lake to *Lux* audiences for the first time. Joining her from the motion picture cast are Ray Milland and William Holden, with Lynne Carver playing Constance Moore's screen role in the story of a pair of Air Force cadets and their relationships with the two girls who complicate their lives. (At the conclusion of the March 23 broadcast, DeMille had announced that Brian Donlevy would be on hand to recreate his movie role, but he is inexplicably absent, and *Lux* semiregular Warren Ashe, who appears in the film version as a cadet, plays his part.)

346. "The Fighting 69th," 4/6/42

Based on the 1940 Warner Bros. film (screenplay by Norman Reilly Raine, Fred Niblo, Jr., and Dean Franklin).

Additional Sound Effects Engineer: Paul Norby.

Cast: Pat O'Brien (Father Duffy), Robert Preston (Jerry Plunkett), Ralph Bellamy (Wild Bill Donovan), Edward Marr (Murphy), Edwin Max (Crepe Hanger), Griff Barnett (Colonel/Doctor), Jack Mather (Big Mike), Charles Seel (Sergeant), Hans Conried (Kilmer), Tyler McVey (Jim), Arthur Gillmore (Lieutenant/Guard), Leo Cleary (Onlooker/MacArthur), Erik Rolf (McManus/Private), Stanley Farrar (Alabama), and Warren Ashe (First Doctor/Managan).

Singers: Morton Scott, Robert Bradford, Phillip Neeley, Allan Watson, Abe Dinovitz, Paul Keast, Ray Linn, Tudor Williams, Delos Jewkes, and Enrico Ricardi.

Commercials: Duane Thompson (Sally).

Although it was made prior to the United States' involvement in World War II, Warner Bros.' 1940 release *The Fighting 69th* is a drama especially well suited to the situation that existed in the spring of 1942. Cast in *Lux*'s typically well-mounted production centering around the world-renowned Irish regiment are Pat O'Brien, repeating his role of Father Duffy from the film version, Robert Preston in James Cagney's screen part, and Ralph Bellamy, who plays George Brent's movie role.

During the curtain call, Ralph Bellamy reads a telegram from the real William J. ("Wild Bill") Donovan, whom he had just portrayed in the radio play.

347. "Northwest Mounted Police," 4/13/42

Based on the 1940 Paramount film (screenplay by Alan LeMay, Jesse Lasky, Jr., and C. Gardner Sullivan).

Cast: Gary Cooper (Dusty Rivers), Paulette Goddard (April Logan), Preston

Foster (Sergeant Jim Brett), Bea Benaderet (Louvette), Fred MacKaye (Ronnie), Cy Kendall (Corbeau), Pedro deCordoba (Big Bear), Vernon Steele (Cabot), Harold Huber (Dan), Verna Felton (Mrs. Burns), Dix Davis (a Boy), Noreen Gammill (Nicole), Leo Cleary (Shorty/Superintendent), Victor Rodman (Riel), Tyler McVey (Constable), Jack Mather (Inspector/Marcel), Warren Ashe (Jerry/Brave), Howard McNear (Orderly/Trooper), Stanley Farrar (Fenton), and Bruce Payne (MacDuff).

Commercials: Duane Thompson (Sally), Jeanne Darrell (Singer), and Paul Norby (assistant, sound effects).

Cecil B. DeMille's 1940 Paramount picture *Northwest Mounted Police* was adapted for *Lux* and presented on April 13. The large-scale and colorful screen production loses something in the translation to radio, but this tribute to the Canadian Mounties comes across as an exciting action drama nonetheless. Gary Cooper, Paulette Goddard, and Preston Foster, all of the film cast, are also on hand for the radio rendering, but while the gentlemen repeat their screen roles, Goddard is heard in Madeleine Carroll's motion picture part of April Logan. (Bea Benaderet assumes Goddard's film role of the scheming Louvette.)

348. "One Foot in Heaven," 4/20/42

Based on the 1941 Warner Bros. film (screenplay by Casey Robinson), in turn based on the book by Hartzell Spence.

Intermission Guest: Camille McLain Anderson, "Lady of Cotton, 1942" (after Act 1).

Cast: Fredric March (William Spence), Martha Scott (Hope Spence), Verna Felton (Mrs. Sandow/Fourth Lady), Leo Cleary (Thurston/Chief), Josephine Whitell (Mrs. Thurston/Second Lady), Griff Barnett (Dr. Romer/MacFarland), Dix Davis (Hartzell, as a

Boy), Leone Ledoux (Baby/Girl), William Melton (Hartzell, as a Young Man), Eugene Forsyth (Hartzell), Noreen Gammill (Louella/Third Lady), Bruce Payne (Haskins), Doris Sederholm (Maid/First Lady), and Priscilla Lyon (Eileen).

Singers: Mildred Carroll, Grace Neilson, Dawn O'Day, Betty Bruce, Barbara Van Brunt, Jan Williams, Henry Kruse, Abe Dinovitz, Homer Hall, and Enrico Ricardi.

The April 20 broadcast turns out to be another entry abridged to 45 minutes due to a special government message. *One Foot in Heaven*, which was based on Hartzell Spence's biography of his father (Methodist pastor William Spence), was directed by Irving Rapper and released by Warner Bros. in 1941. Fredric March and Martha Scott reprise their movie roles in *Lux's* broadcast of April 20, which gives a good account of the story despite the abridged running time.

"One Foot in Heaven" was performed on the *Lux Summer Theatre* on July 27, 1953, and on the *Lux Video Theatre* on February 3, 1955.

349. "Penny Serenade," 4/27/42

Based on the 1941 Columbia film (screenplay by Morrie Ryskind), in turn based on a short story by Martha Cheavens.

Cast: Robert Taylor (Roger), Barbara Stanwyck (Julie), Beulah Bondi (Mrs. Oliver), Edgar Buchanan (Applejack), Griff Barnett (Judge/Man), Duane Thompson (Tommy's Mother), Bobby Larson (Tommy), Warren Ashe (Doctor/Porter), Leone Ledoux (Baby), and Ann Todd (Trina).

Singers: Jeanne Darrell, Betty Rome, Ruth Clark, Betty Bruce, Ethlyn Williams, Stella Harris, Georgia Stark, Jerry Jordan, Mary Modere, and Enrico Ricardi.

Commercials: Lois Collier (Mary),

Eve McVey (Girl), and Torey Carleton (Sally).

Cary Grant and Irene Dunne are the stars of the 1941 George Stevens–directed Colnmbia film *Penny Serenade,* which was performed on *Lux* with real-life husband and wife Robert Taylor and Barbara Stanwyck as the young couple who adopt a child. (Beulah Bondi and Edgar Buchanan repeat their roles from the motion picture.) The story compellingly nnfolds in flashback as the wife listens to an album of phonograph records she and her husband have collected during their courtship and marriage. (The tunes are: "You Were Meant for Me," "I Kiss Your Hand, Madame," and "I Can't Give You Anything but Love" in Act 1; "Soft Lights and Sweet Music" and "Sweet Sue, Just You" in Act 2; and "Memories" and "Happy Birthday" in Act 3.)

"Penny Serenade" was presented again on May 8, 1944, and on the *Lux Video Theatre* on January 13, 1955.

350. "Suspicion," 5/4/42

Based on the 1941 RKO film (screenplay by Samson Raphaelson, Joan Harrison, and Alma Reville), in turn based on the novel *Before the Fact,* by Francis Iles (Anthony Berkeley) (1932).

Cast: Joan Fontaine (Lina), Brian Aherne (Johnnie), Nigel Bruce (Beaky), Jill Esmond (Isobel), Vernon Steele (General McLaidlaw/Clerk), Gloria Gordon (Mrs. McLaidlaw), John Abbott (Melbeck/Burton), Eric Snowden (Inspector Hodgson/Bailey), Claire Verdera (Secretary), and Pax Walker (Ethel).

Commercial: Eve McVey (Sally).

The 1941 Alfred Hitchcock– directed production *Suspicion* by RKO puts less emphasis on the visual than many of Hitchcock's films, and it serves to translate effectively to the audio medium.

Lux's version casts Joan Fontaine in her original screen role (for which she won the Best Actress Oscar) as the apprehensive young wife who gradually comes to suspect that her husband is trying to murder her, while Brian Aherne is heard in Cary Grant's film part of her husband, the likable ne'er-do-well, Johnnie. Nigel Bruce recreates his movie role of Beaky, and Pax Walker, who plays the maid, Phoebe, in the picture, is given the larger role of Ethel in the broadcast.

"Suspicion" was presented again on September 18, 1944.

351. "The Last of Mrs. Cheyney," 5/11/42

Based on the play by Frederick Lonsdale (1925).

Cast: Norma Shearer (Mrs. Cheyney), Walter Pidgeon (Lord Arthur Dilling), Adolphe Menjou (Charles), Frederic Worlock (Lord Kelton), Keith Hitchcock (Willie), Winifred Harris (the Duchess), Jill Esmond (Kitty), Claire Verdera (Maria), John Abbott (George), Eric Snowden (William), Pax Walker (Joan/Maid [Act 3]), Charles Seel (Steward/John), and Anne James (Maid [Act 2]).

Commercials: Doris Sederholm (Mary), James Eagles (Man), Dix Davis (Boy), Barbara Jean Wong (Girl), Fred MacKaye (Man), and Ann Tobin (Voice of Irene Dunne).

Norma Shearer, MGM's leading lady, made her belated *Lux* debut on May 11 as the title character in "The Last of Mrs. Cheyney." Shearer, whose only appearance before the *Lux* microphone this is, does a fine job and gives an animated portrayal of the sophisticated jewel thief, the same role she undertook in the 1929 film version. Walter Pidgeon and Adolphe Menjou are her two leading men, and Winifred Harris (of the 1925 Broadway cast) is the Duchess, an intended victim.

DeMille announces at the conclusion of the program that for the seventh consecutive year, readers of the *Movie-Radio Guide* in their "Star of Stars" poll have voted the *Lux Radio Theatre* the best dramatic show on the air.

See 3/16/36 for information on stage and film productions.

352. "A Man to Remember," 5/18/42
Based on the 1938 RKO film (screenplay by Dalton Trumbo), in turn based on the story by Katharine Haviland-Taylor.

Cast: Lionel Barrymore (John Abbott), Anita Louise (Jean), Glenn Ford (Dick Abbott), Leo Cleary (Sykes), Harlan Briggs (Ramsey), Griff Barnett (Perkins), Charles Seel (Harkness), Francis X. Bushman (Dr. Robinson), Fred MacKaye (Howard Sykes/Man), Bruce Payne (Minister/Man), Duane Thompson (a Patient's Mother/Woman), Dick Elliott (a Stranger/Dr. Palmer), Dix Davis (Dick, as a Boy), Leone Ledoux (Jean, as a Baby), Mary Lou Harrington (Little Girl), Warren Ashe (Johnson), Edward Marr (Raymond/Boy), and Victor Rodman (Superintendent).

Commercials: Doris Sederholm (First Woman/Voice), Jane Morgan (Second Woman), and Janet Waldo (Libby).

For *Lux*'s second offering of "A Man to Remember," Lionel Barrymore gives an excellent performance in the role of kind-hearted, selfless country doctor John Abbott. He is capably assisted by Anita Louise as his loyal adopted daughter and Glenn Ford as his neurologist son.

One Man's Journey, the first film version of Katharine Haviland-Taylor's story "A Man to Remember," had in fact starred Lionel Barrymore, but it is RKO's 1938 film from the same source that is the basis for this *Lux* production (just as it was for the earlier broadcast).

See 12/14/39 for information on film versions.

*353. "Test Pilot," 5/25/42
Based on the 1938 MGM film (screenplay by Vincent Lawrence and Waldemar Young; original story by Frank Wead).

Cast: Robert Taylor (Jim), Rita Hayworth (Ann), Robert Preston (Gunner), Cy Kendall (Drake), Fred MacKaye (Joe), Bea Benaderet (Mrs. Benson/Secretary), Verna Felton (Mrs. Barton), Charles Seel (Announcer), Howard McNear (Grant), Tris Coffin (Benson), Tudor Williams (General), Warren Ashe (Announcer), and Bobby Larson (Boy).

Commercials: Sandra Coles (Woman), Lois Collier (Sally).

The 1938 Victor Fleming–directed aviation drama *Test Pilot* stars Clark Gable, Myrna Loy, and Spencer Tracy, while *Lux*'s version features Robert Taylor, Rita Hayworth, and Preston Foster in the story of two pilots who literally climb to new heights in testing airplanes, and of the girl who figures prominently in both their lives.

*354. "Ball of Fire," 6/1/42
Based on the 1942 Samuel Goldwyn/RKO film (screenplay by Charles Brackett and Billy Wilder).

Cast: Barbara Stanwyck (Sugarpuss O'Shea), Fred MacMurray (Professor Bertram Potts), Felix Vallee (Professor Odely), Griff Barnett (Professor), Leo Cleary (Professor Gurkaroff), Norman Field (Professor Robinson), Bruce Payne (Professor Pearson), Warren Ashe (Joe Lilac), Verna Felton (Miss Flagg), Edwin Max (Pastrani), Frank Penny (Arthur), Arthur Q. Bryan (Justice), Charlie Peck (Newsboy), Tyler McVey (Harry and Waiter), and Lynne Martin (Singer).

Commercials: Doris Singleton (Voice of Madeleine Carroll), Janet Russell

(Mary), Janet Waldo (Voice of Rosalind Russell), and Fred MacKaye (Man).

Ball of Fire, Howard Hawks's 1942 Samuel Goldwyn/RKO comedy, concerns a burlesque queen with gangland connections who hides out with a group of staid college professors, eventually falling in love with one of them. *Lux* brought the story to the airwaves on June 1, with Barbara Stanwyck playing her movie role and Fred MacMurray in the Gary Cooper screen part.

*355. "Arise, My Love," 6/8/42

Based on the 1940 Paramount film (screenplay by Charles Brackett and Billy Wilder; original story by Jacques Thery, Benjamin Glazer, and John S. Toldy).

Cast: Loretta Young (Augusta), Ray Milland (Tom), Cy Kendall (Phillips), Tris Coffin (Shep), John Kennedy (Pink), Howard McNear (Priest/Clerk), Fred MacKaye (Mechanic/Radio), Jose Perez (Guard/Bellboy), Leo Cleary (Governor/Conductor), Tony Martelli (Driver/Steward), Charles Seel (Waiter), Norman Field (Officer), Jack Mather (Porter/Fisherman), and Torey Carleton (Secretary).

Commercials: Janet Waldo (First Woman/Girl), Janet Russell (Second Woman), Arthur Gillmore (Boy), and Lois Collier (Sally).

Mitch Leisen's 1940 Paramount comedy centered around a high-spirited female foreign correspondent and the "soldier of fortune" flyer who are caught up in the doings of World War II. *Lux*'s adaptation starred Loretta Young in Claudette Colbert's film role and Ray Milland in his original screen part. (Future *Lux* announcer John Kennedy appears in a supporting role.)

*356. "You Belong to Me," 6/15/42

Based on the 1941 Columbia film (screenplay by Claude Binyon).

Cast: Merle Oberon (Helen Hunt),

George Brent (Peter Kirk), Thomas Mills (Moody), Fred MacKaye (Gulliver/Second Reporter), Sandra Coles (Nurse), Arthur Q. Bryan (Clerk/Manager), Francis X. Bushman (Doctor/Second Clerk), Boyd Davis (Barrows/Billings), Janet Waldo (Girl), Charles Seel (Driver/Reporter), Verna Felton (Shopper), Tyler McVey (Bob), and James Eagles (Mac).

Commercials: Arthur Gillmore (Man), Janet Russell (Voice of Loretta Young/Girl), and Doris Sederholm (Woman/Voice of Joan Bennett).

In *Lux*'s radio rendering of "You Belong to Me," Merle Oberon and George Brent were given the roles Barbara Stanwyck and Henry Fonda played in the 1941 Columbia film (directed by Wesley Ruggles) in which a female doctor's jealous husband believes that all of her male patients are "on the make."

*357. "Bedtime Story," 6/22/42

Based on the 1942 Columbia film (screenplay by Richard Flournoy), in turn based on a story by Horace Jackson and Grant Garrett.

Cast: Loretta Young (Jane Drake), Don Ameche (Lucius Drake), Truman Bradley (William), Arthur Q. Bryan (Eddie), Ann Doran (Virginia), Verna Felton (Emma), Pinto Colvig (Pop), Ann Tobin (Secretary/Girl), Charles Seel (Collins), Rolfe Sedan (Pierce), Dick Ryan (Mac/Man), Fred MacKaye (Bert/Drunk), Eddie Marr (Mike/Clerk), Torey Carleton (Beulah/Chambermaid), Boyd Davis (Eccles), and Naomi Maher (Betsy/Maid).

Commercials: Sandra Coles (Sally), Joanne Darrell (Singer).

June 22 marked the date of *Lux*'s first airing of the Columbia comedy *Bedtime Story*, which deals with an egocentric playwright who goes to extremes to persuade his estranged wife to star in his latest production. The 1942 Alexander

Hall–directed film was brought to the airwaves with Loretta Young in her original screen role and Don Ameche in the part taken by Fredric March in the motion picture.

The story was presented again on February 26, 1945, and on the *Lux Video Theatre* on November 10, 1955.

358. "The Champ," 6/29/42

Based on the 1931 MGM film (screenplay by Leonard Praskins; original story by Frances Marion).

Cast: Wallace Beery (the Champ), Josephine Hutchinson (Linda), Noah Beery (Tony), Bobby Larson (Dink), Charles Seel (Sponge), Phil Herlick (Jonah), Griff Barnett (Second Reporter/Doctor), Howard McNear (Photographer/Man), Jose Perez (Jose/Third Man), Gwen Delano (Mary), Edward Marr (Photographer/Man), Arthur Q. Bryan (Whitey), Leo Cleary (Guard/Announcer), Stanley Farrar (Louis), Jack Mather (First Reporter/Referee), and Fred MacKaye (Bookie/Second Man).

Commercials: Sandra Coles (Sally), Janet Waldo (Betty/Libby), and Arthur Gillmore (Tom).

Lux's second broadcast of "The Champ" again features Wallace Beery, Josephine Hutchinson, Noah Beery, and Bobby Larson, who starred in the earlier radio production of the 1931 MGM motion picture.

See November 13, 1939, for information on film versions.

359. "Love Affair," 7/6/42

Based on the 1939 RKO film (screenplay by Delmar Daves and Donald Ogden Stewart; original story by Mildred Cram and Leo McCarey).

Cast: Charles Boyer (Michael Marnet), Irene Dunne (Terry McKay), Tris Coffin (Kenneth), Bea Benaderet (the Grandmother/Woman), Ferdinand Munier (Courbett), Griff Barnett (Su-perintendent/Second Man), Edwin Max (Sign Painter/Man), Dix Davis (Boy), Barbara Jean Wong (Girl), Joe Pennario (Boy), Doris Bryan, Gwen Bryan, Betty Bryan (Trio/Ad Libs), Norman Field (Frenchman/Priest), Ann Doran (Miss Lane), Bruce Payne (Doctor/Steward), Torey Carleton (Lois), Eric Snowden (Englishman/Man), Charles Peck (Page Boy/Elevator Boy), Tony Martelli (Photographer/Taxi Driver), and Leo Cleary (Manager/Guide).

Commercials: Sandra Coles (Sally), Arthur Gillmore (Bill), Doris Sederholm (Ann/Mary), and Janet Waldo (Ruth).

"Love Affair" was offered on *Lux* for a second time on July 6, once again with Irene Dunne reprising her movie role, on this occasion opposite her leading man of the screen version, Charles Boyer. The script is the same, even down to Dunne's songs, which are: "Sing, My Heart" (partial; words by Ted Koehler, music by Harold Arlen) and a complete rendition of "Wishing" (words and music by B.G. DeSylva), in which she is once again assisted by the Bryan Sisters.

See 4/1/40 for information on film versions.

360. "H.M. Pulham, Esq.," 7/13/42

Based on the 1941 MGM film (screenplay by King Vidor and Elizabeth Hill), in turn based on the novel by John P. Marquand (1941).

Cast: Hedy Lamarr (Marvis Myles), Robert Young (Harry Pulham), Josephine Hutchinson (Kay Motford), Norman Field (Mr. Pulham), Verna Felton (Mrs. Pulham/Nurse), Fred MacKaye (Bill), Thomas Mills (Hugh), Duane Thompson (Miss Rollo/Miss Percival), Jack Mather (Bo-Jo/Driver), Tris Coffin (Ridge/Artist), Leo Cleary (Bullard/Conductor), Charles Seel (Kaufman), and Eugene Forsyth (Page Boy).

Commercials: Sandra Coles (Sally), Doris Sederholm (Mary), and Janet Waldo (Girl).

The last broadcast of *Lux*'s 1941-42 season spotlights the 1941 MGM film *H.M. Pulham, Esq.* It seems an unusually quiet story on which to end the season, though it is a well-done drama telling of an assertive young lady who helps a troubled young man take charge of his life. Hedy Lamarr and Robert Young reprise their original roles for the broadcast, and Josephine Hutchinson is heard in Ruth Hussey's movie part of Kay.

After the curtain call, a brief tribute is paid to announce that Melville Ruick, who had been with the program for six years, was leaving the show to join the Air Force.

*360a. *The Victory Theatre*, "The Philadelphia Story," 7/20/42
Based on the 1940 MGM film (screenplay by Donald Ogden Stewart), in turn based on the play by Philip Barry (1939).
Cast: Cary Grant (C.K. Dexter Haven), Katharine Hepburn (Tracy Lord), Lieutenant James Stewart (Mike Conner), Ruth Hussey (Elizabeth Imbrie), Virginia Weidler (Dinah Lord), Nicholas Joy (Seth), Janet Beecher (Margaret), Gale Gordon (George), Verna Felton (Librarian), Sandra Coles (Mother), and Leo Cleary, Charles Seel, Norman Field, and Bruce Payne. In public service announcement for war bonds (after Act 2): Verna Felton (Mrs. Brown).

A week after *Lux*'s regular season ended, a special presentation of the U.S. government's *Victory Theatre* was aired to raise money for the war effort. (*The Victory Theatre* ran through the summer of 1942, with each of several CBS series contributing one program.) The show selected for the series premiere was *Lux*'s "The Philadelphia Story," with five members of the 1940 MGM film cast: Cary Grant, Katharine Hepburn, James Stewart, Ruth Hussey, and Virginia Weidler. (The play tells of a society divorcée whose upcoming nuptials are complicated by the presence of the ex-husband who still loves her and by the arrival of the cynical newshound who has been assigned to cover the event.) Although not officially part of the *Lux Radio Theatre* series (there are no commercials for the product), the program follows the *Lux* format closely, and the regular supporting players and production crew are used. (This is also the first show for new *Lux* announcer John M. Kennedy, who would be a part of the series for the next ten seasons.)

George Cukor directed the first film version of *The Philadelphia Story* for MGM in 1940. The 1956 musical version, *High Society*, stars Bing Crosby, Grace Kelly, Frank Sinatra, Celeste Holm, and Lydia Reed, under Cedric Gibbons and Hans Peters' direction.

"The Philadelphia Story" was to be presented as part of the regular *Lux Radio Theatre* series on June 14, 1943.
Additional film version: MGM, 1956 (*High Society*).

Eighth Season
(September 14, 1942–July 12, 1943)

Columbia Broadcasting System, Monday, 9:00–10:00 P.M. *Host*: Cecil B. DeMille. *Announcer*: John Milton Kennedy. *Director*: Sanford Barnett. *Musical Director*: Lou Silvers. *Adaptations*: George Wells. *Sound Effects*: Charlie Forsyth.

361. "This Above All," 9/14/42

Based on the 1941 20th Century–Fox film (screenplay by R.G. Sheriff), in turn based on the novel by Eric Knight (1941).

Cast: Tyrone Power (Clive Briggs), Barbara Stanwyck (Prudence Cathaway), James Kirkwood (Roger), Stuart Robertson (Monte), Claire Verdera (Iris), Norman Field (the Rector), Verna Felton (Sergeant/Nurse), Frederic Worlock (General/Major), Josephine Gilbert (Violet/Nurse), Vernon Steele (Radio/Clerk), Herman Waldeman (Joe/Man), Thomas Mills (Parsons/Farmer), Charles Seel (Artie/Fireman), Barbara Denny (Girl), Colin Campbell (Proprietor/Second Man), Bruce Payne (Waiter/Minister), Eric Snowden (Policeman/Conductor), Fred MacKaye (Sergeant/Bert), Billy Roy (Boy), Vickie Madden, and Ann James (Ad Libs).

Singers: Phillip Neely, Allan Watson, Robert Bradford, and Enrico Ricardi.

Commercials: Arthur Gillmore (Man), Frances Woodward (Voice of Jean Arthur), Janet Waldo (Libby), and Phillip Neely (Singer).

This Above All, 20th Century–Fox's love story set in wartime England, was directed by Anatole Litvak and released in 1941. *Lux*'s intelligent radio version features Tyrone Power of the screen cast and Barbara Stanwyck in Joan Fontaine's movie role in the drama of a troubled deserter and the girl who helps him pick up the pieces of his shattered existence.

During the curtain call, DeMille announces that Power has enlisted in the military.

362. "How Green Was My Valley," 9/21/42

Based on the 1941 20th Century–Fox film (screenplay by Philip Dunne), in turn based on the novel by Richard Llewellyn (1940).

Cast: Walter Pidgeon (Mr. Gruffydd), Donald Crisp (Mr. Morgan), Maureen O'Hara (Angharad), Roddy McDowall (Huw), Sara Allgood (Beth Morgan), Gale Gordon (Narrator), Stewart Robertson (Dai Bando), Joseph Kearns (Cyfartha), Paul Langton (Ianto), Kemball Cooper (Mr. Jonas/Gwilym), Gloria Gordon (Mrs. Nicholas/Second Woman), Frederic Worlock (Mr. Evans), Esta Mason (Enid/Woman), Herbert Evans (Peterson), Fred Mackaye (Man), Claire Verdera (Woman), Norman Field (Man), Stephen Muller, Joe Pennario, Barbara Jean Wong, Antonio Oland, Billy Roy (Ad Libs), and Tudor Williams (Man/Ad Libs).

Singers: Tudor Williams, Robert Bradford, Jon Williams, Stewart Bair, Richard Davis, Allan Watson, David J. Reed, Eddie Davis, Cyril Clare, John Clay Thomas, Will Louis, Reese Williams, and Enrico Ricardi (Coach).

Commercials: Betty Jean Hainey (Jane), Janet Waldo (Mary), Sandra Coles (Sally), and Arthur Gillmore (Man).

It is only fitting that the 1941 film that won five Academy Awards, including best picture, best director (John Ford), and best supporting actor (Donald Crisp), should eventually be produced in a *Lux Radio Theatre* adaptation. The cast of this intriguing drama of a proud Welsh mining family is excellent and includes the five principal players from the motion picture: Walter Pidgeon, Donald Crisp, Maureen O'Hara, Roddy McDowall, and Sara Allgood (the last three making their *Lux* debuts with this broadcast).

The play was presented again on

March 31, 1947, and September 28, 1954.

363. "The Magnificent Dope," 9/28/42

Based on the 1942 Paramount film (screenplay by George Seaton; original story by Joseph Schrank).

Cast: Henry Fonda (Thaddeus Page), Don Ameche (Dwight Dawson), Lynn Bari (Claire Harris), Arthur Q. Bryan (Horace Hunter), Eddie Marr (Messenger/Man Number Two), Bea Benaderet (Mrs. Hunter), Verna Felton (Ma), Fred MacKaye (Radio Announcer), Griff Barnett (Doctor/Reindel), Joe Latham (Mitchell/Man), Bruce Payne (Gordy/Morton), Torey Carleton (Secretary), Mary Raymond (Girl), and Lee Millar, Jr. (Photographer).

Commercials: Arthur Gillmore, Sandra Coles, Jeanne Darrell (Singer), Betty Jean Hainey, and Frances Woodward.

The 1942 20th Century–Fox film *The Magnificent Dope* was *Lux*'s attraction on September 28. Starring in the broadcast are Henry Fonda, Don Ameche, and Lynn Bari, all of whom give fine performances in the roles they created in the Walter Lang–directed movie centering around a naive hick who goes to New York and outwits an exploitative, fast-talking city boy.

364. "Love Crazy," 10/5/42

Based on the 1941 MGM film (screenplay by William Ludwig, Charles Lederer, and David Hertz).

Cast: Hedy Lamarr (Susan), William Powell (Steve), Gale Gordon (Ward), Dorothy Lovett (Isobel), Verna Felton (Mrs. Cooper), Joseph Kearns (Dr. Klugle), Fred MacKaye (Grayson), Arthur Q. Bryan (George), Wally Maher (Attendant/Man Number Two), Eddie Marr (Joe/Cop), Griff Barnett (Judge/Janitor), Ferdinand Munier (Man/Dr. Wuthering), James Bush (Taxi/Mike), Bessie Smiley (Woman/Secretary),

Horace Willard (Butler), Betty Hill (Girl/Operator), Boyd Davis (Dentist), and Norman Field (Man).

Commercials: Sandra Coles (Sally), Janet Waldo (Libby).

The screwball comedy *Love Crazy*, which was another vehicle for William Powell and Myrna Loy, was directed by Jack Conway and released by MGM in the spring of 1941. A year and a half later, the film was adapted by *Lux* without Loy, but with Powell teamed with Hedy Lamarr (who is given the chance to display her seldom used comedic talents) in the tale of a man who attempts to prove himself insane to prevent his wife from being granted a divorce. (Powell greatly amuses the audience by donning a woman's hat during a scene in which the story calls for him to masquerade as a female.)

365. "Morning Glory," 10/12/42

Based on the 1933 RKO film (screenplay by Howard J. Green; original story by Zoe Akins).

Cast: Judy Garland (Eva Lovelace), John Payne (Joseph Sheridan), Adolphe Menjou (Louis Easton), Bea Benaderet (Rita), Norman Field (Hedges), Gloria Blondell (Dance Hall Girl/Secretary), Lillian Bond (Girl), Ann Doran (Moll/Ella), Fred MacKaye (Man Number Two/Charlie), Dick Ryan (Cop/Sailor), Paul Langton (Seymour/Sam), Frank Penny (Counterman/Waiter), Tyler McVey (Man/Joseph), Leo Cleary (Butler/Jake), Lee Arnold (Girl Number Two).

Lux's October 12 broadcast of "Morning Glory" gave Judy Garland a non-musical setting and allowed her to display her abilities as an excellent dramatic actress. In addition to Garland, *Lux*'s version of the drama of a stage-struck girl determined to find success as an actress in New York features John Payne (in Douglas Fairbanks, Jr.'s, film role) and Adolphe Menjou, who repeats his screen part.

Garland does sing one song in Act 3: "I'll Remember April (and Be Glad)" (words and music by Don Raye, Gene de Paul, and Pat Johnson; from the Universal film *Ride 'Em Cowboy*).

Morning Glory, the RKO film for which Katharine Hepburn won an Academy Award, was directed by Lowell Sherman in 1933, while Buena Vista's 1958 version, entitled *Stage Struck*, was directed by Sidney Lumet and featured Susan Strasberg, Henry Fonda, and Christopher Plummer.

Additional film version: Buena Vista, 1958 (*Stage Struck*).

366. "My Favorite Blonde," 10/19/42

Based on the 1942 Paramount film (screenplay by Don Hartman and Frank Butler; original story by Melvin Frank and Norman Panama).

Cast: Bob Hope (Larry Haines), Virginia Bruce (Karen Bentley), Bea Benaderet (Madame Runick/Frederick's Mother), Verna Felton (Mrs. Topley), Edwin Max (Karl), Fred MacKaye (Carleton/Doctor), Eddie Marr (Doorman/Second Newsboy), Duane Thompson (Receptionist/Mother), Wally Maher (First Policeman/Radio Announcer), Dix Davis (Frederick), Charles Seel (Sheriff/Elvin), Leo Cleary (Faber/Conductor), Horace Willard (Newsboy/Porter), Jack Mather (Ulrich/Cop Number Two), Pinto Colvig (Penguin/Driver), and Warren Ashe (Driver/Radio).

Commercials: Sandra Coles (Sally), Janet Waldo (Libby), and Duane Thompson (Girl).

Although by the fall of 1942 Bob Hope was no stranger to *Lux* (he had appeared on four previous occasions), the October 19 broadcast marks the first time the comedian appeared in a *Lux* adaptation of one of his own films. Paramount's *My Favorite Blonde*, the comedic tale of a vaudeville performer who becomes caught up in an international conspiracy, was directed by

Sidney Lanfield and released in 1941. Originally, Ann Sothern had been announced to play the title character (Madeleine Carroll's screen part), but she is absent without explanation, and Virginia Bruce capably plays the role. Even though many events that are only seen in the film have to be described in the broadcast, the adaptation makes up in good spirits what it lacks in smoothness.

367. "Wake Island," 10/26/42

Based on the 1942 Paramount film (screenplay by W.R. Burnett and Frank Butler).

Cast: Brian Donlevy (Major Caton), Robert Preston (Joe), Broderick Crawford (Smacksie), Gale Gordon (Commander Roberts), Griff Barnett (Doctor/Parkman), Howard McNear (Lieutenant Bruce Cameron), Mary Lou Harrington (Cynthia), Edwin Max (Sergeant), Pinto Colvig (Dog/Probenzki), Wally Maher (McCloskie), Fred MacKaye (Announcer/Talker), Paul Langton (Runner), Tyler McVey (Tommy/Man), Hal Gerard (Warren), Lillian Bond (Mrs. Cameron), Jeff Corey (Frank), Charles Seel (Patric), Warren Ashe (Johnson/Lewis), Leo Cleary (Kurusu/Orderly), Janet Russell (Native Girl), Eddie Marr (Sparks), and Jack Mather (Hogan).

Commercials: Duane Thompson (Woman after Act 1/Woman after Act 3), Betty Jean Hainey (Girl after Act 1/Girl after Act 3).

John Farrow's splendidly directed, intelligent 1942 Paramount tribute to the American Marines who died defending Wake Island would earn him the prestigious *New York Times* Critics' Award for 1942. *Lux*'s presentation of "Wake Island" retains the motion picture's documentary feel (with DeMille providing the narration) and features two members of the screen cast in their original roles: Brian Donlevy and Robert

Preston. (Broderick Crawford is heard in William Bendix's film role of Smacksie.)

368. "A Woman's Face," 11/2/42

Based on the 1941 MGM film (screenplay by Donald Ogden Stewart), in turn based on the play *Il était une fois*, by Francis deCroisset.

Cast: Ida Lupino (Anna Holm), Brian Aherne (Dr. Segert), Conrad Veidt (Torsten Barring), Norman Field (Judge), Lillian Bond (Vera Segert), Bobby Larson (Lars-Erik), Griff Barnett (Barring), Aubrey Mather (Prosecutor), Vernon Steele (Defense Attorney), Jeff Corey (Herman Runvick), Jane Morgan (Emma), Josephine Gilbert (Christina/ Nurse), Leo Cleary (Dalvik/Guard), and Charles Seel (Clerk).

Commercials: Janet Waldo (Libby), Stanley Farrar (Man), Mary Raymond (Woman), Sandra Coles (Sally), and Betty Jean Hainey (Patty).

A Woman's Face, which was directed by George Cukor and released by MGM in 1941, stars Joan Crawford as the physically and emotionally scarred woman whose outlook is altered after she undergoes successful plastic surgery. *Lux*'s November 2 broadcast features Ida Lupino, who makes a fine Anna Holm, giving the character just enough sympathy to make her transformation convincing, with Brian Aherne in the part Melvyn Douglas plays in the picture and Conrad Veidt repeating his strong screen characterization of the scheming Torsten Barring. (A Swedish film version, entitled *En Kvinnas Ansikte*, was produced in 1938 and starred Ingrid Bergman in the lead role.)

Additional film version: Swedish, 1938 (*En Kvinnas Ansikte*).

*369. "Sullivan's Travels," 11/9/42

Based on the 1941 Paramount film (screenplay by Preston Sturges).

Cast: Veronica Lake (Girl), Ralph Bellamy (Sullivan), Norman Field (Sergeant), Griff Barnett (Attorney), Joe Latham (Doctor), Frank Penny (Man), Tony Martelli (Convict/Driver), Mady Correll (Mrs. Sullivan), Fred MacKaye (James/Man Number Two), Warren Ashe (Casalsis), Charles Seel (Lebrand), John Laing (Man/Tramp), Arthur Q. Bryan (Hadrian/Man Number Three), Verna Felton (Miss Rains/ Effie), Thomas Mills (Valet), Edwin Max (Charlie), William Philips (Cop), and Graham Denton (Val/Sheriff).

Commercials: Beverly Brown (Girl's Voice), Vyola Vonn (Woman's Voice), Arthur Gillmore (Man's Voice), Paula Winslowe (Voice of Rosalind Russell), and Dorothy Lovett (Libby).

Preston Sturges wrote and directed Paramount's 1941 release *Sullivan's Travels*, an intriguing comedy chronicling the exploits of a pampered movie director (noted for his popular light farces) who insists upon experiencing firsthand the troubles of the down-and-out prior to his making a grim social drama. Veronica Lake of the screen cast was present for the *Lux* production, and Ralph Bellamy filled in for the previously announced George Brent in Joel McCrea's film role. Two of the screen version's most important sequences are enacted with no dialogue, and their absence must have been missed, but George Wells's new scene for the radio play neatly tied together any potential loose ends.

370. "To Mary, with Love," 11/16/42

Based on the 1936 20th Century-Fox film (screenplay by Richard Sherman and Howard Ellis Smith), in turn based on the story by Richard Sherman (1935).

Cast: Irene Dunne (Mary Wallace), Ray Milland (Jack Wallace), Otto Kruger (Bill Hallan), Bea Benaderet (Connie), Dorothy Lovett (Kitty), Fred

MacKaye (First Man/Second Newsboy), Eddie Marr (Bartender/First Newsboy), Howard McNear (Drunk/Cab Driver), Arthur Q. Bryan (Butler/Announcer), Duane Thompson (Operator/Nurse), Doris Singleton (Secretary/Woman), Jane Bierce (Nurse/Second Woman), and Bruce Payne (Elevator Man/Second Man).

Commercials: Marjorie Davies (Libby), Caroline Burke (Sally), Beverly Brown (Girl/Mary), and Duane Thompson (Mother).

Lux's November 16 broadcast offered an adaptation of 20th Century–Fox's *To Mary, with Love*, a drama of marital discord rearing its head in a previously happy marriage. The radio version features Irene Dunne, Ray Milland, and Otto Kruger in the roles created in the 1936 John Cromwell–directed film by Myrna Loy, Warner Baxter, and Ian Hunter.

*371. "The Gay Sisters," 11/23/42

Based on the 1942 Warner Bros. film (screenplay by Lenore Coffee), in turn based on the novel by Stephen Longstreet (1942).

Cast: Barbara Stanwyck (Fiona Gaylord), Robert Young (Charles Barclay), Bobby Larson (Austin), Lois Collier (Susanna), Dorothy Lovett (Evelyn), Leo Cleary (Gibbon), Fred MacKaye (Gig), Griff Barnett (Pedloch), Noreen Gammill (Saskia/Woman), Boyd Davis (Wheeler), Joe Latham (Judge/Doctor), Paul Langton (Gaylord), Jane Bierce (Girl/Nurse), and Joe Pennario (Boy).

Commercials: Marjorie Davies (Betty), Paula Winslowe (Mary), and Caroline Burke (Sally).

Lux's version of Warner Bros.' *The Gay Sisters* featured Barbara Stanwyck in her original screen role as one of the aforementioned siblings (of the title) who dupes a fellow into matrimony so that she may collect her inheritance,

while Robert Young took the part played by George Brent in the 1942 Irving Rapper film.

The *Lux Video Theatre* presented a version on November 22, 1956.

*372. "Broadway," 11/30/42

Based on the 1942 Universal film (screenplay by Felix Jackson and John Bright), in turn based on the play by Phillip Dunning (1926).

Cast: George Raft (George), Janet Blair (Billie), Lloyd Nolan (Dan), Cy Kendall (Steve Crandall), Leo Cleary (Nick), Bea Benaderet (Pearl), Gloria Blondell (Marie), Eddie Marr (Dolph), Mack Gray (Mack/Harvey), Charles Seel (Scar/Adam), Fred MacKaye (Benny/Joe), Griff Barnett (Pete), Norman Field (Wingy/Kerry), Bruce Payne (Newsboy), Julie Bannon (Ruby), Janet Russell, Jane Bierce, and Duane Thompson (Ad Libs).

Singers: Stanley Farrar (for Lloyd Nolan), Ann Tobin (for Janet Blair).

Commercials: Caroline Burke (Sally), Shelby Miller (Man), and Betty Jean Hainey (Girl).

Universal's 1942 drama *Broadway* (which was directed by William A. Seiter) focuses upon life in New York City during the 1920s, and on the turf wars that occur between rival racketeers. Repeating their roles for *Lux* listeners were George Raft and Janet Blair, while Lloyd Nolan was heard in Pat O'Brien's motion picture part.

373. "The War Against Mrs. Hadley," 12/7/42

Based on the 1942 MGM film (screenplay by George Oppenheimer).

Cast: Edward Arnold (Elliot Fulton), Fay Bainter (Stella Hadley), Jean Rogers (Patricia), Van Johnson (Michael), Fred MacKaye (Theodore), Verna Felton (Mrs. Fitzpatrick), Ann O'Neil (Cecilia), Jane Morgan (Mrs.

Winters), Ferdinand Munier (Bennett), Norman Field (Dr. Meecham), Janet Russell (Millie), Jane Bierce (Secretary/Maid), Charles Seel (Radio/Stevens), Graham Denton (Bob/Second Reporter), Stanley Farrar (Peters), Julie Bannon (Reporter/Girl), and Ken Christy (Louie/Soldier).

For the one-year anniversary of the bombing of Pearl Harbor, *Lux* appropriately selected the effective drama "The War Against Mrs. Hadley" to mark the occasion. Fine performances are given by leads Edward Arnold and Fay Bainter as the sage family friend and the selfish clinging vine whose patriotism is kindled by the trials and tribulations of the war. Also present from the cast of the MGM motion picture (which was directed by Harold S. Bacquet) are Jean Rogers and Van Johnson.

374. "Algiers," 12/14/42

Based on the 1938 Walter Wanger/United Artists film (screenplay by John Howard Lawson and James M. Cain), in turn based on the 1937 French film *Pepe Le Moko* (screenplay by Henri Jeanson and Roger D'Ashelbe), from the novel by Detective D'Ashelbe.

Cast: Charles Boyer (Pepe Le Moko), Loretta Young (Gaby), J. Carroll Naish (Inspector Slimane), Gene Lockhart (Regis), Isabel Jewell (Ines), Charles Seel (Janvier/Gendarme), Norman Field (André), Fred MacKaye (Carlos), Noreen Gammill (Hostess), Kelly Flint (Gaby's Friend/Girl), Jeff Corey (L'Arbi), Griff Barnett (Grandpère), Don Peters (Pierrot), and Graham Denton (Man/Man Number Two).

Commercial: Dorothy Lovett (Libby).

"Algiers" returned to *Lux* a year and a half after the first production in July of the previous year. Charles Boyer, the star of both the 1938 Walter Wanger/United Artists film and the earlier broadcast, again recreates his role of the sophisticated criminal Pepe Le Moko, with Loretta Young in the part of Gaby. Character actors J. Carroll Naish, Gene Lockhart (repeating his screen part), and Isabel Jewell round out the cast of principals.

See 7/7/41 for information on film versions.

375. "The Pied Piper," 12/21/42

Based on the 1942 20th Century–Fox film (screenplay by Nunnally Johnson), in turn based on the novel by Nevil Shute (1942).

Cast: Frank Morgan (Howard), Roddy McDowall (Ronnie), Anne Baxter (Nicole), Ralph Morgan (Major Diessen), Dellie Ellis (Sheila), George Sorrel (Aristide), Eric Snowden (Charendon), Leo Cleary (Officer/Aid), Norman Field (Old Frenchman/Aid), Hal Gerard (Second Voice/Rogguet), Alec Harford (Churchill), Claudine LeDuc (Mme. Bonne), Noreen Gammill (Mme. Picard), Merrill Rodin (Willow), Fleurette Zama (Rose), Maurice Tourzon (Pierre), Mary Raymond (Mrs. Cavanagh), Vernon Steele (Mr. Cavanagh), and Barbara Jean Wong (Anna).

Commercials: Paula Winslowe (Girl after Act 2), Julie Bannon (Sally).

Lux's show of patriotism is again evidenced in "The Pied Piper," a topical drama focusing on a kindly Englishman's task of shepherding six war orphans of various nationalities across enemy lines and eventually to safety in the United States. Frank Morgan essays the Monty Woolley screen role, and Ralph Morgan is heard in the Otto Preminger part, while Roddy McDowall and Anne Baxter reprise their motion picture characterizations. Also from the cast of the Irving Pichel–directed motion picture are child actors Merrill Rodin and Fleurette Zama.

The story aired again on November 6, 1944.

376. "A Star Is Born," 12/28/42

Based on the 1937 David O. Selznick/ United Artists film (screenplay by Dorothy Parker, Alan Campbell, Robert Carson, and John Lee Mahin; original story by William A. Wellman and Robert Carson).

Cast: Judy Garland (Esther Blodgett, aka Vicki Lester), Walter Pidgeon (Norman Maine), Leo Cleary (Oliver Niles), Charles Seel (Libby), Verna Felton (Granny), Arthur Q. Bryan (Moon/Cop), Frances Robinson (Anita), Fred Mac-Kaye (Danny McGuire), Jane Morgan (Aunt Mattie/Central Casting Receptionist), Griff Barnett (Judge), Eddie Marr (Guide/Newsboy), Norman Field (Pop/M.C.), Bruce Payne (Bartender/ Photographer), Graham Denton (Butler/ Schraeger), Arthur Gillmore (Silvers), and Jane Bierce (Maid/Waitress).

Commercials: Paula Winslowe (Girl after Act 1/Girl after Act 2).

Lux's revival of "A Star Is Born" provided Judy Garland with another straight dramatic role, and she succeeds in giving a sincere and sympathetic performance as the wide-eyed, star-struck girl who learns that fame almost always has a price, while Walter Pidgeon is heard as the self-destructive Norman Maine. Interestingly, this broadcast presents Garland's Esther Blodgett 12 years prior to her 1954 musical performance in Warner Bros.' version, and Louis Silvers uses a waltz theme from Max Steiner's excellent film score, but the new script contains almost none of the charm or intelligence of the 1937 screenplay (or the earlier radio adaptation).

See 9/13/37 for information on film versions.

Additional film versions: Warner Bros., 1954; Warner Bros., 1976.

377. "The Bugle Sounds," 1/4/43

Based on the 1941 MGM film (screenplay by Cyril Hume).

Cast: Wallace Beery (Sergeant Hap Doan), Marjorie Rambeau (Suzy), Noah Beery (Colonel Laughton), Leo Cleary (Russell), Fred MacKaye (Dillon), Charles Seel (Leech/Sergeant Lane), Norman Field (Nichols/Officer), Eddie Marr (Private), Griff Barnett (Lieutenant Colonel), Tyler McVey (Rank/ Soldier), Arthur Gillmore (Captain), Bruce Payne (Surgeon/Engineer), Horace Willard (Carteret), Lee Millar, Jr. (Recruit/Adjutant), Joe Latham (Clyde), and Herman Waldeman (Man).

Commercials: Paul Langton (Man), Betty Jean Hainey (Girl), and Dorothy Lovett (Libby).

Lux's first broadcast of 1943 features Wallace Beery in "The Bugle Sounds," which focuses upon an older soldier who resists several technological changes. Also featured in the cast of the *Lux* version are Marjorie Rambeau in Marjorie Main's movie role and Noah Beery in the part Lewis Stone plays onscreen. The movie's romantic subplot (concerning characters played by Donna Reed and William Lundigan) has been eliminated from the broadcast version.

378. "She Knew All the Answers," 1/11/43

Based on the 1941 Columbia film (screenplay by Harry Segall, Kenneth Earl, and Curtis Kenyon; original story by Jane Allen).

Cast: Joan Bennett (Gloria Winters), Preston Foster (Max Willows), Eve Arden (Kitty), Fred MacKaye (Randy), Irvin Lee (Benny), Arthur Q. Bryan (Wharton), Eddie Marr (Messenger/ Goof), Verna Felton (Miss Crouch), Harry Fleischman (Cop/Barker), Leo Cleary (Barber/Barker), Stanley Farrar (Man), Bruce Payne (Waiter), and Abe Reynolds (Shieler).

Commercials: Ann Tobin (Second Woman's Voice), Paula Winslowe (First Woman's Voice), Art Gillmore (Man), and Duane Thompson (Woman).

Lux's adaptation of Columbia's Richard Wallace–directed film *She Knew All the Answers* made for an especially entertaining broadcast. The story is set into motion by a wealthy playboy who intends to wed a chorus girl, but when the executor of his father's estate does not approve of the match (even though he has never met the intended bride), the young lady takes a job in the stuffy executive's office to win him over. The outcome may be predictable, but the play abounds in humorous situations that offer splendid opportunities to Joan Bennett and Eve Arden from the film cast, and Preston Foster in Franchot Tone's screen role.

379. "My Gal Sal," 1/18/43
Based on the 1942 20th Century–Fox film (screenplay by Seton I. Miller, Darrell Ware, and Karl Tunberg), in turn based on the book *My Brother Paul*, by Theodore Dreiser (1942).

Cast: Mary Martin (Sally), Dick Powell (Paul), Charles Seel (Fred), Arthur Q. Bryan (Colonel Truckee/Magistrate), Leo Cleary (Pat), Torey Carleton (May), Paula Winslowe (Countess), Ken Christy (McGuire), Eddie Marr (Driver), Fred MacKaye (Harry/Driver), Harry Fleischman (Man/Policeman), Norman Field (Tailor), Noel Mills (Maid), and Lillian Randolph (Ida).

Singers: Ernest Newton, Henry Kruce, Hobart Ebright, Ray Linn, Robert Stevens, Richard Davis, Dave Knight, Harry Stanton, Allen Watson, and Howard Chandler (Arranger).

Commercials: Ann Tobin (First Girl's Voice), Dorothy Lovett (Libby/Second Girl's Voice), and Paula Winslowe (Third Girl's Voice).

Lux's first musical of the year was 20th Century–Fox's *My Gal Sal*, which was very loosely based on Theodore Dreiser's 1942 biography of his brother, songwriter Paul Dresser (1857–1906).

The Irving Cummings–directed film from the same year stars Rita Hayworth (whose singing was dubbed by Nan Wynn) and Victor Mature, while Lux's adaptation stars Mary Martin and Dick Powell, both of whom give fine performances. Two of the songs written for the film (words by Leo Robin and music by Ralph Rainger) are: "On the Gay White Way" (performed by Mary Martin in Act 1) and "Here You Are" (by Martin and Dick Powell in Act 2), while the Paul Dresser (words and music) numbers used are: "Come Tell Me What's Your Answer, Yes or No" (1898) in Act 1, and "On the Banks of the Wabash, Far Away" (1897; Martin and Chorus) and "My Gal Sal" (1905); Martin and Chrous) in Act 3. ("My Gal Sal" also serves as the musical finale, as sung by Powell and Martin at the conclusion of Act 3.)

380. "This Gun for Hire," 1/25/43
Based on the 1942 Paramount film (screenplay by Albert Maltz and W.R. Burnett), in turn based on the novel by Graham Greene (1936), which was based on the British novel *This Gun for Sale*.

Cast: Joan Blondell (Ellen), Alan Ladd (Raven), Laird Cregar (Gates), Jack LaRue (Michael), Charles Seel (Wilson), Gloria Blondell (Annie), Norman Field (Brewster/Ticketman), Arthur Q. Bryan (Baker/Drew), Jeff Corey (Tommy/Mason), Fred MacKaye (Copy/Newsboy), Vickie Lang (Girl), Paula Winslowe (Pearl/Ruby), Jane Bierce (Girl Operator), Leo Cleary (Fletcher/Second Copy), Boyd Davis (Senator), Earl Keen (Cat/Conductor), and Torey Carleton (Waitress/Secretary).

Commercials: Jane Morgan (Woman's Voice in Act 1), Dorothy Lovett (Woman's Voice in Act 1), Ann Tobin (Woman's Voice in Act 2), and Joe Latham.

Paramount's 1942 film *This Gun for Hire* (directed by Frank Tuttle) seems an unlikely choice for presentation on *Lux,* considering its violent storyline. Nonetheless, the box office success of the picture was not ignored, and the story, with Alan Ladd in his original role of the cold and mechanical paid assassin, became the attraction for the January 25 broadcast. The violence is somewhat toned down for the radio version, and Ladd's character is made more sympathetic (especially in the final act), but the play must have shocked many listeners who were accustomed to *Lux*'s family dramas. Joan Blondell also does a good job in her role as Ellen (the character played by Veronica Lake onscreen), and Laird Cregar repeats his picture part of Gates. Jack LaRue (cast against type) plays Police Detective Michael Crane, but the part is so greatly reduced from the photoplay version (where it is played by Robert Preston) that it amounts to little more than a bit.

James Cagney directed Paramount's 1957 version of *This Gun for Hire,* which is entitled *Short Cut to Hell* and featured Robert Ivers, Georgeann Johnson, Murvyn Vye, and William Bishop.

Additional film version: Paramount, 1957 (*Short Cut to Hell*).

381. "The Show-Off," 2/1/43

Based on the play by George Kelly (1924).

Cast: Harold Peary [the Great Gildersleeve] (Aubrey Piper), Una Merkel (Amy), Beulah Bondi (Mrs. Fisher), Paula Winslowe (Clara), Jeff Corey (Joe), Eddie Marr (Fred), Arthur Q. Bryan (Mr. Fisher), Ken Christy (Williams), Sharon Douglas (Secretary), Norman Field (Miller), Leo Cleary (Frank/Sam), Charles Kane (First Cop), Fred MacKaye (Man/Second Cop).

Commercials: Beverly Brown, Eve Arden (Libby). Preview for *The Maltese Falcon*: Charles Seel (after Act 3).

Lux's February 1, 1943, broadcast once again puts a radio star center stage — on this occasion, Harold Peary, who is better known as the Great Gildersleeve to his Wednesday night listeners. The play selected was George Kelly's 1924 Broadway success *The Show-Off,* which had been presented previously with Joe E. Brown when the series was originating from New York. Because of the similarities between the Great Gildersleeve and interfering braggart Aubrey Piper of "The Show-Off," the play is well suited to the comedian's persona and also includes typical Gildersleeve situations. Rounding out the cast are Una Merkel as Aubrey's sweetheart (later wife), and Beulah Bondi as her mother. In addition to Merkel, the cast includes two players who would become regulars on *The Great Gildersleeve*: Arthur Q. Bryan and Ken Christy.

See 12/9/35 for information on stage and film versions.

Film versions: Paramount, 1926; Paramount, 1929 (*Men Are Like That*); MGM, 1934; MGM, 1946.

382. "The Maltese Falcon," 2/8/43

Based on the 1941 Warner Bros. film (screenplay by John Huston), in turn based on the novel by Dashiell Hammett (1931).

Cast: Edward G. Robinson (Sam Spade), Gail Patrick (Brigid), Laird Cregar (Gutman), Charlie Lung (Cairo), Bea Benaderet (Effie), Eddie Marr (Wilmer), Fred MacKaye (Miles Archer), Warren Ashe (Dundy), Charles Seel (Polhaus), Leo Cleary (Bryan), and Norman Field (Jacoby).

Commercials: Duane Thompson (Second Woman in Act 1/Third Girl in Act 2), Paula Winslowe (Third Woman in Act 1/Girl in Act 2), and Ann Tobin (First Woman in Act 1/Girl in Act 2). *Are Husbands Necessary?* promo: Eddie Marr, Bea Benaderet.

Warner Bros.' 1941 hit *The Maltese Falcon* was directed by John Huston (who also wrote the screenplay) and recounts the tale of a private eye who becomes involved in the search for an elusive and valuable statuette. Humphrey Bogart, who found himself a star after his performance of hard-boiled detective Sam Spade, is not present in *Lux*'s version, which instead uses Edward G. Robinson in the leading role. Robinson takes a different approach to the character, seemingly limiting Spade's sense of humor and making him more businesslike. Filling out the cast are Gail Patrick in Mary Astor's film part, Laird Cregar in Sydney Greenstreet's role, and radio actor Charlie Lung as Peter Lorre's screen character.

Warner Bros. first filmed *The Maltese Falcon* in 1931 under Roy Del Ruth's direction, with the leads going to Ricardo Cortez, Bebe Daniels, and Dudley Digges. The 1936 William Dieterle–directed version bears the title *Satan Met a Lady* and stars Warren William, Bette Davis, and Allison Skipworth (in a female equivalent of the Gutman part).

Additional film versions: Warner Bros., 1931; Warner Bros., 1936 (*Satan Met a Lady*).

383. "Are Husbands Necessary?," 2/15/43

Based on the 1942 Paramount film (screenplay by Tess Slesinger and Frank Davis), in turn based on the novel *Mr. and Mrs. Cugat*, by Isabel Scott Rovick (1937).

Cast: George Burns (Jim Cugat), Gracie Allen (Jane Cugat), Arthur Q. Bryan (Mr. Atterbury), Jack Mather (Chuck), Paula Winslowe (Myra), Ruby Dandridge (Millie), Leo Cleary (Mr. O'Toole), Verna Felton (Orphanage Matron), Griff Barnett (Prosecutor), Norman Field (Judge), and Fred MacKaye (Butler).

Commercials: Duane Thompson (Woman), Dorothy Lovett (Libby).

"Are Husbands Necessary?" brought George Burns and Gracie Allen back to *Lux* for the second time in a light comedy very similar to their first outing in "Dulcy," with Allen once again cast as a wacky wife whose various attempts to help her husband invariably end in disaster.

The 1942 Paramount film featured Ray Milland and Betty Field in the roles Burns and Allen play in the broadcast, and was directed by Norman Taurog.

*384. "This Is the Army," 2/22/43

Based on the 1943 Warner Bros. film (screenplay by Casey Robinson and Captain Claude Binyon), in turn based on the Broadway musical (music and lyrics by Irving Berlin; dialogue by James McColl).

Intermission Guest: Major General Irving J. Phillipson, head of Army Emergency Relief (after Act 2).

Cast: Unbilled Soldiers.

Singers: Ernest Newton, Herbert Wright, George Gramlich, Homer Hall, Hubert Reed, Kenneth Rundquist, Robert Bradford, Stewart Bair, George Nickson, and Enrico Ricardi.

Commercials: Lois Collier, Bea Benaderet, and Paula Winslowe.

This Is the Army, Irving Berlin's patriotic musical salute to the U.S. Army, was produced on stage at the Broadway Theatre on July 4, 1942, with a cast consisting of 350 soldiers. The Warner Bros. screen version, filmed the same year, was directed by Michael Curtiz and featured many of that studio's stars playing alongside the servicemen, as well as Berlin himself, who performed his song "Oh, How I Hate to Get Up in the Morning" (1917; originally *Yip, Yip, Yaphank*). Berlin also appeared in the opening and curtain call of *Lux*'s version and sang two numbers in the dramatic portion of the broadcast (based on the stage production), which also featured a cast of 200 soldiers and a chorus of professional singers. The musical numbers performed (all with words and music by Irving Berlin) were: Act 1: "This Is the Army" (chorus), "I'm Getting Tired" (chorus/octette), "Mandy" (first chorus solo and chorus hum/second chorus ensemble and banjo), "That's What the Well-Dressed Man in Harlem Will Wear" (verse and chorus/second chorus ensemble), "The Army's Made a Man Out of Me" (chorus), "American Eagles" (chorus), "Head in the Clouds" (chorus); Act 2: "I Left My Heart at the Stage Door Canteen" (chorus), "Oh, How I Hate to Get Up in the Morning" (Irving Berlin), "Ve Don't Like It" (Irving Berlin), "This Time" (chorus). (The orchestra from the *This Is the Army* stage show is used instead of the regular *Lux* musical staff, but the program was conducted by Lou Silvers with special arrangements by Rudy Schrager.)

Lux donated $15,000 to the Army Emergency Relief Fund for Berlin's permission to air the play, which was performed in two acts instead of the usual three.

385. "The Lady Is Willing," 3/1/43

Based on the 1942 Columbia film (screenplay by James Edward Grant and Albert McCleery; original story by James Edward Grant).

Cast: Kay Francis (Liza Madden), George Brent (Dr. Corey McBain), Arthur Q. Bryan (Ken), Ann Doran (Buddy), Lillian Randolph (Mary Lou), Leone Ledoux (Baby Corey/Nurse), Verna Felton (Mrs. Cummings), Norman Field (Dr. Golding/Workman), Marla Shelton (Frances), Fred MacKaye (Clerk/Victor), Eddie Marr (Newsboy), Wally Maher (Sergeant Bonds), and Charles Seel (Manager/Doorman).

Commercials: Joan Darrell (Act 1), Dorothy Lovett (Libby), and Paula Winslowe (Act 3). *Reap the Wild Wind* preview (after Act 3): Fred MacKaye (Steve), Jack Mather (Man).

Mitchell Leisen produced and directed Columbia's 1942 comedy *The Lady Is Willing*, which stars Marlene Dietrich and Fred MacMurray. Neither the story, which pertains to an insistent young lady who sets out to marry a pediatrician so that she can adopt the foundling to whom she has become attached, nor the dialogue is as humorous as it tries to be, but it makes a pleasant *Lux* vehicle for Kay Francis and George Brent.

*386. "Reap the Wild Wind," 3/8/43

Based on the 1942 Paramount film (screenplay by Alan LeMay, Charles Bennett, and Jesse Lasky, Jr.), in turn based on the novel by Thelma Strobel (1941).

Cast: Ray Milland (Steve), Paulette Goddard (Loxi), John Carradine (King Cutler), Fred MacKaye (Jack), Norman Field (Philpott), Lois Collier (Drusilla), Jack Mather (Dan), Lillian Randolph (Maum Maria), Stanley Farrar (Captain/First Man), Griff Barnett (Judge), Bruce Payne (Leadsman), Leo Cleary (Lawyer/Devereaux), Graham Denton (Clerk/Pixby), Regina Wallace (Mrs. Claiborne), Art Gillmore (Lookout/Farragut), Charlotte Treadway (Mrs. Mottram), Earl Keen (Dog), and Horace Willard (Salt Meat).

Singers: Robert Stevens, Richard Davis, Dave Knight, Harry Stanton, Albert Bryant, Ernest Newton, Stewart Bair, Charles Schrouder, Allan Watson, and Howard Chandler.

Commercials: Betty Jean Hainey (First Girl), Ann Tobin (Second Girl), Dorothy Lovett (Libby), and Duane Thompson (Woman's Voice).

Cecil B. DeMille had the chance to host an adaptation of his own 1942 Paramount film *Reap the Wild Wind* one year after its theatrical release. The radio version of the period piece, which concerns the recovery of sunken ships in nineteenth-century Key West and the treachery perpetrated by unscrupulous salvagers, features Ray Milland and Paulette Goddard in their original screen parts, while John Carradine and *Lux* regular Fred MacKaye take the roles played by Raymond Massey and John Wayne in the film.

387. "Libel!," 3/15/43
Based on the play by Edward Wooll (1935).
Cast: Ronald Colman (Sir Mark Loddon), Edna Best (Lady Enid Loddon), Otto Kruger (Foxley), Frederic Worlock (Sir Wilfred), Alec Harford (Buckingham), George Sorrel (Flordon), Eric Snowden (Judge), Claire Verdera (Waitress/Woman), Thomas Mills (Butler), Norman Field (Associate), and Fred MacKaye (Number 15).
Commercials: Art Gillmore (Man), Dorothy Lovett (Libby), and Paula Winslowe (Sally). Preview of *Each Dawn I Die*: Fred MacKaye (Frank Ross), Warren Ashe (Stacy).
Lux repeated its adaptation of Edward Wooll's play *Libel!* on March 15, again with Ronald Colman as Sir Mark and Otto Kruger as Foxley; on this occasion, however, it is Edna Best who plays Lady Enid, the part that was given to Frances Robinson in the earlier production.
See 1/13/41 for information on stage and film versions.
Film version: MGM, 1959.

388. "Each Dawn I Die," 3/22/43
Based on the 1939 Warner Bros. film (screenplay by Norman Reilly Raine, Warren Duff, and Charles Perry), in turn based on the novel by Jerome Odlum (1938).
Special Guest: Pierre Aumont (during curtain call).

Cast: George Raft (Stacy), Franchot Tone (Frank Ross), Lynn Bari (Joyce), Fred MacKaye (Red/Clerk), Charles Seel (Man/Mason), Norman Field (Warden), Warren Ashe (Gersky), Griff Barnett (Officer/Second Judge), Tyler McVey (Dale), Graham Denton (Deputy/Shake), Leo Cleary (Pete/Italian), Eddie Marr (Limpy/Bud), Mack Grey (Johnny/Second Convict), Stanley Farrar (Second Guard), Art Gillmore (Grayee/First Convict), Ken Christy (Prison Guard/Lockhart), Dick Ryan (Feather), and Boyd Davis (Judge).
Commercials: Janet Russell (Second Woman in Act 3), Dorothy Lovett (First Woman in Act 3), and Doris Singleton (Libby).
William Keighley was at the directorial helm of Warner Bros.' 1939 prison drama *Each Dawn I Die*, which was adapted for radio for the March 22 broadcast. George Raft of the screen cast is on hand to recreate his role of hardened criminal Stacy, while Franchot Tone is Frank Ross (played by James Cagney in the film), the hapless reporter sent to the "big house" for a crime he did not commit. Though the leading lady role is not a large one (portrayed by Jane Brian on the screen), and is even smaller in the broadcast version, Lynn Bari makes the most of her opportunities.
The 20-second preview of the following week's production is missing from its spot just prior to the curtain call—instead, Pierre Aumont is briefly interviewed, then he performs a scene from *Crossroads* in which he would be featured with Lana Turner in the following week's broadcast.

*389. "Crossroads," 3/29/43
Based on the 1942 MGM film (screenplay by Guy Trosper), in turn based on a story by John Kafka and Howard Emmett Rogers.
Cast: Lana Turner (Lucienne), Pierre

Lynn Bari in "Each Dawn I Die" (March 22, 1943) (photo: Photofest).

Aumont (David), Bradley Page (Sarrou), Paula Winslowe (Michele), Norman Field (Dr. Tessier), Regina Wallace (Madame), Victor Rodman (President), Cliff Clark (Attorney), Leo Cleary (Commissaire/Prosecutor), Charlie Lung (Ledue/Clerk), Fred MacKaye (Reporter/Gendarme), and Ferdinand Munier (Albert).

Commercials: Janet Russell (after Act 1 and Act 2).

Jack Conway's intriguing 1942 MGM motion picture *Crossroads* teamed William Powell and Hedy Lamarr in a drama of an amnesiac diplomat who, because of his condition, becomes involved in illicit activities that threaten his future. *Lux*'s adaptation used MGM players Lana Turner and (Jean) Pierre Aumont in the roles played by Lamarr and Powell in the film.

390. "Road to Morocco," 4/5/43

Based on the 1942 Paramount film (screenplay by Frank Butler and Don Hartman).

Cast: Bing Crosby (Jeff Peters), Bob Hope (Turkey Jackson), Ginny Simms (Princess Shalmar), Denis Green (Mullay Kasim), Janet Waldo (Miramarh), Verna Felton (Aunt Lucy), Ferdinand Munier (Hyder Kahn), Leo Cleary (Servant/Proprietor), Charlie Lung (Idiot/Second Arab), Abe Reynolds (Second Vendor), Fred MacKaye (Man/Customer), Norman Field (Vendor/Slave), Charles Seel (Arab Neb Jolla), Ken Christy (Waiter/Guard), Ann Tobin (Ad Libs/Burton), and Jane Bierce (Ad Libs).

Commercials: Paula Winslowe (Mary), Dorothy Lovett (Janet), Janet Russell (Sally).

The third (of seven) films in the popular Bing Crosby–Bob Hope–Dorothy Lamour "Road" series was *The Road to Morocco*, which tells the tale of two pals who meet with a series of adventures after becoming stranded in exotic Morocco. It is in many ways the most intentionally outrageous picture of the batch. *Lux*'s version of the 1942 Paramount film is, unfortunately, unable to employ many of director David Butler's brilliantly bizarre visual touches, but it makes fairly good use of Frank Butler and Don Hartman's screenplay, and it does feature some amusing segments not included in the motion picture (especially the dialogue exchanges that include DeMille at the beginning of Act 3). The one absent member of the film's trio is Dorothy Lamour, whose part is taken in the microphone adaptation by Ginny Simms. The songs from the film score (words by Johnny Burke, music by Jimmy Van Heusen) heard in the

broadcast are: "The Road to Morocco" (Bing Crosby and Bob Hope) in Act 1, and "Constantly" (Ginny Simms) and "Moonlight Becomes You" (Crosby) in Act 2.

391. "Once Upon a Honeymoon," 4/12/43

Based on the 1942 RKO film (screenplay by Sheridan Gibney; original story by Leo McCarey).

Cast: Claudette Colbert (Katie), Brian Aherne (Pat O'Toole), Laird Cregar (Baron von Luher), Albert Dekker (LeBlanc), Charles Seel (Cumberland/Second Nazi), Bea Benaderet (Anna), Fred MacKaye (Cable/Attaché), Regina Wallace (Elsa), Leo Cleary (Announcer/Manager), Denis Green (Radio/First Nazi), Norman Field (Fitter/Official), Stanley Farrar (First Voice/Steward), Griff Barnett (Second Voice/Captain), Cliff Clark (Man/Waiter), Art Gillmore (Attaché/Aide), Ken Christy (Waiter/Taxi), and Barbara Jean Wong (Child Crying).

Commercials: Jane Bierce (Second Girl), Paula Winslowe (Woman), Janet Russell (Sally), and Duane Thompson (Second Girl). *A Night to Remember* preview: Hal Gerard (after Act 3).

Another story of topical interest was "Once Upon a Honeymoon," which was presented by *Lux* on April 12 and concerns a woman who discovers that her new husband is a Nazi official. The 1942 RKO film was directed by Leo McCarey and features Ginger Rogers and Cary Grant in the leading roles, while *Lux*'s intriguing adaptation stars Claudette Colbert and Brian Aherne, with Laird Cregar in Walter Slezak's picture part and Albert Dekker repeating his screen characterization.

392. "A Night to Remember," 4/19/43

Based on the 1943 Columbia film

(screenplay by Robert Flournoy and Jack Henley; original story by Kelly Roos).

Cast: Ann Sothern (Nancy Troy), Robert Young (Jeff Troy), Bradley Page (Turner), Regina Wallace (Mrs. Slater), Lynn Whitney (Polly), Wally Maher (Hanken), Jane Bierce (Ann), Eddie Marr (Bolling), Norman Field (Lingle), Charlotte Treadway (Woman), Frank Penny (Driver/Man), Ken Christy (Kaufman), Fred MacKaye (Scott), Leo Cleary (Waiter/Cop Number Two), Charles Seel (Cop Number One), and Warren Ashe (Murphy).

Commercials: Mel Blanc (Stork), Janet Russell (Sally). *The Lady Has Plans* preview: Fred MacKaye (Ken) (after Act 3).

Columbia's comedy-mystery *A Night to Remember* (which was directed by Richard Wallace) was the play for *Lux*'s April 19 broadcast. This frivolous tale of a young detective–story writer and his energetic wife who move into a Greenwich Village apartment and immediately become entangled in a real murder case stars Ann Sothern and Robert Young in the roles created by Loretta Young and Brian Aherne.

393. "The Lady Has Plans," 4/26/43

Based on the 1942 Paramount film (screenplay by Harry Tugend; original story by Leo Birinski).

Special Guest: Cary Grant (during curtain call).

Cast: Rita Hayworth (Sydney Royce), William Powell (Ken Harper), Neil Madison (Baron), Lynn Whitney (Margot), Fred MacKaye (Announcer/Frank), Denis Green (Ronnie), Charles Seel (Baker), Norman Field (Spencer/Man), George Sorel (Clerk/Aid), Irene Martin (Secretary), Stanley Farrar (Steward/Waiter), Leo Cleary (Driver/Miles), Howard McNear (London/Michael), Julia Warren (Operator), and Bradley Page (Weston/Man Number Two).

Commercials: Paula Winslowe (Mrs. Howard), Art Gillmore (Mr. Howard), and Janet Russell (Sally).

Paramount's *The Lady Has Plans*, which was directed by Sidney Lanfield and released in 1942, is a comedy concerning a female reporter who is mistaken for a Nazi spy. The adaptation comes off well in the hands of *Lux*'s skilled production team, with capable assistance supplied by the excellent performances of Rita Hayworth and William Powell (playing characters created on the screen by Paulette Goddard and Ray Milland).

During the curtain call, special guest Cary Grant makes a speech on behalf of the Second War Loan Drive.

394. "The Navy Comes Through," 5/3/43

Based on the 1942 RKO film (screenplay by Ray Chanslor and Aeneas MacKensie; original story by Borden Chase; adaptation by Earl Baldwin and John Twist).

Special Guest: Frances Rich of the Waves (during curtain call).

Cast: Pat O'Brien (Mallory), George Murphy (Tom), Ruth Hussey (Myra), George Sorel (Croner), Eddie Marr (Sampter), Edwin Mills (Dutson), Warren Ashe (Barringer/Lookout), Griff Barnett (Man Number Two/Judge), Charles Seel (Man/Surgeon), Harry Fleischman (Mate/C.P.O.), Fred MacKaye (Bayliss/Seaman), Noel Madison (Radio/Third Captain), Norman Field (President/Second Man/German), and Leo Cleary (German/Captain).

Commercials: Lynn Martin (Girl), Doris Singleton (Libby).

Warner Bros.' *The Navy Comes Through* (an Edward Sutherland–directed 1942 release) surfaced on *Lux* for the first time on May 3. This modest tribute to the dedication and courage of the U.S. naval forces stars Pat O'Brien and George Murphy of the picture cast and Ruth Hussey in the Ruth Warrick film role. (Hussey stepped in at the last minute to replace Joan Bennett, whose home had burned down the night before the broadcast.)

Frances Rich (daughter of actress Irene Rich) appears during the curtain call to discuss the Waves, a branch of the U.S. service of which she is a member.

Lux presented a second rendering of "The Navy Comes Through" on November 29, 1943.

395. "Now, Voyager," 5/10/43

Based on the 1942 Warner Bros. film (screenplay by Casey Robinson), in turn based on the novel by Olive Higgins Prouty (1941).

Cast: Ida Lupino (Charlotte Vale), Paul Henreid (Jerry Durrence), Dame May Whitty (Mrs. Vale), Albert Dekker (Dr. Jacquith), Mary Lou Harrington (Tina), Fred MacKaye (Elliot Livingstone), Duane Thompson (Miss Trusk/Hilda), Ann Doran (Dora), Claudia Dell (Lisa), Charles Seel (George/Announcer), Stanley Farrar (Mack/Conductor), and June Duprez (Deb).

Commercials: Doris Singleton (Libby), Paula Winslowe (Woman), and Regina Wallace (Woman).

Irving Rapper directed Warner Bros.' 1942 film *Now, Voyager*, the story of an "ugly duckling" long under the thumb of her domineering mother, who escapes to a new life with the assistance of an understanding psychiatrist. Ida Lupino capably plays the role closely associated with Bette Davis (who plays the part in the motion picture as well as in the subsequent *Lux* broadcast) in *Lux*'s effectively concise first rendering, and Paul Henreid resumes his original screen role. Dame May Whitty is heard as Gladys George's movie character, and Albert Dekker takes Claude Rains's screen part.

Lux's second version was aired on February 11, 1946, and the *Lux Video Theatre* presented it on October 4, 1956.

396. "The Talk of the Town," 5/17/43

Based on the 1942 Columbia film (screenplay by Irwin Shaw and Sidney Buchman; adaptation by Dale Van Every; original story by Sidney Harmon).

Cast: Cary Grant (Leopold Dilg), Jean Arthur (Nora Shelby), Ronald Colman (Michael Lightcap), Lynn Whitney (Regina Bush/First Girl), Leo Cleary (Sam Yates), Ken Christy (Judge Grunstadt), Norman Field (Boyd), Horace Willard (Tilsey), Charles Calvert (Second Man/Jake), Robert Harris (Pulaski/D.A.), Warren Ashe (Cop/Bradken), Charles Seel (Cop/Holmes), Fred MacKaye (First Man/Cop), Stanley Farrar (Guy/Officer), and Julia Warren (Second Girl).

Commercials: Lynn Martin (Girl), Doris Singleton (Woman), and Janet Russell (Sally).

The 1942 George Stevens Columbia film *The Talk of the Town* provides interesting roles for its three stars, Cary Grant, Jean Arthur, and Ronald Colman, all of whom reprise their parts for *Lux*'s radio rendering. The comedy-drama focuses on a politically outspoken industrial worker who escapes from prison to avoid being convicted of a crime of which he is innocent, and the spunky schoolteacher and conservative judge (her tenant) with whom he takes refuge. The characters complement each other nicely, and the broadcast adds an extra element by allowing each of the three to serve as first person narrator for one act. The microphone adaptation does alter the emphasis somewhat, with more comedy and less social commentary than the film, which is a decided plus, as the obnoxious radicalism of the Cary Grant screen character is mercifully toned down.

397. "Hitler's Children," 5/24/43

Based on the 1943 RKO film (screenplay by Emmett Lavery), in turn based on the book *Education for Death*, by Gregor Ziemer (1941).

Cast: Bonita Granville (Anna Müller), Otto Kruger (Colonel Henkel), Kent Smith (Professor Nichols), Walter Reed (Karl Bruner), Norman Field (the Bishop), Robert Harris (Dr. Graf/Judge), Verna Felton (Matron Naber), Leo Cleary (Schmidt/Lieutenant), Claudia Dell (Matron), Charles Seel (Sergeant), Griff Barnett (Mr. Müller/Major), Dix Davis (Boy), Regina Wallace (Mrs. Müller), Fred MacKaye (Commentator), Cliff Clark (Franz), Carla Boehm (Mrs. Lenner), and Paul Hilton (Hans).

Singers: Eugene Forsyth, Joe Pennario, Peter Rankin, Paul Hilton, Tommy Lane, Dickie Meyers, Billy Roy, Souyler Standish, and Frank Coghlan, Jr.

Commercials: Janet Russell (Sally), Doris Singleton (Woman's Voice).

Hitler's Children, RKO's hit of 1943 (which was directed by Edward Dmytryk), gave the *Lux* audience a war drama that focuses primarily on the alleged activities of the Hitler Youth. Bonita Granville, Otto Kruger, and Kent Smith all repeat the parts they play on the screen, and another RKO actor, Walter Reed, is heard in the role Tim Holt undertakes in the motion picture. Carla Boehm, who plays Magda in the film, is given the part of Mrs. Lenner in *Lux*'s radio adaptation.

398. "The Major and the Minor," 5/31/43

Based on the 1942 Paramount film (screenplay by Charles Brackett and Billy Wilder), in turn based on the play *Connie Goes Home* (1923) by Edward Childs Carpenter, from the story "Sunny Goes Home" by Fannie Kilburn.

Cast: Ginger Rogers (Susan Applegate), Ray Milland (Major Philip Kirby), Mrs. Leila Rogers (Mrs. Applegate), Paula Winslowe (Pamela), Joan Lorring (Lucy), Arthur Q. Bryan (Mr. Osborne), Peter Rankin (Cadet Wigton), Billy Roy (Cadet Osborne), Frank Coghlan, Jr. (Cadet Moore), Ken Christy (Voice/Conductor Number Two), Fred Mac-Kaye (Ticket Agent), Norman Field (Ticker/the Reverend Doyle), Charlotte Treadway (Mrs. Osborne/Woman), Harry Worth (Announcer/Conductor), and Boyd Davis (Colonel/Ticker).

Commercials: Doris Singleton (Libby), Janet Russell (Sally), and Leone Ledoux (Little Voice).

Billy Wilder's 1943 Paramount comedy *The Major and the Minor* concerns the complications that follow a grown woman's attempt to travel home by train at half fare by posing as an 11-year-old; *Lux*'s broadcast of May 31 reunites three members of the movie cast: Ginger Rogers, Ray Milland, and Mrs. Leila Rogers, who is the former's real-life mother. (Joan Lorring, who plays Lucy in this broadcast, appeared in additional *Luxes* under the name Dellie Ellis.)

399. "My Friend Flicka," 6/7/43

Based on the 1943 20th Century–Fox film (screenplay by Lillie Hayward), in turn based on the novel by Mary O'Hara.

Special Guest: Robert Taylor (during the curtain call).

Cast: Roddy McDowall (Ken), George Brent (Bob), Rita Johnson (Nell), Leo Cleary (Gus), Mary Lou Harrington (Hildy), Fred MacKaye (Tim), Norman Field (Mr. Sargeant), Charles Seel (Doctor), and Earl Keen (Horse Whinny).

Commercials: Janet Russell (Sally), Doris Singleton (Woman). Sound effects assistant: Barbara Sport.

Harold Schuster was the director of *My Friend Flicka*, the fondly remembered 1943 20th Century–Fox tale of a boy's unwavering love for his horse. The *Lux* production features young Roddy McDowall of the screen version, George Brent in Preston Foster's movie role, and Rita Johnson reprising her film part. Missing, of course, is the title character, but *Lux*'s skilled production artists make Flicka's presence very definitely felt and complement the fine performances of the three stars.

Special guest Robert Taylor announces next week's program and informs the listeners that he will begin his service in the Navy Air Corps upon completion of his current motion picture, *Bataan*.

400. "The Philadelphia Story," 6/14/43
Based on the 1940 MGM film (screenplay by Donald Ogden Stewart), in turn based on the play by Philip Barry (1939).
Cast: Robert Taylor (C.K. Dexter Haven), Loretta Young (Tracy Lord), Robert Young (Mike), Roland Drew (George), Mary Lou Harrington (Dinah), Regina Wallace (Margaret), Vicki Lang (Elizabeth), Norman Field (Seth), Verna Felton (Librarian), Fred MacKaye (Mack/Gentleman), Marla Shelton (Secretary), Leo Cleary (Kidd), and Thomas Mills (Edward [the Butler]).
Commercials: Doris Singleton (Second Girl), Paula Winslowe (Girl), Stanley Farrar (Bus Driver), and Art Gillmore (Man).
The first broadcast of "The Philadelphia Story" in *Lux*'s regular series (it had been performed on the special *Victory Theatre* show the season before) aired on June 14 and offered Robert Taylor (heard to excellent advantage as C.K. Dexter Haven), Loretta Young (nicely playing the role of Tracy), and Robert Young (as cynical reporter Mike) the roles created onscreen by Cary Grant, Katharine Hepburn, and James Stewart.

See the *Victory Theatre* broadcast of 7/20/42 for information concerning film and stage versions.

401. "In Which We Serve," 6/21/43
Based on the 1943 Two Cities/United Artists film (screenplay by Noël Coward).
Cast: Ronald Colman (Captain Kinross), Edna Best (Ellen), Pat O'Malley (Walter Hardy), Charlie Lung (Shorty), Claire Verdera (Cath), Gloria Gordon (Mrs. Leeman), Esta Mason (Frieda), Frederic Worlock (Cox'n Number One), Denis Green (Flags), Eric Snowden (Guns), Robert Regent (Stoker), Norbert Mueller (Bobby), Mary Lou Harrington (Lavinia), Fred MacKaye (Lookout/First Announcer), Vernon Steele (Mr. Sawyer/Second Announcer), Alec Harford (Edgecomb), Douglas Grant (Sailor/Reynolds), Anthony Marsh (Coombe/Spencer), Roland Drew (Parkinson/Sailor), Virginia Gordon (Emily), and Raymond Lawrence (Hollett/Man).
Singers: Kenneth Rundquist, Robert Bradford, Homer Hall, Luke Crockett, Paul Keast, Austin Grout, Charles Schrouder, Stewart Bair, Delos Jewkes, and Enrico Ricardi.
Commercials: Doris Singleton (Girl in Act 1/2), Paula Winslowe (Mary/First Woman in Act 2), and Art Gillmore (Man).
Noël Coward wrote, starred in, codirected, and even composed the musical score for the 1943 British production *In Which We Serve*, which was released in the United States by United Artists. The war drama focuses upon the crew of a torpedoed battleship, who, while adrift in a lifeboat, reflect on their relationships with those they left behind. Ronald Colman is a fine choice for the Noël Coward role of the ship's commander, and Edna Best is heard in the Celia Johnson movie part as his wife.

402. "The Great Man's Lady," 6/28/43

Based on the 1942 Paramount film (screenplay by W.L. Rivers), in turn based on an original story by Adela Rogers St. John and Seena Owen, which was based on the story "The Human Side," by Viña Delmar.

Cast: Barbara Stanwyck (Hanna Sempler Hoyt), Joseph Cotten (Ethan Hoyt), Chester Morris (Steely), Fay McKenzie (Girl), Norman Field (Mr. Sempler), Katherine Siley (Woman), Roland Drew (Cadwallader/Second Passenger), Ruby Dandridge (Delilah), Charles Calvert (Assayer/Man), Ernestine Wade (Jerry), Charles Seel (Pierce/Hardy), Fred MacKaye (Quentin/Passenger), Robert McKenzie (Parson/Driver), Leone Ledoux (Baby Ethan), Leo Cleary (Reporter/Frisbee), and Duane Thompson (Bettina).

Singers: Ernest Newton, Henry Kruse, Robert Bradford, Kenneth Rundquist, Stewart Bair, Delos Jewkes, Luke Crockett, Homer Hall, Devona Doxie, Georgia Stark, Virginia Rees, and Elva Lois Kellogg.

Commercials: Doris Singleton (Libby), Paula Winslowe (Mary), Janet Russell (Sally), and Duane Thompson (Woman).

Paramount's 1942 William Wellman–directed drama *The Great Man's Lady* is a story told in flashback by a 109-year-old woman of her life-long devotion to an irresponsible dreamer who rose to become an admired public figure. *Lux*'s adaptation features Barbara Stanwyck of the film cast, Joseph Cotten in the role played by Joel McCrea onscreen, and Chester Morris in Brian Donlevy's motion picture part.

403. "My Sister Eileen," 7/5/43

Based on the 1942 Columbia film (screenplay by Joseph Fields and Jerome Chodorov), in turn based on the play by Joseph Fields and Jerome Chodorov (1940), which is based on the short stories by Ruth McKennie (first published in book form as *My Sister Eileen* in 1941).

Cast: Rosalind Russell (Ruth), Brian Aherne (Robert Baker), Janet Blair (Eileen), Akim Tamiroff (Mr. Appopolous), Roland Drew (Wreck), Ben Alexander (Frank/Second Cadet), Wally Maher (Chick), Jeff Donnell (Helen), Leo Cleary (Craven), Cliff Clark (Cop), Ken Christy (Second Man/Guy), Norman Field (Driver/Sherwood), Verna Felton (Grandma), Fred MacKaye (Man/First Cadet), Louise Arthur (Operator), and Vicki Lang (Receptionist).

Commercials: Janet Russell (Sally), Doris Singleton (Libby).

Columbia's 1942 Alexander Hall–directed hit *My Sister Eileen* was based on the equally successful Broadway play by Joseph A. Fields and Jerome Chodorov (from Ruth McKennie's series of short stories), and stars Rosalind Russell, Brian Aherne, Janet Blair, and George Tobias. *Lux*'s version features three of the film's stars (Akim Tamiroff is heard in Tobias's film part) in an amusing adaptation of the comedy concerning a pair of small town girls hoping to "make good" in the imposing city of New York.

Richard Quine directed a musical version for Columbia in 1955 featuring Betty Garrett, Jack Lemmon, and Janet Leigh.

Additional film version: Columbia, 1955.

404. "Air Force," 7/12/43

Based on the 1943 Warner Bros. film (screenplay by Dudley Nichols and William Faulkner).

Special Guest: Mary Pickford (during curtain call).

Cast: George Raft (Winucki), Harry Carey (Sergeant White), Fred MacKaye (Quincannon), Eddie Marr (Weinberg), Art Gillmore (Williams), Stanley

Farrar (Peterson), Cliff Clark (C.O./ Officer), Leo Cleary (Major Daniels/ Roberts), Vicki Lang (Mary), Mel Blanc (Radio/Major Begley), Charles Calvert (Major Mallory), Duane Thompson (Nurse), Charles Seel (Colonel/Doctor), Louise Arthur (Nurse), Wally Maher (Sergeant/First Marine), Earl Keen (Dog), William Sloan (Moran/ Radio 2), Peter Chong (Jap), Howard McNear (House/Control), Bobby Larson (Kid), Herb Vigran (Callohan/Corporal), Mack Grey (Second Marine), and Bob Haynes (Chester).

Commercials: Doris Singleton (Libby), Janet Russell (Sally).

Lux's 1942-43 season ends with another patriotic story of the American military, "Air Force," which tells of the adventures of the crew of a B-17 just after the bombing of Pearl Harbor on December 7, 1941. The broadcast features George Raft in the role taken by John Garfield in the 1943 Howard Hawks–directed Warner Bros. film, while Harry Carey reprises his original screen part. Special guest Mary Pickford makes an appearance during the curtain call to present DeMille with an award.

Ninth Season
(September 13, 1943–July 3, 1944)

Columbia Broadcasting System, Monday, 9:00–10:00 P.M. *Host*: Cecil B. DeMille. *Announcer*: John Milton Kennedy. *Director*: Sanford Barnett (September 13, 1943–December 27, 1943); Fred MacKaye (January 3, 1944–July 3, 1944). *Musical Director*: Lou Silvers. *Adaptations*: George Wells (September 13, 1943–December 27, 1943); Sanford Barnett (January 3, 1944–July 3, 1944). *Sound Effects*: Charlie Forsyth.

405. "The Phantom of the Opera," 9/13/43

Based on the 1943 Universal film (screenplay by Eric Taylor and Samuel Hoffenstein; adaptation by John Jacoby), in turn based on the novel by Gaston Leroux (1910).

Cast: Nelson Eddy (Anatole), Susanna Foster (Christine), Basil Rathbone (Claudin), Edgar Barrier (Raoul), Bea Benaderet (Biancarolli), Robert Harris (Villeneuve), Norman Field (Lizst/Old Man), Regina Wallace (Aunt/ Woman), Fred MacKaye (Singer/Manager), Helga Moray (Maid), Leo Cleary (Playle), George Sorel (Perretti/Old Man), and Marla Shelton (Georgette).

Chorus: Elva Kellogg, Marshall Sohl, Alexander Hammond, Louis Yaekel, Saul Silverman, Austin Grout, Paul Keast, Freeman High, Robert Franklin, Wynne Hammond, Zaruhi Elmassian, Mary Berman, Georgia Stark, Devona Doxie, and Enrico Ricardi.

Commercials: Doris Singleton (Libby), Sharon Douglas (Girl's Voice).

Lux's ninth season opened not with "Random Harvest," as Cecil B. DeMille had announced on July 12, but with something quite different—an adaptation of Universal's hit *The Phantom of the Opera*. Starring in the broadcast (as in the 1943 motion picture) are Nelson Eddy and Susanna Foster, a splendid actress whose beautiful voice is put to excellent use in this show, while Basil Rathbone (suffering from a case of laryngitis) is heard as the title character (played by Claude Rains onscreen). *Lux*'s presentation actually precedes the film's release, as the Arthur Lubin–directed production was slated to open in New York on October 14 (as is announced by John M. Kennedy). As is a common practice in many motion pictures with an operatic setting, most of the opera selections heard are not from real operas but are arias using well-known instrumental selections and specially constructed lyrics. The musical numbers heard in the *Lux* version are: Act 1: drinking song from Flotow's *Martha* (partial; sung in French by Nelson Eddy); and "Lullaby of the Bells" (Susanna Foster), which was written especially for the film; Act 2: "Operatic Scene," from the opera *Le Prince Masque de la Caucausie* (based on themes from Tchaikovsky's Symphony No. 4 in F Minor [arranged by Edward Ward; words by George Waggner]).

The first *Phantom of the Opera* to reach the screen was Universal's 1925 Rupert Julian–directed production starring Norman Kerry, Mary Philbin, and Lon Chaney. A 1962 British rendering (shot by Hammer and released by Universal-International) featured Thorley Walters, Heather Sears, and Herbert Lom, under Terrance Fisher's direction. Brian DePalma's 1974 musical effort, *Phantom of the Paradise*, had Paul Williams, Jessica Harper, and William Finley in the leads.

Additional film versions: Universal, 1925; Hammer/U-I, 1962; Harbor/Fox, 1974 (*Phantom of the Paradise*).

406. "Flight for Freedom," 9/20/43
· Based on the 1943 RKO film (screenplay by Oliver H.P. Garrett and S.K. Lauren; adaptation by Jane Murfin; original story by Horace McCoy).

Cast: Rosalind Russell (Tonie Carter), George Brent (Randy Britton), Chester Morris (Paul), Marek Wyndheim (Johnny), Charles Calvert (Waiter/Admiral), Charlie Lung (Clerk/Yokohata), Fred MacKaye (Sturges/Second Voice), Norman Field (Official/Connors), Truda Marson (Waitress/Operator), Charles Seel (Mechanic), Eddie Marr (Mac), Herb Vigran (Mike/Announcer), Robert Harris (Official/First Voice), and Howard McNear (Voice/ Man).
Commercial: Janet Russell.

Flight for Freedom, the 1943 Lothar Mendes–directed RKO aviation drama inspired by Amelia Earhart, popped up on *Lux* for the September 20 broadcast. Starring in the radio rendering (as she does in the film) is Rosalind Russell, while the parts which are played in the picture by Fred MacMurray and Herbert Marshall are taken here by George Brent and Chester Morris. Charlie Lung, who plays Yokohata, is also from the motion picture cast.

407. "Ladies in Retirement," 9/27/43
Based on the 1941 Columbia film (screenplay by Reginald Denham and Garrett Fort); play by Edward Percy and Reginald Denham (1939).
Cast: Ida Lupino (Ellen), Brian Aherne (Albert), Dame May Whitty (Miss Fisk), Edith Barrett (Louisa), Bea Benaderet (Emily), Truda Marson (Lucy), Gloria Gordon (Sister Theresa), Claire Verdera (Sister Agatha), and Eric Snowden (Bates).
Commercial: Betty Moran (Girl), Fred MacKaye (First Man), and Stanley Farrar (Second Man).

Columbia's intriguing 1941 Charles Vidor–directed crime drama, *Ladies in Retirement* reached *Lux* two years later as an equally fascinating broadcast in which a desperate woman struggles to suppress a startling secret from the world. Ida Lupino, Dame May Whitty, and Edith Barrett recreate their original roles, while Brian Aherne is heard in Louis Hayward's film part.

The *Lux Video Theatre* presented a version on December 9, 1954.

408. "The Pride of the Yankees," 10/4/43

Based on the 1942 RKO film (screenplay by Jo Swerling and Herman J. Mankiewicz; original story by Paul Gallico).

Cast: Gary Cooper (Lou Gehrig), Virginia Bruce (Eleanor), Edgar Buchanan (Sam Blake), Elsa Janssen (Mom), Griff Barnett (Pop), Hugh Kloss (Lou, as a Boy/First Paperboy), Ken Christy (Policeman/Man), Robert Harris (Doctor/Umpire), Bobby Larson (Billy, as a Kid), Joe Pennario (Joe), Eugene Forsyth (Billy, as an Adult/Second Boy), Stanley Farrar (Conductor/Second Ball Player), Boyd Davis (Mr. Twitchall), Norman Field (Third Man/Doctor), Eddie Marr (Vendor/Photographer), Leo Cleary (Announcer/Huggins), Charles Seel (Coach/Man), Florence Shirley (Nurse/Woman), Fred MacKaye (First Ball Player/Second Man), Charlotte Treadway (Mrs. Fabins), Verna Felton (Mrs. Roberts/Housekeeper), and Dick Ryan (Conductor/Salesman).

Commercials: Bob Haynes (Young Man), Stanley Farrar (First Man), Fred MacKaye (Second Man), Ann Tobin (Girl), and Doris Singleton (Libby).

Samuel Goldwyn's *The Pride of the Yankees* (directed by Sam Wood), the movie biography of baseball great Lou Gehrig (1903–41), reached the screen in 1942 and became one of the most popular attractions of the season. The movie includes a number of well-staged action sequences on the diamond, but the broadcast focuses on dramatic portions. Although some of Gehrig's teammates are important characters in the film (notably Babe Ruth, who plays himself), none are included in *Lux*'s

version (though a few are mentioned in passing). Gary Cooper brings his movie characterization of Lou Gehrig to the *Lux* microphone. Virginia Bruce and Edgar Buchanan are heard in parts taken by Teresa Wright and Walter Brennan in the motion picture.

409. "Heaven Can Wait," 10/11/43

Based on the 1943 20th Century–Fox film (screenplay by Samson Raphaelson), in turn based on the play *Birthday*, by Ladislaus Bus-Fekete.

Cast: Don Ameche (Henry Van Cleve), Maureen O'Hara (Martha), Cliff Clark (Grandfather), Arthur Q. Bryan (His Excellency), Anne O'Neal (Henry's Mother), Roland Drew (Albert), Verna Felton (Mrs. Strabel), Leo Cleary (Mr. Strabel), Robert Harris (Randolph/Butler), Fred MacKaye (Man/Jack), Regina Wallace (Grandmother/Woman), Dorothy Scott (Miss Chivers), Mary Lou Harrington (Child), Dix Davis (Henry, as a Child), Norman Field (Flogdell), Tommy Cook (Jackie, as a Child), Horace Willard (Jasper/Elevator Boy), Paula Winslowe (Peggy), and Alice Mosk (Soloist).

Commercials: Janet Russell (Sally), Bob Haynes (Man), Duane Thompson (First Woman), and Charlotte Treadway (Second Woman).

Lux's version of 20th Century–Fox's *Heaven Can Wait* retold the fantasy of an amiable rake who recounts his life story to the Devil as he waits to have judgment passed on him. Don Ameche re-enacts his part from the Ernst Lubitsch picture, and Maureen O'Hara plays the Gene Tierney role (taking over for Joan Leslie) in *Lux*'s production, which is pleasantly entertaining even if it does not succeed in fully capturing the motion picture's charm.

410. "Mr. Lucky," 10/18/43

Based on the 1943 RKO film (screenplay by Milton Holmes and Adrian

Scott), in turn based on Holmes's novel *Bundles for Freedom*.

Cast: Cary Grant (Joe), Laraine Day (Dorothy), Arthur Hohl (Swede), Verna Felton (Veronica), Eddie Marr (Crank), Ed Emerson (Zepp), Griff Barnett (Priest/Watchman), Arthur Q. Bryan (McDougall), Ken Christy (First Detective), Charles Seel (Second Watchman), Fred MacKaye (Chauffeur/Gaffer), Dorothy Scott (Mrs. Van Every/Woman), Norman Field (Bryant), Catherine Craig (Woman/Nurse), and Boyd Davis (Foster).

Commercials: Janet Russell (Sally), Paula Winslowe (Woman).

The 1943 H.C. Potter–directed RKO comedy-drama *Mr. Lucky* made its way to *Lux* with Cary Grant and Laraine Day resuming their original picture roles. Arthur Hohl (in a rare sympathetic role) appears in Charles Bickford's film part of Swede, who narrates the story of a debonair chiseler who falls in love with an intended victim.

411. "Slightly Dangerous," 10/25/43
Based on the 1943 MGM film (screenplay by Charles Lederer and George Oppenheimer; original story by Ian M. Hunter and Aileen Hamilton).

Cast: Lana Turner (Peggy), Victor Mature (Bob), Gene Lockhart (Burden), Verna Felton (Ba-Ba/Lady), Leo Cleary (Durstin), Florence Halop (Mitzi), Roland Drew (Quill), Walter Soderling (Snodgrass/Proprietor), Robert Harris (Gravet/Stanhope), Ed Emerson (First Paperboy/First Detective), Mason Holtzner (Waiter/Second Man), Griff Barnett (Painter/Hiller), Fred Mac-Kaye (Second Paperboy/Second Detective), Charles Seel (Baldwin), Eddie Marr (Jimmy), Norman Field (Doctor), and Truda Marson (Secretary).

Commercials: Paula Winslowe (Daisy), Betty Moran (Dot), Bob Haynes (Man's Voice, Act 1), Stanley Farrar (Man, Act 3/Elevator Man in Act 1), Norman Field (Man Number Two in Act 1), Charlotte Treadway (Older Woman in Act 1), Fred MacKaye (Man Number Two in Act 3/Bill), Duane Thompson (Mary), and Doris Singleton (Libby).

"Slightly Dangerous," *Lux*'s offering for October 25, brought the popular Lana Turner back to the microphone in the role she created for MGM's 1943 Wesley Ruggles–directed comedy of a young lady who pretends to be the long-lost daughter of a millionaire to gain the inheritance. Originally scheduled to take the leading man's part in the broadcast was Robert Cummings, but in his unexplained absence, Victor Mature (on leave from the Navy) is heard in Robert Young's movie role, while Gene Lockhart plays Walter Brennan's screen part of Mr. Burden.

412. "So Proudly We Hail," 11/1/43
Based on the 1943 Paramount film (screenplay by Allan Scott).

Cast: Claudette Colbert (Janet), Paulette Goddard (Joan), Veronica Lake (Olivia), Sonny Tufts (Kansas), Les Tremayne (John), Fred MacKaye (Captain O'Brien), Norman Field (Dr. Harrison), Regina Wallace (MacGregor), Catherine Craig (Sadie/Betty), Truda Marson (Toni), Dorothy Scott (Irma), Marjorie Davies (Rosemary), Leo Cleary (Colonel Clark/Voice), Boyd Davis (Colonel Mason), Charles Seel (Colonel White), Howard McNear (Soldier/Doctor), and Ed Emerson (Officer/Soldier).

Commercials: Paula Winslowe (First Girl, Act 1), Duane Thompson (Second Girl, Act 1), and Doris Singleton (Libby).

Paramount's tribute to the feminine side of American forces overseas, *So Proudly We Hail*, was presented on *Lux* on November 1. The picture, produced and directed by Mark Sandrich, stars Claudette Colbert, Paulette Goddard,

Veronica Lake, and Sonny Tufts, all of whom repeat their roles in the radio version. The large supporting cast is headed by Les Tremayne in George Reeves's film part.

413. "Salute to the Marines," 11/8/43
Based on the 1943 MGM film (screenplay by Wells Root and George Bruce; story by Robert Andrews).

Cast: Wallace Beery (Bill Baily), Fay Bainter (Jennie), Noah Beery (Colonel), Keye Luke (Flashy), Louise Arthur (Helen), Alex Havier (Native), Charlie Lung (Mr. Agnew/Karitu), Robert Harris (Third Voice/Casper), Paula Winslowe (Mrs. Carson/Woman), Tommy Cook (Frankie), Dix Davis (Jimmy), Fred MacKaye (Lieutenant James), Charles Seel (Second Voice/Preacher), Stanley Farrar (Hanks/Goldberg), Jack Mather (M.P./Adjutant), Ed Emerson (Corporal), Howard McNear (Orderly/Anderson), Roland Drew (Adjutant/Sanders), Griff Barnett (Craig), Tyler McVey (Seaman), and Eddie Marr (Mosely).

Singers: Stewart Bair, Devona Doxie, Zaruhi Elmassion, George Gramlich, Homer Hall, Frank Holiday, Sidney Pepple, Betty Rome, Kenneth Rundquist, Allan Watson, Dorothy Whitson, Jan Williams, and Enrico Ricardi (Chorus Master).

Commercials: Sharon Douglas (Girl's Voice), Doris Singleton (Libby).

S. Sylvan Simon's 1943 MGM war drama *Salute to the Marines* makes for an equally patriotic, inspiring radio presentation. Wallace Beery and Fay Bainter resume their original screen roles as the solid, dependable Marine sergeant major and his half-baked, pacifist wife, respectively. Keye Luke repeats his motion picture part of "Flashy," while Noah Beery (who plays a small part in the film) enacts the role of the colonel (Ray Collins's movie character). The subplot involving the

romance of the sergeant major's daughter, Helen, with a flyer (Marilyn Maxwell and William Lundigan on-screen) is completely eliminated in the broadcast, as is Lundigan's character.

414. "Hello, 'Frisco, Hello," 11/15/43
Based on the 1943 20th Century–Fox film (screenplay by Robert Ellis, Helen Logan, and Richard Macauley).

Cast: Alice Faye (Trudy), Robert Young (Johnny), Eddie Marr (Dan), Bea Benaderet (Bernice), Truda Marson (Beulah), Leo Cleary (Sam), Arthur Q. Bryan (Sharky), Ed Emerson (Turkey/Boy), Cliff Clark (Waiter/Auctioneer), Robert Harris (Burkham/Waiter), Fred MacKaye (Ned), Paul McVey (Cochran), Dorothy Scott (Mrs. Greenwood), Charles Seel (First Barker/Waiter), Ken Christy (Second Barker/Man), and Phil Neely (Soloist).

Commercials: Duane Thompson (Mrs. Jones), Leone Ledoux (Child), Ann Tobin (Girl), and Howard McNear (Man).

Bruce Humberstone directed 20th Century–Fox's 1943 musical *Hello, 'Frisco, Hello*, which features Alice Faye and John Payne in the leads. The feminine half of the team recreates her role of Barbary Coast entertainer Trudy Evans, while Robert Young is recruited to play the man she loves, impresario Johnny Cornell. The story, which is set in the early part of the twentieth century, is successfully atmospheric in *Lux*'s radio recreation of the era, even though, due to time restrictions, most of the period songs that were interpolated into the film are missing from the broadcast. Faye is nevertheless given several opportunities to sing, performing "You'll Never Know" (the hit song written for the motion picture), as well as the following (joined by Robert Young when indicated): Act 1: "Hello, 'Frisco, Hello" (with Young; lyrics by Gene Buck, music

"So Proudly We Hail," which was broadcast on November 1, 1943, reunited Veronica Lake, Claudette Colbert, and Paulette Goddard of the motion picture cast (photo: Photofest).

by Louis A. Hirsh; 1915), "Sweet Cider Time When You Were Mine" (lyrics by Joseph McCarthy, music by Percy Wenrich; 1918), "You'll Never Know" (lyrics by Mack Gordon, music by Harry Warren); Act 2: "They Always Pick on Me" (lyrics by Stanley Murphy, music by Harry von Tilzer; 1911); Act 3: "You'll Never Know" (reprise); Finale: "Hello, 'Frisco, Hello" (with Young).

415. "China," 11/22/43

Based on the 1943 Paramount film (screenplay by Frank Butler), in turn based on the unproduced play *Fourth Brother*, by Archibald Forbes.

Cast: Loretta Young (Carolyn), Alan Ladd (Mr. Jones), William Bendix (Johnny), Philip Ahn (Lin Cho), Barbara Jean Wong (Tan Ying), Lane Tom, Jr. (Lin Wei), Bea Benaderet (Mother), Leone Ledoux (Baby), Helga Moray (Woman/Lin Yung), Fred MacKaye (Jap/Captain), Charlie Lung (Jap/General), Truda Marson (Doris), Marjorie Davies (Nan), Charles Seel, Stanley Farrar, Robert Harris, and Bob Haynes (Ad Libs).

Singers: George Gramlich, Austin Grout, Alan Watson, Kenneth Rundquist, Stewart Bair, Phil Neely, Luke Crockett, Emmett Casey, Clarence Badger, and Enrico Ricardi.

Commercial: Fred MacKaye, Paula Winslowe, Duane Thompson, and Bob Haynes.

The John Farrow–directed Paramount motion picture *China* provided *Lux* with another opportunity to illustrate effectively the wartime situation present in every corner of the globe. Alan Ladd stars in both the film and the broadcast as an American in Japanese-occupied China whose initial uninterest in Japan's quest for territorial advancement is changed by schoolteacher Loretta Young (also in her film role), who champions the cause of the downtrodden Chinese people. William Bendix rounds out the fine cast of principals with a repeat of his screen part as the hero's buddy, and Philip Ahn also resumes his motion picture characterization.

*416. "The Navy Comes Through," 11/29/43

Based on the 1942 RKO film (screenplay by Ray Chanslor and Aeneas MacKensie; original story by Borden Chase; adapted by Earl Baldwin and John Twist).

Cast: Pat O'Brien (Mallory), Ruth Warrick (Myra), Chester Morris (Tom), Fred MacKaye (Man), Charles Seel (Surgeon/Third Captain), Norman Field (President/Second Captain), Leo Cleary (Radio), Cliff Clark (Judge/German), Stanley Farrar (Lookout/C.P.O.), Tyler McVey (Bayliss), Robert Harris (Kroner), Ed Emerson (Berringer), Paul McVey (Nate), Arthur Q. Bryan (Captain), Eddie Marr (Sampter), Bob Haynes (Duttson), Jack Mather (Man Number Two), and Hal Gerard (Sailor).

Commercials: Truda Marson (Dot/Operator in Act 1), Sharon Douglas (Girl), Duane Thompson (Mrs. Cook), Stanley Farrar (Jim), and Paula Winslowe (Nancy/Woman).

Originally planned for the November 29 *Lux* offering were Pat O'Brien and Ruth Warrick in "The Iron Major," the biography of the football coach and war hero Frank Cavanaugh. Legal difficulties, however, caused these plans to be changed at the last minute, and the previously performed "The Navy Comes Through" was substituted. O'Brien and Warrick appeared despite the switch, with Chester Morris rounding out the cast.

See 5/3/43 for information on the film version.

417. "Mrs. Miniver," 12/6/43

Based on the 1942 MGM film (screenplay by Arthur Wimperis, George Froeschel, James Hilton, and Claudine West), in turn based on the novel by Jan Struther (1942).

Cast: Greer Garson (Mrs. Miniver), Walter Pidgeon (Glen), Susan Peters (Carol), Henry Wilcoxon (Vicar), Richard Davis (Vim), Raymond Lawrence (Mr. Ballard), Gloria Gordon (Lady Delton), Tommy Cook (Toby), Mary Lou Harrington (Judy), Duane Thompson (Gladys), Alec Harford (Porter/

Policeman), Charlie Lung (Waiter/ Nobby), Denis Green (Voice/Doctor), Fred MacKaye (German), Vernon Steele (Halliday), and Fred Worlock (Foley).

Singers: Louis Yaekel, Stewart Bair, George Gramlich, Austin Grout, Kenneth Rundquist, Wynne Davis, Betty Rome, Devona Doxie, Virginia Rees, and Enrico Ricardi.

Commercials: Janet Russell (Sally), Doris Singleton (Libby), Paula Winslowe (Girl), Dorothy Scott (Woman), Charlotte Treadway (Woman), and Stanley Farrar (Man).

Metro-Goldwyn-Mayer's Academy Award–winning tribute to the spirit of the British people during the Second World War was presented on *Lux* with both Greer Garson (who won an Oscar for her portrayal) and Walter Pidgeon reprising their roles as the stoic English couple braving various trials and tribulations. *Mrs. Miniver*, which was directed by William Wyler (the recipient of an Academy Award for best direction) in 1942, also features Teresa Wright (winner of a Best Supporting Actress Oscar) in the part of Carol, which is played on *Lux* by Susan Peters, and Henry Wilcoxon in his original part of the Vicar.

418. "Five Graves to Cairo," 12/13/43
Based on the 1943 Paramount film (screenplay by Billy Wilder and Charles Brackett).

Cast: Franchot Tone (Corporal Bramble), Anne Baxter (Mouche), Otto Preminger (Marshall Rommel), J. Carrol Naish (Farid), Fortunio Bonanova (General Sebastiano), Fred MacKaye (Schwegler), Edward Harvey (Fitzung), Charles Seel (Soldier/Officer), Ed Emerson (Second Soldier/Voice), Denis Green (Orderly/Britisher), Norman Field (Major), and Vernon Steele (St. Bride).

Commercials: Duane Thompson

(First and Third Voice in Act 2), Doris Singleton (Libby/Woman in Act 2), and Ann Tobin (Second Woman in Act 2).

The intriguing Billy Wilder/Charles Brackett 1943 Paramount war thriller *Five Graves to Cairo* was capably adapted for *Lux*'s December 13 broadcast. Franchot Tone and Anne Baxter reprise their motion picture parts as the English soldier and fiery French innkeeper who match wits with the Nazis in an isolated desert inn. Otto Preminger takes Erich von Stroheim's role as Field Marshall Rommel, J. Carrol Naish enacts Akim Tamiroff's screen part, and Fortunio Bonanova repeats his original role.

419. "Dixie," 12/20/43
Based on the 1943 Paramount film (screenplay by Karl Tunberg and Darrell Ware; original story by William Rankin; adaptation by Claude Binyon).

Intermission Guest: Lieutenant Junior Grade Helen Rhodes, U.S. Navy Nurse Corps (after Act 2).

Cast: Bing Crosby (Dan Emmett), Dorothy Lamour (Millie), Barry Sullivan (Mr. Bones), Leo Cleary (Mr. Cook), Louise Arthur (Jean), Cliff Clark (Mason), Norman Field (Devereaux/ Head Waiter), Ed Emerson (First Man/ Tenor), Charles Seel (Publisher), Horace Willard (Steward/Driver), Eddie Marr (Pelham/Boy), Griff Barnett (Captain/Manager), and Leo Shorts (Second Man).

Singers: Sidney Pepple, Jan Williams, Henry Kruse, Frank Holiday, Kenneth Rundquist (Soloist), Stewart Bair, Homer Hall, Harry Stanton, George Gramlich, and Enrico Ricardi.

Commercials: Janet Russell (Acts 1 and 2), Doris Singleton (Libby), and Jack Bailey (Voice).

For the rapidly approaching Christmas holiday, *Lux* chose "Dixie," a musical loosely based upon the life of minstrel performer Dan Emmett (1815–1904), who, incidentally, wrote the title song as well as "Old Dan Tucker," a snatch of which is heard during Act 3.

Bing Crosby and Dorothy Lamour repeat their roles from the 1943 Paramount film (directed by A. Edward Sutherland), and Barry Sullivan plays Billy DeWolfe's screen part. Crosby performs the following numbers (all with words by Johnny Burke, music by James Van Heusen, unless otherwise noted): Act 1: "Sunday, Monday, or Always," "Swing Low, Sweet Chariot" (traditional; Crosby with Chorus), "She's from Missouri"; Act 2: "A Horse That Knows His Way Back Home," "If You Please"; Act 3: "Sunday, Monday, or Always" (reprise), "Dixie" (words and music by Dan Emmett; Chorus).

420. "Kathleen," 12/27/43

Based on the 1941 MGM film (screenplay by Mary McCall, Jr.), in turn based on an unpublished story by Kay Van Ripper.

Cast: Shirley Temple (Kathleen), Herbert Marshall (John Davis), Frances Gifford (Angela), Charles Seel (Dr. Foster/Second Moving Man), Bea Benaderet (Lorraine), Griff Barnett (Schoner), Verna Felton (Mrs. Farrell), Norman Field (Jarvis), Ed Emerson (Policeman), and Ken Christy (Moving Man).

Commercials: Paula Winslowe (Woman, Act 2/First Woman, Act 1), Duane Thompson (Second Woman, Act 1), Doris Singleton (Third Woman, Act 1/Woman in Act 3), Dorothy Scott (Fourth Woman, Act 1), and Barbara Jean Wong (Child, Act 2).

Shirley Temple made her first *Lux* appearance in nearly three years in an adaptation of her MGM film *Kathleen*, the story of a neglected girl who is brought closer to her father by her kind-hearted young governess. The 1941 Harold S. Bucquet–directed production makes a pleasant *Lux* comedy,

with very enjoyable performances by the entire cast. Herbert Marshall, also from the movie, repeats his role of the father, and Frances Gifford takes Laraine Day's film part of Angela.

421. "Shadow of a Doubt," 1/3/44

Based on the 1943 Universal film (screenplay by Thornton Wilder, Alma Reville, and Sally Benson), in turn based on a story by Gordon McDonnell.

Special Guest: Jean Bartell, Miss America of 1943 (after Act 2).

Cast: William Powell (Uncle Charlie), Teresa Wright (Charlotte), Ed Emerson (Jack), Regina Wallace (Mrs. Newton), Norman Field (Mr. Newton), Verna Felton (Mrs. Martin/Librarian), Mary Lou Harrington (Ann), Tommy Cook (Roger), Leo Cleary, Charlotte Treadway, Myra Marsh, Buck Woods (Porter), and Charles Seel.

Alfred Hitchcock's 1943 thriller *Shadow of a Doubt* came to *Lux* with Teresa Wright, the "Charlie" of the movie, reprising her characterization for the broadcast. Interestingly, William Powell is cast not in his usual light comedy role but as the deranged murderer (Joseph Cotten in the film) who is idolized by his young and impressionable niece. This broadcast marked Sanford Barnett's debut as adapter.

The *Lux Video Theatre* presented a version on March 24, 1955.

422. "The Constant Nymph," 1/10/44

Based on the 1943 Warner Bros. film (screenplay by Kathryn Scola), in turn based on the play by Margaret Kennedy and Basil Dean (1926), from the novel by Margaret Kennedy (1924).

Cast: Charles Boyer (Louis Dodd), Maureen O'Sullivan (Tessa Sanger), Alexis Smith (Florence Crighton), Walter Kingsford (Charles), Pedro DeCordoba (Sanger), Luis Alberni (Roberto), Duane Thompson (Kate), Joan Lorring (Paula), Truda Marson

"Casablanca" (January 24, 1944), with Alan Ladd, John Loder, and Hedy Lamarr (photo: Photofest).

(Toni), Hans Conried (Fritz), Norman Field (Voice), Gloria Gordon (Lady Long), and Charles Seel (Florist).

Singers: Devona Doxie (Soloist), Betty Stevens (Soloist).

Commercials: Ann Tobin (First Girl), Paula Winslowe (Second Girl), Sharon Douglas (Nancy), and Tyler McVey (Voice).

The 1943 Warner Bros. film *The Constant Nymph* (directed by Edmund Goulding) proved equally successful as a *Lux* broadcast due to the teaming of popular stars Charles Boyer and Maureen O'Sullivan. Boyer reprises his motion picture part of the intensely frustrated composer, and the always natural and sincere O'Sullivan gives an excellent performance as the sensitive young British/Swiss girl, Tessa (played by Joan Fontaine onscreen), who is secretly in love with him. As Tessa is plagued with a valvular lesion that

causes the character to experience frequent dizzy spells, O'Sullivan's subtlety is most effective, for she cleverly delivers her lines in a soft, hushed tone to create intimacy. Alexis Smith rounds out the cast as Florence Crighton, the role she takes in the photoplay.

The 1927 British Gainsborough production features Ivor Novello, Mabel Poulton, and Frances Doble (directed by Adrian Brunel), while the December 9, 1926, New York stage rendering saw Glenn Anders, Beatrix Thompson, and Lotus Robb in the leads.

Additional film version: Gainsborough (British), 1927.

Note: There was no broadcast on January 17, 1944.

423. "Casablanca," 1/24/44

Based on the 1942 Warner Bros. film (screenplay by Julius J. Epstein, Philip

G. Epstein, and Howard Koch), in turn based on the unproduced play *Everybody Comes to Rick's,* by Murray Burnett and Joan Alison.

Cast: Hedy Lamarr (Ilsa), John Loder (Victor Lazlo), Alan Ladd (Rick), Edgar Barrier (Captain Renault), Norman Field (Strasser), Ernest Whitman (Sam), René Gacaire (Casselle), Ed Emerson (Voice), Charles Seel (Carl), Jay Novello (Ugarta), Leo Cleary (Ferrari), and Charles Lung (Sacha).

Commercials: Doris Singleton (Libby), Richard C. Howell (Jim), Paula Winslowe (Peggy), and Dorothy Lovett (Girl).

Warner Bros.' Michael Curtiz–directed film *Casablanca,* one of the surprise hits of 1942, finally surfaced on *Lux* on January 24, 1944. Hedy Lamarr nicely plays Ingrid Bergman's screen role of Ilsa, Alan Ladd plays Humphrey Bogart's part of Rick, and Lamarr's real-life husband, John Loder, plays Victor Lazlo. Edgar Barrier is on hand to enact Claude Rains's picture role of the businesslike but sympathetic police captain, Louis Renault, and Ernest Whitman is heard in the role of Sam. (Whitman performs a partial rendition of "As Time Goes By" during the first act; the Herman Huppeld tune was introduced in the Broadway show *Everybody's Welcome* but became a huge hit after its interpolation into *Casablanca* 11 years later.)

The *Lux Video Theatre* presented a version on March 3, 1955.

424. "Random Harvest," 1/31/44

Based on the 1942 MGM film (screenplay by Claudine West, George Froeschel, and Arthur Wimperis), in turn based on the novel by James Hilton (1941).

Cast: Ronald Colman (Charles), Greer Garson (Paula), Gloria Gordon (Tobacconist Clerk), Joan Lorring (Kitty), Ray Lawrence, Ed Harvey (Kel-

lerman), Eric Snowden, Fred Worlock (Lawyer), Charles Lung, Josephine Gilbert, Vernon Steele, Denis Green, Charles Seel, Richard Nugent, Norman Field, Alec Harford, and Thomas Mills (Shelton).

Commercials: Paula Winslowe (Woman, Act 2), Sharon Douglas (Girl), James Eagles (Man, Act 2), Virginia Gregg (Woman, Act 1), Phil Neely (Singer, Act 1).

Mervyn LeRoy directed MGM's 1942 hit *Random Harvest,* which gave good roles to Ronald Colman and Greer Garson and was presented on *Lux* with both stars in their original roles. The success of the radio adaptation is perhaps limited by the necessity to rush things along a bit, but the performances of Colman and Garson, combined with *Lux*'s usual first-rate production standards, serve at least to remind one of the film's impact.

A second version of "Random Harvest" was performed on April 19, 1948.

425. "His Butler's Sister," 2/7/44

Based on the 1943 Universal film (screenplay by Samuel Hoffenstein and Betty Rheinhardt).

Cast: Deanna Durbin (Ann), Pat O'Brien (Martin), Robert Paige (Charles), Elsa Janssen (Severina), Jay Novello (Popov), Arthur Q. Bryan (Cobb), Truda Marson (Liz), Buck Woods (Porter), Florence Lake (Helen), Josephine Gilbert (Liz), Leo Cleary (Brophy), Charles Seel (Conductor [Boris]), Helga Moray (Lady), and Norman Field (Man).

Commercials: Paula Winslowe (First Voice/Girl), Sarah Berner (Second Voice), Howard McNear (Man), and Janet Russell (Sally).

Lux's February 7 adaptation of the Frank Borzage–directed 1943 Universal release *His Butler's Sister* stars Deanna Durbin of the picture cast in the comedy of a hopeful singer who enlists her half brother's aid in landing an audition with a noted theatrical impresario. Joining her from the screen cast are Pat O'Brien as her sibling and Elsa Janssen as Severina, while Robert Paige rounds out the cast as Charles (the part Franchot Tone plays on-screen). Musical selections performed by Durbin are the 1930 George and Ira Gershwin tune "Embraceable You" (from the musical play *Girl Crazy*) in Act 1, "In the Spirit of the Moment" (words by Bernie Grossman, music by Walter Jurmann) in Act 2, and a reprise of the latter in Act 3.

426. "The Fallen Sparrow," 2/14/44

Based on the 1943 RKO film (screenplay by Warren Duff), in turn based on the novel by Dorothy B. Hughes (1942).

Cast: Robert Young (Kit), Maureen O'Hara (Alma Donne), Walter Slezak (Dr. Scott), Louise Arthur (Barbie), Adele Harrison (Whitney), Johnny McIntyre (Tobin), Bob Burleson (Anton), Charlotte Treadway (Mrs. Lepartino), Griff Barnett (Mr. Lepartino), Howard McNear (Ab), Ed Emerson (Louie), Charles Seel (Robert), René Gacaire (Otto), Norman Field (Waiter/Prince), Jay Novello (Jake), and George Sorrel (Damon).

Commercials: Doris Singleton (Libby), Janet Russell (Sally), Duane Thompson (Second Girl), and Helen Andrews (First Girl).

"The Fallen Sparrow" may not have the benefit of Richard Wallace's suspenseful direction (the high point of the 1943 RKO film), but the story unfolds at a good pace in the capable hands of the *Lux* production team. Robert Young plays Kit, a troubled soldier who returns home from internment in a concentration camp to find his best friend has died under mysterious circumstances. Leading

lady to Young, as she was to John Garfield in the motion picture, is Maureen O'Hara, with Walter Slezak (in his *Lux* debut) as Dr. Scott, the same role he takes in the photoplay.

427. "Wake Up and Live," 2/21/44

Based on the novel by Dorothea Brande (1938), in turn based on the 1937 20th Century–Fox film (screenplay by Harry Tugend and Jack Yellen; story by Curtis Kenyon).

Cast: Frank Sinatra (Eddie), Jimmy Gleason (Marty Hackett), Bob Crosby (Charlie Standish), Marilyn Maxwell (Alice Huntley), James Dunn (Steve), Bea Benaderet (Patsy), Cathy Lewis (Jean), Arthur Q. Bryan (Man on Street/Al), Eddie Marr (Driver), Verna Felton (Operator/Landlady), Charles Seel (Frank), John McIntire (Second Man), Alice Mock (Madame/Soloist), Leo Cleary (Man/Second Thug), Ed Emerson (Herb/First Thug), Stanley Farrar (Man), Norman Field (Stratton), Truda Marson (Third Operator), and Tyler McVey (Man).

Commercials: Janet Russell (Sally), Paula Winslowe (Young Woman/Cindy), and Martha Wentworth (Woman's Voice/Godmother).

Singing star Frank Sinatra appeared in his first dramatic role on February 21 in *Lux*'s "Wake Up and Live," adapted from the 1937 Sidney Lanfield–directed 20th Century–Fox film, which revolves around a timid soul who accidentally becomes a radio singing sensation. Sinatra performs the following selections: Act 1: "I've Heard That Song Before" (words by Sammy Cahn, music by Jule Styne); Act 2: "Embraceable You" (partial; words by Ira Gershwin, music by George Gershwin; from the 1930 Broadway musical *Girl Crazy*), "Dancing in the Dark" (words by Howard Dietz, music by Arthur Schwartz; from the 1930 Broadway musical *The Band Wagon*); Act 3:

"Embraceable You" (reprise), "Wake Up and Live" (brief snatch with Marilyn Maxwell; words by Mack Gordon, music by Harry Revel; incidentally the only song used from the score of the film, which was also heard in an incomplete version as a Marilyn Maxwell solo in Act 1). In addition to leading lady Marilyn Maxwell (in Alice Faye's film role), Frank Sinatra's other costars in the broadcast are James Gleason, Bob Crosby, and James Dunn in roles played in the picture by Walter Winchell, Ben Bernie, and Ned Sparks. Gossip columnist Sidney Skolsky, who was announced on the previous Lux broadcast, did not appear for reasons unexplained.

428. "Guadalcanal Diary," 2/28/44
Based on the 1943 20th Century–Fox film (screenplay by Lamar Trotti; adaptation by Jerry Cady), in turn based on the book by Richard Tregaskis (1943).
Cast: Preston Foster (Father Donnelly), William Bendix (Taxi), Lloyd Nolan (Hook), Richard Jaeckel (Chicken), Herbert Rawlinson (Grayson), Ed Emerson (Davis), John McIntire (Correspondent), Eddie Marr (Man in Prelude), Paul Zuremba (Man), Tom Holland (Steinham), Howard McNear (Jap), Ken Hodge (Sammy), Bob Young (Tex), Charles Seel (Weatherby/Soldier), Charlie Lung (Manuel/Jap), Norman Field (Doctor/Jap), and Gary Brockner (Voice/Second Soldier).
Singers: Sidney Pepple, Robert Tait, Freeman High, Henry Kruse, George Gramlich, Kenneth Rundquist, Stewart Bair, Homer Hall, Delos Jewkes, and Enrico Ricardi (Contractor).
Commercials: Doris Singleton (Libby), Janet Russell (Sally), Paula Winslowe (Mrs. Smith/First Voice), Duane Thompson (Mrs. Jones/Second Voice), Dorothy Lovett (Third Voice), and Harry Lang (Voice).
Guadalcanal Diary, the 1943 Lewis Seiler–directed 20th Century–Fox tribute to the fighting Marines on Guadalcanal, made its way to Lux with four of the principals from the screen cast: Preston Foster, William Bendix, Lloyd Nolan, and Richard Jaeckel. This war drama is a good example of the material popular with Lux audiences during the period, inspiring pride, optimism, and camaraderie with listeners everywhere.

429. "The Letter," 3/6/44
Based on the 1940 Warner Bros. film (screenplay by Howard Koch), in turn based on the play by Somerset Maugham (1927).
Special Guest: Lieutenant Glada Jelinick, U.S. Army nurse (after Act 2).
Adapted for radio by George Wells.
Cast: Bette Davis (Leslie), Herbert Marshall (Robert Crosbie), Vincent Price (Howard Joyce), Charlie Lung (Ong Chi), Bea Benaderet (Chinese Woman), Richard Davis (Withers), Paula Winslowe (Dorothy), Frederic Worlock (Judge), Alex Havier, Regina Wallace, Jo Gilbert (Adele), Eric Snowden (Foreman/Man), and Charles Seel (Policeman).
Commercials: Fay McKenzie (Girl), Duane Thompson (Woman), and Barbara Jean Wong (Chinese Translation).
Lux's second airing of "The Letter" again teams Bette Davis and Herbert Marshall as Leslie and Robert Crosbie. In his Lux debut Vincent Price plays the Howard Joyce role (which was given to James Stephenson in the earlier broadcast as well as in the film), with Charlie Lung portraying Ong Chi instead of Head Boy.
See 4/21/41 for information on film and stage versions.

430. "In Old Oklahoma," 3/13/44
Based on the 1943 Republic film (screenplay by Ethel Hill and Eleanore Griffith; original story by Thomson Burtis).

Cast: Roy Rogers (Dan Summers), Martha Scott (Kathy), Albert Dekker (Jim Gardner), Martha Wentworth (Bessie), Jim Nusser (Cherokee), Ken Christy (Dalton), Stanley Farrar, Eddie Marr, Bob Haynes (Kelter), Noreen Gammill (Mother), Charles Seel (Conductor), Horace Murphy (Man/Charlie), Norman Field (Bartender/Fenton), Leo Cleary (Deeprit), and John McIntire (Big Tree).

Commercials: Ann Tobin (Second Girl, Act 1), Ella Neal (First Girl, Act 1), Robert Clarke (Man), Doris Singleton (Second Girl, Act 2), and Paula Winslowe (First Girl, Act 2).

Roy Rogers made his *Lux* debut in an adaptation of the Albert S. Rogell–directed Republic Western *In Old Oklahoma* on March 13. Rogers takes the part of Dan Summers, which John Wayne plays on the screen, but unlike the originator of the role, he is given the chance to sing two tunes: "I've Learned About Women," in Act 2, and "When My Blue Moon Turns to Gold," in Act 3. Costarring in the broadcast are Martha Scott and Albert Dekker, both in the roles they created in the motion picture.

431. "The Hard Way," 3/20/44

Based on the 1942 Warner Bros. film (screenplay by Daniel Fuchs and Peter Viertel).

Cast: Miriam Hopkins (Helen Chernen), Franchot Tone (Paul Collins), Anne Baxter (Katherine Blane), Chester Morris (Albert Runkel), Griff Barnett (Flores/Conductor), Eddie Marr (Stage Manager), Marion Martin (Lily), Charles Seel (Detective), Norman Field (Doctor/Butler), Leo Cleary (Frenchy), Anne Stone (Waitress/Anderson), Bob Haynes (First Boy), Jack Morrison (Second Boy/Man), Peter Rankin (Johnnie), Truda Marson (Girl), Jay Novello (Wade/Second Man), Ted von Eltz (Shegrun), and Ellen Campbell (Laura).

Commercials: Doris Singleton (Girl), Stanley Farrar (First Voice), Harry Bartel (Second Voice), David Marshall (Bob), and Lynn Martin and Marion Martin (Soloists).

With the radio presentation of the Vincent Sherman–directed 1942 Warner Bros. film *The Hard Way*, *Lux* had the opportunity to feature four stars in a tale of the various dramas that take place behind the footlights. Miriam Hopkins heads the fine cast as the determined "stage sister" who manipulates her naive sibling Anne Baxter in the hopes of helping her achieve stardom. Franchot Tone is the disillusioned actor who provides stability for the girl, while Chester Morris is the actress's tragic first husband (the motion picture featured Ida Lupino, Dennis Morgan, Joan Leslie, and Jack Carson, respectively). Baxter sings snatches (in Act 1) of "Am I Blue" (words by Grant Clarke, music by Harry Akst; from the 1929 film *On with the Show*), and "I'll Get By" (words by Roy Turk, music by Fred E. Ahlert; 1928).

432. "Phantom Lady," 3/27/44

Based on the 1944 Universal film (screenplay by Bernard C. Schoenfield), in turn based on the novel by William Irish (Cornell Woolrich pseudonym) (1942).

Cast: Brian Aherne (Jack), Ella Raines (Carol), Alan Curtis (Scott Henderson), John McIntire (Inspector Burgess), Duane Thompson (Ann Terry), Bea Benaderet (Miss Montiero/Payton/Dr. Chase), Eddie Marr (Cliff), Regina Wallace (Milliner), Jeanette Nolan (Ann), Stanley Farrar (Man), Eddie Emerson (Prosecutor/Second Voice), Charles Seel (Man), Norman Field (Man), Howard McNear (Foreman/Guard), Dick Ryan (Mike/Man), and Ferdinand Munier (Judge/Detective).

Commercials: Janet Russell (Sally), Virginia Gregg (Girl), Dorothy Lovett (First Girl, Act 2), and Ann Tobin (Second Girl, Act 2).

Universal's mystery drama *Phantom Lady* was presented on *Lux* on March 27. The 1944 film was directed by Robert Siodmak and starred Franchot Tone, Ella Raines, and Alan Curtis; two of these three principals repeat their roles in the *Lux* version, with Brian Aherne taking Tone's part. The tightly constructed thriller concerning a secretary who works to clear her boss of a murder charge also provides supporting actor John McIntire with a good role as the police inspector who helps solve the case.

433. "Destroyer," 4/3/44

Based on the 1943 Columbia film (screenplay by Frank Wead).

Cast: Edward G. Robinson (Steve Bolesavsky), Dennis O'Keefe (Mickey), Marguerite Chapman (Mary), John McIntire (Clark), Ed Emerson (Horton), Leo Cleary (Kansas), Eddie Marr (Sailor), Charles Seel (Officer), Norman Field (Officer), Bob Young (Yeoman), Tom Holland (Gillis), Kay Dibbs (Fuller/Radio), Tyler McVey (Dugan/ Casey), and Frank Barton (Man).

John Paul Jones's famous battle cry, "I have not yet begun to fight," provides the theme for *Lux*'s adaptation of William A. Seiter's *Destroyer,* the 1943 Columbia tribute to the loyalty and determination a feisty World War I Navy veteran has for the destroyer that had served him so well in the past. Reprising his motion picture role as the aforementioned veteran is Edward G. Robinson, while Dennis O'Keefe portrays Glenn Ford's screen character and Marguerite Chapman recreates her film role as the former's daughter.

Cecil B. DeMille is heard from Washington, D.C., where he was attending the premiere of his 1944 film *The Story*

of Dr. Wassell, and consequently the narrative at the beginning of each act is handled by announcer John Milton Kennedy.

434. "Happy Land," 4/10/44

Based on the 1943 20th Century–Fox film (screenplay by Kathryn Scola and Julien Josephson); novel by MacKinlay Kantor (1943).

Cast: Don Ameche (Lou Marsh), Frances Dee (Agnes), Walter Brennan (Grandpa), Tommy Cook (Rusty, as a Boy), Leone Ledoux (Rusty, as an Infant/Hilda), Bobby Larson (Todd, as a Boy), Bob Haynes, Joan Lorring, Bill Matile, Charles Seel (Man), Leo Cleary (Ed), Charlotte Treadway (Woman), Dorothy Scott (Voice), John McIntire (Nibby/Voice), Norman Field (Conductor), Fred Barton (Marine/Voice), Norma Nilsson (Jackie), Gloria Fisher (Gretchen/ Girl), and Jack Morrison (Todd).

Commercials: Doris Singleton (Libby), Dorothy Lovett (Girl), and Stanley Farrar (Man).

Happy Land, 20th Century–Fox's Irving Pichel–directed film, translates into an interesting *Lux* drama. The story of a middle-aged couple who lose their son in the war is retold through flashbacks, with the three stars from the movie, Don Ameche, Frances Dee, and Walter Brennan, repeating their roles for the airwaves.

435. "Coney Island," 4/17/44

Based on the 1943 20th Century–Fox film (screenplay by George Seaton).

Cast: Dorothy Lamour (Katie), Alan Ladd (Eddie), Chester Morris (Joe), Eddie Marr (Frankie), Bea Benaderet (Dolly), Boyd Davis (Louie), Joseph Forte (Billy/Second Man), Norman Field (Career), Howard McNear (Pat/ Usher), Truda Marson (Girl/Second Woman), Stanley Farrar (Hot Dog Man/ Second Usher), Charles Seel (Bar Man/ Man), and Doris Singleton (Soloist).

Singers: Henry Iblings, Robert Franklin, Irl Numaker, Robert Tait, Burton Dole, Thomas Clark, George Gramlich, Dudley Kunnell, Tudor Williams, and Enrico Ricardi.

Commercials: Janet Russell (Sally), Doris Singleton (Libby).

For a lighter touch, Walter Lang's 1943 20th Century–Fox musical *Coney Island*, which concerns a turn-of-the-century songbird who is pursued by two men, was chosen for the April 17 broadcast. Dorothy Lamour, Alan Ladd, and Chester Morris take the roles Betty Grable, George Montgomery, and Cesar Romero play in the film, with Lamour singing the following: Act 1: "When Irish Eyes Are Smiling" (partial; words by Chauncey Olcott and George Graff, Jr., music by Ernest R. Ball; from the 1908 musical *Isle o' Dreams*); Act 2: "Cuddle Up a Little Closer" (words by Otto Harbach, music by Karl Hoschna; from the 1908 musical *The Three Twins*), and "Put Your Arms Around Me, Honey" (words by Junie McCree, music by Albert von Tilzer; 1910). Interestingly, none of the songs written specifically for the film (by Leo Robin and Ralph Rainger) appear in this *Lux* version.

Coney Island would be remade at 20th Century–Fox in 1950 as *Wabash Avenue*, a Henry Koster–directed production starring Betty Grable as well as Victor Mature and Phil Harris.

"Coney Island" was repeated on *Lux* on September 30, 1946, and "Wabash Avenue" was performed on November 13, 1950.

Additional film version: 20th Century–Fox, 1950 (*Wabash Avenue*).

436. "This Land Is Mine," 4/24/44

Based on the 1943 RKO film (screenplay by Dudley Nichols).

Cast: Charles Laughton (Albert Lory), Maureen O'Sullivan (Louise Martin), Edgar Barrier (Major von Keller), Regina Wallace (Albert's Mother), Denis Green (George), Ralph Lewis (Paul), Cliff Clark (Professor Sorel), Douglas Wood (the Mayor), Norman Field (Judge), Howard McNear (Railroad Office Clerk), John McIntire (Prosecutor), Charles Seel (Voice), Tyler McVey (Officer/Soldier), and Billy Roy (Edmond).

Commercials: Betty Jean Hainey (Jean), Charlotte Treadway (Mother), Robert Haynes (Bill), Ann Tobin (Betty), and Doris Singleton (Libby).

Lux listeners were certainly in for a memorable evening on April 24 with the radio adaptation of the Jean Renoir–directed 1943 RKO motion picture *This Land Is Mine*. This moving war drama focusing on an anonymous country's fight to overcome oppression through individual participation features excellent performances by the two distinguished stars: Charles Laughton (who repeats his picture role) as the timid schoolteacher who eventually finds his nerve, and Maureen O'Sullivan as the patriotic co-worker who inspires him. (Maureen O'Hara and Walter Slezak play the Louise Martin and Major von Keller roles in the RKO film.)

437. "Appointment for Love," 5/1/44

Based on the 1941 Universal film (screenplay by Bruce Manning and Felix Jackson), in turn based on the story "Heartbeat," by Ladislaus Bus-Fekete. Adapted for radio by George Wells.

Cast: Olivia deHavilland (Jane), Paul Lukas (Andre), Denis Green (Michael), Dorothy Lovett (Edith), Bea Benaderet (Nancy), Arthur Q. Bryan (Hastings), Harold DeBecker (Leary), Duane Thompson (Ethel), Norman Field (Dr. Gunther), Charles Seel (Timothy), Verna Felton (Martha), Eddie Marr (Gus [Elevator Boy]), Stanley Farrar (Man/Waiter), Jack Morrison (Man), Ed

Emerson (Pete), and Eugene Forsyth (Boy/Newsboy).

Commercials: Doris Singleton (Girl), Janet Russell (Sally), Anne Stone (Woman), and John McIntire (Voice).

Two years after *Lux*'s first broadcast of Universal's "Appointment for Love" the story resurfaced, but on this occasion with Olivia deHavilland and Paul Lukas in the leading roles (Myrna Loy and Charles Boyer appeared in the earlier version).

See 2/23/42 for information on the film version; the *Lux Video Theatre* presented an adaptation on November 3, 1955.

438. "Penny Serenade," 5/8/44

Based on the 1941 Columbia film (screenplay by Morrie Ryskind), in turn based on a short story by Martha Cheavens. Adapted for radio by George Wells.

Cast: Irene Dunne (Julie), Joseph Cotten (Roger), Edgar Buchanan (Applejack), Regina Wallace (Miss Oliver), Norma Nilsson (Trina), Charles Seel (Doctor), John McIntire (Judge), Leone Ledoux (Trina, as an Infant), Duane Thompson (Tommy's Mother), and Bobby Larson (Tommy).

Chorus: Stella Fleud, Betty Stevens, Ronnie Lake, Devona Doxie, Georgia Stark, Ethelyn Williams, and Enrico Ricardi.

Commercials: Doris Singleton (Libby), Charlotte Treadway (First Woman), Virginia Gregg (Second Woman), and John McIntire (Second Announcer).

The sentimental story "Penny Serenade" reappeared on *Lux* two years after its first presentation, with Irene Dunne reprising her motion picture role, and Joseph Cotten as her husband.

See 4/27/42 for information on the film version; the *Lux Video Theatre* also presented an adaptation on January 13, 1955.

439. "Action in the North Atlantic," 5/15/44

Based on the 1943 Warner Bros. film (screenplay by John Howard Lawson; additional dialogue by W.R. Burnett and A.I. Bezzarides).

Cast: George Raft (Joe Rossi), Raymond Massey (Captain Jarvis), Julie Bishop (Pearl), Eddie Marr (Johnny), Regina Wallace (Sarah), Bill Martel (Parker), Leo Cleary (Officer), Herb Lytton (Man), Stan Farrar (Reporter), Cliff Clark (Man), Charles Seel (Man/Voice), Ralph Lewis (Monsie), and John McIntire (Man).

Commercials: Janet Russell (Sally), Doris Singleton (Libby).

Lloyd Bacon directed *Action in the North Atlantic*, Warner Bros.' 1943 salute to the Merchant Marines, which became a *Lux* play on May 15. The well-crafted drama stars George Raft in Humphrey Bogart's screen role, while Raymond Massey and Julie Bishop (aka Jacqueline Wells) resume the parts they enact in the film.

440. "Springtime in the Rockies," 5/22/44

Based on the 1942 20th Century–Fox film (screenplay by Walter Bullock; original story by Philip Wylie; adaptation by Jacques Thery).

Cast: Betty Grable (Vicky), Dick Powell (Dan), Carmen Miranda (Rosita), Edgar Barrier (Victor), Verna Felton (Phoebe), Arthur Q. Bryan (Commissioner), Howard McNear (McTavish), Norman Field (Joe), Charles Seel (Clerk), Kelly Flint (Marilyn), Eugene Orrath, Don Gibbs, and Carmen King (Ad Libs). Carmen Miranda and Band: Carmen Miranda, Ivan Lopes (Leader), Jose P. Oliveira, Stanio Osorio, Buster Amarel, Alfonso Osorio, and Oswaldo Gosliano.

Commercials: Doris Singleton (Libby), Betty Moran (Woman), and Stanley Farrar (Man).

Betty Grable's *Lux* debut was marked with a fine performance in a radio adaptation of her 1942 Irving Cummings–directed 20th Century–Fox musical *Springtime in the Rockies,* which concerns a wily musical performer's attempts to win back the affections of his estranged partner/fiancée. Joining Grable from the movie cast is Carmen Miranda, also making her *Lux* debut, while Dick Powell takes the John Payne screen part, and Edgar Barrier plays Cesar Romero's movie character. The entertaining production features the following musical numbers: Act 1: "Run, Little Raindrop, Run" (words by Mack Gordon, music by Harry Warren; sung by Betty Grable and Dick Powell), and "Chattanooga Choo Choo" (Gordon/Warren; originally from the 1941 film *Sun Valley Serenade,* then interpolated into *Springtime in the Rockies* the following year; sung in Spanish by Carmen Miranda and male chorus); Act 2: "I Had the Craziest Dream" (Gordon/Warren; Betty Grable and Dick Powell), and "Tico-Tico" (words by Aloysio Oliveira, music by Zequinha Abreu; 1944; Carmen Miranda); Act 3: finale: "I Had the Craziest Dream" (Grable and Powell).

441. "Old Acquaintance," 5/29/44

Based on the 1943 Warner Bros. film (screenplay by John Van Druten and Lenore Coffee), in turn based on the play by John Van Druten (1940).

Special Guest: Donna Atwood, figure skater, star of Ice Follies of 1944 (after Act 2).

Cast: Alexis Smith (Kit), Miriam Hopkins (Millie), Otto Kruger (Preston), Robert Bailey (Rudd), Gloria Fisher (Deirdre), Bea Benaderet (Mrs. Carter), and Charlotte Treadway (Harriett).

Commercials: Jean Martel (First Girl), Doris Singleton (Second Girl).

Warner Bros.' 1944 release *Old Acquaintance* was directed by Vincent Sherman and starred Bette Davis, Miriam Hopkins, and John Loder. *Lux* brought the interesting story of tangled romances to the airwaves, with Miriam Hopkins in her screen role and Alexis Smith and Otto Kruger costarring. The *Lux Video Theatre* version aired November 29, 1956.

442. "Jane Eyre," 6/5/44

Based on the 1944 20th Century–Fox film (screenplay by Aldous Huxley, Robert Stevenson, and John Houseman), in turn based on the novel by Charlotte Brontë (1847).

Cast: Orson Welles (Edward Rochester), Loretta Young (Jane Eyre), C.S. Ramsey-Hill (Brockelhurst), Janet Scott (Mrs. Fairfax), Mary Lou Harrington (Jane, at ten), Elaine Martin (Adele), Helga Moray (Mrs. Poole), Gloria Gordon (Lady Ingram), Claudia Dell (Blanche), Charles Seel (Mason), Sir Charles Bondi (Minister), and Martha Wentworth (Woman).

Commercials: Doris Singleton (Libby), Helen Andrews (Jane), Duane Thompson (Mary), and John McIntire (Announcer).

The oft-filmed Charlotte Brontë novel *Jane Eyre* (1847) made its way to *Lux* for the second time the same year the most recent screen version (directed by Robert Stevenson for 20th Century–Fox) came to theaters. Orson Welles resumes his photoplay characterization as the emotionally frustrated Edward Rochester, and Loretta Young portrays the world-weary Jane Eyre (Joan Fontaine in the film). In the 1944 *Lux* version, key sequences from Jane's traumatic childhood and her friendship with the Reverend St. John Rivers are deleted, which means the broadcast concentrates almost entirely on her relationship with Edward Rochester.

See 6/27/38 for information on film versions; a third *Lux* rendering was aired on June 14, 1948.

Additional film versions: Whitman Features, 1914; Select Pictures, 1918; Hugo Ballin/Hodkinson Productions, 1921; Monogram, 1934; Sagittarius Productions, 1971.

443. "Naughty Marietta," 6/12/44

Based on the 1935 MGM film (screenplay by John Lee Mahin, Frances Goodrich, and Albert Hackett), in turn based on the 1905 musical production (music by Victor Herbert, book and lyrics by Rida Johnson Young).

Cast: Jeanette MacDonald (Marietta), Nelson Eddy (Dick), Charles Seel (Sailor/Major), Joe Duval (Town Crier/Tom), Verna Felton (Madame), Ferdinand Munier (Captain), Jack Mather (Soldier/Abe), Norman Field (Count), Cliff Clark (Governor), Virginia Gregg (Marie/Third Woman), Betty Moran (First Girl), Ann Tobin (Second Girl/Glenn), Janet Scott (Second Woman), Jay Novello (Rudolf/Butler), Dellie Ellis (Julie), Howard McNear (François), and Regina Wallace (Woman/First Woman).

Chorus: Enrico Ricardi (Singer and Chorus Master), Betty Stevens (Solo), Clarence Badger, Henry Iblings, Earl Hunmaker, Louis Yaekel, George Gramlich, Tom Clarke, Dudley Kunnell, John Knobler, Devona Doxie, and Georgia Stark.

Commercials: Janet Russell (Sally), Helen Andrews (First Woman), Duane Thompson (Second Woman), Doris Singleton (Girl), and John McIntire (Second Announcer).

Victor Herbert's operetta *Naughty Marietta* received its New York premiere on November 7, 1910 (at the New York Theatre), and 25 years later the MGM W.S. Van Dyke–directed film version reached the screen. The motion picture is very well made from many angles and is also remembered as the first production in which Jeanette MacDonald and Nelson Eddy appeared

as a team (the *Lux* broadcast of "Naughty Marietta" served to reunite them on radio, as each had already appeared separately). Interestingly, *Lux's* second version follows the plot of the MGM film, which differs considerably from the stage production and uses some of Gus Kahn's lyrics present in the 1935 photoplay: Act 1: "Day by Day" (Jeanette MacDonald and Chorus), "Tramp, Tramp, Tramp" (Nelson Eddy and Chorus), "'Neath the Southern Moon" (Chorus), "Tramp, Tramp, Tramp" (reprise); Act 2: "Italian Street Song" (Jeanette MacDonald and Chorus), "Falling in Love with Someone" (Nelson Eddy); Act 3: "Ah, Sweet Mystery of Life" (Duet for finale).

See 3/28/38 for information on the film and stage versions.

444. "Lost Angel," 6/19/44

Based on the 1944 MGM film (screenplay by Isobel Lennart; from an idea by Angna Enters).

Cast: Margaret O'Brien (Alpha), James Craig (Mike), Marsha Hunt (Katie), Keenan Wynn (Packy), Griff Barnett (Art), Norman Field (Professor Vincent), Regina Wallace (Woman), Stan Farrar (Reporter), Ed Emerson (Lefty), Lal Chand Mehra (Chinese/Mr. Catty), Charles Seel (Detective/Usher), Herbert Rawlinson (Dr. Mooring), Ferdinand Munier (Cop/Waiter), and Catherine Lewis (Cigarette Girl).

Commercials: Doris Singleton (Libby/First Girl Singing), Dorothy Lovett (Second Girl), and Howard McNear (Joe).

An interesting note concerning the *Lux* adaptation of the Roy Roland–directed 1944 MGM comedy-drama *Lost Angel* was brought to the audience's attention when DeMille mentions that the broadcast is "the first time we've had a star who wasn't born, even, when the first play was presented in this national theatre, by Lux toilet soap."

The actress to whom he is referring is Margaret O'Brien, who (along with James Craig, Marsha Hunt, and Keenan Wynn) repeats her film role as the clinically reared child prodigy who discovers life's simple pleasures through the sympathetic actions of benevolent reporter James Craig.

445. "Christmas in July," 6/26/44
Based on the 1940 Paramount film (screenplay by Preston Sturges).
Guest Host: Lionel Barrymore.
Cast: Dick Powell (Jimmy), Linda Darnell (Betty), Raymond Walburn (Maxford), Howard McNear (Don Harper), Verna Felton (Jimmy's Mother), Griff Barnett (Mr. Zimmerman), Norman Field (Waterbury), Bea Benaderet (Miss Slidewell), Eddie Marr (Jewelry Clark), Abe Reynolds (Schindel), Ken Christy (Policeman), Horace Willard (Sam), Charles Seel (Harry), Leo Cleary (Bill Docker), Eddie Emerson (Charlie), Tyler McVey (Al), Charlie Lung (Baxter), Franklyn Parker (Schmidt), and Norma Nilsson (Sophie).
Commercials: Doris Singleton (Libby), Duane Thompson (Woman, Act 3).
Lux's presentation of Preston Sturges's 1940 Paramount comedy *Christmas in July* was featured on the June 26 program. Dick Powell repeats his film role as Jimmy, the struggling menial employee who is tricked into believing he has won $25,000 in a contest. Linda Darnell gives a fine performance in the role of Betty, which was slightly built up for her *Lux* debut (Ellen Drew plays the part onscreen).

In the absence of DeMille, who was in Chicago for the premiere of *The Story of Dr. Wassell,* the position of host is agreeably filled by Lionel Barrymore.
The *Lux Video Theatre* presented a version on September 9, 1954.

446. "It Happened Tomorrow," 7/3/44
Based on the 1944 United Artists film (screenplay by René Clair and Dudley Nichols).
Cast: Don Ameche (Larry), Anne Baxter (Sylvia), Norman Field (Pop), Eddie Marr (Andy), Griff Barnett (Mr. Gordon), Cathy Lewis (Girl/Lily), Ken Christy (Inspector), Leo Cleary (Lombardi), Ferdinand Munier (Man/Minister), Charles Seel (Man), Franklyn Parker (Proprietor/Officer), Tyler McVey (Man), Ed Emerson (Gambler/Duckie), and Herb Lytton (Man).
Commercials: Janet Russell (Sally), Virginia Gregg (Girl), and Doris Singleton (Libby).
To wrap up *Lux*'s season, producers chose the 1944 René Clair United Artists fantasy *It Happened Tomorrow,* with Don Ameche (in Dick Powell's film role) as the reporter who discovers the advantages (and disadvantages) of knowing tomorrow's news today. Anne Baxter nicely plays the part of his loyal girlfriend, Sylvia (Linda Darnell in the picture).
At the conclusion of the show, DeMille announces that *Lux* is the recipient of the George Foster Peabody Award for "Outstanding Entertainment in Drama."

Tenth Season
(September 4, 1944–June 25, 1945)

Columbia Broadcasting System, Monday, 9:00–10:00 P.M. *Host*: Cecil B. DeMille. *Announcer*: John Milton Kennedy. *Director*: Fred MacKaye.

Musical Director: Lou Silvers. *Adaptations*: Sanford Barnett. *Sound Effects*: Charlie Forsyth.

447. "Maytime," 9/4/44

Based on the 1937 MGM film (screenplay by Noel Langley), in turn based on the 1917 operetta (book and lyrics by Rida Johnson Young, score by Sigmund Romberg).

Cast: Jeanette MacDonald (Marcia), Nelson Eddy (Paul), Edgar Barrier (Nazaroff), Charles Seel (Voice), Cliff Clark (Alex), Arthur Q. Bryan (Opera Director), Boyd Davis (Grant), Ferdinand Munier (Cabby), Virginia Keith (Barbara), Regina Wallace (Ellen), Robert Clarke (Kip), and Jay Novello (Patina).

Chorus: Henry Winkler, Louis Yaekel, Clarence Badger, George Gramlich, Edwin Tunning, Donald Neese, Earl Hunmaker, and Enrico Ricardi.

Commercials: Richard Benedict (Soldier), Julie Bannon (Betty), Doris Singleton (Girl's Voice), and Janet Russell (Emily).

Three months after their initial *Lux* appearance together, Jeanette MacDonald and Nelson Eddy returned to the program in one of their MGM motion picture successes, *Maytime,* a romance between a struggling singer and an opera diva trapped in a loveless marriage to an older man. Most of the Rida Johnson Young/Sigmund Romberg songs from the 1917 stage hit (which featured Peggy Wood) were deleted from the 1937 Robert Z. Leonard–directed film, and an additional three fell by the wayside in the broadcast version. Selections heard in the radio rendering are (the Herbert Stothart numbers were written for the 1937 movie): Act 1: "Reverie" (adapted by Herbert Stothart from Romberg arias; Jeanette MacDonald), "Student Drinking Song" (Stothart; Nelson Eddy), "Le Regiment de Sambre et Meuse" (Robert

Planquette; Nelson Eddy); Act 2: "Carry Me Back to Old Virginny" (James A. Bland, 1876; Eddy and MacDonald), "Jewel Song" (from *Faust,* music by Charles Gounod; MacDonald), "Sweetheart" (Do You Remember?), (words by Rida Johnson Young, music by Sigmund Romberg; Eddy and MacDonald); Act 3: "Czarita" (adapted by Herbert Stothart from themes of Pyotr Ilich Tchaikovsky's Fifth Symphony, libretto by Bob Wright and Chet Forrest), "Sweetheart" (Do You Remember?) (MacDonald and Eddy).

448. "Break of Hearts," 9/11/44

Based on the 1935 RKO film (screenplay by Sarah Y. Mason, Victor Heerman, and Anthony Veiller; original story by Lester Cohen).

Cast: Rita Hayworth (Ann), Orson Welles (Franz Roberti), Griff Barnett (Biorkman), Tom Collins (Johnny), Paula Winslowe (Connie), Arthur Q. Bryan (Orchestra Musician), Eddie Marr (Pianist), Jay Novello (Rico), Charles Seel (Clerk), Paul McVey (Albert), Linda King (Vicky), and Jack Negley (Teckbridge).

Commercials: Janet Russell (Sally), Doris Singleton (Girl).

The *Lux* adaptation of the 1935 Philip Moeller–directed RKO drama *Break of Hearts* served to pair married couple Rita Hayworth and Orson Welles in the story of a promising young composer in love with a self-destructive conductor. Hayworth portrays Ann, the role Katharine Hepburn takes in the film, and Orson Welles plays the Charles Boyer chracter, Franz Roberti.

449. "Suspicion," 9/18/44

Based on the 1941 film (screenplay by

Samson Raphaelson, Joan Harrison, and Alma Reville), in turn based on the novel *Before the Fact*, by Francis Iles (Anthony Berkeley) (1932). Adapted for radio by George Wells.

Cast: William Powell (Johnny), Olivia deHavilland (Lina), Charles Irwin (Beaky), Lois Corbett (Isobel), Vernon Steele (General McLaidlaw/Clerk), Gloria Gordon (Mrs. McLaidlaw), Duane Thompson (Ethel/Headmistress/Girl), Eric Snowden (Inspector Hodgson), and Claire Verdera (Secretary).

Commercials: Doris Singleton (Libby), Helen Andrews (Woman).

For the September 18 broadcast "Suspicion" was brought back, with William Powell taking Cary Grant's picture role, and Olivia deHavilland playing the part created on the screen by her sister, Joan Fontaine.

See 5/4/42 for information on film version; the *Lux Video Theatre* aired a rendering on December 8, 1955.

450. "Lucky Partners," 9/25/44

Based on the 1941 RKO film (screenplay by Allan Scott and John Van Druten; adapted from the story "Bonne Chance," by Sacha Guitry).

Cast: Don Ameche (David), Lucille Ball (Jean), Carlton KaDell (Freddie), Harry Tyler (the Judge), Verna Felton (Aunt Lucy), Noreen Gammill (Elderly Woman), Charles Seel (Wendell), Eddie Marr (Nick Number One/Policeman), Arthur Q. Bryan (Hotel Clerk), Leo Cleary (Elderly Man), and Norman Field (Nick Number Two).

Commercials: Janet Russell (Sally), Doris Singleton (Libby), Duane Thompson (Woman), and Leone Ledoux (Child).

The Lewis Milestone–directed comedy *Lucky Partners* reached *Lux* four years after it premiered on the screen, retelling the story of a carefree artist who purchases a lottery ticket with a ticket with a girl who is a stranger to him. *Lux*'s version features Don Ameche in Ronald Colman's screen part and Lucille Ball (making her *Lux* debut) in the part played in the RKO movie by Ginger Rogers. Although it had been announced at the conclusion of the last week's broadcast that Jack Carson would be on hand to recreate his motion picture role, he does not participate in the proceedings. (Carlton KaDell is heard as Carson's "Freddie" character.)

After Act 3, DeMille notes that *Lux* received an award from the National Safety Council, which was presented by Colonel John Stillwell.

451. "Home in Indiana," 10/2/44

Based on the 1944 20th Century–Fox film (screenplay by Winston Miller), in turn based on a story by George Andrew Chamberlain.

Cast: Walter Brennan (Thunder), Charlotte Greenwood (Penny), Edward Ryan (Sparky), Jeanne Crain (Char), June Haver (Cri-Cri), Clarence Muse (Tuffy), Eddie Marr (Dryer), Carlton KaDell (Bruce), Horace Willard (Man), Charles Seel (Blackdeath), Norman Field (Announcer), Robert Clarke (Doctor), Robert Cole (Tad), Herb Lytton, June Ford, Fred Seward, Bernice Barrett, George Dacos, and Virginia Agnello (Ad Libs).

Commercials: Lieutenant Robert Denham (Man), Stanley Farrar (Older Man), Ann Tobin (Girl in Acts 1 and 3), Janet Russell (Sally), Doris Singleton (Libby), Virginia Agnello (Singer), and Jim Ford (Singer).

"Home in Indiana," adapted from the Henry Hathaway–directed 20th Century–Fox film, brought yet another horse-racing drama to *Lux*. Four players from the movie repeat their characterizations in the broadcast: Walter Brennan, Charlotte Greenwood, Jeanne Crain, and June Haver. Though Edward

Ryan is third-billed among the principals (in a role played by Lon McCallister onscreen), his character is the focal point of the story.

452. "In Old Chicago," 10/9/44
Based on the 1938 20th Century–Fox film (screenplay by Lamar Trotti and Sonya Levien), in turn based on the story "We, the O'Leary's," by Niven Bush.
Cast: Dorothy Lamour (Belle), Robert Young (Dion), John Hodiak (Jack), Cy Kendall (Warner), Janet Scott (Molly), Ruby Dandridge (Hattie), Tom Holland (Bob), Griff Barnett (Driver/Second Man), Eddie Marr (Man/Sergeant), Charles Seel (Pat/Green), Norman Field (Sheridan), Truda Marson (Gretchen/Woman), Leo Cleary (Commissioner/Johnson), Edward J. Begley (Commissioner/Man), Tommy Cook (Dion, as a Boy), Dickie Meyers (Jack, as a Boy/Boy), Bob Martell (Secretary/Corporal), and Herb Lytton (Cop/Brown).
Singers: Homer Hall, Sidney Pepple, Jan Williams, Stewart Bair, and Enrico Ricardi (Singer/Conductor).
Commercials: Julie Bannon (Sally/Peggy), Doris Singleton (Libby), Ann Tobin (Sue), and Tom Hanlon (Second Announcer, Closing).
The 1938 20th Century–Fox production *In Old Chicago* (directed by Henry King) was presented on *Lux* with Dorothy Lamour, Robert Young, and John Hodiak in roles created on the screen by Alice Faye, Tyrone Power, and Don Ameche. Faye was given the chance to perform several musical numbers in the movie, two of which are sung by Lamour in the period piece centering around a mother and her two sons, one of whom becomes a corrupt politician and the other a fervent political reformer: Act 1: "I've Taken a Fancy to You" (partial), and "I'll Never Let You Cry" (both with words by Sidney D. Mitchell, music by Lew Pol-

lack). Although it is of course not possible to bring the spectacular Chicago fire sequences to the radio version, *Lux* adapter Sanford Barnett does a good job making the equivalents of these scenes vivid and exciting.

453. "Seventh Heaven," 10/16/44
Based on the 1927 Fox film (screenplay by Benjamin Glazer), in turn based on the play by Austin Strong (1922). Adapted for radio by George Wells.
Cast: Jennifer Jones (Diane), Van Johnson (Chico), Jean Hersholt (Father Chevillion), Billy Gilbert (Boul), Virginia Gordon (Nana), Norman Field (Brissac), Dick Ryan (Sewer Rat), Charles Seel (Gendarme/Voice), Eddie Marr (Second Gendarme/Man), Jay Novello (Third Gendarme/Manager), Leone Sousa (Madame), and June Ford and Bernice Barrett (Ad Libs).
Commercials: Doris Singleton (Libby), Dickie Meyers (Little Boy), Griff Barnett (Butcher), Julie Bannon (Woman's Voice), and Tom Hanlon (Second Announcer).
The parts of Diane and Chico, which were so splendidly played on the screen by Janet Gaynor and Charles Farrell, are here assigned to Jennifer Jones and Van Johnson. Jean Hersholt turns in a fine performance as Father Chevillion, and comedian Billy Gilbert is heard as Papa Boul. The Austin Strong sentimental favorite "Seventh Heaven" was chosen to commemorate the tenth anniversary of the *Lux Radio Theatre* on October 16.
Other *Lux* versions were performed on October 14, 1934 October 17, 1938, and March 26, 1951; see 10/14/34 for information on stage and film versions.
Additional film version: 20th Century–Fox, 1937.

*454. "The Story of Dr. Wassell," 10/23/44
Based on the 1944 Paramount film

(screenplay by Alan LeMay and Charles Bennett; story by James Hilton), in turn based on the actual accounts by Dr. Wassell and "15 of the wounded soldiers involved."

Cast: Gary Cooper (Dr. Wassell), Carol Thurston (Tremartini), Barbara Britton (Madeline), Reed Hadley (Goggins), Oliver Thorndyke (Andy), Carlton KaDell (Hoppy), Jacqueline DeWitt (Bettina), Howard McNear (Alabam), Ernest Anderson (Corporal/Aide), Ralph Montgomery (Francis), Tyler McVey (Murdock), Stanley Farrar (Sailor/Officer), Norman Field (Admiral), Charles Seel (Radio/Captain), Eddie Marr (Whaley), Bill Marbell (Johnny), Charles Lung (Ping/Bainbridge), Griff Barnett (Holmes), Jerome Sheldon (Wayne), George Neise (Dirk/Driver), Eric Snowden (Carruthers), and Mariah Burns (Mrs. W).

Commercials: Doris Singleton (Girl's Voice), Julie Bannon (Girl's Voice/Janie), Mary Kolda (Sue), Truda Marson (Betty/Second Girl's Voice), Tom Hanlon (Second Announcer), Charles Seel, Norman Field, and Tyler McVey (Men).

Cecil B. DeMille's 1944 inspirational biography *The Story of Dr. Wassell* chronicles the heroic wartime deeds of Dr. Corydon M. Wassell (1894–1958), who rescued and transported injured sailors from Java to Australia while under constant attack by Japanese forces. Gary Cooper reprises his screen role for the broadcast, as does Carol Thurston, while Barbara Britton is heard in Laraine Day's film part.

455. "Standing Room Only," 10/30/44

Based on the 1944 Paramount film (screenplay by Darrell Ware and Karl Tunberg), in turn based on a story by Al Martin.

Cast: Paulette Goddard (Jane Rogers), Fred MacMurray (Lee Stephens), Arthur Q. Bryan (Ira Cromwell), Verna

Felton (Major Cromwell), Norman Field (Mr. Ritchie), Pauline Drake (Alice/Secretary), Doris Singleton (Woman), Earle Ross (Mr. T.J. Todd), Leo Cleary (Man/Farenhall), Charles Seel (Clerk/Admiral), Eddie Marr (Waiter/Second Man), and Sarah Selby (Mrs. R.).

Commercials: Janet Russell (Sally), Dave Marshall (Boy), Julie Bannon (Girl), Margaret Landry (Another Girl), and Tom Hanlon (Second Announcer).

The 1944 Sidney Lanfield–directed Paramount film *Standing Room Only*, which gently pokes fun at the then-topical subject of housing shortages in Washington, D.C., is also a humorous *Lux* broadcast, with Paulette Goddard and Fred MacMurray resuming their motion picture roles, and Arthur Q. Bryan, Norman Field, and Eddie Marr in semilengthy supporting parts.

456. "The Pied Piper," 11/6/44

Based on the 1942 20th Century–Fox film (screenplay by Nunnally Johnson), in turn based on the novel by Nevil Shute (1942).

Cast: Frank Morgan (Mr. Howard), Margaret O'Brien (Sheila), Signe Hasso (Nicole), Cathy Lewis (Mrs. Cavanagh), Noreen Gammill (Madame), Tommy Cook (Ronnie), Vernon Steele (Cavanagh), Eric Snowden (Man), Norman Field (Aide), Jay Novello (Voice Number One/Aristide), Charles Seel (Voice Number Two/Bacquet), Alec Harford (Churchill), Ivette Dognay (Rosi), Leo Cleary (Official), Joel Davis (Man), Mickey Nunn (William), Cyril Ramsey-Hill (Major), and Norma Nilsson (Anna).

Commercials: Doris Singleton (Girl's Voice), Julie Bannon (Janie), Stanley Farrar (Man), Helen Andrews (Woman), Truda Marson (Sue), and Tom Hanlon (Second Announcer).

On November 6, Frank Morgan repeated his *Lux* characterization as the title figure in "The Pied Piper," which he had first performed on the air on December 21, 1942. The most important of the several children's roles in both the film and the earlier *Lux* is that of Ronnie (played by Roddy McDowall); in this version, however, the part of Ronnie's sister, Sheila, is given prominence, with most of the former's lines going to the latter. The obvious reason behind this alteration is the presence of seven-year-old child star Margaret O'Brien, who plays Sheila in the broadcast. Signe Hasso is heard in the leading lady role of Nicole.

See 12/21/42 for information concerning the film.

457. "Magnificent Obsession," 11/13/44

Based on the 1935 Universal film (screenplay by George O'Neill, Sarah Y. Mason, and Victor Heerman), in turn based on the novel by Lloyd C. Douglas (1929). Adapted for radio by George Wells.

Intermission Guest: Frank Sinatra (after Act 1).

Cast: Claudette Colbert (Helen Hudson), Don Ameche (Robert Merrick), Norman Field (Doctor Ramsey), Griff Barnett (Randolph), Regina Wallace (Nancy), Howard McNear (Jimmy/Clerk), Charles Seel (Terry), Gwen Delano (Woman), Norma Nilsson (Child), Julie Bannon (Nurse), Herb Rawlinson (Allan), Jay Novello (Man), and Sharon Douglas (Joyce).

Commercials: Janet Russell (Sally), Doris Singleton (Libby), Truda Marson (Girl's Voice), and Tom Hanlon (Second Announcer).

For *Lux*'s second airing of "Magnificent Obsession," Claudette Colbert and Don Ameche are given the roles played by Irene Dunne and Robert Taylor in the previous broadcast.

See 4/26/37 for information concerning the film versions.

Additional film version: Universal, 1954.

458. "It Started with Eve," 11/20/44

Based on the 1941 Universal film (screenplay by Norman Krasna and Leo Townsend; original story by Hans Kraly).

Cast: Charles Laughton (Jonathan Reynolds), Susanna Foster (Ann), Dick Powell (Johnny), Arthur Q. Bryan (Doctor Harvey), Charles Seel (Clerk/Waiter), Eddie Marr (Bellboy), Griff Barnett (Bishop Maxwell), Norman Field (Roberts), Noreen Gammill (Miss Dimnoggin), Verna Felton (Mrs. Pennington), Doris Singleton (Gloria/Girl), Joe Forte (Thomas/Man), and Franklyn Parker (Conductor/Man Number One).

Commercials: Truda Marson (Betty/Mrs. A), Julie Bannon (Jane/Mrs. B), Lynn Whitney (Mrs. C), Duane Thompson (Woman's Voice), and Tom Hanlon (Second Announcer).

Henry Koster directed Universal's engaging 1941 film *It Started with Eve*, which served as *Lux*'s presentation on November 20 and focuses on a young man who recruits a hatcheck girl to pose as his fiancée in order to humor his supposedly dying father and then must keep up the deception when he recovers. Susanna Foster delightfully plays Deanna Durbin's screen role, Charles Laughton of the film cast is just as amusing on the air, and Dick Powell (who does not sing) agreeably plays Robert Cummings's movie part. The multi-talented Foster beautifully sings the following: "Clavelitus," in Act 2, and "Lullaby of the Bells" (Edward Ward/George Waggner) in Act 3, the latter of which she had sung both in the film and in the *Lux* version of *The Phantom of the Opera*.

Universal's 1964 version, *I'd Rather Be Rich*, was directed by Jack Smith and featured Maurice Chevalier, Andy Williams, and Sandra Dee.

The *Lux Radio Theatre* presented a version on March 29, 1956.

Additional film version: Universal, 1964 (*I'd Rather Be Rich*).

459. "Dark Waters," 11/27/44

Based on the 1944 United Artists film (screenplay by Joan Harrison and Marian Cockrell), in turn based on the *Saturday Evening Post* serial by Frank and Marian Cockrell.

Cast: Merle Oberon (Leslie), Thomas Mitchell (Sidney), Preston Foster (George), Charles Seel (Doctor/Voice), Leo Cleary (Agent/Man), Janet Scott (Aunt Emily), Norman Field (Uncle Norbert), Ruby Dandridge (Florella), Tyler McVey (Man), Gloria Charmley (Cecille), Jane DeLoos (Woman), Mickey Kuhn (Talenques), Horace Willard (Pearson), Norma Nilsson (Ad Libs), and Dickie Meyers (Ad Libs).

Commercials: Janet Russell (Sally), Doris Singleton (Soft Feminine Voice in Act 3/Girl in Act 1), Ann James (First Girl), Julie Bannon (Second Girl), and Herb Lytton (Harsh Voice).

Dark Waters, the Andre de Toth–directed United Artists thriller, centers around a young woman's battle to overcome post-traumatic stress disorder, which was brought about by the effects of surviving a torpedoed ocean liner. Her troubles are further compounded by a group of fortune hunters who pose as family members and attempt to drive her insane for insurance purposes. *Lux* retains both Merle Oberon and Thomas Mitchell from the movie cast, while Preston Foster is heard in the part Franchot Tone plays in the film.

460. "Unguarded Hour," 12/4/44

Based on the 1936 MGM film (screenplay by Howard Emmett Rogers and Leon Gordon), in turn based on Bernard Merival's adaptation of the play by Ladislas Fodor.

Cast: Robert Montgomery (Alan), Laraine Day (Helen), Roland Young (Bunny), Charles Seel (Hilton), Norman Field (Judge), Claire Verdera (Anne/Eloise), Alec Harford (Lord H.), Gloria Gordon (Lady H.), Eric Snowden (Grainger), Raymond Lawrence (Medford), Boyd Irwin (Attorney), Jacqueline DeWitt (Diana), Fred Worlock (General), and Leslie Dennison (Lewis).

Commercials: Janet Russell (Sally), Julie Bannon (Sue), Leone Ledoux (Child), Duane Thompson (Jane), and Doris Singleton (Singer).

Sam Wood was at the directorial helm of the MGM mystery-drama *The Unguarded Hour,* which reached the screen in 1936. The movie roles of Franchot Tone and Loretta Young are taken by Robert Montgomery and Laraine Day in the broadcast, which centers around a woman who holds the key to exonerating an innocent man accused of murder but who cannot come forward because of blackmail threats. (Roland Young is the only one of the principals to reprise his screen character).

461. "Casanova Brown," 12/11/44

Based on the 1944 International film (screenplay by Nunnally Johnson), in turn based on the play *Little Accident,* by Floyd Dell (1928).

Cast: Gary Cooper (Cas), Joan Bennett (Isabell), Thomas Mitchell (J.J.), Verna Felton (Mrs. Dean), Ann O'Neal (Mrs. Drury), Norman Field (Mr. Drury/Man), Dorothy Scott (Operator/Monica), Leone Ledoux (Boy/Infant), Sarah Selby (Nurse), Charles Seel (Charles), Eddie Emerson (Orderly), Jacqueline DeWitt (Woman), and Sharon Douglas (Madge).

Commercials: Janet Russell (Sally), Doris Singleton (Libby), Herb Lytton (First Man), and Charles Seel (Second Man).

Casanova Brown, the 1944 Sam Wood–directed comedy, played on *Lux* with its original star, Gary Cooper, in the title role of a man who tries to reconcile with his estranged wife after discovering that she is expecting a child. Heard in Teresa Wright's screen part is Joan Bennett, while Frank Morgan's film character goes to Thomas Mitchell. Mitchell actually has a lengthier association with the story than any of the other cast members, for he appeared in the original Broadway production with Malcolm Williams and Katherine Alexander in 1928 when it was entitled *Little Accident*. Universal filmed the story twice: first, in 1930 (directed by William J. Craft), starring Douglas Fairbanks, Jr., and Anita Page, then in a rather loose 1939 version (directed by Charles Lamont), featuring Hugh Herbert, Florence Rice, and Richard Carlson.

Additional film versions: Universal, 1930; Universal, 1939.

462. "Berkeley Square," 12/18/44

Based on the play *Berkeley Square* (1929), by John Balderston, from the story "A Sense of the Past," by Henry James.

Cast: Ronald Colman (Peter Standish), Maureen O'Sullivan (Helen Pettigrew), Dorothy Lovett (Kate), Charles Seel (Cabby/Crier), Gloria Gordon (Lady Ann), Leslie Dennison (Thomas), Claire Verdera (Duchess), Jacqueline DeWitt (Marjorie), Colin Campbell (Throstle), Eric Snowden (Clinton), Norman Field (Reynolds), and Gwen Delano (Maid).

Commercials: Doris Singleton (Libby), Julie Bannon (Girl), and Jack Boyles (Man).

The beautifully executed "Berkeley Square" serves as an excellent vehicle with which to showcase the brilliant performances of highly versatile stars Ronald Colman and Maureen O'Sullivan, who play the world-weary twentieth-century aristocrat who longs for the past, and the uncannily clairvoyant

young eighteenth-century girl literally in love with the future (in the person of Ronald Colman). The tender love scenes between O'Sullivan's Helen Pettigrew and Colman's Peter Standish are especially memorable, as is the moving climax in which Helen gently tells Peter (who must return to the future) that they will "be together not in my time, or in yours—but in God's."

The 1933 Fox film (which lacks the sincerity and subtlety of this *Lux* presentation) features Leslie Howard and Heather Angel in the leads.

See 12/9/34 for information on stage and film versions; *Lux* also aired a rendering of "I'll Never Forget You" on September 22, 1952.

Additional film versions: 20th Century–Fox, 1951 (*I'll Never Forget You*).

463. "The Vagabond King," 12/25/44

Based on the musical production, book and lyrics by Brian Hooker and W.H. Post, music by Rudolf Friml (1925), in turn based on the play *If I Were King*, by Justin Huntly McCarthy (1901), from his own novel (1901).

Cast: Dennis Morgan (François Villon), Kathryn Grayson (Lady Katherine), J. Carroll Naish (King Louis XI), Walter Bond (Tristam), Jack Boyles (Taberia), Beverly Brown (Hugenette), Charles Seel (Marshall), Tyler McVey (Harold), Ed Emerson (Captain), and Norman Field (Court Astrologer/Page).

Ad Libs: Virginia Agnello, Ralph Montgomery, Cedric Stevens, George Bacos, and June Ford.

Singers: Robert Tait, Orville Haas, Clarence Badger, Norma Nilsson, Robert Bradford, George Gramlich, Donald Neese, Lee Winter, Jack Law, and Enrico Ricardi (Contractor).

Commercials: Doris Singleton (Girl), Charlotte Treadway (Woman in Acts 1 and 3), and Betty Jean Hainey (Jane).

The second presentation of "The

Vagabond King" features Dennis Morgan and Kathryn Grayson in the roles taken earlier by John Boles and Evelyn Venable. (Grayson also appears in the 1956 Michael Curtiz–directed Paramount film.) Musical selections are as follows: Act 1: "Some Day" (Grayson), "Song of the Vagabonds" (Morgan); Act 2: "Only a Rose" (Grayson and Morgan); Act 3: "Never Try to Bind Me" (Morgan and Grayson), "Only a Rose" (finale; Morgan and Grayson).

See 8/17/36 for information on stage and film versions.

Film versions: Paramount, 1930; Paramount, 1956.

464. "Bride by Mistake," 1/1/45

Based on the 1944 RKO movie (screenplay by Phoebe and Henry Ephorn), in turn based on the 1934 RKO film *The Richest Girl in the World* (screenplay by Norman Krasna).

Special Guest: Bob Hope.

Cast: Laraine Day (Norah), John Hodiak (Tony), Marsha Hunt (Sylvia), Eddie Marr (Lieutenant Corey), Charles Seel (Connors), Norman Field (Man/Butler/Sam), Dorothy Lovett (Harris), Richard Fraser (Donald), Hal Gerard (Wilson), and Carlton KaDell (Philip).

Commercials: Janet Russell (Sally), Julie Bannon (Girl), Jack Boyles (Man), and Doris Singleton (Libby).

Lux's offering for the first day of 1945 was its adaptation of RKO's Richard Wallace–directed comedy *Bride by Mistake.* Playing the same parts they created in the film, which concerns a millionairess who changes places with her paid companion to ensure that her next suitor is not after her money, are Laraine Day and Marsha Hunt, while John Hodiak takes the Alan Marshal movie role. *Bride by Mistake* is actually a version of the 1934 RKO release *The Richest Girl in the World,* which stars Miriam Hopkins, Joel McCrea, and Fay Wray under William A. Seiter's direction.

During the curtain call, Bob Hope makes an appearance in order to promote the next week's broadcast, "I Never Left Home."

Additional film version: RKO, 1934 (*The Richest Girl in the World*).

465. "I Never Left Home," 1/8/45

Based on Bob Hope's personal experiences as recounted in his book of the same title (1944).

Cast: Bob Hope, Frances Langford, Jerry Colonna, Tony Romano, Norman Field (Hotel Manager/Colonel Stevens), Howard McNear (R.A.F. Pilot/Pyle), Eddie Marr (Sailor/Radio Operator), Ken Christy (Red Cross Club Organizer), Charles Seel (Announcer/Eisenhower), Leo Cleary (Davis/Sicilian), Ed Emerson (Vaughn/Choury), Jack Mather (Sergeant/M.P.), Eric Snowden (Room Service/Scott), Tyler McVey (Lieutenant/Cullen), Franklyn Parker (Intern), Herb Lytton (Dowling/Moore), Bob Cole (Invalid/Cast), Herb Rawlinson (Flanagan/Chandler), George Pembroke (Second R.A.F. Pilot), Lee Millar (Bracelet/Ranger), Bob Young (Strickland/Second Ranger), Claire Verdera (Mrs. Kilby), and Dorothy Lovett (Dolores/Reporter).

Commercials: Janet Russell (Sally), Stanley Farrar (First Man/Mr. Smith), Tyler McVey (Second Man), Bob Cole (Third Man), and Duane Thompson (Mrs. Smith).

A different approach to *Lux's* standard broadcast was given with the airing of "I Never Left Home," an autobiographical sketch of Bob Hope's journeys overseas to entertain troops. Joining him from the original tour are Frances Langford, Jerry Colonna, and Tony Romano. Musical selections are as follows: Act 1: "It Had to Be You" (words by Gus Kahn, music by Isham Jones, 1924; performed by Frances Langford); Act 2: "Embraceable You" (words by Ira Gershwin, music by George Gershwin; from

Girl Crazy, 1930; partial rendition by Langford), "Thanks for the Memory" (words by Leo Robin, music by Ralph Rainger; from *The Big Broadcast of 1938*; performed by Bob Hope), "I'm in the Mood for Love" (words by Dorothy Fields, music by Jimmy McHugh; from the 1935 movie *Every Night at 8*; Langford); Act 3: "You Made Me Love You" (words by Joseph McCarthy, music by James V. Monaco, 1913; Langford).

466. "The Master Race," 1/15/45

Based on the 1944 RKO film (screenplay by Herbert J. Biberman, Anne Froelick, and Rowland Leigh; original story by Herbert J. Biberman).

Cast: George Colouris (Colonel von Beck), Nancy Gates (Nina Vallin), Stanley Ridges (Major Carson), Helen Beverly (Martha), Paul Guilfoyle (Catray), Richard Martin (Frank Bartok), Eric Feldberry (Altmeier), Charles Seel, Paul Theodore, Eric Snowden, Norman Field (Lance), Lurene Tuttle (Helena), and George Neise.

Lux's broadcast of RKO's war drama *The Master Race* (directed by Herbert J. Biberman) features five players from the original cast: George Colouris, Nancy Gates, Stanley Ridges, Helen Beverly, and Paul Guilfoyle. The adaptation is arranged in such a way as to give each of the principals roughly an equal share of airtime, with Colouris having slightly more to do as the escaped Nazi officer who attempts to keep the dream of the Third Reich alive. The role of Helena is greatly minimized, and her nameless illegitimate child (the product of rape) has been eliminated; instead (in dialogue created for the radio version), mention is made of the death of a legitimate daughter (which she never had in the film).

467. "Tender Comrade," 1/22/45

Based on the 1943 RKO film (screenplay by Dalton Trumbo).

Cast: Olivia deHavilland (Jo), June Duprez (Barbara), Dennis O'Keefe (Chris), Eddie Marr (Mike), Paula Winslowe (Woman), Charles Seel (Voice/Announcer), Norman Field (Conductor/Doctor), Regina Wallace (Helen), Sharon Douglas (Doris), Leo Cleary (Waldo/Boy), Gwen Delano (Manya/Mother), and Leone Ledoux (Baby).

Commercials: Janet Russell (Sally), Truda Marson (Girl), Robert Clarke (Boy), and Doris Singleton (Girl Number Two).

Cecil B. DeMille's distinguished eight-and-a-half-year position as the *Lux Radio Theatre* host unfortunately came to an unceremonious end with the broadcast of RKO's "Tender Comrade." The Edward Dmytryk–directed drama of the women "left behind" by their soldier-husbands was completely recast by *Lux* producers. They chose Olivia deHavilland, June Duprez, and Dennis O'Keefe to take the screen parts of Ginger Rogers, Ruth Hussey, and Robert Ryan, respectively.

After the broadcast, DeMille announced that the *Lux Radio Theatre* was voted "Outstanding Dramatic Program for 1944" by *Radio Daily*.

468. "Lady in the Dark," 1/29/45

Based on the 1944 Paramount film (screenplay by Frances Goodrich and Albert Hackett), in turn based on the musical play by Moss Hart, music by Kurt Weill, lyrics by Ira Gershwin (1941).

Guest Host: Lionel Barrymore.

Cast: Ginger Rogers (Liza Elliott), Ray Milland (Charley Johnson), Carlton KaDell (Randy), Charles Seel (Father), Verna Felton (Maggie), Doris Singleton (Foster), Herb Rawlinson (Kendall), Charlotte Treadway (Martha), Eddie Marr (Photographer/Man), Norman Field (Man), Ed Emerson

(Man Number Two), Norma Nilsson (Child), Robert Clarke (Pen), Gloria Fisher (Barbara), Jay Novello (Russell/ Man Number Three), Frances Woodward (Girl/Mother), and Howard McNear (Dr. Brooks).

Commercials: Truda Marson (First Girl), Julie Bannon (Girl), Duane Thompson (Woman), Leone Ledoux (Child), and Betty Jean Hainey (Second Girl).

Lux's production of "Lady in the Dark," a rather odd comedy focusing on a career woman's inner struggle for personal happiness (glimpsed through dream sequences and psychoanalysis), reteams Ginger Rogers and Ray Milland of the original 1944 Mitch Leisen–directed film. Moss Hart's 1941 stage play, on which the motion picture is based (and which stars Gertrude Lawrence and Macdonald Carey in the Broadway production), is a musical featuring songs of Ira Gershwin and Kurt Weill. The motion picture deletes most of the score, however, and except for a few bars Ginger Rogers sings during the circus dream sequence, the only Gershwin/Weill selection heard in the broadcast is "My Ship," which Rogers performs in Act 3. Even the well-known "Saga of Jenny" is omitted from the score of the broadcast version.

In this, the first post–Cecil B. DeMille broadcast, Lionel Barrymore is heard as guest host.

"Lady in the Dark" was performed again on February 16, 1953.

469. "Laura," 2/5/45

Based on the 1944 20th Century–Fox film (screenplay by Jay Drather, Samuel Hoffenstein, and Betty Reinhart), in turn based on the novel by Vera Caspary (1943), which was based on her serialized story "Ring Twice for Laura" (*Collier's*, October/November, 1942).

Guest Host: Lionel Barrymore.

Cast: Dana Andrews (Mark McPherson), Gene Tierney (Laura), Vincent Price (Shelby Carpenter), Otto Kruger (Paul Lydecker), Lois Corbett (Ann), Duane Thompson (Maid), Leo Cleary (Crane), Noreen Gammill (Bessie), Charles Seel (Alford/Radio), and Howard McNear (Radio in Act 3).

Commercials: Julie Bannon (Girl), Doris Singleton (Libby), Betty Jean Hainey (Girl), Franklyn Parker (First Man), and Charles Seel (Second Man).

The 1944 Otto Preminger 20th Century–Fox motion picture *Laura* was recreated for *Lux* utilizing the film's three stars, Dana Andrews, Gene Tierney, and Vincent Price, with Otto Kruger taking the part played by Clifton Webb onscreen. The unconventional mystery tells of a detective who, while investigating the past of a supposedly murdered glamorous artist, finds himself falling in love with her.

470. "For Whom the Bell Tolls," 2/12/45

Based on the 1943 Paramount film (screenplay by Dudley Nichols), in turn based on the novel by Ernest Hemingway (1940).

Guest Host: Otto Kruger.

Cast: Gary Cooper (Robert), Ingrid Bergman (Maria), Akim Tamiroff (Pablo), Gale Sondergaard (Pilar), Mikhail Rasumny (Rafael), Tito Renaldo (Augustio), Charles Seel (El Sordo/Colonel), Eddie Marr (Andros/ Second Voice), Norman Field (Anselmo), Howard McNear (Primitive/ Major), Jay Novello (Fernando), Ed Emerson (Gomez), Paul Theodore (Man/Voice), and Joe Granby (Golz).

Commercials: Doris Singleton (Libby), Marrisa Bria (Betty), Clete Lee (Bob), and Betty Jean Hainey (First Girl).

Paramount's *For Whom the Bell Tolls* (directed by Sam Wood in 1943) is faithfully adapted to radio and stars Gary Cooper, reprising his film role of an American fighting against the Fascists in the Spanish Civil War, and three other members of the picture cast: Ingrid Bergman, Akim Tamiroff, and Mikhail Rasumny. Gale Sondergaard is heard in Katina Paxinou's movie role of Pilar, and Otto Kruger appears as guest host.

471. "Sunday Dinner for a Soldier,"
2/19/45

Based on the 1944 20th Century–Fox film (screenplay by Wanda Tuchock and Melvin Levy).

Guest Host: Jesse L. Lasky.

Cast: Anne Baxter (Tessa), John Hodiak (Eric), Charles Winninger (Grandfeathers), Verna Felton (Agatha Butterfield), Patricia Lowrey (Mary), Bobby Larson (Jeep), Billy Roy (Mike), Charles Seel (York/Second M.P.), Eddie Marr (Man/M.P.), Ruby Dandridge (Louella), Dickie Meyers (Boy), Robert Regent (Kenneth/Second Man), Janet Scott (Mrs. Dobson), and Earl Keen (Chicken).

Commercials: Duane Thompson (Woman, Act 1), Julie Bannon (Woman, Act 2), Charlotte Treadway (Second Woman, Act 1), and Herb Lytton (Man).

The 1944 Lloyd Bacon–directed 20th Century–Fox entry *Sunday Dinner for a Soldier* made pleasant fare for February 19. Reprising their screen roles from the original picture cast are Anne Baxter, Charles Winninger, and John Hodiak as the heads of a hospitable rural Florida family and an eternally grateful soldier, respectively.

472. "Bedtime Story," 2/26/45

Based on the 1941 Columbia film (screenplay by Richard Flournoy), in turn based on a story by Horace Jackson and Grant Garrett.

Guest Host: Donald Crisp.

Cast: Greer Garson (Jane), Cary Grant (Luke), Carlton KaDell (Dud-

ley), Arthur Q. Bryan (Eddie), Verna Felton (Emma), Eddie Marr (Mike/Clerk), Ed Emerson (Bert), Linda King (Beulah), Norman Field (Pop), Leo Cleary (Man), Dorothy Scott (Betsy/Maid), Jay Novello (Pierce), Boyd Davis (Keeles), Charles Seel (Collins/Electrician), Doris Singleton (Girl/Secretary), and Colleen Collins (Virginia).

Commercials: Janet Russell (Sally), Charlotte Treadway (Woman), Julie Bannon (Betsy), and Helen Andrews (Nancy).

Lux's February 26 broadcast presented a second rendering of "Bedtime Story," which on this occasion features Greer Garson and Cary Grant in the leads.

See 6/22/42 for information on film.

473. "Disputed Passage," 3/5/45

Based on the 1939 Paramount film (screenplay by Sheridan Gibney and Anthony Veiller), in turn based on the novel by Lloyd C. Douglas (1943).

Guest Host: Brian Aherne.

Cast: Alan Ladd (John), Akim Tamiroff (Professor Forster), Ann Richards (Audrey), Charles Seel (Voice Number Two/Kai), Clete Lee (Anderson/Man), Ralph Lewis (Shelby/Man), Eddie Marr (Chadwick/Man), Truda Marson (Winifred/Phone Girl), Robert Regent (Voice Number One/Britisher), Norman Field (Cunningham), Paul Theodore (Abbott), Lal Chand Mehra (Chang), Jay Novello (La Ferrier), Leone Ledoux (Child/Girl), and Barbara Jean Wong (Nurse/Woman).

Commercials: Doris Singleton (Libby), Janet Russell (Sally), Julie Bannon (First Woman), and Ann Tobin (Second Woman).

The Frank Borzage–directed 1939 Paramount film *Disputed Passage* provided *Lux* listeners with a drama focusing on the never-ending struggle of dedicated surgeons delicately balancing their professional and personal lives. Alan Ladd and Ann Richards play the roles taken by John Howard and Dorothy Lamour in the motion picture, while Akim Tamiroff resumes his screen part of Professor Forster.

474. "The Devil and Miss Jones," 3/12/45

Based on the 1941 RKO film (screenplay by Norman Krasna). Adapted for radio by George Wells.

Guest Host: Brian Aherne.

Cast: Frank Morgan (J.P. Merrick), Linda Darnell (Mary), Gordon Oliver (Joe), Arthur Q. Bryan (Hooper), Griff Barnett (Love), Ferdinand Munier (George), Howard McNear (Thomas Higgins/Conductor), Verna Felton (Store Shopper), Ed Emerson (Eddie), Eddie Marr (Store Detective), Boyd Davis (Waldron), Norman Field (Carlo), Charles Seel (Allyson), Doris Singleton (Girl), Norma Nilsson (Sally), and Lois Corbett (Secretary/Woman).

Commercials: Robert Cole (First Man), Ralph Lewis (Second Man), Julie Bannon (Girl), Helen Andrews (Sue), and Duane Thompson (Mrs. Abbott).

Lux listeners who heard the March 5 broadcast were in for a surprise one week later, for only one of the three announced stars scheduled to appear in "The Devil and Miss Jones" actually participated in the show. Missing were Charles Laughton and Dennis O'Keefe, while Linda Darnell plays Mary as promised. Taking the roles of the absent stars are Frank Morgan and Gordon Oliver.

See 1/19/42 for information concerning the film version.

475. "Grissley's Millions," 3/19/45

Based on the 1944 Republic film (screenplay by Muriel Roy Bolton).

Guest Host: Otto Kruger.

Cast: Pat O'Brien (Joe), Lynn Bari (Katherine), Elisabeth Risdon (Leona), Carlton KaDell (Hayes), Franklyn Parker (Fray), Eddie Marr (Fred), Ann Stone (June/Operator), Gloria Fisher (Maribelle), Earl Keen (Agent), Joe Granby (Grissley), Griff Barnett (Penny), Ed Emerson (Lewis), Horace Murphy (Gatekeeper), Charles Seel (Adams), Gwen Delano (Mattie), Paul Theodore (Albert), and Norman Field (Man).

Lux's March 19 broadcast offered a change of pace with the presentation of the Republic film *Grissley's Millions*. The adaptation of the John English film is a slight murder mystery centering around the will of a cantankerous millionaire and his scheming relatives. Pat O'Brien and Lynn Bari star in the roles played by Paul Kelly and Virginia Grey in the 1944 film, while Elisabeth Risdon resumes her original screen part.

476. "A Tale of Two Cities," 3/26/45

Based on the novel by Charles Dickens (1859).

Guest Host: Frank Craven.

Cast: Orson Welles (Sydney Carton), Rosemary deCamp (Lucie Manette), Denis Green (Charles Darnay), Griff Barnett (Dr. Manette), Verna Felton (Madame Defarge), Norman Field (Lorry), Ken Christy (Jailer/Guard), Charles Seel (Cabelle), Lurene Tuttle (Lisette), Ferdinand Munier (Coachman/President), Jay Novello (Joe/Leader), Robert Regent (Jerry/Journeyman), Eric Snowden (Stryver), Boyd Davis (Attorney/General), Paul McVey (Judge), Alec Harford (Baread), Thomas Mills (Innkeeper), Regina Wallace (Miss Pross), Virginia Gordon (Annette), and Herb Lytton (Sergeant/Defarge).

Commercials: Janet Russell (Sally), Truda Marson (Girl), Ralph Lewis (Boy), and Doris Singleton (Girl).

Charles Dickens's *A Tale of Two Cities* returned to *Lux* on March 26 with Orson Welles as Sydney Carton, a role he had previously played on his own *Mercury Theatre* broadcast of July 25, 1938. The leading feminine part of

Lucie Manette goes to Rosemary deCamp, and the supporting cast is led by Denis Green, Griff Barnett, Verna Felton, and Norman Field.

See 1/12/42 for information on film versions; a third rendering was performed on March 18, 1946.

Film versions: 1917; British, 1925 (*The Only Way*); MGM, 1935; British, 1958.

477. "Swanee River," 4/2/45

Based on the 1939 20th Century–Fox film (screenplay by John Taintor Foote and Philip Dunne).

Guest Host: Walter Huston.

Cast: Dennis Morgan (Stephen Foster), Al Jolson (E.P. Christie), Frances Gifford (Jane McDowell), Charles Seel (Harry), Norman Field (Wilson/Doctor), Eddie Marr (Cedar/ Man Number Three), Janet Scott (Landlady/Woman), Leone Ledoux (Nina/Baby Cry), Leo Cleary (Tumbo/ Manager), Howard McNear (Leader/ Man Number Two), Ed Emerson (Man Number Two in Act 2/Man), Norma Nilsson (Child), Billy Roy (Sam), Earl Taylor Smith (Uncle Joe), and Paul Frees (Man).

Singers: Enrico Ricardi, Sidney Pepple (Soloist), Gene Curtsinger, Robert Tait, Robert Bradford, Clarence Badger, Warren Tipple, George Gramlich, Kenneth Rundquist, Donald Neese, Robert Kiber, Lee Winter, and Frank Chamberlain.

Commercials: Janet Russell (Sally), Truda Marson (First Girl), Julie Bannon (Second Girl), and Doris Singleton (Girl's Voice).

Lux's rendering of "Swanee River," the life story of American songwriter Stephen Foster (1826–64), is actually just an excuse to present a bevy of beloved Foster melodies. Al Jolson of the film cast repeats his role as E.P. Christie, with Dennis Morgan as Stephen Foster and Frances Gifford as Jane McDowell (in the roles played by

Don Ameche and Andrea Leeds in the 1939 Sidney Lanfield–directed 20th Century–Fox film). The musical selections (all with words and music by Stephen Foster) are: Act 1: "Oh, Susanna" (1848), "Camptown Races" (1850; both sung by Al Jolson), "My Old Kentucky Home" (1853; Dennis Morgan); Act 2: "Ring de Banjo" (1851), "Jeannie with the Light Brown Hair" (1854), "Old Black Joe" (1860; all by Dennis Morgan); Act 3: "Old Folks at Home" (1851; Al Jolson).

During the curtain call, Al Jolson sings "April Showers" while *Lux* musical director Lou Silvers (the song's composer) accompanies him on the piano.

478. "The Suspect," 4/9/45

Based on the 1944 Universal film (screenplay by Bertram Millhauser; adaptation by Arthur T. Horman), in turn based on the novel *This Way Out*, by James Ronald (1939).

Guest Host: Thomas Mitchell.

Cast: Charles Laughton (Phillip Marshall), Ella Raines (Mary Gray), Rosalind Ivan (Cora), Denis Green (Gilbert Simmons), Lester Matthews (Huxley), Truda Marson (Sybil), Norman Field (Stanton), Antony Ellis (John), Eric Snowden (Officer/Prentice), Tommy Cook (Marridew), Alec Harford (Cabbie/Barber), Charles Seel (Barkeeper), Claire Verdera (Mrs. Simmons), Gloria Gordon (Waitress), and Beryl V. Collins (Steward).

Commercials: Lila Webb (Woman), Paul Theodore (Man), Betty Jean Hainey (Girl), Doris Singleton (Girl's Voice), and Robert Clarke (Boy).

The Lux adaptation of Robert Siodmak's 1944 Universal thriller *The Suspect* served to reunite original motion picture cast members Charles Laughton, Ella Raines, and Rosalind Ivan in a story concerning a kindly

"Swanee River" (April 2, 1945), with Frances Gifford and Dennis Morgan (photo: Photofest).

office clerk who decides to do away with his shrewish wife.

479. "Only Yesterday," 4/16/45

Based on the 1933 Universal film (screenplay by William Hurlbut, Arthur Richman, and George O'Neil), in turn based on the book by Frederick Lewis Allen (1931). Adapted for radio by George Wells.

Guest Host: Edward G. Robinson.

Cast: Ida Lupino (Mary Lane), Robert Young (James Emerson), Lois Corbett (Aunt Julia), Tommy Cook (Jimmie), Lurene Tuttle (Blanche), Charles Seel (Mr. Lane/Voice), Howard McNear (Doctor/David), Norman Field (Fairchild/Cabby), Eddie Marr (Messenger/Soldier), Ferdinand Munier (Mr. Emerson/Butler), Regina Wallace (Mrs. Lane), Janet Scott (Abby/ Mother), and Truda Marson (Deborah/ Nurse).

Commercials: Doris Singleton (Libby), Julie Bannon (Kay), Betty Jean Hainey (Jane), Ann Tobin (Nancy), and Virginia Gregg (Mary).

The April 16 broadcast brought back yet another play previously aired on *Lux*. This rendering of "Only Yesterday" stars Ida Lupino in Margaret Sullavan's movie part and Robert Young in the role John Boles was assigned in the picture version.

A brief tribute to Franklin Roosevelt, who died on April 12, is delivered by guest host Edward G. Robinson prior to the opening theme music.

See 11/6/39 for information concerning the film version; the *Lux Video Theatre* presented a rendering on September 27, 1956.

480. "The Petrified Forest," 4/23/45
Based on the play by Robert E. Sherwood (1934).
Guest Host: Thomas Mitchell.
Cast: Ronald Colman (Alan Squire), Susan Hayward (Gaby), Lawrence Tierney (Duke Mantee), Norman Field (Gramps), Bill Martel (Boze), Leo Cleary (Linesman/Sheriff), Ed Emerson (Jackie), Eddie Marr (Bugs), Charles Seel (Second Linesman/Radio), Regina Wallace (Mrs. Chisholm), Jay Novello (Ruby), and Herbert Rawlinson (Chisholm).
Commercials: Doris Singleton (Libby), Janet Russell (Sally), Julie Bannon (Nancy), and Truda Marson (June).
Lux's second airing of "The Petrified Forest" is a somewhat more streamlined and superficial telling of the story, bringing in Ronald Colman, Susan Hayward, and Lawrence Tierney to play the leading roles. The original ending, which was discarded in the earlier broadcast, is restored in this more recent rendering.
See 11/22/37 for information concerning the film and stage versions.
Film version: Warner Bros., 1936.

481. "Moontide," 4/30/45
Based on the 1942 20th Century–Fox film (screenplay by John O'Hara), in turn based on the novel by Willard Robertson.
Guest Host: Mark Hellinger.
Cast: Humphrey Bogart (Bobo), Virginia Bruce (Anna), Cy Kendall (Tiny), Norman Field (Nutsy), Griff Barnett (Voice/Wilson), Charles Seel (Brothers), Lal Chand Mehra (Henry), Paul Theodore (Albert/Clerk), Ed Emerson (Clerk/Radio), Billy Roy (Boy), Dorothy Scott (Woman/Nurse), Myra Dell (Second Woman/Mildred), Franklyn Parker (Cop), Jay Novello (Charlie), and Earl Keen (Dog).
Commercials: Doris Singleton (Libby), Duane Thompson (First Woman),

Helen Andrews (Second Woman), and Madeleine Lee (Woman).
Stars Humphrey Bogart and Virginia Bruce were teamed for *Lux*'s broadcast of "Moontide," the story of an abrasive sailor and the emotionally despondent girl whom he protects. Mark Hellinger, the producer of the 1942 Archie Mayo–directed film (which stars Jean Gabin and Ida Lupino), is on hand to serve as guest host.

482. "Sing, You Sinners," 5/7/45
Based on the 1938 Paramount film (screenplay by Claude Binyon).
Guest Host: Mitchell Leisen.
Cast: Bing Crosby (Joe), Joan Caulfield (Martha), James Dunn (David), Elizabeth Patterson (Mrs. Beebe), Charles Seel (Announcer), Billy Roy (Nibs), Eddie Marr (Master of Ceremonies/Pete), Lee Sherin (Waiter/Boy), Earl Taylor Smith (Porter/Filter), Norman Field (Steward), Arthur Q. Bryan (Al), Ed Emerson (Ringner), and Virginia Agnello and Bernice Barrett (Ad Libs).
Commercials: Janet Russell (Sally), Doris Singleton (Libby), Truda Marson (Young Housewife/Second Woman, Act 2), and Lila Webb (First Woman, Act 2).
The second *Lux* offering of an adaptation of the 1938 Paramount film *Sing, You Sinners* utilizes Bing Crosby from the motion picture cast, as well as Joan Caulfield and James Dunn (in roles taken by Ellen Drew and Fred MacMurray in the film), while Elizabeth Patterson is again heard as Mrs. Beebe. (Crosby performs the same songs in this version that he did in the January 15, 1940, broadcast.)
See 1/15/40 for information on the film version.

483. "Alexander Graham Bell," 5/14/45
Based on the 1939 20th Century–Fox

film *The Story of Alexander Graham Bell* (screenplay by Lamar Trotti), in turn based on the story by Ray Harris.

Guest Host: Mitchell Leisen.

Cast: Don Ameche (Alexander Graham Bell), June Duprez (Mabel Hubbard), Truda Marson (Gertrude), Charles Seel (Mr. Sanders), Francis X. Bushman (Mr. Hubbard), Tommy Cook (George), Dickie Meyers (Boy), Regina Wallace (Mrs. Hubbard/Nurse), Myra Dell (Woman), Edwin Rand (Watson), Gwen Delano (Mrs. Sanders), Stanley Farrar (Man/Conductor), Herbert Lytton (Man Number Two/Man), Paul McVey (Man Number Three/Doctor), Ferdinand Munier (Judge), Boyd Davis (Barrows), Griff Barnett (Attorney), and Norman Field (President).

Commercials: Doris Singleton (Libby), Julie Bannon (Barbara), and Betty Jean Hainey (Jane).

"Alexander Graham Bell," which was based on the 1939 20th Century–Fox film biography directed by future *Lux* host Irving Cummings, was presented on May 14. Starring as Alexander Graham Bell (1847–1922) in both the movie and the broadcast is Don Ameche, while June Duprez splendidly plays his love interest, Mabel (Loretta Young in the film). Curiously, those immortal words "Mr. Watson, come here, I want you" have been altered to "*Tom*, come here, I want you," even though the picture version retained the line as (allegedly) first spoken by Bell over the telephone.

A second broadcast was aired on April 26, 1955.

484. "And Now Tomorrow," 5/21/45

Based on the 1944 Paramount film (screenplay by Fred Kohlmar and Raymond Chandler), in turn based on the novel by Rachel Field (1942).

Guest Host: Preston Sturges.

Cast: Alan Ladd (Dr. Merrick Vance), Loretta Young (Emily Blair), Griff Barnett (Dr. Weeks), Charles Seel (Meade), Norman Field (Dr. Sloan), Earl Smith (Porter), Paul Theodore (Man/Peter), Stanley Farrar (Conductor), Janet Scott (Martha), Doris Singleton (Janice), Edwin Rand (Jeff), Ann Tobin (Angeletta/Operator), and Duane Thompson (Woman).

Commercials: Truda Marson (First Girl), Virginia Gregg (Second Girl), Julie Bannon (Girl's Voice/Woman's Voice), Betty Jean Hainey (Girl), and Ralph Lewis (Boy).

Lux's production of "And Now Tomorrow" reteams Alan Ladd and Loretta Young, both of whom also appear in the 1944 Paramount film (which was directed by Irving Pichel). The story focuses on a doctor treating a supposedly incurably deaf patient with whom he inevitably falls in love, and it is done with *Lux*'s usual taste and intelligence.

A second version was aired on June 10, 1946.

485. "Kentucky," 5/28/45

Based on the 1938 20th Century–Fox film (screenplay by Lamar Trotti and John Tainor Foote; story by John Tainor Foote).

Guest Host: Mitchell Leisen.

Cast: Laraine Day (Sally Goodwin), Walter Brennan (Peter Goodwin), Tom Drake (Jack Dillon), Howard McNear (Mr. Goodwin/Marty), Norman Field (Dillon), Herb Rawlinson (Man/Voice), Leo Cleary (Man), Arthur Q. Bryan (Second Man/Doctor Nelson), Haskell Coffin (First Dillon/Official), Ed Emerson (Soldier/Clerk), Horace Willard (Luke/Swipe), Ruby Dandridge (Cleo), Earl Smith (Man), Lillian Randolph (Lily), Charles Seel (First Man/Announcer), Eddie Marr (Chalker/Tom), Robert Cole (Jacky), Hal Dawson (Hollish), Truda Marson (Helen), and Ralph Lewis (Second Soldier).

Commercials: Janet Russell (Sally), Julie Bannon (Janie), and William Martell (Bob).

In keeping with the spirit of the approaching Kentucky Derby, *Lux* chose "Kentucky" for the week of May 28. This effectively presented horse-racing drama involving the trials and tribulations of two feuding Sonthern families stars Laraine Day, Tom Drake (in roles originated by Loretta Young and Richard Greene in the 1938 David Butler 20th Century–Fox film), and Walter Brennan (resuming his Academy Award–winning motion picture role of Peter Goodwin).

486. "Intermezzo," 6/4/45

Based on the 1939 Selznick International/United Artists film (screenplay adaptation by George O'Neil), in turn based on the 1936 Swedish film (screenplay by Gosta Stevens and Gustav Molander; original story by Gustav Molander).

Guest Host: Hal Wallis.

Cast: Ingrid Bergman (Anita), Joseph Cotten (Holga Brant), Paula Winslowe (Margit), Norman Field (Thomas Stenberg), Regina Wallace (Emma/Woman), Norma Nilsson (Ann Marie), Bill Roy (Erich), Boyd Davis (Charles/Conductor), Earl Keen (Waiter/Dog), Eric Snowden (England/Cab), Charles Seel (Doctor), George Sorrel (Paris/Man), and Dickie Meyers and Mary Lon Harrington (Ad Libs).

Commercials: Robert Cole (Boy), Betty Jean Hainey (Girl), Julie Bannon (Girl's Voice), Duane Thompson (First Woman), and Helen Andrews (Second Woman).

Lux's June 4 broadcast of "Intermezzo" stars Ingrid Bergman reprising the role she played in both the Selznick International/UA film and the earlier radio rendering, on this occasion, opposite Joseph Cotten.

See 1/29/40 for information on film versions.

Additional film version: Swedish, 1936.

487. "Murder, My Sweet," 6/11/45

Based on the 1945 RKO film (screenplay by John Paxton), in turn based on the novel *Farewell, My Lovely,* by Raymond Chandler (1940).

Guest Host: Irving Pichel.

Cast: Dick Powell (Philip Marlowe), Claire Trevor (Helen), June Duprez (Ann), Mike Mazurki (Moose Malloy), Cy Kendall (Inspector Randall), Gerald Mohr (Jules Amthor), Robert Regent (Mariott), Norman Field (Grail), Eddie Marr (Bartender/Cab Driver), Doris Singleton (Operator/Girl), Charles Seel (Butler/Sanderberg), Ed Emerson (Nulty/Ross), and Lee Sherin (Mike).

Commercials: Paula Winslowe (Girl's Voice), Duane Thompson (First Woman), Regina Wallace (Second Woman), Trnda Marson (Mary), and Ralph Lewis (Man).

The well-made Edward Dmytryk–directed RKO thriller *Murder, My Sweet* reached *Lux* near the end of the 1944-45 season. Starring as cynical hard-boiled detective Philip Marlowe is Dick Powell, who recreates his film portrayal. Claire Trevor and Mike Mazurki are also present to reprise their screen characterizations, while June Duprez effectively plays Anne Shirley's movie part. Based on Raymond Chandler's novel *Farewell, My Lovely,* the complex story of a private eye's search for an ex-convict's former girlfriend is not easy to follow even in the screen version, but Sandy Barnett's slick adaptation, combined with the cast's enthusiastic playing, makes "Murder, My Sweet" entertaining.

Farewell, My Lovely was actually filmed once prior to the better-known RKO version as the third entry in that studio's *Falcon* series in 1942. Though the names of most of the characters have been changed, the plot of *The Falcon Takes Over* is basically the same as that of Chandler's novel. Starring in that Howard Benedict–directed production are George Sanders, Lynn Bari, Helen Gilbert, and Ward Bond. Britain produced the most recent film version to date, releasing *Farewell, My Lovely* in 1975 with Robert Mitchum, Charlotte Rampling, Sylvia Miles, and John Ireland (directed by Dick Richards).

Additional film versions: RKO, 1942 (*The Falcon Takes Over*); British, 1975.

488. "The Canterville Ghost," 6/18/45

Based on the 1944 MGM film (screenplay by Edwin Blum), in turn based on the story by Oscar Wilde (1887).

Guest Host: Hal B. Wallis.

Cast: Margaret O'Brien (Jessica), Charles Laughton (Sir Simon), Tom Drake (Cuffy Williams), Eric Snowden (Valentine), Boyd Davis (Canterville), Claire Verdera (Mrs. Palverdine), Ed Emerson (Benson), Gerald Mohr (Lieutenant Kane), Gloria Gordon (Mrs. Potter), Eddie Marr (Jordan), Clifton Young (Trigger), Robert Cole (Eddie), Charles Seel (Man), and Norman Field (Butler).

Commercials: Janet Russell (Sally), Truda Marson (Girl/Second Girl, Act 1), Betty Jean Hainey (First Girl, Act 1), Julie Bannon (Kay), and Doris Singleton (Pat).

Metro-Goldwyn-Mayer's Jules Dassin–directed comedy *The Canterville Ghost* made its way to the airwaves with original cast members Margaret O'Brien and Charles Laughton, and with Tom Drake in the role played onscreen by Robert Young. The fantasy concerns a little girl's involvement with a restless seventeenth-century spirit who will remain earthbound until an ancient curse is broken.

489. "The Woman in the Window," 6/25/45

Based on the 1944 RKO/International film (screenplay by Nunnally Johnson), in turn based on the novel *Once Off Guard*, by J.H. Wallis (1942).

Guest Host: Mark Hellinger.

Cast: Edward G. Robinson (Richard Wanley), Joan Bennett (Alice Reed), Dan Duryea (Arthur Heidt), Charles Seel (Jackson), Herbert Rawlinson (Lesley), Norman Field (Charles), Eddie Marr (Paper), Stanley Farrar (Mazard), Ed Emerson (Cop Number One/Man), Haskell Coffin (Williams/Man Number Two), Franklyn Parker (Cop), Duane Thompson (Operator), and Lester Matthews (Barkstone).

Commercials: Janet Russell (Sally), Doris Singleton (Libby), Ann Tobin (Girl, Act 3), Betty Jean Hainey (Second Girl, Act 3), Truda Marson (Joan), Ralph Lewis (Bill), Julie Bannon (Peg), and Virginia Gregg (First Girl, Act 2).

The RKO 1944 thriller *The Woman in the Window* made compelling material for *Lux*'s season finale. Despite the obvious inability to translate Fritz Lang's visual devices to the air, the well-scripted drama is nevertheless impressive. Starring in the *Lux* broadcast, as they do in the motion picture, are Edward G. Robinson as a stodgy professor, Joan Bennett as the young lady who innocently involves him in a murder, and Dan Duryea as a despicable blackmailer.

Eleventh Season (August 27, 1945–June 24, 1946)

Columbia Broadcasting System, Monday, 9:00–10:00 P.M. Vine Street Playhouse, Hollywood, California. *Host*: Various guest hosts, August

26, 1945–October 29, 1945; William Keighley, November 5, 1945–June 24, 1946. *Announcer*: John Milton Kennedy. *Second Announcer*: Thomas Hanlon. *Director*: Fredric MacKaye. *Musical Director*: Louis Silvers. *Sound Effects*: Charlie Forsyth. *Adaptations*: S.H. Barnett (except as otherwise noted). Intermission guests (when present) appear after Act 2 (unless otherwise noted).

490. "Practically Yours," 8/27/45
Based on the 1944 Paramount film (screenplay by Norman Krasna).
Guest Host: John Cromwell.
Intermission Guest: Virginia Wells, Paramount starlet.
Cast: Claudette Colbert (Peggy), Ray Milland (Lieutenant Bellamy), Herbert Rawlinson (Meglin), Arthur Q. Bryan (Albert), Peggy Webber (Mrs. Macy/Girl), Griff Barnett (Uncle Ben/Sumpter), Boyd Davis (Butler), Ed Emerson (Announcer/Man), Stanley Farrar (Man Three), Ramsey Hill (La Grosse), Earl Keen (Dog), Bill Martel (Adams/Man One), Franklyn Parker (Announcer/Harper), Dorothy Scott (Second Girl), Janet Scott (Mrs. Meglin), and Charles Seel (Ellis/Voice).
Commercials: Doris Singleton (Libby), Truda Marson (Girl).
To kick off *Lux*'s twelfth season on a cheerful note, the producers chose to adapt the Mitchell Leisen–directed Paramount film *Practically Yours*. This comedy with dramatic undertones centers around a war hero who (through media hype) is thrown together with a girl who is little more than a passing acquaintance. The broadcast features Claudette Colbert in her original screen role and Ray Milland in the Fred MacMurray picture part.

491. "The Enchanted Cottage," 9/3/45
Based on the 1945 RKO film (screenplay by Herman J. Mankiewicz), in turn based on the play by Sir Arthur Wing Pinero (1922).

Guest Host: Hunt Stromberg.
Intermission Guest: Rita Corday, RKO starlet.
Cast: Robert Young (Oliver Bradford), Dorothy McGuire (Laura Pennington), Noreen Gammill (Mrs. Minnett), Lester Matthews (John), Henry Blair (Danny), Kathleen Fitz (Beatrice), Regina Wallace (Alice), Ralph Lewis (Man One/Private), Harold Davis (Man Two/Corporal), Charles Seel (Man Three/Conductor), Leo Cleary (Freddie), and Lois Corbett (Woman).
Commercials: Doris Singleton (Libby), Truda Marson (Girl).
John Cromwell's RKO picture *The Enchanted Cottage* was released in 1945 and is a tale of two cosmetically imperfect people who overcome their bitterness and shyness through their love for one another.
The September 3 adaptation by Lux of the film cast Robert Young and Dorothy McGuire in their original picture roles.
John S. Robertson directed First National's 1924 production of *The Enchanted Cottage*, which starred Richard Barthelmess and May McAvoy.
Additional film version: First National, 1924.

*492. "Experiment Perilous," 9/10/45
Based on the 1944 RKO film (screenplay by Warren Duff), in turn based on the novel by Margaret Carpenter (1943).
Guest Host: Mark Hellinger.

Claudette Colbert during a rehearsal of "Practically Yours" (August 27, 1945) (photo: Photofest).

Intermission Guest: Audrey Long, RKO starlet.

Cast: George Brent (Dr. Hunt), Virginia Bruce (Allida), Paul Henreid (Nick), Howard McNear (Clag), Norman Field (Frank/Clerk), Kathleen Fitz (Elaine), Charles Seel (Maitland), Duane Thompson (Nurse), George Neise (Gregory), Truda Marson (Girl/Nurse Two), Regina Wallace (Cissie), Dorothy Scott (Deria), and Terry Blair (Alec).

Commercial: Doris Singleton (Libby).

Jacques Tourneur's 1944 RKO drama

George Brent and Virginia Bruce in "Experiment Perilous" (September 10, 1945) (photo: Photofest).

Experiment Perilous came to *Lux* with George Brent in his original picture part of a physician who becomes involved in a murder mystery surrounding a noted philanthropist and his intriguing young wife. Virginia Bruce and Paul Henreid portrayed the characters played by Hedy Lamarr and Paul Lukas in the motion picture, and frequent *Lux* performer George Neise repeated his screen role.

493. "Christmas Holiday," 9/17/45
Based on the 1944 Universal film (screenplay by Herman J. Mankiewicz), in turn based on the novel by W. Somerset Maugham (1939).
Guest Host: William Keighley.
Singing Coach: Enrico Ricardi.
Cast: Loretta Young (Abigail Man-

ette), William Holden (Lieutenant Jerry Mason), David Bruce (Robert Manette), Charles Seel (Man Two), Ed Rand (Johnny/Man in Act 2), Norman Field (Man in Act 1/Cop), Colleen Collins (Girl), Gerald Mohr (Simon), Billy Roy (Bellboy), Ed Emerson (Steve/Eddie), Noreen Gammill (Mother), Anne Stone (Valerie), Devona Doxie (Soloist), and Toby Williams (Soloist).
Commercials: Doris Singleton (Libby), Truda Marson (Girl in Act 2), Julie Bannon (Girl's Voice in Act 2), and Ralph Lewis (Boy).
Though *Lux*'s version of the Robert Siodmak–directed Universal drama *Christmas Holiday* aired some time before the 1945 Yuletide season, the story does not seem out of place because of its non–Christmassy feel and

"Christmas Holiday," with Loretta Young and David Bruce (September 17, 1945) (photo: Photofest).

attitude concerning situations and characters. Loretta Young is heard in Deanna Durbin's screen role of the understanding wife of a murderous weakling, while William Holden (who appears in his first radio broadcast since completing his service in the Army Air Corps) plays the Dean Harens movie part of the sympathetic lieutenant who hopes for a chance with the misguided girl. David Bruce, who plays the supporting role of Gerald Tyler in the film, is elevated to the Gene Kelly photoplay character of the heroine's husband in the broadcast.

William Keighley, who makes his

first appearance as guest host in this program, would seven weeks later be hired as *Lux*'s new permanent host.

*494. "It's a Date," 9/24/45

Based on the 1940 Universal film (screenplay by Norman Krasna), in turn based on a story by June Hall, Frederick Kohner, and Ralph Block.

Guest Host: Irving Pichel.

Cast: Brian Aherne (John), Diana Lynn (Pam), Gale Sondergaard (Georgia), Charles Seel (Kelly/Messenger), Ted Maxwell (Sidney), Peter Witt (Ober), Verna Felton (Sara), Norman Field (Andrews), Leo Cleary (Governor/ Horner), Walter Craig (Steward), Guy Kingsford (Steward/Messenger), and Dorothy Scott (Girl).

Commercials: Doris Singleton (Girl Singer), Truda Marson (Girl's Voice), and Muzzy Marcellino (Soldier [Singer]).

Guest "producer" Irving Pichel was on hand to host the *Lux* broadcast of Universal's 1940 film *It's a Date*, the plot of which follows the complications that arise when a talented teen is given the chance to appear in an important Broadway part originally slated for her mother. The William A. Seiter–directed film features Walter Pidgeon, Deanna Durbin, and Kay Francis, while *Lux*'s presentation cast Brian Aherne, Diana Lynn, and Gale Sondergaard in their roles.

495. "Mr. Skeffington," 10/1/45

Based on the 1944 Warner Bros. film (screenplay by Phillip G. Epstein and Julius J. Epstein), in turn based on the novel by "Elizabeth" (1939).

Guest Host: William Keighley.

Cast: Bette Davis (Fanny Skeffington), Paul Henreid (Job Skeffington), Marjorie Riordan (Young Fanny), Joseph Kearns (George), Charles Seel (Squire/Tyler), Dorothy Scott (Marey), Jack Edwards, Jr. (Trippy), Edward Emerson (Chester/Man One), Guy

Kingsford (Thatcher/Man Three), Gerald Mohr (Morrison/Man Four), Robert Coute (Vance/Waiter), Norman Field (Doctor/Butler), Gloria McMillan (Fanny, age 11), Tyler McVey (Attendant/Man Two), George Neise (Johnny), and Duane Thompson (Nurse).

Commercials: Truda Marson (Alice), Betty Jean Hainey (Sue/Voice), Doris Singleton (Libby), and Helen Andrews (Housewife).

Bette Davis returned to *Lux* on the first of October in another of her popular screen characterizations. In this instance, it was Warner Bros.' *Mr. Skeffington*, a tale of a petty and vain woman who refuses to acknowledge her advancing years and casts off the only man who truly loves her. Playing Claude Rains's screen part of the title character is Paul Henreid, with Marjorie Riordan repeating her movie role as the daughter, and radio actor Joe Kearns taking the Walter Abel film character of Fanny's cousin, George (who narrates the story in this version).

496. "Roughly Speaking," 10/8/45

Based on the 1945 Warner Bros. film (screenplay by Louise Randall Pierson), in turn based on the autobiography of Louise Randall Pierson (1942).

Guest Host: Irving Pichel.

Intermission Guest: Angela Greene, Warner Bros. starlet.

Cast: Rosalind Russell (Louise), Jack Carson (Harold), George Neise (Rodney), Norman Field (Dr. Baldrich/Voice Three), Charles Seel (Loudspeaker/ Doctor), Gloria McMillan (Barbara, age ten), Henry Blair (Johnny, age eight), Donald Barell (Rodney, Jr., age nine), Norma Nilsson (Louise, Jr., age seven/ Frankie, age five), Tommy Cook (Frankie, age 11), Robert Cole (Johnny, age 15), Kathleen Fitz (Barbara, age 24/ Nurse), Lee Millar (John, age 22), Robert Quarry (Rodney, age 23), Truda

Marson (Louise, Jr., age 21), Norman Field (Somlitch), Jay Novello (Tony/ Van Driver), Eddie Marr (Man One/ Man Two in Act 3), Ed Emerson (Voice One/Man Two in Act 2), and Guy Kingsford (Voice Two/Man Three).

Chorus: Kenneth Rundquist, George Gramlich, Lute Crockett, Donald Neese, Betty Rome, Mary Mahoney, Jeanne Dunne, Devona Doxie (Soloist), and Enrico Ricardi (Coach).

Commercials: Doris Singleton (Libby), Janet Russell (Sally), and Julie Bannon (Voice in Act 3/Voice of Maria Montez).

Lux's "Roughly Speaking," which is based on the 1945 Michael Curtiz–directed Warner Bros. film, chronicles the ups and downs in the life of Louise Randall Pierson, author of the story (in a period spanning 1902 to the Second World War). Rosalind Russell and Jack Carson repeat their roles as Louise and Harold, while George Neise plays Tom Tyler's screen part of Rodney.

497. "A Medal for Benny," 10/15/45
Based on the 1945 Paramount film (screenplay by Frank Butler; original story by John Steinbeck and Jack Wagner).

Guest Host: Irving Pichel.

Intermission Guest: Doris Dowling, Paramount starlet.

Cast: Dorothy Lamour (Lolita), Arturo de Cordova (Joe), J. Carrol Naish (Charlie), Mikhail Rasumny (Raphael), Charles Seel (Tailor/Voice), Leo Cleary (Man/Mayor), Franklyn Parker (Walters), Ralph Moody (Jake/Conductor), Evelyn Scott (Toodles), Norman Field (Mibbs), Hal Dawson (Herbert), Eddie Marr (Edgar), Tyler McVey (Red/Second Voice), William Green (General), Mickey Kuhn (Chito), and Noreen Gammill (Mrs. Catalina/ Woman).

Commercials: Doris Singleton (Libby), Ann Tobin (Jerry), Truda Marson (First Girl in Act 3), and Dorothy Irwin (Second Girl in Act 3).

Lux's broadcast of "A Medal for Benny," which chronicles a small town's eagerness to cash in on the fame of a dead war hero, features four principals from the film: Dorothy Lamour, Arturo de Cordova, J. Carrol Naish, and Mikhail Rasumny. Irving Pichel, who directed the 1945 motion picture, serves as guest host.

*498. "Lost Angel," 10/22/45
Based on the 1944 MGM film (screenplay by Isobel Lennart; from an idea by Angna Enters).

Guest Host: Mitchell Leisen.

Intermission Guest: Marissa O'Brien, MGM starlet.

Cast: Margaret O'Brien (Alpha), George Murphy (Mike), Donna Reed (Katie), Eddie Marr (Packy), Griff Barnett (Vincent), Herbert Rawlinson (Dr. Woodring), Regina Wallace (Mrs. Catty), Charlie Lung (Mr. Catty/Chinese), Ed Emerson (Lefty/Second Reporter), Charles Seel (Detective/Loudspeaker), Stanley Farrar (Reporter/ Usher), Lou Merrill (Editor/Popcorn), Franklyn Parker (Cop/Waiter), Velma Caesar (Cigarette Girl), and Dorothy Ellers (Singer).

Commercials: Doris Singleton (Libby), Bob Bruce (Man).

Lux's second radio rendering of MGM's 1944 Roy Roland–directed comedy-drama *Lost Angel* once again featured Margaret O'Brien as the title character, with George Murphy and Donna Reed in the roles taken by James Craig and Marsha Hunt in the film.

See 6/19/44 for information on film version.

499. "The Affairs of Susan," 10/29/45
Based on the 1945 Paramount film (screenplay by Thomas Monroe), Laszlo Gorog, and Richard Flournoy).

Guest Host: Mitchell Leisen.

Intermission Guest: Edith Head, Paramount costume designer (after Act 1).

Cast: Joan Fontaine (Susan Darnell), George Brent (Roger Burton), Don DeFore (Mike Ward), Charles Seel (Uncle Jimmy), Howard McNear (Richard), George Neise (Bill), Dorothy Scott (Nancy/Phone Operator), Anne Stone (Mona/Second Girl), Leo Cleary (Cusp), Eddie Marr (Tommy), and Lynn Whitney (Mrs. Oakleaf).

Commercials: Ann Tobin (Housewife), Truda Marson (Girl).

Joan Fontaine, George Brent, and Don DeFore reprise their movie roles for *The Lux Radio Theatre* version of Paramount's William Seiter–directed *The Affairs of Susan*. The forced comedy tells the tale of a flighty woman who alters her personality to match each of the three distinctly different men with whom she is involved.

The story was performed again on *The Lux Summer Theatre* broadcast of August 24, 1953.

500. "Destry Rides Again," 11/5/45

Based on the 1939 Universal film (screenplay by Felix Jackson, Gertrude Purcell, and Henry Myers), in turn based on the novel by Max Brand (1930).

Intermission Guest: Nancy Gates, RKO starlet (after Act 3).

Cast: James Stewart (Tom Destry), Joan Blondell (Frenchy), Frances Robinson (Janice), Leo Cleary (Wash), Ken Christy (Mayor), Noreen Gammill (Lily Belle), Tommy Cook (Eli), Charles Seel (Claggett/Turner), Dorothy Scott (Mrs. Claggett), Joe DuVal (Gyp), Ruby Dandridge (Clara), Tyler McVey (Creepy/Man Two), Franklyn Parker (Bugsy/Man), and Doris Singleton (Soloist [Frenchy's Singing Voice]).

Commercials: Doris Singleton (Libby), Truda Marson (Voice of Merle Oberon).

The *Lux* production of George Marshall's 1939 Universal comedy-drama *Destry Rides Again* marks the debut of motion picture producer-director William Keighley as permanent host. James Stewart reprises his screen role as the laconic, homespun philosopher Deputy Tom Destry, who attempts to clean up a rugged frontier town without the aid of a gun, and Joan Blondell plays brassy dance-hall girl Frenchy, a part taken by Marlene Dietrich in the film.

Max Brand's novel originally reached the screen in 1932 via Universal's first version, which was directed by Alan James and Ben Stoloff and starred Tom Mix and Claudia Dell. Joel McCrea and Shelley Winters starred in the second remake, *Frenchie*, which was directed by Louis King and released in 1951. The most recent version to date, released in 1955 and entitled *Destry*, served as a vehicle for Audie Murphy, while cast in the leading lady role on this occasion was Mari Blanchard.

Additional film versions: Universal, 1932; Universal, 1951 (*Frenchie*); Universal, 1955 (*Destry*).

501. "Guest in the House," 11/12/45

Based on the 1945 Hunt Stromberg/United Artists film (screenplay by Ketti Frings), in turn based on the play by Hagar Wilde and Dale Eunson (1942).

Intermission Guest: Audrey Young, Paramount starlet.

Cast: Robert Young (Douglas Proctor), Anne Baxter (Evelyn Heath), Charles Seel (John/Clerk), Regina Wallace (Martha), Frances Robinson (Jane), George Neise (Dan), Edith Van Horn (Miriam), Gerald Mohr (Ernest), Norma Nilsson (Lee), and Leora Thatcher (Hilda/Operator).

Commercials: Doris Singleton (Libby), Truda Marson (Voice).

Lux's broadcast of the 1945 John Brahm–directed psychological drama *Guest in the House* was the attraction for November 12. Robert Young takes the part of the happy-go-lucky artist (played by Ralph Bellamy onscreen) and Anne Baxter splendidly reprises her film role as the title character whose neurotic outbursts and various phobias cause plenty of trouble for her generous hosts.

502. "The Keys of the Kingdom," 11/19/45

Based on the 1944 20th Century–Fox film (screenplay by Joseph L. Mankiewicz and Nunnally Johnson), in turn based on the novel by A.J. Cronin (1941).

Intermission Guest: Joyce Elaine MacKenzie, International Pictures starlet.

Cast: Ronald Colman (Father Francis Chisholm), Ann Harding (Mother Maria Veronica), Joseph Kearns (Townsend), Colin Campbell (MacNabb), Eric Snowden (Willie), Alan Napier (Joseph), Ramsey Hill (Angus), Charles Lung (Mr. Chin/Captain), Lal Chand Mehra (Mr. Poo), H.T. Tsang (Hosannah), Barbara Jean Wong (Philomena), Peter Chong (Major), Charles Seel (Fiske), Duane Thompson (Sister Martha/Mrs. Fiske), and Anne Stone (Sister Clothilde).

Commercial: Doris Singleton (Libby).

Lux's adaptation of the 1944 20th Century–Fox drama *The Keys of the Kingdom* chronicles the life of an occasionally unorthodox but thoroughly dedicated Scottish priest who brings Christianity to a remote area of China. Ronald Colman stars in the broadcast, taking the part that is played by Gregory Peck in the John M. Stahl-directed film. Costarring in the relatively small role of Mother Maria Veronica is Ann Harding, playing the part taken by the fourth-billed Rose Stradner in the movie; H.T. Tsang reprises his screen character of Hosannah Wang.

503. "Salty O'Rourke," 11/26/45

Based on the 1945 Paramount film (screenplay by Milton Holmes).

Intermission Guest: Katherine Connors, 20th Century–Fox starlet.

Cast: Alan Ladd (Salty O'Rourke), William Demarest (Smitty), Marjorie Reynolds (Barbara), James Cardwell (Johnny Cate), Charles Seel (Announcer/Cop), Eddie Marr (Babe), Mel Ruick (Baxter), Griff Barnett (Mac), Leora Thatcher (Mother), Robert Cole (Breezer), Jack Carrington (Cop), Herbert Lytton (Herman/Cop Three), Jack Bruskoff, Robert Quarry, Joseph Agnello, Frank Gerstle, and Virginia Agnello (Ad Libs).

Commercials: Doris Singleton (Libby), Truda Marson (Girl).

Lux's adaptation of Paramount's Raoul Walsh–directed horse-racing melodrama *Salty O'Rourke* came to the airwaves with Alan Ladd repeating his screen role as an in-debt fellow who pins his hopes on a fiery horse and an insubordinate jockey. Marjorie Reynolds plays the love interest, a role taken by Gail Russell in the movie, while William Demarest reprises his film role as the hero's sidekick and James Cardwell is heard in the Stanley Clements part of the jockey.

Keighley notes that *Lux*'s studio audience paid for their admission to this broadcast by purchasing war bonds, and that over $2.5 million was raised.

504. "Blood on the Sun," 12/3/45

Based on the 1945 United Artists film (screenplay by Lester Cole; original story by Garrett Fort, from an idea by Frank Melford).

Intermission Guest: Sherry Berger, former dancer and wife of RKO producer Richard Berger (after Act 1).

Cast: James Cagney (Nick Condon), Sylvia Sidney (Iris Hilliard), Charles Seel (Kajioka/Voice), Lou Merrill (Oshima), Paul McVey (Bickett), Lee Gooding (Yamamoto/Johnson), Tristram Coffin (Cassell), Edward Emerson (Ollie), Roland Varne (Yamada), Lal

Chand Mehra (Prince Tatsugi), Jack Carrington (Hijikata), Eddy Fields (Tojo/Gallagher), Robert Bruce (Bugalow/Clarke), Herbert Lytton (Tanaka/Guffey), Frances Robinson (Edith), Tyler McVey (Sprague), Noreen Gammill (Amah), Hugh McArthur (Hayashi/Oshima), Stanley Farrar (Waiter/Man), Barbara Jean Wong (Girl), and José Perez (Purser/Porter).

Commercials: Doris Singleton (Libby), Janet Russell (Sally).

"Blood on the Sun" is a drama centering around an American newspaper editor in pre-war Japan who attempts to expose that government's Tanaka Plan (a drawn proposition for world conquest). The Frank Lloyd–directed United Artists picture stars James Cagney and Sylvia Sidney, both of whom repeat their parts for *Lux*'s December 3 broadcast.

505. "Guest Wife," 12/10/45
Based on the Jack K. Skirball/United Artists film (screenplay by Bruce Manning and John Klorer).

Intermission Guest: Jayne Clyde, Universal-International songwriter (after Act 1).

Cast: Olivia deHavilland (Mary Price), Don Ameche (Joe Parker), Dick Foran (Chris Price), Lou Merrill (Worth), Frances Robinson (Susy), Griff Barnett (Mills), Alexander Gerry (Arnold/Second Conductor), Leo Cleary (Evans/Porter), Charles Seel (Harry/Conductor), Fred Devlin (Reed/Butler), Howard McNear (Clerk), Eddie Marr (Reporter), Anne Stone (Blanche), Colleen Collins (Ginny/Girl), and James Eagles (Man).

Commercials: Doris Singleton (Libby), Janet Russell (Sally).

United Artists' frivolous comedy *Guest Wife*, chronicling the inconveniences a young couple is put through thanks to the husband's tall tale–telling best friend, came to *The Lux Radio Theatre* with the two male members of its starring trio, Don Ameche and Dick Foran, repeating their movie parts. Olivia deHavilland takes the title role, which is played in the Sam Wood-directed screen version by Claudette Colbert.

506. "Made for Each Other," 12/17/45
Based on the 1939 Selznick International film (screenplay by Jo Swerling), in turn suggested by a story by Rose Franken.

Intermission Guest: Jane Nigh, 20th Century–Fox starlet (after Act 1).

Cast: James Stewart (Johnny Mason), Marsha Hunt (Jane Mason), Verna Felton (Mrs. Mason), Lou Merrill (Judge Doolittle), Guy Kingsford (Carter/Denver), Kathleen Fitz (Eunice/Second Nurse), Griff Barnett (Dr. Healy), Eddie Marr (Allentown/Boy), Ernestine Wade (Annie), Tyler McVey (Conway/Man), Ed Emerson (Hatton/Waiter), Alexander Gerry (Butler/Man), Dorothy Scott (Third Nurse), and Leone Ledoux (Baby Cry/Girl).

Commercials: Julie Bannon (Libby), Helen Andrews (Housewife), Betty Jean Hainey (Girl), Vivian Carter (Nancy), and Beverly Brown (Betty).

"Made for Each Other" had a return *Lux* engagement on the December 17 program, with James Stewart reprising his movie role and Marsha Hunt as the Carole Lombard screen character.

See 2/19/40 for information on the film version.

507. "I'll Be Seeing You," 12/24/45
Based on the 1944 Selznick International film (screenplay by Marion Parsonnet), in turn based on the unpublished radio play *Double Furlough*, by Charles Martin.

Intermission Guest: Betty Bryant, wife of novelist (and creator of "The Saint") Leslie Charteris (after Act 1).

Cast: Joseph Cotten (Zachary Morgan),

Dorothy McGuire (Mary Marshall), Regina Wallace (Sarah), John Parrish (Henry), Barbara Drake (Barbara), Ken Christy (Al), Jeff Corey (Man in Act 1/ Man in Act 3), Eddie Marr (Taxi/Man in Act 3), Sanford Bickart (Doctor/Man Two), Charles Seel (Clerk/Conductor), Franklyn Parker (Guard/Man One), and Janet Scott (Second Woman).

Commercials: Truda Marson (Jane), Betty Jean Hainey (Betty), and Ann Tobin (Housewife).

In keeping with the spirit of the holiday season, *Lux* chose the William Dieterle–directed Selznick International drama *I'll Be Seeing You* for its Christmas eve broadcast. This quietly sensitive love story of emotional recovery through trust and kindness stars Joseph Cotten in his original screen role as the shell-shocked soldier on leave, and Dorothy McGuire as the small town girl on furlough from prison (the role Ginger Rogers plays in the film).

508. "Pride of the Marines," 12/31/45

Based on the 1945 Warner Bros. film (screenplay by Albert Matz).

Intermission Guest: Eleanor Broder, secretary to Mitchell Leisen, Paramount Studios (after Act 1).

Special Guest: Al Schmidt (from New York City; during curtain call).

Cast: John Garfield (Al Schmidt), Eleanor Parker (Ruth Hartley), Dane Clark (Lee Diamond), Charles Seel (Announcer/Captain), Frances Robinson (Virginia), Virginia Gordon (Ella), Tyler McVey (Jim), Ann Todd (Loretta), Ben Alexander (Rivers), Edwin Max (Irish/Man), Edward Emerson (Red/Man Two), Herb Vigran (Jack/ Driver), Lou Merrill (Doctor/Conductor), Eddie Marr (Marine), Theodore von Eltz (Uncle/Colonel), Herb Lytton (Jap/Train Announcer), Truda Marson (Girl/Operator), Janet Scott (Woman in Act 1/Woman in Act 2), and Ann Tobin (Girl Two).

Commercials: Janet Russell (Sally), Betty Moran (Marie), and Duane Thompson (Mrs. Evans).

Based on the 1945 Delmar Daves Warner Bros. film about the life of Sergeant Albert A. Schmidt (a young Marine blinded in action), the December 31 broadcast of "Pride of the Marines" captures the motion picture's optimism and sympathy shown by civilians to the physically disabled veterans. John Garfield, Eleanor Parker, and Dane Clark all reprise their screen characterizations, and the real Al Schmidt is heard from New York City during the curtain call.

509. "You Came Along," 1/7/46

Based on the 1945 Paramount film (screenplay by Robert Smith and Ayn Rand; original story by Robert Smith).

Cast: Van Johnson (Bob), Lizabeth Scott (Ivy), Don DeFore (Captain "Shakespeare" Anders), Charles Seel (Colonel Hunt), George Neise (Janoshek), Lou Merrill (Mr. Porter/Soldier), Arthur Gilmore (Bill/Second Reporter), Truda Marson (Frances/Nolan), Frances Robinson (Joyce/Girl in Act 1), Eddie Marr (Desk Clerk/Western Union), Herb Rawlinson (Halliday/Taylor), Jeff Corey (Reporter/Agent), Beverly Brown (Girl Reporter/Girl), Madge Cleveland (Donna/Girl Three), Lee Sherin (Photographer/Waiter), Gloria Holliday (Carol/ Girl Four), Colleen Collins (Girl One), and Betty Bryant (Singer).

Commercials: Doris Singleton (Libby), Ann Tobin (Woman).

Director John Farrow's successful 1945 Paramount drama *You Came Along* was a fine choice for *Lux*'s first broadcast of 1946. This tale of a terminally ill Army captain who distinguishes himself both in the air and on the homefront stars Van Johnson in Robert Cummings's film role, and Lizabeth Scott and Don DeFore recreating their original parts.

510. "The Valley of Decision," 1/14/46

Based on the 1945 MGM film (screenplay by John Meehan and Sonya Levien), in turn based on the novel by Marcia Davenport (1943).

Intermission Guest: Helen O'Hara, MGM starlet.

Special Guest: Louis B. Mayer, MGM executive vice president (in curtain call).

Cast: Greer Garson (Mary Rafferty), Gregory Peck (Paul Scott), Gale Gordon (Jim), Charles Seel (Callahan/ Voice), Norman Field (McCready/ Man), Francis X. Bushman (Scott), Janet Scott (Mrs. Scott), George Neise (Willie), Lurene Tuttle (Louise), Truda Marson (Connie), Sam Edwards (Ted), Gwen Delano (Delia), Dorothy Scott (Julia), Guy Kingsford (Giles), Boyd Davis (Gaylord), Leo Cleary (Pat), Ted Albright, James Floto, Jack George, Clark Kuney, Edwin Mills, and Joseph Worthy (Ad Libs).

Commercials: Doris Singleton (Libby), Ann Tobin (Voice).

Lux's presentation of Tay Garnett's 1945 MGM motion picture *The Valley of Decision* is a faithful (if scaled-down) adaptation of the period romantic drama focusing on a servant's marriage to the scion of a prominent steel mill family, and the problems arising from their conflicting social backgrounds. Greer Garson and Gregory Peck repeat their screen roles in the radio version, which features a special appearance by MGM executive vice president Louis B. Mayer during the curtain call.

511. "Johnny Eager," 1/21/46

Based on the 1941 MGM film (screenplay by James Edward Grant and John Lee Mahin).

Intermission Guests: Mrs. Laverne Stiffler, Hollywood waitress (after Act 1), and Roberta Joney, dancer (after Act 2).

Cast: Robert Taylor (Johnny), Susan Peters (Lisbeth), Van Heflin (Jeff), Cy Kendall (Marco), George Neise (Mark), John Parrish (Farrell), Leo Cleary (Halligan), Edwin Max (Benjy), Jay Novello (Julio), Evelyn Scott (Garnet), Ruth Perrott (Millie/Miss Mines), Ed Emerson (Les Rankin), Marilyn Lowrey (Birdie), Charles Seel (Verne/Cop), Lou Merrill (Tony/Ryan), Helen O'Hara (Judy), and Eddie Marr (Man/ Cop).

Commercial: Truda Marson (Woman).

For Robert Taylor's return to *Lux* (after his service in the Navy was completed), producers chose to present Mervyn LeRoy's 1941 MGM underworld crime melodrama *Johnny Eager*, in which Taylor also stars. Susan Peters plays Lana Turner's screen role, and Van Heflin reprises the part for which he won 1941's Best Supporting Actor Oscar, that of the hero's alcoholic friend. (Cy Kendall, who plays Halligan in the movie, is here heard as Marco.)

512. "The Clock," 1/28/46

Based on the 1945 MGM film (screenplay by Robert Nathan and Joseph Schrank), in turn based on a story by Paul and Pauline Gallico.

Intermission Guest: Ruth Brady, MGM starlet.

Cast: Judy Garland (Alice Mayberry), John Hodiak (Joe Allen), Howard McNear (Clerk Three), Herb Lytton (Guide/Guard Two), Tyler McVey (Sergeant), Franklyn Parker (Man One), Edwin Max (Man Two/Guard Three), Janet Scott (Woman/Mother), Ruth Brady (Girl), Julie Bannon (Girl/Woman), Eddie Marr (Irving), Alex Gerry (Florist/Room Service), Arthur Gilmore (Announcer/Soldier), Jay Novello (Drunk/Bernie), Verna Felton (Mama Henry), Leo Cleary (Conductor/ Hymie), James Eagles (Elevator/Sailor), Dorothy Scott (Receptionist/P.A. Woman), Jack Carrington (Conductor/

"You Came Along" (January 7, 1946), with Lizabeth Scott and Van Johnson (photo: Photofest).

Guard One), William Green (Customer/ Information), Joseph Kearns (Al), George Young (Boy/Little Boy), and Charles Seel (Cop/P.A.).

Commercial: Doris Singleton (Libby).

Lux's version of the 1945 Vincente Minnelli MGM drama *The Clock* tells the engagingly quiet story of a soldier on a 48-hour leave in New York City. John Hodiak appears in Robert Walker's screen part of the soldier, while Judy Garland reprises her movie role of the girl he meets during his furlough. Max Steiner's waltz from *A Star Is Born* is

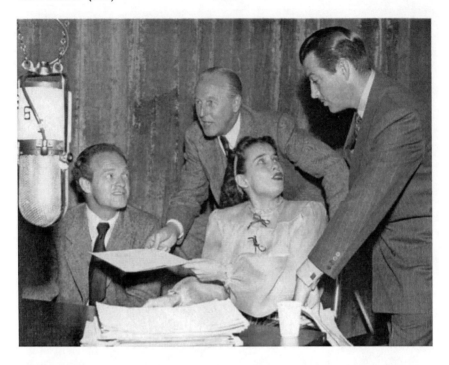

"Johnny Eager" (January 21, 1946) rehearsal with Van Heflin, William Keighley, Susan Peters, and Robert Taylor (photo: Photofest).

effectively put to use as the play's main theme by musical director Louis Silvers.

513. "This Love of Ours," 2/4/46

Based on the 1945 Universal film (screenplay by Bruce Manning, John Klorer, and Leonard Lee), in turn based on the play *Come Prima Meglio di Prima (Floriani's Wife)*, by Luigi Pirandello (1923).

Intermission Guest: Helen Rose, MGM costume designer (played by Ann Tobin).

Cast: Rita Hayworth (Karin), Charles Korvin (Michel Touzac), Sue England (Susette), Joe Kearns (Targel), Regina Wallace (Tucker), George Neise (George), Norman Field (Andrews), Herbert Rawlinson (Bailey), Francis X. Bushman (Barnes), Stanley Waxman

(Paul/Summers), Joseph Granby (Bailey), Charles Seel (Halmer), Noreen Gammill (Woman in Nightclub/Second Woman), Truda Marson (Anna), Duane Thompson (Mumsy/Girl), and Janet Scott (Woman/Housekeeper).

Commercials: Doris Singleton (Libby), Janet Russell (Sally), and Julie Bannon (Woman).

The *Lux* adaptation of the William Dieterle–directed Universal film *This Love of Ours* is a story of estrangement through misunderstandings. Rita Hayworth stars in the Merle Oberon screen part, and Charles Korvin reenacts his original role; child actress Sue England, also of the movie cast, repeats her characterization of their young daughter.

Originally scheduled to appear as a guest between the second and third acts was MGM costume designer Helen Rose, but a last-minute indisposition caused her to miss the broadcast, and radio actress Ann Tobin, introduced as Rose, read her part over the air.

A second film version of the play on which *This Love of Ours* was based was filmed by Universal-International in 1956 under the title *Never Say Goodbye*, with Cornell Borchers and Rock Hudson starring under Jerry Hopper's direction.

Additional film version: Universal-International, 1956 (*Never Say Goodbye*).

514. "Now, Voyager," 2/11/46

Based on the 1942 Warner Bros. film (screenplay by Casey Robinson), in turn based on the novel by Olive Higgins Prouty (1941).

Cast: Bette Davis (Charlotte Vale), Gregory Peck (Jerry), Joseph Kearns (Dr. Jaquith), Janet Scott (Mrs. Vale), Gloria McMillan (Tina), Norman Field (Conductor/Announcer), Duane Thompson (Miss Trask), Melville Ruick (Elliott), Frances Robinson (Deb), Charles Seel (George/Mack), and Dorothy Scott (Lisa/Dora).

Commercials: Doris Singleton (Libby), Truda Marson (Susie).

The February 11 repeat of "Now, Voyager" gives Bette Davis the chance to reprise her screen role and casts Gregory Peck opposite her as her love interest. Appearing in featured supporting roles are Joseph Kearns as the sympathetic psychiatrist and Janet Scott as the heroine's domineering mother.

See 5/10/43 for information on the film version; the story was presented on *The Lux Video Theatre* on October 4, 1956.

515. "Captain January," 2/18/46

Based on the 1936 20th Century–Fox film (screenplay by Sam Hellman, Gladys Lehman, and Harry Tugend), in turn based on a novella by Laura E. Richard (1890). Adapted for radio by George Wells.

Intermission Guest: Lisa Renny, starlet.

Cast: Margaret O'Brien (Star), Lionel Barrymore (Captain January), Cliff Clark (Nazro), Griff Barnett (Winthrop), Duane Thompson (Mrs. Easton), Noreen Gammill (Mrs. Morgan), Tommy Cook (Gerald), Howard McNear (Easton), William Green (Judge/Old Sailor), Jeff Corey (Storekeeper), and Charles Seel (Man/Deeter).

Commercials: Doris Singleton (Libby), Helen Andrews (Mrs. Jones).

Lux's repeat of "Captain January" aired on February 18, with Margaret O'Brien and Lionel Barrymore in the roles taken by Shirley Temple and Charles Winninger in the earlier broadcast.

See 1/27/41 for information on the film version.

516. "Thunderhead, Son of Flicka," 2/25/46

Based on the 1945 20th Century–Fox film (screenplay by Dwight Cummings and Dorothy Yost), in turn based on the novel by Mary O'Hara (1943).

Intermission Guest: Gloria Tucker, usherette at Hollywood's Egyptian Theatre.

Cast: Roddy McDowall (Ken), Preston Foster (Rob), Rita Johnson (Nell), Cliff Clark (Sergeant), Mary Lou Harrington (Hildy), Jeff Corey (Tim), Charles Seel (Announcer), and William Green (Man/Vet).

Commercials: Doris Singleton (Libby), Duane Thompson (Woman).

My Friend Flicka, 20th Century–Fox's popular horse story (released in 1943), which was presented on *Lux* on June 7, 1943, received a follow-up with *Thunderhead, Son of Flicka*, which was presented first on the screen in 1945,

Roddy McDowall and William Keighley in "Thunderhead, Son of Flicka"
(February 25, 1946) (photo: Photofest).

then on *Lux* on February 25, 1946. All three principals from the Louis King–directed movie reprise their roles in the broadcast version, Roddy McDowall as the tenacious youngster who has as much of a challenge raising Flicka's spirited offspring as he did the parent, and Preston Foster and Rita Johnson as his understanding father and mother. Jeff Corey played the role of Tim in *My Friend Flicka* on the screen but was unable to repeat the part in the movie sequel as he was serving in the military at the time. He is, however, on hand to

William Keighley, Gene Tierney, and announcer John Milton Kennedy during rehearsals for "The Amazing Mrs. Holliday" (March 4, 1946) (photo: Photofest).

perform the role in the radio version of "Thunderhead, Son of Flicka."

517. "The Amazing Mrs. Holliday,"
  3/4/46
  Based on the 1943 Universal film (screenplay by Frank Ryan and John Jacoby; adapted by Boris Ingster and Leo Townsend; original story by Sonya Levien).
  Intermission Guest: Beverly Thompson, starlet.
  Cast: Gene Tierney (Ruth), Walter Brennan (Timothy), Edmond O'Brien (Tom), Joseph Kearns (Henderson), Cliff Clark (Commodore), Janet Scott (Louise/Woman), Herb Rawlinson (Edgar), Regina Wallace (Karen), Griff Barnett (Ferguson), Eddie Marr (Jeff/Second Reporter), Dorothy Scott (Lucy/Woman Reporter), Ivan Bruce (Re-porter/Clerk Two), Guy Kingsford (Photographer/Man in Act 2), John Parrish (Clerk/Man), Gloria McMillan (Elizabeth), Ann Whitfield (Winifred), Johnny McGovern (Teddy), Charles Seel (Batson/Clerk Three), and Jerry Farber.

Universal's *The Amazing Mrs. Holliday*, which was directed by Bruce Manning and released in 1943, concerns a young missionary who masquerades as the widow of a deceased commodore in order to provide eight war orphans with a home. Starred in *Lux*'s well-paced adaptation of the comedy are Gene Tierney, taking the part created on the screen by Deanna Durbin, Edmond O'Brien, recreating his movie role, and Walter Brennan, playing the Barry Fitzgerald picture character.

"The Amazing Mrs. Holliday" was

performed on *The Lux Video Theatre* on October 16, 1955.

518. "Presenting Lily Mars," 3/11/46
Based on the 1943 MGM film (screenplay by Richard Connell and Gladys Lehman), in turn based on the novel by Booth Tarkington (1933).
Intermission Guest: Jessica Tandy, actress (after Act 3).
Cast: June Allyson (Lily Mars), Van Heflin (John Thornway), Arthur Gilmore (Owen), Regina Wallace (Mrs. Mars), Frances Robinson (Isobel/Angela), Janet Scott (Mrs. Thornway), Gwen Delano (Sarah/Woman), Eddie Marr (Scotty), Cliff Clark (Mike/Man Three), George Neise (George Hobart), Tommy Bernard (Davey), Gloria McMillan (Elizabeth), Eddie Firestone, Jr. (Charlie/Man), Ed Emerson (Clerk/Man One), Truda Marson (Girl in Act 2/Girl in Act 3), and Charles Seel (Professor Eggleston/Man).
Commercials: Doris Singleton (Libby), Julie Bannon (Woman).
Metro-Goldwyn-Mayer's *Presenting Lily Mars*, a 1943 attraction directed by Norman Taurog and featuring Judy Garland and Van Heflin, was adapted for *Lux*'s March 11 broadcast. The story of a small town girl with fervent aspirations for the New York stage may not be original, but *Lux*'s production with June Allyson (who *does not* sing in Garland's film role) and Van Heflin makes for an entertaining broadcast.

519. "A Tale of Two Cities," 3/18/46
Based on the novel by Charles Dickens (1859). Adapted for radio by George Wells.
Intermission Guest: Betty Howling, starlet.
Cast: Ronald Colman (Sydney Carton), Heather Angel (Lucy Manette), Janet Scott (Madame Defarge), Lurene Tuttle (Lizette), Norman Field (Lorry), Alec Harford (Harand), Eric Snowden

(Stryver), Boyd Davis (Attorney General), William Green (President/Coachman), Guy Kingsford (Jerry/Juryman), Noreen Gammill (Miss Pross), Thomas Mills (Innkeeper), Edwin Max (Defarge/Jailer), Dorothy Scott (Annette), Herbert Bruce (Joe/Leader), and Jeff Corey (Sergeant/Guard).
Commercial: Doris Singleton (Libby).
March 18 found "A Tale of Two Cities" appearing for the third time on *Lux*, on this occasion with Ronald Colman (of the cast of the 1935 film and the first *Lux*) and Heather Angel in the leading roles, with radio actress Janet Scott as Madame Defarge.
See 1/12/42 for information on the film versions; additional *Lux* presentation on March 26, 1945.

520. "Wonder Man," 3/25/46
Based on the 1945 Samuel Goldwyn/RKO film (screenplay by Don Hartman, Melville Shavelson, and Philip Rapp; original story by Arthur Sheekman; adaptation by Jack Jevne and Eddie Moran).
Intermission Guest: Jacqueline White, MGM starlet.
Cast: Danny Kaye (Edwin Dingle/Buzzy Bellew), Virginia Mayo (Ellen), Charles Seel (Grosset/Man One), Frances Robinson (Midge), Carlton KaDell (Monte), Lou Merrill (D.A.), Edwin Max (Chimp), Jay Novello (Torno), Ed Emerson (Jackson), Truda Marson (Girl in Park), Eddie Marr (Sailor), Herb Vigran (Driver/Man Three), Abe Reynolds (Schmidt), Lee Sherin (Passenger/Waiter), Stanley Farrar (Waiter Two/Man Two), Betty Moran (Girl in Club), Allen Meek (Opera Singer), and Joan Barton (Singer).
Commercials: Doris Singleton (Libby), Julie Bannon (Woman).
Lux's adaptation of the Bruce Humberstone–directed comedy-fantasy *Wonderman*, which features Danny Kaye and Virginia Mayo in their original

Wallace Beery with daughter Carol Ann Beery in "Barnacle Bill" (April 1, 1946) (photo: Photofest).

screen roles, is a convoluted tale of a set of twins with very different but equally obnoxious personalities. Kaye performs two songs (both with words and music by Sylvia Fine) from the movie, "Bali Boogie" (in Act 1) and "Opera Number" (in Act 3).

521. "Barnacle Bill," 4/1/46
    Based on the 1941 movie (screenplay by Jack Jevne and Hugo Butler).
    Intermission Guest: Dorothy Patrick, starlet.
    Cast: Wallace Beery (Barnacle Bill), Marjorie Main (Marge Cavendish), Carol

Ann Beery (Virginia), Jay Novello (Pico), Earl Lee (Pop), Edwin Max (Kelly), Duane Thompson (Letty), Jeff Corey (Petillo/Jeff), William Green (Reverend/Man One), Cliff Clark (Mac-Donald/Auctioneer), Tyler McVey (Dixon), and Charles Seel (Man Two/ Coast Guard).

Wallace Beery should have felt right at home in *Lux's* broadcast of Richard Thorpe's popular 1941 comedy-drama *Barnacle Bill*, as it gives him the opportunity once again to portray an irresponsible seafarer who redeems himself in the nick of time. Both Beery and Marjorie Main reprise their original motion picture roles, and Carol Ann Beery (the star's daughter) takes the Virginia Weidler screen part.

Circulating recordings of the show's dress rehearsal, performed on March 31, feature Noah Beery as Adam Kelly, but the actor passed away on the day of the program and his role was taken by Edwin Max.

522. "Honky Tonk," 4/8/46

Based on the 1941 MGM film (screenplay by Marguerite Roberts and John Sanford).

Intermission Guest: Nina Foch, Columbia actress.

Cast: Lana Turner (Elizabeth), John Hodiak (Candy Johnson), Gale Gordon (Brazos), Leo Cleary (Judge), Paula Winslowe (Gold Dust), Tyler McVey (Sniper), Noreen Gammill (Mrs. Varner), Edwin Max (Blackie), Jay Novello (Adams), Brooke Temple (Wells), Cliff Clark (Kendall/Bartender), Dorothy Scott (Mrs. Morgan), Alexander Gerry (Blake/Doctor), Stanley Farrar (Man/ Conductor), and Charles Seel (Desk Clerk).

Commercials: Doris Singleton (Libby), Duane Thompson (Woman), and Franklyn Parker (Seller).

Lux's adaptation of MGM's 1941 Western melodrama *Boom Town* focuses on a cheap crook with a respectable front whose illicit activities involving his burgeoning Nevada boom town inevitably lead to tragedy. The broadcast features Lana Turner in her original screen role of the reformer-wife, and John Hodiak as the corrupt but redeemable "businessman," played by Clark Gable in the Jack Conway–directed film.

523. "Whistle Stop," 4/15/46

Based on the 1946 United Artists film (screenplay by Philip Yordan), in turn based on the novel by Maritta M. Wolff (1941).

Intermission Guest: Virginia Thorne, Goldwyn starlet.

Cast: Alan Ladd (Kenny Dietz), Evelyn Keyes (Mary), Gale Gordon (Lew Lentz), Edwin Max (Gillo), Sammie Hill (Fran), Jane Morgan (Molly), Leo Cleary (Sam), Truda Marson (Jessie/Operator), George Neise (Ernie), Ed Emerson (Barker), Anne Stone (Stella), and Charles Seel (Al).

Commercials: Doris Singleton (Libby), Betty Moran (Woman).

Whistle Stop, United Artists' 1946 Leonide Moguy–directed picture, was translated to the radio for *Lux's* April 15 program. The grim and sordid tale of an embittered wastrel whose shady and irresponsible life-style eventually lands him in the middle of a murder case stars George Raft and Ava Gardner on the screen, and Alan Ladd and Evelyn Keyes in the *Lux* broadcast. Victor McLaglen's movie part of the hero's sidekick is played by radio/movie character actor Edwin Max, and Sammie Hill (a very versatile young radio actress) does a splendid job in her *Lux* debut as the emotionally tortured girl in love with the self-pitying hero (the part played on the screen by Jorja Curtright).

524. "Love Letters," 4/22/46

Based on the 1945 Paramount film

**William Keighley and Evelyn Keyes rehearsing "Whistle Stop" (April 15, 1946)
(photo: Photofest).**

(screenplay by Ayn Rand), in turn based on the novel *Pity My Simplicity,* by Chris Massie (1944).

Intermission Guest: Lila Leeds, Paramount starlet (as played by Wilma Francis).

Cast: Loretta Young (Singleton), Joseph Cotten (Alan), Frances Robinson (Dilly), Janet Scott (Beatrice Remington), Norman Field (Mack), Griff Barnett (Bishop), George Neise (Roger), Boyd Davis (Lawyer), Jay Novello (Jupp), Jeff Corey (Driver/Postman), Guy Kingsford (Clerk), Duane

Thompson (Nurse), and Charles Seel (Doctor).

Commercials: Doris Singleton (Libby), Janet Russell (Sally).

While a story centering around a sensitive soldier's eloquent letters of love ghost-written to the girl of a less-than-gentlemanly fellow serviceman might ordinarily be conceived as comedy, *Lux*'s broadcast of the 1945 William Dieterle drama illustrates the lingering (and far-reaching) tragedy connected with living a lie. Loretta Young gives a fine performance as the long-suffering amnesiac, Singleton, played by Jennifer Jones in the film, and Joseph Cotten resumes his motion picture role as Alan.

Scheduled starlet Lila Leeds was unable to appear because of illness, so Wilma Francis read her part over the air.

The story was telecast on *The Lux Video Theatre* on January 20, 1955.

525. "Gaslight," 4/29/46
Based on the 1944 MGM film (screenplay by John Van Druten, Walter Reisch, and John L. Balderston), in turn based on the play by Patrick Hamilton (1938).

Intermission Guest: Janet Thomas, Paramount starlet.

Cast: Ingrid Bergman (Paula), Charles Boyer (Gregory), Gale Gordon (Cameron), Janet Scott (Elizabeth), Truda Marson (Nancy), Eric Snowden (Williams), Claire Verdera (Lady Dalroy), Raymond Lawrence (Mufflin), Gloria Gordon (Mrs. Thwaites/Woman), and Charles Seel (Voice/Superintendent).

Commercials: Doris Singleton (Libby), June Whitfield (Dottie), and Frances Whitfield (Mother).

Lux's presentation of the 1944 George Cukor MGM psychological thriller *Gaslight* reteams Ingrid Bergman and Charles Boyer in the story of an anguished young wife who is driven to the point of insanity by her greedy, coldly calculating older husband. (Gale Gordon is heard in the Joseph Cotten screen part.) The radio adaptation is very successful in retaining the atmosphere and recreating the suspense of the picture version.

An earlier film version of Patrick Hamilton's play was released in England in 1940 with Diana Wynyard, Anton Walbrook, and Frank Pettingell under Thorold Dickinson's direction. (The film was released in the United States in 1952 under the title *Angel Street*.)

Additional film version: British National Pictures, 1940 (released in the United States as *Angel Street*).

526. "Tomorrow Is Forever," 5/6/46
Based on the 1946 RKO film (screenplay by Lenore Coffee), in turn based on the novel by Gwen Bristow (1943).

Intermission Guest: Elsie Sullivan, secretary of MGM fan mail department (after Act 1).

Cast: Claudette Colbert (Elizabeth Hamilton), Van Heflin (Erich Kessler [John MacDonald]), Richard Long (Drew), Natalie Wood (Margaret), Gale Gordon (Larry), Tommy Cook (Bryan), and Leone Ledoux (Baby).

Commercial: Doris Singleton (Libby).

The familiar plot of a remarried World War I widow whose first husband resurfaces some 20 years later is rehashed in RKO's 1946 drama *Tomorrow Is Forever*. The Irving Pichel–directed film features Claudette Colbert and Orson Welles as the aforementioned, while *Lux*'s version recasts Colbert in her original role and uses Van Heflin in the part taken by Welles onscreen. The broadcast's supporting cast includes Richard Long and Natalie Wood in their movie roles and Gale Gordon in the George Brent film part.

Ingrid Bergman and Charles Boyer during rehearsals of "Gaslight" (April 29, 1946) (photo: Photofest).

527. "Pardon My Past," 5/13/46
Based on the 1945 Columbia film (screenplay by Earl Felton and Karl Lamb; original story by Patterson McNutt and Harlan Ware).
Intermission Guest: Jeff Donnell, Columbia starlet.
Cast: Fred MacMurray (Eddie York/Peanuts), Marguerite Chapman (Joan), Lou Merrill (Arnold), Herb Vigran

(Chuck Gibson), Boyd Davis (Wills), Norman Field (Grandpa), Ed Emerson (Long), Dorothy Lovett (Mary), Edwin Max (Detective), Ann Whitfield (Susan), Hal K. Dawson (Driver/Cop Two), Cliff Clark (Cop in Acts 1 and 3), and Charles Seel (Butler).
Commercials: Doris Singleton (Libby), Julie Bannon (Woman).
Columbia's Leslie Fenton comedy

Pardon My Past tells of a recently discharged soldier whose remarkable resemblance to an irresponsible gambler leads to a series of amusing complications. Starring in this implausible but entertaining broadcast version are Fred MacMurray and Marguerite Chapman, both of whom reprise their screen roles, with radio actors Herb Vigran and Lou Merrill playing the William Demarest and Akim Tamiroff movie characters.

528. "Deadline at Dawn," 5/20/46

Based on the 1946 RKO film (screenplay by Clifford Odets).

Intermission Guest: Martha Hyer, RKO starlet.

Cast: Joan Blondell (June), Paul Lukas (Gus), Bill Williams (Alex), Gerald Mohr (Brady), Jay Novello (Pal), Sammie Hill (Helen), Julie Bannon (Nan), Edwin Max (Dooley), Justin Cooper (Kane), Barney Phillips (Sleepy), Anne Stone (Girl), Stanley Farrar (Waiter), Cliff Clark (Cop in Acts 2 and 3), Tyler McVey (Cabby/Milkman), Lee Sherin (Man [Orangeade Vendor]), Noreen Gammill (Woman), and Charles Seel (Sergeant/Man [at the apartment house]).

Commercials: Doris Singleton (Libby), Truda Marson (Woman).

Deadline at Dawn, RKO's current Harold Clurman murder mystery, made for a well-constructed, suspenseful *Lux* adaptation starring Joan Blondell (in Susan Hayward's screen role) as the world-weary dance-hall girl whose life takes a positive turn after she teams up with an innocent sailor in an effort to clear the boy of murder. Paul Lukas and Bill Williams resume their original screen parts as the kindly cabbie with more than a passing interest in the mystery, and the befuddled sailor in question, respectively. Radio actress Sammie Hill memorably portrays the key role of Helen.

529. "Music for Millions," 5/27/46

Based on the 1944 MGM film (screenplay by Myles Connolly).

Intermission Guest: Mary Stuart, MGM starlet.

Cast: Margaret O'Brien (Mike), Jimmy Durante (Andrews), José Iturbi (Himself), Frances Gifford (Barbara), Marisa O'Brien (Rosalind), Florence Lake (Jane), Norman Field (Uncle), Janet Scott (Mrs. McGuff), Edwin Cooper (Doctor), Eddie Marr (Soldier), Truda Marson (Girl), James Eagles (Elevator), Guy Kingsford (Clerk), and Charles Seel (Colonel).

Commercial: Doris Singleton (Libby).

Music for Millions, MGM's mixture of popular music, concert music, comedy, and drama, was directed by Henry Koster and released in 1944. May 17 saw *Lux*'s version, which features Margaret O'Brien, Jimmy Durante, and José Iturbi from the original cast, plus Frances Gifford in June Allyson's movie part and Marisa O'Brien in the Marsha Hunt film role.

The broadcast's musical selections are: Act 1: "Toscanini, Iturbi and Me" (words and music by Walter Bullock and Harold Spina; sung by Durante), Concerto for Piano and Orchestra in A Minor, opus 16 (1869; Edvard Grieg), an excerpt performed by José Iturbi (piano) and orchestra; Act 2: "Umbriago" (words by Irving Caesar, music by Jimmy Durante; sung by Durante); Act 3: "Clair de lune" (1890; Claude Debussy; from *Suite Bergamasque*; partial; performed by José Iturbi and orchestra).

530. "None but the Lonely Heart," 6/3/46

Based on the 1944 RKO film (screenplay by Clifford Odets), in turn based on the novel by Richard Llewellyn (1943).

Intermission Guest: Myra Dell, RKO starlet.

Cast: Brian Aherne (Ernie Mott), Ethel Barrymore (Ma), June Duprez (Ada), Lester Matthews (Jim), Frances Robinson (Aggie), Norman Field (Ike), Eric Snowden (Twite), Jay Novello (Taz), Gloria Gordon (Mrs. Snowden), Jeff Corey (Cash), Raymond Lawrence (Sergeant), Claire Verdera (Mrs. Chalmers/Nurse), Edwin Cooper (Cop Two), and Charles Seel (Man/Cop).

Commercials: Duane Thompson (Girl), Tyler McVey (Man), and Janet Russell (Sally).

Richard Llewellyn's somber novel of a cockney ne'er-do-well and his dying mother became one of RKO's most impressive releases of 1944 as directed and scripted by Clifford Odets. While Cary Grant (who was originally announced for the *Lux* broadcast) was cast against type in the movie version, the role of Ernie Mott is right up Brian Aherne's alley, and he gives a typically able performance. Repeating her Academy Award-winning portrayal of Ma is Ethel Barrymore (in her only Hollywood *Lux*), and June Duprez, also of the film cast, is an impressive Ada.

531. "And Now Tomorrow," 6/10/46

Based on the 1944 Paramount film (screenplay by Frank Partos and Raymond Chandler), in turn based on the novel by Rachel Field (1942).

Cast: Olivia deHavilland (Emily Blair), John Lund (Merrick Vance), Joseph Kearns (Dr. Weeks), Frances Robinson (Janice), Gerald Mohr (Jeff), Janet Scott (Aunt Martha), Edwin Cooper (Dr. Sloan), Ann Tobin (Operator), Guy Kingsford (Peter/Man), Charles Seel (Reade), Duane Thompson (Girl), Stanley Farrar (Man), and Horace Willard (Porter).

Commercials: Doris Singleton (Libby), Cliff Clark (Al), and Helen Andrews (Woman).

Lux's second presentation of *And Now Tomorrow* features Olivia deHav-

illand and John Lund in the adaptation of the 1944 Irving Pichel drama.

See 5/21/45 for information on the film version.

532. "Fallen Angel," 6/17/46

Based on the 1945 20th Century–Fox film (screenplay by Harry Kleiner), in turn based on the novel by Marty Holland (1945).

Intermission Guest: Gloria Saunders, 20th Century–Fox starlet.

Cast: Linda Darnell (Stella), Maureen O'Hara (June), Mark Stevens (Eric), Lois Corbett (Clara), Gerald Mohr (Judd), Norman Field (Pop), Earle Ross (Madley), Leo Cleary (Ellis/Man), Edward Emerson (Atkins), Charles Seel (Chief/Driver), Cliff Clark (Detective), and Hal Derwin (Singer).

Commercials: Truda Marson (Joan), Julie Bannon (Connie).

Fallen Angel, 20th Century–Fox's Otto Preminger–directed drama, focuses on a small-time chiseler's plan to bilk an innocent girl out of $12,500 in order to marry his abrasive hash-slinging love interest. *Lux*'s June 17 broadcast version features Maureen O'Hara in the role played by Alice Faye on the screen, Linda Darnell in her original motion picture part, and Mark Stevens in the Dana Andrews film role.

533. "State Fair," 6/24/46

Based on the 1945 20th Century–Fox film (screenplay by Oscar Hammerstein II), in turn based on the novel by Phil Stong (1932).

Intermission Guest: Anabel Shaw, 20th Century–Fox starlet.

Cast: Dick Haymes (Wayne), Jeanne Crain (Margy), Vivian Blaine (Emily), Elliott Lewis (Pat), Charles Seel (Abel), Regina Wallace (Ma), Ed Emerson (McGee/Ticket Seller), Dick Ryan (Miller/Al), Eddie Marr (Barker/Storekeeper), George Neise (Marty/Man), Edwin Cooper (Voice [P.A.]), and Earl Lee

(Hippenstahl), Noreen Gammill (Mrs. Hager/Operator), Cliff Clark (Barker Two/Simpson), Stanley Farrar (Thomas/ Fingerling), and Truda Marson (Eleanor).

Singers: Carol Stewart (Soloist [Margy's Singing Voice]), Winona Black, Devona Doxie, Zaruhi Elmassian, Georgia Stark, George Gramlich, Robert Tait, Clarence Badger, Jr., Marion Reese, Robert Bradford, and Enrico Ricardi (Arranger and Coach).

Commercials: Doris Singleton (Libby), Janet Russell (Sally).

Lux closed the 1945-46 season with a presentation of the 1945 Walter Lang–directed Rodgers and Hammerstein screen musical *State Fair*. The story focuses on a family's joys and heartaches involving the greatly anticipated annual state fair, and starring in the broadcast are Dick Haymes, Jeanne Crain, and Vivian Blaine in their original roles, and Elliott Lewis in the Dana Andrews movie part. The characters of Mr. and Mrs. Fiske (played by Charles Winninger and Fay Bainter onscreen) are greatly reduced in size for the radio version and are portrayed by Charles Seel and Regina Wallace. Songs (all written for the film by Oscar Hammerstein II [words] and Richard Rodgers [music]) heard in the program are: "It Might as Well Be Spring" (Carol Stewart), "That's for Me" (Vivian Blaine), and "It's a Grand Night for Singing" (Dick Haymes) in the first act; "It's a Grand Night for Singing" (reprise; ensemble) and "Isn't It Kinda Fun?" (Haymes and Blaine) in Act 2; and "It's a Grand Night for Singing" (finale; Haymes and ensemble) in the final act.

Fox first filmed *State Fair* in 1933 (without songs) under Henry King's direction and featuring a cast headed by Norman Foster, Janet Gaynor, Sally Eilers, Lew Ayres, Will Rogers, and Louise Dresser. A 1962 film was produced by 20th Century–Fox and used several musical numbers from the 1945 version, plus a few new songs with both music *and* words by Richard Rodgers. The stars of that José Ferrer–directed release are Pat Boone, Pamela Tiffin, Ann-Margret, Bobby Darin, Tom Ewell, and Alice Faye.

Twelfth Season
(August 26, 1946–June 23, 1947)

Columbia Broadcasting System, Monday, 9:00–10:00 P.M. Vine Street Playhouse, Hollywood, California. *Host*: William Keighley. *Announcer*: John Milton Kennedy. *Second Announcer*: Thomas Hanlon (August 26, 1946–February 24, 1947). *Director*: Fredric MacKaye. *Musical Director*: Louis Silvers. *Sound Effects*: Charlie Forsyth. *Adaptations*: S.H. Barnett (except as otherwise noted). Intermission guests (when present) appear after Act 2 (unless otherwise noted).

534. "Without Reservations," 8/26/46
Based on the 1946 RKO film (screenplay by Andrew Solt), in turn based on the novel *Thanks, God, I'll Take It from Here*, by Jane Allen and Mae Livingston (1946).

Intermission Guest: Kay Christopher, RKO starlet.

Cast: Claudette Colbert (Christopher Madden), Robert Cummings (Rusty Thomas), Elliott Lewis (Dinky), Charles Seel (Gibbs/Man Two), Cliff

Clark (Baldwin/Man One), Sandra Gould (Connie), Leo Cleary (Peters/Klotch), Eddie Marr (Jerome/Attendant), Dick Ryan (Pood/Mr. Randall), Noreen Gammill (Mrs. Randall/Secretary), Franklyn Parker (Conductor in Act 1/Man in Act 3), Robert Earle (Potter/Announcer in Act 2), Dorothy Scott (Alma/Second Woman), Edwin Cooper (Conductor in Act 2), Janet Scott (Woman/First Woman), Stanley Farrar (Man Three/Man), Tyler McVey (Boy/Announcer in Act 3), Horace Willard (Porter/Redcap), and Janet Russell (Wave/Girl).

Commercial: Doris Singleton (Libby).

Lux's season opener for 1946-47 was RKO's Mervyn LeRoy–directed comedy *Without Reservations*, which was revived with its star, Claudette Colbert, recreating her screen role. *Lux*'s broadcast tells the story of a novelist journeying to Hollywood to adapt her latest book to the screen who meets a pair of Marines en route (one of whom she falls in love with). Also featured are Robert Cummings in John Wayne's movie part, and radio actor Elliott Lewis in Don DeFore's film role.

535. "Our Vines Have Tender Grapes," 9/2/46

Based on the 1945 MGM film (screenplay by Dalton Trumbo), in turn based on the novel *For Our Vines Have Tender Grapes*, by George Victor Martin (1940).

Intermission Guest: Linda Christian, MGM starlet.

Cast: Margaret O'Brien (Selma), Frances Gifford (Viola Johnson), James Craig (Nels), Joseph Kearns (Pa), Griff Barnett (Bjorn Bjornson/Faraasen), Janet Scott (Mrs. Bjornson), Tyler McVey (Peter/Man in Act 1), Cliff Clark (Driver/Man Two), and Charles Seel (Man).

Chorus: Devona Doxie, Betty Rome,

Barbara Chitson, Robert Bradford, George Gramlich, and Enrico Ricardi (Coach).

Commercials: Doris Singleton (Libby), Truda Marson (Woman).

Lux's "Our Vines Have Tender Grapes," which was adapted from MGM's Roy Rowland–directed 1945 motion picture, primarily concerns itself with the adventures of the young daughter of a Norwegian farming family. Three principals from the movie, Margaret O'Brien, Frances Gifford, and James Craig, reprise their roles for the broadcast, while radio actor Joseph Kearns is heard in Edward G. Robinson's film part.

536. "The Barretts of Wimpole Street," 9/9/46

Based on the play by Rudolf Besier (1931).

Intermission Guest: Renee Randall, Paramount starlet.

Cast: Loretta Young (Elizabeth Barrett), Brian Aherne (Robert Browning), Vanessa Brown (Henrietta), Lester Matthews (Mr. Barrett), Janet Scott (Wilson), Frances Robinson (Arabel), Truda Marson (Bella), Charles Seel (Doctor), Vernon Downing (Captain Cook/Bevan), Peter Rankin (Octavius), Guy Kingsford (George), George Neise (Henry), Robert Barrett Mineah (Septimus), Edwin Rand (Charles), Sam Edwards (Alfred), and Frank Milano (Flush [the dog]).

Commercial: Doris Singleton (Libby).

Lux's adaptation of the play *The Barretts of Wimpole Street* features Brian Aherne in his original stage role, plus Loretta Young, Vanessa Brown, and Lester Matthews in the parts taken by Katharine Cornell, Margaret Baker, and Charles Waldron in the Broadway production that opened at the Empire Theatre on February 9, 1931. (Cornell and Aherne also appeared in the 1945 Broadway revival.) Vernon Downing, who plays Captain Cook and Henry Bevan in the broadcast, created the role of Alfred in the stage version.

A faithful, wonderfully effective motion picture version (directed by Sidney Franklin) was produced by MGM in 1934 starring Norma Shearer as the fragile Eliza- beth, Fredric March as Robert Browning, Maureen O'Sullivan as the delightful Henrietta Barrett, and Charles Laughton as the girls' tyrannical father. A 1957 version (again produced by MGM and directed by Sidney Franklin) features Jennifer Jones, Bill Travers, Virginia McKenna, and John Gielgud.

Film versions: MGM, 1934; MGM, 1957.

537. "Madame Curie," 9/16/46

Based on the 1943 MGM film (screenplay by Paul Osborn and Paul H. Rambeau), in turn based on the book by Eve Curie (1937).

Intermission Guests: Helene Stanley, MGM starlet (after Act 1), Merrick Dearborn, president of the National Safety Council, and Charles Luckman, president of Lever Brothers (after Act 2).

Cast: Greer Garson (Madame Curie), Walter Pidgeon (Pierre), Norman Field (Mr. Curie, Sr./First Driver), Janet Scott (the Elder Mrs. Curie), George Neise (David/Man Two), Murray Wagner (Dr. Becquerel/Voice), Fred Howard (Perot/Second Scientist), Ann Whitfield (Child), Charles Seel (Director/Second Driver), Herman Waldman (Roget/Jenkins), John Parrish (Doctor/ Man), and Dorothy Scott (Seamstress/ Woman).

"Madame Curie," *Lux*'s chronicle of the fascinating scientific research of Pierre (1859–1906) and Marie (1867–1934) Curie (whose monumental discovery of radium won them the Nobel Prize in physics in 1903), was the attraction for September 16. Starring on the air, as they did in MGM's 1943 Mer-

vyn LeRoy feature, are Greer Garson and Walter Pidgeon.

The second act intermission features Merrick Dearborn, the president of the National Safety Council, who presents the "award of honor for distinguished service to safety" to Lever Brothers president Charles Luckman.

*538. "Sentimental Journey," 9/23/46

Based on the 1946 20th Century–Fox film (screenplay by Samuel Hoffenstein and Elizabeth Reinhardt), in turn based on a story by Nelia Gardner White.

Intermission Guest: Coleen Gray, 20th Century–Fox starlet.

Cast: John Payne (Bill), Lynn Bari (Julie), Gloria McMillan (Betty), Charles Seel (Detective), Eddie Marr (Don), Stuart Robertson (Dr. Miller), Janet Scott (Miss Benson), Noreen Gammill (Martha), Duane Thompson (Miss McMasters), Al Ebon (Gregg), Guy Kingsford (Judson), Carole Matthews (Ruth), and Lois Corbett (Mrs. Deane).

Commercial: Doris Singleton (Libby).

Sentimental Journey, 20th Century–Fox's sensitive drama of a terminally ill young woman whose dying wish is to adopt a child for the beloved husband she will leave behind, was directed by Walter Lang and reached the screen in 1946 with Maureen O'Hara and John Payne in the leading roles. Payne repeated his picture part for *Lux*, and Lynn Bari was heard in O'Hara's role.

The studio produced a second version in 1958 under the title *The Gift of Love*, which was directed by Jean Negulesco and featured Lauren Bacall and Robert Stack.

Additional film version: 20th Century–Fox, 1958 (*The Gift of Love*).

539. "Coney Island," 9/30/46

Based on the 1943 20th Century–Fox film (screenplay by George Seaton).

Intermission Guest: Yvonne Rob, 20th Century–Fox starlet.

Cast: Betty Grable (Kate Farley), Victor Mature (Eddie Johnson), Barry Sullivan (Joe Rocco), Charles Seel (Keene/Man), Eddie Marr (Frankie), Leo Cleary (Finnigan/Second Man), Stanley Farrar (Billy/Second Usher), Cliff Clark (Louis/Hot Dog Man), June Foray (Dolly/Woman), Dick Ryan (Pat/Usher), Herb Rawlinson (Hammerstein), Truda Marson (Girl/Second Woman), and Doris Singleton (Soloist).

Chorus: Robert Tait, Sidney Pepple, George Gramlich, Clarence Badger, Harry Stafford, Kenneth Stevens, Ronald Bruce, Ray Lina, Homer Hall, and Enrico Ricardi (Coach).

Commercial: Doris Singleton (Libby).

Lux's second offering of "Coney Island" features Betty Grable in her original screen role, with Victor Mature and Barry Sullivan. Grable agreeably performs "When Irish Eyes Are Smiling" (words by Chauncey Olcott and George Graff, Jr., music by Ernest R. Ball; from *Isle o' Dreams*, 1912) during Act 1; and "Cuddle Up a Little Closer" (words by Otto [Hauerbach] Harbach, music by Karl Hoschra; from *The Three Twins*, 1908) and "Put Your Arms Around Me, Honey" (words by Junie McCree, music by Albert von Tilzer, 1910) in Act 3.

See 4/17/44 for information on the film versions; this was performed on *Lux* again as "Wabash Avenue" on November 13, 1950.

540. "Dragonwyck," 10/7/46

Based on the 1946 20th Century–Fox film (screenplay by Joseph L. Mankiewicz), in turn based on the novel by Anya Seton (1943).

Intermission Guest: Mara Carpenter, Warner Bros. script supervisor.

Cast: Gene Tierney (Miranda), Vincent Price (Nicholas Van Ryn), Gale Gordon (Dr. Jeff Turner), Margaret M. Meredith (Johanna), Gloria McMillan (Katrine), Norman Field (Wells), Janet Scott (Magda), Truda Marson (Peggy), Griff Barnett (Otto/Dr. Williams), Jay Novello (DeGrenier/Clergyman), Jeff Corey (Bleecker/Man), Sondra Rodgers (Mother), Herbert Lytton (Driver/Tomkins), and Charles Seel (Dirck/Mayor).

Commercials: Doris Singleton (Libby), Julie Bannon (Jean), and Janet Russell (Betty).

Dragonwyck, a 20th Century–Fox Gothic drama, marked the directorial debut of Joseph L. Mankiewicz, who also adapted Anya Seton's novel to the screen. The story (which takes place in the mid–1840s) concerns a young lady of Connecticut farming stock who travels to an eerie mansion on the Hudson to take up residence with some decidedly odd distant relatives. *Lux*'s adaptation, which features both Gene Tierney and Vincent Price from the motion picture cast, is much more atmospheric than the film, though the abridgment of the screenplay simplifies the characters into rather underdeveloped figures. (Both Tierney and Price, however, make the most of their roles.) Receiving featured billing in the Glenn Langan movie role is radio actor Gale Gordon, whose romantic interest in the heroine is diluted, especially by the deletion of his (and the picture's) last line of dialogue.

541. "To Have and Have Not," 10/14/46

Based on the 1944 Warner Bros. film (screenplay by Jules Furthman and William Faulkner), in turn based on the novel by Ernest Hemingway (1937).

Intermission Guest: Carrie McCord, 20th Century–Fox starlet.

Cast: Humphrey Bogart (Harry Morgan), Lauren Bacall (Mary Browning), Tim Graham (Eddie), George Sorel (Gerard), Jack Kruschen (Inspector Renard), Betty Alexander (Helene), Jack Lloyd (DeBursac), Robin Hughes

(Beauclerc), Stanley Farrar (Emil/ Voice), Herman Waldman (Coyo), Herb Lytton (Albert/Man), and Charles Seel (Johnson).

Commercials: Doris Singleton (Libby), Janet Scott (Grandmother), and Truda Marson (Jane).

It took two years for *Lux* to bring Howard Hawks's 1944 Warner Bros. hit *To Have and Have Not* to the air. Humphrey Bogart reprises his screen role of Harry Morgan, an American fishing boat captain who becomes involved with the Resistance movement in Nazi-occupied Martinique, and Lauren Bacall (who made her movie debut in the film) is also present in her original part of "Slim." The well-done adaptation retains the best-remembered scenes from the motion picture, with just enough continuity in between to keep the complex story from becoming too confusing.

The story was telecast on *The Lux Video Theatre* on January 17, 1957.

542. "Miss Susie Slagle's," 10/21/46

Based on the 1945 Paramount film (screenplay by Anne Froelick and Hugo Butler), in turn based on the novel by Augusta Tucker (1939).

Intermission Guest: Nina Foch, motion picture starlet.

Cast: Joan Caulfield (Gret), William Holden (Pug), Billy DeWolfe (Ben), Griff Barnett (Dr. Howe), Janet Scott (Miss Slagle), Norman Field (Dr. Bone), Clarke Gordon (Lige), George Neise (Bert), Stuart Robertson (Otto/Dr. Bowen), Earl Taylor Smith (Hizer), Truda Marson (Nan), Herman Waldman (Dr. Faber), Charles Seel (Dr. Metz/Dean), Thomas Mitchell (Clay), David Ellis (Irving/Young Man), Robert Cole (Ellis), Joel Davis (Boy), Dorothy Scott (Mrs. Johnson), and Jack Carrington (Anesthetist/Johnson).

Chorus: Robert Bradford, Donald Neese, A. Kenneth Stevens, George Gramlich, Phil Neely, Delmar Porter, and Enrico Ricardi (Coach).

Paramonnt's John Berry–directed production *Miss Susie Slagle's* was the attraction for October 21. This drama of struggling medical students and the kindly landlady with whom they share their various troubles stars Joan Caulfield repeating her screen role, William Holden in Sonny Tufts' movie part, and for comic relief, Billy DeWolfe, also of the picture cast. Top-billed in the film is Veronica Lake, but as the broadcast shifts the story's emphasis to the Joan Caulfield character, Lake's movie role is taken by radio actress Truda Marson. (The title character, which is played by Lillian Gish in the motion picture, is given to Janet Scott for the radio version.)

"Miss Susie Slagle's" was performed on *The Lux Video Theatre* on November 24, 1955.

543. "From This Day Forward," 10/28/46

Based on the 1946 RKO film (screenplay by Hugo Butler, Edith Sommer, and Charles Schnee; adaptation by Garson Kanin), in turn based on the novel *All Brides Are Beautiful*, by Thomas Bell (1936).

Cast: Joan Fontaine (Susie), Mark Stevens (Bill), Eddie Marr (Hank), Charles Seel (Hoffman), Anne Stone (Martha), Leo Cleary (Jake), Norman Field (Judge/Higgler), Herb Butterfield (Yeagan), Noreen Gammill (Ma), Howard Jeffrey (Timmy), Norma Nilsson (Barbara), Thomas Mitchell (District Attorney), Cliff Clark (Detective/Man), Dorothy Scott (Girl/Woman), Julie Bannon (Girl Two).

Commercials: Doris Singleton (Libby), Truda Marson (Woman).

Though Thomas Bell's novel *All Brides Are Beautiful* was purchased in 1940 by RKO, the studio waited six years before filming the social drama as

From This Day Forward. The story (the bulk of which is told in flashback) centers around a young idealistic New York couple whose diet of love hardly sustains them during their daily struggles with poverty. Joan Fontaine and Mark Stevens reprise their screen roles for the *Lux* version of the 1946 John Berry–directed movie.

544. "I've Always Loved You," 11/4/46

Based on the 1946 Republic film (screenplay by Borden Chase, from his original story "Concerto").

Intermission Guest: Olga San Juan, Paramount starlet.

Cast: Joseph Cotten (George), Catherine McLeod (Myra), Otto Kruger (Goronoff), Noreen Gammill (Mrs. Goronoff/Woman), Janet Scott (Mrs. Sampter), Daphne Drake (Paula), Norman Field (Hassman), George Neise (Severin/Man Two), Jay Novello (Nick), Guy Kingsford (Chauffeur/Man), and Charles Seel (Man Three).

Commercial: Doris Singleton (Libby).

Lux's adaptation of Frank Borzage's 1946 Republic drama *I've Always Loved You* details the personal struggles that arise between a conductor and the promising girl pianist who loves him. Joseph Cotten plays the part of the girl's boyfriend from back home, taken by third-billed William Carter in the movie, with Catherine McLeod repeating her screen role of the pianist and Otto Kruger in Philip Dorn's motion picture part of the conductor. The uneventful story of the movie is merely an excuse for the Technicolor production and the parade of concert piano pieces (played on the soundtrack by Artur Rubinstein). Nonetheless, the radio version offers acceptable entertainment, and though none of the musical selections is performed in its entirety, the show does serve as a fine display piece for the versatile *Lux* orchestra, under the direction of Louis Silvers.

Fragments of the following pieces (some very brief, and most at least partially obscured by dialogue) are performed by Ignace Hilsberg (solo piano unless noted): Act 1: Etude in C Minor, op. 10, no. 12 (Frederic Chopin), Sonata no. 23 in F Minor, op. 57 ("Appassionata"; Ludwig van Beethoven), Nocturne no. 5 in F-sharp Major, op. 15, no. 2 (Chopin), Concerto in C Minor for Piano and Orchestra, op. 18 (Serge Rachmaninoff), third movement (Allegro scherzando); Act 2: Rachmaninoff's C Minor Concerto (reprise), finale (with orchestra), Fantaisie-Impromptu in C-sharp Minor, op. 66 (Chopin); Act 3: Symphony no. 9 in E Minor, op. 95 ("From the New World") (Antonin Dvorak), fourth movement (Allegro con fuoco), finale (orchestra only), Rachmaninoff's C Minor Concerto, finale (reprise) (with orchestra).

*545. "Gallant Journey," 11/11/46

Based on the 1946 Columbia film (screenplay by William Wellman and Byron Morgan).

Intermission Guest: Janis Carter, Columbia starlet.

Cast: Glenn Ford (John), Janet Blair (Regina), Jack Kruschen (Father Ball), Norman Field (Father Keaton), Leo Cleary (Logan), Regina Wallace (Mother/Mrs. Logan), Eddie Marr (Marskey), Clarke Gordon (Jim/Man), Robert Cole (Tom), Charles Seel (Mahoney/Man One), Truda Marson (Mary), Henry Howland (Rheinlander/Man Three), George Neise (Walker/Man Two), Paul Marion (Dondaro), and Cliff Clark (Banker/Doctor).

Commercials: Duane Thompson (Girl), Marjorie Riordan (Margaret).

The aerial expertise of multitalented director William Wellman (who was a decorated flyer with the Lafayette Flying Corps and the Black Cat Group during the First World War) made him a fine choice to direct Columbia's 1946 drama *Gallant Journey*. The film, which focuses upon glider experimentation during the latter part of the last century, was adapted for *Lux*, with Glenn Ford and Janet Blair recreating their original screen roles.

546. "O.S.S.," 11/18/46

Based on the 1946 Paramount film (screenplay by Richard Maibaum).

Intermission Guest: Lucille Barkley, Paramount starlet.

Cast: Alan Ladd (Martin), Veronica Lake (Ellen), Gale Gordon (Commander Brady), Joseph Kearns (Meister), Richard Benedict (Bouchet), Charles Seel (Colonel Field), Norman Field (Albert/Scientist), Jay Novello (Brink), Rolfe Sedan (Gates/Engineer), Noreen Gammill (Madame Prideaux/Woman), Ed Emerson (Pilot/Corporal), George Neise (Farmer/First German), Howard Jeffrey (Gerard), Harry Roland (Second German), George Sorel (Archibald/Fireman), Truda Marson (Girl/Woman), and Robert Coute (LeFevre).

Commercial: Doris Singleton (Libby).

Paramount's espionage thriller *O.S.S.* (directed by Irving Pichel) gave *Lux* producers an excuse to reunite the popular screen team of Alan Ladd (of the movie cast) and Veronica Lake (in Geraldine Fitzgerald's screen role). The story of American agents on a clandestine assignment in Nazi-occupied France also offers prominent parts to radio regulars Gale Gordon and Joseph Kearns. (Richard Benedict also repeats his picture portrayal.)

547. "Mrs. Parkington," 11/25/46

Based on the 1944 MGM film (screenplay by Robert Thoeren and Polly James), in turn based on the novel by Louis Bromfield (1943).

Intermission Guest: Dorothy Porter, MGM starlet.

Cast: Greer Garson (Mrs. Parkington), Walter Pidgeon (Major Parkington), Loretta Hillbrandt (Aspasia), Alvina Temple (Jane), Richard Benedict (Ned), Herbert Butterfield (Avery), Regina Wallace (Hattie), Constance Cavendish (Mona), Stuart Robinson (Kinard), Janet Scott (Alice), Marjorie Bennett (Mrs. Graham), Gerald Mohr (Ramsey), Norman Field (Quincy/Manager), Charles Seel (Doctor/Leader), Noreen Gammill (Mrs. Humphrey/Woman), Lois Corbett (Helen), Sandra Rodgers (Madeleine), Jack Edwards, Jr. (Jack), Jay Novello (Cellino/Orlando), and David Laughlin (Singer).

Lux's episodic telling of the 1944 Tay Garnett–directed drama *Mrs. Parkington* chronicles the dubious lives of three generations of nouveau riche Americans. Greer Garson and Walter Pidgeon are featured in their original screen roles as the long-suffering matriarch and ruthless philanderer, respectively.

548. "Meet Me in St. Louis," 12/2/46

Based on the 1944 MGM film (screenplay by Irving Brecher and Fred F. Finklehoffe), in turn based on the *New Yorker* stories and novel by Sally Benson (1942).

Intermission Guest: Lola Dean, MGM starlet.

Cast: Judy Garland (Esther), Margaret O'Brien (Tootie), Tom Drake (John Truett), Gale Gordon (Alonzo), Coleen Gray (Rose), Regina Wallace (Mrs. Smith), Norman Field (Grandpa), Billy Roy (Lon), Noreen Gammill (Katie), Dick Ryan (Costello), Clarke Gordon (Warren), Charles Seel (Braukoff), Truda Marson (Girl in Act 1), Johnny McGovern (Glennie), Joel Davis (Johnny), Jerry Farber (Tommy), Howard Jeffrey (Boy), and Lois Kennison (Girl in Act 2).

Chorus: Robert Bradford (Soloist), Gil Morohan, Harry Stafford, Sid Pepple, Henry Kruse, Muzzy Marcellino,

Gloria Eygard, Dorothy Jackson, Mary Mahoney, Doreen Trydon, Devona Doxie, Ruth Clark, and Enrico Ricardi (Coach).

Commercials: Doris Singleton (Libby), Helen Andrews (Mrs. Green), and Alyn Lockwood (Mrs. Brown).

The Vincente Minnelli–directed musical hit *Meet Me in St. Louis* reached *The Lux Radio Theatre* in time for the 1946 Christmas season. The story, which is set in St. Louis as it prepares for the 1904 World's Fair, offers meaty roles to all of the principals, led by Judy Garland, Margaret O'Brien, and Tom Drake of the MGM film cast. Making a notable contribution in support is Gale Gordon as the bombastic father of the clan (Leon Ames's film role). Judy Garland performs three songs written for the film (all with words and music by Hugh Martin and Ralph Blane): "The Boy Next Door" (in Act 1), "The Trolley Song" (in Act 2), and "Have Yourself a Merry Little Christmas" (in Act 3).

549. "Together Again," 12/9/46

Based on the 1944 Columbia film (screenplay by Virginia Van Upp and F. Hugh Herbert).

Intermission Guest: Jeff Donnell, Columbia starlet.

Special Guest: Jack Benny (in curtain call).

Cast: Irene Dunne (Anne), Walter Pidgeon (George Corday), Jerome Courtland (Gilbert), Jeff Donnell (Diana), Alan Reed (Grandpa), Noreen Gammill (Jessie), Leo Cleary (Buchanan), Eddie Marr (Perc/M.C.), Virginia Gregg (Muriel/Girl), Anne Stone (Gilda/Woman Two), Jay Novello (Leonardo/Man Two), Janet Scott (Woman), Cliff Clark (Cop Two/Conductor), Lillian Randolph (Maid), and Charles Seel (Cop One/Man).

Commercials: Doris Singleton (Libby), Norman Field (Secretary of Agriculture).

Together Again, Charles Vidor's 1944 Columbia comedy, appeared on *Lux's* December 9 broadcast with Irene Dunne of the movie cast and Walter Pidgeon in Charles Boyer's picture role. The story concerns a widowed independent mayor whose family decides she would find more fulfillment as the wife of an ardent New York sculptor. Jerome Courtland also repeats his picture part, while Jeff Donnell (who serves as intermission guest as well) and Alan Reed are heard in the Mona Freeman and Charles Coburn roles.

Comedian Jack Benny makes a surprise appearance during the curtain call to plug the following week's broadcast of "Killer Kates."

"Together Again" was repeated on May 10, 1955.

550. "Killer Kates," 12/16/46

Based on the unproduced Warner Bros. story "The Man They Couldn't Kill."

Intermission Guest: Joan Winfield, Warner Bros. starlet.

Cast: Jack Benny (Jeff Morley), Gail Patrick (Helen), Alan Reed (Al Brady), Gale Gordon (Dr. Alberon), Gerald Mohr (Norton), Ge Ge Pearson (Frances), Norman Field (Mayor), Eric Snowden (Walters), Herbert Vigran (Steve), Eddie Marr (McCall/Hoppy), Ed Emerson (Stanley/Cop), Jay Novello (Blinky/Mario), Dick Ryan (Patch/First Stagehand), Ken Christy (Chief/First Cop), Franklyn Parker (Doorman/Second Stagehand), Charles Seel (Waiter/Second Cop), and Doris Singleton (Singer).

Commercials: Doris Singleton (Libby), Janet Russell (Sally).

Promised for the *Lux Radio Theatre* broadcast of December 16 was Jack Benny in a "dramatic" role. As often happens when a comedian appears in a dramatic program, the play itself finds the comic on more familiar ground than the promise would have us believe. Such is the case with "Killer Kates," in which an actor starring as a cold-blooded gangster in the theatre (though he is quite the opposite in real life), has a breakdown and assumes the identity of his stage character. The story abounds in the sort of situations that one might encounter in a *Jack Benny Program* sketch, though the dialogue is not nearly as amusing. Assisting the radio comedian are Gail Patrick as his wife and Alan Reed as his aggressive manager. (The radio play was based on an unproduced Warner Bros. property.)

551. "Do You Love Me?," 12/23/46
Based on the 1946 20th Century–Fox film (screenplay by Robert Ellis and Helen Logan; original story by Bert Granet).
Intermission Guest: Eve Miller, 20th Century–Fox starlet.
Cast: Maureen O'Hara (Katherine Hilliard), Dick Haymes (Jimmy Hale), Barry Sullivan (Barry Clayton), John McIntire (Herbert Benham), Melville Ruick (Ralph), Ed Emerson (Karl/Man Two), Herbert Vigran (Billy/Man Three), Edwin Max (Taxi), Truda Marson (Girl [Peters]), Janet Scott (Mrs. Crackleton), Norman Field (Waiter/Man), Noreen Gammill (Woman Two), Stanley Farrar (Conductor/Man), Charles Seel (Man One/Man Two), and Jerry Hausner (Bellboy/Messenger).
Chorus: Pauline Byrne Preshaw (and Quintet), Vincent Dugan, Tony Perisi, Howard Hudson, Howard Andrews Williams, Devona Doxie, Ruth Martin, Betty Rome, Mary Mahoney, and Enrico Ricardi (Coach).
Commercial: Doris Singleton (Libby).
Gregory Ratoff's 1946 20th Century–Fox film *Do You Love Me?* provided *Lux* with a musical to cap the Christmas season. Maureen O'Hara and Dick Haymes repeat their screen roles (as the mousy conservatory student who undergoes a transformation after hearing an offhand remark and the "groaner" with whom she eventually finds love), while Barry Sullivan is cast as the somewhat abrasive band leader (Harry James in the motion picture) who avidly pursued the now glamorous lass whom he had earlier offended. Haymes performs "The More I See You" (words by Mack Gordon, music by Harry Warren) and "Do You Love Me?" (words and music by Harry Ruby) in Act 1; "Chestnuts Roasting on an Open Fire" ("The Christmas Song") (words by Robert Wells, music by Mel Tormé) in Act 2; and "Do You Love Me? (reprise) in Act 3.

552. "Crack-Up," 12/30/46
Based on the 1946 RKO film (screenplay by John Paxton, Ben Bengal, and Ray Spencer), in turn based on the story "Madman's Holiday," by Frederic Brown.
Intermission Guest: Jacqueline White, RKO starlet.
Cast: Pat O'Brien (George Steele), Lynn Bari (Terry), Lester Matthews (Traybin), John McIntire (Dr. Lowell), Herbert Butterfield (Barton), Cliff Clark (Cochran), Stanley Waxman (Stevenson), June Whitley (Mary), Eddie Marr (Vendor), Norman Field (Station Agent/Man Two), Dick Ryan (Waiter/Butler), Charles Seel (Johnson), Ed Emerson (Wilson/Man), Tyler McVey (Ticket Agent/Man Three), and Franklyn Parker (Conductor).
Commercials: Doris Singleton (Libby), Duane Thompson (Mother), Stanley Farrar (Father), and Lois Kenison (Girl).
The RKO film *Crack-Up*, a periodically interesting though often confusing drama of an art expert who stumbles upon a forgery operation, came to *The Lux Radio Theatre* with Pat O'Brien in his original role (the victim of the title

situation). Also in the cast are Lynn Bari in Claire Trevor's screen role as the hero's fiancée, and Lester Matthews as the somewhat mysterious Traybin (Herbert Marshall's movie part).

553. "Till the End of Time," 1/6/47

Based on the 1946 RKO film (screenplay by Allen Rivkin), in turn based on the novel *They Dream of Home,* by Niven Busch (1944).

Intermission Guest: Kay Christopher, RKO starlet.

Cast: Laraine Day (Pat), Bill Williams (Cliff), Robert Mitchum (Bill Tabeshaw), Tony Barrett (Perry), Leo Cleary (Mr. Harper), Regina Wallace (Mrs. Harper), Richard Benedict (Soldier/Benny), Norman Field (Waiter), Tyler McVey (Hal), George Neise (Jack), Noreen Gammill (Mrs. Kincellor), and Charles Seel (Mitchell/Man).

Commercial: Doris Singleton (Libby).

Lux opened 1947 on a topical note with the presentation of Edward Dmytryk's 1946 RKO drama *Till the End of Time.* This postwar account of the various physical and emotional traumas of three returning soldiers features Laraine Day in the role Dorothy McGuire plays on the screen, and Robert Mitchum repeating his movie part. Bill Williams, who appears as Perry in the film, plays Guy Madison's picture part in the broadcast, and Tony Barrett is given Williams's screen character. The main theme in Louis Silvers's incidental music is the title song, which was adapted for the movie by Ted Mossman from Chopin's Polonaise in A-flat Major, opus 53.

554. "The Green Years," 1/13/47

Based on the 1946 MGM film (screenplay by Robert Ardrey and Sonya Levien), in turn based on the novel by A.J. Cronin (1944).

Intermission Guest: Lee Wilde, MGM starlet.

Cast: Charles Coburn (Grandfather Gow), Tom Drake (Robert), Beverly Tyler (Alison), Hume Cronyn (Mr. Leckie), Dean Stockwell (Robert, as a Boy), Gale Gordon (Jason Reid), Regina Wallace (Mrs. Leckie), Mary Gordon (Grandma), Frederic Worlock (McKellar), Guy Kingsford (Murdock), June Whitley (Kate), Eric Snowden (Priest), Colin Campbell (Blakely), and Norman Field (Doctor).

Commercial: Doris Singleton (Libby).

The Green Years (directed for MGM by Victor Saville) tells the engaging story of an Irish orphan growing up in Scotland, from his arrival at the home of his new family (strangers to him at the outset), to the point at which he reaches manhood. The film, which even at 127 minutes was forced to condense A.J. Cronin's novel, has been necessarily abbreviated further for *Lux*'s radio version. Reducing the importance of the supporting characters greatly minimizes the effectiveness of a story of this nature, yet the sincere performances of Charles Coburn, Tom Drake, Beverly Tyler, Hume Cronyn, and Dean Stockwell (all in their original roles), combined with an intelligent script, add up to a satisfactory entertainment.

555. "Anna and the King of Siam," 1/20/47

Based on the 1946 20th Century–Fox film (screenplay by Talbot Jennings and Sally Benson), in turn based on the book by Margaret Landon (1944).

Intermission Guest: Hazel Dawn, 20th Century–Fox starlet.

Cast: Irene Dunne (Anna), Rex Harrison (the King of Siam), John McIntire (Kralahome), Jeanette Nolan (Lady Thiang), Constance Cavendish (Tuptim), Jonny Barnett (Louis), Tommy Cook (Prince), Norman Field (Doctor/Colonel Renard), Fred Howard (Interpreter), Herbert Lytton (Alak), Charles

"The Green Years" (January 13, 1947), with Tom Drake and Beverly Tyler (photo: Photofest).

Seel (Captain), Jack Edwards, Jr. (Sir Edward), Noreen Gammill (Beebe), and Truda Marson (Mary Ann).

Commercial: Doris Singleton (Libby).

An unusual drama of 20th Century–Fox's, *Anna and the King of Siam* (di-rected by John Cromwell) is adapted into an interesting *Lux Radio Theatre* presentation. The radio version finds Irene Dunne recreating her film por-trayal as the English schoolmistress who is engaged by the King of Siam

Irene Dunne and Rex Harrison in "Anna and the King of Siam" (January 20, 1947) (photo: Photofest).

(Rex Harrison, also repeating his screen role) to educate the children of his "semibarbaric" country.

The story was repeated on *Lux*'s May 30, 1949, broadcast.

556. "Cluny Brown," 1/27/47

Based on the 1946 20th Century–Fox film (screenplay by Samuel Hoffenstein and Elizabeth Reinhardt), in turn based on the novel by Marjorie Sharp (1944).

Intermission Guest: Barbara Lawrence, 20th Century–Fox starlet.

Cast: Charles Boyer (Adam Bolinski), Olivia deHavilland (Cluny Brown), Alan Reed (Sir Henry), Gale Gordon (Mr. Wilson), Betty Fairfax (Mother), Jack Edwards, Jr. (Andrew), Constance Cavendish (Betty), Eric Snowden (Serett), Earl Hubbard (Ames), Noreen Gammill (Mrs. Wilson/Mrs. Bailey), and Charles Seel (Forrity).

Ernst Lubitsch produced and directed 20th Century–Fox's *Cluny Brown*, a quirky comedy (set in 1938 England) focusing on a bubbly cockney girl with a keen interest in plumbing, and her friendship with an anti–Nazi refugee author. Charles Boyer capably repeats his film role in *Lux*'s amusing adaptation, while Olivia deHavilland gives a lively account of the title character, which was played onscreen by Jennifer Jones.

557. "National Velvet," 2/3/47

Based on the 1944 MGM film (screenplay by Theodore Reeves and Helen Deutsch), in turn based on the novel by Enid Bagnold (1935).

Intermission Guest: Dorothy Patrick, MGM starlet.

Cast: Mickey Rooney (Mi), Elizabeth Taylor (Velvet), Donald Crisp (Mr.

Brown), Janet Scott (Mrs. Brown), Norman Field (Ede), Charles Seel (Joe), Truda Marson (Edwina/Woman), Lois Boniston (Malvolia), Johnny McGovern (Donald), Alec Harford (Greenford), Jack Edwards, Jr. (Tim), Herbert Rawlinson (Constable), George Neise (Doctor/Man), and Jerry Barnes (Dog). *Commercial*: Doris Singleton (Libby).

Originally the property of RKO in 1935, *National Velvet* was purchased in 1941 by MGM, which brought the horse-racing drama to the screen in 1944 under the direction of Clarence Brown. *Lux*'s February 3, 1947, version features three players from the movie cast: Mickey Rooney as the embittered jockey, Elizabeth Taylor as the idealistic farm girl who dreams of glory for her beloved horse, and Donald Crisp as her money-loving father.

558. "Frenchman's Creek," 2/10/47
Based on the 1944 Paramount film (screenplay by Talbot Jennings), in turn based on the novel by Daphne du Maurier (1941).
Intermission Guest: Melle Matthews, 20th Century–Fox starlet.
Cast: Joan Fontaine (Lady Dona), David Niven (the Frenchman), Alan Reed (William), Gerald Mohr (Lord Rockingham), Tom Collins (Harry), Keith Hitchcock (Godolphin), and Charles Seel, Raymond Lawrence, Jay Novello, Norman Field, and Anne Stone.
Commercials: Doris Singleton (Libby), Alyn Lockwood (Betty), Clarke Gordon (Bill).

Daphne du Maurier's controversial best-seller *Frenchman's Creek* reached the screen via Paramount's 1944 Mitchell Leisen–directed release. *Lux*'s version of the movie comes across as a breezy and rather unconvincing love story of a lady whose boredom with the commonplace inspires her to begin an illicit love affair with a pirate. Recreating her film role of Lady Dona is Joan Fontaine, while David Niven makes a sophisticated buccaneer in Arturo de Cordova's screen part.

559. "Devotion," 2/17/47
Based on the 1946 Warner Bros. film (screenplay by Keith Winter).
Intermission Guest: Patricia White, Paramount starlet.
Cast: Jane Wyman (Emily Brontë), Virginia Bruce (Charlotte Brontë), Vincent Price (Mr. Nichols), Norman Field (Mr. Brontë), Alan Reed (Thackery), Janet Scott (Elizabeth/Lady Thornton), Jack Edwards, Jr., June Whitley, Ramsey Hill, and Charles Seel.

Lux's version of Warner Bros.' 1946 drama *Devotion* (which was actually completed in 1943) is a faithful adaptation of an unfaithful screen depiction of the lives of the Brontë sisters. Ida Lupino, who plays the gentle, soft-spoken Emily (1818–48) in the Curtis Bernhardt–directed film, was unable to appear as scheduled in the *Lux* version, so the part was given to Jane Wyman. Virginia Bruce plays the high-spirited Charlotte (1816–55), Olivia deHavilland's screen role, and Vincent Price assumes the Paul Henreid movie character of the man both women love.

560. "Kitty," 2/24/47
Based on the 1946 Paramount film (screenplay by Karl Tunberg and Darrell Ware), in turn based on the novel by Rosamund Marshall (1943).
Intermission Guest: Marilyn Monroe, 20th Century–Fox starlet.
Cast: Paulette Goddard (Kitty), Patric Knowles (Sir Hugh Marcy), Alan Reed (Thomas Gainsborough), Norman Field (Duke), Raymond Lawrence (Selby), Eric Snowden (Dobson/Prison Guard), Gloria Gordon (Lady Susan/Meg), George Neise (Barney/Man), Herb Rawlinson (Doctor), Charles Seel (Lawyer), and Ann Tobin (Molly).

"Cluny Brown" (January 27, 1947), with Charles Boyer and Olivia deHavilland (photo: Photofest).

Commercials: Doris Singleton (Libby), Janet Russell (Sally), Margie Liszt (Mrs. A), Noreen Gammill (Mrs. B), and Regina Wallace (Mrs. C).

Paramount's 1946 period drama *Kitty*, which was directed by Mitchell Leisen, arrived on *Lux* with Paulette Goddard engagingly recreating her screen role as an eighteenth-century British waif who ascends the social ladder with the much needed assistance of an opportunistic rogue. Patric Knowles, who plays suitor Brett Hardwood in the movie (a character who does not appear

Mickey Rooney and Elizabeth Taylor recreated their film roles in "National Velvet" on February 3, 1947 (photo: Photofest).

in the radio play), is given Ray Milland's screen part of the scheming Sir Hugh in the broadcast.

561. "Somewhere in the Night," 3/3/47
Based on the 1946 20th Century–Fox film (screenplay by Howard Dimsdale and Joseph L. Mankiewicz), in turn based on a story by Marvin Borowsky.

Intermission Guest: Ruth Roman, Paramount starlet.

Cast: John Hodiak (George Taylor), Lynn Bari (Christy Smith), Carleton

KaDell (Mike), Bill Johnstone (Kendell), Norman Field (Clerk), Eddie Marr (Joe), and Charles Seel (Voice).

Commercials: Doris Singleton (Libby), Herbert Lytton (Voice).

Joseph L. Mankiewicz directed 20th Century-Fox's thriller *Somewhere in the Night*, which was released in 1946. The tale of an amnesiac ex-serviceman trying to piece together his shady past (which may have included a murder) contains too many twists for a one-hour radio play, which results in a confusing, if eventful, drama. John Hodiak reprises his movie part, and Lynn Bari plays the Nancy Guild screen character.

562. "It's a Wonderful Life," 3/10/47

Based on the 1946 Liberty/RKO film (screenplay by Frances Goodrich, Albert Hackett, Jo Swerling, and Frank Capra), in turn based on the story "The Greatest Gift," by Philip Van Doren Stern (1943).

Intermission Guest: Susan Blanchard, 20th Century-Fox starlet.

Cast: James Stewart (George Bailey), Donna Reed (Mary Hatch), Victor Moore (Clarence), Bill Johnstone (Mr. Bailey), John McIntire (Joseph), Leo Cleary (Uncle Billy), Edwin Maxwell (Potter), Janet Scott (Mother), Noreen Gammill (Voice), Cliff Clark (Man), Norma Jean Nilsson (Baby), and Eddie Marr, Norman Field, Franklyn Parker, Ann Carter, and Charles Seel.

Commercial: Doris Singleton (Libby).

Lux's adaptation of the 1946 Frank Capra dramatic fantasy *It's a Wonderful Life* received a warm reception from the radio studio audience when it was performed on March 10. Both James Stewart and Donna Reed are on hand in their original screen roles, while Victor Moore is given Henry Travers's motion picture part of Clarence. The latter's character (as well as the entire broadcast) is played more for comedy

than in the film, and key incidents (and even characters) of the 127-minute movie are deleted for the microphone version.

563. "Leave Her to Heaven," 3/17/47

Based on the 1945 20th Century-Fox film (screenplay by Jo Swerling), in turn based on the novel by Ben Ames Williams (1944).

Intermission Guest: Martha Hyer, RKO starlet.

Cast: Gene Tierney (Ellen Barrett), Cornell Wilde (George Harland), Kay Christopher (Ruth), Alan Reed (Glen Robie), Gale Gordon (Russell Quinton), Tommy Cook (Danny), Tim Graham (Luke), Louise Lorimer (Mrs. Barrett), Norman Field (Dr. Mason/Judge), Bill Johnstone (Dr. Saunders/Metcalf), Alex Gerry (Conductor/Carlson), and Charles Seel (Guthridge).

Commercial: Doris Singleton (Libby).

Ben Ames Williams's interesting tale of a neurotic young woman fanatically obsessed with a man she "loves too much" made for an intriguing, well-acted *Lux* broadcast on March 17. Gene Tierney recreates her picture part of the emotionally unstable girl, and Cornell Wilde also reprises his movie role as her patient husband. Kay Christopher plays the Jeanne Crain screen character of Ruth.

"Leave Her to Heaven" was performed on *The Lux Summer Theatre* on August 10, 1953.

564. "Smokey," 3/24/47

Based on the 1946 20th Century-Fox film (screenplay by Lily Hayward, Dwight Cummings, and Dorothy Yost), in turn based on the novel by Will James (1929).

Intermission Guest: Laurette Luez, 20th Century-Fox starlet.

Cast: Joel McCrea (Clint Barkley), Constance Moore (Julie), Bill Johnstone (Jeff Hicks), Noreen Gammill

(Gram), Ira Grossel (Frank), Eddie Marr (Peters), Cliff Clark (Bailey), Tim Graham (Jim), June Whitley (Waitress/Woman), and Charles Seel (Bart).

Commercial: Doris Singleton (Libby).

Louis King directed the 1946 20th Century–Fox version of *Smokey*, the simple story of a man's love for a spirited stallion. Joel McCrea stars in *Lux*'s adaptation, playing Fred Mac-Murray's screen part, and Anne Baxter's movie role goes to Constance Moore.

There have been two other films based on Will James's novel *Smokey*. The first was directed by Eugene Forde and released in 1933 with a cast headed by Victor Jory and Irene Bentley. The 1966 20th Century–Fox version was directed by George Sherman, with the leads going to Fess Parker and Diana Hyland.

Additional film versions: Fox, 1933; 20th Century–Fox, 1966.

*565. "How Green Was My Valley,"
    3/31/47
Based on the 1941 20th Century–Fox film (screenplay by Philip Dunne), in turn based on the novel by Richard Llewellyn (1940).

Intermission Guest: Randy Stuart, 20th Century–Fox starlet.

Cast: David Niven (Mr. Gruffydd), Maureen O'Sullivan (Angharad), Donald Crisp (Mr. Morgan), Sara Allgood (Beth Morgan), Gale Gordon (Narrator), Johnny McGovern (Huw, as a Boy), Tony Barrett (Ianto), Clarke Gordon (Davy), Ira Grossel (Dai), Bill Johnstone (Young Spoiler), Frederic Worlock (Dr. Richards), Ramsey Hill (Man), Claire Verdera (Mrs. Nichols), Howard Jeffrey (Boy), June Whitley (Enid/Woman), Charles Seel (Ivor/Man), Carole Sue Leeds, Betty Grannis (Ad Libs), and Norman Field.

Chorus: Robert Tait, Robert Bradford, Sidney Pepple, George Gramlich,

C. Curtsinger, Stewart Bair, Kenneth Rundquist, Donald Reese, Delos Jewkes, Allan Watson, and Enrico Ricardi (Coach).

Commercials: Doris Singleton (Libby), Janet Russell (Sally).

The popular 20th Century–Fox drama *How Green Was My Valley* was presented on *Lux* for a second time on March 31, on this occasion starring David Niven, Maureen O'Sullivan, Donald Crisp, and Sara Allgood. (Frederic Worlock repeated his movie role of Dr. Richards.)

See 9/21/42 for information on the film version; there was an additional *Lux* broadcast on September 28, 1954.

566. "Alexander's Ragtime Band,"
    4/7/47
Based on the 1938 20th Century–Fox film (screenplay by Kathryn Scola, Lamar Trotti, and Richard Sherman).

Intermission Guest: Marian Marshall, 20th Century–Fox starlet.

Cast: Tyrone Power (Alex), Dinah Shore (Stella), Al Jolson (Himself), Dick Haymes (Charlie), Margaret Whiting (Jerry), Eddie Marr (Snapper/Joe), William Johnstone (Driver), Charles Seel (Man One), Lee Sherin (Man Two), Margie Liszt, Kathryn Kane, Holland Morris, and Harold Purvis (Ad Libs).

Commercial: Doris Singleton (Libby).

The reissue of 20th Century–Fox's 1938 film *Alexander's Ragtime Band* in theatres was the occasion for *Lux*'s revival of the musical on April 7. The new script, which features a part for Al Jolson as himself (narrating the story), once again includes several numbers by Irving Berlin (some of which were not performed in the motion picture). Songs heard in the broadcast (all with words and music by Irving Berlin) are: Act 1: "Lazy" (1924; Al Jolson), "Alexander's Ragtime Band" (1911; Dinah Shore), "Now It Can Be Told" (written for the movie, 1938; Dick Haymes); Act 2: "Blue Skies" (from the musical *Betsy,* 1926; Margaret Whiting), "When I Lost You" (1912; Dick Haymes), "Remember" (1925; Dinah Shore); "Cheek to Cheek" (from the film *Top Hat,* 1935), "A Pretty Girl Is Like a Melody" (from *The Ziegfeld Follies of 1919*), "Alexander's Ragtime Band " (reprise; Dinah Shore).

See 6/3/40 for information on the film version.

567. "Monsieur Beaucaire," 4/14/47

Based on the 1946 Paramount film (screenplay by Melvin Frank and Norman Panama), in turn based on the novel by Booth Tarkington (1901).

Intermission Guest: Arlene Dahl, Warner Bros. starlet.

Cast: Bob Hope (Monsieur Beaucaire), Joan Caulfield (Mimi), Carlton KaDell (Duc de Chandre), Luis Van Rooten (Minister), Roland Varno (General Francisco), Eric Snowden (King Louis XV), Bill Johnstone (George Washington), Norman Field (Priest), and Jay Novello, Kay Christopher, Don Morrison, Lois Corbett, Laurette Fillbrand, Anne Stone, Herbert Lytton, and Charles Seel.

Monsieur Beaucaire, the 1946 George Marshall–directed Paramount period piece that pokes fun at the French aristocracy during the reign of Louis XV, was adapted for *Lux* one year later. The plot, which has Bob Hope playing a court barber who exchanges identities with a duke for political purposes, is merely an excuse for a collection of typical Bob Hope comic situations and one-liners (many of which were specially prepared for the broadcast).

Joan Caulfield is also on hand to recreate her motion picture role.

A straight version of "Monsieur Beaucaire" was performed on *Lux* on June 21, 1937; see that entry for information on film and stage versions.

568. "My Reputation," 4/21/47

Based on the 1946 Warner Bros./ First National film (screenplay by Catherine Turney), in turn based on the novel *Instruct My Sorrows,* by Clare Jaynes (pseudonym of Jane Rothschild Mayer and Clara Spiegel) (1942).

Intermission Guest: June Harris, Paramount starlet.

Cast: Barbara Stanwyck (Jessica Drummond), George Brent (Major Landis), Janet Scott (Mother), Frances Robinson (Ginn), Ira Grossel (Gary), Tommy Cook (Keith), Robert Ellis (Kim), Bill Johnstone (George), Noreen Gammill (Anna), Gloria McMillan (Gretchen), Charles Seel (Frank), and Lois Corbett.

Commercial: Doris Singleton (Libby).

After a lengthy absence, Barbara Stanwyck and George Brent returned to the *Lux* program in an adaptation of Curtis Bernhardt's 1946 Warner Bros./ First National drama *My Reputation.* Both players reprise their original screen characterizations: Stanwyck as a lonely widow pressured by her meddling mother and two teenage boys to remain dedicated to her late husband's memory, and Brent as the serviceman who has a romantic interest in her.

569. "My Darling Clementine," 4/28/47

Based on the 1946 20th Century–Fox film (screenplay by Samuel G. Engel; story by Sam Hellman), in turn based on the book *Wyatt Earp, Frontier Marshal,* by Stuart N. Lake.

Intermission Guest: Colleen Townsend, 20th Century–Fox starlet.

Cast: Henry Fonda (Wyatt Earp), Richard Conte (Doc Holliday), Cathy Downs (Clementine), Earle Ross (Clanton), Carlton KaDell (Morgan), Paula Winslowe (Chihuahua), Bill Johnstone (Old Actor), and Cliff Clark, Norman Field, Clarke Gordon, Tim Graham, Eddie Marr, George Neise,

Tyler McVey, Charles Seel, and Edwin Max.

Commercial: Doris Singleton (Libby).

John Ford's film version of the famed gunfight at the OK Corral, and the events leading up to it, became a *Lux* play on April 28. The radio adaptation of *My Darling Clementine* is faithful to the film, though the climactic gunfight is inevitably disappointing. Henry Fonda and Cathy Downs reprise their roles of Wyatt Earp and (the purely fictional) Clementine, while Richard Conte takes the Victor Mature movie part of Doc Holliday. (The real Doc Holliday died in 1887 — six years after the gunfight at the OK Corral.)

570. "The Egg and I," 5/5/47

Based on the 1947 Universal film (screenplay by Chester Erskine and Fred Finklehoffe), in turn based on the novel by Betty MacDonald (1945).

Intermission Guest: Jane Adams, Universal starlet.

Cast: Claudette Colbert (Betty), Fred MacMurray (Bob), Elvia Allman (Ma Kettle), Frances Robinson (Harriet Putman), Bill Johnstone (Pa Kettle), Janet Scott (Mother), Billy Roy (Tom), Tim Graham (Joe/Character), Charles Seel (Sheriff), Noreen Gammill (Maid), Earl Lee (Huntington), Lois Kennison (Girl), Bobby Ellis (Albert), Vance Colvig (Animal Imitations), and Ira Grossel, Norman Field, Cliff Clark, and Howard Jeffrey.

Commercial: Doris Singleton (Libby).

If Universal's 1947 Chester Erskine–directed release *The Egg and I* is not as amusing over the air as it is on the screen, it is no fault of *Lux*'s players or adapter. Much of the humor of the screenplay is simply lost without the visual effect, and some of the picture's most humorous sequences do not translate to the audio medium. Starring in the broadcast, as they do in the film, are Claudette Colbert and Fred MacMurray as the newlywed city slickers who have a go at a chicken farm, with predictable results. The characters of Ma and Pa Kettle made their first movie appearances in *The Egg and I*, memorably played by Marjorie Main and Percy Kilbride. *Lux* producers opted for radio actors Elvia Allman and Bill Johnstone to portray them in the radio version, and both closely imitate the creators of the roles.

571. "Johnny O'Clock," 5/12/47

Based on the 1947 Columbia film (screenplay by Robert Rossen), in turn based on a story by Milton Holmes.

Intermission Guest: Virginia Hunter, Columbia starlet.

Cast: Dick Powell (Johnny), Marguerite Chapman (Nancy Hobbs), Lee J. Cobb (Inspector Koch), Janis Carter (Nell), Bill Johnstone (Chuck Blayden), Jay Novello (Marchettis), Ira Grossel (Charlie), Alvina Temple (Harriet), Edwin Max (Tom), Charles Seel (Clerk/Taxi), Noreen Gammill (Woman), Eddie Marr (Man), Robert Bruce (Cop/Man Two).

Commercial: Doris Singleton (Libby).

Robert Rossen's first directorial effort, *Johnny O'Clock* (a 1947 Columbia release), made a convoluted though entertaining (thanks to the witty dialogue) noir tale on *Lux*'s May 12 program, centering around a hard-boiled gambler's association with mayhem, murderers, and molls. Dick Powell reprises his motion picture role as the title character, and Marguerite Chapman fills in for an indisposed Evelyn Keyes, who had been scheduled to repeat her film part. Heading the supporting cast are Lee J. Cobb, also from the movie, and Janis Carter in Nina Foch's screen role. (Ira Grossel, who plays the unbilled character of Duke in the picture, is heard in the important role of Charlie in the broadcast.)

572. "It Happened on Fifth Avenue," 5/19/47

Based on the 1947 Allied Artists/ Monogram film (screenplay by Everett Freeman and Vick Knight; original story by Herbert Clyde Lewis and Frederick Stephani).

Intermission Guest: Elyse Knox, Monogram starlet.

Cast: Victor Moore (Aloysius P. McKeever), Don DeFore (Jim), Charlie Ruggles (Michael J. O'Connor), Gale Storm (Trudy), Lois Corbett (Mary), George Neise (Whitey), Guy Kingsford (Kane), William Johnstone (Felton), June Whitley (Alice/Woman), Abe Reynolds (Finklehoff), Leone Ledoux (Baby Cry/ Operator), and Charles Seel (Harry).

Commerical: Doris Singleton (Libby).

The postwar housing shortage was the theme for *Lux*'s May 19 broadcast, which was based on Roy Del Ruth's 1947 Allied Artists/Monogram comedy *It Happened on Fifth Avenue.* Four members of the screen cast appear in their original roles: Victor Mature, Don DeFore, Charlie Ruggles, and Gale Storm.

573. "Vacation from Marriage," 5/26/47

Based on the 1945 MGM British/ London film (screenplay by Clemence Dane and Anthony Pelissier).

Intermission Guest: Marilyn Buford, MGM starlet.

Cast: Deborah Kerr (Cathy), Van Heflin (Robert), Frances Robinson (Dizzy), Victor Wood (Scotty), Valerie Cardew (Elena), Tom Collins (Richard), Bill Johnstone (Tom), Eric Snowden (Man), Charles Seel (Jim/Doctor), Helen Geddes (Girl), Virginia Riley (Ad Libs), and Pat Aherne, Gloria Gordon, Norman Field, Herb Rawlinson, and Charles Seel.

Commercial: Doris Singleton.

Alexander Korda's *Vacation from Marriage* in 1947 was a comedy-drama that focuses upon a restless, bored couple who enlist in the Navy, with profound results. Deborah Kerr reprises her screen role in *Lux*'s charming account of the story, while Van Heflin plays the part taken by Robert Donat in the film.

574. "The Jazz Singer," 6/2/47

Based on the play by Samson Raphaelson (1925).

Intermission Guest: Joan Winfield, Warner Bros. starlet.

Cast: Al Jolson (Jack Robin), Gail Patrick (Mary Dale), Ludwig Donath (Cantor Rabinowitz), Tamara Shayne (Sara Rabinowitz), Carlton KaDell (Stevens), Bill Johnstone (Yudleson), Eddie Marr (Jimmy), Charles Seel (Doctor), Bobby Ellis (Boy), and June Whitley (Girl).

The success of Columbia's 1946 release *The Jolson Story* inspired *Lux* producers to revive *The Jazz Singer,* in which Al Jolson had starred on the screen in 1927 and on *The Lux Radio Theatre* in 1936. The source for the *Lux* script is the 1925 play. In addition to Jolson, the radio cast consists of Gail Patrick and from *The Jolson Story*, Ludwig Donath and Tamara Shayne. Al Jolson's musical numbers (all interpolations) are: "Toot-Toot, Tootsie" (words by Gus Kahn and Ernie Erdman, music by Dann Russo; interpolated into *Bombo*, 1922), "I'm Sittin' on Top of the World" (words by Sam Lewis and Joe Young, music by Ray Henderson; 1925), and "Blue Skies" (words and music by Irving Berlin; from *Betsy*, 1926) in Act 1; "Keep Smilin' at Trouble" (words by Al Jolson and Buddy DeSylva, music by Lewis Gensler; from *Big Boy*, 1925), and "Rock-a-bye Your Baby with a Dixie Melody" (words by Sam M. Lewis and Joe Young, music by Jean Schwartz; interpolated into *Sinbad*, 1918) in Act 2. Jolson also performs what he describes as a new composition by himself called "All My Love" in the curtain call.

See 8/10/36 for information on stage and film versions.

*575. "One More Tomorrow," 6/9/47

Based on the 1946 Warner Bros. film (screenplay by Charles Hoffman and Catherine Turney), in turn based on the play *The Animal Kingdom*, by Philip Barry (1932).

Intermission Guest: Maria Palmer, RKO actress.

Cast: Dennis Morgan (Tom), Jane Wyman (Christie), Alexis Smith (Cecilia), Gale Gordon (Jim), Ira Grossel (Pat), Frances Robinson (Fran), William Johnstone (Rufus), Stanley Waxman (Owen/Man in Act 2), Charles Seel (Waiter/Man in Act 3), Edwin Mills, Gordon Gray, Florida Edwards, and Dorothy Garner (Ad Libs).

Commercials: Doris Singleton (Libby), Truda Mason (Sally).

Warner Bros.' *One More Tomorrow*, which was directed by Peter Godfrey, relates the story of a well-to-do young man who marries a glamorous left-wing newspaper editor, temporarily casting aside his faithful girlfriend in the process. *Lux*'s broadcast of June 9 features all three of the movie's stars, Dennis Morgan, Jane Wyman, and Alexis Smith, in their original roles.

Philip Barry's play *The Animal Kingdom* (the source of *One More Tomorrow*) was filmed by RKO under its original title in 1932. Starring in that Edward H. Griffith film are Leslie Howard, Ann Harding, and Myrna Loy.

Additional film versions: RKO, 1932 (*The Animal Kingdom*).

576. "The Other Love," 6/16/47

Based on the 1947 United Artists film (screenplay by Harry Brown and Ladislas Fodor), in turn based on the unpublished story "Beyond," by Erich Maria Remarque.

Cast: Barbara Stanwyck (Karen Duncan), George Brent (Dr. Anthony Stanton), Richard Conte (Paul), Joan Lorring (Celestine), and Frances Robinson, William Johnstone, Regina Wallace, Charles Seel, and June Whitley.

Commercials: Dorothy Lovett (Libby), Truda Marson (Sally).

Andre de Toth's 1947 United Artists drama *The Other Love* was brought to *Lux* the same year, with Barbara Stanwyck recreating her screen role as a seriously ill concert pianist who longs to live life to the fullest. George Brent (in David Niven's film part) plays the physician who loves her, and Richard Conte resumes his original character of the gambler whose romantic interest threatens to shoren her life. (Joan Lorring also repeats her film role.)

577. "Cynthia," 6/23/47

Based on the 1947 MGM film (screenplay by Harold Buchman and Charles Kaufman), in turn based on the play *The Rich Full Life*, by Viña Delmar (1945).

Intermission Guest: Amparo Ballester, MGM starlet.

Cast: Elizabeth Taylor (Cynthia), George Murphy (Larry), Mary Astor (Louise), Gil Stratton, Jr. (Rickey), Bill Johnstone (Professor), Leo Cleary (Fred), Lois Corbett (Carrie/Teacher), Josephine Graham (Stella), Norman Field (Dingle), Billy Roy (Willis), Noreen Gammill (Sadie/Nurse), Stanley Farrar (Man), and Charles Seel (Man).

Commercial: Dorothy Lovett (Libby).

A Rich Full Life, a Viña Delmar Broadway play concerning a sheltered, sickly girl of overly protective parents, was produced for the big screen (under Robert Z. Leonard's direction) as *Cynthia* in 1947. *Lux*'s season closer on June 23 featured its enjoyable adaptation of the story and cast three of the movie players in their original roles: Elizabeth Taylor, George Murphy, and Mary Astor.

1

Lux Presents Hollywood